LORDSHIP AND LANDSCAPE IN NORFOLK

1250–1350

Cartouche of the 1590 map of 'the lordeshippe or mannor of Holkeham' by Thomas Clerke of Stamford Baron St Martin.

RECORDS OF SOCIAL AND ECONOMIC HISTORY
NEW SERIES XX

LORDSHIP AND LANDSCAPE

IN NORFOLK

1250–1350

The Early Records of Holkham

EDITED BY

WILLIAM HASSALL

AND

JACQUES BEAUROY

Published *for* THE BRITISH ACADEMY
by OXFORD UNIVERSITY PRESS

Oxford University Press, Walton Street, Oxford OX2 6DP
Oxford New York Toronto
Delhi Bombay Calcutta Madras Karachi
Kuala Lumpur Singapore Hong Kong Tokyo
Nairobi Dar es Salaam Cape Town
Melbourne Auckland Madrid

and associated companies in
Berlin Ibadan

Published in the United States
by Oxford University Press Inc., New York

British Library Cataloguing in Publication Data
Hassall, W.O
Lordship and Landscape in Norfolk,
1250–1350; Early Records of Holkham.
Records of Social & Economic History,
New Series; No. 20
I. Title II. Beauroy, Jacques III. Series.
942.612
ISBN 0–19–726093–4

Typeset by the Literary and Linguistic Computing Centre, Cambridge
Printed in Great Britain
on acid-free paper by
Bookcraft (Bath) Ltd,
Midsomer Norton, Avon

Foreword

The Holkham estate has been mainly identified in the eyes of the public and economic historians alike with the achievements of the Coke family and improvements in Norfolk agriculture from the seventeenth century onwards. From this perspective the present volume *Lordship and Landscape in Norfolk 1250–1350*, which is the twentieth to be published in the new series of *Records of Social and Economic History*, may appear as part of the 'pre-history' of Holkham. In fact, it sets out the documentary basis of a major medieval estate in its own right, from one of the richest seigneurial archives still in private hands.

The different categories of the documents allow Dr Hassall and Dr Beauroy to analyse both the development of the estate and its modes of operation. Charters concerning land conveyance (which make plain an active market in land during the thirteenth century), terriers which contain detailed descriptions of parcels of land, rentals, lists of tenants, custumals setting out services and rents owed, manorial court rolls which provide much data on social and occupational relationships, the accounts of the officials responsible for different operations on the estates, allow a detailed pattern to be built up. The Neel Cartulary, in particular, offers exceptional data about the functioning of the estate from these sources. While primarily concerning agriculture (the Norfolk system of husbandry in the eighteenth century evidently had medieval origins), the Holkham records contain significant material about such other matters as fishing, ships (Gilbert Neel was in partnership with local merchants using the little port), and women retailers in the local markets.

A second volume is planned to cover the period 1350–1600.

Peter Mathias
*Chairman, Records of Social and
Economic History Committee*

Contents

CONTENTS

List of Illustrations

FRONTISPIECE

Cartouche of the 1590 map of the 'lordeshippe or mannor of Holkeham' by Thomas Clerke of Stamford Baron St Martin (Holkham Hall muniments, Ms. 771, Rack no. 2/1).

MAPS

FICHES   in pocket at the back

(1)   Illustrating Holkham Documents (HD) 1–47, 70–296 and
      Holkham Papers (HP) 995–1006

(2)   Illustrating Holkham Papers (HP) 1007–1060, 1062–1103, 3808

(3)   Illustrating the transformation of Holkham in the
      eighteenth and nineteenth centuries (maps, views, portraits) and
      the seals of the medieval documents (Fiche 3: G1–14)

(For a full listing of the documents reproduced in Fiches 1, 2 and 3, see Appendix 6.)

Preface

The publication of the medieval documents in this volume is designed to study the first well documented century of Holkham's history before the creation of the great estate of the Cokes and the famous Palladian Hall with its treasures and park. Previous research has focused mainly upon the place of Holkham in agricultural history and in the history of art and taste. What was clearly needed was the longer historical perspective which would take us back to the medieval political, social and economic foundations of Holkham, enabling us to get an understanding of the background of the changes which took place in modern times and which appeared to obliterate the past. It reveals Holkham's medieval past, agricultural and social, which made possible the setting of its later developments.

Moreover, our aim in bringing to light these documents, preserved, for their greater part, at Holkham Hall, was to make available an important source for further research into the origins of the economic and social distinctiveness of medieval East Anglia. Agricultural historians will now have at their disposal an earlier and larger documentary base for the study of field patterns and cropping practices in west Norfolk. For the historians of medieval social structure the rather large body of lay seigneurial documents connected with the Holkham manors should be of great use to shed light upon the characteristics of Norfolk medieval society.

The preparation of this edition, which was planned jointly in 1982 and adopted for publication by the Records of Social and Economic History Committee of the British Academy in October 1984, fell in two parts. William Owen Hassall (librarian to the Earls of Leicester, 1937–83) examined and transcribed the medieval archives of Holkham. On his retirement from the Bodleian Library, he had generous help from the Leverhulme Trust and from the British Academy. His preliminary work made this enterprise possible. He undertook to establish the texts of the *Holkham Documents* and of the *Holkham Papers* and their diplomatic and palaeographical aspects. He is responsible for the 'Topography of Holkham'.

For his part, Jacques Beauroy (Centre National de la Recherche Scientifique, University of Paris I Panthéon-Sorbonne) is responsible for the planning of the edition, the writing of the chapters of the Introduction, the study of Holkham's social and agrarian aspects and the prosopography of the unprinted court rolls. He also transcribed part of the texts, revised and completed the edition. There has been much consultation between the editors about their contributions to this joint edition.

Numerous debts have been incurred in the making of this volume. William Hassall, firstly, wishes to remember his seniors, A.E. Popham and Francis

Wormald of the British Museum for introducing him to the third Earl of Leicester, grandson of Coke of Norfolk, who invited him to explore the treasures of Holkham Hall; Charles Johnson and Hillary Jenkinson of the PRO; Hilda Johnstone and Eliza Jeffries Davis at the Institute of Historical Research; W.A. Pantin and H.E. Salter of Oxford. Among the living, he appreciates the help of colleagues in Oxford, especially at the Bodleian Library, and of foreign scholars, especially Dr. Yuri Ulyanov, who confirmed his belief in the significance for historians of the survival of so many secular medieval sources *in situ* at Holkham. He thanks the fourth and fifth Earls of Leicester for their continuing support, for allowing much photography and microfilming and for letting him have the use of William Kent's Temple in the Park.

Both of us are very grateful to Viscount Coke and to the Trustees of the Holkham Estate for their generous hospitality and for allowing publication of the medieval documents and the photographs (of which they retain the copyright) on the microfiches. Thanks are due to Miss Kathleen Major for recommending the inclusion in the edition of both the original charters and their summaries from the Neel Cartulary, to Dr. Brian and Kate Ward-Perkins, sometime librarians at Holkham, to Mrs. Hiskey, archivist, and to Mr. Frederick Jolly, administrator of Holkham Hall, for their kind help and patience. Mr Malcolm Parks kindly discussed the chronology of the handwritings of the deeds on Fiche 1 and 2. We wish to express our special thanks to Dr. Marjorie Chibnall and Dr. Richard Smith for the supervision of this edition for the British Academy.

Jacques Beauroy is particularly grateful to Professor Georges Duby for his guidance and amicable support and to Professor Rodney Hilton for first leading him to the study of medieval East Anglia, and wishes to thank the Economic and Social Research Council for their research grants, over the years, which made this work possible. The hospitality of the Cambridge Group for the History of Population and Social Structure has also provided him with the greatest encouragement.

We also wish to express our gratitude to Mr. James Rivington, Publications Officer of the British Academy, for his generous advice. We are grateful to the following for the drawing of the map of medieval Holkham: Mr. Ralph Goldsmith and Mrs. Eleanor Beard, and the Archaeological Units of Norfolk and Oxford; and to the Courtauld Institute, the Map Department of the British Museum, Mr. E.E. Swain, and the National Building Record, whose photographs made possible the study of Holkham early estate maps.

We wish to thank Dr. John Dawson and Mrs. Beatrix Bown of the Literary and Linguistic Computing Centre of the University of Cambridge for producing camera-ready copy of this volume and for creating the index from the computerized text. We are also grateful to Mr. Nigel Le Page of

Microform Academic Publishers for the making of the three microfiches. At the Norfolk Record Office in Norwich, Paul Rutledge and Susan Maddock were always very helpful, and at the Public Record Office in Chancery Lane, the staff kindly assisted in the search for the Norfolk Feet of Fines relating to Holkham.

We wish to express our thanks to the following for the making and the use of photographs for reproduction on Fiche 3: Leopold Schmidt of Freiburg-im-Breisgau (Fiche 3: C3; D1, 11; E1, 6, 7); the Cambridge University Collection and the Director of Aerial photography (Fiche 3: A10–14); Graham Pooley (14 seals on Fiche 3: G1–14); Sidney Braybrooke of the Bodleian Library for enlargements of seals; Peter Eden (details of working map on Fiche 3: E5); the Curators of the Bodleian Library (Model Farm, Fiche 3: B3); Major R.L. Coke, D.S.O., M.C.D.L. and Mrs Coke (Portrait of the 2nd Earl of Leicester by the Hon. J. Collier, Fiche 3: B12); the Aurora Publishing House and B. Piotrovsky, Director of the Hermitage Museum of St. Petersburg (the earliest view of the lake, Fiche 3: D5); Mrs. F.C. Howlett (Fiche 3: F7); Professor Yoko Miyoshi (Fiche 3: B11; F8, 9).

Finally thanks are due to Jennifer Paxton of Harvard University for reading parts of our manuscript, to the late Mrs. Vera Read, to Mrs. Dorothy Hartley of Stoke Poges and to Mrs. D.H. Bayliss of South Creake for their typing, to the trustees of the Mark Fitch Fund and to the Direction des Relations Culturelles du Ministère des Affaires Etrangères (Paris) for making it possible to employ Humaira Ahmed, Deborah McGovern and Judy Winchester for retyping; and also to Mr. Dickerson of the Forestry Department who helped to make intelligible the hardest document of all, the palimpsest presented by Holkham Park itself, by locating ancient pits used as medieval landmarks, now hidden by trees.

Abbreviated References

NOTE: Works cited here are not listed in the Bibliography

Add.   Additional

BD   Burnham Document

BL   British Library

Blomefield, *Norfolk*   F. Blomefield and C. Parkin, *An Essay Towards a Topographical History of the County of Norfolk*, 11 vols, London, 1805–10

Brabner, Gazetteer   J.H.F. Brabner, *The Comprehensive Gazetteer of England and Wales*, London, 1894

Brettingham   M. Brettingham, *The Plans, Elevations and Sections of Holkham in Norfolk, the Seat of the Late Earl of Leicester*, Atlas in Folio (33), London, 1761

Cal. Close   *Calendar of the Close Rolls Preserved in the Public Record Office*, London, 1900–63

Cal. IPM   *Calendar of Inquisitions Post Mortem and Other Analogous Documents Preserved in the Public Record Office*, London, 1904–55

Cal. Inq. Misc.   *Calendar of Inquisitions Miscellaneous (Chancery) Preserved in the Public Record Office*, London, 1916–68

Cal. Patent   *Calendar of the Patent Rolls Preserved in the Public Record Office*, London, 1901–86

Cart. of Dereham   Cartulary of the Abbey of West Dereham, BL Ms. Add. 46353

Cart. of Creake   *Cartulary of Creake Abbey*, ed. A.L. Bedingfield, Norfolk Record Society, XXXV, Norwich, 1966

Cart. of Walsingham   Cartulary of the Priory of Walsingham, BL Ms. Cotton Nero E VII

Davis   G.R.C. Davis, *Medieval Cartularies of Great Britain, a Short Catalogue*, London, 1958

DNB   *Dictionary of National Biography*, 63 vols, London, 1885–1900; suppl., 18 vols, London-Oxford, 1901–1986

Dodwell, *Fines*   B. Dodwell, *Feet of Fines for the County of Norfolk from the Reign of Richard I to the Reign of John, 1198–1215*, 2 vols, PRS, ns., 27, 32, London, 1952–6

Dugdale, *Monasticon*   W. Dugdale, *Monasticon Anglicanum*, revised edn, J. Caly, H. Ellis and B. Bandinel, eds, 8 vols in 6, London, 1817–30

EPS   English Place-Name Society

Farrer	W. Farrer, *Honors and Knight's Fees*, 3 vols, London, 1923–5
Feudal Aids	*Inquisitions and Assessments Relating to Feudal Aids With Other Analogous Documents Preserved in the Public Record Office*, London, 1898–1919
GEC, *Peerage*	*The Complete Peerage of England, Scotland and Ireland*, ed. G.E. Cokayne, revised edn, 13 vols in 14, London, 1910–59
HD	Holkham Documents. The numbers refer to items described in catalogues compiled by H.A. Davidson
HMC	Royal Commission on Historical Manuscripts
HP	Holkham Papers. The numbers refer to items described in catalogues compiled by E.J.L. Scott
Moor, *Knights*	C. Moor, *Knights of Edward I*, 5 vols, Harleian Society, LXXX–LXXXIV, London, 1929–32
NCC	Norwich Consistory Court
Neel Cart.	Neel Cartulary, Holkham Hall Muniments HD 22a
NRA	National Register of Archives
NRO	Norfolk Record Office
NRS	Norfolk Record Society
n.s.	new series
OED	Oxford English Dictionary
OS	Ordnance Survey
PRO	Public Record Office
PRS	Pipe Rolls Society
Red Book	*The Red Book of the Exchequer*, ed. H. Hall, 3 vols, Rolls Series, London, 1896
Rot. Hund.	*Rotuli Hundredorum tempore Henrici III et Edwardi I in Turr' Lond' et in Curia Receptae Scaccarii Westm.*, 2 vols, London, 1812–18
Rye, *Norfolk Fines*	W. Rye, *A Short Calendar of the Feet of Fines for Norfolk from the Reign of Richard I to the Reign of Richard III*, 2 vols, Norwich, 1885–6
Scots Peerage	*The Scots Peerage*, ed. Sir James Balfour Paul, 9 vols, Edinburgh, 1904–14
TRHS	Transactions of the Royal Historical Society
VCH	Victoria History of the Counties of England

Bibliography

Allison, K.J., 'The Sheep-Corn Husbandry of Norfolk in the 16th and 17th Centuries', *Agricultural History Review*, V (1957), 12–30

–   'The Lost Villages of Norfolk', *Norfolk Archaeology*, XXI (1955), 116–62

Astill, G., Grant, A., eds, *The Countryside of Medieval England*, Oxford, 1988. Pp. 300

Aston, M., *Interpreting the Landscape: Landscape Archaeology in Local Studies*, London, 1985. Pp. 168

Aston, M., ed., *Medieval Fish, Fisheries and Fishponds in England*, Oxford, 1988. Pp. 484

Aston, M., Austin, D., Dyer, C., eds, *The Rural Settlements of Medieval England, Studies Dedicated to Maurice Beresford and John Hurst*, Oxford, 1989. Pp. 318

Aston, T.H., ed., *Landlords, Peasants and Politics in Medieval England*, Cambridge, 1987. Pp. 446

Aston, T.H., Philpin, C.H.E., eds, *The Brenner Debate, Agrarian Class Structure and Economic Development in Pre-Industrial Europe*, Cambridge, 1985. Pp. 339

Aston, T.H., Coss, P.R., Dyer, C., Thirsk, J., eds, *Social Relations and Ideas: Essays in Honour of R.H. Hilton*, Cambridge, 1983. Pp. 337

Bailey, M., *A Marginal Economy: East Anglian Breckland in the Late Middle Ages*, Cambridge, 1989. Pp. 350

–   'Sand into Gold: The Evolution of the Foldcourse System in West Suffolk, 1200–1600', *Agricultural History Review*, XXXVIII (1990), 40–57

Baker, A.R.H. and Harley, J.B., *Man Made the Land: Essays in English Historical Geography*, Newton Abbot, 1973. Pp. 208

Baker, A.R.H., Biger, G., eds, *Ideology and Landscape in Historical Perspective: Essays on the Meaning of some Places in the Past*, Cambridge, 1992. Pp. 356

Baker, A.R.H., Billinge, M., eds, *Period and Place: Research Methods in Historical Geography*, Cambridge, 1982. Pp. 377

Baker, A.R.H., Butlin, R.A., eds, *Studies of Field Systems of the British Isles*, Cambridge, 1973. Pp. 702

Baker, A.R.H., Gregory, D., eds, *Explorations in Historical Geography: Interpretative Essays*, Cambridge, 1984. Pp. vii, 252

Baker, J.H., *The Third University of England: The Inns of Court and the Common Law Tradition*, Selden Society Lecture, London, 1990. Pp. 50

Barg, M.A., 'The Social Structure of Manorial Freeholders: An Analysis of the Hundred Rolls of 1279', *Agricultural History Review* XXXIX (1991), 108–15

Bayliss-Smith, T., Owens, S., eds, *Britain's Changing Environment from the Air*, Cambridge, 1990. Pp. 256

Bean, J.M.W., *From Lord to Patron: Lordship in Late Medieval England*, Manchester, 1989. Pp. 279

Beauroy, J., *Vin et Société à Bergerac du Moyen Age aux Temps Modernes*, Stanford French and Italian Studies 4, Saratoga, 1976. Pp. 293

– 'Offices Manoriaux et Stratification Sociale à Heacham (Norfolk), 1285–1324', *Flaran* 4 (1982), 237–44

– 'La Conquête Cléricale de l'Angleterre', *Cahiers de Civilisation Médiévale* XXVII (1984), 34–48

– 'Family Patterns and Relations of Bishop's Lynn Will Makers in the Fourteenth Century', *The World We Have Gained, Essays Presented to Peter Laslett* (L. Bonfield, R.M. Smith, K. Wrightson, eds), Oxford, 1986, 23–42

– 'Analyse Quantitative d'une Seigneurie Anglaise: Offices Manoriaux, Activités Marchandes et Structure Sociale dans le Norfolk Occidental à la Fin du XIIIe Siècle', *Histoire et Mesure*, III (1988), 515–25

– 'Sur la Culture Seigneuriale en Angleterre au XIVe Siècle: Un Poème Anglo-Normand Inédit dans le Cartulaire des Barons de Mohun (Somerset)', *Mélanges Georges Duby* (C. Amado, G. Lobrichon, eds), forthcoming, Paris-Bari, 1993

Beauroy, J. et al., eds, *The Wolf and the Lamb: Popular Culture in France from the Old Regime to the Twentieth Century*, Stanford French and Italian Studies 3, Saratoga, 1977. Pp. 253

Beckett, J.V., 'The Peasant in England: A Case of Terminological Confusion?' *Agricultural History Review*, XXXII (1984), xxxvi, 113–23

Bedingfield, A.L., ed., *Cartulary of Creake Abbey*, N.R.S., XXXV (1966). Pp. xxxvi, 146

Beresford, M.W. and St. Joseph, J.K.S., *Medieval England: An Aerial Survey*, Cambridge, 1979. Pp. 286

Beresford, M.W., Hurst, J.G., eds, *Deserted Medieval Villages*, London, 1971; new edn, Gloucester, 1989. Pp. 340

Beresford, M.W., *The Lost Villages of England*, Gloucester, 1987. Pp. 445

Blake, W.J., 'Norfolk Manorial Lords in 1316', *Norfolk Archaeology*, XXX (1952), 234–85

Bloch, M., *Caractères Originaux de l'Histoire Rurale Française*, 2 vols, t. 1, Oslo-Paris, 1931; new edn, Paris, 1955; t. 2, Paris, 1956. Pp. 261; 230

– *Mélanges Historiques*, 2 vols, Paris, 1963. Pp. 1108

Bridbury, A.R., *England and the Salt Trade in the Later Middle Ages*, Oxford, 1955. Pp. 198

Britnell, R.H., 'Minor Landlords in England and Medieval Agrarian Capitalism', *Past and Present*, LXXXIX (1980), 3–22

Britton, E., *The Community of the Vill*, Toronto, 1977. Pp. 291

Brooke, C.N.L., Postan, M.M., eds, *'Carte Nativorum', a Peterborough Abbey Cartulary of the Fourteenth Century*, Oxford, 1960. Pp. 261

Brown, Ph., ed., (gen. ed. J. Morris), *Domesday Book*, XXXIII, Norfolk, 2 vols, Chichester, 1984 (photostat reproduction of the 1783 edition)

Butlin, R., 'Georgian Britain, c. 1714–1837', *Historic Landscapes of Britain from the Air* (R.E. Glasscock, ed.), Cambridge, 1992, pp. 154–185

Cam, H., *The Hundred and the Hundred Rolls,: An Outline of Local Government in England*, London, 1930; new edn, 1963. Pp. 296

Cameron, K., *The Place-Names of Lincolnshire*, EPS, vols LXIV/LXV, part two: Lincolnshire, Lindsey, North Riding, the Wapentake of Yarborough, Nottingham, 1991. Pp. 326

Campbell, B.M.S., 'The Regional Uniqueness of English Field Systems? Some Evidence from Eastern Norfolk', *Agricultural History Review*, XXIX (1981), 16–28

— 'The Complexity of Manorial Structure in Medieval Norfolk: A Case Study', *Norfolk Archaeology*, XXXIX (1986), 225–61

— 'Towards an Agricultural Geography of Medieval England', *Agricultural History Review*, XXXVI (1988), 87–98

— 'Land, Labour and Productivity Trends in English Seignorial Agriculture, 1208–1450', *Land, Labour and Livestock, Historical Studies of European Agricultural Productivity* (B.M.S. Campbell, M. Overton, eds), Manchester, 1991, 144–82

Campbell, B.M.S., ed., *Before the Black Death: Studies in the Crisis of the Early Fourteenth Century*, Manchester, 1991. Pp. 232

Cantor, L., ed., *The English Medieval Landscape*, London, 1982. Pp. 225

Chibnall, A.C., *Sherington: Fiefs and Fields of a Buckinghamshire Village*, Cambridge, 1965. Pp. 304

Clanchy, M.T., *From Memory to Written Record, England 1066–1307*, London, 1979. Pp. 330

Colvin, H., *The White Canons of England*, Oxford, 1951. Pp. 459

Cosgrove, D.E., *Social Formation and Symbolic Landscape*, London, 1984. Pp. 293

Cosgrove, D.E., Daniels, S., eds, *The Iconography of Landscape: Essays on the Symbolic Representation, Designs and Use of Past-Environments*, Cambridge, 1988. Pp. ix, 318

Cosgrove, D.E., Petts, G., eds, *Water, Engineering and Landscape: Water Control and Landscape Transformation in the Modern Period*, London, 1990. Pp. xiv, 214

Coss, P., *Lordship, Knighthood and Locality: A Study in English Society c. 1180–c.1280*, Cambridge, 1991. Pp. 361

Cozens-Hardy, B., *The History of Letheringsett; with Extracts from the Diary of Mary Hardy (1773–1809)*, Norwich, 1957. Pp. 172

Darby, H.C., *The Medieval Fenland*, Cambridge, 1940; new edn, Newton Abbot, 1974. Pp. 200

– *The Domesday Geography of Eastern England*, Cambridge, 1971. Pp. 400

– *Domesday England*, Cambridge, 1977. Pp. 430

Darby, H.C., ed., *A New Historical Geography of England Before 1600*, Cambridge, 1973. Pp. 767

Denholm-Young, N., *Richard of Cornwall*, Oxford, 1947. Pp. 187

Dodgshon, R.A., *The Origin of British Field Systems: An Interpretation*, London, 1980. Pp. xiv, 165

Dodgshon, R.A., *The European Past: Social Evolution and Spatial Order*, Basingstoke, 1987. Pp. xi, 403

Dodwell, B., 'Holdings and Inheritance in Medieval East Anglia', *Economic History Review* XX (1967), 53–66

Douglas, D.C., *The Social Structure of Medieval East Anglia*, Oxford Studies in Social and Legal History, IX (1927). Pp. 288

Duby, G., *La Société au XIe et XIIe Siècles dans la Région Mâconnaise*, Paris, 1953. Pp. 688

– *Guerriers et Paysans: Essai sur la Première Croissance Économique de l'Europe*, Paris, 1973. Pp. 308

– *Hommes et Structures du Moyen Age*, Paris, 1973. Pp. 424

– *Les Trois Ordres ou l'Imaginaire du Féodalisme*, Paris, 1978. Pp. 428

– *The Knight, the Lady and the Priest: The Making of Modern Marriage in Medieval France* (transl. from the French), Harmondsworth, 1983. Pp. 311

– *William Marshal: The Flower of Chivalry* (transl. from the French), London, 1985. Pp. 155

– *L'Histoire Continue*, Paris, 1991. Pp. 221

Dyer, C., *Standards of Living in the Later Middle Ages*, Cambridge, 1989. Pp. 297

Dymond, D., *The Norfolk Landscape*, London, 1985. Pp. 279

Eden, P., 'Land Surveyors in Norfolk, 1550–1850', Pt. I, 'The Estate Surveyors', *Norfolk Archaeology*, XXXV (1973), 474–82

– 'Land Surveyors in Norfolk, 1550–1850', Pt. II, 'The Surveyors of Inclosure', *Norfolk Archaeology*, XXXVI (1975), 119–48

– 'Three Elizabethan Estate Surveyors: Peter Kempe, Thomas Clerke and Thomas Langdon', *English Map-Making 1500–1650: Historical Essays* (S. Tyacke, ed.), London, 1983, 68–84

Emden, A.B., *A Biographical Register of the University of Cambridge to 1500*, Cambridge, 1963. Pp. 695

Farmer, D.H., *The Oxford Dictionary of Saints*, Oxford, 1987. Pp. 478

Field, J., *English Field Names*, Newton Abbot, 1972. Pp. 291

Fossier, R., *La Terre et les Hommes en Picardie jusqu'à la Fin du XIIIe Siècle*, 2 vols, Paris-Louvain, 1968. Pp. 817

– *La Société Médiévale*, Paris, 1991. Pp. 464

Foxall, H.D.G., *Shropshire Field Names*, Shrewsbury, 1980. Pp. 98

Gelling, M., *Signposts to the Past: Place-Names and the History of England*, London, 1978. Pp. 256

– *Place-Names in the Landscape*, London, 1984. Pp. ix, 326

Glasscock, R.E., ed., *The Lay Subsidy of 1334*, Oxford, 1975. Pp. xxxvii, 516

– *Historic Landscapes of Britain from the Air*, Cambridge, 1992. Pp. 256

Gray, H.L., *The English Field Systems*, London, 1915; new edn, 1959. Pp. 568

Gregory, T., Gurney, D., *Excavations at Thornham, Warham, Wighton and Caistor St Edmund, Norfolk*, Gressenhall, 1986. Pp. 62

Hadfield, M., *A History of British Gardening*, 1960; new edn, Harmondsworth, 1985. Pp. 509

– *Landscape with Trees*, London, 1967. Pp. 199

– *The English Landscape Garden*, London, 1977. Pp. 72

Hall, C.P., Ravensdale J.R., eds, *The West Fields of Cambridge*, Cambridge, 1976. Pp. 168

Hall, D., *Fenland Landscapes and Settlements Between Peterborough and March*, Cambridge, 1987. Pp. 72

Hallam, H.E., 'Some Thirteenth-Century Censuses', *Economic History Review*, X (1958), 340–61

– *Settlement and Society: A Study of the Early Agrarian History of South Lincolnshire*, Cambridge, 1965. Pp. 277

– *Rural England, 1066–1348*, London, 1981. Pp. 309

– 'The Climate of Eastern England', *Agricultural History Review*, XXXII (1984), 124–32

Hallam, H.E., ed., *The Agrarian History of England and Wales*, vol. 2 (1042–1350), Cambridge, 1988. Pp. 1086

Hanawalt, B.A. ed., *Crime in East Anglia in the Fourteenth Century: Norfolk Gaol Delivery Rolls, 1307–16*, N.R.S. XLIV, Norwich, 1976. Pp. 150

– *Women and Work in Pre-industrial Europe*, Bloomington, 1986. Pp. 233

Harper-Bill, C., ed., *English Episcopal Acta VI Norwich 1070–1214*, Oxford, 1990. Pp. lxxxviii, 439

Harvey, P.D.A., ed., *The Peasant Land Market in England*, Oxford, 1984. Pp. 375

Hassall, W.O., 'Views from the Holkham Windows', *Tribute to an Antiquary, Essays Presented to Mark Fitch* (E. Emmison, R. Stephens, eds), London, 1976, 305–19

Hassall, W.O., ed., *Cartulary of St Mary Clerkenwell*, Camden 3rd ser., LXXI, London, 1949. Pp. 358

– *A Catalogue of the Library of Sir Edward Coke*, Yale Law Library Publications 12, London-Oxford, 1950. Pp. 98

– *The Holkham Bible Picture Book*, London, 1954. Pp. vii, 152 with 42 plates

– *The Holkham Library: Illuminations and Illustrations in the Manuscript Library of the Earl of Leicester*, The Roxburghe Club, Oxford, 1970. Pp. xii, 48, 160 plates

Higounet, C., *Paysages et Villages Neufs du Moyen Age*, Bordeaux, 1975. Pp. 486

– *Villes, Sociétés et Economies Médiévales*, Bordeaux, 1992. Pp. 600

Hill, D.R., *A History of Engineering in Classical and Medieval Times*, London, 1984. Pp. 263

Hillier, B. and Hanson, J., *The Social Logic of Space*, Cambridge, 1984. Pp. 281

Hilton, R.H., *The English Peasantry in the Later Middle Ages and Related Studies*, The Ford Lectures for 1973, Oxford, 1975. Pp. 256

– *A Medieval Society: The West Midlands at the End of the Thirteenth Century*, 1967; new edn, Cambridge, 1983. Pp. 305

– *Class Conflict and the Crisis of Feudalism*, 1985; new edn, London, 1990. Pp. 255

– 'Medieval Market Towns and Simple Commodity Production', *Past and Present*, CIX (1985), 1–36

– *English and French Towns in Feudal Society*, Cambridge, 1992. Pp. 174

Hilton, R.H., Aston, T.H., eds, *The English Rising of 1381*, Cambridge, 1984. Pp. vi, 220

Hindle, B., *Medieval Roads*, Aylesbury, 1982. Pp. 62

Holt, R.A., *The Mills of Medieval England*, Oxford, 1988. Pp. x, 202

Homans, G.C., *English Villagers of the Thirteenth Century*, 1941; new edn, New York, 1975. Pp. 478

Hooke, D., *Medieval Villages: A Review of Current Work*, Oxford, 1985. Pp. 223

– *The Anglo-Saxon Landscape: The Kingdom of Hwicce*, Manchester, 1985. Pp. 270

Hooke, D., ed., *Anglo-Saxon Settlements*, Oxford, 1988. Pp. 320

Horwood, A.J., *Ninth Report of the Royal Commission on Historical Manuscripts*, part one, Report and Appendix, 'The Earl of Leicester', xvi–xvii, 1883, and part two, Appendix and Index, 'The Manuscripts of the Right Honourable the Earl of Leicester, Holkham Hall, Norfolk', 357–375, London, 1884

Hoskins, W.G., *The Midland Peasant*, London, 1957. Pp. 322

– *Provincial England*, London, 1963. Pp. 236

– *Local History in England*, 1959; new edn, London, 1972. Pp. 268

– *The Making of the English Landscape*, London, 1955; Harmondsworth, 1970. Pp. 327; 1988 (with an introduction and commentary by C. Taylor); London, 1992 (paperback). Pp. 256

Hunt, J.D., Willis, P., eds, *The Genius of the Place: The English Landscape Garden 1620–1820*, Cambridge (Mass.), 1990. Pp. 392

Jellicoe, G. and S., *The Landscape of Man: Shaping the Environment from Prehistory to the Present Day*, 1975; revised edn, London, 1987. Pp. 400

Jessopp, A., *Historical Manuscripts Commission, Report on Manuscripts in Various Collections*, 'Charters, Early Conveyances, Court Rolls, etc. of the Right Honourable the Earl of Leicester, preserved at Holkham Hall, Norfolk', IV, London, 1907, 313–325

Jones, A., 'Land Measurement in England 1150–1350', *Agricultural History Review*, XXVII (1979), 10–18

Kealey, E.J., *Harvesting the Air: Windmill Pioneers in Twelfth Century England*, Woodbridge, 1987. Pp. 307

Kent, N., *General View of the Agriculture of the County of Norfolk with Observations on the Means of Improvement*, London, 1794. Pp. 56

Kerridge, E., *The Agricultural Revolution*, London, 1967. Pp. 428

Kershaw, I., 'The Great Famine and Agrarian Crisis in England, 1315–22', *Past and Present*, LIX (May 1973), 3–50

Kosminsky, E.A., *Studies in the Agrarian History of England in the Thirteenth Century* (R.H. Hilton, ed.), Oxford, 1956. Pp. 370

Kussmaul, A., *Servants in Husbandry in Early Modern England*, Cambridge, 1981. Pp. xii, 233

Langdon, J., *Horses, Oxen and Technological Innovation: The Use of Draught Animals in English Farming from 1066 to 1500*, Cambridge, 1986. Pp. lxvi, 329

– 'Water-mills and Windmills in the West Midlands, 1086–1500', *Economic History Review*, XLIV (1991), 424–44

Laslett, P., *The World We have Lost: Further Explored*, London, 1983. Pp. 353

Lawson, A.J. et al., eds, *Barrow Excavations in Norfolk, 1950–82*, Gressenhall, 1986. Pp. 125

Leadam, I.D., 'The Inquisition of 1517. Inclosures and Evictions', Pt. II, *T.R.H.S.*, NS, VII (1893), 127–292

Le Roy Ladurie, E., *Les Paysans de Languedoc*, 2 vols, Paris, 1966. Pp. 1035

– *Montaillou, village occitan de 1294 à 1324*, Paris, 1975. Pp. 642

Mac Farlane, A., *The Origins of English Individualism*, Oxford, 1978. Pp. 216

Maitland, F.W., *Domesday Book and Beyond: Three Essays on the Early History of England*, Cambridge, 1897; new edn, 1987. Pp. 527

Maitland, F.W., ed., *The Court Baron with Select Pleas from the Bishop of Ely's Court of Littleport*, Selden Society, IV, London, 1891. Pp. 158

Marshall, W., *The Rural Economy of Norfolk, Comprising the Management of Landed Estates, and the Present Practice of Husbandry in that County*, 2 vols, London, 1787. Pp. xvii, 400; ix, 392

Miller, E., ed., *The Agrarian History of England and Wales*, vol. 3 (1348–1500), Cambridge, 1991. Pp. xxv, 982

Mingay, G.E., *A Social History of the English Countryside*, London-New York, 1990. Pp. 246

Oman, C., ed., *The Great Revolt of 1381*, Oxford, 1906; new edn, 1969. Pp. 219

Owen, D.M., *The Making of King's Lynn: A Documentary Survey* R.S.E.H., n.s. IX, Oxford, 1984. Pp. 513

Palgrave, F., ed., *The Parliamentary Writs and Writs of Military Summons*, 2 vols in 5, London, 1827–34

Parker, R.A.C., 'Coke of Norfolk and the Agrarian Revolution', *Economic History Review*, VIII (1955), 156–66

– *Coke of Norfolk, a Financial and Agricultural Study*, Oxford, 1975. Pp. 222

Penning-Rowsell, E.C., Lowenthal, D., eds, *Landscape Meanings and Values*, London, 1986. Pp. 160

Pickering, F.P., ed., *The Anglo-Norman Text of the Holkham Bible Picture Book*, Oxford, 1971, Pp. ccv, 136

Poos, L., Smith, R.M., 'Legal Windows onto Historical Populations?: Recent Research on the Demography and the Manor Court in Medieval England', *Law and History Review*, II (1984), 128–52

– 'Shades Still on the Window?: A Reply to Zvi Razi', *Law and History Review*, III (1986), 409–29

Postan, M.M., *The Medieval Economy and Society*, London, 1972. Pp. 296

Postgate, M.R., 'Field Systems of East Anglia', *Studies of Field Systems of the British Isles* (A.R.H.. Baker and R.A. Butlin, eds), Cambridge, 1973, 281–324

Powicke, F.M., *King Henry III and the Lord Edward: The Community of the Realm in the Thirteenth Century*, 2 vols, Oxford, 1947. Pp. 858

   – *Stephen Langton*, London, 1928; new edn, 1965. Pp. 227

Pye, K., ed., *A Scientific Bibliography of the North Norfolk Coast*, Cambridge, 1991. Pp. 14

Ravensdale, J.R., *Liable to Floods: Village Landscape on the Edge of the Fens, 450–1850*, Cambridge, 1974. Pp. 206

Ravensdale, J.R., Muir, R., *East Anglian Landscapes: Past and Present*, London, 1984. Pp. 256

Razi, Z., *Life, Marriage and Death in a Medieval Parish: Economy, Society and Demography in Halesowen, 1270–1400*, Cambridge, 1980. Pp. 162

   – 'The Use of Manorial Court Rolls in Demographic Analysis: A Reconsideration', *Law and History Review*, III (1985), 191–200

   – 'The Demographic Transparency of Manorial Court Rolls', *Law and History Review*, V (1987), 524–35

Réville, A., *Le Soulèvement des Travailleurs d'Angleterre en 1381*, Paris, 1898. Pp. 346

Riches, N., *The Agricultural Revolution in Norfolk*, London, 1967. Pp. 194

Roberts, B.K., *Rural Settlement in Britain*, London, 1979. Pp. 221

   – *The Making of the English Village: A Study in Historical Geography*, Harlow, 1987. Pp. 234

Roberts, B.K., Glasscock, R.E., eds, *Villages, Fields and Frontiers: Studies in European Rural Settlement in the Medieval and Early Modern Periods*, Oxford, 1983. Pp. xvii, 433

Round, J.H., ed., *Rotuli de Dominabus et Pueris et Puellis de xii Comitatibus [1185]*, PRS, XXXV, London, 1913. Pp. 132

Rowley, T., ed., *The Origins of Open Field Agriculture*, London, 1984. Pp. 258

Russell, J.C., *British Medieval Population*, Albuquerque, 1948. Pp. 389

Rye, W., *Scandinavian Names in Norfolk. Hundred Courts, Mote Hills, Toothills and Roman Camps and Remains in Norfolk*, Norwich, 1920. Pp. 56

Sanders, I.J., *English Baronies: A Study of Their Origin and Descent 1086–1327*, Oxford, 1960. Pp. 203

Sawyer, P.H., ed., *Medieval Settlement: Continuity and Change*, London, 1976. Pp. 357

Schmidt, L., *Holkham Hall, Studien zur Architektur und Ausstattung*, Ph.D. Diss., Freiburg-im-Breisgau, 1980. Pp. 158, 54 plates

   – *Thomas Coke, 1st Earl of Leicester, an Eighteenth-Century Amateur Architect*, Freiburg-im-Breisgau, 1980. Pp. 20, 31 plates

Schofield, R.S., 'The Geographical Distribution of Wealth in England, 1354–1649', *Economic History Review*, XVIII (1965), 483–510

Simpson, A., 'The East Anglian Foldcourse: Some Queries', *Agricultural History Review*, VI (1958), 87–96

Slicher Van Bath, B.H., *The Agrarian History of Western Europe, 500–1850*, London, 1963. Pp. 364

Smith, R.M., 'Coping with Uncertainty: Women's Tenure of Customary Land in England, c. 1370–1430', *Enterprise and Individuals in Fifteenth Century England* (J. Kermode et al., eds), Far Thrupp Stroud (Gloucs.), 1991, 43–67

Smith, R.M., ed., *Land, Kinship and Life-Cycle*, Cambridge, 1984. Pp. xiii, 547

Stephens, N., ed., *Natural Landscapes of Britain from the Air*, Cambridge, 1990. Pp. 288

Stroud, D., *Capability Brown*, London, 1950; new edn, 1975. Pp. 262

Taylor, C., *Fields in the English Landscape*, London, 1975; new edn, 1982. Pp. 174

– *Roads and Tracks of Britain*, London, 1979; new edn, 1982. Pp. 210

– *Village and Farmstead: A History of Rural Settlement in England*, London, 1983. Pp. 254

Thomas, K., *Man and the Natural World: Changing Attitudes in England, 1500–1800*, Harmondsworth, 1983. Pp. 246

Thirsk, J., ed., *The Agrarian History of England and Wales*, vol. 4 (1500–1640), Cambridge, 1967. Pp. xl, 919

Venn, J., and, J.A., *Alumni Cantabrigenses*, part I, Cambridge, 1924. Pp. 504

Wade-Martins, P., 'The Origins of Rural Settlement in East Anglia', *Recent Work in Rural Archaeology* (P.J. Fowler, ed.), London, 1975, 137–57

– 'The Archaeology of Medieval Rural Settlement in East Anglia', *The Rural Settlements of Medieval England: Studies Dedicated to Maurice Beresford and John Hurst* (M. Aston, D. Austin, C. Dyer, eds), Oxford, 1989, 149–65

Wade-Martins, P., ed., *Norfolk from the Air*, photographs principally by D.A. Edwards, Norwich, 1987. Pp. 168

Wade-Martins, S., *A Great Estate at Work: The Holkham Estate and its Inhabitants in the Nineteenth Century*, Cambridge, 1980. Pp. 288

Williams, R., *The Country and the City*, London, 1973; new edn, 1985. Pp. 335

Williamson, J., 'Norfolk: Thirteenth Century', *The Peasant Land Market in England* (P.D.A. Harvey, ed.), Oxford, 1984, 31–102

Willis, D., ed., *The Estate Book of Henry de Bray*, Camden 3rd ser., XXVII, London, 1916. Pp. 159

Wood, M., *The English Medieval House*, London, 1981. Pp. 448

Wrigley, E.A., 'City and Country in the Past: A Sharp Divide or a Continuum', *Historical Research*, LXIV (1991), 107–20

Wrigley, E.A., Schofield, R.S., *The Population History of England, 1541–1871: A Reconstruction* (with contributions from R. Lee and J. Oeppen), Cambridge, 1989. Pp. 779

Young, A., *General View of the Agriculture of Norfolk, Drawn up for the Consideration of the Board of Agriculture and Internal Improvement*, London, 1813. Pp. xx, 532

INTRODUCTION

Chapter 1

The Holkham Hall Muniments

The medieval records of Holkham printed in this book are the earliest documents, preserved at Holkham Hall, among the family and estate papers of the Coke family, Earls of Leicester.[1] These documents constitute the medieval foundation of the Holkham Hall muniments, kept in the new archive rooms located in the Kitchen Wing of the Palladian Hall. The Holkham seat of the Earls of Leicester is situated on the north-west coast of the County of Norfolk.

We consider the Holkham Hall muniments, as to the quality of their medieval holdings, to be one of the richest seigneurial archives in England held privately. We wish to express formally our gratitude to the Right Honourable Viscount Coke, to his predecessors and to his ancestors, as lords of Holkham, for keeping their muniments so well and so carefully. The chance and fruitful encounter of two scholars and the authorization of the noble owner of these records made possible their publication hereunder presented.

THE CATALOGUE OF THE MUNIMENTS AND OUR EDITION

It was in 1610 that the first connection of the Coke family with Holkham was established. Sir Edward Coke (1552–1634), Lord Chief Justice, bought in that year Neel or Lucas manor for £3,400 to house his fourth son, John, of the Inner Temple. Two years later John Coke married Meriel Wheatley, the heiress of Hillhall Manor in Holkham (1612). Neel Manor in Holkham was one of the many estates in many counties which the great lawyer assembled for the endowment of his family. He recorded the process in his *Great Book of Conveyances* (Holkham Ms. 764). The *Great Book* ignored the medieval records in the evidence room of the old house of Hillhall. Other local estates (with such earlier title deeds as survived) were systematically absorbed during the next two centuries. Another 'Evidence Chamber' is mentioned in 1653 at Godwick (Holkham General Estate Deed 30).

With the extinction of various families of the heirs of Sir Edward Coke, the remains of his 'Great Estate' were eventually reunited in the conscientious hands of the guardians of Thomas Coke (1697–1759), builder of Holkham Hall and first Earl of Leicester (cr. 1744). In February and

---

1   Cf. NRA no. 12332, Coke family, Earls of Leicester, family and estate papers: Contents, catalogues and 2 vols of transcripts.

March 1707 the guardians employed Messrs. Jacombe and Gibson to examine all the writings of the Estate, make catalogues of them and 'that account be taken of what are enrolled'.[2] In 1708 Mr. Christopher Bedingfield made an 'abstract of the most material deeds' about Norfolk and Suffolk. He ignored medieval deeds. Matthew Brettingham (1699–1769) illustrated a short-lived counting house on the front of the Hall and Lady Leicester's inventory of 1774 listed its furniture.[3] But in the time of Coke of Norfolk (1754–1842), second 'first' Earl of Leicester (recr. 1837), Francis Blaikie, his agent, kept his papers beneath the 'Strangers Wing'.

A new system of recording was begun in 1851–2 by the second Earl's agent, H.W. Keary. In 1854 new stables, west of the house, formed a complex which included a new estate office. This had a purpose-built strong-room, where the muniments were kept in tin trunks on iron frames, reaching the lofty ceiling. The muniments stayed in the strongroom of the estate office until 1985. In 1985 Lord Coke, while Nicholas Pickwoad of Norwich was engaged on conservation of the Holkham Books, had the tin trunks taken upstairs in the Kitchen Wing to newly converted archive rooms arranged by Mrs. Hiskey.[4]

Between 1890 and 1916 the two series of Holkham catalogues which ordered the title deeds and estate papers, and thus the medieval documents printed here, were compiled. E.J.L. Scott's catalogue is dated 1890 and was made as a consequence of A.J. Horwood's report on the manuscript library for the Royal Commission on Historical Manuscripts of 1884.[5] It is arranged in one long numerical series of documents. The documents were grouped alphabetically, by county, and subdivided by parish. Wills were placed together at the end. H.A. Davidson continued Scott's work between 1912 and 1916 and, as his predecessor, arranged the documents in chronological order.

We decided to print the documents in the same numerical order as is given in the two series of Holkham catalogues. Numbers allocated by

---

2   Holkham Ms. 743: Minutes of the proceedings of the Hon. Charles Bertie, Esq., Sir Edward Coke, Bart., Sir John Newton, Bart., and John Coke, Esq., appointed guardians of Thomas Coke, Esq., of Holkham in the County of Norfolk, pp. 51 (17 Feb. 1707) and 54 (5 March 1707).

3   Matthew Brettingham (1699–1769), architect, pupil of William Kent (1658–1748). After the death of William Kent he completed the erection of Holkham Hall (1734–64). He published, in 1761, *The Plans, Elevations and Sections of Holkham in Norfolk, the Seat of the Late Earl of Leicester*, Atlas in Folio. The work of Leopold Schmidt shows that the main architect of Holkham was actually Thomas Coke, Earl of Leicester, himself. Cf. *Thomas Coke, 1st Earl of Leicester, an Eighteenth-Century Amateur Architect*, 1980, and *Holkham Hall, Studien zur Architektur und Ausstattung*, Ph. D. Diss. (Freiburg im Breisgau, 1980).

4   N. Pickwoad, Report on the Books at Holkham Hall, 5 May 1983, *Archives*, p. 24, (typescript at Holkham Hall).

5   A.J. Horwood, HMC, Ninth Report, Pt. II, Append., 1884, pp. 344–5. The findings of the commission were summarized in 1907 by Augustus Jessopp in a report on the Holkham Estate office, HMC, Various Collections, iv, pp. 313–25.

Davidson and Scott are used as references and the abbreviations HD (Holkham Documents) and HP (Holkham Papers) are used to designate the series described by Davidson and Scott respectively.[6]

Inevitably, in the cataloguing process some documents were assigned to the wrong parish or century. This has meant that a few documents in the numerical series were excluded from our texts. HD 15 to 17 were omitted, as they were wrongly dated by Davidson. HD 39 related to Burghwodehall in Godwick, not to Burghall, and should have been placed among Tittleshall and not among Holkham documents. HD 19a was a late sixteenth century transcript about Knight's Fees in North Greenhoe and was omitted, as it is printed in *Feudal Aids 1284–1432*, and reproduced in Fiche 1: B6.[7] HD 80 was omitted, as it is a summary of suits about folds and wrecks in Burghall and Wighton leets, 1325–1576, but it was reproduced in Fiche 1: E12. The texts of the Burghall rental and of the Feodary were superior in the Neel Cartulary (HD 22a) to that in HD 4a and 4b and HD 5a and 5b. These latter were omitted, and their variants were relegated to footnotes, while the better copies in the cartulary were printed. For the Peterstone terrier in Holkham (1315) the best text, kept in the Burnham Box as BD 28, was included here and collated with the texts of HD 205 and HD 300.

Davidson made separate parcels for charters and for court rolls within his series for each century. This explains the omission of HD 48–78, except for an excerpt from HD 75 listing lords of Hillhall. HD 155 was placed with HD 75 because it was an alternative version of the same document containing supplementary information. The only irregularity in the numerical series made by Scott was the omission of HP 1061. No such document ever existed. The chronological sequence of documents sometimes failed to correspond to the order in the catalogue, as Davidson had wrongly placed some early fourteenth century charters in the thirteenth century parcels. The cause of this was that the regnal year given in the Mss. occasionally confused Edward I and Edward II through the omission of 'filii Edwardi' or 'secundi'.

THE STRUCTURE OF THE EDITION

The documents are grouped under 159 reference numbers. They all belong to the Holkham Hall muniments series of HD and HP, except for our last two documents which belong to the Public Record Office. In fact, our 159

---

6   Edward John Long Scott (1840–1918) was Assistant in the Department of Manuscripts, British Museum, 1868, Keeper, 1888, latterly Keeper of Muniments at Westminster Abbey. H.A. Davidson was the son of a Scottish game keeper. He deplored his inability to read early handwriting and the insufficiency of his Latin. Inside the tin trunks, E.J.L. Scott had white cardboard (acid free) boxes such as the British Museum used. But H.A. Davidson had to be content with brown paper parcels. Scott evidently had clerical help, as it has been observed that the catalogue was not in his handwriting.

7   *Feudal Aids*, vol. 3, p. 54.

reference numbers include a larger collection of single documents. In some cases, several documents of different types are gathered under the same numerical reference. First among these 'multiple' documents is, obviously, the Neel Cartulary (HD 22a), which alone contains 267 items, of which we are printing 259. But no. 260 of the cartulary, Lucas's Gazetteer, itself includes 107 different entries, referring, summarising, surveying, dating and locating purchases of land in 107 different purchase operations, corresponding, in fact, to 107 other original documents. HD 6, HD 14, HD 20, HD 79, HD 81, HD 82 are also 'multiple' items. HD 6 is a fourteenth-century copy or summary, made at Holkham, of 29 West Dereham Abbey charters for the early part of the thirteenth century. HD 14 includes 3 manor court records of the manor of Hillhall in Holkham (1312 and 1322) and one list of tenants in 1312. HD 20 contains the rental of the manor of Peter le Bret (1302) and also seven short manor courts of Peter and Eustace le Bret (later Neel), and the first surviving court of Richard Neel (20 Nov. 1314). HD 79 includes 6 courts of Richard Neel, lord of the new manor (1322, 1325, 1324, 1327, 1329, 1329), in the order of their position on the membrane. HD 81 includes four documents: one agenda arising from Neel manor court of 1329, a list of tenements in Holkham acquired by the Neels (1329), another agenda from the Neel manor court of 1329, and an account of the rents due for the dower lands of Katerine Neel in Burnham (1329). HD 82 includes a Burghall manor court (3 July 1332), a Burghall collector's account (June–Sept. 1332) and the Burghall leet court of 22 July 1332. The two courts were written on the same membrane, and the account of Richard Blakeman was sewn over the leet court, with the obvious intention of linking them closely, in the manorial records and archive at the time.

Part I   HD 1–HD 21, c. 1250–1322:
16 reference numbers, charters and manorial documents, 8 grants, 2 quit-claims, 1 final concord, 3 series of manor courts, 3 rentals.

Part II   HD 22a, Neel Cartulary, 1414–c.1460:
55v folios (paper), 1 reference number including 267 numbered copies of documents of which 259 are printed here, 1 inquisition, 1 feodary, 1 rental, 1 pedigree, 251 summaries or copies of charters, 1 copy of a presentation charter, 1 alphabetical gazetteer and 2 terriers. (Cf. description of HD 22a at the beginning of the text of the Neel Cartulary.)

Part III   HD 22b–HD 205, c. 1291–1352:
31 reference numbers, charters and manorial documents, 14 grants, 1 confirmation, 4 letters of attorney, 1 final concord, 3 hayward's accounts, 1 collector's account, 1 terrier, 1 rental, 2 courts baron, 1 leet court, 2 court agendas, 1 list of tenements purchased, 1 account of dower lands, 1 sub-escheator certificate, 1 acquittance from the Officiality of Norwich.

Part IV   HP 995–HP 1103, HP 3808, c. 1270–1350:
109 reference numbers, charters and miscellaneous documents, 72 grants, 16 quitclaims, 9 confirmations, 6 letters of attorney, 1 manorial lease indenture, 4 bonds, 1 will with probate.

Part V   PRO E 179/149/9 m. 32 (1332–3), PRO C 47/2/25 no. 18 (1336–7):
2 reference numbers, royal documents, 1 lay subsidy return for Holkham, 1 inquisition on Holkham ships.

THE TYPES OF DOCUMENTS

As we have just shown, our volume includes a variety of medieval documents, but a very large proportion of them belonged to the category of original charters or grants as instruments of land conveyance. Our edition is constituted, for its larger part, by original charters, grants and their supporting documents, as quitclaims, confirmations or letters of attorney (132). The number of charters included is even greater if we add to the original charters all the summaries of grants included in the Neel Cartulary. Far behind, in second position, come manorial documents of different kinds as originals or as copies (36). There are also four bonds and other 'miscellaneous' documents (8), and the remaining few documents emanated from the Exchequer, the Chancery or other royal courts (9). But our centrepiece is the Neel Cartulary (1) whose exceptional features provide, with this first edition of Holkham medieval records, the opening of new and fruitful perspectives on the problem we had aimed to investigate at the outset: the origins of the economic and social distinctiveness of medieval East Anglia. The Neel Cartulary and the other seigneurial registers and terriers of the medieval muniments of Holkham Hall led us to an immediate, and perhaps facile, answer: the East Anglian distinctiveness relied, in part, on the relatively high cultural level attained by its lay seigneurial group, especially at the local level, in the early fifteenth century, with its evident consequences for adept estate-management and agricultural productivity.[8]

---

[8]   On medieval Norfolk as a populated and highly developed county, cf. H.E. Hallam, ed. *The Agrarian History of England and Wales*, 1988, vol. 2, pp. 139–40, 272–98, 508–16, 594–603.

Charters and supporting documents *(originals)*

Grants	Quitclaims	Confirmations	Letters of Attorney
94	18	10	10

Total: 132

Manorial documents *(originals and copies)*

Courts	Rentals	Terriers	Accounts
18	5	4	4

Total: 31

Related manorial documents *(originals)*

Court agenda	Account of dower lands	Lease Indenture	List of Lords
2	1	1	1

Total: 5

Miscellaneous Documents *(originals)*

Bonds	Wills	Probate	Acquittance by Officiality
4	1	1	1
	Pedigree		
	1		

Total: 8

Royal documents *(originals and copies)*

Final Concords	Feodary	Inquisitions	Lay subsidy return
4	1	2	1
	Subescheator Certificate		
	1		

Total: 9

Cartulary
1

Total: 1

Overall Total: 186

Our original charters (with quitclaims and confirmations) were chronologically distributed in two groups of almost equal size. The first group, between 1250–1310, included 61 charters with its concentration in the decade 1290–1300 (39), and only three charters in the decade 1300–10. The second group of original charters, with 59 charters, were dated between 1310 and 1350, 27 of them between 1314 and 1320. In addition, all our nine letters of attorney were dated between 1316 and 1337. Before 1300 a number of our charters did not have a dating clause, but this was not the case for the period after 1300, where almost all of them were dated. Most of the charters of the period before 1310 concerned the family of le Bret (Geoffrey, Adam, Peter, John) and their manors, while the second group of charters, between 1310 and 1350, concerned the Neel family of Burnham Norton, Richard and Katerine Neel and their sons Thomas and Gilbert Neel, new lords in Holkham. Thirty two charters, five quitclaims, one confirmation and seven letters of attorney had Richard and Katerine or Katerine Neel alone (after 1336) as parties, generally as grantees and buyers of land, i.e. 73% of all the original charters in this second group. The Holkham charters, after the Statute 'Quia emptores' of 1290, registered changes in formulation and generally replaced the 'Habendum et Tenendum de me' clause by an 'Habendum et tenendum de Capitalibus dominis feodi' clause. These transfers were sales of land which were not to be effected by way of sub-infeudation, as used to be the case before 1290.

One of the remarkable features of our *corpus* of documents is, that most of these 132 original charters were summarised and referred to in the Neel Cartulary, which we are also printing. The cartulary associated a repertory of documents organized chronologically with a survey of manorial lands by locations organized alphabetically, with dates of acquisition placed in the margin. Its author sought to have instant information on the location and history of each of his parcels, as the marginalia of his alphabetical gazetteer quoted, with Roman or Arabic numerals the year (only) of issuance of the original title deed. The medieval landowners were not using maps as their sixteenth-century counterparts were to do. Cartularies and terriers, and even charters with all their abuttals and location indications, were operating as maps or plans. Dealing with these manorial and estate-management documents implied, necessarily, a long training on the spot in the actual and very complex fields described.[9]

---

9   For the modern estate maps see Peter Eden, 'Land Surveyors in Norfolk, 1550–1850' Pt. I, *Norfolk Archaeology*, 1973, pp. 474–82; Pt. II, *Norfolk Archaeology* 1975, pp. 119–48, and *idem* 'Three Elizabethen Estate Surveyors: Peter Kempe, Thomas Clerke and Thomas Langdon', *English Map-Making 1500–1650: Historical Essays*, 1983, pp. 68–84.

The fact that such a number of original medieval charters of the thirteenth and first part of the fourteenth centuries, preserved in close relationship to the cartulary which had used them in the early part of the fifteenth century, remained in their original place over seven hundred years and in the same and still seigneurial muniments, is perhaps a unique circumstance. It allows us to get nearer to an understanding of the practical use of medieval records in their own time and their own setting and of their meaning for their medieval authors, as medieval records were and are much more than simply sources for the social historians of today.

MANORIAL DOCUMENTS

There were several manors in medieval Holkham. Our documents illustrate the most important ones. Except for the manor court rolls between 1330 and 1350, relatively incomplete and scattered over these twenty years, we print here all the manorial documents which have survived. To retain the valuable information contained in the manor courts, we have elaborated a prosopography of the tenants during these two latter decades, which we publish in Appendix 1.

In this volume we print the first eighteen Holkham manor courts which have survived, dated between 1312 and 1332, for three Holkham Manors: Hillhall, Bret-Neel and Burghall (HD 14, HD 20, HD 79, HD 82). Among them is one leet court of 1332, prerogative of the lord of Burghall Manor. These manor courts had the formal characteristics of seigneurial courts of smaller secular estates. Sometimes very short, their business was not ordered with the care shown in the series of court rolls of the larger manors of religious houses.

The rentals and lists of tenants of various dates between 1250 and 1350 which have survived concern four Holkham manors: Hillhall, Bret, Burghall and Peterstone. The most detailed and thoroughly informative is the Burghall rental of c. 1273 (no. 255 in Neel Cartulary), and the three rentals of Bret Manor (HD 11, 1293–4, HD 20, 1302, HD 21, 1311–14) were fundamental for the history of the Neel Manor which was its direct successor. We have a few documents later than 1350, especially in the Neel Cartulary, itself a fifteenth-century document (1414–1460), among which one is difficult to define strictly: No. 261 in the Neel Cartulary, *Terra solidata per nativos in manus Gilberti Neel et heredum suorum* (c. 1390), is a list of former freehold lands held for cash rent by three bond tenants. The document, which is no. 262 of the Neel Cartulary, *Terre nativorum tenencium in manus domini de Feodo Gilberti Neel in Holkham* (c. 1390), is a terrier, as it describes exclusively lands, parcel by parcel. The first of three Hillhall manor courts, of 1 May 1312 (HD 14), has an interesting list of tenants.

Terriers as 'descriptions of lands that follow a topographical arrangement, proceeding parcel by parcel through the fields' are the great strength of the Holkham Hall muniments from the fourteenth to the sixteenth century. We plan to print the most important of them with a selection of charters, accounts and court rolls in a second volume of Holkham records (1350–1600) to document English social structure and the evolution of English medieval seigneurial agriculture and productivity in a crucial period. We are able, in this first volume of records, to publish the specially detailed terrier of Peterstone Priory in Holkham fields (1315, HD 205 VIIa), where ninety-nine and a half acres in fifty-four parcels are described with their crops. This document shows precisely the crop rotation system in use in Holkham at the beginning of the fourteenth century. Finally, the Neel Cartulary (HD 22a), our central item, is in fact also a systematically organized terrier for the managing purposes of an adept and diligent small secular lord of the first half of the fifteenth century.

We are printing here the four manorial official accounts which survive for Holkham from before 1352, three hayward's accounts for the manor of Hillhall (1349–52) and the first collector's account for the manor of Burghall in 1332, when Richard Neel with three partners took the manor of Burghall in Holkham at farm from the Earl of Atholl (HD 45, 46, 47, 82). We do not, unfortunately, have any reeve's account for the period of demesne farming at Burghall Manor before 1332.

MISCELLANEOUS AND ROYAL DOCUMENTS

We can place in the category of miscellaneous documents the four bonds or contracts of cash payments (1337–46, HP 1095, 1096, 1100, 1101). They concern the Neel family, whose rise to gentry status in Holkham, from Burnham Norton, can perhaps be related to mercantile and maritime fortune. The investment in merchant capital, which placed Gilbert Neel in partnership with two merchants, William de Barney and Benedict Scot of Horning, perhaps using the port of Holkham (1345, 1347, HP 1100, 1101), was undoubtedly indicative of the Neel family's social origins. However, the will of Thomas Neel (1350, HP 3808), elder son of Richard and Katerine Neel, which is the only one of our documents to follow the Annunciation style of reckoning, says very little. It is very different, in its brevity of style and contents, from the wills of the merchants of Bishop's Lynn nearby for the same period.[10]

---

10   Cf. Jacques Beauroy, 'Family Patterns and Relations of Bishop's Lynn Will Makers in the Fourteenth Century', in L. Bonfield, R.M. Smith, K. Wrightson, eds, *The World We Have Gained, Essays Presented to Peter Laslett*, 1986, pp. 23–42.

As for documents emanating from royal officials and courts, there are only four final concords, of which only one is an original (1341, HD 41), and a related subescheator certificate (1338, HD 40), the lay subsidy return for Holkham (1332, PRO E 179/149/9 m. 32), the inquisition on Holkham ships (1336, PRO C 47/2/25 no. 18), and the inquisition on folds (1306, HD 22a, no. 1), all particularly informative about the social structure of Holkham. We believe also that the Feodary (HD 22a, no. 253) is related to the Hundred Rolls inquiry of Edward I (1279–80).

THE NEEL CARTULARY

The choice of 1350 as a 'terminus ad quem' for this first volume of Holkham records was determined, primarily, by what appeared to be the main seigneurial event happening in Holkham in the first part of the fourteenth century, as told by an exceptional document.

The Neel Cartulary tells us the story of the creation of a new Holkham Manor between 1314 and 1345. The exceptional feature about it is the fact that, while it concerns a single manor and one landowning family only, it allows, by its sheer comprehensiveness, its elegant organization and the judicious selection of fundamental documents, the study of the whole of medieval Holkham, where there were several other co-terminous manors and lords. In itself it is clearly the fundamental medieval document of the muniments and the key to the history of medieval Holkham.

Godfrey Davis in his catalogue of medieval cartularies of Great Britain (1958) listed 1185 cartularies of religious houses and 159 secular cartularies – 1344 cartularies in all – among which the Neel Cartulary was no. 1299.[11] Most of these 159 secular cartularies concerned the upper layer of the knightly class and the baronial group. One consequence of this fact is that these cartularies were very rarely confined to the limits of one parish. While the Neel Cartulary focused exclusively on Holkham, its manors and its fields, other cartularies and registers copied or summarised charters and manorial documents scattered over several parishes and counties. The closest in scope among the five other secular cartularies listed for Norfolk are perhaps the Petigard Cartulary (Davis, no. 1307) concerning the parish of Sporle (and others in its vicinity) and the Fincham Cartulary (NRO, Hare of Stow Bardolf Collection, no. 199, 185 x 4) for Barton Bendish, Fincham and Should-hamthorpe, but their organization was absolutely conventional. The other three known Norfolk secular cartularies, the Narford Cartulary (Davis, no. 1298), the Thorp Cartulary (Davis, no. 1327) and the Norwich Cartulary

---

11   Davis, p. 151, no. 1299. The entry for the Neel Cartulary in Davis's catalogue is erroneous in many respects and is made obsolete by our edition.

(Davis, no. 1302) concern baronial possessions spread over the two counties of Norfolk and Suffolk.[12]

In the frontispiece of the text of the Neel Cartulary we provide a detailed description of the five quires of the register, written on 55 folios of imported paper bound with a parchment cover. The six different watermarks in filigrane point to Italian and Southern French sources of supply. It was composed and written by one author, Edmund Lucas, '*Domicellus*' of East Dereham, lord of Neel Manor in Holkham through his wife, between 1414 and 1435, with a few later interpolations in quires four and five.[13] The original composition, the ordering and the kind of documents copied or summarised, the reference system used to survey and thus to manage his land, makes it an exceptional document of medieval estate-management. It also constitutes a source for the study of the mind and culture of a small Norfolk lord in the early fifteenth century.

The holdings of the Holkham Hall muniments for the period 1250–1350 which we are printing here, were the working archive of Edmund Lucas. His cartulary was a 'systematic' terrier which he associated with the original reference charters found in his muniments chest in order to understand the descent of his land, gather the titles to their acquisition and direct to their precise location within the three great fields of medieval Holkham. The alphabetical repertory (HD 22a no. 260) which he organized between folios 41 and 50 showed his sense of rational management. Also, there was an attractive aspect in the historian's manner by which he reconstructed the legal base of his possessions in two main chapters. Using the original charters at his disposal, which he transcribed in summary and to which he gave a reference number, he placed, in the twelve first folios, 150 charters of the late thirteenth and early fourteenth centuries concerning the preceding manor of Bret. In folios 13 to 24 he placed the charters of the Neel purchases from 1314 to 1345. At folio 30 he placed the Neel pedigree (HD 22a no. 254), starting with the grandparents of his wife, founders of Neel Manor, and ending with his grandchildren. He had a clear cursive hand, and his capacity

---

12   It does seem that laymen in England started to practice cartulary-making in the thirteenth century. (M.T. Clanchy, *From Memory to Written Record, England 1066–1307*, 1979, p. 80) The earliest surviving lay cartulary is the Constable Cartulary from Yorkshire (Davis, no. 1224), dating from the 1200s. Four other early survivors are from Northamptonshire (second half of the thirteenth century and early fourteenth century): Richard Hotot's estate book (Davis, no. 1256), Ralph Basset's roll (Davis, no. 1188a), the Braybrooke Cartulary (Davis, no. 1206), and the Estate Book of Henry de Bray (Davis, nos. 1203, 1204), edited by Dorothy Willis in 1916 (Camden, third series, vol. 27). The social status of its author and the scope and contents of Henry de Bray's estate book bear some comparison with the Neel Cartulary, except for the fact that the Neel Cartulary was essentially a sophisticated estate-management instrument and not, like Henry de Bray's estate book, a family remembrancer.

13   Edmund Lucas made his will on Monday 25 April 1435, and died before Thursday 17 Nov. 1435, when his will was proved in Norwich, NCC, Fo. 185v Surflete.

for handling and relating all these Latin charters and documents and his fluent writing of Latin pointed to a literate, legal and administrative training.

THE HOLKHAM HALL MUNIMENTS

Medieval Holkham could well be the best documented parish in Norfolk, which is recognized to be 'one of the best documented counties in the country and in the Middle Ages further distinguished by a high density of population and relatively intense system of husbandry'.[14] The importance of Holkham in the modern phase of English social and agricultural history undoubtedly has a medieval foundation, which we aim to expound and explain. Edmund Lucas's cartulary is rather representative of several other Holkham seigneurial registers found in the Holkham Hall muniments from the second half of the fourteenth century to the sixteenth century. They form the basis for a second volume of records (1350–1600) which we plan to edit while engaged on a monograph on the social history of medieval Holkham.

Thomas Grigges's Hillhall Book of 114 folios (c. 1470, HD 75, HD 155) was certainly the most important of these Holkham registers following the Neel Cartulary. Most of the manors we have started to document in the present volume had, from the second half of the fourteenth century to the end of the sixteenth century, numerous rentals, terriers and accounts with further court rolls and charters. The fuller accounts concerned Burghall Manor for 1460–82 (HD 142). An essential source for sixteenth-century and medieval Holkham is constituted by the *Book of Edmund Newgate* (1549, HD 296) and by *John Pepy's Sheep and Shepherd's accounts* (1530–36, HD 253, 255) and his rentals and courts for Neel and Burghall Manors (1542–50, HD 274). All the Peterstone Priory medieval documents are in the Holkham Hall muniments, and most of them were associated in the same registers with the Walsingham Priory Holkham terriers and rentals for the fourteenth and fifteenth centuries (HD 205, HD 300). The medieval holdings of the Holkham Hall muniments also concern many other parishes in west Norfolk.[15]

---

14 Cf. Bruce Campbell, 'Land, Labour, Livestock and Productivity Trends in English Seignorial Agriculture, 1208–1450', in Bruce M.S. Campbell and Mark Overton, eds, *Land, Labour and Livestock, Historical Studies of European Agricultural Productivity*, 1991, p. 151. For the modern period cf. N. Riches, *The Agricultural Revolution in Norfolk*, 1967; R.A.C. Parker, *Coke of Norfolk, a Financial and Agricultural Study 1707–1842*, 1975; S. Wade-Martins, *A Great Estate at Work, The Holkham Estate and its Inhabitants in the Nineteenth Century*, 1980.

15 The Holkham Hall muniments hold substantial medieval documentation for the following: Wells-next-the-Sea, the Burnhams, Wighton, Quarles, Creake, Warham, Egmere, Waterden, Tittleshall-cum-Godwick, Castle Acre, Fulmodestone, Dunton, Billingford, Bintry, Longham, Lexham, Flitcham (now kept at the NRO), Sparham, Massingham, Weasenham (now kept at Weasenham Hall), Wellingham.

APPENDICES

This edition is completed by six appendices:

Appendix 1 is the *Prosopography of Holkham 1330–1350*, which aims at assembling the names of the tenants in Holkham before 1350, using the court rolls not printed here, thus supplementing the names found in our printed documents.

Appendix 2 includes four genealogical sketches of four families of Holkham lords occurring in the documents we print here.

Appendix 3 contains 27 commentaries interpreting the text of the *Feodary* of 1279–80 as transcribed by Edmund Lucas in the Neel Cartulary, HD 22a, Fos. 27–29v no. 253.

Appendix 4 is the *Topography of Holkham 1250–1350* illustrated by two maps of medieval Holkham. The Holkham documents yielded a mass of field names and of medieval toponyms, hitherto unknown, in use in Holkham medieval parish before they disappeared, buried under the great enclosure and park. Historical geography, landscape and linguistic history profit from this research.[16]

Appendix 5 lists all the Feet of Fines relating to Holkham and to individuals holding land in Holkham from 1198 to 1406 preserved in the Public Record Office.

Appendix 6 lists the contents of the three microfiches which accompany the volume of documents and aim to illustrate the hands of scribes and the lay-out of our original charters and of the Neel Cartulary (Fiches 1 and 2). Fiche 3 seeks to illustrate the radical transformation of Holkham in the modern period from the vanished medieval landscape which we now bring to light to the great Palladian hall and the park of the eighteenth and nineteenth centuries.

---

[16] Cf. K. Cameron, *The Place-Names of Lincolnshire*, EPS vols LXIV/LXV, Pt. II, 1991; J. Field, *English Field Names*, 1972; H.D.G. Foxall, *Shropshire Field Names*, 1980; C.P. Hall, J.R. Ravensdale, eds, *The West Fields of Cambridge*, 1976.

Chapter 2

The Neel Cartulary and the
Seigneurial Registers of Holkham

The particular wealth of the Holkham Hall muniments is constituted by the large number of terriers describing several of the main manorial holdings of Holkham. These terriers date mostly from the fifteenth and sixteenth centuries. They were written in Latin by the owners or farmers of the described lands, who composed whole paper registers with the information contained in charters, rentals and terriers, which they copied or summarized. Among these estate-management documents were the *Peterstone* and *Walsingham Books* (HD 205, HD 300, BD 0), which concerned the lands of Peterstone and Walsingham Priories in the parish. As for Peterstone (Austin Canons), these terriers concerned all the medieval possessions of this priory, of which the Holkham Hall documents are the main source. For the Burghall Manor in Holkham, the *Burghall Book* (HD 120), made by John Waylond and which later belonged to Lady Anne Gresham, associated rentals and terriers. Together with the accounts (HD 142) of John Waylond, Edmund Waylond, Geoffrey Porter and William Cobbe, *'firmarii'* of Burghall Manor, John Waylond's Book showed the structure of land-holding and the appropriation of Holkham space and fields by the tenants in the largest of the Holkham manors.

In the sixteenth century, the *Book of Edmund Newgate* (HD 296, 1549), composed by the heir to the Northerne family, prominent in fourteenth-century Holkham, described not only his lands in the Church Field (*Campus Occidentalis de Holkham*), the Stathe Field (*Campus Orientalis de Holkham*), but also the land of all the occupiers of the South Field (*Campus Australis de Holkham*). The area covered by Newgate's survey in the South Field and in the Church Field amounted to 1,472 acres and 2 roods, dispersed among 1,001 different strips and sixty individual tenants. Forty-two estates had less than 10 acres in 1549, and among the eighteen remaining estates, the five larger ones were the Burghall Manor holding of 225 acres in 141 pieces, the Hillhall Manor holding of 209 acres in 129 pieces, the Peterstone Priory holding of 195 acres in 59 pieces, the Neel Manor holding of 157 acres in 95 pieces and Gunnor's holding of 108 acres in 50 pieces. The *Book of Edmund Newgate* used the word *stadium* for a furlong which was given a specific name, and whose area varied from approximately 30 to 100 acres. *Pecia* described one or more strips. A strip often contained several *selions*. It was clear that these registers of terriers were composed and written by these Holkham lords with the aim of understanding the whole field system in which their lands were embedded. In the absence of cartographical instruments and of estate maps, the systematic learning of the names of furlongs, of the names of the tenants of individual *pecie* and of their precise area, boundaries and abuttals, was all the more necessary if the lord was a non-resident.[17]

The fifteenth century, in Holkham, was particularly well documented, as Thomas Grigges's Hillhall Book (HD 75, HD 155, 1460–94) supplements the Neel Cartulary. Edmund Lucas of East Dereham and Thomas Grigges of Wells-next-the-Sea, authors of the two main fifteenth-century seigneurial registers of Holkham, needed to compile them because they were, at least partially, absentee landlords in Holkham. The composition of these two estate-management instruments enabled them to find their way in the maze of the ownership of *pecie* in the Holkham furlongs. Their social status and culture were rather comparable.[18] Thomas Grigges, lord of the manor of Hillhall, was the younger of the two, as he succeeded to his father John Grigges in 1436 and died in 1494. He was a member of the Middle Temple Inn and, among other gentlemen, was sued for dues in 1479 and 1486. His son and heir, Aubrey, was 19 years old in 1494.[19] The Hillhall Book was compiled between 1460 and 1490. Edmund Lucas started to compose his cartulary in 1415. In a document he copied in 1430 he called himself *Domicellus de Est Derham*.[20] The last documents contained in the Neel Cartulary were dated 1449 and 1457. They were added by John Waylond, his brother-in-law.

A comparison of the wills of members of the Lucas family over three

---

17   Cf. C.P. Hall, J.R. Ravensdale, eds, *The West Fields of Cambridge*, 1976; A. Jones, 'Land Measurement in England 1150–1350', *Agricultural History Review*, 1979.

18   On the broad matter of seigneurial attitudes and economic ethos, see Jacques Beauroy, 'Sur la Culture Seigneuriale en Angleterre au XIVème Siècle: Un Poème Anglo-Normand Inédit dans le Cartulaire des Barons de Mohun (Somerset)', in *Mélanges Georges Duby* (C. Amado, G. Lobrichon, eds), forthcoming, 1993.

19   PRO, Plea Rolls, CP 40/870, mm. 440 and 530 (1479) and CP 40/895, m. 252 (1486); *Cal. IPM*, 10 Henry VII, vol. I, no. 1033 (24 Oct. 1494), p. 442. Thomas Grigges died on 12 August 1494. Aubrey Grigges, aged 19, was his son and heir. 'Norfolk Manor of Hyl Halle in Holkham, held of the King, as of the Manor of Wighton, parcel of the duchy of Lancaster, by fealty and 5s. rent at Easter and Michaelmas yearly, for all service. A messuage, 100 acres arable land and 20 acres pasture in Holkham worth 40s., held of William Boleyn, knight, as of the manor called "Borow Halle" in Holkham, by fealty and 2s.'

20   HD 22a, Fo. 37v no. 258, Presentation of Letheringsett, 23 April 1430.

generations seems to show some sort of upward mobility.[21] Edmund Lucas died in 1435, between Monday 25 April 1435, when he made his will, and Thursday 17 November 1435, when his will was proved by the Official of the Bishop of Norwich. His sister-in-law, Margaret Neel, eldest daughter of Gilbert Neel, had married John de Quarles of Holkham, who was given by Edmund's father, Roland Lucas de Estderham, in his will of Thursday 22 June 1391, a tunic of ankle length, striped and lined with fur. The wills of Roland Lucas (1391) and of Edmund Lucas (1435) are comparable in their style and content. They are relatively brief, do not mention any land precisely, and contain mainly religious clauses and bequests and names of executors. The will of Edmund Lucas (1435) omits even the name of his eldest son and principal heir who inherited the bulk of the Neel family estate in Norfolk through his mother, Mary Neel, the last Neel heiress. The Official noted the small amount of Edmund's estate ('*propter exilitatem bonorum dicti defuncti*').[22] After having called himself in a presentation charter of 1430 '*domicellus de Estderham*', in his will of 1435 he was simply 'of Holkham', and could not claim a special burial place in the church of Holkham, while his son Thomas (1447) specified that he wanted to be buried in St. Withburga's church in the chapel of St. Thomas martyr, next to the tomb of his mother Mary Neel. By contrast with his father and grandfather, Thomas Lucas (1447) bequeathed with great precision all his lands in Norfolk, among which was the Neel Manor in Holkham, to his wife Etheldreda for her life, and to Elizabeth, his only surviving daughter and heir. His two brothers, Stephen Lucas and Richard Lucas, the rector of Horningtoft church, were mentioned as his heirs if his daughter should die without heirs of her body.

In their wills, the two elder Lucases, Roland (1391) and Edmund (1435) did not give themselves any title, while Thomas Lucas (1447) was styled '*armiger*'. The third Lucas, Thomas, heir of the Neels of Holkham, was thus a degree higher on the social scale than his father or his grandfather. By its extraordinary amount of detail, the will of Thomas Lucas showed the higher status reached by the third generation of the Lucas family after the

---

21 Will of Roland Lucas, NCC, Register Harsyk, Fo. 146, 22 June 1391, *prob.* 10 July 1391. Will of Edmund Lucas, NCC, Register Surflete, Fo. 185v, 25 April 1435, *prob.* 17. Nov. 1435. Will of Thomas Lucas, NCC, Register Wilbey, Fo. 133, *ultima voluntas* 7 March 1447, *prob.* 20 April 1447. The Neel Pedigree (HD 22a, Fo. 30 no. 254) indicates that Thomas Lucas also had two sons, who must have died in childhood as he only mentions, as his heir, his daughter Elizabeth in 1447. See Appendix 2 for the pedigree of the Neel family and the text of the three Lucas wills (1391, 1435, 1447).

22 Edmund Lucas and his brother-in-law John de Quarles were holding their Holkham estate in the name of their wives, the Neel heiresses, daughters of Gilbert, as stated by the inquisition of 1401/2: '*Hundredum de North Greenhowe, ... Johannes Wharles et Edmund Lucas, de jure uxorum suarum, heredum Gylberti Neel tenent in Holkham j. quart. f.m. de domina Dionisia de Monte Caniso, et eadem de uxore Radulphi Cromwell, militis, et eadem de rege.*' Women were, in this case, both mesne tenants and tenants-in-chief.

Black Death, and how the marriage of Edmund with Mary Neel had enhanced the status of this family, whose mobility, in the late fourteenth century, seemed particularly associated with clerical careers and church property.

Edmund Lucas came to Holkham to manage the estate of the Abbey of West Dereham in the parish.[23] His brother, his sons and his cousin pursued clerical careers and held prebends in Cambridge, in London and in Norfolk.

The Lucas family had close ties with the University of Cambridge. Thomas Lucas, elder son of the author of the Neel Cartulary and the will-maker of 1447, had been admitted to King's Hall in July 1409. We know that he left Cambridge in 1415, before marrying Etheldreda, daughter of Nicholas de Castello. Stephen Lucas, the second son, was also admitted to King's Hall, Cambridge, on 25 August 1415, after the resignation of his elder brother in his favour. Richard Lucas, the third son, rector of Horningtoft, Norfolk, must have been a student in Cambridge after his two older brothers, i.e. between 1420 and 1430. Another Richard Lucas of East Dereham had earlier been a student at Pembroke Hall, Cambridge (Lic. A, 1388; M.A., 1390; B.Th., 1399). He was the brother of Edmund and thus the uncle of Thomas, Stephen and Richard Lucas. Another prominent Cambridge *alumnus* was called Richard Dereham (1367–1417) and was a cousin: he became warden of King's Hall (1399–1413 and 1415–17).[24] With such numerous and close family ties with Cambrige, it is not surprising that Edmund Lucas himself composed and wrote his *Cartulary* so effectively and elegantly in Latin. He obviously had a literate, legal and administrative training, and it seems that he had been the bailiff of the Abbot of West Dereham in Holkham, before marrying Mary Neel. In our view the fact that Edmund Lucas and Thomas Grigges, both lords in Holkham and both authors of remarkable seigneurial registers in Latin for two of Holkham's notable manors in the fifteenth century, were connected with the University of Cambridge and with the Inns of Court, the 'Third University of England', demonstrates the high cultural level attained by the smaller and middling lay seigneurial group of Norfolk at the local level, with its consequences for efficient estate-management and agricultural productivity.[25] These small lords actually laid down the medieval basis of the celebrated Norfolk system of husbandry of the modern period.

The Neel Cartulary had, in the mind of its author, several purposes. It constituted a guide to the Neel Manor muniments and title deeds; on the

23   Cf. HD 194, 22 July 1410, and note 49, p. 34 *infra*.

24   Cf. J. and J.A. Venn, *Alumni Cantabrigenses*, part I, 1924, and A.B. Emden, *A Biographical Register of the University of Cambridge to 1500*, 1963.

25   John H. Baker, *The Third University of England: The Inns of Court and the Common Law Tradition*, 1990.

other hand it was to operate as a topographical guide to the fields of
Holkham, to identify and locate the several hundred parcels of land which
made up the land of Neel Manor. The rigorous mind of Edmund Lucas was
particularly apparent in the selection of the material, its ordering and in the
reference system he used. He went as far back as possible, and placed the
Bret charters (late thirteenth and early fourteenth century) before the
purchases made by the grandparents of his wife in the first half of the
fourteenth century, thus making a fundamental distinction between the
original Bret nucleus and the new acquisitions of Richard and Katerine Neel
between 1314 and 1345, the foundations of the new fourteenth century Neel
Manor. His principal aim in localising all the parcels of his manor in the
fields of Holkham was shown in the marginalia accompanying the documents
he copied and summarized. They started with document no. 2, on Folio 2,
while the first document he copied on Folio 1v, about the folds of Holkham
in 1306, was a relevant topographical and seigneurial introduction to the
landscape of Holkham fields from the salt marshes in the north to the South
Field, detailing twenty different sheep runs with their courses and the names
of their owners.

The Neel Cartulary contains no fewer than 220 different Holkham field
names, and it is in great part thanks to this number of field names collected
by the systematic terrier of Edmund Lucas, that the two maps of Holkham
we include in this volume could be drawn.[26] Associated with the Hillhall
Book and several of the later terriers and especially the 1549 *Book of
Edmund Newgate*, the Neel Cartulary is, because of the specific bias of
Edmund Lucas towards naming Holkham medieval place-names, fields,
landmarks, roads etc., a uniquely rich source. The marginalia, placed by
Edmund Lucas in the margin of each of his entries in the *Cartulary*, were
chosen from among the elements of localisation of his parcels of land
provided by the charters he copied. The pieces were bound by named roads
and tracks and belonged to named furlongs or *quarentene*. The *pecia* or strip
varied from 1/2 rood to 11/2 acres on average, though there were much larger
pecie, e.g. the *pecia* of 9 acres in the furlong named 'Gonyeswong' to the
south-west of the parish, granted by Nicholas son of Richard de Barking, to
William Craske (HD 22a, no. 140). The headlands (*forere*) were often
mentioned as boundaries, as well as the names of the tenants of neighbouring
pieces.

The marginalia sometimes designate the nature and the use of the land, as
for instance *Bruera* (HD 22a, no. 7), or *Quaedam acra cum domo* (HD 22a,
no. 51) or *Molendinum venticum* (HD 22a, no, 64). Most of the time, though,

---

26   For our two maps, Holkham Fields 1250–1350 and Holkham Town 1250–1350, see
      Appendix 4, Topography of Holkham 1250–1350.

Edmund Lucas chose a furlong name, but there are exceptions, e.g. 'Northfeld' (HD 22a, no.11), a translation of *Campus Aquilonalis.* 'Northfeld' also seemed to be a place-name in the East Field, to the east of Burgate croft. As a guide to the location of his parcels, his choice of details from the charters in the marginalia reflect Lucas's personal acquaintance with the Holkham landscape.

The *Cartulary* was used as a note-book, as a report for further inquiry and as an agenda about legal problems with neighbours on the ground. A number of the charters summarized were to be examined and checked against the actual pieces of land in the fields. Four main devices were used to indicate further action to be taken. The word which Edmund Lucas placed most often in the margin of his summaries was *inquiratur.* He meant that he would inquire on the spot about the land in question, seeing it and asking neighbours about it. The inquiry was necessitated, no doubt, by the rather uncertain control over the piece of land by the Neel estate, when he wrote in the margin of HD 22a, no. 34, *inquiratur qui sunt tenentes,* or, as in HD 22a, no. 25, *inquiratur quia Prior de Walsingham occupat vs. dominum ut dicitur.* Other marginal injunctions were used, such as *examinatur, memorandum* and the drawing of an index finger. These latter three seemed to be somewhat less imperative than the more common *inquiratur.* Ninety-three summaries in quire 2 were given numbers in sequence, and the corresponding number was inscribed on the original charter in his muniments, which made any search for an original document easy and swift. As it was usual for the new lord to inquire and learn about his rights, it is obvious that the compendium of summaries of charters and of title deeds was composed to enable Edmund Lucas to recover lost or encroached land and lost or forgotten rights. Seigneurial rights over bondmen were perhaps his concern when he wrote *Perquisicio Nativorum* in the margin of HD 22a, nos. 103 and 104, about the serfs bought by Simon Hammond from John le Bret in 1295 and 1296, and who in turn, with their 'sequele', were bought by Richard and Katerine Neel in 1314 and came into the Neel estate. The will to recover all his rights led Edmund Lucas to place an *inquiratur* about all the aspects entailed by the transfer of the Bret Manor to the Neels in 1314, *inquiratur, Quietaclamacio de mesuagiis Neles, dominiis, faldagiis et serviciis liberorum et nativorum,* HD 22a, no. 195. Richard and Katerine Neel had bought a piece of 3 acres of land in Holkham from Bartholomew Pay on 12 January 1316, and the piece was situated at Billesmere furlong, abutting on its eastern side on Quarlesgate, and on its western side on the land of the Prior of Walsingham. In a firm marginal comment, Edmund Lucas claimed this lost piece of land, *Prior de Petyrston injuste occupat et continet iij acras ... memorandum,* HD 22a, no. 160. The most striking comment made in the margin by Edmund Lucas, and which signified the main aim of the *Cartulary,* concerned the last

Neel charter: a grant of 13 acres for a service of 23d. yearly, made on 16 May 1317 by Richard and Katerine Neel to Warin, Prior of Peterstone (HD 22a, no. 252). A hundred years later Edmund Lucas decided to revoke this grant made by the grandparents of his wife and to have the 13 acres seized, with the following statement in the left margin: *Petyrston, preceptum seisire quia nullus prior neque confratres ibidem existunt.*

The Feodary of 1279–80 (HD 22a, no. 253) and the Burghall Rental of 1273–1303 (HD 22a, no. 255) were placed by Edmund Lucas in the third quire of the *Cartulary*, along with some other documents he deemed important: the Neel pedigree, the presentation of Letheringsett and three terriers. The Feodary (no. 253) was copied from the Hundred Rolls return and re-ordered for clarity. Each Holkham fief was given a title, and the names of the current lords and tenants in the fifteenth century were added in the margins. Thus, for the sub-manor of the Burghall Manor held by Geoffrey le Bret in 1279–80 the marginal comment was: *Edmund Lucas et parcenarij ejus tenent et vocatur Neles.* In his copy of the Burghall Rental (no. 255), Edmund Lucas did not intervene as much, and seemed to have been mainly interested in the names of the Holkham tenants of the late thirteenth century. He recognized in the margin some of their holdings as *Terra Biscop* or *Terra Dusyng.* It is clear that he was looking into the nature of customary labour services and of their commutation in Burghall Manor, the largest Holkham manor, which Richard Neel took on as farmer, with a consortium, in 1332 from the Earl of Atholl.

The Gazetteer (HD 22a, no. 260), entitled in Middle English 'Purchase londys', placed in quire 4, constituted an ingenious system, devised to gain time in the research process on the ground and in the muniments, and to identify all the parcels acquired by the Neels. The alphabetical ordering referred to Holkham fields, place-names or roads. Each parcel was preceded in the margin by the date of acquisition, couched in regnal year reckoning, in Arabic or in Roman numerals. The marginalia referred these dates to the specific original charters which he must have classified in his muniments according to regnal years. The quick localisation of his parcels in the field and of their title deeds in his archives was the concern. Edmund Lucas had also in mind the control of their actual possession as lord of Neel Manor, for he added in the margin the word *habet*, which meant that the parcels were in his hands. At other times he added *inquiratur*. Having misplaced a 'Greyston' parcel in the letter T he added *Require in G.* In each entry the name of the vendors from whom the Neels bought their land in the first part of the fourteenth century were mentioned. Names of fields and places in Holkham, names of the vendors and the names of Richard and Katerine Neel, who bought the parcels, were often emphasized by pressing on his quill, in order to leave a bolder trace on the paper. We have attempted to reproduce these intentions of the author with bolder characters in our edition of the Gazetteer. Our edition of the Gazetteer shows systematically the relationship of its entries with the numbered summaries or the original charters which have survived.

The characteristics of the Neel Cartulary which we described above, reflect the mind of a small Norfolk lord able to devise a time-saving search tool for all his parcels of land in the complex fields of Holkham at the beginning of the fifteenth century. Not narrowly focused on the Neel Manor, the Neel Cartulary expressed a wider intelligence of the historical and legal basis of Holkham's manorial landscape. The Hillhall Book for the Holkham Hillhall Manor can be compared with the Neel Cartulary, which it complements as an important source for the medieval landscape of Holkham.

The Hillhall Book of Thomas Grigges (HD 75, HD 155), who died in 1494, was composed between 1460 and 1490. It was started nearly forty years after the Neel Cartulary. Hillhall Manor and Neel Manor had their *sita manerij* facing each other at the centre of Holkham Town. Neel Manor was situated to the west of the Common and of Crossgate; Hillhall Manor's 'Great Close' was situated to the east of Crossgate and of the Common. In the first thirteen folios Thomas Grigges placed 9 documents which had significant historical importance for Hillhall. Among these were the list of the lords since Baldwin and Thomas d'Akeny in the second half of the thirteenth century (Fos. 3–3v), the first parcels of Holkham land acquired by the Grigges family of Wells-next-the-Sea in 1390, and the rental of the 9 *tenementa* liable for the office of *messor* (Fos. 4–10v).

In the second section (Fos. 14–39), Thomas Grigges placed the description of 42 freeholds dependent on Hillhall in 1467–8. While Edmund Lucas was essentially concerned with the large number of demesne lands acquired by Richard and Katerine Neel, the Hillhall Book was explicit about the small freeholders. In its third section (Fos. 41–69r), Thomas Grigges presented a fully detailed terrier of the Hillhall Manor lands (1486–7) in the North Field, the South Field and the Church Field. This is especially important for the study of the medieval landscape of Holkham and brings out topographical information as well as social information on the tenant population and on the pattern of settlement. The final section (Fos. 69v to 114v) includes 19 leases of Grigges's land in Holkham conceded to various individuals (1487–90) and thirteen supplementary terriers (1477–83).

The Hillhall Book, more than twice the length of the Neel Cartulary, lacks the latter's great elegance of composition. Thomas Grigges, in the ordering of his material, followed a simple chronological order. The centre-piece was the terrier of 1486–7, which covered a large part of the Holkham fields and was an especially important source. Its material was, on the whole, less varied and it did not include fundamental documents for the whole parish as the

Feodary of 1279–80 did in the Neel Cartulary. The Hillhall Book relied less on original charters, but was very informative on the expansionary strategies of Thomas Grigges as lord in Holkham. As an estate-management tool, the Neel Cartulary was, undoubtedly, easier to handle.

Chapter 3

Lordship and Landscape in Norfolk

Holkham Park is the end-product of repeated purchases and improvements of local land since the beginning of the seventeenth century, made possible by the gradual reconcentration of the wealth dispersed among the heirs of Chief Justice Coke. It was created in the eighteenth century, but clever realignments of roads gradually enlarged it to its present size. The rebuilding of houses at the Stathe and the gradual destruction of Holkham Town, the creation of the lake and other fashionable garden features, which were modified with the changing fashions of successive decades, eliminated nearly all traces of the medieval hamlets, their gardens, closes and fields with their port on the North Sea.

The medieval landscape of Holkham was determined by a complex manorial structure which organized the space of a specific coastal site. A large front of salt marshes did not prevent access to the sea and the development of a port. The place-name of Holkham has an Old-English element, 'Holc', which seems to indicate a hollow, a cavity. It could originally have designated the natural depression dividing the Church Field and the Stathe Field, which was fed by seven springs and flowed into the tidal creek of the Stanre marsh, on its north side. The damming of this depression in the eighteenth century allowed the creation of the present lake. To the south of the salt marshes, the land of Holkham is formed of chalk covered by light, sandy loams, which provide good arable land, easily marled from local pits in the Middle Ages. It is typical of the 'Good Sands' agricultural region of Norfolk, so called by Arthur Young in the eighteenth century.[27]

The area covered by the parish of Holkham and by the fields and *feoda* of medieval Holkham is illustrated here in our maps 'Holkham Fields 1250–1350' and 'Holkham Town 1250–1350', and amounts to approximately 4,000 acres. Brabner's Gazetteer mentions the figure of 4,000 acres for Holkham, while Kelly's Directory (1912) mentions 4,618 acres which include the area of the tidal marshes reclaimed in the modern period, in 1720 and 1860. The Gazetteer of the British Isles (John Bartholomew, 1966) mentions

---

27   W.G. Hoskins *The Making of the English Landscape*, (1st edn. 1955), paperback edition, 1992, p. 154. W.G. Hoskins was mistaken when he stated that Coke of Norfolk transformed 'heathland into cornfields'. Holkham's sandy loams have provided good cornfields since the medieval period. See also R.A.C. Parker, 'Coke of Norfolk and the Agrarian Revolution', *Economic History Review*, VIII, 1955, pp. 156–66.

4,717. The present park, within its walls, covers about 3,000 acres. The Coke
estates in Norfolk amounted to 42,000 acres in the nineteenth century. But at
the death of the 4th Earl of Leicester (1949), 17,000 acres were sold, and it
amounts now to 25,000 acres, including land in the Burnhams and in Castle
Acre. The present Holkham Estate, including land in Warham, in Burnham
(Peterstone) and the foreshore, amounts to 5,000 acres.

Medieval Holkham demonstrated a highly complex manorial structure. We
are fortunate enough to have at our disposal a copy of what we believe to be
a return of the Hundred Rolls Commissioners of 1279–80: the *Feodarium de
Dominiis in Holkham et de eorum tenentibus*, which Edmund Lucas placed in
his *Cartulary* (HD 22a, Neel Cartulary, Fos. 27–29, no. 253). It can be
compared with other returns of the same royal inquiry of 1279–80 for seven
villages adjacent to Holkham: Burnham Thorpe, Kettlestone (with
Fulmodestone and Croxton), North Barsham, Waterden, Sculthorpe, West
Barsham and East Barsham.[28] An analysis of the complexity of manorial
structure in west Norfolk can thus rely on the analysis of eight Hundred
Rolls returns. The Hundred Rolls return for Hevingham in east-central
Norfolk, studied by Bruce Campbell (1986), seem to show no more
complexity nor greater division of lordship than Holkham or some of its
neighbouring villages.[29] The study of manorial structure has to rely on a
detailed *feodarium* or survey, and cannot be based on the erratic and
incomplete *Nomina Villarum* of 1316, or on the sketchy notations by
Blomefield.

In 1086 Domesday Book described six manors, and some characteristics
which were already there in the eleventh century can be identified two
centuries later. Holkham was still dependent upon Wighton which was then
in royal domain, and consequently referred to, in 1279, as 'ancient demesne
manor'. Domesday Book associated Holkham with the other *berewics* of
Wighton, Quarles, Wells and Warham. In the thirteenth and fourteenth
centuries it was at Wighton that the court of the Hundred of North Greenhoe
sometimes met.[30] In 1086, royal domain at Holkham was assessed at four
carucatae (one carucata = 80–120 acres), with one part not assessed for
taxation, *vastata*. In the Feodary of 1279–80 we find again three fiefs created
by the Norman Conquest and individually named in Domesday Book: The

---

28   University of London Library, Fuller Collection, 7/5, 15 membranes: Burnham Thorpe
     (mm. 1–2), Kettlestone with Fulmodestone and Croxton (mm. 3–4), North Barsham (mm.
     5–7), Waterden (mm. 8–9), Sculthorpe (mm. 10–11), West Barsham (mm. 12–13), East
     Barsham (mm. 14–15).

29   Bruce Campbell, 'The Complexity of Manorial Structure in Medieval Norfolk: A Case
     Study', *Norfolk Archaeology*, 1986, pp. 225–261.

30   NRO, Hamond Coll., S 11 6B, Hundred of North Greenhoe court rolls, 1315, 1322–3,
     1324, 1324–5, 1325–6, 1327–9, 1328–9, 1332, 1346, 1349–50, 1351–2. The hundred
     court held its three-weekly session at Wighton or Quarles, Walsingham, Holkham,
     Warham, Stiffkey, Cockthorpe, Thursford, Hindringham, Dalling, and Egmere, in rotation.

fief of Alan of Brittany reappearing as that of Richmond, the fief of Warenne under the same name, and the fief of the Bishop of Thetford under the name of that of Norwich, since the see was removed to Norwich in 1094–6. The principal manor in 1086 was apparently that held before the Conquest by Ketel, and attributed to Tovi, companion of the Conqueror. Two *villani* were counted on the 3 *carucatae*, with 8 *bordarij*, 3 *servi*, and 18 *sokemanni*, besides 5 pigs and 300 sheep. In describing Holkham, Domesday Book gave the lion's share to the *sokemanni*, i.e. privileged tenants. The Feodary's vocabulary used the word *sokemanni* only in its description of the 3 first fiefs (Wighton, Noyon and Dakeny), where it was always qualified by the phrase '*qui tenent in villenagio*'. It would appear that the wording of the document of 1279 reflected the decline and disappearance of Domesday Book's class of *sokemanni*, at least under its specific legal definition. The use of *qui tenent in villenagio* or villein tenure corresponded to the more precise definition of customary tenure in the thirteenth century. A large part of the *villani* were free, having replaced the *sokemanni*, but were holding villein land. On the other hand, among the numerous *liberi tenentes* of 1279 holding in socage, there was certainly a good number of descendants of the former *sokemanni*. Finally, in the Feodary of 1279, the *coterelli ... qui tenent cum suis cotagiis in villenagio* replaced the *bordarij* of Domesday Book.[31]

It is possible to argue that the main outlines of the nexus of authority and of the social bonds at Holkham as defined in Domesday Book had not been fundamentally altered in the course of the ensuing two hundred years. But the expansion of the population and of the economy during the twelfth and thirteenth centuries had the special consequence of a multiplication of the sub-infeudations. Beneath the level of the mesne tenants of knightly rank, *armigeri* and the *homines ad arma*, the market in free land encouraged the growth of a large group of *liberi tenentes*. The Feodary suggests that there were 35 on the 15 fiefs between which it distinguishes. Actually there seem to have been more. Lay lordship continued to predominate and there was still only limited growth in the new monastic properties of West Dereham, Creake, Walsingham and Peterstone as a result of acquisition largely in frankalmoign.

---

31   *Domesday Book, Norfolk* (John Morris, Phil. Brown, eds), 2 vols, 1984: King, 1, 34, 41. Count Alan, 4, 20. Warenne, 8, 118. Bishop of Thetford, 10, 13, 26. Peter de Valognes, 34, 19. Tovi, 48, 2.

THE MANORIAL STRUCTURE OF HOLKHAM

The 1279–80 Hundred Rolls return for Holkham identified no less than eight head tenants, holding in chief from the King: Geoffrey de Lusignan (*capitalis dominus*), Ralph de Tosny, Robert de Tattershall, Mary de Nevile, Gilbert de Clare, the Bishop of Norwich, the Master of Carbrooke and Earl Warenne. Since Kosminsky's classic study, manorial types and relative strength of lordship have been used to differentiate among English medieval regions.[32] The main Holkham holdings showed great variety in size and structure.

Wighton

Holkham was subject to the royal manor of Wighton. In 1279 a minor, the ward of John d'Harcourt, held it. He was Geoffrey de Lusignan, son of Henry III's half-brother. The lord Edward had received it as a grant from his father and had given it in turn to Geoffrey de Lusignan the elder, Geoffrey's father.[33] The actual share of Wighton's demesne at Holkham was small: 6 *sokemanni* with 8 acres of arable. Yet Geoffrey de Lusignan, according to the Feodary was *Capitalis Dominus de Holkham*. As the Hundred of North Greenhoe was in the hands of the bailiff of Wighton, the overriding jurisdiction of Wighton involved not only the *visus franciplegij* but also the right of wreck and of tolls in the port and market of Holkham. These royal rights set Wighton's jurisdiction above that of Burghall, a manor held by Denise de Montchesney who held the right to hold a court leet with *visus franciplegij* within the boundaries of Holkham. Lower down the scale, Thomas d'Akeny held a *curia baronis* for his manor of Hillhall with three 'laghedays' a year at Kyngishil, a name which is not found in later documents and which may have been the original name of the hill on which Hillhall was built, and which may have been the site of the burgh, to which the old road from Wells (called Burgate) ran.[34] Geoffrey le Bret was an example of another of the *feoda tenentes* who held a court for his tenants.

Two *feoda* or manors in the Holkham of 1279 were subordinate to Geoffrey de Lusignan, tenant-in-chief and lord of Wighton. First, there was the *feodum* of Ralph Noyon (or Nuggon) of Salle, a knight, with 136 acres held in *villenagio* by 23 *sokemanni* and 3 *coterelli*. This passed to the Prior of Peterstone, who held courts for them. Two *liberi tenentes* were attached,

---

32 E.A. Kosminsky, *Studies in the Agrarian History of England in the Thirteenth Century*, (ed. R.H. Hilton), 1956. R.H. Britnell, 'Minor Landlords in England and Medieval Agrarian Capitalism', *Past and Present*, LXXXIX, 1980, pp. 3–22. See also M.A. Barg, 'The Social Structure of Manorial Freeholders: An Analysis of the Hundred Rolls of 1279', *Agricultural History Review*, 1991, pp. 108–15.

33 *Rot. Hund.*, vol. 1, p. 483; H. Cam, *The Hundred and the Hundred Rolls*, London, 1930, p. 196.

34 HD 22a, Neel Cart., Fo. 12 no. 150, *Copia carte Thome filij Baldewyni de Akeny*.

John Godewyne with 40 acres and 1 fold, and John Silk with 3 acres and 1 rood. The acquisition of Noyon by the Prior of Peterstone was probably effected towards the end of our period.[35] Another vassal of Lusignan at Holkham was Hubert de Wighton, with a fief of 31 acres and 3 roods held by *villani*, but also by 4 *liberi tenentes*, among whom were Bartholomew de Burgate and John Silk.

Hillhall

The second fief, to keep to the order in the Feodary of 1279, was a manor called Hillhall. Ralph de Tosny had been its tenant-in-chief. Thomas d'Akeny held it of his brother, John d'Akeny, yielding a silver ring for a sparrow-hawk. Under Henry III their father, Baldwin d'Akeny, obtained for his manor of Hillhall the privilege of a weekly market, to be held on Mondays, and of a fair on August 29.[36] He had been one of the 32 knights in the train of Richard of Cornwall at his election as King of the Romans in 1257.[37] In the demesne of Hillhall Thomas d'Akeny had a messuage, 14 acres and a mill. There were also 36 *sokemanni* holding *in villenagio*, with messuages and 130 acres, and 3 cottars with their cottages and 3 acres. His sub-feudatories were 5 *liberi tenentes*: The Prior of Peterstone (42 acres, 1 fold), the Abbot of Creake (49 acres, 1 fold), Robert le Heyre (40 acres), Bartholomew de Burgate (14 acres), and Ralph Hacun (24 acres, 1 fold). In the sub-infeudation, John Silk held three times as a *liber tenens* of Hillhall: of Robert le Heyre (4 acres), of Geoffrey le Bret of Warham (3 acres), and of Ralph Hacun for his whole holding (24 acres, 1 fold and a marsh). Altogether there were 314 acres, 3 folds and a marsh at Hillhall.

At the court of 1 May 1312, payments were registered for the dubbing of Thomas d'Akeny. Some indication of the social structure of the tenants of the manor of Hillhall emerged from the list: There were 70 *villani*, presumably *nativi*, and 30 *liberi tenentes*, male and female, making allegiance.[38] The Feodary of 1279 was, then, an outline of the seigneurial structure of Holkham which only mentioned the upper layer of the *liberi tenentes*.

---

[35]   HP 1006, 5 Sept. 1293, Dominus Ralph Noyon (or Nugion) was witness of a charter of John son of Geoffrey le Bret (also in HD 22a, Neel Cart., Fo. 7, no. 85); Thomas Noyon, son of Ralph, and Richard Noyon are mentioned as grantors of 2 parcels of 1/2 acre to the Abbey of Creake, Cart. of Creake, nos. 190, 191. Most of the cottages of the manor of Noyon, later Peterstone, were grouped together in Westgate, in Holkham Town, but at least once in the fifteenth century the court was held in a dwelling at the Stathe, not at Peterstone.

[36]   Blomefield, *Norfolk*, vol. 9, p. 233. Henry III granted Monday market and a fair on the Decollation of John the Baptist (29 Aug.). To ratify an exchange of land, Baldwin d'Akeny gave Peter le Bret an exemption of all tonnage in his market and fair in Holkham, HD 22a, Neel Cart., no. 151.

[37]   C. Moor, *Knights of Edward I*, vol. 1, 1929, p. 261; N. Denholm-Young, *Richard of Cornwall*, 1947, p. 91.

[38]   HD 14 (Hillhall), 5 April 1277.

Looking at the other end of the social scale, Bartholomew de la Dale answered, on January 15 1287, for the chevage payments of 8 *anlepimen*, landless and unmarried bondmen.[39] As a local reflection of the Hundred Rolls inquiry, a 'charter of liberties' of Thomas d'Akeny (c. 1275) defined the services and customs owed by his men. Perhaps similar 'charters of liberties' were granted elsewhere, following up the general definition of rights in the Hundred Rolls. The Hillhall Manor Charter was especially devoted to the limits of seigneurial taxation. Reliefs on succession to holdings were never to exceed the total of a year's rents, *'quantum reddit per annum de redditu assise'*. Free tenants, marrying outside the manor, were not to pay more than 10s. for licence to marry, and their payment was to be graded according to their abilities up to that maximum. For marriage within the manor the maximum was set at 5s. and varied beneath that level in accordance with the wealth of the couple. Thomas d'Akeny undertook to select each year *collectores* only from the tenants of the manor. The royal writs enacting taxes on towns and cities throughout the kingdom should apply to Holkham on the same occasions and in the same way as at Wighton. Thomas d'Akeny was allowed 3 annual courts at the 'laghedays' at Kingishil, and his tenants owed him no further suit of court. Each *anlepiman* was to pay an annual chevage limited to 11/2d. Finally, Hillhall tenants were exempted from the obligation to use the manorial mill, one of several at Holkham. This thirteenth century Hillhall 'charter of liberties' was seen by Edmund Lucas, when he copied it in his *Cartulary* in 1415, as giving a significant account of manorial custom and of lord and tenant relationships in Holkham.[40]

Burghall

Burghall, the most important of the Holkham fiefs, and the most extensive manor, was held in 1279 by Denise de Montchesney as part of the Honor of Arundel. Robert de Tattershall was tenant-in-chief. The manor of Denise de Montchesney was assessed at half a knight's fee. She held, in addition to the ordinary court baron of Burghall, a *curia leta* each year for the *villata* on 22 July, the feast day of St Mary Magdalen.[41] She had the right of tumbrell, wreck, mill and warren. According to the Hundred Rolls, William de Montchesney and his mother Denise had exercised the assise of bread and ale which normally went with the *curia leta*, and the *visus franciplegij* for the

---

39   HD 14 (Hillhall), 15 April 1287.
40   HD 22a, Neel Cart., Fo. 12 no. 150, *Copia carte Thome filij Baldewyni de Akeny*.
41   Four Burghall leet courts are extant up to 1350: HD 82, 22 July 1332; HD 84, 22 July 1334; HD 86, 22 July 1337; HD 87a, 22 July 1350. William de Montchesney, lord of Burghall, died in 1287. His mother Denise acquired wardship of his lands while his daughter Denise was in her minority. Denise de Montchesney, daughter of William, became the wife of Hugh de Vere before 1301. She died in 1313. Her heir was her cousin, Aymer de Valence. Cf. Farrer, vol. 3, p. 108.

past 26 years, and there was some overlap between the Burghall leet and the Wighton leet which reduced the right of the king.[42]

Burghall Manor had a demesne of 248 acres, whereof 120 acres were arable, and another 120 acres of marsh with 8 acres of meadow and a fold. The meadow lay north of Hillhall, on the east side of the long depression which Thomas Coke was to make into a lake. As to the tenants, 36 *villani* held 252 acres with their messuages. The Feodary also mentioned 3 *coterelli* (3 acres), and 15 acres held directly by the Prior of Peterstone. Burghall had 3 dependent manors.

a) Le Bret (Neel Manor after 1314)

The biggest of the 3 manors associated with Burghall was that of Geoffrey le Bret, destined to become the nucleus of the manor of Richard Neel in the early fourteenth century. From this came the large number of the Bret *feoffamenta* dating from the second half of the thirteenth century, which Edmund Lucas transcribed in the first section of his *Cartulary*. The manor of Geoffrey le Bret owed the service of one quarter of a knight's fee. It had a demesne of 120 acres and a fold. The dependent holdings *in villenagio* amounted to 60 acres. The tenants were obliged to come together to render suit of his manorial court twice a year, also to attend the meetings of the Hundred Court once every 3 weeks, and the two annual sheriff's tourns. Geoffrey le Bret had 7 *liberi tenentes*: Bartholomew de Burgate, Ralph Mariot and William le Meir with holdings of 1 acre, while John Goldwyne had a bigger holding (16 acres), Adam Carpenter a messuage and 6 acres, John Silk 41/2 acres, and Ralph Rymour one cottage. The rental of Geoffrey le Bret (c. 1295) mustered 45 tenants, and those of Peter le Bret (c. 1303) 27 tenants, of whom 20 were *custumarij*.[43]

b) Hacun

Also attached to Burghall, the fee of Ralph Hacun was worth 1/16th of a knight's fee and consisted of a messuage, 30 acres and a fold. Some *villani* held 20 acres with their messuages. The *liberi tenentes* of Ralph Hacun's fief numbered 10, among whom John Silk reappeared on this new account for 5 acres. The Priors of Walsingham and Peterstone held 41 acres and 13 acres respectively. The total came to about 115 acres.[44]

---

42 *Rot. Hund.*, I, pp. 483, 526.
43 HD 11, Rental of Geoffrey le Bret of Holkham, c. 1293–4; HD 20, Rental of Peter le Bret, before 1303; HD 21, *Redditus assis' Tenentium Petri le Bret de Holkham*.
44 Ralph Hacun, Grant to the Abbey of West Dereham of all his marsh called Stande; Cart. of Dereham, Fo. 263 no. xii; Ibid., Fo. 51v no. cxxii; Cart. of Walsingham, Fo. 54v no. clii; *Cart. Creake*, no. 197. Ralph Hacun was witness of 17 charters (1270–1294–6) published here, Richard Hacun, 1 charter, Robert Hacun, 2 charters, and Walter Hacun, his nephew, 27 charters (1291–1304).

c) Burgate

Bartholomew de Burgate was a witness to 51 of the charters printed here,
dating from 1272 to 1302. He had a *feodum* dependent on Burghall in 1279,
whose name is perpetuated in Burgate furlong, shown east of Hillhall in the
map of 1590.[45] In contrast with the sub-manor of Geoffrey le Bret, this
feodum was not assessed for any contribution to the royal host. It consisted
of a messuage, 40 acres and a fold. The tenant was bound to attend the
meetings of the *curia* of Burghall, and every three weeks those of the
Hundred, and twice annually those of the Shire, '*bis in anno ad comitatum
Norwici*'. Scutage of 5d. for 20s. was typical of free tenure, but there was an
additional labour service of 3 *precaria cum caruca ad cibum domini*. It
numbered 3 *liberi tenentes*, whose holdings did not exceed 2 acres. The
tenure of Bartholomew de Burgate had its origin in the ancient tenure of
Bertram le Verdoun, and one should note certain elements of service *in
villenagio* which it was required to give.[46]

Bret-Tobers

Two other *feoda* depended on the Honor of Arundel held by Robert de
Tattershall, without being connected with Burghall. Firstly, the manor of John
le Bret was held under a mesne tenant, Roger Broun, and consisted of 60
acres and a fold. The Hillhall Book showed that it passed from John, son of
John and grandson of Adam le Bret, to John Tobers of Wiveton, who bore
the canting arms of two bears.[47] There were also 32 acres occupied by 5
villani. Among 4 *liberi homines* the most significant was the Prior of
Walsingham with 46 acres and a fold. The whole came to about 160 acres.
Also in Tattershall's fief Peter le Vewtre had a tenure of 16 acres. This, in
conjunction with his fief of Burnham, amounted to the service of one
knight's fee.[48]

Hindringham

The part of the Honor of Richmond unquestionably had its origin in the fief
of Alan of Brittany in Domesday Book. It was held by Geoffrey of

---

45   Burgate furlong, on the map of 1590, was bounded on the north by a road from Wells,
      which joined the old road from Burnham to Wighton at Hillhall, and seems to have no
      connection with the Borough, which is the name of a pasture surrounded by an iron age
      rampart toward the east end of the saltmarsh in the foldcourse of Burghall.
46   Bartholomew de Burgate: no. 199, *Cart. of Creake*. Thomas, son of Bartholomew de
      Burgate: no. XXV, Fo. 266, Cart. of Dereham, no. CXX, Fo. 51v; Cart. of Walsingham.
47   The manor of Bret-Tobers, in 1369-70, passed from Robert, son of John de Kirkham, to
      John Andrew, under whom the lordship was united with that of Hillhall. Its house stood
      on the south-west side of the Great Close of Hillhall, on the north side of the Burnham-
      Wighton road which Thomas Coke buried under his park. The name is preserved in
      Tubbins wood.
48   Many Vewtre deeds are in the PRO among the *Ancient Deeds*.

Hindringham, whose name was that of a village nearby. In the first half of the fourteenth century an Adam and a Thomas of Hindringham, perhaps of the same family, were among the *milites de Comite Norfolci*.[49] Geoffrey de Hindringham was the vassal of Humphrey de Wighton, who held directly from Mary de Neville, tenant-in-chief and the lady of the Honor of Richmond. The holding of Geoffrey de Hindringham represented 18 acres, occupied by 3 *villani* and their messuages. He also had 3 *liberi tenentes*: Geoffrey Goodwyne with his messuage, 12 acres and a fold, John Curson, who had a messuage and 41/2 acres for an annual rent of 2s. 1d. and a basket of peas and John Roberd, who had 1/2 acre, paying 3d. annual rent.

Caly-David

In the part of the Honor of Warenne at Holkham, held by James de Thorp under John, Earl Warenne (1231-1304), we find Everard Caly, who witnessed 9 charters (1270-1304), and Humphrey David who witnessed 34 charters (1274-1309). They jointly held 24 acres and a fold. One *villanus* and 2 *coterelli* had holdings which came to 6 acres. In the same fee, Bartholomew de Burgate had a messuage and 12 acres (occupied by 2 *villani*), and John Silk had a diminutive holding of 3 roods.

Burton Lazars

In the Honor of Clare, seven *liberi tenentes* shared in the 31 acres which the Brothers of Burton Lazars in Leicestershire had received in free alms under Gilbert de Clare (1243-1295), tenant-in-chief. Thomas Leffe (witness in 5 charters, 1272-1284) had a messuage and 8 acres, and the Prior of Peterstone held of him half a fold. Gilbert Souter and Humphrey David had 12 acres with their messuages and held, together, the other half of the fold. In the same fee, Bartholomew the smith and Lucy Lange held a messuage and 5 acres. Mariota Bendyng had a messuage and 6 acres.

Bacon

In the fee of the Bishop of Norwich, Roger Bacon was the vassal of William Bardolf for a holding of 15 acres. With his possessions at Cockthorpe, Roger's holding at Holkham amounted to half a knight's fee. Here, Bartholomew de Burgate kept 15 acres and a fold, while the Prior of Peterstone, his only tenant, held 8 acres. The total came to 38 acres.

---

49 *Parliamentary Writs and Writs of Military Summons*, ed. F. Palgrave, 2 vols in 5, 1827-1834, vol. 2, Div. II, p. 641.

Carbrooke

The only commandery of the Hospitallers of St John of Jerusalem in Norfolk was that of Carbrooke near Watton. At Holkham this had a holding occupied by 2 *liberi tenentes*: Bartholomew Underclynt with a messuage and 1/2 acre, and Bartholomew de Burgate with a messuage and 12 acres of marsh, held in sub-infeudation by the Prior of Walsingham.

The Church

The Feodary of 1279–80 concluded with an account of the position of the parish church under the title *De advocacione Ecclesie de Holkham*. It was dedicated to St Withburga, the daughter of King Anna and sister of St Etheldreda of Ely. John Lackland gave half the church to the Abbey of Viterbo. This was eventually reunited with the other half, which had been given with the advowson by William de Montchesney to the Abbey of West Dereham. The Abbey of West Dereham eventually managed the whole estate from its grange at Huncrundel, south-west of the church.[50] The endowment of the two parts represented a rectorial estate of 49 acres. West Dereham Abbey possessed much more land in Holkham, and it seems that the Feodary did not take account of the extent of the possessions of the Premonstratensians of West Dereham in the late thirteenth century. The Dereham Cartulary contained grants of land to the Abbey by several Holkham tenants, probably dating from the second half of the thirteenth century.[51] West Dereham was tenant of a fold *juxta mariscum saleficum*. An account of John Denny, Dereham's agent at Holkham, survives for 1366-7 and describes a sizable demesne. Edmund Lucas, himself *domicellus de Est Derham*, was originally the administrator of West Dereham's demesne at Holkham before he became lord of Neel Manor through marriage to its heiress. A terrier of 1542 counted about 110 acres in the estate, mostly in pieces of land on the western side of the parish.[52]

The three other Norfolk monasteries with lands at Holkham, the priories of Walsingham, Peterstone and Creake, belonged to the order of Augustinian canons. As shown above, the best endowed seems to have been Walsingham with 53 acres of marsh, 46 acres of land and a fold. Indeed the survey of folds in 1306 ascribed 2 folds to the Priory of Walsingham, one of the 9

---

50   Dereham grange, at Huncrundel, stood at the junction of a Roman road which formed the western parish boundary between Holkham and Burnham Thorpe, and the road which once ran from Burnham to Wighton, bounding Holkham South Field.

51   Cart. of Dereham, Fos. 258v to 267.

52   HD 53, *Compotus Johannis Denny servientis Abbatis de Derham*, Sept. 1366-Sept. 1367. HD 194: Edmund Lucas was referred to as bailiff of 'Hondcrondale', the grange of the Abbot of West Dereham, for default of suit at the leet of Burghall, 22 July 1410; HD 284, *The Abbot of Dereham's dragge in Holkham fylde*, c. 1542.

faldae communes and the other within the salt marshes.[53] The Walsingham Cartulary gave a register of 39 charters in its Holkham portion and, most noteworthy, the gift to the Priory by Ralph, son of Silvester, on 25 November 1250, of 32 acres of arable and 25 acres of marsh.[54] A terrier of 1430 described pieces of arable amounting to some 86 acres.[55] Peterstone Priory, situated at Burnham Overy, a little west of Holkham, possessed 80 acres and a fold according to the Feodary. But two terriers of the first decade of the fourteenth century enumerated the pieces of land owned by Peterstone at Holkham which included over 140 acres of arable.[56] A rental of 1337 listed 28 *liberi tenentes* with holdings in the manor.[57] The survey of folds in 1306 showed Peterstone as holding 2 folds, a *falda communis*, and a fold called Cotesfold, opened between the festivals of St James (25 July) and St Martin (11 Nov.), in partnership with Humphrey David.[58]

The third convent of Augustinian canons, the Abbey of Creake, had, according to the Feodary, 40 acres and a fold at Holkham. The 28 Holkham documents in the Creake Cartulary gave a list of grants of land in the second half of the thirteenth century amounting to about 90 acres. The area of some of the pieces was not indicated.[59]

The Folds

The location and ownership of folds formed one of the more significant aspects of seigneurial structure at Holkham. Those who had folds and therefore had flocks of sheep, were the chief lay and ecclesiastical lords and *liberi tenentes* of Holkham. The Feodary of 1279–80 showed that each of the manors had at least one fold. The total number of folds was 16, including the two halves of the manor of Burton Lazars held by the Prior of Peterstone and Gilbert Souter and Humphrey David. Three *liberi tenentes* of Hillhall had folds (Peterstone, Creake and Silk). There were four folds dependent on Burghall (Denise de Montchesney, Geoffrey le Bret, Ralph Hacun and Bartholomew de Burgate). Bartholomew de Burgate himself was holding 3 folds. The Prior of Peterstone and Humphrey David were mentioned twice as

53   HD 22a, Neel Cart., Fo. 1v no 1, 16 April 1306, inquiry copied by Edmund Lucas as a significant document at the beginning of his *Cartulary*.

54   Cart. of Walsingham, no. CIV, Fo. 48: *Carta Radulfi filij Silvestri de uno messuagio et XXXII acris terre arabilis et XXV acris marisci.* HD 3 is a copy of the final concord of 25 Nov. 1250 (PRO, CP 25(1) 157/80, no. 1159) confirming the grant to Walsingham.

55   HD 127, Terrier of the Priory of Walsingham renewed ... 1430-1, renewed 1467-8.

56   HD 205 Fo. 15, *Visus terrarum Prioratus de Peterstone facta anno regis Edwardi filij Edwardi VIII*, 1314-15 and *BD 28*, same terrier in the same year but with details of crops.

57   HD 205 no. xiii, d, Fo. 18v, Free rental of Peterstone in Holkham, c. 1337.

58   HD 22a, Neel Cart., Fo. 1v no. 1, An Inquisition on the Folds of Holkham, 16 April 1306, *videlicet falde Prioris de Petra et Humfredi Davyd conjunctim qui habent cursum inter Haddedowe et Thorpmere.*

59   *Cart. of Creake*, no. 175, Fo. 203.

owners of folds. The survey of folds in 1306 was more exact, both on the three kinds of fold (9 *communes*, 5 *juxta mariscum saleficum*, 6 *cotesfoldes*) and on their owners (see Table 1).[60] West Dereham had only one fold within the limits of the marsh. In all, in this special inquiry, 20 folds were delimited, and they had 16 tenants. The names of *liberi tenentes*, proprietors of folds, according to the 1306 survey, appeared in the original charters summarized by Edmund Lucas, as the most frequent witnesses: Martin Goldwyn, 44 times between 1274 and 1317, John Aynild, 34 times between 1274 and 1347, Richard le Northerne, 43 times between 1274 and 1322, William Silk, 46 times between 1284 and 1343. Sometimes, of course, a father had the same name as his son and heir.

MANORIAL COMPLEXITY AND DIVIDED LORDSHIP

On the whole, the manorial structure of Holkham was particularly complex, and divided and weak lordship allowed smaller competing freeholders to dominate the scene and to animate the land market in free tenures.

The Holkham *feodum* of Wighton, held by Geoffrey de Lusignan, was a smaller manor of 219 acres with two foldcourses. There was no demesne, and the two sub-manors of Ralph Noyon de Salle (136 acres) and of Hubert de Wighton (31 acres) were connected with manorial centres situated elsewhere. The first of these two sub-manors had 23 *sokemanni* or freemen holding villein land, and the second had 6 freeholds.

The d'Akeny-Hillhall Manor had a very small demesne, a messuage with 14 acres, but it was endowed with important seigneurial prerogatives in Holkham town, port and fields (Cf. 22a, Neel Cart., nos. 150 and 151). The lord, Thomas d'Akeny had a court baron, a market and a fair. He also had a windmill and 3 foldcourses. Its dependent holdings of 143 acres of villein land were held by 36 *sokemanni* and 3 cottars. But a larger portion of the manor, 173 acres, was held by six freeholders. Here a slightly larger 'small' manor, 323 acres according to Kosminsky's scale, had its larger portion (54%) held by freeholders.[61]

---

60   HD 22a, Neel Cart., Fo. 1v no. 1, An Inquisition on the Folds of Holkham, 16 April 1306.

61   Cf. E.A. Kosminsky, *Studies in the Agrarian History of England in the Thirteenth Century*, (R.H. Hilton, ed.).1956, pp. 95–130.

Table 1

FOLDS AT HOLKHAM IN 1306

I (9) *FALDAE COMMUNES currentes undique in campis et brueris ejusdem ville et non plures*

Dominus **Hugh de Veer**
Abbas de **Crek**
Prior de **Walsingham**
Martin Goldewyn
Prior de **Petra**
John le Bret
John Ayneld (ex dimissione **Walteri Hakun**)
John Hammond (ex dimissione **Galfridi le Bret**)
John Godwyne

II (5) *SUNT ET ALIE FALDE JUXTA MARISCUM SALEFICUM ibidem et juxta campum adjacentem annuatim currentes*

Dominus **Hugh de Veer**
Prior de **Walsingham**
Abbas de **Derham**
Richard le Northerne (ex dimissione **Bartholomei de Burgate**)
William Silk (ex dimissione **Payn Wolleman**)

III (6) *SUNT ALIE FALDE QUE VOCANTUR 'COTESFOLDES' que habent cursum suum in campis ejusdem ville in locis diversis que debent levari circa festum Sancti Iacobi [25 Jul.] et habent cursum suum usque festum Sancti Martini [11 Nov.]*

Prior de **Petra** **Humphrey David**	Conjunctim currens inter **Hadehowe** et **Thorpmere** vocata **Hammestalefolde**
Bartholomew de Burgate	empta de **Bartholomeo** de **Wighton** currens inter **Thorpmere, Creykgate** et **Coppinge**
Humphrey David et parcennari sui loco **Eborardi Caly**	currens inter **Clynt** et **Hadehowe**
Bartholomew Adam et parcennari sui	currens inter **Gibbesgate** et **Hadehowe**
Geoffrey Poysun et parcennari	quam emit **W. Wake** de feodo **Hakonis** currens inter Aulam de **Monchensy** et **Creyksty**
Bertrammus le Verdoun (quondam)	currens in campis de **Holmys** inter **Hundecroundeldrove** et **Millehil** et viam regiam

Source: HD 22a, Fo. 1v no. 1

According to Kosminsky's scale, the manor of Burghall, the largest Holkham manor, was of medium size, with approximately 900 acres. Its manorial structure was of a classic pattern. It had a substantial demesne: 28% of its land (248 acres) was under direct seigneurial farming, 37% was villein land (337), and the freeholds amounted to 35% (319 acres). Among these, the Bret sub-manor, holding court for its tenantry, accounted for 210 acres. In 1314, the successor sub-manor of Neel expanded its holding by buying out other freeholders of several Holkham manors, using a very active intra-manorial land market in freeholds.

The Bret-Tobers manor, sub-manor of the Tattershall fee through Roger Brown, had a demesne of 60 acres (38%), a small area (32 acres) of villein land held by 5 'villani', and freeholds representing 42%, i.e. the larger part of its area. On the other hand, the Burton Lazars holding of 62 acres, directly held from Gilbert de Clare, himself tenant-in-chief, had a demesne of 31 acres with the other 31 acres held by freeholders.

All the other small Holkham holdings had rather irregular patterns: The Vewter holding of the Tattershall Honour had only 16 acres of villein land held by his villeins; the Hindringham holding of the Nevile fee had 18 acres of villein land held by 3 villeins and 16 1/2 acres held by 3 free tenants; Roger Bacon's fee had 15 acres of villein land, 23 acres of freeholds and no demesne; the Carbrooke fee and the Caly and David fee of the Warenne Honour had only freeholds, and the Holkham church of St Withburga held 40 acres, equally from two tenants-in-chief, and 9 acres of villein land.

Smaller and irregular manors and freeholders (35) dominated the Holkham landscape in 1279–80. Complexity and division of lordship seemed the main feature, here as in Hevingham. The necessarily communal organisation of the foldcourses induced some sort of collective lordship, associating manorial lords and the main '*liberi tenentes*'.

THE REGIONAL CONTEXT

A comparison of Holkham's manorial structure with the manorial structures of the other seven west Norfolk villages whose Hundred Rolls returns have survived will place its specific landscape in its medieval regional context. In spite of its fragmentary nature, the return of Burnham Thorpe, immediately to the west, shows that there were, in 1279–80, four tenants-in-chief, William de Calthorpe, Earl Warenne, Earl Roger Bigod, the Countess of Arundel with 9 sub-manors. These had generally small demesnes and numerous small holdings. There were four foldcourses.[62]

---

62   Fuller Collection, 7/5, mm. 1–2, Burnham Thorpe.

In Kettlestone, to the south-east (5 km east of Fakenham), the *capitalis dominus* was Thomas de Hauvyle with only 4 acres in demesne, a windmill, a foldcourse, liberty of bull and boar, and the view of frankpledge. He had 217 acres held by his villeins, and 4 freeholders with medium and small size messuages. One of them, Matilda, daughter of Roger Godeholt, had 9 free sub-tenants and a foldcourse. The other tenant-in-chief was Earl Warenne: two main holdings depended on the Warenne fee, the manors of Geoffrey de Hindringham (also a lord in Holkham), and the manor of Walter de Grantcourt who was also the lord of the two dependent hamlets of Fulmodestone and Croxton. The manor of Geoffrey de Hindringham had a very small demesne of 1 acre, a windmill and a foldcourse, liberty of bull and boar and 2 cottars, but it had 19 freeholders who had 34 sub-tenants holding 51 sub-tenancies. None of the freeholders held more than 10 acres. Most of the sub-tenants held from 3 acres to 1 rood. The whole of Geoffrey de Hindringham's holding amounted to little more than 120 acres.

The manor of Walter de Grantcourt in Kettlestone was much more substantial as a seigneurial holding, as it had a demesne of 115 acres, free warren, liberty of bull and boar and also view of frankpledge. It had 70 acres of villein land held by 15 villeins with 15 messuages. Walter de Grantcourt was the patron of Kettlestone's church, where Payn de Grantcourt, a brother or a cousin, was rector. In the hamlets of Fulmodestone and Croxton he was '*capitalis dominus*' and the largest landlord, while the Hospitallers of Carbrooke and the Prior of Castle Acre had smallholdings. He had a large demesne of at least 480 acres, comprising 5 *carucatæ* of arable land (one *carucata* = 80–120 acres), 23 acres of meadow, 32 acres of pasture, 25 acres of wood, a windmill, free warren, liberty of bull and boar, and view of frankpledge. Thirty villeins and seven cottars held 151 acres in villeinage, and 32 acres were held by seven freeholders. The demesne of Walter de Grantcourt was relatively large and represented twice the size of the villein lands and freeholds combined.[63]

In North Barsham, which, in the Hundred Rolls of 1279–80, was the most fully covered village, with 198 entries, the *capitalis dominus* was Thomas Trivet, under Earl Warenne, as tenant-in-chief. There were five main head tenants, and three principal manors. Trivet Manor had 100 acres as demesne, liberty of bull and boar, a foldcourse and a water mill shared with William Braunche. There were 92 acres of villein land held by 15 villeins and their messuages, 8 cottars and 13 freeholders with their sub-tenants who held approximately 40 acres. The second manor in North Barsham was held by William son of Nicholas, holding his land from William de Wauncy. He had a demesne of 59 acres, with 56 acres of arable, 3 acres of meadow, a water

---

63   Ibid., mm. 3–4, Kettlestone with Fulmodestone and Croxton.

mill, liberty of bull and boar and a foldcourse. Villein land amounted to 22 acres only, held by 3 villeins and 3 cottars. His manor was characterized by an extremely large number of freeholders whose lands amounted to nearly 260 acres: sixteen main tenants held 97 plots held by other freeholders. In all, the manor of William son of Nicholas, comprised more than 342 acres. A third manor, held by John son of Henry le Syre, had as demesne 63 1/2 acres, the half of a water mill, liberty of bull and boar and one foldcourse. There were two villein messuages of 10 acres each, and seven cottars holding 5 acres and 1 rood. There were also 31 freeholds, amounting to more than 80 acres. Hamo son of Richard and 11 freeholders held the Walpole-Bardolf-Warenne fee in North Barsham. He had 12 acres and one foldcourse as demesne. Most of the freeholders held their land here from John, son of Henry le Syre (35 acres). Queen Eleanor, the King's mother,[64] had a manor of 27 acres held by 16 freeholders. It did not have any demesne nor villein land. Gilbert le Danterre had a holding of 10 acres and a foldcourse, and Hervey de Stanhowe held a water mill. The rector of the church of North Barsham was John Trivet, a relative of the 'capitalis dominus' as in Kettlestone, and his church was endowed with 44 acres. The manor of the Priory of Castle Acre had one free tenant holding 13 acres. The remaining small plots of land were held by other free tenants.[65]

Divided lordship and a complex structure characterized East Barsham too in 1279–80, though Earl Warenne was tenant-in-chief for the whole vill. The fee of Thomas de Hauvyle included two manors. The manor of Roger de Prigetone had a demesne of 62 acres, two thirds of a foldcourse and liberty of bull and boar. Sixteen villeins held 107 acres, and 15 acres were divided between three freeholders. The second sub-manor of the Hauvyle fee was that of Roger de Wolferton with, as demesne, a messuage of 40 acres, a water mill and one third of a foldcourse. Eight villeins held 47 acres and there were three freeholders, one holding 3 roods and the two others 2 curtilagia. In the Bardolf-Warenne fee, Roger de Saint Martin was the lord of the manor with a demesne of 81 acres, liberty of bull and boar, a foldcourse and a court regulating the assize of bread and ale. Twenty-one villeins were holding 101 acres of villein land, nine cottars held 2 1/2 acres, and five freeholders held 16 acres. A sub-manor of Roger de Saint Martin was held by John de Salle with a demesne of 52 acres and seven main freeholders who themselves had freeholders as sub-tenants. Henry de Warham's manor was held from Robert Bole, with Earl Warenne as tenant-in-chief. The demesne included 66 acres, one foldcourse and liberty of bull and boar. Ninety seven acres were held by 15 villeins. Thirteen main freeholders with a number of sub-tenants held 124

---

64   Eleanor of Provence, 1217–91, widow of Henry III, was the mother of Edward I.
65   Ibid., 7/5, mm. 5–7, North Barsham.

acres. Among them, the most important was the Prior of Coxford, who held a messuage of 54 acres, liberty of bull and a foldcourse. The Priory of Castle Acre had the advowson of the church of East Barsham, and Earl Warenne had three free tenants who had a number of sub-tenants. There were two small manors directly held from Earl Warenne. The fact that he was tenant-in-chief of all the manors did not prevent complexity and actual division of lordship in the manorial landscape. Roger de Burnham's holding of 15 acres was held by Walter Mast, and Jordan Foliot's manor of 23 acres was held by four villeins with 4 messuages.[66]

The manorial landscapes of West Barsham and Sculthorpe perhaps corresponded most to a so-called north-west Norfolk pattern of relatively strong lordship. The *capitalis dominus* in West Barsham was William de Wauncy, tenant of Earl Warenne. The single manor had a demesne of 327 acres, a windmill, liberty of fold, of warren, of bull and boar, view of frankpledge and the fair in autumn (29 August). 440 acres of villein land were held by fifty villeins with their messuages. The rest of the vill was held by numerous free tenants and their free sub-tenants. Among the larger holdings, the Priory of Castle Acre had 120 acres, a foldcourse, the advowson of the church, and 10 villeins holding 36 acres, Nicholas son of Ralph le Herre held 71 acres and the Priory of Fakenham 36 acres. Sculthorpe itself was held directly by Earl Warenne, tenant-in-chief holding the Hundred of Gallow. He had a demesne of 330 acres, a water mill, a fish pond and 34 villeins holding 460 acres and 35 *cottarij* holding 27 acres with their cottages. The rest (456 acres) was held by the 24 main freeholders and their sub-tenants. William de Wauncy, the Prior of Castle Acre, the Prior of Fakenham and Ralph Capellanus held the four foldcourses of West Barsham and Sculthorpe.[67]

Lastly Waterden, directly adjoining Holkham on its south-east boundary, had two main manors under Earl Warenne as tenant-in-chief. The *capitalis dominus* was Roger de Saint Martin. He had 67 acres as demesne lands, the advowson of the church, a foldcourse, liberty of bull and boar, the assize of bread and ale, and the view of frankpledge. The villein lands amounted to 107 acres held by 17 villeins and 2 cottars. He had a manor house situated outside his messuage. The freeholders were very numerous: Richard Adylwald, Nicholas de Frenge, Roger de Waterden and Roger Simenel were the most important, with many sub-tenants. The second manor was held by William son of Nicholas who held a manor in North Barsham from William de Wauncy and Earl Warenne. He had a very small demesne and mainly a large number of freeholders with small parcels. There were also 6 other

---

66 Ibid., 7/5, mm. 14–15, East Barsham
67 Ibid., mm. 12–13, West Barsham; mm. 10–11, Sculthorpe.

freeholds, from 15 to 30 acres each, with a number of free sub-tenants. Here, as in Holkham, the Hospitallers of Carbrooke had a small holding, and the Priory of Castle Acre had the advowson of the church. In Waterden there were 5 foldcourses and 2 windmills.[68]

Holkham had 2 windmills and 9 'common foldcourses', 5 others on the salt marshes, and 6 other temporary ones, called 'cotesfoldes'. It also had a port and an important market. Its features comparable to most of the seven other vills, described in the surviving returns of the Hundred Rolls of 1279–80, are the number of smaller lords and freeholders which accounted for the complexity of its manorial structure.

FEODA TENENTES AND LIBERI TENENTES OF HOLKHAM

The Holkham documents throw a vivid light on the middling and lesser *feoda tenentes* and their *liberi tenentes* who dominated the local scene in the late thirteenth century. Among those whom fourteenth century nomenclature would describe as *armigeri* or *servientes* might one, perhaps, class Geoffrey le Bret, Roger Bacon, John le Bret and Ralph Hacun? Their tenure was subject to military service, but armorial seals were absent from the many sealed documents of the Brets. From all the members of this little group of *feoda tenentes* the Brets were outstanding because of the fact that our records centered round the *Cartulary* of the Neels as successors of the Brets. The le Brets were principal parties in 67 of the charters summarized in the Neel Cartulary. Indeed they had the biggest of the 3 subordinate manors of Burghall, a fact which ranked them next after Burghall and Hillhall on the local stage. The cartularies of Dereham, Creake and Walsingham showed that no other Holkham family was as generous as the Brets with their 17 grants in free alms for religious houses.[69] The absence of a cartulary for the Priory of Peterstone makes it impossible to know whether it would have told the same story. According to the Feodary of 1279–80 Geoffrey le Bret had eight *liberi tenentes*. When Peter le Bret conveyed his fief to Richard and Katerine Neel in August 1314, he enumerated his 20 *liberi tenentes*.[70] The rules of inheritance of this elite followed the principle of primogeniture in the male line.[71] Eight members of the family of le Bret were witnesses on 115 occasions here, and John le Bret, son of Geoffrey le Bret, witnessed 51 of our original deeds between 1284 and 1330.

---

68   Ibid., 7/5, mm. 8–9, Waterden.
69   Le Bret family: *Cart. of Creake*, nos. 182, 183, 189, 198, 201, 203; Cart. of Dereham, nos. XVI, XIX, XX, XXVI, XXVII; Cart. of Walsingham, nos. CV, CVI, CII, CVIII, CIX, CX, CXXV, CXXIX.
70   HD 22a, Neel Cart., Fo. 17v no. 191, 19 Aug. 1314.
71   HD 7, Geoffrey le Bret to his son, John le Bret, 23 May 1284.

Ralph Hacun, another *feodum tenens*, but of lower status, at least in Holkham, held his small fee in 1279 as a dependency of Burghall (1 messuage, 30 acres, 1 fold). He had nine *liberi tenentes*, among whom were the Prior of Walsingham and the Prior of Peterstone. He was also a tenant of the manor of Hillhall (24 acres, 1 fold and 1 marsh) under John Silk. He was the sole grantor in 2 charters, and with his nephew Walter he granted 6 *pecie* of land to Simon Hammond.[72] Ralph and Walter Hacun were well represented in the cartulary of Dereham, and in those of Walsingham and Creake. In the Holkham charters published here, they acted often as witnesses, Ralph in 17 charters (1270–1294–6) and Walter Hacun in 27 charters (1291–1304).

Bartholomew de Burgate, on the other hand, had tenures in most of the Holkham manors as sub-tenant, but he held his own *feodum* directly from Denise de Montchesney, lady of Burghall (40 acres, 1 messuage, 1 fold). No obligation to military service was attached to it. He was the only holder of three folds in 1279. His son Thomas was a tenant of West Dereham and a benefactor of Walsingham.[73] Bartholomew de Burgate made 4 grants and appears as a witness in 51 charters in this edition (1272–1302). His son, John de Burgate, was a capital pledge named at the leet of July 1350.[74]

Liber tenens, but not *feodum tenens* like the Brets, Hacun and Burgate, John Silk had holdings in most of the Holkham manors in 1279–80. He was listed 9 times as a tenant in the Feodary. His most important holding was held under Ralph Hacun in the manor of Hillhall. He purchased more land than he sold, and was a grantee in a series of enfeoffments, especially on the part of Geoffrey le Bret. He had three sons, Adam, Gilbert and William, and father and sons were witnesses together in certain charters. Gilbert Silk borrowed 5 marks in June 1289 from Saleman, son of Deulecres, Jew of Norwich.[75] William Silk witnessed 46 of our grants between 1274 and 1315. A John Silk witnessed 43 charters between 1284 and 1343, and it is reasonable to believe that a John Silk senior was the witness of the 31 grants of 1284 to 1296, and that John, son of William Silk, was the witness in 12 grants from 1319 to 1343.

---

72 HD 22a, Neel Cart., Fo. 5v nos. 68, 69; Fo. 6v no. 80.
73 Cart. of Dereham, no. XXV, Fo. 266; Cart. of Walsingham, no. CXX, Fo. 51v.
74 HD 87a, Burghall leet court, 22 July 1350.
75 PRO, E 101 250/7, 1291/2, *Gilbertus Silk filius Johannis Silk de Holkham de Comite Norfolci debet Salemanno medico filio Deulecres de Norwico Judeo XX quart. frumenti vel in quinque marcas per unam obligacionem cuius data est die mercuri infra septimanam pentecost, anno regni Regis E. XVII* (Wed. 8 June 1289).

THE NEW NEEL MANOR

The charters collected by Edmund Lucas in 1415 and then transcribed and
calendared in his *Cartulary*, illustrated the genesis and evolution of a
seigneurial inheritance in the first half of the fourteenth century. There was a
very active land market at work in Holkham from the second half of the
thirteenth century, and maybe well before. The process of social
differentiation in the group of *liberi tenentes* was fostered by the use of this
market in free tenures, the purchase and sale of pieces of land with the
charter Lucas called *feoffamentum* as its tool. It was this market in holdings
which allowed Richard Neel, coming from Burnham Norton, to create a new
manor in Holkham.

   In the first group of documents, which he put together between Fo. 2 and
Fo. 12v (151 items), the majority dealt with the holdings of the manor of
Geoffrey le Bret, which passed to the Neels by the conveyance of 1314.[76]
Among the 82 vendors were 10 members of the Bret family. Geoffrey le Bret
and his son John were, by themselves, responsible for 32% of all the sales.
Of 19 sales by Geoffrey, 13 (68%) went to a single purchaser, Simon
Hammond. Simon took the same proportion of the 27 sales of John le Bret,
i.e. 19 (67%). After them came Adam le Bret with 4 sales. Bartholomew de
Burgate, Walter Hacun, Adam Hammond, William Silk and Bartholomew
Smith fell into the category which made 3 sales. The rest of the vendors
made 1 or 2, like Walter de Calthorpe, lord of the manor of Burnham
Thorpe, Holkham's western neighbour, or Everard Caly and Humphrey
David, chief tenants of the fief of Warenne. As deeds of enfeoffment and
sales of land, these grants formed the legal instrument of relationships within
the group of *liberi tenentes*.

   Just as Geoffrey and John le Bret were outstanding among the ranks of
the grantors, so on the parts of the 57 grantees one single individual was
prominent: Simon Hammond (*filius Hamonis*) was the one who gained by
34% of all the conveyances. It was from John le Bret that he received the
main grants in 1295 and 1296. These sales often did not state the precise
areas of land transferred: *tenementum* or *pecia* had to suffice. Serfs were sold
the same way.[77] Simon Hammond became one of the chief *liberi tenentes* of
the Brets in the last two decades of the thirteenth century even though he
appeared only once in the Feodary of 1279-80, as the tenant of Ralph Hacun.
Far behind him in the group of purchasers came John Silk with 8
acquisitions, William Craske with 7 and William Curson with 5. Secular
clerks were included in the ranks of the purchasers: Richard de Barking,

---

76   HD 22a, Neel Cart., Fo. 17v no. 191, 19 Aug. 1314.
77   Ibid., Fo. 8v no. 104, John le Bret to Simon Hammond, ... *Gilbertum Gurle et Elvinam
      Daleman nativos meos.*

rector of Egmere, Walter de Mundene, perpetual vicar of Holkham, the *capellani* of Holkham, William de Heveringlond and Robert de Knapton, and William Horsford, rector of Stiffkey.[78]

The second set of transcripts in the Neel Cartulary, from Fo. 13 to Fo. 24v and in his *Gazetteer*, from Fo. 41 to Fo. 50v, rehearsed the purchases made by the grandparents, uncle and father of Edmund Lucas's wife, Mary Neel. It was the history of the construction, piece by piece, of the manor of Neel at Holkham. Between 1314 and 1445, 4411/2 acres had been bought. The centrepiece of the new manor was the old manor of Geoffrey le Bret, left to his son John in 1284.[79] In April 1302, the manorial court was held in the name of Eustace le Bret, and between 1311 and 1313 in that of Peter le Bret, another brother of John.[80] The first court of Richard Neel was dated 1314-15.[81]

It was possible to identify 112 acts of purchase made by the Neels between 1314 and 1345. Among the 39 vendors we found a score of purchasers in the first series of grants analysed above. The Neels bought from 4 chief vendors: the Brets and three *liberi tenentes*, Adam Craske, William Roteney, and Thomas le Northerne.[82] The conveyance of the *feodum* and *dominium* of Peter le Bret, Geoffrey's heir, occurred in various stages. Five deeds calendared by Edmund Lucas recorded the process. First that of August 1314, executed at Burnham, transferred to Richard and Katerine Neel 1/2 acre and *totam croftam suam cum pertinenciis in Holkham*. The same conveyance included 2 *nativi*, Henry and Christiana Underhowe, and 20 *liberi tenentes*. Of these he made a nominal roll.[83] In the following year 3 deeds, at some months' interval, transferred to the Neels the heart of the possessions of Peter le Bret: first, on 5 April 1315, the messuage which he held of his father Geoffrey, and 3 *pecie* of land; then, on 19 May 1315, a *pecia terre cum pertinenciis* with 4 *nativi*, John Thurbern and Reynald son of Roger Thurbern, and Matilda and Mabel Ernald. On 18 August 1315 Peter le Bret made a general confirmation of all the sales by an act of *relaxacio* and *quieta clamacio*.[84] Eustace le Bret, rector of Tasburgh, on 6 May 1317 gave up to the Neels any rights which he might claim in the *dominium* of the Brets at Holkham.[85] Edmund Lucas summarised at the head of the list of the Neel

78   Ibid., nos. 6, 19, 22, 50, 85, 138, 139, 148.
79   HD 7, Geoffrey le Bret to his son John, 23 May 1284.
80   HD 20, 3 Aug. 1311, 6 Aug. 1312.
81   HD 20, 21 Nov. 1314.
82   HD 22a, Neel Cart., Fos. 13–24v nos. 151–252, *Copia cartarum de perquisitione Ricardi Neel de Holkham et Katerine uxoris ejus Thome Neel et Gilberti filiorum predictorum Ricardi et Katerine*, and the alphabetical gazetteer, Fos. 41–50v.
83   Ibid., Fo. 17v no. 191, Peter le Bret to Richard and Katerine Neel, 19 Aug. 1314.
84   Ibid., Fo. 18 no. 193, 19 May 1315; no. 194, 5 April 1315 and 18 Aug. 1315.
85   Ibid., Fo. 18 no. 195, 6 March 1317.

purchases what was certainly the final stage of the transfer, a deed of
confirmation made on 18 July 1329.[86]

After the Brets, the most important vendors to the Neels were three *liberi
tenentes*: Adam Craske (22 sales), William Roteney (11) and Thomas le
Northerne (22). This trio accounted for 44% of all the transactions. The
Neels bought 32 acres, and half a fold in 22 purchases from Adam Craske.
From Thomas le Northerne the Neels bought 67 acres in 16 transactions,
between 1332 and 1336. From William Roteney, in 1323–4, they had bought
25 acres in 27 pieces belonging to different furlongs which William held
principally in the fee of Adam le Bret. Roteney's holding was very
fragmented. It is one example of the free tenures which the Neels amassed in
the course of manorial concentration. A number of purchases were described
as adjoining pieces which already belonged to the Neels.[87]

The Neels succeeded to the Brets in all their possessions in Norfolk, not
only at Holkham but also at Surlingham and Swainsthorpe, south of Norwich.
One may conjecture that the wealth of the Neels of Burnham was new at the
beginning of the fourteenth century and that their purchases at Holkham,
Surlingham and Swainsthorp confirmed their rise to the gentry. At Holkham
their rise was connected with the existence of a long standing, very active
market in free tenures fuelled by a numerous group of *liberi tenentes*. The
question arises: were the Neels examples of a new gentry rising in the first
half of the fourteenth century, or was the establishment of a new manor of
Neel, absorbing smaller ones, simply due to the downward mobility of the
Bret family?

THE ECONOMY

To understand the system of peasant holdings, their size, services and rents,
and the practical organization of agriculture at Holkham towards the close of
the thirteenth century, the best source is the document transcribed by Edmund
Lucas under the rubric, *Tenementa de Burghall in Holkham*.[88] It is a
custumal, dating from 1273, and listing the tenants with a description of their
services and rents in relation to the size of their holdings. The 3 rentals of
the Brets of the turn of the century can also provide useful indications, but

---

86 Ibid., Fo. 13 no. 152, 18 July 1329.
87 HD 81, mm. 2, *Tenementa que Ricardus Nel et Caterina uxor adquisierunt de Willelmo
    Roteney in Holkham*. About 24 acres in 27 different *pecie* among which there were two
    of 4 acres. As for the rest, most parcels were of 1/2 acre to 1 acre. The smaller measured
    1 rood.
88 HD 22a, Neel Cart., Fos. 31–34v no. 255. In fact the Neel Cartulary copy is entitled:
    *Rentale de Burghall in Holkham, Rotulus de tenemento quod fuit Domini Warini de
    Monte Caniso de Redditibus* and *consuetudinibus tam liberorum quam villanorum in
    Holkham*. HD 4 and HD 4a are original parchment rolls of 1272–3 and 1303, from which
    the copy was made.

we do not have any accounts before 1330.[89] It is by a retrospective use of documents of the second half of the fourteenth century, and of the fifteenth and even sixteenth centuries, that light is thrown on many aspects. The court rolls between 1277 and 1332 have only survived in pitiable numbers, some 18 courts for the manors of Hillhall, Bret and Neel. After 1332 the series of rolls begins to give better cover for the manor of Burghall.[90]

According to the custumal of 1273, which appears to be the updating of an older document started about 1248, in the time of Warin de Montchesney, the free and servile holdings of Burghall, taken as a whole, extended over 670 acres. It listed the holdings of 79 tenants. Among the first 10 were found the names of the tenants of the *feoda* and of the *liberi tenentes* of the fee of Denise de Montchesney: Ralph Hacun, Peter, Thomas and Adam le Bret, and also Bartholomew de Burgate, Richard Mariot, Geoffrey Goodwin and the rest. For them it was a question of payment of rents and of some services commuted into cash. If one limits the analysis to 62 tenures extending over 3711/2 acres and forming the heart of the peasant holdings, one can arrive at an idea of their average size and of the conditions of rents and services to which they were subjected (cf. Table 2).

Table 2

PEASANT HOLDINGS AT BURGHALL (HOLKHAM)

c. 1250–1273

	12 ac	6 ac.	3 ac.	2 ac.	1 ac.	1/2 ac.	
number	17	19	12	6	3	5	62
%	27	31	20	9	5	8	100%
area (ac.)	204	114	36	12	3	21/2	3711/2

---

[89]   HD 11, Rental of Geoffrey le Bret, c. 1295; HD 20 and HD 21, Rentals of Peter le Bret, c. 1303.

[90]   Cf. Appendix 1 for list of court rolls.

More than half of the holdings were of 6 or 12 acres (58%). At Brancaster
and Binham one usually found the unit of a 12 acre holding called toftland,
erving or manloth.[91] The *tenementa* of 12 acres occupied, at Burghall, over
half the area.

The *tenementa* were normally held by several people. The tendency
towards fragmentation of units of tenure was the product of the pressure of
increasing population, which was the reason for the existence of tenures of 2
acres and less. The custumal of Burghall showed clearly the internal fission
of *tenementa*, which, however, did not prevent them remaining working units
in the agricultural system. We find 5 *parcenarij* holding 6 acres called after
Thurild, and in the case of the *terra Bisshop* 3 acres were divided between 9
parcenarij, while the lord held 10 acres. In each *tenementum* the demesne
formed a part of which the size varied. Partible inheritance certainly played a
role in this fragmentation. The Hillhall Book described in detail 9 fragmented
tenements of 6 acres, liable in turn for the service of *messor* in 1467-8,
which showed one of the tenemental unit's traditional functions.[92]

There was little difference at Burghall in relation to the size of the
holdings between the kinds of rent and labour services exacted, and
everything was translated into its monetary equivalent and commuted. The
table of rents and boonworks showed a certain scaling of rents, up to a
holding of 24 acres (cf. Table 3). The holdings were charged both with the
tax of *faldagium* for the right of participation in the seigneurial fold, and
with a tax which corresponded to the supply of a half measure of dung
(*fimus*). With the *precaria cum caruca*, labour services in autumn were the
heaviest. The custumal concluded with a total in money for all the rents and
commuted works, but it also reckoned the total of days of work due on the
lands for the various services. It was a mixed system: a paid work force was
employed on the demesne but it was also possible, according to requirements,
to mobilise a part of the labour of the tenants.

On the manor of Geoffrey le Bret, a first rental of about 1295 enumerated
the tenants, whether *liberi* or *custumarij*, without distinction. A second rental
of Peter le Bret of about 1303 listed seven *liberi tenentes* and 18 *custumarij,
nativi et villani*.[93]

---

91   D.C. Douglas, *The Social Structure of Medieval East Anglia*, 1927, p. 43; B. Dodwell,
      'Holdings and Inheritance in Medieval East Anglia', *Economic History Review*, 1967, pp.
      53–66; P.D.A. Harvey, ed., *The Peasant Land Market in England*, 1984, Introduction, pp.
      1–28; Janet Williamson, 'Norfolk: Thirteenth Century', ibid., pp. 31–102.
92   HD 75, The Hillhall Book, Fos. 4-10v, detailed description of 9 customary tenements
      liable for the office of *messor*, 1467-8.
93   HD 11, Rental of Geoffrey le Bret, c. 1295 and HD 21, Rental of Peter le Bret, c. 1303.

Table 3

RENTS AND BOONWORKS AT BURGHALL (HOLKHAM)
1250–1273

	3ac.	6 ac.	12 ac.	24 ac.
AVERAGIUM	2d.	3d.	3d.	3d.
CAR. AUT.	6d.	3d.	3d.	3d.
AVENA	–	6d.	12d.	21d.
BRASEUM	–	3 ob.	3d.	3d.
CENSA	4d.	8d.	14d.	28d.
FALDAGIUM	1d.	3d.	4d.	6d.
FIMUS	1 ob.	1 ob.	4d.	4d.
FLAGELLATIO	4d.	8d.	16d.	16d.
GALLINE	1d.	1d.	2d.	4d.
OPER. AUT.	8d.	16d.	18d.	24d.
PREC. AUT.	6d.	–	–	3d.
PREC. ET CARUC.	3d.	6d.	6d.	6d.
SARCLATIO	3 ob.	3 ob.	3 ob.	3 ob.
STAGNUM	1d.	1d.	1d.	1d.
WARDESE	1 ob.	–	–	1 ob.
WODELODE	–	–	–	–
Summa	3s.2d.ob.	4s.10d.ob. quadr.	7s.3d.ob.	10s.7d.
	WILLIAM ASKETEL	WILLIAM SON OF ROGER	GEOFFREY PAYN	GEOFFREY LE GRENE

Source: HD 22a, Neel Cart., Fos. 31–34v no. 255

In 1314 the same Peter le Bret conveyed his possessions at Holkham to
Richard and Katerine Neel and specified the homages and services of all his
20 free tenants.[94] It can be deduced from these documents, that about half the
tenants in the manor of the Brets at Holkham in 1300 were of free status.
Among the 16 customary holdings only one exceeded 12 acres, but it was
shared by several tenants. The holding of 5 acres owed 3 days work in
autumn and 1 *precaria cum caruca*, here called *ploubere.*

The surviving accounts from before 1350 for the manors of Burghall and
Hillhall are few, jejune, and do not deal with direct management.[95] Since
1332, Burghall had actually been taken at farm by Richard Neel, Gilbert and
Henry Burgeys and William de Waterden.[96] In taking Burghall, the chief
manor at Holkham, at farm with partners, Richard Neel continued his policy
of deliberate aggrandizement, which he had pursued for the past 15 years by
means of land purchases and the creation of Neel Manor. The annual returns
registered by John Mey, collector and agent of the 4 farmers, reached a total
of £20 3s. 10d. They included the fixed quit rents of the tenants (*redditus
assise*) at 5 terms and, above all, the profits of 8 *curie* during the year and of
the leet, which produced about half the grand total received (Sept. 1332–3,
Sept. 1334–5). The rest of the receipts came from the commutation of labour
services and the letting of certain portions of the demesne. The cereals
mentioned were barley and oats. Outgoings were recorded very briefly and
consisted of payments for the fees of manorial officers deducted from the
receipts. The earliest account rolls of Hillhall date from 1349; they are briefer
still, confining themselves to the *redditus assise* (70s. 3d.), the profits of the
market, and those of the jurisdiction of the manor court (79s. 9d.). As at
Burghall, this was the most important source of income. The total receipts at
Hillhall in 1349–50 amounted to £7 11s., the income of Burghall in 1333
was three times as high.

The most detailed and precise account was that of the demesne of the
manor of West Dereham under the direct management of the abbey's agent at
Holkham, John Denny, for the year 1366. In spite of its late date, a
retrospective use of it is necessary to arrive at a clearer picture of the rural
economy before 1350.[97] The system of flexible cropping shifts which ruled at

---

94   HD 22a, Neel Cart., no. 191, 19 Aug. 1314.
95   HD 82, *Compotus Ricardi Blakeman collectoris*, 24 June 1332–29 Sept. 1332; HD 84,
      mm. 2d., *Compotus Johannis Mey collectoris*, 29 Sept. 1332–1333; HD 84, mm. 8d.,
      Compotus Johannis Mey collectoris in terra Comitis, 29 Sept. 1334–29 Sept. 1335, for
      Burghall. For Hillhall: HD 45, *Compotus Thome Clerk, messoris*, 29 Sept. 1349–29 Sept.
      1350; HD 46, *Compotus Hervei Pope, messoris* 29 Sept. 1350–29 Sept. 1351.
96   HP 1080, Indenture of Dom. David de Strabolgy Earl of Atholl, and Richard Neel of
      Burnham, Gilbert Burgeys of Titchwell, Henry Burgeys of same, and William de
      Waterden, 30 May 1332. Confirmation of the lease of Burghall to Richard Neel and his
      associates, 11 June 1332 at Woodstock, *Cal. Patent*, 1330-1334, p. 306.
97   HD 53, *Compotus Johannis Denny servientis Abbatis de Derham*, Sept. 1366–Sept. 1367.

Holkham was a complicated triennial system which involved an alternation of the cereals sown in autumn, wheat and rye or maslin, and the spring cereals like barley and oats, with leguminous plants, peas and beans. A terrier of the Holkam lands of the Prior of Peterstone in 1315 gave accurate details on the crops which were sown and on the land lying fallow.[98] Among the 54 Peterstone pieces of land scattered in the South Field, 56% were under cultivation and the rest (44%) lay fallow. The 47 acres 3 roods sown comprised 6 different crops: 18 acres 3 roods of barley, 13 acres of oats, 7 acres 1 rood of rye, 4 acres 2 roods of peas, 3 acres 3 roods of wheat and 2 roods of maslin (wheat and rye). The rotation was organized within the groups of *tenementa* situated in the same area, and not according to the 3 great fields into which the area was divided. In terms of the volume of production, barley seemed to have come first and was turned into malt locally. The fallow portion was used for the open tracts of the foldcourses. The breeding, in particular of sheep, but also of pigs, cattle and horses, completed the system. John Denny was especially exacting in dealing with the demands of the organization and upkeep of the folds, the purchase of 48 wattle hurdles or mobile fences and an iron post. He paid for the work of permanent *famuli* and of seasonal labourers.[99]

There is no doubt that sheep-corn husbandry, as described by K.J. Allison for the 'good-sand' region of Norfolk, existed at Holkham as far back as the thirteenth century.[100] It linked the pastoral economy based on the practice of multiple and concurrent foldcourses closely with cereal production characterized by flexible cropping shifts. This system was in full swing in the second half of the thirteenth century and must have had behind it a well established tradition. As stated earlier, the *Feodarium* of 1279 counted 16 folds attached to various manors and holdings. The custumal of Burghall of 1273 mentioned the tax of *faldagium* and the transport of loads of dung, which suggested the systematic practice of enriching the soil and also, perhaps, individual livestock management.

---

98 *Visus terrarum Prioratus de Peterston*, HD 205 no. VIIa, Fos. 15–15v, Terrier of Peterstone Priory lands in Holkham, 16 or 23 Jan. 1315.

99 HD 53, *Compotus Johannis Denny*, Sept. 1366–Sept. 1367.

100 K.J. Allison, 'The Sheep-Corn Husbandry of Norfolk in the 16th and 17th Centuries', *Agricultural History Review*, 1957, pp. 12–30; M. Bailey, *A Marginal Economy, East Anglian Breckland in the Later Middle Ages*, 1989. M. Bailey, 'Sand into Gold: The Evolution of the Foldcourse System in West Suffolk, 1200–1600', *Agricultural History Review*, 1990, pp. 40–57; Bruce Campbell, 'The Regional Uniqueness of English Field Systems? Some Evidence from Eastern Norfolk', *Agricultural History Review*, 1981, pp. 16–28; H.L. Gray, *The English Field Systems*, 1915, edn. 1959, pp. 326–331; H.E. Hallam, 'The Climate of Eastern England', *Agricultural History Review*, XXXII, 1984, pp. 124–32; M.R. Postgate, 'Field Systems of East Anglia', ch. 7, pp. 313–324, in A.R.H. Baker and R.A. Butlin, *Studies of Field Systems of the British Isles*, 1973. A. Simpson, 'The East Anglian Foldcourse: Some Queries', *Agricultural History Review*, 1958, pp.87–96;

The inquiry into folds in 1306 gave a picture of conditions already prevalent in the thirteenth century, and emphasized the number of folds. Throughout the whole year 9 *falde communes* used both the lands left fallow and the common heath or *bruara* with the common part of the marsh. The Lyng, a great stretch of moor in the South Field towards the south-east side of the land of Holkham, formed the chief area of pasture for summer, completing the annual folds. There were 5 other private folds, using the northern sector of the land of Holkham within the bounds of the coastal marshes, *juxta mariscum saleficum*. In all, 20 folds were in concurrent active use in the territory of Holkham, if one adds to the 14 annual folds the 6 little temporary folds, *alie falde que vocantur cotes foldes*, opened from the 25 July to 11 November, before the winter corn was sown. Some fold owners, like the Prior of Walsingham, opened their folds too early and were fined by the manor court.[101] In 1590, by contrast, 4 fold courses had replaced the score of folds of the early fourteenth century. The reduction to 4 fold courses from the great number existing in the early fourteenth century gives a yardstick for the process of concentration at work in the fifteenth and sixteenth century.[102]

From our documents it is possible to obtain a detailed picture of Holkham's medieval fields. The *pecia* was a common term used in the grants to describe one or more strips. A strip often contained several selions, but the word *selio* does not appear in our documents. A group of contiguous *pecie* composed a *cultura* (or *stadium*) which carried its own name to indicate its whereabouts. *Quarentena* or *cultura* were synonyms meaning the same as furlong. There could be considerable variations in the areas included in the *pecie*. Two examples of sales of groups of *pecie* in 1295 and 1309 give an idea of their irregular size. On 30 April 1295, Geoffrey le Bret granted a group of 8 *pecie* situated in different *culture*, to Simon son of Hamon: three of these *pecie* were of 3 or 4 acres, the other five varied between 1/2 and 1/4 acres.[103] When Helewise, widow of John le Bret, on 4 May 1309, gave to her son Gilbert a holding divided into 7 *pecie*, the biggest measured 21/2 acres, the smallest less than 1/2 acre, three extended over 1/2 acre, two over 11/4 acres.[104]

We know in detail the composition of the properties of three free tenants in the second half of the thirteenth century. They had been preserved in exactly the same form until the second half of the fifteenth century. The

---

101   HD 86, 22 July 1337.
102   Holkham Hall, Ms. 771, Holkham Map 1, 1590, North foldcourse, Newgate foldcourse, Caldowe foldcourse, Wheatley's foldcourse, quoted by M.R. Postgate, 'Field Systems', *op. cit.*, p. 316.
103   HP 1011, 30 April 1295, summarized by Edmund Lucas in HD 22a, Neel Cart., Fo. 4 no. 46.
104   HD 24, 4 May 1309.

holding of Ralph, son of Silvester, granted to Walsingham in 1250, comprised two pieces of great size, one of 7 acres and the other of 3 acres, and all the other eighteen pieces varied between 1/4 and 11/2 acres. They lay in most cases in the south-east part of the South Field.[105] Another example, the holding granted in 1278 by Ralph Hacun to John Silk, comprised 19 acres and *unam liberam faldam*. It had pieces in the Stathe Field and in the Church Field. Most of the pieces, except for one of 41/2 acres, had areas between 1/2 and 3/4 acres at most. Half the pieces (10) measured 3 roods.[106] Finally the holding of Bartholomew de Burgate, in the fee of Roger Bacon, was described in 1482–3 as it was in 1279. It had kept its integrity through inheritance: 15 acres with pasture and a fold. It was almost all situated in the Stathe Field on the edge of the salt marsh, with 61/2 acres concentrated in the same *stadium* or *quarentena* near Marshgreene. Of its ten component pieces four had 2 acres or more and the other six varied between 1/2 and 11/2 acres.[107] Smaller tenures in villeinage showed the same fragmentation of *pecie* scattered in different *culture*, as in the case of John Beneyt and his brood, who settled in 1333 on a holding of 33/4 acres, which comprised a cottage and nine *pecie* of which the largest measured 1 acre and the smallest 1/2 rood.[108]

There were also a number of much larger and often enclosed holdings, closes and crofts, which contributed to the diversification of Holkham's agricultural landscape. This was certainly the case with the *sita manerij*, the land adjacent to the centres of the numerous manors, around the *aula* of Montchesney (Burghall), the Tobers close of 8 acres and 1 rood, or the close of Hillhall extending over 16 acres.[109] We do not know the size of the messuage or croft of Geoffrey le Bret, but it must have been surrounded by a sufficiently large piece of land to allow free entry and exit, and it gave the basis for the Neel manorial *situm*.[110] The large consolidated holding of 80 acres belonging to Burghall called *magna pecia de Burghall nominata le IIII^{xx} ac.*,[111] which must have existed before 1350, confirmed the character of irregularity in the field pattern and the trend towards individualism already present in medieval Holkham. We consider that the numerous crofts that bear their owner's name, mentioned as abuttals or even as field-names, or

---

105   HD 75, *The Hillhall Book*, Fo. 13.
106   Ibid., Fo. 30v.
107   Ibid., Fo. 80v.
108   HD 84, 1 July 1333.
109   HD 75, *The Hillhall Book*, Fos. 41 bis, 42, 1486–7, described a number of closes at Hillhall, including Tobers close.
110   HD 7, Grant by Geoffrey le Bret of Holkham to his son John, 23 May 1284: ... *mesuagium meum cum libero introitu et exitu et cum edificiis et arboribus superstantibus et cum omnibus pertinenciis...*
111   HD 296, The *Book of Edmund Newgate* (1549), Fo. 5v: *Stadium incipiens ad magnam peciam de Burghall nominatam le IIII^{xx} ac.*, situated on the west side of Gibbesgate.

connected with a landmark, are of particular significance in the medieval landscape of Holkham.

We establish here that the sandy loams of Holkham constituted good arable land yielding good barley and corn crops from the thirteenth century at least, and that marling[112] was a current medieval practice. The 'Norfolk system of husbandry' of the eighteenth and nineteenth centuries crowned a long series of improvements which had outstanding medieval foundations in Holkham, as in the rest of northwest Norfolk. In the eighteenth century the building of the Palladian Hall and the creation of the great park of the Earls of Leicester transformed the landscape of Holkham, but the farming practices of Coke of Norfolk were not fundamentally new. They were inherited from a long tradition of intensive cultivation. The mistake of W.G. Hoskins (1955), who thought that Holkham was a waste area of heathland occupied by rabbit warrens before Coke of Norfolk transformed it, has been repeated since by several authors, and recently by R. Butlin in his study of the Georgian landscape of Britain (1992). Our book proves without a doubt that such a view is wrong.[113]

---

112   See *infra*, Topography, Appendix 3: Marllond
113   Cf. W.G. Hoskins, *The Making of the English Landscape* (1st edn. 1955), (paperback, 1992), p. 154; R. Butlin, 'Georgian Britain c. 1714–1837', in R.E. Glasscock, ed., *Historic Landscapes of Britain from the Air*, p. 167–71.

Chapter 4

Aspects of Social Structure

The court rolls for the Holkham manors which have survived from before 1350 contain substantial information about the social life of the community, especially about the interaction of tenants in the land market (sale, purchase and letting of parcels of land), and about their relationships as creditors or debtors in numerous pleas of debt and detinue. They illustrate the social context of the documents printed here, and shed light on a number of Holkham tenants mentioned in the charters. There remain records of some 68 courts, unevenly spread between 1277 and 1350. From the 54 courts between 1330 and 1350 it has been possible to identify 724 individuals, among whom were 197 women.[110]

In the earliest group of courts, between 1277 and 1329, which concerned the manors of Hillhall and Bret-Neel, over half the business of the *curia* dealt with the redistribution of *pecie* of land. Conveyances of *pecie* between tenants were above all effected by the procedure *ad opus*. All the phases of the family cycle, entry into adult life, marriage, retirement or death, involved the conveyance of parcels of land. In some instances, purchases of *pecie* were the acts of adult sons or daughters who were establishing their position in the community with the help of their parents. In 1317 a young man, John le Meyre, bought 3 1/2 roods from John Peye and 1 rood from Alice Andrew with the help of his mother Helewise; if John were to die without an heir these two parcels would revert to his mother.[111] In 1277, an older couple, John Edrich and his wife, sold their messuage and lands to John Carpe and his wife Cecily, who were presumably newly married and related to the Edriches. The latter granted again to the former owners *unam domum edificatam in dicto messuagio cum libero introito and exitu ad terminum vite eorum.*[112] Furthermore, through purchases, sales or letting of land, freemen and villeins alike expanded their holdings and their revenue either in the form of money or in the form of yearly crops (*vestura*).

The average in these transfers of parcels was 1 rood, i.e. 1/4 acre. Apart from the sale and purchase of parcels, the courts of Hillhall showed that the letting of parcels between tenants was current practice in the second half of the thirteenth century, and the examination of the 1330–50 courts showed

---

110   Cf. Appendix 1, Prosopography of Holkham, 1250–1350, for list of court rolls and the biographical index of persons in the court rolls 1330-1350.

111   HD 14, 1 Feb. 1322.

112   Ibid., 5 April 1277.

that the movement intensified in a very distinct way.[113] The first court of 1277 gave, by itself, 8 instances of letting.[114] The sizes of the parcels varied between 1 and 2 roods and the lengths of the leases between 2 and 10 years. The indebtedness of the lessor was probably in some cases the reason for the lease, and the lessee recovered his outlay out of the crop on the parcel of land. Through the *curia* the lord also provided holdings for newcomers. As elsewhere, the *curia* in Holkham checked the title of all tenants to their tenures in order to control default of payment of services.

After the transfer of parcels, debt litigation and settlement represented the highest proportion of the cases which occupied Holkham courts. There were problems of debts within families, between neighbours, craftsmen, hucksters and clients about land, foodstuffs, drink and other essential supplies of everyday living and work. And there were also all those which arose round commercial activity connected with the harbour traffic and with the market of Holkham. A number of suitors had disputes with other tenants or aliens about fishery affairs and the export of corn and wool. Apart from the satisfaction of local demands, Holkham was also in touch with the trade along the coast as well as with overseas trade which gave a means of employment and profit to a certain number of merchants, shipowners and mariners.[115] Merchandizing involved all degrees of the social structure of the community. Two acknowledgements of debts showed that one of the sleeping partners or investors for commercial purposes was Gilbert Neel, son of Richard and Katerine, who advanced money and took a share in the enterprises of William de Barney (1345) and Benedict Scot (1346) *ad marcantizandum.*[116]

The manorial officers of Holkham appear in a clearer light in the court rolls which survived for the period 1330–1350 in so far as they include 4

---

113   Cf. numerous examples of letting between 1330 and 1350 in the Prosopography, Appendix 1.

114   HD 14, 5 April 1277.

115   PRO, C 47/2/25, no. 18, see *infra*, last document printed. There were nine fishing boats of some importance at Holkham in 1336: three of 20 tons and six of 12 tons. John de Bilney was master of three fishing vessels, two of 20 tons, *la Haga* and *la Katerina* and one of 12 tons called *la Plente*. Walter Osbern was master of *la Katerina* of 12 tons, William Dollon was master of a *Cogge* (12 tuns). John Speller was master of *le Christofer* (20 tons) and of *la Welyfair* (12 tons). Richard Silk was master of *la Charité* (12 tons), Richard Speller was master of *le Nicholas* (12 tons). John de Bilney, master of 3 fishing boats, was logically the richest tax payer of Holkham, after Richard Neel, in the Lay Subsidy of 1332-3, with 10s (cf. p. 451). The other masters of fishing boats, John Speller (6s. 8d.) and Richard Speller (4s.) and Walter Osbern (4s.) were also in the upper half of the subsidy payers.

116   HP 1100, 2 Oct. 1345, Bond from William de Barney to Gilbert Neel; HP 1101, 18 Aug. 1346, Bond from Benedict Scot to Gilbert Neel. The sums which Gilbert Neel advanced as credit for merchandizing were 20s. sterling in the case of William de Barney and £3. sterling in the case of Benedict Scot.

Burghall *curie lete*.[117] But in the late thirteenth-century courts for Hillhall, the *collector* seemed to be the chief officer elected by the community. In 1277 Richard Payn was *collector*, and in 1287 it was John Edrych and Cecily Carpe who were elected to the office.[118] The offices of *messor* and of *prepositus* appeared in the first courts of Richard Neel, where in 1327 a woman, Agnes Hoddes, was elected as *messor*.[119] Between 1326 and 1329 the manorial community was taxed for the ineffectiveness of its officers, or because it failed to elect them. A collective fine of 11s. was inflicted on the tenants because of the arrears of payment to the lord on the part of the *prepositus* over 8 successive years.[120] In the 1330s, at Burghall, election to the office of *prepositus* required a 12 acres *tenementum*, generally divided among several tenants, while the election to the office of *messor* required a 6 acres *tenementum* only.[121] There was an obvious reluctance to assume manorial responsibilities among the Holkham tenantry. Since the first half of the fourteenth century at least, lords had recourse to compulsion and collective responsibility when faced with the small attraction given by the offices and the risks involved. It is probably to this period that one should attribute the date of the establishment of nine *tenementa* of 6 acres of *terra nativa* which, at Hillhall, took in turn the collective burden of the office of *messor*.[122]

The leet court of Burghall, which took place once a year on July 22 (feast of St. Mary Magdalen), gave the names of 12 *capitales plegij*. At the same time 2 *afferatores* and 2 *probatores cervisie* were elected. As elsewhere, one can see despite the paucity of the surviving leet courts, that a good number of these *capitales plegij* held the position for many years.[123] These manorial officers were, naturally, particularly active at the manorial court, as were

---

117 Cf. Jacques Beauroy, 'Offices Manoriaux et Stratification Sociale à Heacham (Norfolk) (1285–1324)', in *Les Communautés Villageoises en Europe Occidentale du Moyen Age aux Temps Modernes*, Flaran 4, 1982, pp. 237–244; Idem, 'Analyse Quantitative d'une Seigneurie Anglaise: Offices Manoriaux, Activités Marchandes et Structure Sociale dans le Norfolk Occidental à la Fin du XIIIème Siècle', *Histoire et Mesure*, III, 1988, pp. 515–25.

118 HD 14, 5 April 1277 and 16 Jan. 1287: *Totum homagium eligit in officio collectoris hoc anno suo periculo Johannem Edrych et Ceciliam Carpe parcennarium suum ad faciendum officium.*

119 HD 79, 2 Dec. 1327 and 30 Jan. 1329: *Memorandum quod...recepit dominus hoc die de Agneta Hoddes messore de anno preterito viij s. v d. ob...*

120 HD 79, 27 Nov. 1326 and 30 Jan. 1329.

121 HD 82, 22 July 1332; HD 84, 22 July 1334.

122 HD 75, *The Hillhall Book*, Fos. 4–10v, rental of 9 customary *tenementa* liable for the office of *messor*, 1467–8.

123 HD 82, 22 July 1332; HD 84, 22 July 1334; HD 86, 22 July 1337; HD 87a, 22 July 1350. In the 1332, 1334, 1337 leet courts we find mostly the same as *capitales plegij*: John Mey (3 times), John Crane (3 times), Godman Burgoine (3 times), Simon Burgoine (3 times), Roger de Repps (3 times), Roger Odes (3 times), John Joudy (3 times), Roger Crane (3 times), John le Smith (3 times), Peter de Langham (twice), Roger de Ketleston (twice).

Richard Blakeman, John Mey or John le Smith, pledging for others, but also buying and selling land or involved in debt pleas. The richest one was Peter de Langham, taxed at 8s. on the Lay subsidy list of 1333.[124] Roger de Repps, the baker, was capital pledge between 1332 and 1337, and the Crane family with their relations, the Burgoines, seemed to find some advantage in holding office as capital pledges.

The recording of marriages in the available court rolls was meagre: 3 marriages between 1277 and 1329, and 18 between 1330 and 1350. Some parents paid the sums due for the *licentia maritandi* of their children. Such was the case of Richard Payn, the *collector* of Hillhall who paid 7d., on 1 May 1312 for the marriage of his son.[125] Mabel Ernald, on her part, paid 12d. in 1325 for a licence for her daughter Matilda to marry.[126] We know the value of a dowry or *maritagium* of a freeholder's daughter around 1284: Agnes le Heire received from her father, Robert le Heire of Morston, 3 acres of land when she married William Curson.[127] Generally the women themselves paid for their *licentia maritandi* or for the fine incurred for marrying without licence. Couples could also pay their liabilities jointly: Richard Blakeman, a prominent villager, married Agnes Bulwer, widow of John Bulwer, and together they paid the large sum of 1/2 mark (6s. 8d.) on 25 January 1334.[128] At the same date the marriage of William Bere demonstrated the nexus between succession and a decision to marry, for he paid, on the same day, a heriot of 32d. for succession to paternal holdings and a fine of 24d. for a simultaneous marriage.[129] For sexual activity out of wedlock, leyrwite and childwite, women were liable to a *gersuma* of 32d. Alice Carpe and Margaret Slopere both paid such a fine several times between 1334 and 1337, having given birth to illegitimate children. Matilda Hecheman in 1342, Matilda Paye in 1345, and Cecily de Howgate in 1350, paid a *gersuma* for leyrwite.[130]

Portions for widows were often the subject of litigation and settlements. Isabel de Barsham, the widow of John de Barsham, was involved in two disputes about debt in 1333–4 with other women, Beatrice Huberd and Agnes

---

124   PRO, E 179/149/9, m. 32, Lay Subsidy 6 E. III (1332–1333). Among the 53 subsidy payers, most of the *capitales plegij* were mentioned. Cf. text printed *infra*, pp. 449–50.
125   HD 14, 1 May 1312.
126   HD 79, 16 Dec. 1325.
127   HP 1039, c. 1284, HD 22a, Neel Cart., Fo. 6 no. 70, Conveyance from Robert le Heire to William Cursun.
128   HD 84, 25 Jan. 1334.
129   Ibid., 25 Jan. 1334, followed immediately by William Bere's heriot and marriage licence payments, Margery de Scharneton (Sharrington) paid a heriot for succeeding to her father, Geoffrey. It is reasonable to assume that the two heirs got married.
130   Alice Carpe: HD 84, 25 Jan. 1334, HD 85a, 8 Jan. 133; SC 2 193/1, 16 Feb. 1337. Margaret Slopere: HD 84, 1 Nov. 1334; SC 2 193/1, 11 Sept. 1337. Matilda Hecheman, SC 2 193/1, 12 Oct. 1342. Matilda Paye, SC 2 193/1, 15 April 1345. Cecily de Howgate, HD 83, 7 July 1350.

Bulwer, wife of Richard Blakeman, while she abandoned to Alice Dersi all her dower and her claims on the *tenementa* of her deceased husband.[131] On her part, Agnes Bulwere was involved, through the fact of her remarriage to Richard Blakeman, in a prolonged legal battle with the family of her former in-laws. After a suit which had invoked the assise of novel disseisin, she established that her dower should be confirmed to her by Richard Bulwer, a relation of her former husband (28 March 1335). This meant half a messuage and 20 acres of land which should remain the property of her new husband if Agnes should die first, instead of reverting to the Bulweres.[132]

The Lay Subsidy of 1332 for the *villata* of Holkham listed ten women out of fifty-three tax payers. Two of these women, Matilda Charle (60d.) and Isabel de Barsham (36d.) paid more than the average (33d.).[133] From a study of the women who appeared most frequently in the *curia*, a clear conclusion emerges that their public life was connected with commercial affairs in the local market. Indeed, far and away the majority of the fines they paid concerned the assize of bread and ale. The majority of the pleas in which they found themselves related to debts presumably contracted from their important role as retailers and from their participation in the world of petty commodity production.[134] As to the land market, women sold or let parcels more often than they bought them. Alice Dersi had inherited, on 28 March 1335, from her father, Walter Dersi, a messuage and 9 acres: she let 3 acres on leases varying from six to eight years before the 10 December 1348, when she married William Mariot.[135] Margaret Slopere, in December 1334, bought from her parents a messuage and 3 acres in eight pieces, regranting this holding to them with use rights for their life, and between 1335 and 1348 she sold or let five pieces.[136] The women who had made savings as retailers, members of families of well-to-do tenants and widows or heiresses of holdings, offered lands for sale or parcels to rent to increase their incomes. Finally, cases of violence described in the leet courts sometimes presented a picture of women in conflict with other women. In the five cases of *hamsoken* in which women were parties, three women had three other women as their victims. In the two other cases, Margaret Crane was successful as defendant against her own son, and Catherine Leman joined a man, John Crane, to assault another man.[137]

---

131 HD 84, 6 May 1333, 21 June 1334, 21 Oct. 1334.

132 Ibid., 25 Jan. 1334, 22 June 1334, 28 March 1335.

133 PRO, E 179/149/9, m. 32. Cf. *infra*, pp. 00.

134 R.H. Hilton, 'Medieval Market Towns and Simple Commodity Production', *Past and Present*, no. 109, pp. 3–23 and B.A. Hanawalt (ed.), *Women and Work in Pre-industrial Europe*, 1986, especially pp. 1–36.

135 HD 87a, 10 Dec. 1348.

136 HD 84, 8 Dec. 1334.

137 HD 84, 22 July 1334; HD 85a, 22 July 1347; HD 87a, 22 July 1350.

Method of Editing

Original charters, which constitute the bulk of this edition, have been transcribed as accurately as possible with their peculiar punctuation. The occurrence of occasional indeterminate capital letters and punctuation make any such text an unreliable guide to the usage of some originals, even if record type were employed. Microfiches are, however, available, and references to these are given after the summaries of the printed texts. Doubtful extensions are indicated by italics, and conjectural interpolations by square brackets. For brevity, line numbers and indications of the ends of lines were omitted. *U* and *v* are standardised by the adoption of *v* initially and *u* medially. *I* is used both for the long and short forms of the letter, but *j* has been used at the end of words and of numerals. We transcribed the Middle English forms of *Katerine* and *Caterine* whenever we encountered them in the Latin texts, and reproduced them in our English summaries. Abbreviations have been expanded. After each charter, comments are made on the seals, if any, on hands, on medieval endorsements, letters, figures and marks.

Marginalia are indicated by angle brackets, and interpolations by scribes are printed between oblique strokes. Capitals and punctuation have been standardised in the 252 charters transcribed by Edmund Lucas in the Neel Cartulary. Space has been allowed to print the texts of both the cartulary and, in their numerical positions, in the HD or HP series, such originals as survive. The cartulary retains topographical details, but omits names of witnesses.

We have transcribed court rolls and manorial documents and Lucas's alphabetical gazetteer with a particular care, so as to make sure that the marginalia stood out in the printed text and preceded the entries to which they referred. Roman numerals in the texts have been transcribed in lower case and punctuation in the courts or rentals has been standardised. However, in the Neel Cartulary we have transcribed the copies made of the Feodary and of the Burghall Rental as they were copied by Edmund Lucas, without punctuation. We made sure that all the marginalia stood out well for clarity of reading and interpretation.

HOLKHAM DOCUMENTS: HD 1 – HD 21

c. 1250–1322

HD 1 – HD 21

HD 1

Grant from Roger, son of Ralph, to Robert Hacun of all his lands and tenements in Holkham, 17 acres in the marsh of Stanre. [c. 1250]

Cf. HD 6 (XII)
Fiche 1: A2

Sciant presentes et futuri quod Ego Rogerus filius Radulfi concessi et dedi et hac mea carta presenti et sigillo meo confirmaui Roberto Hacun et heredibus suis pro homagio suo et seruicio suo et pro viginti solidis quos mihi dedit in gersumam totam terram meam et [t]otum tenementum meum quod habui in Holgham in marisco de Stanre de dono domini Galfridi filio Petri cum omnibus pertinenciis suis sine aliquo retinemento pro septem decim acris terre habendum . et totam meam partem de duobus solidatis de reditu de victun'. Illi et heredibus suis tenendum de me et heredibus meis in feodo et hereditate . libere . quiete . honorifice . in bono et pace. Reddendo inde annuatim triginta quatuor denarios . ad istos terminos. Scilicet ad pasca . septem decim denarios ad festum Sancti Michahelis septem decim denarios pro omni seruicio . consuetudine . et exactione ad me pertinentibus. Et predictus Robertus Hacun et heredes sui facient seruicium capitalium dominorum. Et ego prenominatus Rogerus filius Radulfi et heredes mei warantizabimus prenominato Roberto Hacun et heredibus suis prenominatam terram et tenementum predictum per prenominatum seruicium contra omnes homines. Hiis testibus. Ricardo de Bradeker. Petro de Holgham. Ricardo Hacun. Radulfo de Vilethen. Nicholao de Nughun. Radulfo de Stiuekeye. Ricardo Mundi. Roberto Hacun. Roberto de Binetre. Galfrido le sire de Massi[n]gham. Galfrido de Bradeker. Adam filio Walteri de Hogham. Johanne fratre suo et multis aliis.

Seal: missing.

HD 2

*Grant from John, son of Simon of Quarles, to the Hospital of St. Nicholas
between Holkham and Burnham. Gift of 3 acres in 2 plots in Quarles.*

[early 13th century]

Fiche 1: A3

Sciant presentes et futuri quod ego Iohannes filius Simonis de Warfes
Concessi dedi et hac carta mea confirmaui pro salute anime mee et pro
animabus antecessorum et successorum meorum deo et hospitali Sancti
Nicholai quod situm est inter Burnham et Holcham et fratribus ibidem
commorantibus tres acras terre cum pertinenciis in campis de Warfles in
duabus peciis . quarum vna pecia iacet inter Holchamgate et terram ecclesie
de Warfles et abbutat super culturam Bartholo[mei] filij Martini apud
Wodegate et alia pecia iacet versus aquilonem a comuni puteo de W...
aquilonem et abuttat super culturam eiusdem Ba[rtholomei] ... et
successoribus in liberam puram et perpetuam elemosinam ... predictas tres
acras terre cum pertinentiis predictis fratribus et successoribus eo[rum] ...
[inper]petuum et deffendemus . et in huius rei testimonium presenti [carta] ...
. munitam. His testibus. Iohanne de Nerford' milite Barth[olomeo] de . ...
Hamone Mundi. Symone filio Huberti. Bartholomeo filio Step[hani] ... [filio]
Walteri de Wucton'. Thoma de Holkham. Willelmo fratre eius. Henrico filio
....

Seal: missing.

NOTE: Bottom left portion missing.

HD 3

*Final concord, Ralph, son of Silvester of Walsingham, to William, Prior of
Walsingham of a messuage and thirty two acres of land in Holkham.*

25 Nov. 1250

Cf. PRO CP 25(1) case 157 file 80 no. 1159, Appendix 5, no. 20
Fiche 1: A4

Hec est finalis concordia in curia domini Regis apud Norwicum; a die Sancti
Martini. In Quindecim dies. Anno regni regis Henrici filij Regis Iohannis
tricesimo quinto coram Henricum de Bathon'. Iohanne de Gatesden'. Roberto
de Brywes. Gilberto de Preston'. Magistro Simone de Wanton et Willelmo de
Wilton' Iustic' Itinerantibus et aliis domini Regis fidelibus tunc ibi

presentibus. Inter Willelmum priorem de Walsingham querentem per fratrem Alanum del Orchard' canonicum suum positum loco suo ad lucrandum vel perdendum et Radulfum filium Siluestri de Walsingham inped' de uno mesuagio et triginta et duabus acris terre cum pertinenciis in Holkham. Vnde placitum Warantie carte sumonitum fuit inter eos in Eadem Curia scilicet quod predictus Radulfus recognouit predictum mesuagium et terram cum pertinenciis esse Ius ipsius Prioris et ecclesie sue de Walsingham. Vt illa que Idem prior et ecclesia sua predicta habeat de dono predicti Radulfi. Et preterea idem Radulfus dedit et concessit eidem priori Viginti et Quinque acras marisci cum pertinenciis in eadem villa que Iacent ex opposito predicti messuagij versus Boream. Habendum et tenendum eidem priori et successoribus suis et ecclesie sue predicte de predicto Radulfo et heredibus suis in liberam et perpetuam elemosinam imperpetuum. Reddendo inde per annum duos solidos et sex denarios ad duos terminos. Scilicet ad Natale domini duodecim et octo denarios pro omni seruicio consuetudine et exaccione ad predictum Radulfum et heredes suos pertinente. Et facit inde capitalibus dominis feodi illius pro predicto Radulfo et heredibus suis omnia alia seruiciaque ad predictum mesuagium pratum et mariscum pertinent. Et predictus Radulfus et heredes sui warantizabunt eidem priori et successoribus suis et ecclesie sue predicte predict' messuag' terram et mariscum cum pertinenciis suis in liberam et perpetuam elemosinam suam per predicta seruicia contra omnes homines imperpetuum. Et pro hac recognicione . donacione . concessione war'. fine et concordia dictus prior dedit predicto Radulfo viginti marcas argenti.

NORFF'

NOTE: The two texts differ only in punctuation. This estate was held by Walsingham of Tobers Manor (later part of Hillhall Manor). The scattered strips which composed this estate are described in detail in Thomas Grigges's Hillhall Book (c.1460–90), HD 75 Fo. 13. Ralph Silvester's close was in Southgate opposite the messuage of William Waylond, HD 75 Fo. 98. The estate included an early enclosure in the Lyng named, in the map of 1590, White Ollond. None of the land is in the western half of the parish, furthest from Walsingham. This grant with a confirmation by Adam le Bret and Robert son of William of Walsingham is in the Walsingham Cartulary, BL Ms. Cotton Nero E VII, nos. CIII, CIV.

HD 4a and 4b　　　　　　　　　　　**HD 5a and 5b**

Burghall rental.　　　　　　　　　　*Feodary*

Not printed　　　　　　　　　　　　　Not printed
Cf. HD 22a, no. 255.　　　　　　　　　Cf. HD 22a, no. 253.
Fiche 1: A5 and A6.　　　　　　　　　Fiche 1: A7 and A8.

HD 6

West Dereham Abbey Holkham charters.　　　　　　　[thirteenth century]

Fiche 1: A9

NOTE: A quire of 16 leaves on fifteenth century paper made by an administrator of West Dereham Abbey grange at Holkham from the unpublished fourteenth century cartulary, BL Ms. Add. 46353. The first seven pages contain a copy of the Holkham Feodary which is printed from a similar but better arranged text in HD 22a, no. 253. Then follow seven pages with the text of one Dereham charter followed by summaries of 29 others. On the last page: *Haec due scedulae exscriptae ex libro veteris Abbatis de Dereham in Custodia Magistri Dereham vel Magistri Gurton. qui liber est in membrana et Continet omnes Cartas dicti Abbatis et Conuentus.* These copies of charters throw some light on Holkham in the generation before the *corpus* of Holkham documents edited here. The original excerpts are reproduced with the addition in brackets of amplifying details from the Dereham Cartulary. Unfortunately the names of witnesses are omitted. The summary gives descriptions of lands granted as in the cartulary. The Roman figures are taken from the cartulary.

[I] Carta domini Willelmi de Monte Caniso de medietate ecclesie de Holkham quantum ad patronum pertinet.

Omnibus Sancte matris ecclesie filiis ad quos presens scriptum peruenerit Willelmus de Montecaniso Salutem in domino. Nouerit vuniuersitas vestra me intuitu dei et pro salute anime mee et vxoris mee et heredum meorum et omnium antecessorum et successorum meorum dedisse et concessisse in puram et perpetuam elemosinam et quietam deo et ecclesie Sancte Marie de Derham et canonicis ibidem deo seruientibus medietatem ecclesie de Holkham quantum ad patronum pertinet cum omnibus ad ipsam pertinentibus in perpetuum pacifice possidendam et alterius quoque medietatis ius omne quod habeo vel habiturus sum cum omni ad eam pertinentibus similiter eiusdem Canonicis in puram et perpetuam elemosinam concessi et dedi. Hec igitur habet mea tam concessio quam donacio perpetue stabilitatis Robur optineat eam presentis scripti et sigilli mei apposicione confirmaui. Inhibeo autem nequis heredum meorum contra hanc piam donacionem meam presumat. Quod si fecerit malediccionem omnipotentis dei et meam incurrat. Hiis testibus.

[II]   Confirmacio Iohannis Episcopi Norwicensis de medietate ecclesie de Holkham in vsus proprios.

Ita quidem quod dicti Abbas et Canonici ecclesiam cum vacuerit in vsus proprios perpetuo possideant salua honesta sustentacione vicarij quod nobis et successoribus nostris assignandam reseruauimus et salua reuerencia obediencia et debitis consuetudinibus Sancte Norwicensis ecclesie.

NOTE: Bishop John I of Oxford (1175-1200).

[III]   Confirmacio Iohannis Norwicensis episcopi de medietate ecclesie de Holkham cum omnibus ad illam pertinentibus in proprios vsus sustentacionem perpetuo possidendam salua vicaria perpetua decem marcarum in certam porcionem dicte medietatis a nobis et successoribus nostris assignandam ad presentacionem dicti *Abbatis* vicario in eadem medietate perpetuo ista ministraturo post decessum Huberti de Montecanisio eiusdem medietatis vicarij perpetui qui quamdiu vixerit eis inde soluet duos Byzantos nomine pensionis. Salua eciam auctoritate Sancte Norwicensis ecclesie et nobis et successoribus nostris in perpetuum iure pontificali et parochiali. Etc.

NOTE: Bishop John II de Gray (1200–14) recites and confirms a charter from his predecessor Bishop John I of Oxford (1175–1200) to the new *plantacio* of West Dereham (which Hubert Walter, Dean of York, later Archbishop of Canterbury founded in 1188). See *English Episcopal Acta VI Norwich 1070–1214*, 1990, nos. 427–9.

[IV]   Confirmacio Norwicensis Iohannis episcopi Norwicensis[a] de medietatis ecclesie Holkham cum omnibus ad illam medietatem pertinentibus in proprios vsus ad suam sustentacionem perpetuo possidendam salua vicaria perpetua decem marcarum certa porcione dicte medietatis a nobis et successoribus nostris assignandam ad presentacionem dictorum *Abbatis* et *canonicorum* vicario in eadem medietate perpetuo ministraturo post decessum Huberti de Montecaniso eiusdem medietatis persone. Salua auctoritate Sancte Norwicensis ecclesie iure pontificali etc.

NOTE: Bishop John II de Gray (1200–14).

VARIANT: [a] The cartulary text also repeats *Norwicensis* as here.

[V]   Confirmacio Huberti archiepiscopi Cantuariensis cartarum Iohannis Norwicensis episcopi de ecclesia de Holkham.

NOTE: In the cartulary the confirmation by Archbishop Hubert Walter (d. 1205) concerns Ringland church as well as Holkham. In the title the cartulary only mentions Ringland, as it does too in the title of no. VI.

[VI] Confirmacio prioris Sancte Trinitatis Norwicensis de ecclesia de Holkham.

NOTE: Prior Simon's *inspeximus* of charters of Bishop William Raleigh (1239–1243) confirming grants from Bishops John I of Oxford and John II de Gray and Thomas de Blunville (1226–36) of half Holkham church with Thorpe and Ringland to the Abbot of West Dereham.

[VII] Ordinacio Abbatis de Thorneia et de burgo de controuersia inter *Abbatem* de *Derham* et Philippum de Brunham militem.

[VIII] Composicio inter nos *Abbatem* de *Derham* et priorem de Walsingham super decimis piscarie de Holcham de ecclesie Sancti Clementis de Brunham vt patet in carta.

NOTE: Agreement made at Peterstone, 1273, that if a Burnham boat with a Holkham master lands at Burnham, Walsingham is to have the tithes in right of St. Clement's church, Burnham, and Walsingham's agent is to pay half to Dereham. If a Holkham boat with a Burnham master lands at Holkham, the agents of Dereham and Viterbo are to take the tithes in right of Holkham church. Each year account is to be rendered at Peterstone on the feasts of St. Margaret and St. Martin as above. If a Burnham boat with a Burnham master lands at Holkham, Holkham church gets nothing even if all the sailors are of Holkham. If a Holkham boat with a Holkham master lands at Burnham, St. Clement's church gets nothing even if all the sailors are Burnham men.

[IX] Conuencio inter priorem et conuentum de Castelacra et *Abbatem* de *Dereham* super duabus partibus decimarum garbarum de Holkham in campo de Holkham.

NOTE: [John Prior of] Castle Acre agrees with Simon Abbot of West Dereham to grant for 40s. rent payable on St. John Baptist's day at Castle Acre two parts of tithe of what was the demesne of Warin de Montchesney. The penalty for failure to pay at any term is 20s. The Priory of Castle Acre may distrain on any land held by the Abbey of West Dereham of the fee of Earl Warenne in Norfolk, taking any goods and chattels until 40s. rent and the 20s. penalty is paid (23 July 1304).

[X] Confirmacio Domini Iohannis Regis Anglie de donacione Willelmi de Monte Caniso de medietate ecclesie de Holkham.

NOTE: John's grant includes any right West Dereham Abbey may have or obtain later to the other half of the church at Holkham and also Ringland.

[XI] Heruicus Leffe de Holcham dedit et concessit abbati de *Derham* vnam peciam terre sue cum pertinenciis in campis de Holkham vnam peciam terre sue cum pertinenciis in campis de Holkham iacentem in loco vocato Aduboteme inter terram dicti Abbatis de Derham ex parte australi et terram Gilberti filij Bartholomei de Holcham ex parte Boreali et caput versus occidentem abbutans super regiam viam que ducit apud Quarles Reddendo inde annuatim obolum ad ij terminos videlicet *Sancti* [Michaelis] et Pascham pro omni seruicio.

NOTE: Harvey Leffe witnesses HP 999 and 1042, c. 1270.

[XII] [Ego] Radulfus Hacun de Holkham concessi et dedi totum illum mariscum meum in villa de Holkham qui quondam fuit Bertrami de Holkham qui vocatur Standre et iacet inter mariscum Domini Warini de Monte Canisio et mariscum que fuit quondam Bertrami de Holkham quem vendidit domino Warino in liberam puram et perpetuam elemosinam.

NOTE: Cf. HD 1, a grant of 17 acres of marsh of Stanre to Robert Hacun. It is Stondel marsh in HD 24 and Stander marsh in Burghall account in HD 84.

[XIII] Reginaldus filius Gilberti [de Hoga] de Holkham concessit ecclesie quinque rodas terre de feodo ecclesie de Holkham que abbutant ad capud orientale super Dalegate et vnam rodam et dimidiam ad Hevedacre iacentes iuxta terram dictorum Abbatis de D*erham* et canonicorum ex parte australi et capud orientale super Creplegate siue in predictis peciis habeatur plus siue minus in puram elemosinam.

NOTE: The annual rent is 1/2d. at Easter. Cf. XXIV for this land paying 3d.

[XIV] Willelmus filius Iohannis de Holkham concessit etc. vnam peciam terre cum pertinenciis quae iacet in campo de Holkham apud Endaker et terram Petri le Bret et terram Eborardi filij Margarete Reddendo annuatim quatuor denarios *Michaelis* et Pasche.

NOTE: A Peter le Bret is a grantor in 1314–6 but an earlier namesake was of the mid-thirteenth century and was son of a third Peter. See XXVI.

[XV] Ricardus filius Radulfi Goldewine de Holkham confirmauit vnam peciam terre cum pertinenciis que iacet in Campo de Holkham apud Endaker inter terram Petri le Bret et terram [Eborardi] filij Margarete quam habuit ex dono Willelmi filij Iohannis in puram elemosinam.

NOTE: The rent is 4d. half at Michaelmas and half at Easter.

[XVI] Adam le Breth filius Ade le Bret de Holkham dedit ecclesie totum homagium et seruicium Reginaldi filij Willelmi de Holmes cum toto tenemento quod de me tenuit in Campo de Holcham vocato Suthfeylde inter feodum Abbatis de D*erham* et terram prioris de Walsingham et caput orientale abuttat super Hadowgate cum octo denariis annui redditus quos percipere solebat de dicto Reginaldo ad quatuor terminos anni videlicet

Micaelis ij d. etc. 7 rodas terre iacentes inter terram predictam et terra abbatis de Derham et ad scutagium domini regis cum venerit etc. cum warda releuiis eschetiis et omnibus aliis pertinentibus ad dictum tenementum pertinentibus in perpetuam elemosinam Reddendo inde sibi et heredibus predictum scutagium.

[XVII]   Charta Thome le [N]uiun de Salle dedit etc. vj d. ob. annui redditus quos percipere solebam de Rogero filio Elfrici Frost de Holkham ad duos terminos videlicet Michaelis iij d. et ob. etc. Christi iij d. de quatuor peciis terre iacentibus in Holkham.

> NOTE: The pieces of land were: (1) a plot between lands of Reginald le Breth and Robert de Howegate abutting west on land of Bartholomew son of Agnes; (2) between lands of William Alberd to the south and Gilbert *ad pratum* to the north, abutting west on Hadhowegate. The grantor's surname is obscurely written in HD 6 but is clearly written twice in the Dereham Cartulary, Fo. 264v.

[XVIII]   Carta Henrici filij Roberti de Holkham dedit ecclesie vnam peciam terre in Campo de Holkham qui vocatur Suthfylde apud le Vtgong qui iacet inter terram Thome del Hil et terram Bartholomei filij Petri et abbuttat versus orientem super terram dicti Thome et versus occidentem super Adhowegate. Reddendo inde annuatim mihi j d. ad ij terminos videlicet Michaelis et Pasche.

[XIX]   Carta Galfridi filij Angnetis le Breth de Warham concessit et dedit vnam peciam terre in Holkham [in campo] qui vocatur Claylond inter terram Abbatis de Dereham et terram Gilberti filij Dauid et abbuttat versus austrum super terram de Peterston. In puram elemosinam. Reddendo ij d. sibi.

> NOTE: Grant for 2d. payable half at Easter and half at Michaelmas.

[XX]   Quietaclamacio Galfridi le Breth de Warham relaxauit totum ius in seruicio duorum denariorum redditus quos iure de eis percipere solebam.

> NOTE: The abbot pays a certain sum of money down. The rent is due from a certain unspecified piece of land.

[XXI]   Carta Clementis filij Henrici de Nortona dedit ecclesie duas acras terre cum pertinentiis in Brunhamthorpe qui iacent apud Mikellhelles in tribus locis inter terras fratrum de Peterston et terram filij Ricardi filij Fretherici quarum due pecie abuttant super terram Petri le Breth et tertia pecia terre abuttat super terram Heruei Leffe apud Thorpmere. Reddendo iiij d. sibi etc.

> NOTE: Grant in free alms, rent due half at Michaelmas, half at Purification of BVM.

[XXII] Carta Clementis rectoris ecclesie omnium Sanctorum de Brunhamthorpe dedit ecclesie duas acras terre cum pertinenciis in Campo de Brunhamthorpe que iacent apud Mikellehelles in tribus locis inter terram fratrum de Peterston et terram Ricardi filii Fretherici quarum due pecie iacent et abuttant super terram Petri le Breth et tercia pecia abuttat super terram Heruei Leffe apud Thorpemere.

NOTE: Grant in free alms for 4d. rent due half at Michaelmas and half at Purification of BVM.

[XXIII] Carta Willelmi filij Iohannis Mercatoris de Holkham dedit ecclesie septem acras terre et dimidiam cum pertinenciis que iacent in campo de Holkham qui vocatur Suthfeylde inter terram Reginaldi filij Galfridi et terras Ade le Brethe de Holkham. Reddendo vj d. sibi etc.

NOTE: Grant in free alms. Rent due at Christmas.

[XXIV] Carta Reginaldi filij Gilberti de Hoga de Holkham dedit ecclesie quinque rodas terre de feodo ecclesie de Holkham qui abuttant super Dalegate versus orientem et vnam rodam et dimidiam ad Hevedaker iacentes iuxta terras abbatis de Derham ex parte australi et abuttant ad vnum capud super Crexgate versus orientem. Reddendo iij d. sibi etc.

NOTE: Grant in free alms. Rent due half at Easter, half at Michaelmas . Cf. XIII for the land paying 1/2d. at Easter.

[XXV] *Abbas* de *Derham* confirmauit Thome filio Bartholomei de Holkham pro homagio et seruicio totam liberam terram ad medietatem nostram ecclesie de Holkham pertinentem quam Willelmus filius Iohannis de Holkham mercatoris quondam tenuit de nobis in Campis de Holkham. Reddendo nobis xvj d. per annum.

NOTE: This is the first of four grants of free land by Angerus, *dei patiencia abbas*, all undated but perhaps about 1250. The rent is due, half at Michaelmas and half at Easter. For 7 acres in South Field granted for 6d. rent by William son of John the merchant, see XXIII.

[XXVI] *Abbas* de *Derham* confirmauit etc. Petro le Breth filio Petri le Breth de Holkham tres acras libere terre ad medietatem nostram de Holkham pertinentes quas predictus Petrus senior tenuit de nobis in campo de Holkham reddendo per annum xxx d. xv d. ad *Michaelis* xv d. ad *Pascha*.

NOTE: The rent is 12d. not 15d. at the two terms in a summary of this deed in the Neel Cart., HD 22a, no. 90. The 12d. is written in darker ink, as if deliberately.

[XXVII] A*bbas* de D*erham* confirmauit etc. Ade le Breth de *Holkham* filio Radulfi le Breth pro homagio suo et seruicio quod nobis fecit septem rodas libere terre ad medietatem nostram ecclesie de Holkham pertinentis in Campo de Holkham quas dictus Radulfus quondam tenuit de nobis: reddendo nobis annuatim xvj d. viii ad M*ichaelis* et viii ad P*ascha*.

[XXVIII] A*bbas* de D*erham* confirmauit Roberto filio Willelmi de Walsingham sex acras libere terre in Holkham pro homagio et seruicio suo quod fecit nobis de feodo : que vj acre pertinent ad medietatem nostram ecclesie de Holkham et quas Magister Adam de Walsingham tenuit de nobis. Reddendo annuatim nobis etc. xl d. ad S*ancti* M*ichaelis* xx d. et ad Pascha xx d.

[XXIX] Finalis Concordia inter Alanum filium Simonis de Wyghton et inter A*bbatem* de D*erham* de dimidia acra terre [ad] portas Grangie A*bbatis* de D*erham* in Holkham versus orientem. Et sic finis libri illius.

NOTE: *orientem* is a copyist's error for *occidentem* which is correctly transcribed in the Dereham Cartulary, Fo. 267. The original foot of fine is PRO CP 25(1) case 154 file 26 no. 350. Cf. Appendix 5, no. 3 (8 Aug. 1206). 8 August 1206. The abbot's grange is on the western parish boundary of Holkham at Huncrundel, on the site of Model Farm. The abbot had paid 2 marks for a quitclaim in free alms. In HD 6 the final concord is followed by XXX, a slightly expanded repetition of X. Cf. HD 22a, no. 253.

HD 7

Grant from Geoffrey le Bret of Holkham to his son John of what later became Neel Manor. 23 May 1284

Fiche 1: A10

Sciant presentes et futuri quod ego Galfridus filius Petri le Bret de Holkham . concessi . dedi . et hac presenti carta confirmaui Iohanni filio meo primogenito pro homagio et seruicio suo . mesuagium meum cum Libero introitu et exitu et cum edificiis et arboribus superstantibus et cum omnibus pertinenciis iacens in villa de Holkham cum tota terra mea sicud iacet in diuersis peciis cum tota vestura et totum ius et clamium quod habui vel habere potui in terris arabilibus . in pratis . mariscis . viis . semitis aquis molendinis . ouilibus . redditibus . homagiis . wardis releuiis et Eschaetis cum omnibus pertinenciis que mihi pertinent . vel pertinere poterunt in villa et campis de Holkham sine aliquo retinemento. Tenend' et habend' de me et heredibus meis vel meis assignatis . sibi et heredibus suis de corpore suo legitime procreatis . libere . quiete . bene in pace . in feodo et hereditate .

Cuicumque vel quandocumque . predictum mesuagium et totam predictam terram cum omnibus pertinenciis . dare . vendere vel assignare voluerit . except' domui relligionis. Reddend' inde et faciend' inde annuatim . pro me et heredibus meis dominis feodorum debita seruicia et consueta . que pertinent ad predictum mesuagium . et ad predictam terram . cum omnibus pertinenciis. Et michi annuatim in tota vita mea . decem libras argenti . scilicet ad festum Sancti Michaelis . pro omnibus seruiciis consuetis exaccionibus sectis curie et pro omnibus secularibus demandis. Et ego predictus Galfridus . et heredes mei . vel mei assignati . warantizabimus acquietabimus . et deffendemus predictum mesuagium cum tota predicta terra et cum omnibus aliis pertinenciis . predicto Iohanni et heredibus suis . de corpore suo legitime procreatis . per predictum seruicium contra omnes imperpetuum. Et si predictus Iohannes discedat sine herede de corpore suo generato'. predictum mesuagium et tota predicta terra cum omnibus aliis pertinenciis . remaneat Petro fratri suo et heredibus suis. Et si predictus Petrus discedat sine herede de corpore suo generato'. predictum mesuagium cum tota terra predicta cum omnibus pertinenciis . remaneat Eustacio suo fratri . et sic de fratre ad fratrem et heredibus suis. In cuius rei testimonium . huic presenti scripto sigillum meum apposui. Hiis testibus. Domino Iohanne Dekeny milite. Fratre Rogero priore de Petriston. Radulfo Hacun de Holkham. Iohanne filio Ade le Bret de eadem. Bartholomeo de Burgate. Simone filio Hamonis. Vnfrido Dauid. Willelmo Crak'. Rogero Dillingg' et multis aliis. Dat' apud Holkham . die martis proxima post ascensionem domini. Anno regni Regis Edwardi Duodecimo.

Seal: missing.
Endorsement: none

HD 8

Grant from Adam, son of Adam le Bret of Holkham, to William son of Gilbert Curthun of Holkham of 1 plot.   [c. 1272–5]

Cf. HD 22a, Fos. 3 no. 21, 4v no. 49, and 7 no. 86.
Fiche 1: A11

Sciant presentes et futuri quod ego Adam filius Ade le Bret de Holcham concessi dedi et hac presenti carta mea confirmaui Willelmo filio Gilberti Curthun eiusdem ville. pro homagio et seruicio suo et pro triginta solidis argenti quos mihi dedit premanibus: vnam peciam terre mee cum pertinenciis Jacentem in campis de Holcham inter terram que fuit Heruey del Hil versus austrum et terram que Katerina de Egemere tenet in dote versus aquilonem. et capud occidentale abuttat super Caldousty. Illi et heredibus suis . habendam et tenendam de me et heredibus meis libere quiete . bene . in pace . iure et hereditarie . cuicumque . et quando eam dare legare vendere vel assignare voluerit siue in egritudine constitutus siue extra. Reddendo inde annuatim mihi et heredibus meis vnum denarium scilicet ad Natiuitatem Iohannis Baptiste pro omni seruicio consuetudine exaccione secta curie et omni seculari demanda.ᵃ Ego vero predictus Adam et heredes mei warantizambimus ac aquietabimus et omnino deffendemus prenominatam peciam terre cum pertinenciis prefato Willelmo et heredibus suis vel eius assignatis sicut predictum est per predictum seruicium contra omnes christianos et Iudeos inperpetuum. In huius rey testimonium presenti carta pro me et heredibus meis sigillum meum apposui. Hiis testibus. Petro le Bret. Radulfo Hacun . Bartholomeo de Burgate . Iohanne Goldwyn' . Galfrido Goldwyn' . Radulfo Mariot . Iohanne filio Reginaldi . Dauid Man . Thoma filio Heruey Leffe . Ada filio Bartholomei carpentarij et multis aliis.

Seal: missing.
Hand: Cf. HP 999, 1000, 1001, 1039, 1042.
Endorsement: none

VARIANT: ᵃ Written as two words.

HD 9

Grant from Everard Underhowe of Holkham to Roger Calwere of Holkham of 3/4 rood.   1 Dec. 1291

Cf. HD 22a, Fo. 2v no. 14.
Fiche 1: A12

Sciant presentes et futuri quod ego Eborardus sub Hoga de Holcham concessi dedi et hac presenti carta mea confirmaui Rogero Calwere de eadem villa pro homagio et seruicio suo et pro viginti solidis quos mihi dedit premanibus. dimidiam rodam et quartam partem vnius rode terre iacentem in camp' de Holcham inter terram abbatis de Krec ex parte occident' is et terram Willelmi le Meyre ex parte orientis. Et abuttat versus aquilonem super Wellegate. Tenendam et habendam predictam terram dicto Rogero et heredibus suis de me et heredibus meis libere quiete iure et hereditarie . vel cuicumque vel quandocumque mihi illam dare vendere vel assignare voluerit. Reddendo inde annuatim mihi et heredibus meis vnum obolum ad pascha . pro omnibus seruiciis curiarum sectis et secularibus demandis. Et ego vero predictus

Eborardus et heredes mei warantizabimus et defendemus predictam peciam terre contra omnes homines imperpetuum. In cuius rei testimonium huic carte sigillum meum apposui. Hiis testibus. Iohanne le Bret . Bartholomeo de Burgate . Iohanne Silk' . Willelmo filio eius . Gilberto le Bret . Simone Hamund . Willelmo Crasc . Waltero Hakun . Ricardo le Northerne . Humfrido Dauid et aliis. Reddendo inde ad commune auxilium quando venerit in soka de Withtune ad viginti solidos vnum quadrantem ad plus plus ad minus minus. Dat' apud Holcham in crastino Sancti Andree anno regni regis Edwardi vicesimo.

Seal: Circular white seal 1 in. diam. Fleur de lys in garter. Sigill. Eborardi.

Endorsement: *Dimidia Roda et quart' vnius rode ex parte occid' Abbatis de Creyk abbut' super Wellegate versus aquilonem.* T[ranscriptum] in hand of Edmund Lucas.

HD 10

Quitclaim from John, son of Geoffrey le Bret of Holkham, to Simon Hamund of Holkham of 7½ acres in 4 plots. 10 Nov. 1294

Cf. HD 22a, no. 127.

Fiche 1: A13

NOTE: These 4 plots plus another 4 were granted in HP 1011, 30 April 1295 = HD 22a, Fo. 4 no. 46.

Sciant presentes et futuri quod ego Iohannes filius Galfridi le Bret de Holkham Concessi Confirmaui et pro me et heredibus meis inperpetuum quietum Clamaui Simoni Hamund eiusdem wille et heredibus suis totum ius et Clamium meum quod habui . vel aliquo modo . habere potui in quatuor peciis terre cum pertinenciis iacentibus in Campis de Holkham quarum Prima pecia in se Continens Septem Rodas terre iacet apud Greyston . et Secunda pecia in se Continens quatuor acras terre Iacet apud Duuspeyt . et Tercia pecia in se Continens . vnam acram terre Iacet apud Grenegate . et Quarta pecia in se Continens tres rodas terre Iacet ad Capud orientale illius pecie terre predicte que vocatur Grenegate. Quas quidem quatuor pecias terre predictas dictus Simon adquisiuit de me Infra Annos mee Etatis legitime . Ita quod nec ego Iohannes nec heredes mei . nec mei assignati de Cetero aliquid Iuris vel Clamij . de predictis quatuor peciis terre cum pertinenciis Exigere vel vendicare poterimus. Istam autem Concessionem et quietam Clamacionem feci ego Iohannes predicto Simoni et heredibus suis in seysina ipsius Simonis de toto tenemento predicto pro Triginta solidis argenti quos mihi dedit. Et ego predictus Iohannes et heredes mei vel assignati warantizabimus et omnino defendemus totum tenementum predictum cum pertinenciis predicto

Simoni et heredibus suis et assignatis suis Contra omnes homines inperpetuum. In cuius Rei testimonium huic presenti scripto sigillum meum Apposui. Dat' apud Holkham die mercurij proxima ante festum Sancti Martini Episcopi Anno Regni Regis Eadwardi vicessimo secundo. Hiis testibus. Bartholomeo de Burgate . Iohanne filio Ade le Bret . Iohanne Sylke . Willelmo Silke . Martino Goldwyne . Galfrido Godwyne . Iohanne Aynild . Willelmo Craske . Gilberto le Bret . Waltero Hakun . Roberto le Marschall . Humfrido Dauid et aliis multis.

> Seal: Circular seal of white wax (formerly coated with reddish paint). An eight-pointed star with globular points within an inscription: Iohis Fil. Galfridi. 1¹/₂ in. diam.
> Hand: Cf. HD 22b, HP 1009, 1010, 1024.
> Endorsement: T[ranscriptum] in hand of Edmund Lucas.

HD 11

Rental of Geoffrey le Bret of Holkham.　　　　　　　　　　　[c. 1293–4]

> Cf. HD 20 for rental of Peter le Bret.
> Fiche 1: A14

REDITUS ASS' TENENTIUM GALFRIDI LE BRET DE HOLKHAM

Ad festum Sancti Michaelis.		Ad Pascam.[b]	
Iohannes Silke	iiij d. ob.	Petrus filius Ade le Bret	i d.
Rogerus Belneye	vj d. ob. q[a].	Iohannes Silke	xj d. ob.
Willelmus Curstun	j d.	Rogerus Elurich	j d. qr.
Simon Amund	vj d. ob. q[a].	Herueus Byleman	j d.
Erueus Buleman	j d.	Bartholomeus de Burgate	j ob.
Rogerus Elurich	iij d. ob.	Radulfus Mariot	iij d.
Bartholomeus de Burgate	j ob.	Willelmus le Meyre	iij d.
Prior de Peterston	xj d. et ob.	Prior de Petereston	xj d. et ob.
Adam Carpentarius	xij d.	Adam Carpentarius	xij d. ob.
Willelmus Mere	iij d.	Ricardus Wlmer	j ob.
Radulfus Marut	iij d. et j caponem	Radulfus Rutur	iij d.
Ricardus Wlmer	j ob.	Simon Scharles	j ob.
Willelmus Duc	j d.	[name erased]	j d. ob.
Simon Schales	j ob.	Willelmus Duc	ij d.
Willelmus filius Bete	j d. ob.	Willelmus Bete	ij d.
Robertus Ape	j d. ob.	Robertus Ape	ij d.

Matilda Ernald	j d. ob.
Gilbertus Gurle	j d. ob.
Rogerus Thurbern	j d.
Eborardus sub Monte	j d. ob.
Gilbertus Daleman	j d.
Emma de Campo	ij d.
Reginaldus Digge	j d. ob.
Rogerus Ernald	iiij d.
Ricardus le Norne	vj d. ob.
Tomas Warin	iij d.
Iohannes Ide	vij d.
Adam Dersi	ij d.
Auuisa Rutele	ij d.
Gilbertus Gant	ij d. [struck out]
Ricardus Olnie	j d.
Iohannes Gerard	ij d. ob
Radulfus Rutur	iij d.
Gilbertus Payn	j d.
Emma le Colt	iij d. ob.
Willelmus Craske	j d.
Robertus filius Emme^a	ij d. ob.
Iohannes Aynild	j d.
Rogerus Spellere	j d.
Warinus de Quarles	j d.
Rogerus filius Emme	ij d.
Willelmus de Hyndryngham	j d.
Herueus Quytbred	j d.
Humfridus Dauy	j ob.
Iohannes le Ward de Dalling'	j ob.

Eborardus sub Monte	j d. ob.
Matilda Ernald	j d. ob.
Gilbertus Gurle	j d. ob.
Rogerus Thurbern	j d. q^a.
Gilbertus Daleman	j d. q^a.
Emma de Campo	ij d.
Reginaldus Digge	j d. ob.
Rogerus Ernald	iiij d.
Ricardus le Norne	j ob.
Tomas Warin	iij d.
Iohannes Ide	iij d.
Adam Dersi	ii d.
Robertus filius Emme	ij d. ob.
Gilbertus Gant	ij d.
Rad. Hacun pro terra Norne	j d.
Symon Hamund	ob. q^a.
Rogerus Belney'	j d. ob.
Iohannes Aynild^c	j d.
Rogerus filius Emme	vij d.
Willelmus de Hyndryngham	j d.
Herueus Quytbred	j d.
Symon filius Hamonis	j ob.
Gilbertus Dalle	j d.

Ad festum Sancti Andree.

Willelmus Bete	ij d.
Robertus Ape	iij d.
Eborardus sub Monte	j d. ob.
Matilda Ernald	j d. ob.
Gilbertus Gurle	j d. ob.
Rogerus Thurbern	ij d.
Gilbertus Daleman	j d. q^a
Emma de Campo	ij d.
Rogerus Ernald	iiij d.

Ad Pentecosten.

Willelmus Bete	ij d.
Robertus Ape	ij d.
Eborardus sub Monte	j d. ob.
Matilda Ernald	j d. ob.
Gilbertus Gurle	j d. ob.
Rogerus Thurbern	j d. q^{ae}.
Gilbertus Daleman	j d. q^a
Emma de Campo	j d
Rog' Berkar' et	

Matilda vxor eius de Torp   j ob.^{f}

Willelmus Craske   ob. et q^a.

Rogerus Raund   j ob.

Rogerus Speller'^{d}.   j q^a.

Ad Natiuitatem Sancti Iohannis Baptiste

Scutagium domini Regis

Willelmus Craske   ob. et q^a.

Symon Hamund   j d.

Herueus Wytbred   ij d.

Rogerus Belneye ad scutagium
domini Regis quando venerit
ad xx sol. q^a. ad plus plus
ad minus minus.
Petrus filius Ade le Bret
ad scutagium domini Regis
quando venerit ad xx s. q^a.
ad plus plus ad minus minus.
Simon Amund ad scutagium
domini Regis quando venerit
ad xx s. j ob. ad plus
ad minus minus.
Willelmus Curstun ad Scutagium

Ad Natale domini

domini Regis quando venerit
ad xx s. q^a. ad plus plus

Petrus filius Ade le Bret   j d.

ad minus minus.

Gilbertus Aynild   j. ob.

Rogerus Elurich ad scutagium

Rogerus Elurich   j d.

domini Regis quando venerit

Iohannes Silke   j d.

ad xx s. iij q^a. ad plus plus ad

Gilbertus le Bret   j. ob.

minus minus.

Herueus Quytbred^e iij d.

Adam Carpentarius ad scutagium
domini ad xx s. iij d. ad plus
plus ad minus minus.
Herveus Buleman ad scutagium
domini ad xx s. ob. ad plus
plus ad minus minus.
[Name Erased] ad viginti solid.
iij d. ob. et ad plus plus et ad
minus minus.
Radulfus Hacun ad viginti solid.
pro terra Norne iij d.
Prior de Peterston ad xx sol. ob.
et ad plus plus et ad minus
minus.

Willelmus Craske ad xx solid.
ob. et ad plus plus et ad minus
minus.
Johanes filius Ade le Bret ad xx
solid. [no sum stated]
Isabella Godwine ad xxti. s. ob.
ad plus plus ad minus minus.
Rogerus Elueric ob. ad plus plus
ad minus.

Willelmus filius Bete et Robertus Ape facient vnum ploubere.

Eborardus sub Monte et Gilbertus Gurle et Matilda Ernald facient vnum ploubere.

Rogerus Thurbern et Gilbertus Daleman et Rogerus de Campo facient vnum ploubere.

Thomas Warin faciet vnum ploubere.

Iohannes Ide faciet vnum ploubere.

Dorse

The top six inches of the roll are badly rubbed. After listing ten small payments including Rogerus Elueriche iij d., Robertus Meyr iij d., Radulphus Mariot iij d., Robertus Ape j d. ob., Robertus filius Emme ij d. ob. and (in place of Iohannes Goldewin struck out) the prior of Peterstone xxiij d. *ad festum Sancti Michaelis et ad Pentecosten* it proceeds:

Iohannes de Belneye tenuit quondam et nunc tenet Rogerus Belneye apud Sexacres vij acras terre apud Scu.s..botme iiij acras apud Billesmere iij acras .... de .... per annum vij d. ob. Iohannes le Wright tenet ex parte orientali ecclesie dimidiam acram quondam Iohannes de Dallyngge.

Walterus filius Radulfi de Olneye tenuit et quondam Willelmus Curzoun apud Adhowe j acram j rodam terre. Reddendo per annum ij s.

Rogerus Eluerich' tenuit quondam apud Wichescroft j acram j rodam terre. Et apud Waterslades siue Claylond dimidiam acram. Reddendo iiij d. per annum.

Bartholomeus de Burgate tenuit quondam et nunc tenet Willelmus Wake in crufta sua j acram. Reddendo per annum vj d. et j capon'.

Iohannes Goldewyne tenuit quondam et nunc tenet Prior de Peterstone xvj acras terre vnde etc. Reddendo xviiij d.

Willelmus le Meire tenuit quondam et nunc tenet Heilota le Meyre j mesuagium cum crufta continenti j acram terre. Reddendo vj d.

Radulfus Mariot quondam et nunc Iohannes Bulwere Heilota Meire et Willelmus filius Alicie j acram terre in quadam crufta. Reddendo vj d. et j capon'.

Radulfus Wulmere tenuit quando et nunc tenet j cotagium. Reddendo j d.

Emma de Campo tenuit quondam et nunc tenet Claricia de Hogate per virgam dimidiam rodam apud Bondescroft reddendo ob. Et Reginaldus le Sheppard tenet dimidiam acram in duabus peciis apud Westbondescroft j rodam dimidiam et Claylond dimidiam rodam. Reddendo j d. ob. Set vetus rentale dicit de iiij d. Ideo distring' pro arreragiis.

Robertus filius Emme quondam et nunc tenet Bartholomeus filius Margerie ij acras terre in vna pecia vocata Iamescroft. Reddendo v d.

Heredes Iohannis Aynild tenent j acram terre vnde inquirendum. Reddendo iij d. ob.

Adam Aynild tenuit quondam et nunc Walterus Aynild j rodam et dimidiam terre quondam Hawisie Powel in Estgate. Reddendo ob.

Rogerus Spellere quondam postea et nunc Ricardus Spellere tenet apud Bondescroft j acram terre. Reddendo ij d. q^a.

Heredes Rogeri filij Emme tenent. Reddendo iij d.

Willelmus de Hindringham tenuit quondam et nunc Robertus Mayn vnde inquirendum reddendo ij d. Herueus Qwytbred quondam tenuit nunc tenet Iohannes de Belneye apud Sexacres ij acras terre. Reddendo iiij d.

Humfridus Dauy quondam et nunc Emma filia eius apud Wardeshou Sty dimidiam acram. Reddendo ob.

...... Halle tenuit quondam et nunc heredes sui apud Burgate j rodam terre. Reddendo j d.

Willelmus Craske tenuit quondam set quantum et per seruicium inquirendum et dicitur quod debet reddere iiij d. q^a sicut patet per vetus rentale ..... pro pascellis.

Iohannes Broun tenuit quondam et nunc Mariota Gibbes tenet in Hougate dimidiam acram. Reddendo j d.

Ricardus Northerne quondam tenuit et nunc Thomas filius eius pro tenemento quondam Iohannis Ide et pro terra Rotele vnde et vbi inquirendum. Reddendo j d.

Ricardus filius Rogeri Eluerich quondam et nunc Rogerus filius eius tenet j acram dimidiam in crufta de Hogate. Reddendo inde domino j d. Et pro domino j libram piperis.

Petrus filius Ade le Bret quondam et nunc Hugo Otes tenet j mesuagium suum et cruftam. Reddendo ij d.

Willelmus Silke tenet etc. set quid et per quod seruicium inquirendum.

Willelmus Duk tenet set quid et per quod seruicium inquirendum.

Herveus Buleman tenuit etc. set per quod seruicium et quod feodum etc. inquirendum.

Reginaldus Digge tenuit set quid etc.

Simon Scharles tenuit etc. set per quod seruicium et quod feodum inquirendum.

Radulfus Hakun tenuit quondam de terra Norne videlicet j acram in Nornescroft. Reddendo j d.

Iohannes filius Ade le Bret quondam terram quondam Eborardi sub monte set quantum vbi et per quod seruicium inquirendum.

Rogerus Bercar' de terra quondam Emme atte Feld in duabus peciis vna j roda et dimidia apud Bondescroft et aliam dimidia roda apud Cleylond. Reddendo j d. ob.

Rogerus Rauen tenuit et nunc Henricus Anger tenet j cotagium. Reddendo ob.

Greyston vnam acram et tres rodas terre.

Deuspest iiij acras terre.

Grenegate vnam acram et tres rodas terre.

Adowe Brest iij acras terre.

Ryngwarislond vnam acram et tres rodas terre.

Hadowe iij acras terre.

NOTE: The last seven items of HD 11 correspond in order and area with lands granted by Geoffrey le Bret's son John on 10 Nov. 1294 in HP 10 (HD 22a, no. 127). This suggests that the date of this rental of Geoffrey le Bret is earlier. In support of this is the fact that John le Bret gave Gilbert Gurle to Simon Hammond on 16 July 1296 (HD 22a, no. 104); furthermore John son of Geoffrey le Bret gave to Humphrey David 2d. which he used to receive of William Ducke on 5 June 1295 (HP 1012). The Neel manor court of 1329 ordered inquiries into the doubtful points about these holdings (HD 81).

VARIANTS: [a] This and the next eight names, except Quytbred, are added in a paler ink. [b] Pasca repeated in Ms. [c] This and the following five names are added in paler ink. [d] Added in very pale ink. [e] The name is almost erased. [f] This line was added later.

HD 12

*Grant from John Charlys senior of Holkham to Simon Hamund of Holkham
of 1 rood.*   5 May 1295

Cf. HD 22a, Fo. 7v no. 94
Fiche 1: B1

Sciant presentes et futuri quod ego Iohannes Charlys senior de Holkham
Concessi dedi et hac presenti Carta mea Confirmaui Simoni Hamund et
heredibus suis eiusdem wille pro septem solidis Argenti quos mihi dedit in
gersumam vnam rodam terre mee iacentem in Campis de Holcham apud
Sladaker inter terram meam ex parte Aquiloni. et terram predicti Simonis ex
parte australi et Capud orientale abuttat super terram prioris et Conuentus de
Peterston et Capud occidentale abuttat super Hadhoweheuedes . habend' et
tenend' de Capitalibus Dominis feodi illius et heredibus suis vel suis
assignatis . Libere . quiete . bene . in pace . iure . et hereditarie . Cuicumque
vel quandocumque eam dare . vendere . vel assignare voluerit exceptis
domibus Religionis . faciend' Inde Annuatim pro me et heredibus meis
Capitalibus dominis feodi illius vnum denarium ad Natiuitatem Sancti
Iohannis Baptiste pro omnibus seruiciis . Consuetudinibus . et exaccionibus .
Sectis Curie et secularibus demandis. Et Ego predictus Iohannes et heredes
mei vel mei assignati warantizabimus et omnino defendemus predictam
Rodam terre predicto Simoni et heredibus suis vel suis assignatis Contra
omnes homines inperpetuum. In Cuius rei testimonium huic Carte sigillum
meum Apposui. Dat' apud Holcham Die Iouis proxima post Inuencionem
Sancte Crucis Regni Regis Edwardi vicessimo tertio. Hiis testibus .
Bartholomeo de Burgate . Iohanne filio Ade le Bret . Iohanne Sylke .
Willelmo filio suo . Martino Goldwyne . Galfrido Goldwyne . Waltero Hakun
. Willelmo Craske . Iohanne Aynild . Ricardo le Northerne . Iohanne Rutur .
Roberto Le Marschall et aliis multis.

Seal: Circular seal 1¹/₂. in diam. of white wax (formerly coated with reddish paint).
Flower head. In Aug. 1982 the seal was found detached.
Hand: Cf. HP 995, 1007, 1008, 1011, 1012, 1014, 1015, 1016, 1017, 1019 (1294–6).

HD 13

Grant from John Charlys senior of Holkham to Simon Hamund of Holkham of a plot of 11/2 acres.   12 Dec. 1296

Cf. HD 22a, Fo. 7v no. 95
Fiche 1: B2

Sciant presentes et futuri quod ego Iohannes Charlys senior filius Simonis Charlys de Holkham Concessi . dedi . et hac presenti Carta mea Confirmaui . Simoni Hamund eiusdem wille et heredibus suis pro quadam summa pecunie quam mihi dedit in gersumam . vnam peciam terre mee in se continentem vnam acram et dimidiam terre iacentem in campis de Holkham in quarentena que vocatur Shladeacre inter terram meam ex parte Aquilon' . et terram quondam Radulfi Chelys ex parte australi . et caput orientale abuttat super terram prioris et Conuentus de Peterston. Habend' et tenend' de Capitalibus Dominis feodi illius . illi et heredibus suis Libere . quiete . bene . et in pace . Iure . et hereditarie . faciend' inde Annuatim pro me et heredibus meis Capitalibus Dominis feodi illius quatuor denarios et obolum . videlicet ad festum Sancti Andree vnum denarium et obolum . ad Annunciacionem Beate Marie Virginis vnum denarium et obolum . et ad Natiuitatem Sancti Iohannis Baptiste vnum denarium et obolum . pro omnibus seruiciis Consuetudinibus . exactionibus . Sectis Curie . et secularibus demandis. Et ego predictus Iohannes et heredes mei warantizabimus predictam peciam terre . predicto Simoni et heredibus suis contra omnes homines inperpetuum. In Cuius Rei testimonium. Huic Carte sigillum meum apposui. Hiis testibus . Bartholomeo de Burgate. Iohanne filio Ade Le Bret . Martino Goldwyne . Galfrido Godwyne . Willelmo Silke . Willelmo Craske . Ricardo Le Northerne . Iohanne Aynild . Waltero Hakun . Gilberto Le Bret . Iohanne Rutur . Humfrido Dauyd et Aliis. Dat' apud Holkham die Mercurij proxima post festum Sancti Nicholai episcopi. Anno regni regis Edwardi vicesimo quinto.

Seal: missing. Seal tag is a scrap of parchment made of piece of a deed in same handwriting.
Hand: Cf. HP 1070
Endorsement: T[ranscriptum] in the hand of Edmund Lucas. *Sladacer ... J Waylond* in later hand.

HD 14

Court Rolls of Hillhall Manor.   1312 and 1322

Fiche 1: B3

Mem. 1

HOLKHAM CURIA TENTA DIE LUNE PROX. POST OCTAB' PASCH.
ANNO REGNI REGIS EDWARDI*ᵃ* QUINTO.   1 May 1312

<Vacat quia non expectat [di]em>
Robertus de Swanton' def. versus Thomas de Schengham de placito debiti
per Galfridum atte Sloo pleg' Gilbertus Meyn et Galfridus Thorebarre.
<Vacat quia non expectat diem   Preceptum est>
Hugo Sutor de communi – per Radulfum Cheterel pleg' Willelmus Sutor
et Godman Sutor .
<Preceptum est>
Adhuc preceptum est retinere in manu domini j rodam terre quam
Galfridus Daulin obiit seisitus . quousque etc. et respondere de exitu . etc.
<Preceptum est>
Adhuc preceptum est retinere in manu domini j rodam terre que fuit
Rogeri Aloise quia non facit seruicia. Et respondere de exitu etc.
<Finis . viij . d.>
Godmannus Sutor reddit sursum in manu domini . j . rodam terre ad opus
Willelmi Sutor et Isabelle vxoris sue. Et dat pro ingressu habendo.
<Preceptum est>
Adhuc preceptum est retinere in manu domini dimidiam acram terre quam
Willelmus Osebern acquisiuit de heredibus Heruei Balle et respondere de
exit*u*.
<Finis . vj . d.>
Godmannus Sutor reddit sursum in manu domini j rodam terre iacentem
apud Scamelond' ad opus Hugonis Otes . ad terminum . x . annorum et dat
domino pro termino habendo.
<Finis . vj . d.>
Radulfus Daulyn per licenciam domini . dimisit Hugoni Hotes dimidiam
acram terre ad terminum . v . annorum iacentem apud Scothogate et domino
pro termino habendo. Pleg' Gilbert' Main et Ricard' Pain . vj. d.
<Finis . iiij . d.>
Rogerus filius Faber*ᵇ* dimisit Hugoni Otes . j . rodam terre apud
Scothogate ad terminum v annorum. Et dat domino pro termino habendo vj
d. Pleg' predictorum.

<Misericordia . xij . d. Preceptum est>

De Roberto de Swantone et pleggiis suis ad respondendum videlicet Willelmo le Heiward et Ricardo Payn . quia non veniunt ad respondendum Thome de Schengham in placito debiti in misericordia. Et preceptum est ponere predictum Robertum per meliores plegios.

Helewysia le Northerne habet licenciam de domino ad seminandum . j . rodam terre que capta fuit in manu domini pro defalta seruiciorum subtractorum. Ita quod dicta Helewysia non metet dictam . terram nec habebit vesturam dicte terre quousque satisfecit domino et balliuis suis de omnibus amerciamentis et debitis.

<Preceptum est>

Preceptum est retinere in manu domini dimidiam rodam terre post mortem Cristine Cage . et respondere de exitu quousque etc.

<Misericordia xij . d. Preceptum est>

De Hugoni Toli et plegiis suis scilicet Galfrido Smart et Radulfo de Oleneye quia non veniunt ad respondendum domino. Ideo in misericordia. Preceptum ponere per meliores plegios.

<Misericordia . iij . d.>

Walterus Pain et Berta vxor Willelmi de Warham per licenciam concordati sunt ita quod dicta Berta ponit se in misericordia. Et dicta Berta ponit se in misericordia. Et dicta Berta dabit dicto Waltero . xv d. soluend' . medietatem ad festum Sancti Michaelis et aliam medietatem ad festum Sancti Martini. Plegij Galfridus Thurbern et Iohannes Reinold.

<Querela . Preceptum est>

Iohannes filius Rogeri \Fabri/ queritur de Radulfo Daulyn et Godman filio suo de placito terre. Plegij de prosequendo Rogerus filius Fabri et Radulfus de Oleneye.

<Finis . vj . d.>

Alicia Briche dimisit dimidiam acram terre iacentem iuxta Le Lyng*s* Radulfo Cursun ad terminum . vij . annorum. Et dat domino pro dicta terra tenenda ad terminum predictum. Pleg' Radulfi de Oleneye vj d.

<Misericordia ij . s. j . d.>

Presentant quod Henricus Wainflet iij . d. Simon Esterild iiij . d. Geffrei^c Esterild . Willelmus de Warham iij . d. Iohannes de Creik iij . d. Gilbertus Crane nil Gilbertus Maniard iij . d. Hugo Sutor iij . d. Isabella filia Simonis filij Radulfi et Bartholomeus atte Dale iij . d. Ricardus Olf iij . d. faciunt defaltam. Misericordia.

Willelmus de Warham dimisit Godmanno filio Radulfi Daulin dimidiam acram terre ad terminum . x annorum . et dominus non tenetur . ad warantiam.

<Querela. Misericordia . iij . d.>

Willelmus Sutor queritur de Godmanno Sutor' de placito debiti. Plegij de prosequendo Radulfus de Oleneye et Iohannes Reynold' . eo quod . dictus Godmannus debet dicto Willelmo . xix . s. et adhuc detinet. Dictus Godmannus in plena curia dedicit predictum Willelmum et negat ei debere predictos xix . s. Et ponit se in inquisicionem. Qui dicunt . quod predictus Godmannus tenetur dicto Willelmo in predictos . xix s. Et . noluit invenire pleg. de predicto debito. Ideo.

<Preceptum est. Querela.>

Willelmus filius Henrici queritur de Godmanno Sutor' de placito debiti. Plegij de prosequendo. Radulfus de Oleneie et Reginaldus Cocus. Et preceptum est distringere predictum Godmannum quousque attach. etc.

<Querela Preceptum est.>

Willelmus filius Henrici queritur de Radulfo Daulyn de placito debiti. Plegij de prosequendo. Reginaldus Cocus et Radulfus de Olneye. Et preceptum est distringere predictum Radulfum . quousque . etc.

<Respectum>

Abbas de Crek habet diem vsque ad proximam curiam ad satisfaciendum domino de viij . denariis annui redditus vel ad returnandum vnam districcionem. Plegij Iohannes Godcock et Hugo Otes.

<xx s.>

Ad hanc curiam venit Iohannes Edrich in plena curia et reddit sursum in manum domini vnum mesuagium cum pertinenciis iac' iuxta terram Iohannis Aynild ex parte occidentali et mesuagium Agnete Briche ex parte orientali ad opus Iohannis Carp Cecilie vxoris sue heredum eorum et assignatorum faciend' . seruicia secundum consuetudinem Manerij. Et dat domino pro ingressu habendo xx . s. Pleg. Radulfi de Olneye. Et tradita est eis seysina. Et preterea predicti Iohannes Carp et Cecilia vxor sua . veniunt et reconcedunt dicto Iohanni Edrich' et Wolueue vxori sue vnam domum edificatam in dicto mesuagio cum libero introitu et exitu ad terminum vite eorum. Ita quod dicta Wolueue vxor dicti Iohannis Edriche non potest calumpniare aliam dotem post discessum predicti Iohannis viri sui nisi dictam domum. Et post mortem predicte Wolueue predicta domus remaneat predictis Iohanni Carp et Cecilie vxori sue et heredibus eorum imperpetuum.

Dorse

Much faded and partly illegible.

Ad huc de Curia precedenti
<[finis] vij . d.>
De Ricardo Pain pro filio suo maritando . vij . d.
<[auxilium] xx . s.>
De toto homagio[1] de dono pro milite domino faciendo . vt in carta eorum ex feofamento domini Thome de Akeney allocatur per dominum et suis balliuis xx . s.
<Memorandum de onere. Preceptum est.>
Memorandum quod Ricardus Pain collector oneratus fuit pro execucione ad extremam curiam de xx s. pro duobus amerciamentis videlicet de Gilberto filio Iohanne Selke quod se maritauit sine licencia domini . x . s. et de Berta filia Iohanne Selke sorore sua pro eodem . x s. Qui dicit quod non [potuit] distringere superdictos quod nil habent. Et etiam \Iohanna/ mater eorum non debet respondere pro filiis suis eo quod dicta Iohanna mater dictorum [..dicit quod ..] fecit finem cum domino ut numquam .. .. pro ratione filiarum suarum vt patet in curia tenta in festo Sancti Mathei Apostoli anno. Edwardi quarto. Et quia dicta Iohanna ...... vnam acram terre vnde fecit finem cum domino ut predictum est ideo ponatur in respectum quousque plus inquiratur.

Summa xlviij s. j d.

List of Hillhall Manor tenants

Gilbertus Edrich' fecit fidelitatem . et Iur'.
Ricardus Payn . similiter.
Rogerus filius Fabri similiter Iur'.
Galfridus Thurbern similiter Iur'.
Walterus Pay[n] fecit similiter et Iur'.
Hugo Sutere non venit pro contemptu.[d]
Rogerus Iendy fecit similiter . et Iur'.
Iohannes de Folsham similiter.
Bartholomeus atte dale.
Agneta Oddes.
Iohanna filia Simonis filij Radulfi.
Mathilda . soror eius.
Isabella . soror eius. | R
Helewisia soror eius.
Mariota soror eius.
Rogerus Carpentarius.

Godmannus Dawly.
Walterus Pay.
Willelmus de Warles.
Hugo Sutere.
Thomas frater eius.
Edmundus Suture.
Willelmus Sutere.
Henricus Waynflad.[e]
Alicia Godgrom.
Cristiana Godgrom.
Galfridus Estrild.
Simon frater eius.
Iohannes Porron.
Alicia Ernyes.[d]
Iohannes Schrudy.[e]
Iohannes Andreu.

---

1   Cf. HD 22a, Fo. 12 no. 150 for services and customs due to the d'Akenys.

Stephanus Attetuneshende.
Ricardus Attetuneshende.[e]
Gilbertus Maynard.[e]
Gilbertus Crane.
Wluuua Dawes.
Oylota soror eius.
Mariota que fuit vxor Gilberti
filij Roberti.[e]
Robertus filius Gilberti.
Alicia Bryche.

Iohannes filius Gilberti.
Alicia Andrew.
Galfridus Thurburn.
Iohannes Reynald.
Willelmus Elsy.
Agneta Elsy
Rogerus filius Fulconis.
Iohannes de Folsham.
Gilbertus Mayn.
Iohannes Carpe.
Mariota Crask.

<Vacat>

Iohannes Edrich'. – quia alibi.
Agneta Belahe.
Gilbertus Maynard
Rogerus Vheles.
Sabina Payn.
Iohanna de Orchard.
Elewisia de Creyk.[e]
Louegold Wallet.
Alicia soror eius.
Rogerus Ioudy.[d]
Ricardus Rutour
Ricardus Payn.
Radulfus Daulyn.
Richardus Hieler.
Helewysia Cage.
Memorandum de Ada filia Iohannis Selk.

Anlepimen[2]

Iohanna filia Edrich.[e]
Emma soror eius.[e]
Mariota Rutour.[e]
Isabella Elsy[e]
Margareta filia Radulfi Daulyn.[e]
Alicia filia Radulfi Attedale.[e]

---

2   F.W. Maitland explained *Anelepyman* as a description of a man who was no householder, *The Court Baron with Select Pleas from the Bishop of Ely's Court of Littleport*, 1891, pp. 146, 149. They were there helping harvest. Anelepymen paid a capitation called *chevage* and had come from outside the manor for work. All six are here female. On 1 Sept. 1360 two out of a similar gang of six at Hillhall were female and half shared the same surname. They paid 11/2d. each, HD 89a. Others worked for Burghall, HD 84. At Littleport too there were *anelepywymmen*. References occur in various East Anglian manors (e.g. Heacham). See also G.C. Homans, *English Villagers of the Thirteenth Century*, 1941, p. 211–12, Edward Britton, *The Community of the Vill*, 1977, p. 136–7, and D.C. Douglas, *The Social Structure of Medieval East Anglia*, 1927, p. 31. Also, cf. C.N.L. Brooke, M.M. Postan, eds, *'Carte Nativorum', A Peterborough Abbey Cartulary of the Fourteenth Century*, 1960, p. xl, anlepemen, peasant's servants, undersettles.

Libere tenentes

Abbas de Creyk.

Prior de Peterston

Iohannes le Heyr

Radulfus Curthon.

Thomas Curthon.*e*

Iohannes Godkot.

Marg' Haye.

Robertus de Swanton.

Galfridus le Eyward. Fecit fidelitatem.

Radulfus Reve.*e*

Cecilia Ernys.

Iohannes Aynild.

Willelmus Silk.

Robertus de Gristone. Fecit fidelitatem.

Mariota Craske.*d*

Gilbertus Northerne.

Reginaldus Aldyyn.

Hugo Red.

Mariota Leman.

Claricia de Hogate fidelitatem.

Emma Deryng.

Mariota Skynnere.

Iohanna Andr' vnder Clynt per Thomam filius eius.

Iohn Maye.

Iohannes Parsone fidelitatem.

Adam Aynild.

Mariota que fuit vxor Gilberti filij Radulfi.

Willelmus de Warham.

Hugo Toly.

Iohannes Thurbern.

[*There follows a short list of about eight small plots of land, including one rood at the mill.*]

Mem. 2

HOLCHAM

CURIA IBIDEM DE TERMINO SANCTI ANDREE TENTA DIE MERCURIJ PROXIMA POST FESTUM SANCTI HILLARIJ ANNO REGNI REGIS EDWARDI QUINTODECIMO   20 January 1322

<Fidelitas>

Heruicus Boleman fecit fidelitatem domino pro tenura quam clamat tenere in Holkham de domino pro s[eruiciis] etc.

<Misericordia . iij. d.>

De primis plegiis Rogeri Jowdy quia ipsum non habet \ad prosequendum / versus Iohannem Silke in placito debiti. Et preceptum est ipsum facere per meliores.

<Misericordia . iij. d.>

De Bartholomeo le Marchall quia non est prosequend' . versus Iohannem Leyr in placito debiti.

<Misericordia>

Laurencius Bylaghe qui petit terciam partem vnius rode terre de vna dimidia acra terre de bassa tenura quod Galfridus Julyan habet adhuc termino duorum annorum. Ideo predictus Laurencius in misericordia.

<Misericordia . iij . d.>

Compertum est per inquisicionem quod Miriella mater Iohannis filij Rogeri numquam fuit seisita de tribus Rodis terre quas petit versus Philippum filium Radulphi. Ideo consideratum est quod dictus Iohannes sit in misericordia et predictus Philippus teneat dictam terram in pace et hereditarie etc.

<Releuium . vj . d.>

Ad istam Curiam venit Galfridus filius Gilberti Mayn et petit admitti cum Roberto fratre suo ad medietatem hereditatis \post mortem patris sui et admittatur in hered' et fecit domino fidelitatem et releuium videlicet dupplicabit redditum suum post mortem patris sui tenend' dictam medietatem hereditatis de domino. Fac' domino seruicia etc. Saluo iure etc.

<Releuium . vj . d.>

Conpertum est per inquisicionem quod tenementum Ade Crokkere videlicet vnum mesuagium cum vij . rodis terre sunt de libero tenemento istius manerij et Bartholomeus Calwere et parcenarij sui reddunt domino pro dicto mesuagio et tenemento xij d. ad terminos vsuales. Et predictus Bartholomeus Calewere dat domino pro auxilio habendo de predicto redditu leuando.

<Finis . iij . d.>

Vna roda terre que capta fuit in man*um* domini quam Matil*da* Here de Brunham tenet liberatur eidem ad cust' quousque ostendat cartam suam. Et dat domino pro custodia predicta.

<Finis . xij. d.>

Berta filia Gilberti reddit sursum in man*um* domini vnam rodam terre cum pertinenciis ad opus Bartholomei filij Godmanni filij Radulfi tenend*am* sibi et Heredibus suis reddendo domino seruic*ia* etc. Saluo iure cuiuslibet etc. Et dat domino pro ingressu habendo in dicta roda terre etc.

<Finis . iiij . d.>

De Willelmo filio Reginaldi Bercar' pro termino suo habendo in tertia parte vnius domus quam alloc. de Iohanne filio Gilberti Edrych' ad terminum quatuor annorum termino incipiente ad festum Sancti Petri Ad vincula vsque ad idem in quatuor annos.

<Soluend*um* Finis . iij . d.>

De Radulpho de Olneye pro termino suo habendo in vna roda terre ad terminum quinque annorum quam habet ex dimissione Margarete filie Simonis termino incipiendo ad Natale domini vltimo preterit*um*. Et dat domino etc. Et dicta Margareta faciet interim seruicia etc.

<Finis . iij . d. Misericordia . iij . d.>

Conpertum est per inquisicionem quod Iohannes filius Rogeri detinuit dimidiam rodam terre de hereditate Custancie Miryold' iniuste. Ideo consideratum est quod dicta Constancia habeat et teneat predictam dimidiam rodam terre sibi et heredibus suis etc. fac. domino etc. Saluo iure etc. Et cepit sursum per virgam et dat domino.

<Finis . vj . d. Misericordia>

De Willelmo Cat et Matilda ad capud ville pro perambulacione habenda inter ipsos de iiij^{or} pedibus terre in latitudine et longitudine . xx . ped. videlicet de Willelmo Cat . iij . d. et de dicta Matilda et matre eius iij d.

<Finis . iij . d.>

Iohannes Shrudy reddit sursum in man*um* domini j quarterium vnius rode terre ad opus Iohannis Andreu tenend' sibi et heredibus suis et habet inde seisinam et dat domino pro ingressu. Pleg. Bartolomei de la Dale.

<Releuium>

Gilbertus le Soutere Anlepimannus[3] domini fecit fidelitatem domino de cheuagiis suis et arreragiis et quod non subtraet de domino etc.

<Misericordia . ii . d.>

Conpertum est per inquisicionem quod Bartolomeus Calwere verberauit Bertam Gilberd et male tractauit ad damnum suum vj d. . Ideo consideratum est quod predicta Berta recuperet versus predictum Bartholomeum predictas vj d. Et predictus Bartholomeus in misericordia.

<Finis . xij . d.>

Hugo le Soutere reddit sursum in man*um* domini vnam rodam terre ad opus Rogeri Ester tenend' sibi et heredibus suis imperpetuum saluo iure etc.

---

3   See footnote on page 88.

fac' domino seruicia etc. Et dat domino pro ingressu habendo plegio collectore.

<Eleccio collectoris>

Totum homagium eligit in officium collectoris hoc anno suo periculo Iohannem Edryche et Ceciliam Carpe parcennarium suum ad faciendum officium.

<Anlepimanni>[4]

Bartholomeus de la Dale respondet de cheuagiis Anlepimannorum de termino preterito scilicet de . viij . anlepimannorum.

<Finis . vi . d.>

Laurencius de Belaghe dat in excambium Beatrici Northerne et Isabelle Northerne terciam partem vnius rode terre pro medietate vnius domus et medietate vnius curie tenend' eidem Laurencio et heredibus suis et tenend' terciam partem predicte rode terre predicte Beatrici et Isabelle et heredibus eorum. Et dant domino ex vtraque parte.

<Preceptum est>

Preceptum est retinere vnam rodam terre in manu domini quam Philippus filius Radulphi clamat vt ius et hereditatem suam. Et satisfacere eidem Philippo interim de proparte et Matilde Taye de dote etc.

<Preceptum est>

Certificare ad proximam curiam de omnibus tenementis et feodis pertinentibus ad dictum manerium et de omnibus feodis.

CURIA IBIDEM TENTA DIE LUNE PROXIMA ANTE FESTUM PURIFICACIONIS BEATE MARIE ANNO REGNI REGIS EDWARDI FILIJ EDWARDI [XV?]ᶠ   1 Feb. 1322?

<Preceptum est>

Sicut alias capere in manus domini . j . rodam terre quam Matildis Here de Brunham tenet quousque ostendat cartam suam.

<Preceptum est>

Preceptum est retinere sicut prius in manus domini j rodam terre quam Iohannes filius Radulfi clamat in hereditate vt ius suum.

<Preceptum est>

Adhuc preceptum est certificare ad proximam curiam de omnibus tenementis et feodis pertinentibus ad manerium et de omnibus feodis.

<Preceptum est>

Attachiare Roisiam Buleman quod sit ad proximam curiam ad respondendum Hugoni Otes de placito debiti plegiis de prosequendo Iohanne Carpentario et Collectore.

---

4   See footnote on page 88.

<Preceptum est>
Preceptum est capere in manus domini totam terram quam Iohannes filius Rogeri tenet de domino et mesuagium suum quousque reddat se iusticiand' domino pro \contemptu/ despectu facto domino et quousque inuenerit plegios ad respondendum Mabilie de Kedestone de placito debiti et aliis conquerentibus super eundem Iohannem in diuersis querelis de placito debiti.
<Preceptum est>
Preceptum est distringere Simonem le Ropere quod sit ad proximam curiam Iohanni Ioudy de placito debiti plegiis de prosequendo Iohanne Gelneye et Collectore.
<Finis iij . s. et vj d.>
Iohannes Peye reddit sursum in manus domini tres rodas \et dimidiam/ terre ad opus Iohannis le Meyre tenend' sibi et heredibus suis saluo iure etc. reddend' domino etc. et dat domino pro ingressu habendo iij s. vj d. et data est ei seisina in plena curia. Et si predictus Iohannes obiat sine herede de corpore suo predicte tres rode et dimidia reuertentur in manus Helewysie le Meyr matris dicti Iohannis.
<Finis . xij . d.>
Idem Iohannes in manus domini reddit sursum . vnam rodam terre ad opus Rogeri de Erpingham tenend' sibi et heredibus suis saluo iure etc. reddend' domino etc. et dat domino pro ingressu habendo . xij . d.
<Preceptum est>
Preceptum est retinere in manu domini dimidiam rodam terre quam Custancia Muriel vendidit Iohanni filio Rogeri quousque idem Iohannes veniat et dat domino pro ingressu habendo et faciat domino quod ius etc.
<Finis . xij . d.>
Iohannes Shrudy et Alicia vxor sua reddunt sursum in manus domini vnam Rodam terre ad opus Willelmi Osbern tenend' sibi et heredibus suis saluo etc. reddend' etc. et dat domino pro ingressu habendo . xij . d.
<Finis . xij . d.>
Alicia Andreu reddit sursum in manus domini vnam rodam terre ad opus Iohannis Le Meyre tenend' sibi et heredibus suis etc. saluo iure etc. Reddend' domino etc. et dat domino pro ingressu habendo . xij . d. Set si idem Iohannes moriatur sine herede de corpore suo predicta terra reuertetur Helewysie matri sue et heredibus suis etc.
<Finis . ij .s.>
Iohannes filius Gilberti reddit sursum \in manus domini/ quamdam porcionem in mesuagio quo in parte Australi ad opus Willelmi Osbern tenend' sibi et heredibus suis etc. saluo iure etc. Reddend' etc./ et dat domino pro ingressu habendo. ij . s. iacent' iuxta mesuagium Abbatis de Crek ex australi parte et continet iuxta viam regalem in latitudine versus orientem xiij . pedes. Et ad capud occidentem in latitudine. xxiiij . pedes . et in longitudine continet . v^{xx} pedes . et tres pedes.

<Finis . vj . d.>

Beatrix le Northerne reddit sursum in manus domini vnam dimidiam rodam terre ad opus Berte le Speller' tenend' sibi et heredibus suis etc. saluo etc. et dat domino pro ingressu habendo.

<Misericordia . iij . d.>

Robertus Mayn in misericordia quia cecidit versus Hugonem Otes in querela dicti Hugonis \versus ipsum/ de placito debiti et ideo preceptum est leuare de dicto Roberto pro dicta misericordia.

Mabilia de Ketlestone fecit attornatum suum \Dyonisium de Wython'/ in plena curia versus Iohannem filium Rogeri . de placito debiti . pleg' Collector'.

<Querela. Inquisicio. Misericordia . iij . d.>

Berta filia Rogeri \Roberti/ Euerard' queritur super Iohannem Le Meye de placito debiti eo quod iniuste detinet ei vt asserit j . quarterium ordei pro \acra/ j Roda terre quas idem^g Iohannes tenet de hereditate sua ei dimissa a festo sancti Michaelis anno regni . regis . Edwardi xij^o in tres annos. Venit predictus Iohannes et contradicit. Vnde inquisicio dicit quod dictus Iohannes tenetur ei in predicto quarterio. Et ideo preceptum est leuare dictum quarterium ordei ad opus predicte Berte pro dampno eiusdem Berte preceptum est leuare ad opus Berte vj denar'.^{h} Et predictus Iohannes in misericordia pro falsa detentione.

<Inquisicio>

Robertus Mayn inuenit pleg*ios* ad soluendum Hugoni Otes debitum quod ei debet. Pleg' Adam Crask*e*' et Collector' secundum conuencionem comunem et fidem inter eos prestit' ad arbitrium aliorum in inquisicione.

<Misericordia . iij . d.>

Galfridus Iulian in misericordia pro defalta secte curie.

<Misericordia . iij . d.>

Iohannes filius Rogeri pro eodem et pro \contemptu/^{i} facto domino.

<Misericordia . iij . den.>

Willelmus Cat*e* pro eodem.

    [Then follows an entry of 2 lines which is rubbed out and illegible]

Summa ix s. vij d.

VARIANTS: ^{a} filij Edwardi is omitted after Edwardi here and in HD 20. The date is therefore 1312, not 1277. This is compatible with the names of some of the tenants, such as Robert de Swanton. ^{b} Sic in Ms. ^{c} Iohannes struck out. ^{d} Struck out in Ms. ^{e} Inserted in Ms., added later. ^{f} Davidson reads 5 Edward II. ^{g} ijdem in Ms. ^{h} Underlined in Ms. ^{i} despectu struck out.

HD 15 and 16

These two rolls are much faded and rubbed and are dated in H.A. Davidson's Catalogue of Holkham Documents 'c. 1300'. Davidson's catalogue is arranged chronologically but both rolls contain some names which are found in the court rolls of the reign of Richard II and in the first half of the fifteenth century. Both contain the heirs of Ralph Crow who was still alive in 1409 (HD 94) and of Robert Docking who died in 1458 according to a monumental inscription in Holkham church.

HD 17

Does not exist and H.A. Davidson struck it out of his catalogue.

HD 18

Quitclaim from Simon of London and Agnes Scule his wife, daughter of Robert Hakun of Holkham, to Robert Angry of Egmere of all her rights in Holkham. [c. 1294]

Fiche 1: B4

Sciant presentes et futuri quod ego Simon de Londoniis manens in villa de Sancta Fide et Agnes Scule vxor mea filia Roberti Hakun de Holkham . vnanimi assensu . Concessimus . remisimus et omnino quietum clamauimus pro nobis et heredibus nostris inperpetuum. Roberto Angry de Hegemere et heredibus suis et suis assignatis totum ius et clamium quod vmquam habuimus vel aliquo modo habere potuimus . videlicet in omnibus tenementis cum mariscis et aysiamentis libertatibus et pertinenciis suis qui descendebant predicte Agneti Scule Iure hereditarie post mortem Radulfi Hakun fratris predicte Agnetis Scule in villa de Holkham sine vllo retenemento . Habend' et tenend' predicto Roberto et heredibus suis et suis assignatis . aut cui . quibus . et quando predicta tenementa cum pertinenciis . dare . vendere . vel assignare . voluerit . in quocumque statu fuerit libere . quiete . bene . in pace . et hereditarie inperpetuum. Ita silicet quod nec nos predicti Simon . Agnes nec heredes nostri nec assignati nostri . nec aliquis per nos vel nomine nostro . aliquod ius vel clamium in predictis tenementis cum mariscis libertatibus aysiamentis et pertinenciis suis sicut predictum est de cetero exigere vel vendicare poterimus inperpetuum. Pro hac autem concessione . remissione . et quiettaclamancia . predictus Robertus dedit nobis quatuor marcas argenti premanibus. Reddendo inde annuatim dominis feodi seruicia debita. In cuius rei testimonium huic scripto sigilla nostra apposuimus. Hiis Testibus Dominis

Iohanne de Walsingham . Ricardo de Walsingham militibus . Iohanne le Bret
. Bartholomeo de Burgate . Galfrido Godwyne . Roberto le Mareschal .
Simone Hamund*a*. Gilberto Aynild . Petro de Grantoun . Ada clerico et aliis.

> Seals: two seals missing.
> Hand: cf. HP 997, 998. Capital S resembles that in HD 8.
>
> VARIANT: *a* These six witnesses (Le Bret to Hammond) came together in dated deeds
> of 1294–6.

HD 19

*Grant from Richard Payn of Holkham to Richard Neel of Burnham and
Katerine his wife of a headland in Holkham.*   [c. 1318]

> Cf. HD 22a, Fo. 15 no. 173 (Lucas no. 22). The related letter of attorney is HD 98.
> Fiche 1: B5

Sciant presentes et futuri quod ego Ricardus Payn de Holcham concessi dedi
et hac presenti carta mea confirmaui Ricardo Neel de Brunham et Katerine
vxori eius et heredibus de corporibus eorumdem legitime procreatis ac rectis
heredibus predicti Ricardi Neel si predicti Ricardus Neel et Katerina sine
herede de corporibus eorumdem legitime procreatis obierint ·' vnam peciam
terre mee iacentem in campis de Holcham et est vna forera et iacet iuxta
terram Iohannis Godwyne ex parte occidentali . habend' et tenend' predictam
peciam terre cum omnibus pertinenciis predictis Ricardo Neel et Katerine
vxori eius et heredibus de corporibus eorumdem legitime procreatis ac rectis
heredibus predicti Ricardi Neel' ·' si predicti Ricardus Neel et Katerina sine
herede de corporibus eorumdem legitime procreato obierint . de capitali
domino feodi per seruicia debita et consueta libere quiete in feodo et
hereditarie.Et ego predictus Ricardus Payn et heredes mei predictam peciam
terre cum pertinenciis predictis Ricardo Neel et Katerine vxori eius et
heredibus de corporibus eorumdem legitime procreatis ac rectis heredibus
predicti Ricardi Neel ·' si predicti Ricardus et Katerina sine herede de
corporibus eorumdem legitime procreato obierint contra omnes gentes
imperpetuum warantizabimus et defendemus. In cuius rei testimonium huic
presenti carte sigillum meum apposui. Hiis testibus. Iohanne Bret . Iohanne
Godwyne . Hugoni Otes . Martino Rust . Thoma Large de Creyk et aliis.

> Seal: missing.
> Hand: The same scribe writes HD 19, 98, HP 1004, 1065,1068, 1069, 1070.
> Endorsement: *Carta Ricardi Payn j pecia terre iuxta terram Iohannis Godwyne.
> Goldwinis croft.* T[ranscriptum] in the hand of Edmund Lucas. A summary of this deed
> numbered 22 in the hand of Edmund Lucas in the margin, in a hand similar to that of the
> endorsement, is in HD 22a, Fo. 15 no. 173.

HD 19a

HD 19a is a 1581 transcript of the 'Book of the knight's fees of North Greenhoe', see *Feudal Aids 1284–1431*, vol. 3.

HD 20

Rental of Peter le Bret of Holkham and Court Rolls of Peter and Eustace le Bret and Richard Neel.

1302–21

Cf. HD 11 for Geoffrey le Bret
Fiche 1: B7

NOTE: The roll consists of one membrane 7¹/₄ in. wide. The bottom of the dorse is much faded.

REDDITUS ANNUALIS PETRI LE BRET DE HOLKHAM

Ad festum Sancti Michaelis.		Ad Pascham.	
Johannes Silke	iij d.	Petrus filius Ad. le Bret	j d.
Rogerus de Belneye	v d. qa.	William Silke	iij d.
Willelmus Curchun	j d.	Rogerus Eluerich	j d. qa.
Symon Hammund (struck off)	vj d. ob. qa.	Herveus Buleman	j d.
Herveus Buleman (struck off)	i d.	Bartholomeus de Burgate	j d.
Rogerus Eluerich	iij d.	Radulfus Maryot	iij d.
Bartholomeus de Burgate	j ob.	Willelmus le Meyre	iij d.
Johannes Goldewyne	viij d.	Johannes Goldewyne	viij d.
Adam Carpentarius	xij d.	Adam Carpentarius	xij d. ob.
Willelmus le Meyre	iij d.	Ricardus Wolmere	j ob.
Radulfus Maryot	iij d. et i capon.	Radulfus le Rymour	iij d.
Ricardus Ulmer	j d. ob.	Symon Charles	j ob.
Willelmus Duc (struck off)	j d.	Willelmus Duc	j d.
Simon Charles	j d. ob.	Robertus Ape	ij d.
Robertus Ape	j d. ob.	Matilda Ernald	j d. ob.
Matilda Ernald	j d. ob.	Gilbertus Gurle	j d. ob.
Gilbertus Gurle	j d. ob.	Rogerus Tuurben	j d. qa.
Rogerus Thurben	j d. qa.	Gilbertus Daleman	j d. qa.
Gilbertus Daleman	j d.	Emma de Campo	ij d.
Emma de Campo	ij d.	Reginald Dige	i d. ob.
Reginald Dige (struck off)	j d. ob.	Johannes Ide	iij d.
Johannes Ide	vij d.	Robertus filius Emme	ij d. ob.
Ricardus Cline	j ob.	Radulfus Hacon	
		pro terra Norne	j d.

Radulfus le Rymour	iij d.
Gibertus Payn	j d.
Robertus filius Emme	ij d. ob.
Johannes Aynild	j d.
Rogerus Speller	j d.
Warinus de Warles	j d.
Rogerus filius Emme	ij d.
Willelmus de Hyndryngham	ij d.
Herveus Wytbred	j d.
Humfridus Davyd	j ob.
Johannes le Warde de Dallinge	
Gilbertus Balle	
Willelmus Craske	j d.
Bartholomeus le Mareschall	j ob.
Johannes Brun	j d.
Ricardus le Northerne	j d.

Summa vj s. vj d. ob. qa.

Rogerus le Belneye	j d. ob.
Johannes Aynild	j d.
Rogerus filius Emme	ij d.
Willelmus de Hindringham	j d.
Herveus Wytbred	j d.
Symon filius Hamonis	j d.
Johannes Brun	j d.
Bartholomeus le Mareschall	j d.
Johannes filius Ade le Bret pro terra Eborardi sub monte	j ob.

Summa v s. vj d. qa.

Ad Festum Sancti Andree

Robertus Ape	ij d.
Matilda Ernald	j d. ob.
Gilbertus Gurle	j d. ob
Rogerus Thurbern	ij d.
Gilbertus Daleman	j d. qa.
Emma de Campo	ij d.
Willelmus Craske	j ob. qa.
Rogerus Spellere	j qa.

Ad Pentecosten.

Robertus Ape	ij d.
Matilda Ernald	j d. ob.
Gilbertus Gurle	j d. ob.
Rogerus Thurbern	ij d. qa.
Gilbertus Daleman	j d. qa.
Emma de Campo	i d.
Reginaldus Berkarius	j d. ob.
Rogerus Raven	j ob.

Ad Natale Domini.

S. Johan. Baptiste.

Petrus filius Ade le Bret	j d.
Johannes Aynild	j ob.
Rogerus Eluerich	j d.
Erveus Buleman	j ob.
Gilbertus le Bret	j ob.
Herveus Wytbred	ij d.
Symon Hammund vnum clavum Gilofere	
Willelmus Sylk	iij d.

Summa bij d.

Ad Festum Nativitat.

Symon filius Hamonis	j d.
Herveus Wytbred	ij d.
Willelmus Craske	j ob. qa.
Radulfus Pay	j d. ob.

Summa iij d. ob. qa.

Summa xiiij s. et iij d. qua.

<plouben.>

Willelmus filius Bette et Robertus Ape facient unum ploubene.

Eborardus Sub Monte Gilbertus Gurle et Matilda Ernald facient unum ploubene.

Rogerus Thurbern Gilbertus Daleman et Rogerus de Campo facient unum ploubene.

Johannes Ide faciet unum ploubene.

<scutagium>

Rogerus le Belneye ad scutagium domini Regis quando venerit ad xxti. s. ob. qa. ad plus plus et ad minus minus.

Petrus filius Ade le Bret ad scutagium domini Regis quando venerit ad xxti. sol. quando ad plus etc.

Symon Hamund ad xxti s. qa. et ad plus etc.

Prior de Petrestone ad xxti. s. j d. ad plus etc.

Willelmus Curthun ad xxti. s. qa. et ad plus etc.

Reginaldus Eluerich ad xxti. s. j d. ob. qa. etc.

Item Adam Carpentarius ad xxti. s. i d. j ob. etc.

Item Herveus Buleman ad xxti. s. j ob. etc.

Item Radulfus Hacon ad xxti. s. pro terra Northerne ij d. etc.

Item Willelmus Craske ad xxti. s. j ob.

Item Isabella Goldwyne ad xxti. s. j ob.

Item Roger Eleurych ad xxti. s. j ob. etc.

Rogerus Sceward ad xxti. s. iij d.

Dorse

CUSTUMARIJ

Robertus Ape tenet vnum mesuagium et v acras terre et reddit per annum vij d. et ob . scilicet ad quatuor terminos ad festum Sancti Andree iij d. ad Pasch' iij d. ad pentecosten ij d. ad festum Sancti Michaelis j d. ob . et facit iij dies in autumno ad cibum [et] pascham et habet pro quolibet die iij billing'[5] et faciet vnum diem amoris ad cibum et ipse et parcenarius eius faciet vnum ploubene.

---

5   A *billy* is a half sheaf (dialect).

CURIA DOMINI EUSTACHIJ LE BRET TENTA APUD HOLCHAM DIE
LUNE PROXIMA POST DOMINICAM PALMARUM ANNO REGNI
REGIS EDWARDI XXX°.*a*   16 April 1302

Adam carpentarius cognouit se tenere vnum mesuagium et . ix . acras
terre. Reddit ij . s. ob. per annum et ad scutagium domini regis xx . s. iiij . d.
ad plus . etc. et fecit fidelitatem.

Rogerus Eluerich'.

Willelmus le Meyre cognouit se tenere vnum mesuagium, et vnam acram
terre et reddit . per annum vj d. et fecit fidelitatem.

CURIA DOMINI EUSTACHIJ LE BRET APUD HOLKHAM . IN VIGILIA
APOSTOLORUM PETRI ET PAULI . ANNO . REGNI REGIS EDWARDI
XXX°.   28 June 1302

De tota Curia pro respectu Curie habendo ij . s . iij . d.

CURIA DOMINI EUSTACIJ LE BRET APUD HOLCHAM DIE BEATE
MARIE MAGDELENE ANNO REGNI REGIS EDWARDI*b* QUINTO.
                                                       22 July 1312

De tenent' terrarum que fuerunt Willelmi le Meyre pro defalta.

Terre Golwyne facit faltam.

Terra Bartholomei de Burga[te] facit faltam.

Terra que fuit Radulfi Mariot facit faltam.

CURIA PETRI LE BRET APUD HOLKHAM DIE MARTIS PROXIMA
POST FESTUM SANCTI PETRI WINCULA ANNO REGIS EDWARDI*b*
QUINTO.   9 Aug. 1311

<Respectu curie habend'>

De tota curia pro secta habenda. ij s.

CURIA PETRI LE BRET APUD HOLKHAM DIE DOMINICA ANTE
FESTUM SANCTI LAURENCIJ ANNO REGNI REGIS EDVARDI*b*
SEXTO.   6 Aug. 1312

De tota curia pro secta habenda. ij s.

CURIA RICARDI NEL APUD HOLKHAM DIE IOUIS IN FESTO SANCTI EDMUNDI REGIS ANNO REGNI REGIS EDWARDI FILIJ REGIS EDWARDI OCTAUO.[6]   20 Nov. 1314

Ricardus Spellere fecit fidelitatem et habet diem ad ostendendum ad proximam curiam cartas suas.

Helywisa le Meire fecit fidelitatem et habet diem ad ostendendum cartas hic ad proximam Curiam.

Emma Curtun fecit fidelitatem et habet diem ad ostendendum cartas ad proximam cur[iam].

Gilbertus Edwy tenuit de domino die \quo obiit/ vnum mesuagium et j acram terre cum pertinenciis et habuit heredem Mariotam Edwy sororem que fecit releuium et fidelitatem pro tenemento predicto. Et Iohannes vir predicte Mariote fecit fidelitatem.

Lovegold Payn fecit fidelitatem pro vna roda terre de terre Willelmi le Dersy. Ponitur in respectum vsque ad proximam curiam.

Eylwisa filia Andree fecit fidelitatem et habet diem ... ad ostendendum cartam. Et ostendit cartam.[c]

Muriela Mariot fecit fidelitatem et habet [ad ostendendum] etc.

Gilbertus Eluerych fecit fidelitatem et habet ad ostendendum et clamat j acram et dimidiam.

Bartholomeus filius Roberti fecit fidelitatem et habet ad ostendendum et clamat tenere v acras.

Henricus Anger fecit fidelitatem et habet ad ostendendum.

Iohannes Belneye fecit fidelitatem domino pro xj acris et dimidia quas clamat tenere de eo.

Bartholomeus Paye fecit fidelitatem post mortem Radulfi Paye cuius heres ipse est et dat releuium.

Ricardus Youyte Wild tenet de domino j . croftam et ij . acras terre in villenagio et fecit fidelitatem.

<Vendidit>

Iohannes le Baker reddit sursum in manum domini j dimidiam acram terre ad opus Ricardi Yutekyl' et heredibus suis et dominus sursum dat eidem predictam terram habend' et tenend' de se et heredibus suis in villenagio per seruicia etc. saluo iure cuiuslibet et dat pro ingressu habendo xij d.

Willelmus filius Thome fecit fidelitatem pro iiij rodis terre cum pertinenciis et habet diem ad ostendendum.

---

6   Perhaps error for *nono* as Thursday fell on St. Edmund's Day, 20 Nov. in 1315 – 1st court of Richard Neel.

CURIA RICARDI NEEL APUD HOLCHAM . DIE VENERIS PROXIMA
POST PASCHA ANNO REGNI REGIS EDWARDI FILIJ REGIS
EDWARDI QUARTODECIMO.   24 April 1321

Agneta Elweriht tenet de domino dimidiam acram terre ad terminum vite
sue cum Iohanne filio Ricardi Elweriht et fecit fidelitatem. Idem Iohannes
nondum fecit fidelitatem. Ideo preceptum est atachiare.

Dominus dat Iohanni Thuorbern et Reginaldo fratri suo vnum cotagium et
duas acras terre et duas \et dimidiam/ rodas et terciam partem Vnius rode
terre . habend' et tenend' sibi et heredibus suis in vilenagio per seruic*ia* etc.
saluo iure cuiuslibet et dant pro ingressu quadranginta solidos de quibus
predictus Iohannes et Reginaldus soluerunt xx^{ti} solidos et habeant diem de
residuo vsque ad festum Sancti Martini in hyeme proxime in futurum.

Elwisia filia Andree ostendit cartas suas et tenet de domino pro iiij d.

<Preceptum est>
Preceptum est attachiare Ricardum Speller' pro fidelitate facienda.

<Preceptum est>
Preceptum est attachiare Martinum Mone pro fidelitate facienda et ad
ostendendum cartas suas ad proximam curiam.

<Preceptum est>
Preceptum est attachiare Henricum Aunger quod sit ad proximam curiam
ad ostendendum cartas suas.

<Preceptum est>
Preceptum est [attachiare] Willelmum filium Thome ad ostendendum
cartas suas ad proximam curiam.

[*Four words worn away.*]
Margareta Gibbus fecit fidelitatem.

<Preceptum est>
Preceptum est attachiare Bartolomeum [*two lines worn away*]

<Preceptum est>
Preceptum est distringere Willelmum filium Alicie ad ostendendum
qualiter ...

[*Last three lines worn away*]

VARIANTS: ^{a} Written in same hand and ink as above. ^{b} filij regis Edwardi omitted
in Ms. ^{c} Added later.

HD 21

Rental of Peter le Bret.   [c. 1280]

Fiche 1: B8

NOTE: HD 22a, Fo. 47 no. 263, in Neel's Gazetteer, an interpolation between N and D is 'Dominium Petri le Bret' (also Fo. 17v no. 191, of 19 Aug. 1314) when Richard Neel acquired Peter le Bret's manor. No. 191 must be considerably later than HD 21 as there seems to be a later generation in it.

HOLCHAM
REDDITUS ASSIS' TENENTIUM PETRI LE BRET DE HOLCHAM

Bartholomeus de Burgate tenet per cartam . in crofta sua j acram et reddit per annum . vj den' . ad duos terminos . scilicet . ad Pasch' iij d. et ad festum Sancti Michaelis . iij d. et j . caponem ad natale domini.

Radulfus Mariot tenet per cartam in crofta sua . j . acram et reddit per annum . vj . d. ad predictos terminos et . j . caponem ad prescriptum terminum.

Willelmus Meyre tenet . j . acram in crofta sua et redit . vj . d. ad predictos terminos.

Iohannes Golwine tenet/ nunc tenet prior de Petr*aston*/ . xvj . acras terre et reddit per annum xxiij d.

Adam Carpentarius tenet j mesuagium et [*space*] et reddit per annum . ij . s. et . j . d. ad predictos terminos.

Ricardus Wlmer tenet . j . piteil et reddit j . d. ad predictos terminos.

Radulfus Rimur tenet . j . mesuagium et reddit vj . d. ad predictos terminos.

<Custumarij.>

Ricardus Olnie fecit fidelitatem domino die Iouis proxima ante festum Sancte Margarete anno rengni regis Edwardi quarto. [Thursday, 16 July 1276]

<Set alienatur in diuersis manibus>

Willelmus filius Bete tenet . j . mesuagium et . v . acras terre et reddit per annum . vij . d. et ob. ad quatuor terminos . scilicet . ad festum Sancti Andree . ij . d. . ad pasch' . ij . d. ad Pentecosten . ij . d. et ad festum Sancti Mikaelis . j . d. et ob . et facit . iij . dies in autumpno . ad vnum repastum et habebit quolibet die ad vesperas . iij . billinges[7] et faciet vnum diem amoris . ad cibum domini . et ipse parcenarius eius . scilicet . Robertus Ape . facient vnum plochbene et . dabit vnam gallinam ad natale domini . et dabit quolibet

---

7   Cf. HD 20.

alio anno . j quadr. de wardse.[8] et dabit quolibet alio anno . ad auxilium vicecomitis . j . d. . quadr.

<Set rem'>

Robertus Ape parcenarius tenet vnum mesuagium et v . acras terre . et reddit per annum . vij . d. ob. ad predictos terminos et facit in omnibus sicud Willelmus Bete in omnibus seruiciis et dabit quolibet quarto anno . j . quadr . de Wardse et dabit quolibet alio anno ad auxilium vicecomitis . j . d. . quadr.

<Set alienatur in diuersis manibus>

Eborardus sub monte tenet . iiij . acras et reddit . vj . d. ad predictos terminos et facit . iij . dies in autumpno ad . j . repastum et habebit iij billingis pro quolibet die et faciet . j . diem amoris ad cibum domini et ipse et Gilbertus filius Willelmi et Matilda Ernald[9] facient vnum plocbene . et . ipse/ dabit vnam gallinam ad natale domini . et ad auxilium vicecomitis . ob . et ad . wardse . quadr. quolibet quarto anno.

<Set rem'>

Matilda Ernalde tenet . iiij . acras terre et reddit . vj . denarios . ad predictos terminos et facit . iij . dies in autumpno ad vnum repastum et habebit . iij . billinges pro quolibet die et faciet vnum diem amoris ad cibum domini et ipsa et Eborardus predictus . et Gilbertus filius Willelmi facient vnum plothbene . et ipsa dabit vnam gallinam ad natale et ad auxilium vicecomitis . ob . et quolibet quarto anno . j . quadr. ad Wardse.

<Set rem'>

Gilbertus filius Willelmi Gurle tenet . iiij . acras terre . et reddit . vj . d. ad predictos terminos et facit . iij . dies in autumpno et omnia seruicia sicud Eborardus . et Matilda parcenarij sui.

<Set rem'>

Rogerus Turnbern. tenet . iij . acras . et j . rodam . et tertiam partem. j . rode . terre . et reddit per annum . v . d. ad predictos terminos . et faciet vnum diem in atumpno ad vnum repastum et habebit . iij . billinges . et quolibet tertio anno vnum diem amoris ad cibum domini . et ipse et duo parcenarij sui facient vnum plocbene et dabit quolibet tercio anno . vnam gallinam ad natale . et dabunt mihi . ad auxilium vicecomitis . j . d. quadr . et quolibet alio anno . j . quadr . ad Wardse.

<Set rem'>

Gilbertus Daleman . tenet sicud Rogerus Turbern . et reddit et facit in omnibus sicud predictus Rogerus.

---

8   Cf. HD 4, (= HD 22a, Fos. 31–4v no. 255); F.W. Maitland, *Domesday Book and Beyond*, 1987 edn., p. 240.
9   Cf. HD 22a, Fo. 18 no. 193.

<In diuersis manibus>.

Rogerus de Campo . tenet et facit in omnibus sicud predicti Rogerus et Gilbertus.

<Alienatur et nihil modo>.

Reginaldus Digge \Eredes R[eg'] facient xxj dies ad vnum repastum domini . sine dinario tenet/ . j . acram et . j . rodam et reddit . iij . d. ad duos terminos scilicet ad Pasch' j d. ob. et ad festum Sancti Michaelis . j. d. ob. et facit . xx . dies . scilicet . xvij . cum . dinario et vno repasto ad nonam . et . iij . dies . ad vnum repastum domini . et habebit pro quolibet die . iij . billinges . et ad natale domini . j . gallinam et ad auxilium vicecomitis . ob . Et sarclabit per j dimidium diem sine cibo. Memorandum quod dictus . R[eginaldus] . calumpniatus fuit de vno die in autumpno . et fecit pacem in vita Petri domini sui et in vita sua pro . iij . s.

<Preceptum est inquirere qui sunt tenentes>

Rogerus Ernald . tenet . xij . acras . terre et reddit . xvj . d. ad iiij predictos terminos . et facit . vj . dies in autumpno . scilicet . iij . cum dinario et vno repasto ad nonam . et . iij dies ad vnum repastum et habebit pro quolibet die . iij . billinges . et faciet vnum diem amoris ad cibum domini et dabit ad natale domini . iij . gallinas et vnum gallum . et ad auxilium vicecomitis ob . quadr . et ad Wardse quadr.

Ricardus Norne tenet . j . acram terre . et reddit ad festum Sancti Michaelis . vj . d. et facit . iij . dies in autumpno ad vnum repastum et capiet pro quolibet die . iij billinges . et faciet vnum diem amoris ad cibum domini et dabit ad natale domini . ij . gallin*as*. Idem reddit pro terra Rutele vnum ob . ad festum Sancti Michaelis et ad Pasch' vnum ob .

Thomas Warin tenet . vj . acras terre et reddit . vj . d. ad. ij . terminos . scilicet . ad Pasch' . iij . d. et ad festum Sancti Michaelis . iij . d. et facit .ij . dies . ad vnum repastum in die . et habebit . pro quolibet . die . iij . billinges et quolibet alio anno . vnum diem . \amoris/ ad cibum domini . et dabit quolibet alio anno . ij . gallin*as* . et quolibet alio anno . j gallum . et ad auxilium vicecomitis . ob . quadr . et ad Wardse quadr . ad Pentecosten . et faciet vnum plothbene.

Iohannes filius . Ide . tenet . vj . acras . terre et reddit et facit in omnibus sicud predictus Thomas.[10]

Emma in Campo fecit pacem domino Tenend' terram suam ad terminum vite sue pro viij denariis per annum ad predictos terminos pro omnibus seruiciis in tota vita sua et dedit domino ij s.

---

10   In 1294 John le Bret granted John son of Ide (Hyde) and family to Richard le Northerne, HD 22a, Fo. 10v no. 132.

Dorse

Adam Dersy tenet . j . rodam . et reddit per annum . iiij . d. scilicet . ad Pasch' . ij . d. et ad festum Sancti Michaelis . ij . d. et facit . iij . dies . in autumpno . ad vnum repastum . et . habebit . iij . billinges pro quolibet die et ad natale domini . j . gallinam.

Hadhewisa Rutele tenet . iij . acras terre . et reddit per annum . iiij . d. ad duos terminos . scilicet . ad Pasch' . ij . d. et ad festum Sancti Michaelis . ij . d. et facit in autumpno . x . dies ad vnum repastum et habebit pro quolibet die . iij . billinges . et vnum diem amoris ad cibum domini . et sarclabit pro . j . dimid' die sine cibo . et ij . gall' ad natale . et ad auxilium vicecomitis . ob.

Gilbertus Gant . tenet . j . acram terre cum *parcenariis* . et reddit . iiij . d. ad duos terminos . scilicet ad Pasch' ij . d. et ad festum Sancti Michaelis . ij . d. et facit . iij . dies in autumpno . ad vnum repastum et habebit pro quolibet die . iij . billinges . et vnum diem amoris ad cibum domini . et dabit ad natale domini . ij . gallinas et ad auxilium vicecomitis . ob .

Ricardus Olnie tenet . j . rodam . et dimidiam terre de terra Rutele . et reddit . per . annum . j . d.

Rogerus molendinarius tenet . iij . acram^a terre et reddit per annum . v . d. et facit . v . dies in autumpno et j diem amoris et sarclabit dimidiam diem et dabit . j . gallinam ad natale domini.

Memorandum quod omnes custumarij dabunt ad auxilium domini sui quolibet anno ad voluntatem domini sui.

NOTE: On the top of the dorse of the membrane written upside down:
Curia Galfridi le Bret die Jovis proxima ante festum Margarete anno Regni Regis .....
(year illegible)
Jurati dicunt quod
Adam ..... in misericordia domini quia non venit.
Tota curia elegit Rogerum Ernald ad prepositum.
Tota curia dat ad auxilium domino v s. vj d. unus quisque alterius plg. et die veneris proxima pacandi.

VARIANT: ^{a} Sic in Ms.

HOLKHAM DOCUMENT HD 22a:

Neel Cartulary

c. 1415–60

NEEL CARTULARY

This cartulary was composed and written by Edmund Lucas. It consists of five quires, each devoted to a different type of document relating to lands at Holkham inherited by the author. Except for a parchment leaf on the outside of quire 5, it was written on paper imported from the Continent in the late fourteenth or early fifteenth century. The tops of many pages were damaged by damp soon after having been written. Some were recopied.

Quire 1, Fos. 1v–12 nos. 2–151   *an inquisition on the folds, Fo. 1v, Fiche 1: B9 (no. 1), precedes copies of 150 charters, of which the last two relate to Hillhall. The copy made in 1414–5 is about the property of the Brets and other families whose lands later came to Richard and Katerine Neel and their heirs. Most are of the time of Edward I.*

Quire 2, Fos. 13–26v nos. 151–252   *contains copies of the 100 title deeds of the Neel family. Only no. 250 is later than 1350, a grant from Gilbert Neel to his children. Some charters of the time of Edward II are dated with no indication that they relate to the second, not the first Edward. Fiche 1: B10 and B11 show specimen pages, Fo. 16v nos. 184–7. Edmund Lucas has numbered these copies (summaries) in the margin with serial numbers. The serial numbers are sometimes endorsed on the original charters, of which many survive, in the same hand. Fos. 24v–26v are blank, except for a short memorandum of 1485.*

Quire 3, Fos. 27–40v nos. 253–259   *is a miscellany of fundamental documents: Fo. 27, Feodary of Holkham (no. 253); Fo. 30, Neel pedigree, Fiche 1: B12 (no. 254); Fo. 31, Burghall rental, Fiche 1: B13 (no. 255); Fo. 35, William de Calthorpe's terrier, perhaps 1449, Fiche 1: B14 (no. 256), not printed; Fo. 36, Walsingham priory land leased to Edmund Lucas, Fiche 1: C1 (no. 257), not printed; Fo. 37v, presentation of Letheringsett, Fiche 1: C2 (no. 258); Fo. 38, terrier of Gilbert Neel, Fiche 1: C3 (no. 259), not printed. Fos. 40–40v are blank.*

Quire 4 (on thicker paper), Fos. 41–50v nos. 260–263   *Edmund Lucas's gazetteer of furlongs, with dates of acquisitions, with separate pages for each initial letter. Later interpolations use blank spaces left available, Fiche 1: C4 (no. 260); Fo. 44v* Terra solidata per nativos in manus Gilberti Neel, *Fiche 1: C5 (no. 261); Fo. 45–45v,* Terre nativorum tenencium in manus domini de feodo Gilberti Neel, *(no. 262);* Dominium Petri le Bret, *Fiche 1: C6 (no. 263).*

Quire 5, Fos. 51–55v nos. 264–267 *Fo. 51–52v, Terrier of Walsingham, Fiche 1: C7 (no. 264), not printed; Fos. 53–54, Terrier of Peterstone, Fiche 1: C8 (no. 265), not printed; Fo. 54v–55v, Rental of Peterstone, Fiche 1: C9 (no. 266), not printed; Fo. 55,* Peterstone Feodum Noion, *Fiche 1: C10 (no. 267), not printed.*

NOTE ON WATERMARKS: Six varieties occur.

1) A tripartite mount surmounted by a cross, Fos. 2, 8, 16, 20. Cf. Edward Heawood, *The Library,* 4th ser., vol. 10, 1930, 'Sources of Early English Paper-supply', p. 297, fig. 67, p. 304, Italy.

2) Two cock's heads addorsed like the unicorn's heads, Fos. 22, 27, 28, 32 (very clear on blank paper). Cf. Charles-Moïse Briquet, *Les Filigranes, Dictionnaire historique des Marques du papier dès leur apparition vers 1282 jusqu'en 1600,* 4 vols., Amsterdam, 1968, iv, nos. 15839–43 (of 1369–98), Italy, Southern France, Low Countries.

3) A basilisk or wyvern, Fos. 28, 32, 35. Cf. C.-M. Briquet, *op. cit.,* iii, as nos. 2674–2680, especially 2675 (of 1389) and 2677 (of 1416–18), Italy.

4) St. Luke's ox with halo and wing holding his gospel, Fo. 40. Cf. C.-M. Briquet, *op. cit.,* iii, not the same as Briquet 2743–45 (of 1376–99).

5) Capital P surmounted by a cross, Fos. 42, 44, 45, 48 and 50. Cf. C.-M. Briquet, *op. cit.,* iv, as no. 8487 (of 1389), France (Troyes, Blois).

6) An ox (without halo, wing or book), the horns bent outward. Cf. C.M. Briquet, *op. cit.* iii, not among nos. 2748–2760 (of 1348–1448), Italy (Lombardy) or Southern France (Montpellier).

HD 22a

NEEL CARTULARY

HOLKHAM. COPIA ANTIQUARUM ET NOUARUM CARTARUM ET ALIARUM EVIDENCIUM TRANSCRIPT' PER EDM. LUCAS ANNO REGNI REGIS HENRICI QUINTI SECUNDO (1414–5) QUONDAM GILBERTI NEL DE EADEM IN HOLKHAM REYNHAM ET WESENHAM DE TERRIS TENEMENTIS ET REDDITIBUS IN VILLIS PREDICTIS.

NOTE: In spite of the mention of Raynham and Weasenham in the heading, the Neel Cartulary contains copies of charters and documents about Holkham only. This heading is written on the inside cover of the parchment binding of the Cartulary.

(Quire 1) **Fo. 1**

Contains miscellaneous notes about rents added partly as late as 1512.

1   *An Inquiry into sheep folds.*   16 May 1306

Fiche 1: B9

Fo. 1v Memorandum quod die lune proxima post festum assencionis domini ad ecclesiam de Holkham anno regni regis Edwardi filij regis Henrici tricesimo quarto coram Simone Caperony attornato Rogeri Cosyn senescallo domini Hugonis de Veer et magistro Reginaldo de Waterdene senescallo Walteri de Calthorp et Roberto de Botune fratre domini Philippi prioris de Walsingham et coram aliis ibidem existentibus in presencia Iohannis le Warner balliui hundredi de Northgrenehowe qui extunc erat in manu domini regis facta fuit ista inquisicio de faldis de Holkham per Ricardum Hauene Willelmum le Messor Eborardum Underhowe Gilbertum Cocche Martinum Rust Galfridum Thurbern Rogerum Slopere Radulfum Daulyn Iohannem filium Emme Iohannem Leuare Clementem Permelay et Iohannem Euerich' qui dicunt super sacramentum suum quod nouem sunt falde communes currentes vndique in campis et in brueris eiusdem ville et non plures: videlicet falda domini Hugonis de Veer abbatis de Crek prioris de Walsingham prioris de Petra Martini Goldewyn Iohannis le Bret Iohannis Ayneld ex dimissione Walteri Hakoun Iohannis Hammond ex dimissione Galfridi le Bret et falda Iohannis Godwyne. Sunt et alie falde iuxta mariscum saleficum ibidem et iuxta campum adiacentes annuatim currentes videlicet falda domini Hugonis de Veer prioris de Walsingham abbatis de Derham Ricardi le Northerne ex dimissione Bartholomei de Burgate et Willelmi Silke ex dimissione Payn Wolleman. Sunt alie falde que vocantur Cotesfoldes que habent cursum suum in campis eiusdem ville in locis diuersis que debent leuari circa festum Sancti Iacobi apostoli et habent cursum suum vsque festum Sancti Martini: videlicet falda Prioris de Petra et Humfredi Dauyd coniunctim que habent cursum suum inter Hadehowe et Thorpemere: alia que vocatur Hamestalfolde quam emit Bartholomeus de Burgate de Bartholomeo filio Simonis de Wychton' currens inter Thorpmere et Creykgate et Coppynge: tercia Humfredi Dauyd et parcennorum suorum loco Eborardi Cayly currens inter Clynt et Hadehowe: quarta Bartholomei Adam et parcenn[orum] suorum currens inter Gibbesgate et Hadehowe: quinta Galfridi Poysun et parcenn[orum] suorum quam emit Willelmus Wake de feodo Hakonis currens inter aulam de Monchensi et Creyksty: sexta habet quondam Bertrammus le Verdoun currens in campis de Holmys inter Hundecroundeldroue et Millehil et viam regiam.

> NOTE: An important survey of folds at Holkham made on 16 May 1306. Among these folds that of Everard Caly was granted by his son Everard to William Craske of Holkham about 1284 (cf. no. 66, HP 1038), and Craske's son Adam Craske of Holkham granted it to Richard and Caterine Neel on 14 Oct. 1326 (no. 185). The Neels also received a fold from John son of Harvey de Burgh and Cecily his wife released by Adam son of Simon Hammond on 8 April 1316 in no. 230, and by Peter le Bret on 10 April in no. 229. Geoffrey le Bret had released a fold to John Hammond (no. 1). The fold bought by William Wake is mentioned in no. 233 when Thomas son of Richard Neel acquired it in 1347. Another copy, made for Walsingham priory, is in BL Ms. Cotton Nero E VII. It has minor variants of spelling and (in margin) *Memorandum quod ista inquisicio patet in feodario super dorsum eiusdem in principio.* Cf. Table 1, *supra*, p. 37.

Fos. 2–12 Owners before Neel

> Summaries of Charters: the top ten lines of the first 12 folios containing about two paragraphs are rendered illegible by damp stains. These almost obliterate the middle of the third charter from the top of most leaves.

Fo. 2 COPIA ANTIQUARUM CARTARUM TERRE NUPER GILBERTI NEEL IN HOLKHAM TRANSCRIPTA PER EDMUNDUM LUCAS ANNO REGNI REGIS HENRICI QUINTI POST CONQUESTUM PRIMO.

[21 March 1413–20 March 1414]

2 *William, son of Bartholomew Mariot of Holkham, grants his brother Richard 3 plots.*   [c. 1284]

Original: HP 1040

<Wellegate>
Ex feoffamento Willelmi filij Bartholomei Mariot de Holkham facto Ricardo

fratri suo tres pecias terre [iacentes] in campis de Holkham quarum vna pecia [est] medietas crufte dicti [Willelmi filij Bartholomei] ...

3 *Geoffrey, son of Peter le Bret of Holkham, grants Geoffrey Silk a plot of land* [c. 1276]

<Wightongate, Scrulescroft>

Damaged by damp: recopied no. 62 below.

4 *John, the Parson of Holkham, grants Bartholomew Calwere a plot at Langfurlong* [c. 1276]

<Scothowgate>
Ex feoffamento Iohannis persone de Holkham facto Bartholomeo Calewer' vnam peciam terre in campis de Holkham que iacet super Langfurlong inter terram que fuit Iohannis Cook ex parte orientali et terram que fuit Gilberti Balle ex parte occidentali et abbuttat versus aquilonem super Scothoggate. Anno regni regis Edwardi filij regis Edwardi nono.

5 *Ralph, son of William at the Gateshende of Brisley and Margaret his wife, grant Simon Mous of Kettlestone and Cecily his wife 1/2 acre.*

27 Nov. 1329

Original: HP 1077. Cf. no. 9

<examinatur, Scamlond>
Ex feoffamento Radulfi filij Willelmi a le Gateshende de Brisele et Margar' vxoris eius facto Simoni Mous de Keteleston et Cecilie vxori eius dimidiam acram terre iacentem in Campo occidentali de Holkham loco vocato Scamelond inter terram Rogeri Carpentarij ex parte occidentali et terram Iohannis Mere ex parte orientali cuius caput australe abbuttat super terram Willelmi filij Alicie et caput boriale abbuttat super terram dicti Radulfi. Anno regni Edwardi tertij post conquestum tercio.

NOTE: This cannot be the same Scamlond as that described elsewhere as in the Stathe Field for Stathe Field could only be called the East Field. Both Scamlonds occur together in a Hillhall rental of 1467, HD 55 Fo. 22v where it, as in the 1590 map, abuts on Wellegateway. Cf. Appendix 4, Topography.

6   *John, son of John le Bret of Holkham, grants William of Heveringlond*
and Robert de Knapton, chaplains, 1 plot of 1³/4 acres   6 Feb 1330

   Original: HP 1079

<Collesmere>
Ex feoffamento Iohannis filij Iohannis Bret de Holkham facto dominis
Willelmo de Heueringlond et Roberto de Knapton' capellanis vnam peciam
terre iacentem apud Collesmere continentem in se septem rodas terre videlicet
inter terram Ade Crasc' ex parte aquilonali et terram Willelmi Grys ex parte
australi cuius caput occidentale abbuttat super Caldowgate. Anno regni
Edwardi tercij a conquestu quarto.

7   *Thomas Likkesalt and Katerine his wife grant Bartholomew Calwere*
1 acre.   31 Oct. 1312

      Original: HP 1003

<Bruera>
Ex feoffamento Thome Likkesalt et Katerine vxoris sue facto Bartholomeo
Calewier' vnam acram terre in campo orientali de Holkham inter terram
Iohannis Godwyne versus orientem et terram Gilberti Huberd versus
occidentem cuius capud australe abbuttat super Brueram etc. apud aquilonale
abbuttat super terram Iohannis Ayneld. Anno regni Edwardi sexto.

8   *John, son of Geoffrey le Bret of Holkham, grants Simon son of Hamo*
3 plots.   [c. 1294–6]

      Original: HP 1043

<Greiston, Grenegate, Heuedlondlond>
Ex feoffamento Iohannis filij Galfridi le Bret de Holkham facto Simoni filio
Hamonis tres pecias terre quarum vna pecia iacet apud Greyston inter terram
que fuit Rogeri Super Campum ex parte australi et terram Iohanne Thurbern
ex parte aquilonali caput occidentale abuttat super terram prioris de
Pet*erstone* et alia pecia iacet inter terram Radulfi de la Dale ex parte
aquilonali et viam que vocatur Grenegate ex parte australi caput occidentale
abbuttat super terram Bartholomei Vnderclynt et tercia pecia que vocatur
Heuedlondlond iacet inter terram que fuit Simonis Peper et caput australe
abuttat super viam que vocatur Grenegate. Nulla data.

   NOTE: The witnesses and the handwriting of HP 1043 suggest c. 1294–6.

9   *Ralph, son of William at the Gateshende of Brisley, and Margery his*
wife grant Simon Mous of Kettlestone and Cecily his wife 1 acre.

[c. 1329]

Cf. HP 1077 and no. 5

\<Schamelond\>

Ex feoffamento Radulfi filij Willelmi a le Gateshende de Brisele et Margerie
vxoris eius facto Simoni Mous de Ketelstone et Cecilie vxori eius vnam
sacram terre iacentem in campis occidentalibus de Holkham in loco vocato
Schamelond iuxta terram quondam Simonis Hammond ex parte boriali cuius
caput occidentale abbuttat super terram Andree Underklynt. Anno regni regis
Edwardi tercij a conquestu tercio.

10   *Bartholomew, son of Henry the Smith of Holkham, grants Simon, son of*
Hamo, 1¹/₂ roods.   [c. 1283–93]

Fo. 2v   \<Westgate\>
Ex feoffamento Bartholomei filij Henrici Fabri de Holcham facto Simoni filio
Hamonis de eadem vnam rodam ibidem et dimidiam terre iacent' in Holcham
Westgate*ᵃ* inter croftam Ade de Brunham ex parte orientali et cruftam
Katerine Kinge ex parte occidentali et caput australe abbuttat super terram
Henrici Dauy et caput aquilonale abbuttat super terram Willelmi Henrici
reddendo ob. Nulla data.

NOTE: The earliest dated grant to Simon may be later than this undated one.

VARIANT: *ᵃ* Westgate repeated in Ms.

11   *Bartholomew, son of Henry the Smith of Holkham, grants Simon, son of*
Hamo, 1 plot.   [c. 1283–1293]

\<Northfeld\>
Ex feoffamento Bartholomei filij Henrici Fabri de Holcham facto Simoni filio
Hamonis vnam peciam terre in campo aquilonali eius ville inter terram
Helewisie Rutele de Burnham versus orientem et terram Reginaldi Thurbern
versus occidentem et abbuttat versus austrum super cruftam Helewisie Rutele
et caput aquilonale super terram Matilde Sabas reddendo j quadr. Nulla data.

12   *Release from John [le Bret?] to Bartholomew, son of Henry the Smith*
of Holkham and to Simon, son of Hamo, 2 plots.   [c. 1283–9]

<[Howesty]>
Relaxacione Johannis [le Bret?] Bartholomeo filio Henrici Fabri de Holcham
et Simoni filio Hamonis de ij pecijs terre ex parte occidentali et caput
australe abbutat super [mesuagium Henrici Dauy] et alia [iuxta] terram que
fuit Reginaldi Thurbern ex parte occidentali et caput [australe abbuttat super]
Howesty.

13   *Geoffrey, son of Peter le Bret of Holkham, grants Simon, son of Hamo,*
1 plot of 1 rood.   [c. 1294–6]

> Original: HP 996

<Northfeld apud le Dale>
Ex feoffamento Galfridi filij Petri le Bret de Holkham facto Simoni filio
Hamonis de eadem villa peciam terre continentem vnam rodam terre inter
terram Rogeri Eluerich ex parte orientali et terram Willelmi Grigge ex parte
occidentali et caput australe abbuttat super terram Gilberti Nicol et caput
aquilonale abbuttat super semitam que ducit de horreo abbatis de Derham in
Holkham ad ecclesiam de Holkham reddendo obolum per annum. Nulla data.

> NOTE: The barn of the Abbot of West Dereham was at Huncroundale which became the
> 'parsonage' of the owner of the rectorial tithes after the Dissolution. Geoffrey son of
> Peter le Bret occurs on 23 May 1284 (HD 7) and 6 Oct. 1296 (no. 102).

14   *Everard Underhowe grants Roger de Calwere 3/4 rood.*   1 Dec. 1291

> Original: HD 9

<Wellegate, inquiratur>
Ex feoffamento Eborardi sub hoga de Holkham facto Rogero de Calewer'
dimidiam rodam et quartam partem vnius rode inter terram abbatis de Crek
ex parte occidentali et terram Willelmi Meire ex parte orientali et abbuttat
versus aquilonem super Wellegate reddendo obolum per annum. Anno regni
regis Edwardi vicesimo.

> NOTE: Cf. court of 8 Oct. 1449, HD 194a for this inquiry.

15   *Isabel, daughter of Ralph le Bret of Holkham, grants William Craske*
1 plot of 1/2 acre.   [c. 1284]

<Caldowgate>
Ex feoffamento Isabelle filie Radulfi Bret de Holkham facto Willelmo Crask'
vnam peciam terre mee continentem dimidiam acram terre iacentem in
campis de Holkham inter terram Gilberti filij Matilde' ex parte australi et
terram Willelmi Flippyng ex parte aquilonale et caput orientale abbuttat super
Caldowgate et caput occidentale abbuttat super terram Gilberti Hayneld
reddendo tres obolos. Nulla data.

NOTE: *Inquiratur* struck out. G. Gonthrop, added in red ink.

16   *Thomas, son of Isabel, daughter of Ralph le Bret, grants William*
Craske 1/2 acre.   [c. 1284]

Original: *HP 1037*

<Collesmere, Eggemergate>
Ex feoffamento Thome filij Isabelle filij Radulfi le Bret facto Willelmo
Craske dimidiam acram terre ad Collismere inter terram Willelmi Curson' ex
parte aquilon' et terram predicti Thome filij Isabelle ex parte australi et caput
occidentale abbuttat super regalem viam que ducit de Holkham ad Eggemer'
reddendo j . d. et ob. per annum. Nulla data.

NOTE: Cf. court of 8 Oct. 1449, HD 194a

17   *Martin Goldewene grants William, son of Robert de Dunwich of*
Walsingham, 1 acre.   3 May 1315

Original: *HP 1052*

<Fulmersgate>
Ex feoffamento Martini Goldewen' facto Willelmo filio Roberti Donewych'
de Walsyngham vnam acram terre in campo de Holkham apud Fulmersgate
iuxta terram Iohannis le Bret ex vna parte et terram Alicie Tutte ex altera
parte et abbuttat super regiam viam. Anno regni regis Edwardi octauo.

18   *Roger le Norne of Holkham grants Simon, son of Hamo, 1¹/₂ roods.*
27 June 1295

Original: HP 1013

<Nortfeld>
Ex feoffamento Rogeri le Norne de Holkham facto Simoni filio Hamonis
vnam rodam et dimidiam terre in camp' de Holkham inter terram Iohannis
Edrich' ex parte aquilonali et terram Thome filij Iohannis ex parte australi et
caput occidentale abbuttat super viam que ducit de la dale apud Thorpe
reddendo obolum. [Die Lune proxima ante festum apostolorum Petri et Pauli]
Anno regis Edwardi vicesimo tercio.

19   *Walter de Mundene, perpetual vicar of half of Holkham church and
Alice his sister, grant to Robert de Knapton, chaplain, 3 acres in 2 plots*
23 Oct. 1330

Original: HD 37

<Wytheriswong, Gibbesgate, Lambulbotme>
Ex feoffamento Walteri de Mundene perpetui vicarij medietatis ecclesie de
Holkham et Alicie sororis eius facto domino Willelmo de Heuerynglond
rectori medietatis ecclesie de Holkham et domino Roberto de Cnapeton
capellano tres acras terre iacentes in duabus peciis in campo australi de
Holkham quarum vna acra et dimidia iacet in vna quarentena que vocatur
Wytheryswong iuxta terram Iohannis le Bret versus aquilonem cuius caput
orientale abbuttat super Gibbesgate et alia acra et dimidia iacet super vnam
culturam que nuncupatur Lambulbotme iuxta terram que fuit Edmundi
Athewald per partem australem et caput orientale abbuttat super communem
viam ducentem de Holkham erga Eggemer'.

20   *William Curthun grants William Craske 1 plot of 1³/₄ acres.*
[c. 1291–8]

Original: HD 36

Fo. 3   <Caldowsty>
Ex feoffamento Willelmi Curthun facto Willelmo Craske vnam peciam terre
continentem septem rodas terre iacentes apud Caldowsty inter terram Iohannis
Bret ex parte aquilonali et terram Cristiane Talbot ex parte australi et caput
orientale abbutt' super terram Gilberti Ayneld [et] caput occidentale abbuttat
super Caldowsty. Reddendo j d. Nulla data .

21 *Adam le Bret grants William, son of Gilbert Curthun, 1 plot.*

[c. 1272–5]

Original: HD 8. Cf. no. 49

\<Inquiratur, Caldowsty\>
Ex feoffamento Ade filij Ade le Bret de Holkham facto Willelmo filio
Gilberti Curthun vnam peciam in campis de Holkham inter terram que fuit
Heruei de la Hil versus austrum et terram quam Caterina Eggemere [ten]et in
dotem versus aquilonem et caput occident' abbuttat super Caldowesty
Reddendo j d. Nulla data.

NOTE: This page was perhaps damaged soon after being written as Edmund Lucas
recopied this deed as no. 49, and no. 22 as no. 50 on the verso of the very next leaf.

22 *John le Bret releases gift by his brother Gilbert to above Walter de*
Mundene and Alice his sister, 1 plot.   6 May 1328

Original: HD 35. Cf. no. 50

\<Lambullbotme\>
Relaxacio Iohannis le Bret facto domino Waltero [de Mundene] vicario
medietatis ecclesie de Holkham et Alicie sorori sue vnam peciam terre de
feodo domini Iohannis Bret iac' in camp' de Holkham in quadam quarentena
que nuncupatur Lambulbotme quam donacionem Gilbertus frater meus fecit
dicto domino Waltero et Alicie reddendo j d. anno regni regis Edwardi filij
Edwardi [secundi].

23 *William, son of John Elwys of Holkham, grants Simon Hamo 1/2 acre.*

[c. 1283–1293]

\<Adowgate, drawing of an index finger\>
Ex feoffamento Willelmi filij Iohannis Elwys de Holkham facto Simoni
Hamonis de eadem dimidiam acram terre iacentem in camp' de Holkham
inter terram Humfredi Dauid ex parte orientali et viam regiam que vocatur
Adowgate versus occidentem et caput aquilonale abbuttat super croftam
Willelmi Simonis caput australe abbuttat super terram que fuit Gilberti
Mundy reddendo obolum per annum. Nulla data.

NOTE: This is not HP 1066.

24   *William, son of John Elwys of Holkham, grants Simon Hammond*
1 plot.   [c. 1283–93]

<Adowgate, drawing of an index finger>
Ex feoffamento Willelmi filij Iohannis Elwys de Holkham facto Simoni
Hammond vnam peciam terre iacentem in camp' de Holkham inter terram
Iohannis Rutele ex parte australi et terram Simonis Laxman ex parte
aquilonali. Caput occidentale abbuttat super regalem viam que ducit de
Holkham apud Creeke et Caput orientale abbuttat super Adowgate. Reddend'
j denar'. Nulla data.

25   *Walter de Calthorpe grants Bartholomew le Caluere of Holkham*
2³/4 roods.   [c. 1278–1300]

<Dedquenepit, Elsiscote, inquiratur quia Prior de Walsyngham occupat versus
dominum vt dicitur>
Ex feoffamento Walteri de Calthorp facto Bartholomeo le Caluere de
Holkham duas rodas et dimidiam et quartam partem vnius rode iacentem in
campis de Holkham in quarentena vocata Dedquenepit inter terram quondam
Willelmi Haye ex parte australi et terram Willelmi clerici ex parte aquilonali
et caput orientale abbuttat super Elsiscote et caput occidentale abbuttat super
terram Amicie le Bret reddendo j d. ob per annum. Nulla data.

> NOTE: This inquiry was made on 22 April 1449. Neel court roll, HD 194a. The 2³/4
> roods are in Dedquenepytt abutting on Elsyescoote. The earliest dated grant to
> Bartholomew le Calwer is 1278. This is granted to Richard and Caterine Neel by Gilbert
> le Calewer of Holkham, no. 246 (1338–9).

26   *Roger Chele of Holkham grants William of Walsingham 2 plots.*
                                                                     6 Dec. 1315

Original: HD 25. Cf. no. 96

<Dalegate, Lethirpitgate, inquiratur>
Ex feoffamento Rogeri Chele de Holkham facto Willelmo de Walsingham
duas pecias terre iacentes in camp' de Holkham quarum vna pecia iacet apud
Dalegate iuxta terram Rogeri Iondy versus austrum et terram Willelmi filij
Alicie per partem aquilonem et abbuttat versus orientem super terram
Iohannis le Bret et caput occident' super terram Ade Crask' et continet in se
septem rodas terre. Alia pecia iacet apud Creyksty iuxta terram hered' Ade
Hammond per partem australem cuius caput orientale abbuttat super
Lethirpitgate et continet vnam rodam terre. Anno regni regis Edwardi Nono.

> NOTE: 9 Edward II not I.

27   *John, son of Geoffrey le Bret of Holkham, grants Ralph Pay 1 plot
bought from Emma Field.*   1295–6

Cf. no. 180 of 1316

<Billesmere>
Ex feoffamento Iohannis filij Galfridi le Bret de Holkham facto Radulfo Pay
de eadem vnam peciam terre quam adquisiuit de Emma super Campum et
iacet in camp' de Holkham apud Billesmer' inter terram Rogeri filij Emme
ex parte australi et terram Hunfredi Dauyd ex parte aquilonali et caput
orientale abbuttat super Quarlesgate et caput occidentale super terram prioris
et conuentus de Walsingham reddendo j d. ob. per annum. Anno regni regis
Edwardi xxiiij°.

NOTE: This land acquired by Ralph Pay was acquired by the Neels from Bartholomew
Pay in 1316, no. 180.

28   *Stephen, son of William Osbern of Holkham, grants Simon Charles
1 rood.*   [c. 1280]

<Bondeswong, Gibbesgate, inquiratur>
Ex feoffamento Stephani filij Willelmi Osbern de Holkham facto Simoni
Charles vnam rodam terre in campis de Holkham apud Bondeswong' inter
terram prioris de Petirston ex parte australi et terram predicti Simonis Charlys
ex aquilone et caput orientale abbuttat super Gibbesgate reddendo vnum
obolum per annum. Nulla data.

NOTE: Simon Charles may have been the father of John Charles who occurs in 1295–6,
nos. 94–5. His tenement is mentioned in no. 65 perhaps about 1272–3 as it was held of
Mariota Bendyng who is not found in later documents. Before c. 1270–80, cf. no. 29.

29   *Matilda Chounde grants Simon Charle of Holkham 2 plots.*   [c. 1280]

<Middilgate, inquiratur>
Ex feoffamento Matild*is* Chounde facto Simoni Charle de Holkham duas
pecias terre iacentes in campis de Holkham inter terram Gilberti de Bintre ex
parte orientali et terram Radulfi Chidekil ex parte occidentali et abbuttat
super terram Christiane filie Bete vsque aquilonem. Et altera pecia iacet inter
terram Willelmi Osbern ex parte orientali et terram meam quam emi de
Iohanne Petir apud Middilgate ex parte occidentali reddendo j d. Nulla data.

NOTE: Another grant to Simon Charles containing names which do not occur in the
dated deeds.

30   *Geoffrey le Bret of Holkham grants Simon Hammond 1 plot.*
                                                                [1283–93]

Fo. 3v   \<Creikgate\>
Ex feoffamento Galfridi le Bret de Holkham facto Simoni Hammond vnam peciam terre iacentem in camp' de Holkham inter terram prioris de Walsingham et dicti Galfridi versus austrum et terram Mariothe versus aquilonem et caput occidentale abbuttat super Krei[yk]gate reddendo obolum per annum. Nulla data.

> NOTE: Like no. 10, probably within the ten years before the earliest dated grant to Simon son of Hamo, i.e. c. 1283–93.

31   *Geoffrey, son of Peter le Bret of Holkham, grants Simon, son of Hamo, 1 plot of 13/4 acres.*   [c. 1294–5]

> *Original: HP 1031*

\<Greyston\>
Ex feoffamento Galfridi filij Petri le Bret de Holkham facto Simoni filio Hammonis vnam peciam terre continentem septem rodas terre apud Greyston inter terram Rogeri super Campum ex parte australi et terram Iohanne Thurbern ex parte aquilonali et caput occidentale abbuttat super terram prioris de Petirston reddendo obolum. Nulla data.

> NOTE: Before no. 46, which is 30 April 1295.

32   *John, son of Gilbert of Bintry, grants Simon, son of Hamo, 1 plot.*
                                                                [c. 1283–93]

> *Original: HP 998*

\<Terra abbuttat super terram Prioris de Peterston\>
Ex feoffamento Iohannis filij Gilberti de Byntre facto Simoni filio Hamonis vnam peciam terre iacentem in campis de Holkham inter terram Willelmi Osbern versus orientem et terram Simonis Charle versus occidentem et caput australe abbuttat super terram prioris de Petirston reddendo obolum per annum. Nulla data.

33   *Thomas of Holkham grants Peter, son of Peter le Bret of Holkham,*
1 plot.   [c. 1250]

<Sennigranesaker>
Ex feoffamento Thome de Holkham facto Petro filio Petri le Bret de
Holkham vnam peciam terre in Holkham inter terram Galfridi Halfpening et
Roberti Husebonde et vocatur Sennigranesaker reddendo annuatim sex
denarios. Nulla data.

> NOTE: Probably early, Halfpening and Husebonde do not occur in any of the other
> deeds.

34   *Agnes, daughter of Simon Charle, grants William, son of Robert de*
Dunwych of Walsingham, 2½ roods in 2 plots.   1315–16

<Blakelond, Dalegate, inquiratur qui sunt tenentes>
Ex feoffamento Agnete filie Simonis Charle facto Willelmo filio Roberti
Dunwych de Walsyngham duas pecias terre iacentes in campis de Holkham
quarum vna pecia iacet super Blakelond iuxta terram quondam Radulfi Schele
et caput orientale abbuttat super Caldousty et continet vnam rodam et
dimidiam terre. Alia pecia iacet iuxta terram quondam Simonis Scherle ex
parte aquilonali et caput orientale abbuttat super Dalegate et continet vnam
rodam terre. Anno regni regis Edwardi filij regis Edwardi nono.

> NOTE: Scherle (and perhaps Schele) may be the same as Charle.

35   *John, son of Geoffrey le Bret of Holkham, grants Simon Hammond and*
Cecily his wife 6 acres in 1 plot.   [c. 1294–6]

> *Original: HP 1032*

<Adowe>
Ex feoffamento Iohannis filij Galfridi le Bret de Holkham facto Simoni
Hammond et Cecilie vxori sue sex acras terre in vna pecia in campis de
Holkham apud Hadowe inter terram Ade Carpentarij ex parte australi et
terram Iohannis Godman ex parte aquilonali et caput occidentale abbuttat
super Ryngewareslond et caput orientale abbuttat super Hadowegate. Nulla
data.

36   *John le Bret of Holkham grants Simon Hammond and Cecily his wife*
4 acres in one plot.   1298–9

<Creykgate>
Ex feoffamento Iohannes le Bret de Holkham facto Simoni Hammond et
Cecilie vxori sue quatuor acras terre iacentem in vna cultura in camp' de
Holkham inter terram Matild*e* Rutell' ex parte aquilonali et terram Martini
Goldewyne ex parte australi. Caput orientale abbuttat super terram Humfredi
Dauyd. Anno regni regis Edwardi filij regis Henrici vicesimo septimo.

> NOTE: HP 1030 reads 6 instead of 4 acres and the locations are not the same. It is a
> different grant.

37   *Geoffrey, son of Peter le Bret of Holkham, grants Simon, son of Hamo,*
1 plot of 3 acres.   [c. 1294–6]

> *Original: HP 995*

<Qwarlesgate>
Ex feoffamento Galfridi filij Petri le Bret de Holkham facto Simoni filio
Hamonis vnam peciam terre in camp' de Holkham continentem tres acras
terre et iacentem inter terram Ade Carpentarij ex parte australi et terram
meam ex parte aquilonali et caput occidentale abbuttat super terram dicti
Simonis et caput orientale abbuttat super regalem viam que ducit de Holkham
apud Qwarles. Nulla data.

38   *Ralph Colt of Holkham grants John, son of Richard the smith, 1 plot.*
                                                                       [c. 1284]

> *Original: HP 1103*

<Cleygraues, Qwarlesgate>
Ex feoffamento Radulfi [Co]lt de Holkham facto Iohanni filio Ricardi Fabri
vnam peciam terre iacentem in camp' de Holkham apud Cleygraues inter
terram Godmanni del Fen ex parte australi et terram Iohannis filij Emme ex
parte aquilonali et abbuttat super regiam viam que ducit se apud Quarles ad
caput occidentale reddendo obolum per annum. Nulla data.

> NOTE: Witnesses suggest date similar to no. 70, c. 1284. Cf. HP 1036, 1037, 1038,
> 1039.

39   *Adam, son of Adam le Bret, grants John, son of Geoffrey Silk, 2 plots.*
[c. 1272–3]

<Caldousty>
Ex feoffamento Ade filij Ade le Bret facto Iohanni filio Galfridi Silke duas pecias terre iacentem in camp' de Holkham quarum vna pecia terre [iacet] inter terram Godmani de parte versus austrum et terram Heruej filij Thome versus aquilonem et caput occidentale abbuttat super Caldousty et alia pecia iacet inter terram Godmanni de parte versus austrum et terram Stephani Sutoris versus aquilonem et caput orientale abbuttat super Caldousty reddendo obolum per annum. Nulla data.

40   *Geoffrey, son of Peter le Bret of Holkham, grants Simon, son of Hamo,*
1 plot.   [c. 1283–93]

Cf. no. 13

Fo. 4   Ex feoffamento Galfridi filij Petri le Bret de Holkham facto Simoni filio Hamondi vnam peciam terre iacentem in camp' de Holkham inter terram que fuit Iohannis filij Eluisie ex parte orientali et regalem viam ex parte occidentali et caput australe abbuttat super terram predicti Simonis filij Hamondi et caput aquilonale abbuttat super terram que fuit Radulfi capellani reddendo j d. per annum [Nulla data].

NOTE: The date may be earlier than the earliest dated grant to Simon son of Hamo, but Geoffrey son of Peter le Bret makes an undated grant to him in no. 41 with seven out of eight witnesses who occur together c. 1294–6.

41   *Geoffrey, son of Peter le Bret of Holkham, grants Simon, son of Hamo,*
13/4 acres in 2 plots and another plot.   [c. 1294–6]

Original: HP 1027

<Grenegate, Hewedlondlond>
Ex feoffamento Galfridi filij Petri le Bret de Holkham Simoni filio [Hamonis] de eadem duas pecias terre in Holkham continentes in se septem rodas terre iacentes inter terram Radulfi de la Dale ex parte aquilonali et viam que vocatur Grenegate ex parte australi et caput occidentale abbuttat super terram Bartholomei Vnderclint. Et alia pecia que vocatur Heuedlondlond iacet inter terram Simonis Pepir ex parte orientali et caput aquilonale abbuttat super terram que fuit Iohannis filij Hide. Et caput australe abbuttat super viam que

vocatur Grenegate. Reddendo dominis feodi quindecim denarios ad festum [Sancti Michaelis] et Pascham et predicto Galfrido Bret j clauum gariofili pro omnibus aliis seruiciis. Nulla data.

NOTE: Seven out of eight witnesses occur together in deeds dated 1294–6.

42   *Geoffrey, son of Peter le Bret, grants Simon, son of Hamo, 1 plot.*

[c. 1294–6]

Original: HP 1028

\<Qwarlesgate\>
Ex feoffamento Galfridi filij Petri le Bret facto Simoni filio Hamonis vnam peciam terre in campis de Holkham inter terram Iohannis Fabri ex parte australi et terram que quondam fuit Nicholai in Campis ex parte aquilonali et abbuttat versus occidentem super viam que ducit de Holkham vsque Qwarles reddendo per annum j quadrantem. Nulla data.

NOTE: Eight out of ten witnesses occur together in deeds dated 1294–6.

43   *John, son of Adam le Bret of Holkham, releases to Simon Hammond right in 2 plots, which he inherited from Simon his kinsman, son of Isabel Fraunceis.*   24 Dec. 1295

Original: HP 1017

Relaxacio Iohannis filij Ade le Bret de Holkham facta Simoni Hammond totum ius et clamium quod habuit in duabus peciis terre que sibi contingebant per descensum hereditatis quondam Simonis consanguinei sui filij Isabelle Fraunceis in quas predictus Simon non habuit ingressum nisi per Stephanum Osbern et Heruum Fabrum saluo seruicio domini Regis videlicet ad Schirrenesscot et Wodewellehot secundum exigenciam predictarum terre et mihi et heredibus meis singulis annis vnum denarium et quadrantem. Dat' apud Holkham die Sabbati proxima ante Natiuitatem domini anno regni regis Edwardi vicesimo quarto.

44   *Helewise, widow of Geoffrey le Bret of Holkham, releases to John atte Faldegate of Burnham and Cecily his wife all rights of dower in the free tenement of Geoffrey, her former husband, in 1/3 of 3 plots.*   21 Nov. 1302

Original: HP 1044

\<Adowbrest, Schortlond, Greiston\>
Relaxacio Helwysie vxoris quondam Galfridi le Bret de Holkham facto Iohanni atte Faldegate de Brunham et Cecilie vxori eius ius quod habuit nomine dotis de libero tenemento dicti Galfridi quondam viri mei videlicet in

tercia parte trium peciarum prout iacent' in campis de Holkham in diuersis culturis et quarentenis scilicet apud Adowebrest Schortlond et Greiston. Dat' apud Holkham die Mercurij proxima ante festum Sancte Katerine virginis anno regni regis Edwardi filij regis Henrici tricesimo primo.

45 *Geoffrey le Bret of Holkham grants Simon Hammond of Holkham 1 plot of 4 acres.* 24 Dec. 1293

Original: *HP 1009*

<Gonyeswong>
Ex feoffamento Galfridi le Bret de Holkham facto Simoni Hammond eiusdem ville vnam peciam terre que continet quatuor acras inter terram Henrici Dauyd ex parte australi et terram Iohannis filij Rogeri le Belneye ex parte aquilonali et caput orientale abbuttat super terram Radulfi Hakun et caput occidentale abbuttat super Gonyeswong'. Dat' apud Holkham die Iouis proxima ante Natiuitatem domini anno regni regis Edwardi vicesimo secundo.

NOTE: In Scott's catalogue the date is misread as being the Nativity of St. John the Baptist.

46 *John, son of Geoffrey le Bret, grants Simon, son of Hamo, 15³⁄₄ acres in 8 plots.* 30 April 1295

Original: *HP 1011*

<Greiston, Duuespit, Grenegate, Hadowbrest, Ryngwaleslond, Skuclif, Adowe>
Ex feoffamento Iohannis filij Galfridi le Bret facto Simoni filio Hamonis quindecim acras et tres rodas terre iacentes in campis de Holkham in octo peciis terre quarum prima pecia continet vij rodas terre [et] iacet apud Greiston, secunda pecia continet quatuor acras terre [et] iacet apud Duuespyt, tercia pecia continet vnam acram terre [et] iacet apud Grenegate quarta pecia continet iij rodas terre [et] iacet ad caput orientale predicte terre que vocatur Grenegate, quinta pecia continet tres acras terre [et] iacet apud Hedhowbrest, sexta pecia continet septem rodas terre [et] iacet apud Ringewaleslond, septima pecia continet duas rodas terre [et] iacet apud Schukelif, octaua pecia continet tres acras terre [et] iacet apud Hadowe inter terram predicti Iohannis filij Galfridi Bret ex parte aquilonali et caput occidentale abbuttat super terram predicti Simonis [et] caput orientale abbuttat super Adowegate. Dat' apud Holkham die Sabbati proxima post festum Sancti Marci*ª* Euangeliste. Anno regni regis Edwardi vicesimo tercio.

NOTE: The first four of these eight plots were granted by John son of Geoffrey le Bret on 10 Nov. 1294 (HD 10). These 8 plots correspond in area and order to lands in the rental of Geoffrey le Bret (HD 11) held by Henry Anger, formerly Roger Rauen.

VARIANT: [a] Marce in Ms.

47   *John atte Faldegate of Burnham and Cecily his wife grant to William, son of Robert de Dunwich of Walsingham, 1/2 plot of 2 1/4 acres.*

13 April 1314

Original: HP 1048

Fo. 4v   <Duuespit>
Ex feoffamento Iohannis atte Faldegate de Brunham et Cecilie vxoris eius facto Willelmo filio Roberti de Walsyngham medietatem pecie terre que vocatur Duuesped et continet duas acras terre et vnam rodam iacentem ixuta terram predicti Willelmi ex parte australi et caput occidentale abbuttat super semitam que vocatur Lethirpithefde et caput orientale super terram Ade Cresk'. Dat' apud Brunham die Sabbati in septimana Pasche anno regni regis Edwardi filij regis Edwardi septimo.

48   *Geoffrey, son of Peter le Bret of Holkham, grants Simon Hammond 3 acres.*   [c. 1283–1293]

<Hangande Adowe>
Ex feoffamento Galfridi filij Petri le Bret de Holkham facto Simoni Hammond tres acras terre in camp*is* de Holkham inter terram prioris de Walsyngham ex parte occidentali et terram meam ex parte orientali et caput aquilonale abbuttat super terram dicti Simonis et caput australe abbuttat super terram Rogeri filij Berte et intitulatur super dorsum quod vocatur Hangandeadowe. Nulla data.

NOTE: This note uses information from the dorse of the lost original to indicate a location which the text fails to do. This is confirmation by Geoffrey of a grant by his son John in no. 124.

49   *Adam, son of Adam Bret of Holkham, grants William, son of Gilbert Curthun, 1 plot.*   [c. 1272–5]

Original: HD 8

<Caldowsty>

NOTE: Copy by Edmund Lucas of no. 21. Nos. 49 and 50 repeat the text of nos. 21 and 22 which was damaged by damp.

50   *John le Bret grants Walter de Mundene, vicar of half Holkham church,*
and Alice his sister, 1 plot.   **6 May 1328**

> *Original: HD 35.* Duplicate of no. 22 [illegible]

\<Lambulbotme\>

Ex concessione Iohannis le Bret terram quam Gilbertus frater suus fecit
domino Waltero de Mundene vicario medietatis ecclesie de Holkham et
Alicie sorori sue de vna pecia terre in campo de Holkham que est de feodo
dicti Iohannis Bret in quadam quarentena que nuncupatur Lambulbotme
reddendo prefato Iohannni Brett et heredibus suis vnum denarium anno regni
regis Edwardi filij regis Edwardi secundi secundo.

51   *Alice, widow of William de Briggate, grants Gilbert, son of John le*
Bret, 1 acre with a house.   **23 June 1316**

> Cf. no. 108 for dimensions of messuage

\<quaedam acra cum Domo\>

Ex feoffamento Alicie que fuit vxor Willelmi de Briggate facto Gilberto filio
Iohannis le Bret donum quod idem Gilbertus quondam fecit predicto
Willelmo et michi de vna acra terre in Holkham cum quadam domo in eadem
sita prout iacet in longitudine et in latitudine inter mesuagium Willelmi
Troude ex parte orientali et mesuagium quod fuit quondam Gilberti Barker ex
parte occidentali et abbuttat versus austrum super regiam viam et versus
aquilonem super terram eiusdem Gilberti. Dat' in vigilia Natiuitatis Sancti
Iohannis Baptiste anno regni regis Edwardi filij regis Edwardi nono.

> NOTE: The measurements occur in nos. 52 (of same date) and in no. 108 of c. 1272–5 in
> which Gilbert Trude and Richard Barker are the predecessors of William Troude and
> Gilbert Barker.

52   *Robert de Briggate grants Alice Reed of Holkham a messuage of 51 ft.*
length and a width of 25 ft. in the south and 23 ft. in the north, with a
house.   **21 June 1316**

\<vnum mesuagium cum Domo\>

Relaxacione Roberti de Briggate facto Alicie Reed de Holkham de vno
mesuagio cum vna domo in eodem sita et iacenti in Holkham inter
mesuagium quod fuit Gilberti Barkar' ex parte occidentali et abbutat super
regiam viam versus austrum et super croftam Gilberti le Bret versus
aquilonem quod quidem mesuagium continet in longitudine quinginta et
vnum pedes et in latitudine ad caput australe viginti et quinque pedes et ad

caput aquilonale viginti et tres pedes. Dat' die Lune proxima ante festum Natiuitatis Sancti Iohannis Baptiste anno regni regis Edwardi filij regis Edwardi nono.

NOTE: The dimensions recur in no. 108.

53 *John, son of Geoffrey le Bret of Holkham, grants Bartholomew Marschall of Holkham 1 plot.*   31 Jan. 1295

<examinatur, terra abbutat super terram prioris de Walsingham>
Ex feoffamento Iohannis filij Galfridi le Bret de Holkham facto Bartholomeo Marschall' eiusdem wille vnam peciam terre iacentem in campis de Holkham inter terram Hunfredi Dauyd ex parte aquilonali et terram que fuit Willelmi Walter ex parte australi et caput occidens abbuttat super terram prioris et conuentus de Wals*ingham*. Dat' die Lune proxima ante Purificacionem beate Marie anno regni regis Edwardi vicesimo tercio.

NOTE: Bartholomew son of William Marschall grants this plot with two others to Richard Neel of Burnham and Caterine his wife in no. 219 nearly 23 years later.

54 *John, son of Warin of Walsingham, grants Bartholomew, son of William le Marschall, 1/2 acre.*   2 Oct. 1294

Original: HP 1024

<examinatur, Ryngewaleslond>
Ex feoffamento Iohannis filij Warini de Wals*ingham* facto Bartholomeo filio Willelmi le Marschall' vnam dimidiam acram terre in camp' de Holkham apud Ringewaleslond inter terram Roberti le^a Leuere ex parte australi et terram Willelmi Chollyng ex parte aquilonali et caput orientale abbuttat super Crekgate [et] caput occidentale abbuttat super terram Bartholomei de Burgate reddendo j d. pro omnibus seruiciis. Dat' die Sabbati proxima post festum Sancti Michaelis anno regni regis Edwardi vicessimo secundo.

NOTE: This is the *pecia* in Ringewaleslond next to the land, late of William Chollyng, granted by Bartholomew son of William Marcharle to the Neels in no. 219 in 1318, 24 years later.

VARIANT: ^{a} Reve struck out.

55 *John, son of Geoffrey le Bret, grants Bartholomew, son of William le Marschall, 1 plot.*   29 Nov. 1294

Original: HP 1020

Fo. 5 <examinatur>
Ex feoffamento Iohannis filij Galfridi le Bret facto Bartholomeo filio

Willelmi le Marschall' vnam peciam terre in camp' de Holkham inter terram
Ricardi [Trippe] ex parte aquilon*ali* et terram que fuit Matild*e* Godkoc ex
parte australi et caput occidentale abbuttat super terram Rogeri Eluerich
reddendo obolum pro omnibus seruiciis. Dat' die Lune proxima post festum
Sancte Katerine virginis anno regni regis Edwardi vicesimo tercio.

NOTE: This plot was granted with two others (nos. 53 and 54) by Bartholomew son of
William le Marcharle to the Neels in 1318 (no. 219).

56   *John le Bret of Holkham grants Hugh Otes of South Creake 3 plots.*
25 March 1308

\<examinatur, Dalegate\>
Ex feoffamento Iohannis le Bret de Holkham facto Hugoni Otes de
Southcreyk tres rodas terre in camp' de Holkham apud Dalegate quarum vna
pecia terre iacet inter terram prioris et conuentus de Peterston ex parte Boriali
et terram que quondam fuit Edmundi Athewald ex parte australi et caput
occidentale abbuttat super Dalegate. Et alia pecia terre iacet iuxta terram
Ricardi Northerne ex parte australi et caput occidentale abbuttat super
Dalegate. Tercia pecia iacet iuxta terram que fuit Heruei Calye ex parte
australi et caput occidentale abbuttat super Dalegate tenend' de dominis feodi.
Dat' in festo Annunciacionis Beate Marie anno regni regis Edwardi filij regis
Edwardi primo.

NOTE: These three plots with a fourth were granted by Edmund son of Hugh Otes to
Richard Neel and Caterine his wife in 1331 (no. 215).

57   *Geoffrey, son of Peter le Bret, grants William Craske 1 plot.*
12 March 1283

\<Dalegate\>
Ex feoffamento Galfridi filij Petri le Bret facto Willelmo Crask' vnam peciam
terre in campo de Holkham inter terram prioris et conuentus de Petirston ex
parte aquilonali et terram predicti Galfridi et terram que fuit Iohannis
Goldewyne abbuttant*em* super partem australem et caput orientale abbuttat
super Dalegate caput occidentale abbuttat super terram Simonis Charles et
super terras de Hogate reddendo duos denarios pro omnibus seruiciis. Dat'
die Sancti Gregorij Pape anno regni regis Edwardi vndecimo.

NOTE: Adam son of William Craske made grants in 1318–33. One of several abutting E.
on Dalegate resembled no. 57 as it was next to the land of Peterstone on the north. This
was called Marlond in 1327 (no. 189) but not in 1283. If the identification is correct it
suggests that marling was carried out between the two dates at this spot.

58   *Geoffrey le Bret of Warham grants John Silk of Holkham 2 plots.*
[c. 1260]

<Bruara>

Ex feoffamento Galfridi le Bret de Warham facto Iohanni Silk*e* de Holkham duas pecias terre iacentes in camp' de Holkham quarum vna pecia terre iacet inter terram Galfridi Godwyn' et Stephani Molendinarij caput orientale abbuttat super Bruar*am*. Alia vero pecia iacet ad caput dicte pecie inter terras Willelmi Rauen et Simonis Carpe reddendo iiij denarios pro omnibus seruiciis. Nulla data.

> NOTE: Geoffrey le Bret of Warham's land in the *bruara* lay on the west side of Holkham parish in the direction of Warham. Geoffrey son of Peter le Bret is often called 'of Holkham'. Geoffrey son of Agnes le Bret of Warham gave West Dereham Abbey land, BL Ms. Add. 43353 Fo. 265. In no. 63 Geoffrey son of Peter grants it (described as at Wadland) to John son of Geoffrey Silk. William Silk gave John Silk's grant to the Neels in 1315-6 (no. 260 Fo. 41v).

59   *William Silk grants Thomas Chartre of Holkham a 'place' of 5 1/2 perches by 5 1/2 perches and 6 ft.*   5 Jan. 1316

<de mesuagio>

Ex feoffamento Willelmi Silk*e* facto Thome Chartr' de Holkham quinque perticatas et dimidiam terre a regia via ex parte australi vsque ad terram meam vsque aquilonem et in latitudine quinque perticatas et dimidiam et sex pedes a mesuagio Radulfi Mone per partem orientalem vsque ad terram Iohannis le Bret ex parte occidentale, videlicet vnam placeam terre iacentem contra mesuagium quod quondam erat Gilberti Payn. Dat' die Lune in vigilia Epiphanie anno regni regis Edwardi [secundi] nono.

> NOTE: Thomas Chartre granted this to the Neels in no. 224 which is undated.

60   *Geoffrey Wynde of Holkham grants John Silk 1 plot.*   [c. 1260]

<Bruara>

Ex feoffamento Galfridi Wynde de Holkham facto Iohanni Silk*e* vnam peciam terre iacentem in campis de Holkham inter terram que fuit Willelmi Wynde versus aquilonem et terram Petri le Bret versus austrum et Caput orientale abbuttat super Bruaram. Reddendo j quadrantem et ad commune auxilium quando venerit in sokna de Wytton' videlicet ad xl s. vnum quadrantem pro omni seruicio. Nulla data.

> NOTE: The next three summaries (of which the first is also from John son of William Wynde) are to John son of Geoffrey Silk. John's father is omitted in no. 60. Only for no. 63 does the original survive to give us a list of witnesses. They suggest a date of about 1284. The unfamiliarity of Wynde's name suggests that he might be earlier.

61   *John, son of William Wynde, grants John, son of Geoffrey Silk of Holkham, 1 plot.*   [c. 1265]

\<Wadelond, Bruara\>
Ex feoffamento Iohannis filij Willelmi Wynde facto Iohanni filio Galfridi Silk' de Holkham vnam peciam terre iacentem in camp' de Holkham que vocatur Wadlondes et caput oriens abbuttat super Brueram et caput occid' abbuttat super terram Bartholomei de Burgate et per partem aquilonalem iacet terra prioris de Wals*ingham*. Reddendo j quadrantem. Nulla data.

NOTE: See note on no. 60.

62   *Geoffrey, son of Peter le Bret, grants John, son of Geoffrey Silk of Holkham, 1 plot.*   [c. 1276]

Duplicate no. 3

\<Scrulescroft, Estgate\>
Ex feoffamento Galfridi filij Petri le Bret facto Iohanni filio Galfridi Silk*e* de Holkham vnam peciam terre mee que vocatur Scrulescroft et iacet in Holkham Estgate inter terram Iohannis le Bret et terram Ricardi de Narrynghis et caput australe abbuttat super regalem viam que ducit apud Wyttone et caput aquilonale abbuttat super terram que fuit Ricardi Fraunceys reddendo j denarium ad Pascha pro omnibus seruiciis. Nulla data.

NOTE: This deed is the same as no. 3 which has been rendered practically illegible by damp. William Silk (probably the William who often witnesses with his father John) gave this land to Richard and Caterine Neel in 1316 in no. 226.

63   *Geoffrey, son of Peter le Bret, grants John, son of Geoffrey Silk, 1 plot.*   [c. 1284]

Original: HP 1025

Fo. 5v   \<Wadelond\>
Ex feoffamento Galfridi filij Petri le Bret facto Iohanni filio Galfridi Silk vnam peciam terre iacentem in camp' de Holkham apud Wodelonde inter terram que fuit Iohannis Goldewine ex parte australi et terram predicti Iohannis Silk ex parte aquilonali et caput orientale abbuttat super Brueram et caput occidentale abbuttat super terram prioris de Wals*ingham* reddendo i[j] denarios. Nulla data.

NOTE: The plot of John, son of Geoffrey Silk, in Wodelonde next to John Goldewine's plot, abutting east on the *Bruara* and west on the Prior of Walsingham's land, seems to be included with three other plots in William Silk's grant of 30 Dec. 1315 to the Neels when Martin has succeeded John Goldewine in no. 225 and HP 1056.

64   *Isabel, daughter of William de Upgate, releases to Geoffrey, son of*
Peter le Bret of Holkham, all rights to a windmill with its profits.   [c. 1284]

\<molendinum venticum\>
Ex concessionis Isabelle filie Willelmi de Upgate in Waterden facto Galfrido
filio Petri le Bret de Holkham totum [ius et] clamium quod habuit in vno
molendino ad ventum cum exitibus multura sectis situ et cum in omnibus
aliis pertinenciis predicto molendino spectantibus et predictus Galfridus
remisit prefate Isabelle homagia et seruicia inde annuatim. Nulla data.

> NOTE: If the windmill of Geoffrey son of Peter le Bret was near his close which passed
> to Richard Neel, a convenient site would have been on the Howe. The windmill of
> Burghall was on the ridge inland from the Stathe. The other reference to a windmill (cf.
> no. 1, 1306) is Millehil, separated by the fields of Holmys from Hundecroundeldroue in
> the northwest corner of the parish. See below, Appendix 4, Millestede.

65   *Mariota Bendyng of Holkham grants Peter le Bret of Holkham homage*
and 1d. annual rent from Simon Charles.   [c. 1272–3]

\<j d. redditus\>
Ex feoffamento Mariote Bendyng de Holkham facto Petro le Bret de eadem
homagium et annuum redditum vnius denarij quem solebat percipere de
Simone Charles pro quodam tenemento quod tenuit de predicta Mariota in
Holkham de vna pecia terre iacenti iuxta croftam dicti Petri ex parte aquilon'
cum homagio releuio wardis seu excaetis. Nulla data.

> NOTE: Peter le Bret is probably the father, not the son, of Geoffrey le Bret. Peter holds
> 100 acres of Warin de Montchesney in 1272–3, no. 255. Mariota Bendyng of Holkham
> does not occur in the later dated documents. She held 6 acres of the brothers of Burton
> Lazars. (Cf. Feodary, no. 253.)

66   *Everard, son of Everard le Caly of Holkham, grants William Craske of*
Holkham 1 plot of 2 acres with half a fold.   [c. 1284]

Original: HP 1038

\<Dalegate cum medietate vnius falde, ij acre cum falda\>
Ex feoffamento Eborardi filij Eborardi le Caly de Holkham facto Willelmi
Craske de eadem vnam peciam terre iacentem in camp' de Holkham inter
terram predicti Willelmi ex parte australi et terram que fuit Warini de Monte
Caniso \Borough Hall/ ex parte aquilone et caput orientale abbuttat super
Dalegate et concessit medietatem vnius falde quam habuit cum Radulfo
capellano currentem in villa et camp' de Holkham cum omnibus libertatitbus
ad medietatem dicte falde pertinentibus reddendo prefato Eborardo vnum

obolum et ad scutagium domini regis pro omnibus seruiciis. Nulla data. Et dicta pecia continet duas acras per nouam cartam.

> NOTE: Warin de Montchesney died in 1255. The land is described as Burghall's in nos. 67 and 185. Everard Caly's fold is included in the survey of folds in no. 1. William Craske's son Adam granted it to the Neels on 14 Oct. 1326 (no. 185), with lands which included the piece with Burghall land on the north defining it as 2 acres. William Craske's land on the south had passed to West Dereham Abbey. The West Dereham Abbey Cartulary (BL Ms. Add. 46353) does not contain a benefaction from any Craske.

67 *Margery Craske of Holkham releases to Adam her son 1 plot held as dower.* 28 Sept. 1326

> Original: HP 1073

<Dalegate>

Ex relaxacione Margerie Craske de Holkham facto Ade filio suo de vna pecia terre quam tenuit nomine dotis de hereditate predicti Ade apud Dalegate iuxta terram Burghalle ex parte boriali cuius caput orientale abbuttat super Dalegate. Dat' die Dominica proxima ante festum Sancti Michaelis Archiangeli, anno regni regis Edwardi filij regis Edwardi vicesimo.

> NOTE: Margery Craske's dower land in Dalegate next land of Burghall is the same land as that described as next that once of Warin de Montchesney in no. 66. Her son Adam granted it to the Neels on 14 Oct. 1325, no. 185.

68 *Walter Hakun of Holkham grants Simon Hammond 2 plots of 2 1/2 acres.* 26 March 1295

<Steynhil, Steynhilcrundell>

Ex feoffamento Walteri Hakun de Holkham facto Simoni Hammond duas pecias terre in campis de Holkham apud Steynhil quarum prima pecia terre iacet inter terram domini Willelmi de Caletorp' ex parte occidentali et terram que fuit Galfridi Goylde ex parte orientali et caput australe abbuttat super Steynhilcrundel et caput aquilonale abbuttat super terram Iohannis Aleyn et alia pecia iacet ad caput australe predicte pecie terre inter terram domini Willelmi de Caletorp' ex parte occidentali et terram Iohannis Burgonye ex parte orientali et caput australe abbuttat super terram predicti Willelmi et caput aquilonale super terram predictam reddendo vnum clauum gariofili pro omni seruicio. Dat' die Sabbati proxima post annunciacionem Beate Marie anno regni regis Edwardi xxiij°. Et continet ij acras et dimidiam vt scribitur in dorso carte.

> NOTE: At the south western corner of Holkham parish was a close which in 1590 belonged to a successor of the Calthorpes and not to any of the Holkham manors. This deed suggests that Steynhilcrundell' may be the most southerly of the great pits which lie within the Burnham Thorpe boundary. John Aleyn and Matilda his wife grant half an

acre and had half rood north of the land of Simon, son of Hamo, at Steynhilcrundell in no. 114. In no. 67 John Aleyn holds adjoining land on the south of the plot given to Simon Hammond. A Walter Hacun was Eleanor of Castile's bailiff in Norfolk, PRO *List and Indexes*, XV, *Ancient Correspondence* (revised) p. 54. At Holkham Walter Hacun made three grants to Simon Hammond in nos. 68, 69 and 100. He was one of the usual witnesses in deeds dated between 1294 and 1304. His predecessor, Ralph Hacun, had been one too, but never occurs in the dated deeds. Ralph was the son of Robert Hacun of Holkham and brother of Agnes Scule. He had died by about 1294–6, HD 18. Both a grantor and a witness called Walter occur in no. 100 (HP 1007).

69   *Ralph Hakun of Holkham grants Simon Hamund 1 plot of 3½ roods.*
[c. 1283–93]

Ex feoffamento Radulfi Hakun de Holkham facto Simoni Hamondi vnam peciam terre cum pertinenciis in Holkham inter terram Gilberti Nicol ex parte occidentali et terram Agnet' filie^a Warini ex parte orientali et abbuttat super terram Roberti Ardy ad caput australe et super terram Petri le Bret ad caput aquilonale reddendo prefato Radulfo ij d. pro omni seruicio et ad scutagium domini regis. Nulla data. Et continet iij rodas terre et dimidiam vt scribitur in dorso carte.

NOTE: Edmund Lucas again quotes the dorse of the original for information additional to that given in the deed about the quantity of land conveyed.

VARIANT: ^{a} filij in Ms.

70   *Robert le Heire of Morston grants William Curson and Agnes his daughter 3 acres as dowry.*
[c. 1284]

Original: HP 1039

Fo. 6   <Wyghtongate>
Ex feoffamento Roberti le Heire de Merston' facto Willelmo Cursun et Agnete filie dicti Roberti in maritagio tres acras terre iacentes in campo de Holkham inter terram abbatis de Creic ex parte occidentale et terram que fuit Ade Gilion ex parte orientali et caput australe abbuttat super viam que vadit de Burnham ad Wighton et caput aquilonale abbuttat super terram Iohannis le Bret reddendo mihi et heredibus meis tres denarios et dimidiam sceppam frumenti pro omni seruicio consuetudine secta curie et demanda etc. Nulla data.

NOTE: Agnes Curthon regrants this land to Richard and Caterine Neel in no. 218.

71   *Geoffrey, son of Ralph, son of Geoffrey Lune of Holkham, grants John,*
son of Geoffrey Silk, of Holkham 1 messuage. [c. 1284]

\<Burgate\>

Ex feoffamento Galfridi filij Radulphi filij Galfridi [Lune] de Holcham facto
Iohanni filio Galfridi Silk de eadem totum illud mesuagium quod tenui in
Holkham et iacet in Burgate cum omnibus edificiis in eo *situatis* et cum vna
crofta ad dictum mesuagium pertinente sine aliquo retinemento quod iacet
inter mesuagium et croftam heredum Alexandri de Burgate versus occidentem
et terram domini abbatis et conuentus de Creik versus orientem et vnum
caput abbuttat super quamdam viam que vocatur Burgate versus aquilonem et
caput australe abbuttat super terram Galfridi filij Reginaldi reddendo prefato
Galfrido filio Radulfi filij Galfridi Lune xij d. pro omni seruicio consuetudine
et seculari demanda etc. Nulla data.

> NOTE: Gilbert son of William Silk regrants this land to Richard Neel in 1319 in no. 209.
> No. 211 gives the dimensions, 9 perches by 61/2 perches.

72   *Bartholomew de Burgate of Holkham grants Gilbert Huberd 11/4 acres.*
22 Dec. 1298

\<Wyghtongate\>

Ex feoffamento Bartholomei de Burgate de Holkham facto Gilberto Huberd
quinque rodas terre cum suis pertinenciis iacentes in camp' de Holkham
collateraliter iuxta terram dicti Bartholomei ex parte orientali et caput australe
abbuttat terram Matilde Pozon ex parte occidentali et caput aquilonale
abbuttat super terram quondam Simonis de Merlawe et caput australe abbuttat
super regalem viam que ducit de Holkham apud Wighton' reddendo
capitalibus dominis duos denarios. Dat' die Lune proxima post festum Sancti
Thome Apostoli anno regni regis Edwardi filij regis Henrici vicesimo
septimo.

> NOTE: This five roods given to Gilbert Huberd abutting on Wightongate in the south
> may be the same as the 11/4 acres given to Richard and Caterine Neel by John Huberd in
> 1328 in no. 241.

73   *William Silk of Holkham grants Gilbert Silk his son 1 messuage and*
croft. 3 Oct. 1316

Original: HP 1058

\<Burgate\>

Ex feoffamento Willelmi Silk de Holkham facto Gilberto Silk filio suo vnum
mesuagium et croftam super eundem abbutantem cum pertinenciis in
Holkham iacentem inter terram abbatis et conuentus de Creik' ex parte

orientali et terram Agnet*e* Briche ex parte occidentali et abbuttat versus aquilonem super regalem viam que vocatur Burgate et versus austrum super terram Ade Ayneld. Dat' die Dominica proxima post festum Sancti Michaelis anno regni regis Edwardi filij regis Edwardi decimo.

>   NOTE: Cf. HP 1071 and HP 1085.

74   *Peter le Bret, son of Geoffrey le Bret of Holkham, grants to William Wake 2s. annual rent had from Gilbert Carpenter.*   **24 Sept. 1314**

<ij s. annui redditus vocat' Erneys>
Ex feoffamento Petri le Bret filij Galfridi le Bret de Holkham concessi dedi et hac presenti carta mea confirmaui Willelmo Wake duos solidos annualis redditus quos percipere solebam de Gilberto Carpentario pro tenemento suo quod Adam Carpentarius tenuit et quod quidem tenementum Rogerus de Foxelee nunc tenet ad duos anni terminos videlicet ad festum Sancti Michaelis duodecim denarios et ad festum pascha xij d. cum homagiis wardis releuiis et omnibus aliis escaetis ad redditum pertinentibus. Dat' die Martis proxima post festum Sancti Mathei Apostoli anno regni regis Edwardi filij regis Edwardi octauo.

>   NOTE: William Wake having acquired this 2s. rent in 1315, gave it to Thomas son of
>   Richard Neel in 1347 in no. 233, wherein it is described as due from lands held by
>   Cecily Erneys. This rent was causing trouble as late as 1563 in Neel court roll, HD 473.

75   *Bartholomew de Burgate de Holkham grants Richard Payn of Holkham and Lewegolda his wife 1 plot.*   **[c. 1276–82]**

<Goldewynescroft>
Ex feoffamento Bartholomei [de] Burgate de Holkham facto Ricardo Payn de eadem et Lewegolde vxori eius vnam peciam terre iacentem in campis de Holkham inter terram Iohannis Godwyne ex parte orientali et terram prioris de Pet*erston* et Ade Lakeman abbutantem super predictam terram versus occidentem cuius caput australe abbuttat super terram Galfridi Thurbern et caput aquilonale abbuttat super terram quondam Heruei Fabri quam tenuit ad voluntatem domini Thome de Snytercham reddendo capitalibus dominis duos denarios per annum pro omnibus seruiciis sectis curie, etc. Nulla data.

>   NOTE: Cf. Goldewyne, no. 260.

76 *Margery Craske, widow of Ralf atte Gateshende of Brisley, grants Simon Ide of Kettlestone 1 plot.*   8 Dec. 1330

Fo. 6v <Brunhamgate>
Ex feoffamento Margerie Craske quondam vxoris Radulfi atte Gateshende de Brisle facto Simoni Ide de Keteleston' \vnam peciam terre/ iacent' in camp' occident' de Holkham inter terram prioris et conuentus de Peterston ex parte orientali et terram Willelmi Rectoris medietatis ecclesie de Holkham ex parte accidentali apud boreale abuttat super Brunhamgate dat' die Sabbati in festo concepcionis beate Marie anno regni regis Edwardi tercij post conquestum quarto.

> NOTE: Simon Ide is probably the same man as Simon Mous of Holkham (no. 238) also called 'of Kettelstone' (nos. 76, 174, and 232). Cf. no. 238.

77 *Richard, son of Ralph Goldwyne, grants William, son of Geoffrey Silk of Holkham, 3 plots.*   [c. 1270]

Original: HP 999

<Duuesty, Wellegate>
Ex feoffamento Ricardi filij Radulfi Goldwyne facto Willelmo filio Galfridi Silk' de eadem tres pecias terre mee iacentes in camp' de Holkham quarum vna pecia iacet apud Duuesty inter terram Reginaldi filij Gilberti ex vna parte et terram Iohannis Ossemod ex altera parte. Et altera pecia terre [iacet apud] Wellegate inter terram Thome de Burgate ex parte orientali et terram Ricardi No[rtherne] ex parte occidentale. Et tercia pecia iacet inter terram Eborardi filij Pagani ex orientali et terram de Thome de Burgate ex occidentali reddendo annuatim predicto Ricardo filio Radulfi octo denarios et ad commune auxilium in forinseca sokna de Wycton' ad xx s. j d. et ad plus plus et ad minus minus pro omni seruicio. Nulla data.

78 *William, son of Ralph Bendyng of Holkham, grants William, son of Geoffrey Silk, 1 plot.*   [c. 1275–95]

<Bendyng>
Ex feoffamento Willelmo filij Radulfi Bendyng de Holkham facto Willelmo filio Galfridi Silke vnam peciam terre iacentem in campo de Holkham que iacet inter terram Gilberti Edwy versus austrum et terram Ricardi Bendyng versus aquilonem et caput occidentale abbuttat super croftam Ricardi Goldwyne reddendo annuatim j d. prefato Willelmo filio Radulfi Bendyng' pro omni seruicio etc. Nulla data.

79   *Gilbert, son of William Nicol of Holkham, grants Simon, son of Hamo*
of Holkham, 1/2 rood.   [c. 1294–6]

Original: HP 1041

<Cleylond>
Ex feoffamento Gilberti filij Willelmi Nicol de Holkham facto Simoni filio
Hamonis de eadem vnam dimidiam rodam terre mee iacentem in campo de
Holkham super Cleylond inter terram Rogeri Thurbern ex parte orientali et
terram dicti Simonis filio Hamonis ex parte occidentali et caput aquilonale
abbuttat super terram Iohanne Thurbern. Caput australe abbuttat super
croftam Iohannis Aleyn reddendo annuatim prefato Gilberto j obolum pro
omni seruicio. Nulla data.

80   *Ralph Hakun of Holkham grants Walter Hakun his nephew 3 plots.*
                                                                          [c. 1275–94]

<Lethirpittes, Steynhil>
Ex feoffamento Radulfi Hakun de Holkham facto Waltero Hakun nepoti suo
tres pecias terre iacentem in campo de Holkham quarum vna pecia iacet apud
Lethepittes iuxta terram Prioris de Wals*ingham* versus aquilonem et terram
Martini Rust versus austrum. Alia pecia iacet apud Steynhil iuxta terram
domini Willelmi de Calthorp versus occidentem et terram Iohannis Burgoyne
versus orientem cuius caput australe abbuttat super terram Willelmi Calthorp
predicti. Tercia pecia iacet apud Steynhil iuxta terram domini Willelmi
Calthorp versus occidentem. Reddendo annuatim predicto Radulfo vnam
radicem Gingeb*r*is pro omnibus seruiciis etc. Nulla data.

> NOTE: When this land is granted to Simon Hamund on 17 March 1294 (no. 100, HP
> 1007) the first piece is described as 13/4 acres. In the Walsingham Cartulary, BL Ms.
> Cotton Nero E VII, Fo. 54 no. 141, Walsingham's land called Tungeland lies next to
> common pasture in the south, land of Richard Godwine in the north and abuts west on
> the royal road and east on common pasture. This suggests that more land was under
> cultivation by 1294 than previously.

81   *John, son of Geoffrey le Bret of Holkham, grants Simon Hamond of*
Holkham 81/2d. p.a.   15 Oct. 1295

Original: HP 1015

<Relaxacio octo d. ob>
Ex relaxacione Iohannis filij Galfridi le Bret de Holkham facto Simoni
Hamond de eadem octo denarios et obolum annui redditus quos percipere
solebat de predicto Simone pro tenemento quod predictus Simon adquisiuit de
Galfrido patre suo ita quod nec heredes mei etc. aliquid ius etc. in predictis
octo denariis et obolo de cetero exigere clamare vel vendere etc. Dat' die

Sabbati proxima ante festum Sancti Luce euangeliste anno regni regis Edwardi xxiij°.

82   *Thomas Selone of Wells and Matilda his wife grant Bartholomew Calewere 1 plot.*   **9 May 1304**

>   *Original: HP 1046*

<Scothoghgate>
Ex feoffamento Thome Seloue de Welles et Matilde vxoris eius facto Bartholomeo Calewere vnam peciam terram iacentem in campo de Holkham inter terram Iohannis Eyr que quondam fuit Bartholomei de Burgate ex parte orientali et terram Gilberti Silk ex parte occidentali et abbuttat versus austrum super viam que vocatur Scothoghgate. Dat' die Sabbati proxima post festum Sancti Iohannis ante portam Latinam anno regni regis Edwardi filij regis Henrici tricesimo secundo.

83   *Gilbert de Langley grants Philip, son of Matthew of Candos, and heirs 2 acres held of William de Montchesney for 1 lb of pepper next to the ancient messuage of Hubert de Montchesney.*   [c. 1250]

Fo. 7   <examinatur, j libr. piperis>
Ex feoffamento Gileberti de Langele facto Philippo filio Mathei de Candos duas acras terre quas ego teneo de domino Willelmo de Monte Can*isio* in villa de Holkham tenendas de prefato Gilberto et heredibus suis pro eodem seruicio quo ipsas predictas acras a predicto Willelmo teneo scilicet pro vna libra piperis pro omni consuetudine et seruicio que vero acre terre iacent inter antiquum mesuagium quod fuit Huberti de Monte Canisio et terram Matildis Bendyng vidue. Nulla data.

>   NOTE: The ancient messuage of Hubert de Montchesney is evidently the old manor house of Burghall which had vanished before the 1590 map was drawn.

84   *Thomas, son of Peter le Bret of Holkham, grants John, son of Helewise de Bathley, 2 acres with messuage in Holkham.*   [after 1255]

<j lib. piperis>
Ex feoffamento Thome filij Petri le Bret de Holkham facto Iohanni filio Heylewisie de Bathele duas acras terre cum mesuagio in Holkham que iacent inter cruftam que fuit Radulfi Bendyng' et terram que fuit domini Warini de Munchensy reddendo predicto Thome et heredibus suis libram piperis ad festum Sancte Margarete virginis. Nulla data.

85   *John, son of Geoffrey le Bret of Holkham, grants Richard de Barking,*
rector of half Egmere church, 1 plot called Gonyeswong.   5 Sept. 1293

Original: *HP 1006*. Cf. nos. 138 and 139

<Gonyeswong>
Ex feoffamento Iohannis filij Galfridi le Bret de Holkham facto Ricardo de
Berkyng rectori medietatis ecclesie de Eggemer' vnam peciam terre in
Holkham que vocatur Gonyswong' inter terram Dionisie de Mounchansy ex
parte australi et terram prioris de Wals*ingham* ex parte aquilonali et abbuttat
ad vnum caput super terram prioris de Petirston vsque occidentem et aliud
caput super terram dicti Iohannis vsque orientem. Dat' die Sabbati proxima
ante Natiuitatem Beate Marie Virginis anno regni regis Edwardi xxj°.

NOTE: Richard de Barking was also rector of half Holkham church and as such received
a similar grant on the same day (no. 138) from Geoffrey le Bret the father of John. John
regranted the plot to Nicholas son of Aveline of Little Witchingham, HP 1021.

86   *Adam, son of Adam le Bret of Holkham, grants William, son of Gilbert*
Curthon, 1 plot.   [c. 1272–5]

Original: *HD 8*. Cf. nos. 21 and 49

<Langebutehil', Gibbesgate>
Ex feoffamento Ade filij Ade le Bret de Holkham facto Willelmo filio
Gilberti Curthon' vnam peciam terre cum pertinenciis iacentem in camp' de
Holkham super Langebuthelhil inter terram Iohannis Asty del Hil versus
austrum et terram que Katerina de Eggemere tenet in dote versus aquilonem
et caput boreale abbuttat super Gibbesgate reddendo annuatim prefato Ade et
heredibus suis vnum denarium pro omnibus seruiciis consuetudinibus sectis
curie etc. Nulla data.

NOTE: Nos. 21 and 49 both read Caldowesty for Gibbesgate.

87   *Richard, son of Alexander Bendyng, grants William, son of Gilbert*
Curthun of Holkham, 1 plot.   [c. 1250]

<Mariotescroft>
Ex feoffamento Ricardi filij Alexandri Bendyng' facto Willelmo filio Gilberti
Curthun de eadem vnam peciam terre iacentem in campis de Holkham inter
terram Iohannis Asty vsque occidentem et terram Soufue ad molendinum
vsque orientem et caput australe abbuttat super croftam Bartholomei Mariot
reddendo inde prefato Ricardo vnum denarium pro omni seruicio
consuetudine etc. Nulla data.

88   *Bartholomew de Burgate of Holkham grants Simon Hammond of*
Holkham 2¹/₂ acres.   27 Oct. 1299

   Original: HP 1022

<Wyghtongate>
Ex feoffamento Bartholomei de Burgate de Holkham facto Simoni Hammond
de eadem duas acras et dimidiam terre in campis de Holkham inter terram
Galfridi Godwyn' ex parte orientali et terram Galfridi Carpentarij ex parte
occidentali et capud australe abbuttat super regalem viam que ducit de
Holcham apud Wyctone et caput australe abbuttat super terram Iohannis
Balteys faciendo capitalibus dominis feodi seruicium debitum et
consuetudinem videlicet vnum obolum pro omni seruicio consuetudine
exaccione secta curie et seculari demanda. Dat' in vigilia apostolorum
Simonis et Iude anno regni regis Edwardi xxvij°.

89   *John, son of Geoffrey le Meyre of Holkham, dwelling in Bungay, grants*
Simon, son of Hamo, 1 plot.   [c. 1283–93]

   <Quichegift, Grenegate>
Ex feoffamento Iohannis filij Galfridi le Meyre de Holkham manentis in
Bungeye facto Simoni filio Hamonis de eadem vnam peciam terre iacentem
in camp' de Holkham ad Quichegift inter mesuagium et croftam Iohannis filij
Ricardi Fabri ex parte orientali et terram predicti Simonis ex parte occidentali
et caput aquilonale abbuttat super viam que vocatur Grenegate reddendo
annuatim prefato Iohanni tres denarios pro omnibus seruiciis etc. Sine data.

90   *Angerus Dei Paciencia, Abbot of West Dereham, grants to Peter le Bret*
of Holkham 3 acres of free land belonging to half Holkham church.
                                                          [c. 1250]

   Omnibus Christi fidelibus presens scriptum visuris vel audituris Angerus
Dei Paciencia abbas de Derham et eiusdem loci conuentus salutem. Noueritis
nos vnanimi assensu capituli nostri concessisse dedisse et hac presenti carta
nostra confirmasse Petro le Bret filio Petri le Bret de Holkham tres acras
libere terre ad medietatem nostram ecclesie de Holkham pertinentem quas
predictus Petrus senior tenuit aliquando de nobis in campis de Holkham
tenend' de nobis et successoribus nostris reddendo inde annuatim duodecim
denarios ad pascha et [festum] Sancti Michaelis pro omnibus seruiciis
consuetudinibus etc. Hiis testibus etc. Nulla data.

   NOTE: There is an *inspeximus* of a charter from Peter le Bret son of Peter le Bret of
   Holkham to Abbot Angerus in the West Dereham Cartulary, BL Ms. Add 46353. In it the
   payment is 30d. at two terms viz 15d. at Easter and 15d. at Michaelmas. See HD 6
   (XXVI).

91 *James de Clare grants Geoffrey Mundi of Wighton for homage and service and 40s. given to fabric of St. Wythburga's church, 21/2 acres and 1/2 rood in 8 plots.* [c. 1250]

Fo. 7v <Brunhamgate, Stowecroft>

Ex concessione Iacobi de Clar' facto Galfrido Mundi de Wichton pro homagio et seruicio suo et pro xl solidis quod dedit ad fabricam ecclesie Sancte Wiburge tres acras terre vna roda minus tenendas de ecclesia Sancte Wyburge et de prefato Iacobo et de heredibus suis reddendo annuatim pro omni seruicio et consuetudine sex denarios ad pascha et [festum] Sancti Michaelis. Huius autem terre vna roda et dimidia iacet iuxta metam de Brunham et tres rode iuxta viam [versus Brunham] et dimidia roda iuxta croftam Matildis vidue et roda et dimidia iuxta terram Galfridi le [Kynge] et vna roda iuxta terram Galfridi le Bret et vna roda et dimidia in Stowecroft dimidia roda iuxta terram Roberti Fabri et vna roda quam Lecent dedit ecclesie. Hec autem pecie terre iacent versus [ecclesiam?] iuxta terram quam Hubertus de Monte Canisio dedit Petro le Bret de Holkham. Hiis testibus etc. Nulla data.

NOTE: Hubert de Montchesney was sheriff of Essex 1257–9, PRO, *List of Sheriffs*, p. 43. The lands are the same in HD 92. See pedigree in Appendix 2.

92 *Hubert de Montchesney grants Peter le Bret of Holkham and heirs land which Harvey Kippe held of St. Wythburga's church and of himself of 21/2 acres 1/2 rood in 8 plots.* [c. 1250]

<Brunhamgate, Stowecroft>

Ex concessione Huberti de Monte Can*isio* facto Petro le Bret de Holkham terram quam Herueus Kippe ex donacione mea tenuit sibi et heredibus suis tenend' de ecclesia Sancte Wytburge et de prefato Huberto reddendo annuatim pro omni seruicio et consuetudine sex denarios ad pascha et [festum] Sancti Michaelis. Huius autem terre vna roda et dimidia iacet iuxta metam de Brunham et tres rode iuxta viam versus Brunham et dimidia roda iuxta croftam Matild*is* vidue. Et roda et dimidia iuxta terram Galfridi le Kynge, vna roda iuxta terram ipsius Petri et vna roda et dimidia in Stowecroft et dimidia roda iuxta terram Roberti Fabri et vna roda quam Lecent dedit ecclesie etc. Hiis testibus. Nulla data.

93   *Lovegolda and Alice, daughters of Gilbert, son of Richard Payn of Holkham, grant William Roteney of Holkham 1 1/2 acres.*   29 May 1317

Original: HP 1078

<Sladaker>

Ex feoffamento Louegolde et Alicie filiarum Gilberti filij Ricardi Payn de Holkham facto Willelmo Roteney de eadem vnam acram et dimidiam terre iacentem collateraliter in campo de Holkham apud Sladaker inter terram dicti Willelmi versus austrum et terram Rogeri Ode per partem aquilonem et caput orientale abbuttat super terram prioris et conuentus de Pet*erston* reddendo prefato Louegolde et Alicie iiij d. et obolum pro omni seruicio etc. Dat' die Dominica in festo Sancte Trinitatis anno regni regis Edwardi decimo.

94   *John Charles senior of Holkham grants Simon Hammond of Holkham 1 rood.*   5 May 1295

Original: HD 12

<Sladaker>

Ex feoffamento Iohannis Charles senioris de Holkham facto Simoni Hammond de eadem vnam rodam terre iacentem in camp*o* de Holkham apud Sladaker inter terram dicti Iohannis ex parte aquilonali et terram predicti Simonis ex parte australi. Caput orientale abbuttat super terram prioris et conuentus de Peterston caput occidentale abbuttat super Adowehefdes reddendo pro predicto Iohanne capitalibus dominis feodi vnum denarium per annum pro omni seruicio secta curie etc. Dat' die Iouis proxima post invencionem Sancte Crucis anno regni regis Edwardi xxiij°.

95   *John Charles senior, son of Simon Charles of Holkham, grants Simon Hammond 1 plot of 1 1/2 acres.*   12 Dec. 1296

Original: HD 13

<Sladaker>

Ex feoffamento Iohannis Charlys senioris filij Simonis Charles de Holkham facto Simoni Hammond vnam peciam terre continentem vnam acram et dimidiam terre iacentem in camp*is* de Holkham in quarentena vocata Sladaker inter terram dicti Iohannis ex parte aquilon*ali* et terram quondam Radulfi Cheles ex parte australi. Caput orientale abbuttat super terram prioris et conuentus de Petirston. Reddendo annuatim capitalibus dominis feodi quatuor denarios et obolum pro omni seruicio etc. Dat' die Mercurij proxima post festum Sancti Nicholai Episcopi anno regni regis Edwardi xxv^to.

96   *Roger Chele of Holkham grants William de Walsingham 1 rood in exchange for another rood*   **6 Dec. 1315**

     Original: HD 25. Cf. no. 26

<Sladaker>

Ex feoffamento Rogeri Chele de Holkham facto Willelmo de Walsingham vnam rodam terre arabilis in campis de Holkham iuxta terram predicti Willelmi ex parte aquilonali et terram Iohannis Charle ex parte australi et iacet dicta roda terre apud Sladaker in excambium pro j roda terre iacenti iuxta terram meam ex parte aquilonali et terram Roberti de Gristone que sibi accidit per escaetam de terra Thome Birche ex parte australi reddendo capitalibus dominis etc. Dat' die Sabbati in festo Sancti Nicholai Episcopi anno regni regis Edwardi filij regis Edwardi nono.

97   *Adam Hammond of Holkham grants William, son of Robert de Dunwich of Walsingham, 2 roods in 2 plots.*   **1 Feb. 1314**

     Original: HP 1047. Cf. no. 112

<Sladaker>

Ex feoffamento Ade Hammond de Holkham facto Willelmo filio Roberti de Donewich' de Walsingham duas pecias terre iacentes in Holkham quarum vna pecia iacet apud Sladaker iuxta terram Rogeri Chele ex parte boriali et terram Alicie Briche ex parte australi et continet in se vnam rodam terre et alia pecia iacet apud Litelhowe iuxta terram Iohannis Deye ex parte australi et continet j rodam terre tenend' de capitalibus dominis. Dat' die veneris proxima ante festum Purificacionis beate Marie anno regni regis Edwardi filij Edwardi septimo.

     NOTE: Cf. nos. 111 and 112 for other transactions between the same parties.

98   *William Bulleman of Holkham grants Simon Hammond 11/2 acres and 1/2 rood in 4 plots.*   **[c. 1291–3]**

     Original: HP 1023

Fo. 8   <Hungerhil, Caldowgate, Dalegate>

Ex feoffamento [Willelmi] Bulleman de Holkham facto Simoni Hammond quatuor pecias terre continentes vnam acram dimidiam acram et dimidiam rodam terre in camp' de Holkham quarum vna pecia terre iacet apud Hungerhil inter terram Willelmi Cursun ex parte australi et terram quam Elwysia vxor quondam Gilberti Payn tenet ex parte aquilonali et caput orientale abbuttat super Caldowegate [Secunda vero pecia iacet] apud Dalegate inter terram prioris de Walsingham [ex parte australi et terram que fuit] Iohannis Busshop ex aquilonali et caput occidentale abbuttat super Dalegate. Tercia pecia iacet inter terram Roberti Marchal ex parte orientali et terram quam Elwysia vxor quondam Gilberti Payn tenet in dote ex parte occidentali. Quarta pecia iacet apud Dalegate inter terram Willelmi Craske ex parte australi et terram quam dicta Elwysia tenet in dote ex parte aquilonali et caput orientale abbuttat super Dalegate. Reddendo j denarium prefato Willelmo pro omni seruicio. Nulla data.

99   *Gilbert, son of John Brun of Holkham, grants Simon, son of Hamo,*
1 plot of 1 acre.   [c. 1283–93]

> *Original: HP 997*

\<Grenegate\>
Ex feoffamento Gilberti filij Iohannis Brun de Holkham facto Simoni filio Hamonis vnam peciam terre iacentem in Holkham inter terram dicti Simonis versus occidentem et terram Iohannis Asty versus orientem et caput aquilon*ale* abbuttat super Grenegate reddendo ij denarios prefato Gilberto et ad commune auxilium quando venerit in forinseca sokun de Wyghton' ad xx s. vnum obolum pro omni seruicio. Nulla data. Et continet j acram vt scribitur in dorso carte.

100   *Walter Hakun of Holkham grants Simon Hammond 1 plot of 1³/4 acres*
and 2 other plots.   17 Mar. 1294

> *Original: HP 1007.* Cf. no. 80

\<Steynhil\>
Ex feoffamento Walteri Hakun de Holkham facto Simoni Hammond tres pecias terre iacentes in camp' de Holkham quarum prima pecia terre continens in se vij rodas terre iacet inter terram prioris de Wals*ingham* ex parte aquilonali et terram que fuit Martini Rust ex parte australi. Secunda pecia terre iacet inter terram que fuit domini Willelmi Caltorp' ex parte occidentali et terram que fuit Galfridi Golde ex parte orientali. Et tercia pecia iacet ad caput australe predicte terre inter terram domini Willelmi Calthrop' ex parte occidentali et terram Iohannis Burgoyne ex parte orientali. Dat' die Mercurij proxima post festum Sancti Gregorij Pape anno regni regis Edwardi xxij°.

NOTE: No. 80 describes the first piece as Letherpitte and does not say it is 7 roods. HP 1007 (unlike no. 80 and the marginal catchword of no. 100) does not name Steynhil.

101   *William, son of John Silk of Holkham, grants Edmund Adelwalde of South Creake and Christiana his daughter 6³/4 acres ¹/2 rood in 3 plots.*
[c. 1272–8]

<Dalegate, Hungerhill, Caldogate, Dedquenepit, Adowegate>
Ex feoffamento Willelmi filij Iohannis Silke de Holkham facto Edmundo Adelwald' de Southcreyk et Cristiane filie sue sex acras tres rodas et dimidiam rodam terre in camp' de Holkham quarum vna pecia terre iacet apud Dalegate iuxta terram Willelmi Craske ex parte australi et terram Iohannis Bret ex parte aquilon*ali* et caput occidentale abbuttat super Dalegate, secunda pecia terre iacet apud Hungerhil iuxta terram prioris de Petirston ex parte boriali et terram Iohannis Bret ex parte australi et caput orientale abbuttat super Caldowgate, tercia pecia iacet apud Dedquenepit iuxta [terram] Iohannis filij Simonis Hammond ex parte boriali et caput occidentale abbuttat super Adowgate. Nulla data.

102   *Geoffrey, son of Peter le Bret of Holkham, grants Simon Hammond of Holkham and Cecily his wife 3 acres with 1 fold.*   6 Oct. 1296

<Falda cum tribus acris terre>
Ex feoffamento Galfridi filij Petri le Bret de Holkham facto Simoni Hammond eiusdem ville et Cecilie vxori sue tres acras terre cum vna falda cum omnibus libertatibus apud predictam faldam spectantibus videlicet in pascuis pasturis fugaciis campis brueris viis semitis et omnibus aliis libertatibus aysiamentis extra villam et infra tam innominatis quam nominatis quibuscumque ad predictam faldam spectantibus eisdem statu et forma quibus ego et predecessores mei aliquibus temporibus tenuimus tempore quo fuit in manibus nostris et iacent predicte terre in campis de Holkham cum libertatibus predictis falde in eodem campo orientali. Dat' die Sabbati proxima post festum sancti Michaelis anno regni regis Edwardi xxiiii ^{to}.

NOTE: Cf. nos. 1, 101, 102 and 107.

103   *Acquisition of serfs [too damaged to read].*   12 Nov. 1295

Fo. 8v   <Perquisicio Natiuorum>
Ex feoffamento ... Gilbertum Gurle et Elueuam Daleman nativos meos ... [*8 lines illegible*] aliis seruiciis que ... predecessores mihi vel predecessoribus meis [fecerunt] vel facere consueuerunt. Dat' die Sabbati proxima post festum Sancti [Martini] anno regni regis Edwardi xxiiij^{to}.

104   *John, son of Geoffrey le Bret of Holkham, grants to Simon Hammond of Holkham and Cecily his wife, Gilbert Gurle and Elwina Daleman, his serfs, with their broods.*   16 July 1296

<Perquisicio Natiuorum>
Ex feoffamento Iohannis filio Galfridi le Bret de Holkham facto Simoni Hammond eiusdem ville et Cecilie vxori sue Gilbertum Gurle et Elwiuam Daleman natiuos meos cum totis sequelis suis procreatis et procreandis et omnibus catallis in villa et in campis de Holkham que predic*tus* Gilbertus et Elwiua de predicto Iohanne tenuerunt in villenagio cum omnibus seruiciis et consuetudinibus de predicto villenagio exeuntibus videlicet in cheuagio heriet' et allegancia eorum et liberorum suorum precariis aueragiis gallinis redditibus talliagiis et omnibus aliis seruiciis quibuscumque tam innominatis quam nominatis ad predicta villenagia spectantibus quod predictus Gilbertus et Elwiua et eorum predecessores mihi vel meis predecessoribus aliquo tempore fecerunt vel facere consueuerunt. Dat' die Lune proxima ante festum Sancte Margarete Virginis anno regni regis Edwardi vicesimo quarto.

> NOTE: Gilbert Gurle is mentioned in Geoffrey le Bret's rental, HD 11, and in Neel court roll of 1322, HD 79.

105   *William, son of Simon Hamo of Holkham, grants Walter de Helweton, perpetual vicar of Holkham, the messuage once of John de Bintry of Holkham and 14 acres and 1/2 rood in 19 plots.*   18 April 1313

<Skuckelif, Duuescrundell, Bakonescrundell, Lethrgraues, Millestede, Warledowesty, Feldhous, Slyngeshowe, Dalegate, Pilman, Larkesscote, Litelhowe, Sladaker, examinatur>
Ex feoffamento Willelmi filij Simonis Hamonis de Holkham facto Waltero de Helweton' perpetuo vicario de Holkham totum illud mesuagium quod fuit Iohannis de Byntre in Holkham cum domibus edificiis in eodem sitis preter quamdam longam domum in eodem mesuagio edificatam versus austrum et solum in quo situatur cum aisiamento contra domum videlicet in coop*er*icione et factura parietum et quatuordecim acras et dimidiam rodam terre iacentes in villa et in campis de Holkham in diuersis peciis: quarum vna pecia terre iacet in crofta Iohannis de Byntre. Altera pecia terre iacet apud Skukkelif iuxta terram prioris et conuentus de Wal*singham* ex parte aquilon'. Alia pecia terre iacet in eadem quarentena iuxta terre que fuit Eborardi vnder Howe ex parte aquilon' et australi. Alia pecia iacet in eadem quarentena iuxta terram Willelmi Leflod ex parte aquilon'. Alia pecia terre iacet apud Duuescrundel iuxta terram Thome filij Iohannis filij Hyde ex parte australi. Alia pecia terre iacet apud Bakonescrundel iuxta terram Iohannis de Bylneye ex parte australi. Alia pecia terre iacet apud Lethrgraues iuxta terram Iohannis Fabri. Alia

pecia terre iacet apud Millestede iuxta terram Matild*is* Talbot. Alia pecia terre iacet ad portam Mabilie Hardy iuxta terram Helweue Daleman. Alia pecia terre iacet apud Warldehousty iuxta terram Gilberti Gurle. Alia pecia terre iacet apud Feldhous iuxta terram Iohannis Bylneye. Alia pecia terre iacet apud Shugeshowe iuxta terram Martini Rust. Alia pecia terre iacet apud Dalegate terram Wlwine Pernson. Alia pecia terre iacet apud Pilleman iuxta terram Willelmi de Hyndringham. Alia pecia terre iacet apud Larkesscote iuxta terram Iohannis Carpenter. Alia pecia terre iacet in eadem quarentena iuxta terram Willelmi Silk'. Alia pecia terre iacet apud Litelhowe iuxta terram Mariote Redekyn. Alia pecia terre iacet apud Sladaker' iuxta terram Iohannis Charles et alia pecia terre iacet in eadem quarentena iuxta terram eiusdem Iohannis Charles ex parte aquilonis. Dat' die Mercurij proxima post festum Tiburti et Valeriani martirum anno regni regis Edwardi filij regis Edwardi sexto.

NOTE: Walter the perpetual vicar who here receives John of Bintry's messuage on 18 April 1313 regrants it on 15 Oct. to William son of Robert de Dunwich of Walsingham in no. 106. See also HD 205 no. XIII (1).

106 *Walter de Helweton, vicar of half Holkham church, grants William, son of Robert de Dunwich de Walsingham, the messuage once of John de Bintry and plots as above but numbered 1 to 19.* **15 Oct. 1313**

Fo. 9 <Scuckelif, Duuescrundell, Bakonescrundell, Leyrgraves, Millestede, Warldehousty, Feldhous, Slyngeshowe, Dalegate, Pilman, Larkescote, Litelhowe, Sladaker, examinatur>
Ex feoffamento Walteri [de Helweton capellani] et vicarij medietatis ecclesie de Holkham facto Willelmo filio Roberti Dunewych de Walsyngham totum illud mesuagium quod fuit Iohannis de Byntre [etc.*as in no. 105 except that the plots of land are numbered from* prima *to* nonodecima]. Dat' die Lune proxima post festum Sancti Dionisij anno regni regis Edwardi filij regis Edwardi septimo.

107 *John, son of Geoffrey le Bret of Holkham, grants Simon Hammond 1 acre with fold.* **16 July 1296**

<Falda cum una acra terre, Creykgate, Warledousty>
Ex feoffamento Iohannis filij Galfridi le Bret de Holkham facto Simoni Hammond vnam acram terre cum vna falda et omnibus libertatibus ad predictam faldam spectantibus videlicet in chaceis in campis in bruer*a* viis semitis et omnibus aliis libertatibus et aysiamentis tam innominatis quam nominatis quibuscumque ad predictam faldam spectantibus eisdem statu et forma quibus ego et predecessores mei aliquibus temporibus tenuimus et iacet

predicta acra terre in campis de Holkham inter terram meam ex parte
aquilonali et terram Clementis Daleman ex parte australi et caput occidentale
abbuttat super Creykgate et caput orientale super Warledehousty. Dat' die
Lune proxima ante festum Sancte Margarete Virginis anno regni regis
Edwardi xxiiij[to].

NOTE: See note on no. 102 for this fold.

108   *Geoffrey, son of William de Hindringham, grants John Brein of*
Holkham 1 'place' of 51 ft. length and a width of 25 ft. in the south and 23
ft. in the north, with a house.   [c. 1272–5]

<De quadam domo>
Ex feoffamento Galfridi filij Willelmi de Hindryngham facto Iohanni Brein
de Holkham vnam placeam terre cum quadam domo in eadem sita
continentem in longitudine L et vnum pedem terre et in latitudine ad caput
australe xxv pedes et ad caput aquilonale xxiij pedes terre et iacet in villa de
Holkham iuxta mesuagium Gilberti Trude versus orientem et mesuagium
Ricardi Barker' versus occidentem et abbuttat versus austrum super viam
regiam et versus aquilonem super terram Iohannis Bret, reddendo capitalibus
dominis feodi ij d. obolum pro omnibus seruiciis. Nulla data.

NOTE: This messuage and the measurements (51 ft. long by 25 ft. at the southern end
and 23. ft. at the northern end) are also mentioned in nos. 51 and 52, where William
Troude and Gilbert Barker are in the places of Gilbert Trude and Richard Barker.

109   *Final Concord, Geoffrey de Stiffkey quitclaims to Peter le Bret 1 mes-*
suage and 40 acres.   29 April 1257

Original: PRO CP 25(1) case 158 file 88 no. 1360. Cf. Appendix 5 no. 22.

Fo. 9v   <Finis>
Hec est finalis concordia facta in curia domini regis [apud Norwic'] a die
Pasche in tres septimanas anno regni regis Henrici filij Iohannis xlj[o] coram
Gilberto de Preston et aliis iusticiariis itinerantibus inter Galfridum de
Stiuekeye petentem et Petrum le Bret tenentem de vno mesuagium [et xl
acris terre cum pertinenciis in Holkham] vnde placitum fuit inter eos in
eadem curia scilicet quod [predictus Galfridus remisit et quietum clamauit] de
se et heredibus suis predicto Petro et heredibus suis [totum ius et clamium
quod habui in] predicto mesuagio cum pertinenciis in perpetuum. [Et pro hac
remissione quietaclamacione fine et concordia idem Petrus dedit predicto
Galfrido decem libras Sterlingorum].

NOTE: The text is much faded and has been completed with the aid of the original.

110   *Ralph, son of [Thovey Powel] of Holkham, grants Simon, son of*
Charles del Hil of Holkham, 1 plot.   [c. 1270]

Original: HP 1042

<Warledhousty>
Ex feoffamento Radulfi filij [Thovey Powel] de Holkham facto [Simoni filio
Karoli] del Hil eiusdem ville vnam peciam terre in campis de Holkham inter
terram [Eborardi Thurbern] ex parte australi et terram Simonis ex parte
occidentali et super Warledehousty, reddendo vnum solidum per annum pro
omni seruicio. Nulla data.

111   *Adam Hammond of Holkham grants William, son of Robert de*
Dunwich of Walsingham, 1 acre 1/2 rood.   24 June 1314

Original: HP 1050

<Ryngewareslond>
Ex feoffamento Ade Hammond de Holkham facto Willelmo filio Roberti
Dunewych' de Wals*ingham* vnum acram terre et dimidiam rodam iacentem in
camp' de Holkham apud Ringwareslond iuxta terram Cecilie matris predicte
Ade ex parte boriali et caput occidentale abbuttat super viam que vocatur
Lethirpitgate et caput orientale abbuttat super terram predicte Cecilie quod
tenet nomine dotis. Dat' die Natiuitatis Sancti Iohannis Baptiste anno regni
regis Edwardi filij regis Edwardi septimo.

NOTE: This deed shows that Adam Hammond of Holkham and his mother Cecily were
both alive on 24 June 1314: if Katerine Neel was the heiress she did not inherit until
after that date.

112   *Adam Hammond of Holkham grants William, son of Robert de*
Dunwich of Walsingham, 1/2 a plot of of 2 acres 1 rood.   1 Feb. 1314

Original: HP 1047.

<Duuesped, Lethirpithefedes>
Ex feoffamento Ade Hammond de Holkham facto Willelmi filio Roberti
Dunewych' de Wals*ingham* medietatem vnius pecie terre que vocatur
Duuesped continentem ij acras et j rodam terre et iacet iuxta terram Henrici
Daui ex parte australi et caput occidentale abbuttat super semitam que
vocatur Lethirpithefdes et caput orientale super terram Ade Craske. Dat' die
veneris proxima ante festum Purificacionis beate Marie anno regni regis
Edwardi filij regis Edwardi septimo.

NOTE: No. 97 is of the same date and has the same parties, but the land is different.

113 *Harvey, son of Godwyn on the Hill, grants Philip, son of Matthew de Candos, 1 plot of 1 acre and 2 other plots.* [c. 1250 or earlier]

Cf. no. 83

<Wychegift, Bondeswong>
Ex feoffamento Heruey filij Godwyni super Montem facto Philippo filio Mathei de Candos tres pecias terre in campis de Holkham quarum vna acra terre iacet super Wychegift et due alie pecie iacent apud Bondeswong' reddendo viij d. Nulla data.

NOTE: In 1170, as stated by the return for Norfolk of the Inquest of Sheriffs, some of Mahew or Matthew de Candos's sheep were seized by the bailiffs of the Earl of Arundel, William d'Aubigny, son of the 'Pincerna'. *Red Book of the Exchequer*, cclxix, quoted by Farrer, vol. iii, p. 103.

114 *John Aleyn of Holkham and his wife Matilda grant Simon, son of Simon Hammond, and Cecily his wife 1/2 acre and 1/2 rood.* [c. 1283–93]

<Steynhilcrundell>
Ex feoffamento Iohannis Aleyn de Holkham et Matild*is* vxoris sue facto Simoni filio Simonis [Hammonis] et Cecilie vxoris sue dimidiam acram et dimidiam rodam terre in campis de Holkham apud Steynhilcrundell' inter terram Iohannis filij Emme ex parte orientali et terram domine Dyonisie de Monte Caniso ex parte occidentali et vnum caput abbuttat super terram predicti Simonis versus austrum et super terram domine Dyonisie de Monte Caniso ex parte occidentali et vnum caput abbuttat super terram predicti Simonis versus austrum et super terram domine Dyonisie de Monte Caniso versus aquilonem, reddendo vnum obolum capitalibus dominis. Nulla data.

NOTE: No. 68 of 26 March 1295 suggests that John Aleyn's land had not yet been given to Simon Hammond.

115 *Geoffrey, son of Peter le Bret, grants Simon Hammond and Cecily his wife 4 acres in 1 plot.* [c. 1283–93]

<Creykgate>
Ex feoffamento Galfridi filij Petri le Bret facto Simoni Hammond et Cecilie vxori sue quatuor acras terre in vna cultura in campis de Holkham inter terram Matildis Rutell' ex parte aquilonali et terram Martini Goldewen' ex parte australi et caput orientale abbuttat super Creykgate caput occidentale abbuttat super terram Humfredi Dauyd. Nulla data.

NOTE: The absence of a date suggests that this is one of the earlier grants to Simon and Cecily Hammond – but Cecily was still alive as late as 1314 in no. 111.

116   *Geoffrey, son of Peter le Bret of Holkham, grants Simon Hammond*
6 acres in 1 plot at Adowe.   [c. 1294]

    Original: HP 1030

<Adowe, Ringewareslond>
Ex feoffamento Galfridi filio Petri le Bret de Holcham facto Simoni
Hammond sex acras terre cum pertinenciis iacentes in Camp' de Holkham in
vna pecia apud Adowe inter terram Ade Carpentarij ex parte australi et
terram Iohannis Godman ex parte aquilonali caput occidentale abbuttat super
Ringeswareslond et caput orientale super Adowgate. Nulla data.

> NOTE: This grant of Geoffrey son of Peter is really a confirmation of a grant by his son
> Peter, HP 1032. It is regranted with two other plots in no. 126 on 17 March 1294.

117   *John, son of Geoffrey le Bret of Holkham, grants Simon Hammond*
1/2 acre.   14 March 1296

    Original: HP 1019

<Adowgate>
Ex feoffamento Iohannis filij Galfridi le Bret de Holkham facto Simoni
Hammond vnam dimidiam acram terre iacentem in camp' de Holkham inter
terram meam ex parte aquilon*ali* et terram predicti Simonis ex parte australi
cuius caput orientale abbuttat super Adowegate. Dat' die Mercurij proxima
post festum Sancti Gregorij pape anno regni regis Edwardi xxiiij^{to}.

118   *John, son of Geoffrey le Bret of Holkham, grants Simon Hammond*
1 acre.   12 Dec. 1295

    Original: HP 1016

Fo. 10   <Adowgate>
Ex feoffamento Iohannis filij Galfridi le Bret de Holkham facto Simoni
Hammond vnam acram terre iacentem in camp' de Holkham inter terram
dicti Galfridi ex parte aquilonali et terram predicti Simonis ex parte australi
cuius caput orientale abbuttat super Adowgate et caput occidentale abbuttat
super terram predicti Simonis, reddendo vnum clauum gariofili pro omni
seruicio. Dat' vigil' Sancte Lucie Virginis anno regni Edwardi vicesimo
quarto.[1]

119   *John, son of Geoffrey le Bret of Holkham, grants Simon Hammond of Holkham 1 plot.*   [c. 1291–3]

Original: HP 1033

<Creykgate>
Ex relaxacione Iohannis filij Galfridi le Bret facto Simoni Hammond de [eadem vnam peciam] terre in camp' de Holkham inter terram prioris de Wals*ingham* versus austrum et terram [Mariore] in Campo versus aquilon*ali* et caput orientale abbuttat super terram dicti Galfridi caput occidentale super Creykgate. Nulla data.

120   *John, son of Geoffrey le Bret, grants Simon, son of Hamo, 1 plot of 3 acres.*   [c. 1294–6]

Cf. HP 995 and no. 37

<Qwarlesgate>
Ex feoffamento Iohannis filij Galfridi le Bret facto Simoni filio Hamonis vnam peciam terre continentem in se tres acras terre et iacentem in camp' de Holkham inter terram Ade Carpentarij ex parte australi et terram meam ex parte aquilonali et caput occidentale abbuttat super terram dicti Simonis et caput orientale super regalem viam que ducit de Holkham apud Qwarles, reddendo obolum pro omni seruicio. Nulla data.

NOTE: This grant is confirmed by John's father Geoffrey son of Peter le Bret (no. 37). The original confirmation (HP 995) quotes no. 116 as the *carta feoffamenti* by gift of John.

121   *John, son of Geoffrey le Bret, grants Simon Hammond 1 plot of 4 acres and 1 other plot.*   24 Dec. 1293

<Duuesped, Gonyeswong>
Ex feoffamento Iohannis filij Galfridi le Bret facto Simoni Hammond duas pecias terre iacentem in camp' de Holkham quarum prima pecia in se continens quatuor acras terre iacet apud Duuesped inter terram Henrici Dauyd ex parte australi et terram Iohannis filij Rogeri Belneye ex parte aquilon*ali* et caput orientale abbuttat super terram que fuit Radulfi Hakon et caput occidentale abbuttat super Gonyeswong. Et alia pecia iacet inter terram prioris de Wals*ingham* ex parte occidentale et terram meam ex parte orientali caput aquilonale super terram predicti Simonis caput australe abbuttat super terram Rogeri filij Berte. Reddendo j quadrantem pro omni seruicio. Dat' die Iouis proxima ante Natiuitatem domini anno regni regis Edwardi vicesimo secundo.

NOTE: These 2 plots are regranted on 17 March 1294 in no. 126.

122　*John, son of Geoffrey le Bret, grants Simon, son of Hamo, 1/2 acre.*
16 Feb. 1296

Original: HP 1018

\<Adowegate\>
Ex feoffamento Iohannis filij Galfridi le Bret facto Simoni filio Hammonis vnam dimidiam acram terre iacentem in camp' Holkham inter terram dicti Simonis ex parte australi et terram meam ex parte aquilonali et caput occidentale abbuttat super terram dicti Simonis caput orientale abbuttat super viam que vocatur Hadougate, reddendo vnum clauum gariofili pro omnibus seruiciis. Dat' die Veneris proxima post festum Sancti Valentini anno regni regis Edwardi xxiiij^{to}.

NOTE: This grant of 17 Feb. 1296 seems to be a repetition of one of 29 Nov. 1295 (no. 125).

123　*John, son of Geoffrey le Bret, grants Simon son of Hamo 51/4 acres in 3 plots.*
18 Dec. 1294

Original: HP 1010

\<Adowebrest, Ryngewaleslond, Scokelif\>
Ex feoffamento Iohannis filij Galfridi le Bret facto Simoni filio Hammonis tres pecias terre iacentes in camp' de Holkham quarum prima pecia continens in se tres acras terre iacet apud Hadowbrest et secunda pecia terre in se continens vij rodas terre apud Ryngewaleslond et tercia pecia in se continens duas rodas terre iacet apud Skokelif. Dat' die Sabbati proxima ante festum Sancti Thome Apostoli anno regni regis Edwardi xxiij°.

124　*John, son of Geoffrey le Bret, grants Simon Hammond 3 acres in 1 plot.*
[c. 1294–6]

Original: HP 1034

\<Hangande Adowe\>
Ex feoffamento Iohannis filij Galfridi le Bret facto Simoni Hammond tres acras in vna cultura iacenti in camp*is* de Holkham inter terram prioris de Wals*ingham* ex parte occidentali et terram meam ex parte orientali caput aquilonale abbuttat super terram dicti Simonis et caput australe super terram Rogeri filij Berte. Nulla data et vocatur Hangande Adowe.

NOTE: Confirmed by John's father, Geoffrey son of Peter (no. 48).

125   *John, son of Geoffrey le Bret, grants Simon, son of Hamo, 1/2 acre.*

16 Nov. 1295

\<Adowe\>

Ex feoffamento Iohannis filij Galfridi le Bret facto Simoni filio Hamonis vnam dimidiam acram terre iacentem apud Hadowe inter terram meam ex parte aquilon*ali* et terram predicti Simonis ex parte australi cuius caput orientale abbuttat super Hadhowgate et caput occidentale abbuttat super terram predicti Simonis, reddendo vnum clauum gariofili pro omnibus seruiciis. Dat' vigilia Sancti Andree apostoli anno regni regis Edwardi xxiiij^{to}.

NOTE: This grant of 29 Nov. 1295 seems to be repeated on 17 Feb. 1296 (no. 122).

126   *John, son of Geoffrey le Bret, grants Simon Hammond 1 plot of 4 acres, 1 plot of 5 acres and another plot.*   17 Mar. 1294

Original: HP 1008

\<Duuesped, Adowgate\>

Ex feoffamento Iohannis filij Galfridi le Bret facto Simoni Hammond tres pecias terre in campis de Holkham quarum prima pecia continet in se quatuor acras terre iacentes apud Duuespit inter terram Henrici Dauyd ex parte australi et terram Iohannis filij Rogeri Bilneye ex parte aquilonali caput orientale abbuttat super terram que fuit Radulfi Hakoun. Secunda pecia iacet inter terram prioris et conuentus de Wals*ingham* ex parte occidentali et terram meam ex parte orientali caput aquilonale abbuttat super terram dicti Simonis. Tercia pecia iacet inter terram meam ex parte aquilon' et terram Ade Carpentarij ex parte australi et caput orientale abbuttat super Adowegate et continet v acras terre. Dat' die Mercurij proxima post Sancti Gregorij pape anno regni regis Edwardi xxij°.

NOTE: The first two plots had been granted (HD 22b) on 24 Dec. 1293. The third plot had been granted (no. 116) by Geoffrey son of Peter (in confirmation of his son John's grant in HP 1032).

127   *John, son of Geoffrey le Bret quitclaims Simon son of Hamo 71/2 acres in 4 plots.*   10 Nov. 1294

Original: HD 10

Fo. 10v   \<Griston, Duuesped, Grenegate\>

Ex [concessione et] quiet*a* clamacione Iohannis filij Galfridi le Bret facto Simoni filio Hamonis quatuor pecias terre cum pertinenciis iacentes in camp' de Holkham quarum prima pecia continens vij rodas terre iacet apud [Greiston], secunda pecia continens quatuor acras terre iacet apud Duuespyt, tercia pecia continens vnam acram terre iacet apud Grenegate, quarta pecia continens iij rodas terre iacet ad caput orientale alterius pecie terre que vocatur Grenegates. Dat' die Mercurij ante festum Sancti Martini epsicopi anno regni regis Edwardi xxij°.

NOTE: These four plots of land are the first four out of seven renamed in a grant from John son of Geoffrey le Bret dated 30 April 1295 in no. 46 (HP 1011).

128   *Lawrence Bendyng of Holkham grants Lawrence Skinner of Holkham 1 plot.*   **28 April 1339**

Original: HP 1097. Cf. HP 1099 and HP 1106 (not printed)

\<Bendyng\>
Ex feoffamento Laurencij Bendyng de Holkham facto Laurencio Skynner' de eadem vnam peciam terre iacentem in villa de Holkham inter terram Matilde Charle ex parte australi et terram Willelmi Crask ex parte aquilon*ali* et caput orientale abbuttat super croftam Laurencij Bendyng et caput occidentale abbuttat super placeam terre Matil*de* Charle. Dat' apud Holkham die Mercurij proxima post festum Sancti Marci Euangeliste anno regni regis Edwardi tercij post conquestum tercio decimo.

NOTE: Lawrence Skinner regrants this land to Gilbert Neel of Burnham 5 years later (no. 178, HP 1099). The plots of Christina Bendyng and Robert son of Lawrence Skinner abut on the common marsh in the west (HP 1106); the land mentioned in no. 128 seems to lie in Crosgate.

129   *Adam Gant of Holkham quitclaims to William de Hindringham 1 plot*
                                                                          [c. 1284]

\<Dalegate, Caldowgate\>
Quieta clamacio Ade Gant de Holkham facto Willelmo de Hyndryngham in vna pecia terre iacenti in camp' de Holkham inter terram Iohannis Dusyng ex parte aquilonali et terram Iohannis Fabri ex parte australi cuius caput occidentale abbuttat super Dalegate et caput orientale abbuttat super Caldowgate. Nulla data.

NOTE: John Dusyng is mentioned in the Burghall rental (no. 255).

130   *Helewise, daughter of Roger Othehil, grants Richard Blakeman of Walsingham a curtilage of 50 ft. length and 24 ft. width and 1 plot lying apart (diuisim) in vill and field.*   **23 Nov. 1321**

\<vnum Curtilagium, Vesthowe\>
Ex feoffamento Helewysie filie Rogeri Othehil de Holkham facto Ricardo Blakeman de Magna Wals*ingham* vnum curtilagium et vnam peciam terre

iacent diuisim' in villa et in campis de Holcham de quibus curtilagium iacet iuxta Ripam inter terram Rogeri Wryghte ex parte occidentali et communem semitam que ducit de Ripa de Holkham versus Welles ex parte orientali et continet in longitudine quinquaginta pedes et in latitudine viginti quatuor pedes. Et predicta pecia terre iacet apud Vesthowe iuxta terram Umfredi Dauy ex parte orientali et iuxta terram quondam Ricardi le Wryghte ex parte occidentali. Quod quidem curtilagium cum predicta pecia terre ego dicta Helewysia adquisiui in viduitate mea de Thoma filio Iohannis de Holcham. Dat' die Lune in festo Sancti Clementis pape et martiri anno regni regis Edwardi filij regis Edwardi quintodecimo.

NOTE: This curtilage lies at the Stathe next to the shore between the land of Roger le Wright and the path from Holkham Stathe to Wells.

131   *Thomas, son of John of Holkham, grants Helewise Othehil as above.*
14 July 1320

<Curtilagium, Vesthowe>
Ex feoffamento Thome filij Iohannis de Holcham facto Helewysie Othehil vnum curtilagium [*etc. as above, but reads in* diuersis locis *for* diuisim]. Dat' die Lune proxima post festum Translacionis Sancti Thome martiris anno regni regis Edwardi filij regis Edwardi quartodecimo.

132   *John, son of Geoffrey le Bret, grants Richard le Northerne all claims in the tenements or in the bodies of Thomas, Roger, Richard and Matilda, children of John, son of Hyde, and in their broods.*   19 Dec. 1294

<Quietaclamacio Natiuorum>
Quietaclamacione Iohannis filij Galfridi le Bret facto Ricardo le Northerne totum ius et clamium quod habuit vel aliquo modo habere potuit ratione natiuitatis siue tenementorum in tenementis et in corporibus Thome Rogeri Ricardi et Matild*is* fil' Iohannis filij Hyde et in eorum sequelis procreatis et procreandis et in eorum catallis siue tenementis predicto Ricardo et heredibus suis vel suis assignatis sine aliqua contradiccione seu calumpnis mei vel heredum meorum. Dat' die Dominica proxima ante festum Sancti Thome apostoli anno regni regis Edwardi vicesimo tercio.

NOTE: John son of Hyde may be John Ide (HD 21).

133   *Everard Underhowe of Holkham grants Bartholomew the miller*
1 rood   **20 July 1295**

>   *Original: HP 1014*

Fo. 11   <Caldougate>
Ex feoffamento Eborardi Vndirhowe de Holkham facto Bartholomeo le
[Muner] vnam rodam terre iacentem in camp' de Holkham inter terram
Roberti le Marchal ex parte aquilonali et terram que fuit Willelmi Curthun ex
parte australi cuius caput occidentale abbuttat super Caldowgate reddendo
vnum obolum capitalibus dominis feodi et ad auxilium quando evenerit in
forinseca sokna de Wycton' ad xxs. vnum quadrantem pro omni seruicio.
Dat' die [Sancte Margarete] anno regni regis Edwardi vicessimo tercio.

>   NOTE: See also no. 198.

134   *John, son of Adam le Bret of Holkham, grants Bartholomew the miller*
1 rood.   [c. 1294–6]

>   *Original: HP 1035*

<Schortlond, Caldowgate>
Ex feoffamento Iohannis filio Ade le Bret de Holkham facto Bartholomeo
Molendinario vnam rodam terre quam adquisiuit de Roberto Fulmere [nativo
suo] iacentem in campis de Holcham apud Schortlond inter terram predicti
Bartholomei ex parte australi et terram Iohannis Ayneld ex parte aquilonari et
caput occidentale abbuttat super terram Iohannis Curthun et caput orientale
abbuttat super Caldowgate, reddendo obolum predicto Iohanni filio Ade le
Bret pro omni seruicio. Nulla data.

135   *Robert Fulmer of Holkham quitclaims to Bartholomew the miller*
1 rood.   **18 Oct. 1296**

<Caldowgate>
Ex concessione et quietaclamacione Roberti Fulmer' de Holkham facto
Bartholomeo molendinario totum ius quod habuit in j roda terre iacenti apud
Schortlond inter terram dicti Bartholomei ex parte australi et terra Iohannis
Ayneld ex parte aquilonali caput occidentale abbuttat super terram Iohannis
Curthun caput orientale abbuttat super Caldowgate. Dat' die Sancti Luce
euangeliste anno regni regis Edwardi vicesimo quarto.

>   NOTE: This grant is made by Robert Fulmer who is called *natiuus meus* by John son of
>   Adam le Bret, the lord of the fee, in no. 134.

136   *Thomas, son of John of Holkham, grants Bartholomew, son of Stephen,*
1 plot.   [c. 1291–1300]

Original: HP 1026

Ex feoffamento Thoma filij Iohannis de Holcham facto Bartholomeo filio
Stephani vnam peciam terre iacentem in camp' de Holcham inter terram
Guylde Capenote versus austrum et terram Roberti Fulmer' versus aquilonem
caput orientale abbuttat super regalem viam, reddendo obolum et ad
scutagium domini regis quando euenerit in sokna de Wycton' ad xx s. vnum
quadrans pro omni seruicio. Nulla data.

NOTE: Bartholomew son of Stephen (nos. 136 and 137) may be the same as the
Bartholomew the miller (nos. 133–135). There had been a miller called Stephen (no. 58).

137   *Guylda Capenota of Holkham grants Bartholomew, son of Stephen,*
2 plots.   [c. 1291–1300]

<Schortlond, Dalegatescote>
Ex concessione et feoffamento Guylde Capenote de Holkham facto
Bartholomeo filio Stephani duas pecias terre iacentes in camp' de Holkham
quarum vna pecia iacet apud Schortlond inter terram Thome filij Iohannis ex
parte aquilonali et terram que fuit Galfridi Sutoris ex parte australi et capud
orientale abbuttat super regalem viam et alia pecia iacet inter terram que fuit
Galfridi Sutoris versus austrum et terram qui fuit Gilberti filij Guylde versus
aquilonem et caput orientale abbuttat super Dalegatescote, reddendo vnum
denarium et ad scutagium quando euenerit in forinseca sokna de Wyctone ad
xx s. vnum quadrans pro omni seruicio. Nulla data.

138   *Geoffrey le Bret of Holkham grants Richard de Barking, rector of half*
Holkham church, the land called Goneyswong.   5 Sept. 1293

Cf. HP 1006 and nos. 85 and 139

<Gonyeswong>
Ex feoffamento Galfridi le Bret de Holcham facto Ricardo de Berkyngg'
rectori medietatis ecclesie de Holkham illam peciam terre que vocatur
Gonyeswong quam predictus Ricardus emit de Iohanne filio meo inter terram
Dionisie de Muntchauncy ex parte australi et terram prioris de Wals*ingham*
ex parte aquilonali. Dat' die sabbati proxima ante festum natiuitatis beate
Marie virginis anno regni regis Edwardi vicesimo primo.

NOTE: The grantor is Geoffrey le Bret, the father of John the grantor in no. 85. Both
deeds are of the same date.

139　*Richard de Barking, rector of half church of Egmere, grants Nicholas, son of Aveline of Little Witchingham, 1 plot acquired from John le Bret and Geoffrey his father.*　　　　　5 Dec. 1296

\<Gonyeswong\>

Ex feoffamento Ricardi Berkyng' rectori medietatis ecclesie de Eggemere facto Nicholao filio Aueline de Parua Wychingham vnam peciam terre mee quam adquisiui de Iohanne le Bret et Galfrido patre suo iacentem in camp' de Holcham inter terram Dionisie de Munchansy ex parte australi et terram prioris de Wals*ingham* ex parte aquilonali et abbuttat ad vnum caput super terram prioris de Petirston versus occidentem et aliud caput super terram predicti Iohannis et Galfridi versus orientem et vocatur Gonyeswong. Dat' die sabbati proxima ante festum Sancti Thome Apostoli anno regni regis [Edwardi] filij regis Henrici vicesimo quinto.

> NOTE: Richard de Barking regrants what he had acquired in no. 85 in 1293 from John le Bret and Geoffrey his father three years later. No. 140 explains that this was 9 acres when it is passed to William Craske. William Craske's son grants it to Richard and Caterine Neel on 6 May 1318 no. 164.

140　*Nicholas, son of Richard de Barking, grants William Craske of Holkham 1 plot of 9 acres.*　　　　　[c. 1296–1300]

\<Gonyeswong\>

Ex feoffamento Nicholai filij Ricardi de Berkyng' facto Willelmo Crask*e* de Holkham et heredibus suis vnam peciam terre continentem ix acras terre iacentem in campis eiusdem ville in quarentena vocata Gonyeswong' iuxta partem australem vnius pecie terre quam domina Dionisia de Monte Caniso tenet in dote et terram prioris et conuentus de Wals*ingham* versus aquilonem cuius caput orientale abbuttat super terram quondam Simonis Hammond et caput occidentale super terram prioris et conuentus de Petirston et Willelmi Wake. Nulla data.

> NOTE: This is given by Adam son of William Craske to Richard and Caterine Neel in 1318 (no. 164). Lucas's Gazetteer, no. 260 Fo. 44, describes the area of land as 9 acres.

141　*Matthew the carpenter and his daughter Agnes grant Roger, son of Osbern, 1 plot of 3/4 acre.*　　　　　[?c. 1265]

Fo. 11v　\<Schortlond, Schotowgate\>

Ex feoffamento Mathei Carpentarij facto Rogero filio Osbern et cum Agneta filia dicti Mathei vnam peciam terre iacentem apud Schortlond inter terram Thome de Burgate versus orientem et terram [Henrici Noteman] versus occidentem et caput australe abbuttat super Schotowgate et continet iiij rodas terre, reddendo prefato Matheo tres denarios pro seruiciis. Nulla data.

142 *Richard Thorne of Holkham grants John Cocus of Barney 1 plot.*
[c. 1272–95]

<Adowe, Duuescrundell>
Ex feoffamento Ricardi Thorne de Holcham facto Iohanni Coco de Berneye
vnam peciam terre in campo de Holkham iacentem in quarentena que vocatur
Adowe videlicet inter terram quondam Iohannis Ide ex parte australi et terram
Simonis Hammond ex parte aquilonali et caput orientale abbuttat super
terram Simonis Charle et caput occidentale super viam regalem apud
Duuecrundell, reddendo per annum prefato Ricardo obolum et quando
euenerit auxilium regis etc. pro omnibus seruiciis. Nulla data.

> NOTE: Nos. 142 and 143 relate to the same plot of land. The grantee's widow grants it
> on 30 Oct. 1326 to Richard and Caterine Neel in no. 159.

143 *John le Bret of Holkham grants Edmund de Kettlestone and his wife
Matilda Peper of Holkham 1 plot.*   2 Feb. 1320

<Adowe, Duuescrundell>
Ex feoffamento Iohannis le Bret de Holcham facto Edmundo de Keteleston'
et Matilde Peper vxori sue de Holkham vnam peciam terre iacentis in camp'
de Holkham super vnam quarentenam que vocatur Adow videlicet que^a
impetraui de Iohanne le Cu de Berneye sicut iacet prope terram Willelmi
Roteney per partem aquilonis cuius caput occidentale abbuttat super regalem
viam apud Duuescrundell. Dat' die Sabbati in festo Purificacionis beate Marie
anno regni regis Edwardi terciodecimo.

> NOTE: See no. 142.

144 *Harvey the smith of Holkham and Matilda his wife grant John Aynild
of Holkham 1 plot of 3/4 acre.*   25 Feb. 1345

<Schotowgate, occupatur per Iohannem Bret>
Ex feoffamento Heruei Fabri de Holcham et Matilde vxoris eius facto Iohanni
Ayneld de eadem vnam peciam terre iacentem apud Scothowgate inter terram
dicti Iohannis ex parte orientali et terram Cecilie Sweyn ex parte occidentali
et caput boreale abbuttat super Scothowgate. Dat' die Martis proxima post
carnepriuium anno regni regis Edwardi tercij post conquestum xix° et
continet per nouam cartam iij rodas terre.

> NOTE: John Aynild, the grantee, gives this to Gilbert Neel on 13 September 1345 in no.
> 237, i.e. *before* no. 144.

145 *Godeman Sutor of Holkham grants Margery, widow of William Craske,*
1/2 rood. 21 Feb. 1309

Original: HD 23

<Adowe>
Ex feoffamento Godemanni Sutoris de Holkham facto Margerie quondam
vxoris Willelmi Crask*e* vnam dimidiam rodam terre iacentem in campo de
Holcham in quadem quarentena que vocatur Adowe inter terram Thome
Crask*e* ex parte aquilonali et terram Henrici Dauyd ex parte australi et caput
orientale abbuttat super terram que quondam fuit Simonis Charle et caput
occidentale abbutat super Adowegate. Dat' die Veneris proxima ante festum
Sancti Mathei apostoli anno regni regis Edwardi secundo.

146 *Humphrey, son of David and Amice his wife of Holkham, grants*
William Craske 2 plots. [c. 1284]

Original: HP 1066

<Dalegate, Adowe>
Ex feoffamento Humfredi filij Dauid et Amicie vxoris eius de Holkham facto
Willelmo Crask*e* duas pecias terre iacentem in campo de Holkham quarum
vna pecia iacet inter terram Gilberti Ayneld ex parte aquilonali et abbuttat
versum orientem super Dalegate. Et alia pecia iacet apud Adowe inter terram
Bartholomei de Burgate ex parte australi et terram Iohannis Rutele ex parte
aquilonali et abbuttat versus occidentem super Adowegate reddendo prefato
Humfredo duos denarios et scutagium. Nulla data.

147 *Geoffrey le Bret of Holkham grants Simon, son of Hamo of Holkham,*
a plot of 13/4 acres. [c. 1283–93]

Original: HP 1029

<Endaker>
Ex feoffamento Galfridi le Bret de Holkham facto Simoni filio Hamonis de
eadem vnam peciam terre que vocatur Endaker continentem vnam acram et
dimidiam et vnam rodam iacentem in campo de Holkham inter terram abbatis
de Derham ex parte australi et terram prioris de Wal*singham* ex parte
aquilonali et caput orientale abbuttat super viam que vocatur Crekgate et
caput occidentale abbuttat super terram prioris de Wal*singham*, reddendo
prefato Galfrido jd. et ad sc*u*tagium pro omnibus seruiciis etc. Nulla data.

148　*Simon Mous of Holkham and Cecily his wife grant William Horsford, rector of St. John Baptist in Stiffkey, and Robert atte Milne of Wighton 1¹/₂ acres in 2 plots.*　21 April 1335

<terra abb*uttat* super terram Andree Vnderclynt apud West Scamelond>
Ex feoffamento Simonis Mous de Holkham et Cicilie vxoris eius facto domino Willelmo Horsforde rectori ecclesie Sancti Iohannis Baptiste de Stivekeye et Roberto atte Milne de Wighton' duas pecias terre iacentes in camp' de Holkham quarum vna pecia vnius acre iacet iuxta terram Andree Vnderklint ex parte boriali et caput orientale abbuttat super terram Iohannis Meye. Et alia pecia dimidia acre iacet inter terram Iohannis atte Droue ex parte orientali et terram Robert Wrighte ex [parte] occidentali et caput austral abbuttat super terram Willelmi filij Thome. Dat' die Veneris proxima post festum Tiburti et Valeriani anno regni regis Edwardi tercij ix°.

149　*Thomas, son of Henry Leffe of Holkham, grants to William, the clerk of Holkham, 1 plot.*　[c. 1283–93]

　　Original: HP 1000. Cf. no. 199

Fo. 12　Ex feoffamento Thome filij Henrici Le[ffe] de Holkham facto Willelmi clerico de Holcham vnam peciam terre iacentem in camp' de Holkham inter terram Reginaldi Osmod ex parte australi et terram Gilberti Sutoris de Westgate ex parte aquil*onari* et abbuttat super terram prioris de Wals*ingham* versus orientem et super Thor*peme*re versus occidentem, reddendo prefato Thome j d. pro omnibus seruiciis. Nulla data.

　　NOTE: William le Clerk grants this land to Richard and Caterine Neel in no. 199.

Liberty of Homage of Akeny in Holkham.

150　*Charter of Thomas son of Baldwin de Akeny referring to inquisition (1274–5) about services and customs of his men in Holkham which used to be in royal hands. Thomas ratifies these customs. They and their heirs may have these customs forever with release from the suits of the mill for which he had sued them.*　[c. 1275–80]

COPIA CARTE THOME FILII BALDEWYNI DE AKENY

<Libertas homagij Dakeny in Holkham> [left margin]
<Libertas homagij de Akeny> [right margin]
Data per copiam. Omnibus Christi fidelibus hoc scriptum visuris vel audituris

Thomas filius Baldewyni de Akeny salutem in domino. Quia intellexi per inquisicionem nuper factum anno regni regis Edwardi tercio per breue eiusdem domini regis per Willelmum de Aungr', Ricardum le Cheuer', Iohannem le Ray, Iohannem Grene, Herueum Buleman, Willelmum Charles de hundredo de Galehothe, Adam Crabbe, Bertram le Nuiun, Radulfum de Reydham, Iohannem de Warham, Galfridum Godwyne et Gilbertum Payn de hundredo de Northgrenhooh de seruiciis et consuetudinibus hominum meorum in Holkham qui solebant esse in manibus predecessorum dicti domini regis Anglie: qui iurati dixerunt per sacramentum suum quod dicti homines mei tempore quo fuerunt in manibus predecessorum dicti domini regis facere consueuerunt preter redditum assisum de seruiciis et consuetudinibus scilicet pro releuiis terrarum suarum post mortem antecessorum suorum debet quilibet quantum reddit per annum de redditu assiso. Item pro allegianciis liberorum si extra manerium maritare debent dabunt decem solidos argenti ad plus et minus secundum eorum facultates. Si infra manerium dabunt quinque solidos forma predicta. Item habebunt collectores annuatim tantum de dicto homagio meo. Item quando dominus rex talliat burgos suos vel ciuitates ita quod manerium de Wyghton per breue domini regis tunc talliatur debent talliari. Item debent venire apud Kyngggishil ad tres curias per annum que vocantur Laghedayes. Item vnusquisque anlepiman dabit per annum denarium et obolum pro cheuagio. Et ego predictus Thomas pro me et heredibus meis omnia predicta ratificans et concedens hoc scripto meo confirmaui predictis hominibus meis quod ipsi et eorum heredes vel assignati eorum filij et filie ista seruicia et consuetudines habeant et teneant imperpetuum vna cum relaxacione sectarum molendini quam ab eis faciendum calumpniaui. Ita quod nec ego nec heredes mei nec aliquis nomine nostro decetero alia seruicia vel consuetudines de predictis hominibus et eorum heredibus vel assignatis exigere vel vendicare poterimus imperpetuum. In cuius rei testimonium huic scripto sigillum meum apposui. Hiis testibus. Radulfo Hacoun . Galfrido le Bret de Holkham . Bartholomeo de Burgate . Iohanne filio Ade le Bret . Bertrammo le Nuioun . Iohanne filio Galfridi de Warham . Bartholomeo filio Simonis . Ricardo Mundy . Petro ad molendinum de Wichton*e* . Ricardo Curben . Radulfo de Styweky . Adam de Nouer's . Michaele le Bret . Galfrido Godewyne . Gilberto Payn . Galfrido de Bretaine et aliis.

NOTE: The marginal captions are in both margins. This relates to the manor of Hillhall. This and no. 151 are the first charters for which the names of witnesses have been transcribed. They conclude the first part of the cartulary. Witnesses are also given for no. 250 in the second part. Kynggishil has not been found in later Holkham documents. It may have become Hill Hall, the d'Akeny Manor house at the west end of Holkham Hall.

151   *Peter le Bret and Baldwin de Akeny, knight, agree that Peter and his heirs granted Baldwin and his heirs 1 plot 5 perches wide and 13 perches long. Baldwin de Akeny granted Peter le Bret a plot in exchange and agreed that his heirs and men be quit of all tonnages in his market and his fair in Holkham.*   [c. 1260–79]

\<Conuencio Akeny\>

Hec est conuencio facta inter Petrum le Bret ex vna parte et dominum Baudewynum de Akeny militem ex altera videlicet quod dictus Petrus concessit pro se et heredibus suis imperpetuum dicto domino Baudewyne et heredibus suis vnam peciam cum pertinenciis iacentem iuxta quamdam viam que vocatur Hadowgate et continet in se in latitudine quinque perticatas et in longitudine tresdecim perticatas et abbuttat super viam regalem versus aquilonem et caput australe abbuttat super terram predicti Petri le Bret: ita quod dictus dominus Baudewynus concessit dicto Petro pro se et heredibus suis imperpetuum vnam peciam terre cum pertinenciis in escambio iacentem iuxta cruftam quondam Dauyd le Klynt versus austrum et caput orientale abbuttat super Hogate. Et vt ista concessio rata et stabilis permaneat prenominatus Baudwynus concessit prefato Petro et heredibus suis et omnibus homagiis suis sibi pertinentibus in villa de Holkham esse solut' et quiet' de omnibus tonnagiis in mercato meo et feriam in Holkham imperpetuum. In huius rei testimonium presenti scripto ad modum cirographi confecto alter alteri scripto sigillum suum apposuit. Hiis testibus. Radulfo Hacoun . Ada le Bret . Bartholomeo de Burgate . Roberto de Warfeles . Iohanne Goldewyne . Euerardo le Kayly . Nicholao de Warfeles et aliis.

Fo. 12v   [blank]

Fos. 13–24   Neel Purchases

(Quire 2) **Fo. 13**

COPIA CARTARUM DE PERQUISICIONE RICARDI NEEL DE HOLKHAM ET KATERINE VXORIS EIUS THOME NEEL ET GILBERTI FILIORUM PREDICTORUM RICARDI ET KATERINE

> NOTE: Many of the following copies were numbered by Edmund Lucas in the right margin and the numbers not only entered in the margin of the cartulary but also on the original documents, many of which survive in the series.

152   *Lordship of Bret in Holkham Surlingham and Swainsthorpe. Peter, son of Geoffrey le Bret of Holkham, grants Richard Neel of Burnham and Caterine his wife all homages, services and burdens, of all his tenants.*
16 July 1329

\<Neel\>
\<examinatur, Dominium de Bret in Holkham Surlingham et Sweynesthorpe\>
Ex feoffamento Petri filij Galfridi le Bret de Holkham facto Ricardo Neel de Brunham et Caterine vxori eius omnia et singula homagia seruicia et onera omnium et singulorum tenencium meorum de feodo et dominio meo cum suis pertinenciis in villis de Holkham Surlyngham et Sweynethorp' vt in redditibus sectis scutagiis et omnibus aliis redditibus seruiciis et oneribus simul cum wardis releuiis marritagiis escaetis et omnibus aliis proficuis et appruamentis ad huiusmodi feodum [et] dominium meum pertinentibus et michi qualitercumque spectantibus absque omni inde retenemento mei vel heredum meorum decetero imperpetuum. Dat' apud Holkham die dominica proxima ante festum Sancte Margarete Virginis anno regni regis Edwardi tercij post conquestum tercio.

> NOTE: Lucas 1. Peter le Bret held for 1/4 knight's fee 100 acres in Holkham, Swainsthorpe and Surlingham (Norfolk) according to Burghall rental, no. 255.

153   *Richard, son of Simon the smith of Holkham, grants Thomas Neel of Holkham 1 plot of 11/2 roods.*   18 March 1345

\<Adowe\>
Ex feoffamento Ricardi filij Simonis fabri de Holkham facto Thome Neel de eadem vnam peciam terre mee cum pertinenciis iacentem in campis de Holkham apud Adowgate continentem vnam rodam et dimidiam siue habeatur in dicta pecia maius siue minus et iacet inter terram Iohannis Treupage ex parte australi et terram predicti Thome Neel ex parte aquilonali et caput orientale abbuttat super communem viam que ducit de Holkham vsque ad

Qwarles. Dat' apud Holkham die Veneris in festo Sancti Edwardi regis et martiris anno regni regis Edwardi tercij post conquestum nonodecimo.

NOTE: Lucas 2. Cross-reference in Lucas's Gazetteer no. 260 Fo. 41.

154   *Adam, son of William Craske of Holkham, grants Richard Neel of Burnham and Katerine his wife 1 plot of 13/4 acres.*   **29 Oct. 1326**

Original: HP 1075

<Longe Adowe>
Ex feoffamento Ade filij Willelmi Craske de Holkham facto Ricardo Neel de Brunham et Katerine vxori eius vnam peciam terre cum pertinenciis in Holkham que continet in se vnam acram et tres rodas et iacet apud Hadehowe inter terram predicti Ricardi ex parte australi et terram Iohannis Rutele ex parte aquilonali et abbuttat versus occidentem super Hadehogate. Dat' apud Holkham die Mercurij proxima post festum apostolorum Simonis et Iude anno regni regis Edwardi filij Edwardi vicesimo.

NOTE: Lucas 3. Cross-reference in Lucas's Gazetteer no. 260, Fo.41.

155   *Cecily Hammond jun. of Holkham grants Richard Neel of Burnham and Katerine his wife 11/2 roods and the reversion of 11/2 roods.*
25 Aug. 1332

<Hangande Adowe>
Ex feoffamento Cicilie Hamond iunioris de Holkham facto Ricardo Neel de Brunham et Katerine vxori eius vnam rodam et dimidiam iacentem in camp' de Holkham apud Hangandehadhowe inter terram Simonis atte Cros ex parte orientali et terram predicti Ricardi ex parte occidentali vna cum reuersione vnius rode terre et dimidie post mortem Agnetis matris mee quam tenet in dote et iacet in campo de Holkham in loco predicto iuxta terram predicti Ricardi ex parte occidentali cuius caput boriale abbuttat super terram predicti Ricardi. Dat' die Martis proxima post festum Sancti Bartholomei apostoli anno regni regis Edwardi tercij post conquestum vj^{to}.

NOTE: Lucas 4. Cross-reference in Lucas's Gazetteer no. 260 Fo. 44v.

156   *Adam, son of Simon Hamond, grants Richard Neel of Burnham and Katerine his wife 5 acres in 4 plots.*   **5 Nov. 1314**

Original: HP 1051

Fo. 13v   <examinatur, Steynhil, Aldelose, Adowbotme, Dalegate>
Ex feoffamento Ade filij Simonis Hamond facto Ricardo Neel de Brunham et Katerine vxoris eius quinque acras terre cum pertinenciis in Holkham prout

iacet in diuersis peciis videlicet apud Steynhil, Aldelose, Hadehowbotme et apud Dalegate. Dat' die Martis proxima post festum Omnium Sanctorum anno regni regis Edwardi filij regis [Edwardi] octauo.

NOTE: Lucas 5. Cross-reference in Lucas's Gazetteer no. 260 Fo. 41. The Gazetteer reads *Edwardi secondi viij*°. The original reads *Edwardi filij Regis Edwardi octauo*.

157 *Simon atte Cruche and Cecily his wife grant Richard Neel and Katerine his wife 1¹/₄ acres in 2 plots and the reversion of 1¹/₂ roods.*

21 Dec. 1332

\<Greiston, Thorpgate, Hangande Adowe\>
Ex feoffamento Simonis atte Cruche et Cecilie vxoris sue facto Ricardo Neel et Katerine vxoris eius duas pecias terre iacentes in campo de Holkham quarum vna iacet apud Greyston iuxta terram dicti Ricardi ex parte aquilon*ali* et terram Rogeri le Reue ex parte australi et continet tres rodas terre et dimidiam cuius caput occidentale abbuttat super Thorp'gate: altera pecia iacet sub Hangandhowe et continet in se vnam rodam terre et dimidiam vna cum reuersione vnius rode terre et dimidie iuxta terram dicti Ricardi ex parte occidentali et terram Rogeri le Reue ex parte orientali abbuttat super illam versus orientem quam quidem rodam terre et dimidiam Agnes Hamond nouerca predicte Cecilie tenet in dote. Dat' apud Holkham in festo Sancti Thome apostoli. Anno regni regis Edwardi tercij post conquestum sexto.

NOTE: Lucas 6. Cross-reference in Lucas's Gazetteer, no. 260 Fos. 50, 44, 44v.

158 *Margery, widow of William Craske of Holkham, grants Richard Neel of Burnham and Katerine his wife 1/₂ acre.*

20 Dec. 1327

Original: HD 33

\<Longe Adowe\>
Ex feoffamento Margerie quondam vxoris Willelmi Crask*e* de Holkham facto Ricardo Neel de Brunham et Katerine vxoris eius vnam dimidiam acram terre in Holkham et iacet apud Hadowe iuxta terram Rogeri le Wrytte ex parte australi et capud occidentale abbuttat super Hadowgate. Dat' apud Holkham in vigilia Sancti Thome apostoli anno regni regis Edwardi tercij post conquestum primo.

NOTE: Lucas 7. Cross reference in Lucas's Gazetteer no. 260 Fo. 41. Same dates for grants by mother, no. 158, and son, no. 185.

159   *Matilda Peper of Holkham, widow of Edmund de Kettlestone, grants Richard Neel of Burnham and Katerine his wife 1 rood.*   30 Oct. 1326

<Longe Adowe, Duuescrundell>

Ex feoffamento Matild*is* Peper de Holkham quondam vxoris Edmundi de Keteleston' facto Ricardo Neel de Brunham et Katerine vxori eius vnam rodam terre in campis de Holkham super vnam quarentenam que vocatur Hadowe iuxta terram dicti Ricardi ex parte boriali cuius caput occidentale abbuttat super regalem viam apud Duuecrundell. Dat' apud Holkham die Iouis proxima post festum apostolorum Simonis et Iude anno regni regis Edwardi filij regis Edwardi vicesimo.

NOTE: Lucas 8. Cross-reference in Lucas's Gazetteer no. 260 Fo. 41. Matilda Peper and her husband obtained this land on 2 Feb. 1285 (no. 143).

160   *Simon atte Cros and Cecily his wife of Warham grant Katerine, widow of Richard Neel of Burnham, 1/2 acre in 2 plots*   29 Nov. 1337

<Cleylond, Grenegate, Rusteshowe, Marketst(y)>

Ex feoffamento Simonis atte Cros et Cecilie vxoris eius de Warram facto Katerine [quondam] vxori Ricardi Neel de Brunham duas pecias terre iacentes in camp' de Holkham quarum j pecia vnius rode et dimidie iacet apud Cleylond iuxta terram dicte Katerine ex parte occidentali et caput australe abbuttat super Grenegate. Alia pecia dimidie rode iacet apud Rusteshowe iuxta terram predicte Katerine ex parte occidentali et caput boriale abbuttat super le Markesty atte Howe. Dat' apud Holkham in vigilia Sancti Andree anno regni regis Edwardi tercij post conquestum xj°.

NOTE: Lucas 9. Cross-reference in Lucas's Gazetteer no. 260 Fos. 41, 49. In 1451-2 the Neel Terrier includes 1/2 rood at Rustes[howe] abutting on Marketsty at le Howe and 11/2 roods at Cleylond next land of Caterine Neel abutting on Grengate (S), HD 128.

161   *Thomas, son of Richard le Northerne, grants Katerine, widow of Richard Neel of Burnham, 13/4 acres and also 51/2 acres in 4 plots. Thomas Palmer of Burnham Norton releases to Henry Jolif of Holkham 1 plot given by Gilbert Neel.*   20 July 1336 and 24 Feb. 1372

   Originals: HP 1091 and HP 1110 (not printed)

<[Cl]aylond, examinatur, Dalegate, Caldhowe, Bramlond, Wellegate>

Ex feoffamento Thome filii Ricardi Northerne facto Katerine que fuit vxor Ricardi Neel de Brunham quod vna acra et tres rode terre quas Willelmus Wake tenet in Holkham ex dimissione Ele que fuit vxor Bertholomei de Burgate ad terminum vite eiusdem Ele et quas eadem Ela prius tenuit in dotem de Hereditate mea apud Claylond cum pertinenciis in Holkham et que post decessum eiusdem Ele ad prefatum Thomam filium Ricardi Northerne et heredibus ipsius Thome reuerti debuerunt post mortem

Fo. 14 eiusdem Ele prefate Katerine quiete integre remaneant. Concessi etiam prefate Katerine Neel quinque acras et dimidiam terre iacentes in quatuor peciis et in seysina eiusdem Katerine adhuc existentes vt illas quas prius habuit de dono et feoffamento meo cum pertinenciis in Holkham quarum vna pecia duarum acrarum et dimidie iacet apud Dalegate iuxta terram quondam Iohannis Tuber versus boream. Alia pecia vnius acre et vnius rode iacet apud Caldhowe iuxta terram domini prioris de Peterston versus boream. Tercia pecia dimidia acre iacet similiter ibidem iuxta terram Walteri Osbem' versus boream . Quarta pecia vnius acre et vnius rode iacet apud Bramlond iuxta terram domini prioris predicti versus occidentem. Dat' apud Holkham in festo Sancte Margarete Virginis anno regni regis Edwardi tercij post conquestum decimo. Et sequitur relaxacio Thome Palmer' de Brunham Norton' facto Henrico Iolif de Holkham de vna pecia terre quam habuit ex dono et feoffamento Gilberti Neel iacentem in Holkham apud Wellegate iuxta terram Hugonis Smyth' de Welles ex occidente et terram Iohannis Manaunt de Holkham ex parte orientali. Dat' apud Brunham Norton' die Martis proxima post festum Sancti Petri in cathedra anno regni regis Edwardi tercij xlvjto.

NOTE: Lucas 10. Cross-references in Lucas's Gazetteer no. 260 Fos. 41v, 42. Cf. no. 187. See no. 162 note. We do not print HP 1110.

162   *Thomas, son of Richard le Northerne of Holkham, grants Caterine, widow of Richard Neel of Burnham 9½ acres in 5 plots.*   18 Jan. 1336

Original: HP 1087

\<Cleylond, Wellegate, Daulyn\>
Ex feoffamento Thome filij Ricardi le Northerne de Holkham facto Caterine que fuit vxori Ricardi Neel de Brunham quinque pecias terre iacentes in camp' de Holkham apud Cleyelond quarum vna pecia que continet tres acras terre et dimidiam iacet inter terram quondam Iohannis Ayneld ex parte occidentali et terram Gilberti Calewer ex parte orientali cuius caput boriale abbuttat super terram quondam Iohannis Charle. Alia pecia terre iacet ad caput australe earundem inter terram Radulfi Grigge ex parte occidentali et terram Clericie de Howgate ex parte orientali et caput boreale abbuttat super terram eiusdem Thome et continet in se septem rodas terre. Tercia pecia iacet fere ibidem inter terram Thome Escher' ex parte occidentali et terram heredum Willelmi Cat ex parte orientali cuius caput australe abbuttat super terram abbatis et conuentus de Creyke et continet in se septem rodas terre. Quarta pecia continet in se vnam acram terre iacentem prope ibidem inter terram Iohannis Spellere ex parte orientali et terram Iohannis Daulyn ex parte occidentali cuius caput boreale abbuttat super Wellegate. Quinta pecia iacet

ibidem inter terram Roberti Andrehu ex parte orientali et terram quondam Roberti Mayn ex parte occidentali cuius caput boriale abbuttat super Wellega*t*e et continet in se vnam acram terre et dimidiam. Dat' apud Holkham xv kalendas Februarij anno regni regis Edwardi tercij post conquestum nono.

NOTE: Lucas 11. Five cross-references in Lucas's Gazetteer no. 260 Fo. 42. Nos. 161 and 162 are both quoted in Neel court roll of 22 Oct. 1449, HD 194a, as part of the title to the land occupied by Juliana Patryk and John Newgate (19 acres 1 rood). It also quotes no. 167 (33 ac. 1 rood), against which an index hand is drawn in the cartulary. Distraint is taken on Patryk and Newgate to show their title. Cf. no. 187.

163 *William Wake of Holkham recites above, and by virtue of a grant from Thomas, son of Richard Northerne of Holkham, to Caterine Neel, attorns her.*
22 July 1336

Original: HP 1092

<examinatur, Cleylond>

Vniuersis presens scriptum visuris vel audituris Willelmus Wake de Holkham salutem in domino. Cum Thomas filius Ricardi Northerne de Holkham nuper per cartam suam concesserit Caterine que fuit vxor Ricardi Neel de Brunham quod vna acra et tres rode terre quas ego teneo ad totam vitam Ele que fuit vxor Bartholomei de Burgate ex dimissione eiusdem Ele et quas eadem Ela prius tenuit de hereditate predicti Thome in dotem apud Cleylond cum pertinenciis in Holkham et que post decessum eiusdem Ele ad prefatum Thomam et heredes reuerti debuerunt post mortem eiusdem Ele prefate Caterine quiete et integre remaneant habend' et tenend' prefate Caterine heredibus et assignatis suis imperpetuum: noueritis quod ego virtute concessionis predicte Thome predicte Caterine me attornaui et ei feci fidelitatem de essendo eidem Caterine heredibus et assignatis suis de cetero intendens vt eorum tenens de tenemento predicto in forma predicta. Dat' apud Holkham die Lune in festo Sancte Marie Magdalene anno regni regis Edwardi tercij post conquestum decimo.

NOTE: Lucas 12. Cross-reference in Lucas's Gazetteer no. 260 Fo. 42. The particulars about Ela are recited in no. 187 called Thomas Northern's 'charter' by William Wake in HP 1092. Ela daughter of Thomas le Northerne married first Bartholomew de Burgate and then (before 1336) William Wake.

164   *Adam, son of William Craske of Holkham, grants Richard Neel of Burnham and Caterine his wife 1 plot of 9 acres.*   17 Sept. 1317

Fo. 14v   <Gonyeswong>
Ex feoffamento Ade filij Willelmi Craske de Holkham facto Ricardo Neel de Brunham et Caterine vxori sue vnam peciam terre iacentem in camp' de Holkham inter terram domini Heymeri le Walawns ex parte australi et terram prioris de Wals*ingham* ex parte aquilon*ali* et vnum caput abbuttat super terram prioris de Petra versus occidentem et aliud caput super terram quondam Galfridi le Bret versus orientem et vocatur Gunyeswong. Dat' apud Holkham die Sabbati proxima post festum Sancte Crucis in autumpno anno regni regis Edwardi filij regis Edwardi vndecimo et continet ix acras terre.

> NOTE: Lucas 13. Cross-reference in Lucas's Gazetteer no. 260 Fo. 44. This describes the land as 9 acres. William Craske received 9 acres in furlong called Gonyeswong from Nicholas son of Richard of Barking in no. 140. For le Walawns see note on Aymer de Valence, lord of Burghall, on no. 177.

165   *Richard Silk of Holkham and Cecily his wife grant Richard Neel of Burnham and Katerine his wife 3 acres.*   14 Dec. 1318

<Bondeswong>
Ex feoffamento Ricardi Silk*e* de Holkham et Cecilie vxoris eius facto Ricardo Neel de Brunham et Katerine vxori sue tres acras terre iacentes in camp' de Holkham apud Bondescroft inter terram Iohannis de la Dale ex parte aquilon*ali* et terram Iohannis Wrighte ex parte australi et caput occidentale abbuttat super regiam viam caput orientale super terram nostram. Dat' apud Holkham die Iouis proxima post festum Sancte Lucie Virginis anno regni regis Edwardi filij regis Edwardi duodecimo.

> NOTE: Lucas 14. Cross-reference in Lucas's Gazetteer no. 260 Fo. 41v. The location is there called Bondescroft, as in the deed, not Bondeswong. Land within it consisted of strips with different occupiers. This was the condition of land in other crofts and meant that, whatever the croft may have been originally, it had become indistinguishable from any furlong or 'wong'.

166   *Adam, son of William Craske of Holkham, grants Richard Neel of Burnham and Caterine his wife 6 acres in 2 plots.*   12 April 1318

Original: HP 1004

<Wodegate, Wardehowe>
Ex feoffamento Ade filij Willelmi Crask' de Holkham facto Ricardo Neel de Brunham et Caterine vxori sue sex acras terre iacentem in Camp' de

Holkham videlicet apud Wodegate tres acras terre et apud Warldhowh' tres acras terre. Dat' apud Holkham die Mercurie proxima ante dominicam Ram' palmarum anno regni regis Edwardi vndecimo.

NOTE: Lucas 15. Cross-reference in Lucas's Gazetteer no. 260 Fo. 50v. The hand of HP 1004 is the same as that of 1065, 1068 and 1070 which are all of 1319 and 1320. The witnesses of 1004 suggest a similar date.

167 *Adam Craske of Holkham grants Richard Neel of Burnham and Caterine his wife 2 plots.* 6 June 1329

Original: *HP 1076*

<examinatur, Dalegate>
Ex feoffamento Ade Craske de Holkham facto Ricardo Neel de Brunham et Caterine vxoris eius duas pecias terre iacentes apud Dalegate cum pertinenciis in Holkham quarum vna iacet iuxta terram predictorum Ricardi et Caterine ex parte australi et alia iuxta eamdem terram eorum ex parte boriali. Dat' apud Holkham vj^{to} die Iunij a° regni regis Edwardi tercij post conquestum tercio.

NOTE: Lucas 16. Cross-reference in Lucas's Gazetteer no. 260 Fo. 42v. Original document, HP 1076, reads *terre mee iacentes.*

168 *Adam Craske of Holkham grants Richard Neel of Burnham and Katerine his wife 3 acres in 2 plots.* 18 June 1333

<Dalegate, inquiratur, Caldehowgate>
Ex feoffamento Ade Craske de Holkham facto Ricardo Neel de Brunham et Katerine vxoris eius duas pecias terre iacentes in camp' de Holkham quarum vna pecia que continet vnam acram terre et plus iacet apud Dalegate inter terram Iohannis Tuber ex parte vna et terram prioris de Walsingham ex altera parte cuius caput occidentale abbuttat super Dalegate. Alia pecia \inquiratur/ terre iacet apud Caldehowgate inter terram Iohannis Tuber ex parte vna et terram Walteri Bolewar' ex parte altera que continet in se duas acras et caput occidentale abbuttat super Caldehowgat'. Dat' apud Holkham xiiij kalend' Iulij anno regni regis Edwardi tercij post conquestum septimo.

NOTE: Lucas 17. Cross-reference in Lucas's Gazetteer no. 260 Fo. 42v (first piece) and 42 (second piece). The corresponding letter of attorney dated 18 June 1333 is HP 1081.

169   *Adam Craske of Holkham grants Richard Neel of Burnham and Katerine his wife 31/2 acres in 2 plots, of which one of 21/2 acres is a headland.*   5 Oct. 1319

Original: HP 1065

<[St]eynhill, [Bi]l[e]smer, Qwarlesgate>
Ex feoffamento Ade Craske de Holkham facto Ricardo Neel de Brunham et Katerine vxori eius tres acras terre et dimidiam iacentem in camp' de Holkham in diuersis peciis videlicet apud Steynhil duas acras et dimidiam terre iuxta terram Bartholomei filij Maddi de Campo ex parte occidentali et est vna forera. Et apud Billesmere vnam acram terre inter terram predicti Ricardi et terram Elueue Dalman et caput occidentale abbuttat super Quarlesgate. Dat' apud Holkham die Veneris proxima post festum Sancti Michaelis Archangeli anno regni regis Edwardi filij regis Edwardi terciodecimo.

NOTE: Lucas 18. Cross-reference in Lucas's Gazetteer no. 260 Fos. 41v, 48v, 49v.

170   *Joan, widow of Adam Craske of Holkham grants Caterine Neel of Holkham 1 plot of 3 acres.*   20 Nov. 1336

Fo. 15   <inquiratur, Dalegate>
Ex feoffamento Iohanne que fuit vxoris Ade Craske de Holkham facto Caterine Neel de Holkham vnam peciam trium acrarum terre iacentem apud Dalegate cum pertinenciis in Holkham inter terram prioris de Walsyingham ex parte australi et terram prioris de Petra*ston* ex parte boriali et caput occidentale abbuttat super terram predicte Caterine. Dat' apud Holkham vicesimo die Nouembris anno regni regis Edwardi tercij post conquestum decimo.

NOTE: Lucas 19. Cross-reference in Lucas's Gazetteer no. 260 Fo. 42v.

171   *Adam Craske of Holkham grants Richard Neel of Burnham and Katerine his wife 1 plot.*   13 Nov. 1332

<Collesmer, Caldowgate>
Ex feoffamento Ade Craske de Holkham facto Ricardo Neel de Brunham et Katerine vxori eius vnam peciam terre iacentem in camp' de Holkham apud Collemer inter terram predicti Ricardi ex parte aquilon' et terram Willelmi Grys ex parte australi et caput occidentale abbuttat super Caldhowgate. Dat' apud Holkham die Veneris proxima post festum Sancti Martini anno regni regis Edwardi tercij post conquestum sexto.

NOTE: Lucas 20. Cross-reference in Lucas's Gazetteer no. 260 Fo. 42.

172   *Gilbert Silk of Holkham grants Richard Neel and Caterine his wife of Burnham Norton 13/4 acres in 2 plots.*   31 March 1317

<Goldewynescroft>
Ex feoffamento Gilberti Silk de Holkham facto Ricardo Neel et Caterine vxori eius de Brunham Norton' duas pecias terre iacentes in camp' de Holkham quarum vna pecia terre iacet inter terram quondam Gilberti Edwich ex parte australi et terram Henrici Anger' ex parte boriali et caput occidentale abbuttat super croftam Martini Goldewyne et continet in se tres rodas et dimidiam. Alia pecia iacet inter terram Ade Silk' versus aquilonem et terram Edmundi Athelwald versus australe et continet in se tres rodas terre et dimidiam. Dat' apud Holkham die Cene anno regni regis Edwardi filij regis Edwardi decimo.

NOTE: Lucas 21. Cross-reference in Lucas's Gazetteer no. 260 Fo. 44. The foundation of the priory of Peterstone, the only friary (Austin) between Lynn and Yarmouth, suggests the relative commercial importance of Burnham in the thirteenth century.

173   *Richard Payn of Holkham grants Richard Neel of Burnham and Katerine his wife 1 headland.*   [c. 1318]

Original: HD 19

<Goldewyne>
Ex feoffamento Ricardi Payn de Holkham facto Ricardo Neel de Brunham et Katerine vxori eius vnam peciam terre iacentem in campis de Holkham et est vna forera et iacet iuxta terram Iohannis Goldewen' ex parte occidentali. Nulla data.

NOTE: Lucas 22. This is not the headland next to John Goldewyne's land in no. 75 given to Richard Payn for that is on the east as is repeated in Lucas's Gazetteer no. 260 Fo. 44.

174   *Simon Mous of Kettlestone and Cecily his wife grant Katerine, widow of Richard Neel of Burnham, 1/2 acre.*   9 Feb. 1336

Original: HP 1084

<Schamelond>
Ex feoffamento Simonis Mous de Ketelston' et Cecilie vxoris sue facto Katerine que fuit vxor Ricardi Neel de Brunham vnam dimidiam acram terre iacentem in camp' de Holkham apud Schamelond inter terram Rogeri Carpentarij ex parte occidentali et terram Iohannis Mey ex parte orientali cuius caput australe abbuttat super terram Willelmi filij Alicie. Dat' apud Holkham nono die Februarij anno regni regis Edwardi tercij post conquestum decimo.

NOTE: Lucas 23. Cross-reference in Lucas's Gazetteer no. 260 Fos. 41v, 49v. See also no. 232.

175   Roger Heyward of Holkham grants Richard Neel of Burnham and
Katerine his wife 1 plot.   17 May 1317

Original: HD 27

<Billesmere, Qwarlesgate>
Ex feoffamento Rogeri Heyward de Holkham facto Ricardo Neel de Brunham
et Katerine vxori eius vnam peciam terre iacentem in camp' de Holkham
apud Billesmere inter terram abbatis de Creyke ex parte australi et caput
occidentale abbuttat super Qwarlesgate. Dat' apud Holkham die Martis
proxima post festum Assencionis anno regni regis Edwardi filij regis Edwardi
decimo.

NOTE: Lucas 24. Cross-reference in Lucas's Gazetteer no. 260 Fos. 41v, 48v.

176   Rose, widow of Elias Crane of Holkham, grants Richard Neel of
Burnham and Katerine his wife 1 1/2 roods and the reversion of 1 1/2 roods.
                                                             11 May 1322

Original: HD 30

<Wyghtongate>
Ex feoffamento Rose vxoris quondam Helie Crane de Holkham facto Ricardo
Neel de B[runham] et Katerine vxori eius vnam rodam et dimidiam terre cum
reuersione vnius rode et dimidie terre quam mater mea Sibilla Buleman tenet
de me nomine dotis iacentem in ead[em villa] de Holkham inter terram
predicti Ricardi ex parte orientali et terram quondam Heruei Bule[man] ex
parte occidentali et caput australe abbuttat super regiam viam que ducit [de]
Wycton' versus Brunham. Dat' apud Holkham die Martis proxima post
festum Iohannis ante portam latinam anno regni regis Edwardi filij regis
Edwardi quintodecimo.

NOTE: Lucas 25. Not identified in Edmund Lucas's Gazetteer.

177   Bartholomew, son of Robert of Holkham, grants Richard Neel of
Holkham and Katerine his wife 1 plot.   20 Aug. 1322

Original: HP 1005

Fo. 15v   <Steynhil>
Ex feoffamento Bartholomei filij Roberti de Holkham facto Ricardo Neel de
eadem et Katerine vxori eius vnam peciam terre iacentem apud Steynhil inter
terram predictorum Ricardi et Katerine et caput aquilonare abbuttat super
terram domini Adomari de Valencia. Dat' die Veneris proxima [post] festum
assumpcionis beate Marie anno regni regis Edwardi sextodecimo.

NOTE: Lucas 26. Cross-reference in Lucas's Gazetteer no. 260 Fo. 49. Aymer de
Valence succeeded to Denise de Montchesney's estates in 1313 and died in 1324, Farrer,
vol. iii, p. 108. The gazetteer wrongly reads *Edwardi primi 16*.

178   *Lawrence Skinner of Holkham grants Gilbert Neel of Burnham*
1 plot.   9 Aug. 1344

   Original: HP 1099

<Bendyng>
Ex feoffamento Laurencij Skynner' de Holkham facto Gilberto Neel de
Brunham vnam peciam terre iacentem in villa de Holkham inter terram
Matildis Charle ex parte australi et terram Willelmi Craske ex parte
aquilonali et caput orientale abbuttat super croftam Laurencii Bendyng et
caput occidentale abbuttat super quamdam placeam terre Matildis Charle.
Dat' apud Holkham die Lune in vigilia Sancti Laurencij anno regni regis
Edwardi tercij post conquestum octauodecimo. Et iacet in crofta Sewale.

   NOTE: Lucas 27. In no. 128 Lawrence Skinner was granted this land five years before.
   In the fifteenth century, the close of Agnes Sewal lay in the Church Field between the
   closes of Neel Manor and of the Master of St. John of Carbrooke (called Official yard)
   on the west side of the common marsh called Le Moore (towards the north end of the
   body of the present lake), see HD 155, Fo. 39.

179   *Simon atte Cros and Cecily his wife of Holkham grant Katerine Neel*
1/2 acre.   12 March 1337

   Original: HP 1093

<Qwytewong>
Ex feoffamento Simonis atte Cros et Cecilie vxoris eius de Holkham
concessimus dedimus et hac presenti carta nostra confirmauimus Katerine
Neel de eadem vnam dimidiam acram terre apud Qwythewong' cuius caput
orientale abbuttat super regiam viam que ducit apud Qwarles et iacet inter
terram Willelmi Wake ex parte australi et terram dicte Katerine ex parte
boriali. Dat' apud Holkham in die Sancti Gregorij pape anno regni regis
Edwardi tercij a conquestu vndecimo.

   NOTE: Lucas 28. Cross-reference in Lucas's Gazetteer no. 260 Fo. 48v.

180   *Bartholomew Pay of Holkham grants Richard Neel of Burnham and*
Katerine his wife 1 plot.   12 Jan. 1316

<Prior de Petyrston iniuste ocupat et continet iij acras>
<Billesmere, Qwarlesgate, memorandum>
Ex feoffamento Bartholomei Pay de Holkham facto Ricardo Neel de
Brunham et Katerine vxori eius vnam peciam terre iacentem in camp' de
Holkham apud Billesmere inter terram quondam Humfredi Dauyd ex parte

aquilonali et caput orientale abbuttat super Quarlesgate et caput occidentale abbuttat super terram prioris et conuentus de Walsingham. Dat' apud Holkham die Lune proxima post Epiphaniam domini anno regni regis Edwardi filij regis nono.

NOTE: Lucas 29. Cross-reference in Lucas's Gazetteer no. 260 Fos. 41v, 48v. Ralph Pay acquired this land from John son of Geoffrey le Bret in 1295–6, no. 27.

181   *William Athewald of South Creake grants Richard Neel of Burnham and Caterine his wife 3 acres.*   **25 March 1318**

\<examinatur, Wodegate\>
Ex feoffamento Willelmi Athelwald de Southcreyke facto Ricardo Neel de Brunham et Caterine vxori eius tres acras terre in Holkham iacentes apud Wodegate iuxta terram abbatis de Creyke. Dat' apud Brunham in festo Annunciacionis beate Marie anno regni regis Edwardi vndecimo.

NOTE: Lucas 30. Cross-reference in Lucas's Gazetteer no. 260 Fo. 50v. This is not Edward I.

182   *Adam, son of William Silk of Holkham, grants Richard Neel of Burnham and Caterine his wife 1 plot.*   **26 Nov. 1317**

\<Bramlond\>
Ex feoffamento Ade filij Willelmi Silk' de Holkham facto Ricardo Neel de Brunham et Caterine vxori sue vnam peciam terre iacentem in camp' de Holkham apud Bramlond inter terram Roberti atte Gronge et terram Rogeri Kaysche et caput occidentale abbuttat super terram Roberti Marchal. Dat' apud Brunham die Sabbati proxima ante festum Sancti Andree anno regni regis Edwardi vndecimo.

NOTE: Lucas 31. Cross-reference in Lucas's Gazetteer no. 260 Fo. 41v. This is not Edward I.

183   *Adam Craske of Holkham grants Richard Neel of Burnham and Caterine his wife 1 1/4 acres.*   **23 April 1332**

\<Collesmer, Caldehowgate\>
Ex feoffamento Ade Craske de Holkham facto Ricardo Neel de Brunham et Caterina vxori eius quinque rodas terre iacentes in camp' de Holcham apud Collesmere inter terram rectoris de Holkham ex parte australi et terram Heylote le Meyre ex parte boriali cuius caput occidentale abbuttat super

Caldehowegate. Dat' apud Holkham ix kalend' Maij anno regni regis Edwardi tercij post conquestum sexto.

NOTE: Lucas 32. Cross-reference in Lucas's Gazetteer no. 260 Fos. 50v, 42.

184 *Adam Craske of Holkham grants Richard Neel of Burnham and Caterine his wife 5 acres.* **13 Oct. 1332**

Fiche 1: B10

Fo. 16 <Bondescroft>
Ex feoffamento Ade Craske de Holkham facto Ricardo Neel de Brunham et Caterine vxori eius quinque acras terre iacentes in campis de Holkham apud Bondescroft iuxta terram Agnetis Bolewer' ex parte orientali et pars occidentalis est quoddam forarium cuius caput australe abbuttat super terram Willelmi Wake. Dat' apud Holkham tercio idus octobris anno regni regis Edwardi tercij post conquestum sexto.

NOTE: Lucas 33. Cross-reference in Lucas's Gazetteer no. 260 Fo. 41v.

185 *Adam, son of William Craske of Holkham, grants Richard Neel of Burnham and Caterine his wife 2½ acres in 2 plots and half a foldcourse.* **14 Oct. 1326**

Fiche 1: B10

<examinatur, inquiratur, Dalegate, Hungerhil, Caldowgat', et med[ietas], vnius falde>
<memorandum pro abbate de Derham> [right margin]
Ex feoffamento Ade filij Willelmi Craske de Holkham facto Ricardo Neel de Brunham et Caterine vxori eius duas pecias terre cum pertinenciis in Holkham quarum vna pecia continet in se duas acras iacentes inter terram domini abbatis de Derham ex parte australi et terram de Burghalle ex parte boriali et caput orientale abbuttat super Dalegate. Et alia pecia \prior de Walsyngham iniuste ocupat/ continens in se dimidiam acram iacet apud Hungerhil inter terram predicti Ricardi ex parte boriali et terram Iohannis Ayneld ex parte australi et caput orientale abbuttat super Caldowegate: cum medietate vnius faldesoke currentis in camp' de Holkham et omnibus libertatibus ad predictam medietatem spectantibus qualitercumque, quam quidem faldesokam Eborardus filius Eborardi de Cally \Burhowehall/ de Holkham quondam habuit cum Radulfo capellano ibidem. Dat' apud Holkham xiiij° die Octobris anno regni regis Edwardi vicesimo.

NOTE: Lucas 34. Cross-reference in Lucas's Gazetteer no. 260 Fo. 43v. One of a series of grants from Adam Craske to Richard Neel 1318–33. Of two plots *prior de Walsyngham iniuste occupat* the second one. For Everard de Caly's former sheepfold see nos. 1 and 66. The Gazetteer rightly ascribes this to Edward II's reign. The corresponding letter of attorney is HP 1074 of even date.

186　*William Roteney of Walsingham grants Richard Neel and Caterine his wife of Burnham 29 acres in 27 plots.*　　　　　　4 Nov. 1323

Cf. Letter of Attorney, HD 32
Fiche 1: B10

<Duuspet, Scuckelif, inquiratur, Baconescrundel, Endaker, inquiratur, Slyngeshow, Ryngewareslond, Hardyesgate, Sladacre, inquiratur, Larkescote, inquiratur, Duuescrundel, Pilman, Dalegate, Lethrgraues, Warlehousty, Dalegate, inquiratur, Fulmersgate, Millestede, Blakelond>

Ex feoffamento Willelmi Roteney de Walsingham facto Ricardo *N*eel et Caterine vxori eius de Brunham quedam tenementa cum pertinenciis in Holkham in diuersis peciis terre subscriptis: quarum vna pecia quatuor acrarum et dimidie iacet apud Duuspet iuxta terram Iohannis Tydy. Alia pecia iacet apud Scuckelif iuxta terram Willelmi filij Alicie et continet in se quatuor acras. Alia pecia vnius acre iacet fere ibidem iuxta terram prioris de Walsingham. Alia pecia vnius acre fere ibidem iuxta terram Iohannis de Hougate. Alia pecia fere ibidem iuxta terram Iohannis Bulwer et continet in se j rodam et dimidiam. Alia pecia dimidie acre iacet apud Baconescrondel iuxta terram Iohannis de Bulewer'. Alia pecia dimidie acre iacet apud Enedaker' iuxta terram abbatis de Derham. Alia pecia terre iacet apud Slyngeshowe iuxta terram Hugonis Otes et continet in se vnam acram et vnam rodam. Alia pecia vnius acre et dimidie rode iacet apud Ryngewareslond iuxta terram predicti Ricardi Neel. Alia pecia dimidie acre iacet ad portam quondam Hardy iuxta terram Reginaldi de Hougate. Alia pecia apud Sladacre iuxta terram Rogeri Ode et continet in se duas acras. Alia pecia vnius rode fere ibidem iuxta terram abbatis de Derham. Alia pecia vnius rode fere ibidem iuxta terram Iohannis de Deye. Alia pecia fere ibidem iuxta terram Gilberti Puysoun et continet vnam rodam. Alia pecia dimidie acre apud Larkescote iuxta terram predicti Ricardi Neel. Alia pecia dimidie acre fere ibidem iuxta terram predicti abbatis. Alia pecia dimidie acre et dimidie rode iacet apud Duuescrondel iuxta terram Bartholomei le Sutere. Alia pecia vnius acre et vnius rode iacet apud Pilman iuxta terram Hugonis Otes. Alia pecia vnius acre iacet apud Dalegate iuxta terram Gilberti Puysoun. Alia pecia dimidie acre et dimidie rode iacet apud Leyrgraues

Fo. 16v iuxta terram domini comitis de Penbrok'. Alia pecia vnius rode et dimidie iacet fere ibidem iuxta terram Simonis Fabri. Alia pecie vnius rode iacet apud Warldehousty iuxta terram Bartholomei Suter. Alia pecia vnius acre et trium rodarum iacet apud Dalegate iuxta terram Rogeri Ioudy. Alia pecia vnius rode iacet fere ibidem iuxta terram Ade Craske. Alia pecia*ᵃ* vnius acre iacet apud Fulmeresgate iuxta terram Simonis Fabri. Alia pecia vnius rode et dimidie iacet apud Millestede ex transuerso semite ibidem. Et vna pecia vnius rode et dimidie iacet apud Blakelond iuxta terram Hugonis Otes. Dat' apud Holkham quarto die Nouembris anno regni regis Edwardi filij regis Edwardi decimo septimo.

NOTE: Lucas 35. The numerous tenements acquired from William Roteney are cross-referenced in Lucas's Gazetteer no. 260 Fos. 42v, 49v, 41v, 42v, 48v, 44, 49v, 46, 42v, 48, 46, 56v, 43v, 46v, 41v. See also HD 81: Roteney's lands are scattered in the South Field.

VARIANT: *ᵃ* inquiratur in the margin.

187　*Thomas, son of Richard Northerne of Holkham, grants Caterine, widow of Richard Neel of Burnham, 33 1/2 acres in 44 plots.*　　30 April 1336

Fiche 1: B11

<examinatur, memorandum, Mundiesaker, Algerescrofteshend, Gondes-heftlond, Saltergate, Fulmerscrofteshende, Cheker, Estgatecroft, Cleylond, [Po]piwong, Wellegate, Scothougate, Longfurlong, Scothowgate, Scamlond, Schortlond, Scothougate, Clynt, Dalegate, Caldowe, Caldhowegette, Bramlond, Scothowgate, Langefurlong, Scothowgate, Cleylond>
Ex feoffamento Thome filij Ricardi Northerne de Holkham facto Caterine que fuit vxor Ricardi Neel de Brunham triginta tres acras terre et dimidiam acram cum pertinenciis in Holkham: quarum vna pecia vnius acre et vnius rode iacet apud Mundiesaker' et sic vocatur cuius caput occidentale abbuttat super terram Iohannis Leuere. Alia pecia trium rodarum iacet apud Algerescrofteshende et caput occidentale abbutat super viam que ducit versus Statham. Alia pecia trium rodarum iacet per eamdem viam ex parte orientali et caput orientale abbuttat super viam predictam. Alia pecia quinque rodarum iacet inter terram Willelmi Eyres ex parte australi et vocatur Gondeseflond. Alia pecia vnius acre iacet apud Saltergate et caput boriale abbuttat super Wellegate. Alia pecia dimidie rode et quarte partis*ᵃ* vnius rode iacet ad caput australe eiusdem acre inter terram quondam Willelmi Dersy ex parte occidentali et regalem viam que ducit apud Estrgronge ex parte orientali. Alia pecia vnius rode et dimidie iacet apud Fulmerecroftesende et abbuttat super Fulmerescroft versus austrum: vna pecia vnius rode et quarterij vnius rode iacet fere ibidem et abbuttat super eamdem croftam versus austrum. Alia pecia trium rodarum iacet in eadem quarentena inter terram Iohannis Tuber

ex parte occidentali et terram Iohannis de Bilneye ex parte orientali et caput boreale abbuttat super terram Ricardi Calwer'. Alia pecia dimidie acre iacet apud le Cheker' inter terram Iohannis Bilneye ex parte australi et terram Iohannis Charle ex parte boriali. Alia pecia vnius rode et dimidie iacet in eadem quarentena et caput orientale abbuttat super Harueum Buleman. Alia pecia vnius rode iacet ibidem inter terram prioris et conuentus de Petra*ston* ex parte australi et terram abbatis et conuentus de Creyk ex parte boriali. Alia pecia trium rodarum iacet in Estgatecroft iuxta terram Willelmi Wake et caput australe abbuttat super viam regiam que ducit apud Wyghton'. Alia pecia vnius acre et dimidia iacet apud Cleylond et caput australe abbuttat super croftam Caterine relicte Ricardi Neel. Alia pecia vnius rode iacet fere ibidem inter terram quondam Iohannis Charle ex parte occidentali et terram quondam Roberti Mayn ex parte orientali. Alia pecia vnius rode et dimidie iacet ibidem, iuxta terra Thome Cuper' ex parte orientali et caput boriale abbuttat super terram Rogeri Ioudy. Alia pecia vnius acre iacet apud Wellesgat' iuxta terram Ade Ayneld' ex parte occidentali et caput australe abbuttat super Wellegate. Alia pecia vnius rode et dimidie iacet fere ibidem iuxta terram Gilberti Chapman ex parte occidentali iuxta terram Bartholomei le Miller' ex parte orientali et abbuttat super eamdem viam ad caput australe. Alia pecia vnius rode et dimidie iacet apud Popiwong' iuxta terram Thome filij Gilberti le Northerne ex parte orientali et caput australe abbuttat super eamdem

Fo. 17 viam. Alia pecia dimidie acre iacet in alia cultura fere ibidem iuxta terram Iohannis Daulyn ex parte orientali et caput boriale abbuttat super Wellegate. Alia pecia dimidie acre iacet apud Scothowgate iuxta terram Walteri Osbern ex parte occidentali. Alia pecia vnius rode et dimidie iacet fere ibidem iuxta terram Iohannis Speller' ex parte occidentali et caput boriale abbuttat super Scothowegate. Alia pecia dimidie acre et dimidie rode iacet apud Longfurlong' inter terram Thome filij Gilberti le Northerne ex parte occidentali et caput boriale abbuttat super Scothowgat'. Alia pecia vnius rode et dimidie iacet ibidem iuxta terram Thome Brun ex parte occidentali et caput boriale abbuttat super eamdem viam. Alia pecia dimidie acre et dimidie rode iacet ibidem iuxta terram Willelmi Eyr' ex parte orientali et caput boriale abbuttat super eamdem viam. Alia pecia vnius rode et dimidie iacet ibidem iuxta terram Thome filij Gilberti Northerne ex parte occidentali et caput boriale abbuttat super eamdem viam. Alia pecia trium rodarum iacet ibidem iuxta terram Willelmi Dollon ex parte orientali et caput boriale abbuttat super eamdem viam. Alia pecia dimidie acre et dimidie rode iacet apud Scamlond et caput boriale abbuttat super terram Radulfi Grigge. Alia pecia iacet apud Schortlond iuxta terram Henrici Champlynn ex parte orientali et continet vnam rodam et dimidiam et caput australe abbuttat super Scothowgate. Alia pecia vnius acre et dimidie iacet ibidem iuxta terram

Rogeri Ester ex parte orientali et caput australe abbuttat super eamdem viam. Alia pecia vnius acre et vnius rode iacet ibidem iuxta terram Willelmi Eyr' ex parte orientali et caput australe abbuttat super eamdem viam. Alia pecia vnius rode iacet fere ibidem iuxta terram hered' Gilberti Crane ex parte occidentali. Alia pecia trium rodarum iacet ibidem iuxta terram Ricardi Daulyn capellani ex parte occidentali. Alia pecia dimidie acre iacet ibidem iuxta terram Thome Ester' ex parte orientali. Alia pecia dimidie acre iacet apud le Clynt iuxta terram Willelmi Randolf et abbuttat super mariscum. Alia pecia dimidie acre et dimidie rode iacet ibidem et est forera. Alia pecia duarum acrarum et dimidie iacet apud Dalegate iuxta terram Iohannis Tuber ex parte boriali et caput occidentale abbuttat super Dalegate. Alia pecia quinque rodarum iacet apud Caldhowe iuxta terram prioris et conuentus de Petra. Alia pecia dimidie acre iacet ibidem iuxta terram Walteri Osbern ex parte boriali et caput occidentale abbuttat super Caldowegate. Alia pecia quinque rodarum iacet apud Bramlond iuxta terram prioris de Petra ex parte occidentali et abbuttat super quamdam terram Ricardi Neel ad caput boriale. Alia pecia vnius rode et dimidie iacet super Scothowgat' iuxta terram Seman Abraham ex parte occidentali et caput australe abbuttat super Scothowegate. Alia pecia vnius rode iacet ibidem iuxta terram Iohannis Calewer' et caput australe abbuttat super eamdem viam. Alia pecia dimidie acre et dimidie rode iacet apud Langfurlong' iuxta terram Gilberti Chapman ex parte orientali et caput boriale abbuttat super Scothowgate. Concessi etiam eidem Caterine quod vna acra et tres rode terre quas Willelmus Wake tenet ad totam vitam Ele que fuit vxor Bartholomei de Burgate ex dimissione eiusdem Ele quas eadem Ela nuper tenuit de hereditate mea in dotem apud Cleylond cum pertinenciis in Holkham et que post decessum eiusdem Ele ad me et heredes meos reuerti debuerunt post mortem eiusdem Ele prefate Caterine quiete et integre remaneant habend' et tenend' eidem Caterine heredibus et assignatis suis imperpetuum de capitalibus dominis etc. Dat' apud Holkham vltimo die Aprilis anno regni regis Edwardi tercij post conquestum decimo.

NOTE: Lucas 36.The numerous tenements acquired from Thomas Northerne are cross-referenced in Lucas's Gazetteer no. 260 Fos. 46v, 41, 44, 49v, 43v, 42, 40v, 42, 50v, 49v, 42, 49v, 42v, 41v, 41v, 49v, 42. See also nos. 161–163. Juliana Patryke and John Newgate cite HD 161–162 and 187 as evidence of title at Neel court of 8 Oct. 1449, HD 194a. Thomas Northerne's grand-daughter Juliana was the mother of John Newgate who conveyed 2 messuages at the Stathe with 50 acres of arable and 80 acres of marsh with a sheep fold to his son Thomas Newgate on 4 Jan. 1461, HD 145. John Coke acquired the estate of Edmund Newgate Gent. in 1659. It mostly lay like the Northerne's estate in Stathe Field towards the North.

VARIANT: *a* parte in Ms.

188   *Bartholomew the miller of Holkham grants Richard Neel of Burnham*
and Caterine his wife 1 plot of 3/4 acres.   12 April 1316

Cf. HP 1057

Fo. 17v   <memorandum, Schortlond, Caldougate>
Ex feoffamento Bartholomei Molendinarij de Holkham facto Ricardo Neel de
Brunham et Caterine vxori eius vnam peciam terre mee continentem \tres
rodas Robertus/ Gunnore iniuste ocupat*a* in camp' de Holkham apud
Schortlond inter terram Iohannis Ayneld ex parte aquilonali et terram Galfridi
Sutoris ex parte australi et caput orientale abbuttat super Caldowgate'. Dat'
apud Holkham die Lune post Pascha anno regni regis Edwardi filij regis
Edwardi nono.

> NOTE: Lucas 37. Cross-reference in Lucas's Gazetteer no. 260 Fos. 42, 46v, 49v. No.
> 188 is quoted in answer to an inquiry in Neel court roll of 8 Oct. 1449 HD 194a. HP
> 1057 is a letter of attorney for Martin Rust of Holkham to deliver seisin, dated 12 April
> 1316 like no. 188. Robert Gunnor was a tenant and capital pledge of Burghall (HD 120,
> 194), a free tenant of Hillhall (HD 52), of Neel Manor (HD 194a) and of Wighton (HD
> 71) and a tenant of Peterstone (HD 114) and Walsingham (HD 120). On 27 April 1458
> he is described as of Burnham 'marchaunt', *Cal. Patent* 1452–61, p. 380.

> VARIANT: *a* an index finger, possibly drawn in 1449, points to this interlineation.

189   *Adam, son of William Craske of Holkham, grants Richard Neel of*
Burnham and Caterine his wife 1 plot. There follows release from Margery,
widow of William Craske, to Adam her son of same plot, called Marlond.
                                                            25 Sept. 1327

Cf. HD 29

<examinatur, Marlond, Dalegate, examinatur>
Ex feoffamento Ade filij Willelmi Craske de Holkham facto Ricardo Neel de
Brunham et Caterine vxori eius vnam peciam terre in Holkham que vocatur
Marlond et iacet inter terram prioris et conuentus de Petirston ex parte boriali
et terram predicti Ricardi Neel ab*buttantem* super partem australem cuius
caput orientale abuttat super Dalegate. Dat' apud Holkham die Veneris
proxima post festum Sancti Mathei apostoli et euangeliste anno regni regis
Edwardi tercij a conquestu primo. Et sequitur ibidem relaxacio Margerie
quondam vxoris Willelmi Crask' facta Ade filio suo de pecia predicta quam
tenuit nomine dotis de hereditate predicto Ade et vocatur Marlond etc.

> NOTE: Lucas 38. Cross-reference in Lucas's Gazetteer no. 260 Fos. 42v, 46v. HD 29,
> reads *Le Marledelond.* Marling is mentioned in contemporary wills. Over four centuries
> later Coke of Norfolk's marling was hailed as an innovation.

190   *Final concord about a messuage, toft and 24 acres. John, son of Harvey Underburgh of Burnham and Cecily his wife grant to Richard Neel of Burnham and Caterine his wife, the tenement.*   21 Jan. 1316

   Original: PRO CP 25(1) 162/132/500. Cf. Appendix 5, no. 29

\<Finis de tofto et xxiiij acr' terre\>
Hec est finalis concordia facta in curia domini regis apud Westmonasterium in octabis Sancti Hillarij anno regni regis Edwardi filij regis Edwardi nono coram Willelmo de Bereford' Roberto de Trimingham, etc. inter Ricardum Neel de Brunham et Caterinam vxorem eius querentem et Iohannem filium Heruici Vnderburgh de Brunham et Ceciliam vxorem eius deforc*iantes* de vno mesuagio et j tofto et viginti quatuor acris terre cum pertinenciis in Holkham vnde placitum conuencionis summonitum fuit in eadem curia scilicet quod predictus Ricardus recognouit dictum tenementum cum pertinenciis esse ius ipsius Cecilie. Et pro hac recognicione fine et concordia iidem Iohannes et Cecilia concesserunt predictis Ricardo et Caterine predicta tenementa cum pertinenciis et illa eis reddiderunt in eadem curia habend' et tenend' eisdem Ricardo et Katerine et heredibus imperpetuum per ser*uicia que* ad illa tenementa pertinent imperpetuum: cum clausula warantie etc. Et habetur ibidem alia pars finis predicte etc.

   NOTE: Lucas 39.Cross-reference in Lucas's Gazetteer no. 260 Fo. 43v. No. 191 shows that the deforciants, John son of Harvey Underburgh of Burnham and Cecily, were serfs of Peter le Bret granted to Richard and Caterine Neel in 1314.

191   *Peter le Bret of Holkham grants Richard Neel of Burnham and Caterine his wife 1/2 acre and his croft with all his bondmen, villeins and free tenants in Holkham.*   19 Aug. 1314

   Fiche 1: C6

\<examinatur, De natiuis et eorum villenagiis et de seruiciis liberorum tenencium\> [left margin]
\<inquiratur.\> [right margin]
Ex feoffamento Petri le Bret de Holkham facto Ricardo Neel de Brunham et Caterine vxori sue dimidiam acram terre et totam croftam suam cum pertinenciis in Holkham vna [cum] Henrico Vnderhoghe et Cristiana Vnderhoghe natiuis et villanis meis cum tota sequela sua et cum eorum villenagiis et seruiciis bonis et catallis omnibus et cum homagiis et seruiciis omnibus omnium libere tenencium meorum in predicta villa de Holkham videlicet homagia et seruicia Iohannis de Belneye, Willelmi Curssoun, Gilberti Eluerich', Martini Goldewyne, Willelmi le Meyre, Radulfi Mariot, Willelmi Alistessone, Gilberti Edwy, Roberti filij Emme, Ricardi Speller',

Willelmi Wake, Iohannis Dauy, Rogeri filij Emme, Ade Crask', Henrici Anger, Hugonis Otes, Iohannis le Bret, Reginaldi le Bercher, Radulfi Paye et Radulfi Holneye cum omnibus wardis maritagiis releuiis et escaetis omnibus. Dat' apud Brunham proxima [die] Lune post assumpcionem beate Marie. Anno regni regis Edwardi filij regis Edwardi octauo.

> NOTE: Lucas 40. Another copy is no. 263, Fo. 47, under the heading of *Dominium Petri le Bret.*

192 *Walter, son of Richard Mariot de Mundene, vicar of half Holkham church, grants Richard Neel of Burnham and Katerine his wife 1 messuage of 7 perches 9 ft. long in the south, 8 perches long in the north, 6 perches wide in the east and 5 perches wide in the west.*   11 Feb. 1317

<[De] parcella mesuagij Neles>
Ex feoffamento Walteri filij Ricardi Mariot de Mundene vicarius medietatis ecclesie de Holkam facto Ricardo Neel de Brunham Katerine vxori sue vnum mesuagium cum pertinenciis iac' in Holkham iuxta mesuagium dictorum Ricardi et Katerine et caput occidentale abbuttat super regalem viam et continet in longitudine ex parte australi septem perticatas et nouem pedes terre et ex parte aquilon' octo perticatas et in latitudine ad caput orientale sex perticatas et ad caput occidentale quinque perticatas. Dat' apud Holkham die Veneris proxima ante festum Sancti Valentini martiris anno regni regis Edwardi filij regis Edwardi decimo.

> NOTE: Lucas 41.

193 *Peter le Bret of Holkham grants Richard Neel of Burnham and Caterine his wife 1 plot in his croft, 3½ perches 3 ft. wide and 25 perches long, together with his serfs and their broods etc.*   19 May 1315

Fo. 18   <De parcella mesuag' Neles et de Natiuis et eorum villenagiis>
Ex feoffamento Petri le Bret de Holkham facto Ricardo Neel de Brunham et Caterine vxori sue vnam peciam terre cum pertinenciis in villa de Holkham iacentem in crufta predicti Petri cuius caput occidentale abbuttat super regiam viam et caput orientale abbuttat super mesuagium predictorum Ricardi et Katerine et que continet in se de latitudine tres perticatas et dimidiam et tres pedes et de longitudine viginti quinque perticatas vna cum Iohanne Thurbern et Reginaldo Thurbern filiis Rogeri Thurbern natiuis meis cum tota sequela eorum et cum tota sequela predicti Rogeri et cum Matilda Ernald et Mabilia Ernald natiuis meis cum tota sequela eorum et cum omnibus villenagiis suis que de me habent in predicta villa de Holkham cum eorum seruiciis consuetudinibus omnimodis et cum eorum omnibus bonis et catallis et cum tota sequela predicta Rogeri Thurbern vt predictum est. Dat' apud Brunham die Lune in festo Sancti Dunstani archiepiscopi anno regni regis Edwardi filij Edwardi octauo.

NOTE: Lucas 42. The royal road, evidently running north and south towards the church (on the west side of Neel manor house) is called Howgate in HD 111. The tenants of the messuage of the Ernalds do the office of *messor* in Neel court roll of 12 Nov. 1333, HD 83. Quit rents from Roger Thurbern and Roger Ernald were listed in Geoffrey le Bret's rental, HD 11.

194   *Peter le Bret of Holkham grants Richard Neel of Burnham and Caterine his wife 1 messuage and 3 plots, and quitclaims all his lands in Holkham.*   5 April and 18 Aug. 1315

<De mesuag' Neles *quondam Petri Brett*, quietaclamacio de terris et faldagiis>
Ex feoffamento Petri le Bret de Holkham facto Ricardo Neel de Brunham et Caterine vxori sue vnum mesuagium cum omnibus suis pertinenciis in villa de Holkham quod quidem mesuagium quondam fuit Galfridi le Bret patris mei et tres pecias terre cum pertinenciis in predicta villa de Holkham. Dat' apud Holkham die Sabbati proxima post festum Sancti Ambrosij episcopi anno regni regis Edwardi octauo. Et sequitur relaxacio et quietaclamacio predicti Petri le Bret facta Ricardo Neel et Caterine vxori eius totum us et clameum quod habuit vel aliquo modo habere poterit in omnibus terris et tenementis mesuagiis faldagiis pasturis et communis omnibus que unquam fuerunt mihi Petro seu antecessoribus meis in villa de Holkham que habent et tenent ex dono et feoffamento meo siue ex dono et feoffamento alterius cuiuscumque. Dat' apud Holkham die Lune proxima post festum assumpcionis beate Marie anno regni regis Edwardi filij regis Edwardi nono.

NOTE: Lucas 43. *Petri Brett* was added in 16th century. Cross-reference in Lucas Gazetteer no. 260 Fo. 47. The position of Neel manor house is shown on the 1590 map.

195   *Eustace le Bret, rector of Tasburgh, releases to Richard Neel and Katerine his wife all his rights as John, son of Geoffrey le Bret, gave them to him.*

6 March 1317

<inquiratur, Quietaclamacio de mesuag' Neles dominiis faldag' et seruiciis liberorum et natiuorum>
Ex relaxacione Eustachi le Bret rectoris ecclesie de Tasseburgh' facta Ricardo Neel de Brunham et Katerine vxori eius totum us et clameum quod habuit seu quouismodo habere poterit in omnibus mesuagiis gardinis stagnis terris et tenementis cum suis pertinenciis omnibus pascuis pasturis bruariis faldagiis homagiis liberorum tenencium et eorum redditibus seruiciis omnibus villanis et eorum villenagiis catallis et eorum sequelis omnibus in villa de Holkham absque vllo retenemento mei vel heredum meorum adeo integre sicut et ea michi dedit Iohannes filius Galfridi le Bret de Holkham etc. Dat' apud

Brunham die Dominica proxima post festum Sancti Wynewalei anno regni regis Edwardi filij regis Edwardi decimo.

NOTE: Eustace was the son of Geoffrey le Bret and a younger brother of John and Peter (HD 7). Tasburgh is 8 miles south by west of Norwich.

196 William of Hindringham grants Richard Neel of Burnham and Caterine his wife 1 acre.   1 Aug. 1315

<Dalegate, Caldowgate, drawing of an index finger>
Ex feoffamento Willelmi de Hindryngham facto Ricardo Neel de Brunham et Caterine vxori eius vnam acram terre mee cum pertinenciis iacente in campis de Holkham iuxta terram prioris de Petirston [ex parte boreali] et terram Roberti de Swanton' ex parte australi et caput occidentale abbuttat super Dalegate et caput orientale super Caldowgate. Dat' apud Holkham die Veneris proxima post festum Sancti Iacobi apostoli anno regni regis Edwardi filij regis Edwardi nono.

NOTE: Lucas 44. Cross-reference in Lucas's Gazetteer no. 260 Fo. 42v.

197 Walter de Mundene, vicar of half Holkham church, grants Richard Neel and Katerine his wife 3/4 acres.   10 Feb. 1332

Fo. 18v <examinatur, Dalegate>
Ex feoffamento Walteri de Mundene vicarius medietatis [ecclesie] de Holkham facto Ricardo Neel de eadem et Katerine vxori eius tres rodas terre cum pertinenciis iacentes in camp' de Holkham apud Dalegate iuxta terram predicti Ricardi ex parte boriali et terram prioris de Petirston ex parte australi cuius caput occidentale abbuttat super Dalegate. Dat' apud Holkham iiij^{to} Idus Februarij' anno regni regis Edwardi tercij post conquestum sexto.

NOTE: Lucas 45. Cross-reference in Lucas's Gazetteer no. 260, Fo. 42v.

198 Bartholomew the miller [le Munere] of Holkham grants Richard Neel of Burnham and Caterine his wife 1 rood with its crop.   1 Aug. 1315

Original: HP 1055

<inquiratur, Caldowgate>
Ex feoffamento Bartholomei le Munere de Holkham facto Ricardo Neel de Brunham et Caterine vxori sue vnam rodam terre cum tota vestura et omnibus pertinenciis iacentem in campis de Holkham inter terram Roberti le Marchall' ex parte aquilonali et terram Willelmi Fabri ex parte australi cuius caput occidentale abbuttat super Caldowgate. Dat' apud Holkham die Veneris proxima post festum Sancti Iacobi Apostoli anno regni regis Edwardi filij regis Edwardi nono.

NOTE: Lucas 46. Bartholomew's letter of attorney to Martin Rust is HP 1057. See also no. 133 where William Curthun, not William the Smith, is the neighbour.

199   *William le Clerk of Holkham grants Richard Neel of Burnham and Caterine his wife 1 plot*   [c. 1315–20]

Cf. no. 149 and HP 1000

\<Thorpemere\>
Ex feoffamento Willelmi le Clerk de Holkham facto Ricardo Neel de Brunham et Caterine vxori eius vnam peciam terre iacentem in camp' de Holkham inter terram Reginaldi Osmod et terram Gilberti Sutoris de Westgate et vnum caput abbuttat super terram prioris de Walsingham et alium caput super Thorpemer. Nulla data.

NOTE: Lucas 47. Cross-reference in Lucas's Gazetteer no. 260 Fo. 50. William *clericus* acquired the land in no. 149. Cf. nos. 217, 218 and HP 1098.

200   *Adam Craske of Holkham grants Richard Neel of Burnham and Caterine his wife 1 plot of 1³/₄ acres.*   10 April 1333

\<Lambulbotme, Gibbesgate\>
Ex feoffamento Ade Craske de Holkham facto Ricardo Neel de Brunham et Caterine vxori eius vnam peciam terre iacentem in camp' de Holkham apud Lambul'botme inter terram Petri Couper' de Rudham ex parte australi et terram Gilberti Poysun ex parte aquilon' cuius caput orientale abbuttat super Gibbesgate et continet in se septem rodas terre cum pertinenciis. Dat' apud Holkham quarto Idus Aprilis anno regni regis Edwardi tercij post conquestum septimo.

NOTE: Lucas 48. Cross-reference in Lucas's Gazetteer no. 260 Fo. 46.

201   *Geoffrey, son of Julian of Holkham, grants Richard Neel of Burnham and Caterine his wife 3¹/₂ roods.*   13 Aug. 1319

\<inquiratur, Douwesty\>
Ex feoffamento Galfridi filij Iuliane de Holkham facto Ricardo Neel de Brunham et Caterine vxori eius tres rodas et dimidiam terre iacentes in camp' de Holkham apud Douwesty inter terram predicti Ricardi et Katerine ex parte australi et terram quondam Iohannis Haynild ex parte boriali. Dat' apud Holkham die Lune proxima post festum Sancti Laurencij Martiris anno regni regis Edwardi iunioris terciodecimo.

NOTE: Lucas 49. Cross-reference in Lucas's Gazetteer no. 260 Fo. 42v.

202   *Henry Anger of Holkham and Isabel his wife grant Richard Neel of Burnham and Katerine his wife 1¹/₂ roods.*   22 March 1318

Original: HD 28

<inquiratur, Goldewynescroft>

Ex feoffamento Henrici Anger de Holkham et Isabelle vxoris mee facto Ricardo Neel de Brunham et Katerine vxori eius vnam rodam terre et dimidiam iacentem in camp' de Holkham iuxta terram predicti Ricardi et Katerine ex parte aquilonal' et caput occidentale abbuttat super cruftam que quondam fuit Martini Goldewyne et caput orientale abbuttat super cruftam Iohannis Silke. Dat' apud Holkham die Mercurij proxima ante festum Annunciacionis beate Marie anno regni regis Edwardi filij regis Edwardi xj°.

NOTE: Lucas 50. Cross-reference in Lucas's Gazetteer no. 260 Fo. 44.

203   *William the smith of Gresham and Emma his wife grant Richard Neel of Burnham and Katerine his wife 1 rood.*   7 July 1317

Original: HP 1059

Ex feoffamento Willelmi Fabri de Gressham et Emme vxoris sue facto Ricardo Neel de Brunham et Katerine vxori eius vnam rodam terre iacentem in camp' de Holkham inter terram Willelmi de Walsingham ex parte australi et terram predicti Ricardi ex parte aquilon'. Dat' apud Holkham in translacione Sancti Thome martiris anno regni regis Edwardi filij regis Edwardi decimo.

NOTE: Lucas 51. The name of the grantor William *Faber* of Gresham suggests that William of Gresham in no. 219 may be the same as William *Faber* in no. 198. No. 235 shows that his wife is Emma Curson.

204   *Thomas, son of John of Holkham, grants Richard Neel of Burnham and Katerine his wife 1 rood.*   16 March 1321

<Gonyeswong>.

Ex feoffamento Thome filij Iohannis de Holkham facto Ricardo Neel de Brunham et Katerine vxori eius vnam rodam terre iacentem in camp' de Holkham apud Gonyeswong' inter terras predicti Ricardi ex vtraque parte et caput orientale abbuttat super terram prioris de Walsingham et caput occidentale abbuttat super terram Willelmi Wake. Dat' apud Holkham die Lune proxima post festum Sancti Gregorij pape anno regni regis Edwardi iunioris quartodecimo.

NOTE: Lucas 52.

205   *Joan, widow of Henry Hammond of North Barsham, grants Richard Neel of Burnham and Katerine his wife 1 plot of 3 acres.*   1 July 1315

   Original: HP 1053

Fo. 19   <Scotbarbles>
Ex feoffamento Iohanne quondam vxoris Henrici Hammond de Northbarsham facto Ricardo Neel de Brunham et Katerine vxori sue vnam peciam terre in camp' de Holkham apud Scotbarbles que continet in se tres acras terre et iacet iuxta terram Willelmi Craske ex parte australi. Dat' apud Brunham die Martis proxima post festum apostolorum Petri et Pauli anno regni regis Edwardi filij regis Edwardi octauo finiente.

   NOTE: Lucas 53. Cross-reference in Lucas's Gazetteer no. 260 Fo. 49v. Cf. HP 1053 and 1054 (no. 208).

206   *Adam, son of Simon Hammond of Holkham, grants Richard Neel of Burnham and Katerine his wife 2 plots.*   29 March 1315

<Hoselestunge, Thorpgate, Endakere, Lethirpitgate>
Ex feoffamento Ade filij Simonis Hammond de Holkham facto Ricardo Neel de Brunham et Katerine vxori eius duas pecias terre iacentes in camp' de Holkham apud Hoselestunge quarum vna pecia terre iacet iuxta terram Iohannis de Bilneye ex parte orientali et caput boriale abbuttat super terram que quondam fuit Humfredy Dauy et altera pecia abbuttat super Thorpegate. Item aliam peciam abbuttantem super Hendaker inter terram predicti Ricardi ex parte boriali et terram abbatis de Derham ex parte australi et caput orientale abbuttat super Lethirpitgate. Dat' apud Brunham die Sabbati proxima post festum annunciacionis domini anno regni regis Edwardi filij regis Edwardi octauo.

   NOTE: Lucas 54. Cross-reference in Lucas's Gazetteer no. 260 Fos. 44v, 50.

207   *Adam, son of William Craske of Holkham, grants Richard Neel and Caterine his wife of Burnham Norton 11/2 acres in 2 plots.*   1 May 1323

   Original: HP 1072

<Scotbarbles, Nortpilman>
Ex feoffamento Ade filij Willelmi Craske de Holkham facto Ricardo Neel et Caterine vxori eius de Brunham Nortone duas pecias terre iacentes in camp' de Holkham quarum vna pecia iacet apud Scotbarbles inter terram predictorum Ricardi et Katerine ex parte australi et continet in se quinque rodas terre cum pertinenciis. Alia pecia iacet apud Nortpilman iuxta terram predictorum Ricardi et Katerine ex parte orientali et continet in se vnam

rodam cum pertinenciis. Dat' apud Holkham in festo apostolorum Philippi et
Iacobis anno regni regis Edwardi filij regis Edwardi sextodecimo.

NOTE: Lucas 55. Cross-reference in Lucas's Gazetteer no. 260 Fos. 47, 49v.

208 *William, son of Henry Hammond of North Barsham, grants Richard*
Neel of Burnham and Katerine his wife 1 acre and the release of 3 acres.
15 July 1315

Original: HP 1054

Ex feoffamento Willelmi filij Henrici Hammond de Nortbersham facto
Ricardo Neel de Brunham et Katerine vxori sue vnam acram terre cum
pertinenciis in villa de Holkham cum pertinenciis. Dat' apud Brunham die
Martis proxima post festum apostolorum Petri et Pauli anno regni regis
Edwardi filij regis Edwardi octauo. Et sequitur ibidem relaxacio Willelmi et
Hamonis filij Henrici Hammond de Northbar[s]ham facta Ricardo Neel de
Brunham et Katerine vxori eius totum ius et clameum que habuerunt in tribus
acris terre cum pertinenciis in Holkham quas habent ex dono et feoffamento
Iohanne matris predictorum Willelmi et Hamonis. Dat' apud Brunham die
Martis proxima ante festum Sancte Margarete virginis anno regni regis
Edwardi filij regis Edwardi nono incipiente.

NOTE: Lucas 56. No cross–reference in Lucas's Gazetteer no. 260. The three acres were
granted on the same day as the 1 acre. They were at Scotbarbles, no. 205.

209 *Gilbert, son of William Silk of Holkham, grant Richard Neel of*
Burnham his croft.
25 Feb. 1320

Original: HP 1064

<Burgate, inquiratur>
Ex feoffamento Gilberti filij Willelmi Silk de Holkham facto Ricardo Neel de
Brunham totam cruftam meam cum pertinenciis iacentem in Burgate inter
terram quondam Alexandri de Burgate versus occidentem et terram domini
abbatis et conuentus de Creyk' versus orientem et capud aquilonale abbuttat
super mesuagium meum. Dat' apud Holkham die Lune proxima post festum
Sancti Mathei apostoli anno regni regis Edwardi filij regis Edwardi
terciodecimo.

NOTE: Lucas 57. Cross-reference in Lucas's Gazetteer no. 260 Fo. 41v.

210   *John le Bret releases to Richard Neel of Burnham and Katerine his wife all his rights in 1 plot with house thereon as granted by Gilbert, son of John le Bret his father.* 17 Feb. 1333

<Quietaclamacio de pecia terre et domo>
Ex relaxacione Iohannis le Bret de Holkham facto Ricardo Neel de Brunham et Katerine vxori eius totum us et clameum que habeo seu aliquo modo habere potero nomine alicuius recti in vna pecia terre iacenti in villa de Holkham cum quadam domo supersita prout in quadam carta feoffamenti quam habent de dono Gilberti filij Iohannis le Bret patris mei plenius specificatur. Dat' apud Holkham xiij° Kalend' Martij anno regni regis tercij post conquestum septimo.

NOTE: No Lucas number. See nos. 51 and 108.

211   *Gilbert, son of John Silk of Holkham, grants Richard Neel of Burnham 13d. yearly from his messuage measuring 9 perches in length and 6 1/2 in width.* 3 March 1320

Original: HP 1070

Fo. 19v   <xiij d. annui redditus, habet Gonthorp>
Ex[a] feoffamento Gilberti filij Iohannis Silk' de Holkham facto Ricardo Neel de Brunham tresdecim denarios annuatim imperpetuum percipiend' videlicet de mesuagio meo \modo non edificato/ in Holkham inter mesuagium quondam Alexandri de Burgate et terram abbatis et conuentus de Creyke et caput boriale abuttat super Burgate et caput australe abbuttat super terram predicti Ricardi et continet in se dictum mesuagium in longitudine nouem perticatas terre in latitudine sex perticatas et dimidiam terre. Dat' apud Holkham die Lune proxima post festum Sancti Mathei apostoli anno regni regis Edwardi filij regis Edwardi terciodecimo.

NOTE: Lucas 58. John son of Geoffrey Silk acquired this messuage in no. 71 about 1284. This house disappeared between 1319 when Richard Neel acquired it from Gilbert son of John Silk and the date when *modo non edificato* was interlineated in the fifteenth century.

VARIANT: [a] Relaxacione struck out.

212   *Thomas le Northerne of Holkham grants Katerine, widow of Richard Neel of Burnham, 1 'place'.* 11 Nov. 1335

Original: HP 1085

<Burgate, drawing of an index finger>
Ex feoffamento Thome le Northerne de Holkham facto Katerine que fuit vxor

Ricardi Neel de Brunham vnam placeam terre iacentem in camp' de eadem apud Burgate iuxta terram abbatis de Creyk ex parte orientis et terram Agnet' Briche ex parte occidentali cuius caput australe abbuttat super terram predicte Katerine et caput aquilonale abbuttat super viam regiam que ducit de villa de Welles versus Holkham in festo Sancti Martini confessoris anno regni regis Edwardi tercij post conquestum nono.

> NOTE: Lucas 59. Cross-reference in Lucas's Gazetter no. 260 Fo. 41v. Gilbert Silk of Holkham granted this to Thomas le Northerne in 1321, HP 1071. William Silk had granted it to Gilbert in 1318 in HD 73.

213 *Adam, son of Simon Hammond of Holkham, grants Richard Neel of Burnham and Katerine his wife 1 rood.*   [c. 1315]

Ex feoffamento Ade filij Simonis Hammond de Holkham facto Ricardo Neel de Brunham et Katerine vxori eius vnam rodam terre. [*Five lines left blank in Ms.*].

> NOTE: Lucas 60. Cf. no. 206.

214 *Edmund, son of Hugh Otes of Holkham, grants Richard Neel of Burnham and Katerine his wife 1 acre.*   16 March 1330

<examinatur, Pilman, Qwarlesgate>
Ex feoffamento Ed*mundi* filij Hugonis Otes de Holkham facto Ricardo Neel de Brunham et Katerine vxori eius vnam acram terre iacentem in camp' de Holkham apud Pilman inter terras predicti Ricardi ex vtraque parte cuius caput occidentale abbuttat super Qwarlesgate. Dat' apud Holkham die Veneris proxima post festum Sancti Gregorij pape anno regni regis Edwardi tercij a conquestu quarto.

> NOTE: Lucas 61. Cross-reference in Lucas's Gazetteer no. 260 Fo. 48. For more land from this grantor and for its origin see no. 215.

215 *Edmund, son of Hugh Otes of Holkham, grants Richard Neel of Burnham and Katerine his wife 2 1/2 roods in 2 plots and 2 other plots. Richard, son of John Bulwer releases to Richard and Katerine Neel all his rights in 5 plots acquired from Edmund, son of Hugh Otes.*   17 April 1331

<examinatur, Dalegate, Litelhowe, Dalegate, Litelhowe, Pilman>.
Ex feoffamento Ed*mundi* filij Hugonis Otes de Holkham facto Ricardo Neel de Brunham et Katerine vxori eius quatuor pecias terre iacentes in camp' de Holkham quarum vna pecia iacet inter terram prioris et conuentus de Petirston ex parte boriali et terram quondam Ed*mundi* Athewald ex parte australi et caput occidentale abbuttat super Dalegate. Secunda pecia iacet inter

terram Thome le Northerne ex parte australi et terram Rogeri Ode ex parte boriali que continet in se vnam rodam terre et caput occidentale abbuttat super Dalegate. Tercia pecia iacet iuxta terram Ricardi Bulewere ex parte boriali que continet in se vnam rodam terre et dimidiam et caput occidentale abbuttat super Dalegate. Quarta pecia terre iacet apud Litelhowe inter terram quondam Rogeri Cheles ex parte australi et terram Simonis Fabri ex parte boriali et caput occidentale abbuttat super terram Ricardi Neel. Dat' apud Holkham die Benedicti Sancti abbatis in quadragesima. Anno regni regis Edwardi tercij a conquestu quarto. Et sequitur relaxacio Ricardi filij Iohannis Bolewere de Holkham facto Ricardo Neel de Brunham et Katerine vxori eius totum us et clameum quod habuit in quinque peciis terre quas idem Ricardus et Katerina

Fo. 20 nuper adquisierunt de Edmundo filio Hugonis Otes cum pertinenciis in Holkham. Quarum vna pecia iacet prope Dalegate inter terram prioris de Petirston ex parte borialie et terram quondam Edmundi Athewald ex parte australi. Alia pecia iacet inter terram Thome Northerne ex parte australi. Alia pecia iacet inter terram Thome Northerne ex parte australi et terram Rogeri Ode ex parte boriali et caput occidentale abbuttat super Dalegate. Quarta pecia iacet apud Litelhowe inter terram quondam Rogeri Cheles ex parte australi et terram quondam Simonis Fabri ex parte boriali. Quinta pecia iacet apud Pilman inter terras predictorum Ricardi et Caterine ex vtraque parte. Dat' apud Holkham xvij die Aprilis anno regni regis Edwardi tercij a conquestu quinto.

NOTE: Lucas 62. Cross-reference in Lucas's Gazetteer no. 260 Fo. 46. In no. 56 (1308) John le Bret granted these three plots to Hugh Otes, father of the grantor of no. 215 (1331).

216   *Simon atte Cros of Holkham grants Katerine, widow of Richard Neel of Burnham, 1/2 acre with their release.*   **20 Nov. 1336**

Original: HD 38

\<inquiratur, Grenegate\>
Ex feoffamento Simonis atte Cros de Holkham facto Katerine que fuit vxoris Ricardi Neel de Brunham dimidiam acram terre iacentem collateraliter ex parte boriali de Grenegate cuius caput orientale abbuttat super terram predicte Katerine. Dat' apud Holkham vicesimo die Nouembris anno regni regis Edwardi tercij post conquestum decimo. Et sequitur relaxacio predicti Simonis et Cecilie vxoris eius de dimidia acra predicta facto prefate Katerine Neel eiusdem date etc.

NOTE: Lucas 63. Cross-reference in Lucas's Gazetteer no. 260 Fo. 44.

217   *Roger Marchal of Holkham grants Richard Neel of Burnham and Katerine his wife 3 acres.*   [c. 1319]

   Original: HP 1068

<Warramgate>

Ex feoffamento Rogeri Marchal de Holkham facto Ricardo Neel de Brunham et Katerine vxori eius tres acras terre iacentes in Holkham inter terram abbatis de Creyk' et terram que fuit Ade Gylyon et caput australe abbuttat super viam que ducit de Holkham ad Warram et caput boriale abbuttat super terram Iohannis le Bret. Nulla data.

   NOTE: Lucas 64.

218   *Agnes Curthon of Holkham grants Richard Neel of Burnham and Katerine his wife 3 acres with their release.*   [c. 1300]

<examinatur>

Ex feoffamento Agnetis Curthon de Holkham facto Ricardo Neel de Brunham et Katerine vxori eius tres acras terre iacentes in camp' de Holkham inter terram abbatis de Creyke et terram que quondam fuit Ade Gylyon. Nulla data. Et sequitur relaxacio et quietaclamacio Willelmi de Gressam facto Ricardo Neel de Brunham et Katerine vxoris eius totum us et clameum in tribus acris terre predicte prout iacent inter terram abbatis de Creyke et terram Ade Gylion sine data.

   NOTE: Lucas 65. Gressam's quitclaim, HP 1067, reads *Gillyon*. Agnes Curthun obtained this land on marriage from her father, no. 70. Cf. no. 235 for Agnes, widow of William Curson.

219   *Bartholomew, son of William Marcharle of Holkham, grants to Richard Neel of Burnham and Katerine his wife 3 plots.*   20 Jan. 1318

   Original: HP 1062

<examinatur, Ringwaleslond, Creykgate>

Ex feoffamento Bartholomei filij Willelmi Marcharle de Holkham facto Ricardo Neel de Brunham et Katerine vxori eius tres pecias terre iacentes in camp' de Holkham quarum vna pecia iacet apud Ringwaleslond iuxta terram que quondam fuit Willelmi Chollyng ex parte aquilonali et caput orientale abbuttat super Creykgate. Altera pecia iacet iuxta terram que quondam fuit Matild*is* Godkot ex parte australi et caput occidentale abbuttat super terram que quondam fuit Rogeri Elwerich. Tercia pecia iacet iuxta terram que quondam fuit Humfredi Dauid ex parte aquilonali et caput occidentale abbuttat super terram prioris et conuentus de Wals*ingham*. Dat' apud Holkham die Veneris in festo Sanctorum*ᵃ* Fabiani et Sebastiani anno regni regis Edwardi filij regis Edwardi vndecimo.

NOTE: Lucas 66. Cross-reference in Lucas's Gazetteer no. 260 Fos. 42, 49. Cf. nos. 53–55.

VARIANT: *a* Sancti in Ms.

220   *John, son of William Silk of Holkham, grants Richard Neel of Burnham and Katerine his wife 2 plots.*   22 Nov. 1317

   Original: HP 1060

Fo. 20v   <Gibbesgate>
Ex feoffamento Iohannis filij Willelmi Silk de Holkham facto Ricardo Neel de Brunham et Katerine vxori eius duas pecias terre iacentes in camp' de Holkham quarum vna pecia iacet iuxta terram prioris et conuentus de Petirston et caput occidentale abbuttat super viam que vocatur Gibbesgate. Altera pecia iacet inter terram Iohannis Bret ex parte australi et caput occidentale abbuttat super viam que vocatur Gibbesgate. Dat' apud Holkham die Martis proxima ante festum Sancti Clementis anno regni regis Edwardi filij regis Edwardi vndecimo.

   NOTE: Lucas No. 67. Cross-reference in Lucas's Gazetteer no. 260 Fo. 44.

221   *Thomas, son of Richard le Northerne of Holkham, grants Richard Neel of Holkham and Caterine his wife 1/2 acre and all lands held by five of his tenants together with four serfs.*   6 April 1332

<Dalegate cum seruiciis et consuetudinibus natiuorum tenencium et cum natiuis et sequelis terris bonis et catallis suis>
Ex feoffamento Thome filij Ricardi Northerne de Holkham facto Ricardo Neel de Holkham et Caterine vxori eius medietatem vnius acre terre iacentem apud Dalegate iuxta terram eiusdem Ricardi et omnes terras et omnia alia tenementa que Iohannes le Wryghte de eadem Willelmus Godwyne de eadem, Cecilia atte Hil de eadem, Berta vxor Iohannis Spellere de eadem et Amisius filius Willelmi filij Radulfi de Wals*ingham* coniunctim vel diuisim de me tenent ad voluntatem meam per virgam cum pertinenciis in Holkham. Concessi etiam et dedi prefato Ricardo et Caterine Agnetam et Helwysiam filias Thome filij Iohannis Ide de Holkham, Amisiam et Ceciliam filias Ricardi filij Iohannis Ide de eadem natiuas meas cum omnibus sectis et sequelis earum terris suis bonis et catallis earum. Dat' apud Holkham sexto die Aprilis anno regni regis Edwardi tercij post conquestum sexto. Et sequitur alia carta eiusdem.

   NOTE: Lucas 68. Cross-reference in Lucas's Gazetteer no. 260 Fo. 42v. On 24 April 1332 Neel court roll notes homages lately acquired from Thomas son of Richard Northerne giving locations of strips for which fealty is done or required. On 10 Nov. 1335 the collector's account of Christina Rutele adds into the total of rents of assise due the rents newly acquired from Thomas le Northerne. The five copyholders and the four granddaughters of John Ide occur in the court rolls (HD 83).

222   *Thomas, son of Richard Northerne, grants Richard Neel of Burnham and Katerine his wife 1 plot of 1/2 acre and all lands of John Ide and his sons Thomas and Richard, together with the latter's daughters and broods.*

6 April 1332

Ex feoffamento Thome filij Ricardi Northerne facto Ricardo Neel de Brunham et Katerine vxori eius vnam peciam terre iacentem apud Dalegate iuxta terram predicti Ricardi et continet in se medietatem vnius acre. Concessi etiam prefato Ricardo et Caterine omnes terras et omnia tenementa que aliquando fuerunt Iohannis Ide de Holkham Thome et Ricardi filiorum eiusdem Iohannis cum pertinenciis in eadem villa et Agnetam et Helewysiam filias predicte Thome filij Iohannis Amisiam et Ceciliam filias predicti Ricardi filij Iohannis cum tota secta et sequela sua bonis et catallis earum terris et tenementis suis cum omnibus pertinenciis. Dat' apud Holkham sexto die Aprilis anno regni regis Edwardi tercij post conquestum sexto.

NOTE: No Lucas number. Cross-reference in Lucas's Gazeteer no. 260 Fo. 42v.

223   *William Silk of Holkham grants Richard Neel of Burnham and Caterine his wife 1 plot of 11/4 acres and 3 other plots.*   23 Dec. 1315

Original: HD 26

<Wadelond, Bruera, Wellelond, inquiratur, Cathil>
Ex feoffamento Willelmi Silke de Holkham facto Ricardo Neel de Brunham et Caterine eius vxori quatuor pecias terre in camp' de Holkham quarum vna pecia iacet apud Wadlond iuxta terram Martini Goldewyne cuius caput orientale abbuttat super brueram et caput occidentale super terram prioris de Walsingham. Et vna pecia que vocatur Wellelond et iacet iuxta terram Matild' Choud' ex parte occidentali et continet in se quinque rodas terre cuius caput australe abbuttat super terram Iohannis Carpentarij. Et tercia pecia iacet apud Cathil cuius caput orientale abbuttat super terram Willelmi Asty et caput occidentale super predictam peciam que vocatur Wellelond. Et quarta pecia iacet in eadem quarentena cuius caput orientale abbuttat super terram predictam Willelmi Asty et caput occidentale sup[er] [pre]dictam terram que vocatur Wellelond et iacet inter terras Thome Idessone. Dat' apud Brunham in die Martis proxima post festum Sancti Thome apostoli anno regni regis Edwardi filij regis Edwardi nono.

NOTE: Lucas 69. Cross-reference in Lucas's Gazetteer no. 260 Fo. 50v.

224   *Thomas Chartre of Holkham grants Richard Neel of Burnham and*
Katerine his wife 1 plot.   [c. 1300]

Fo. 21 <examinatur>
Ex feoffamento Thome Chartre de Holkham facto Ricardo Neel de Brunham
et Katerine vxori eius vnam peciam terre cum pertinenciis iacentem in
Holkham inter terram Iohannis Bret et terram Radulfi Mone et vnum caput
abbuttat super terram predicti Ricardi et aliud caput super regiam viam. Nulla
data.

> NOTE: Lucas 70. Thomas Chartre acquired this land between lands of John Bret and
> Ralph Mone in no. 59.

225   *William Silk of Holkham releases to Richard Neel of Burnham and*
Katerine his wife 4 plots.   9 March 1316
> *Original: HP 1056*

<Wadelond, Wellelond, inquiratur, Cathil>
Ex relaxacione Willelmi Silk de Holkham facto Ricardo Neel de Brunham et
Katerine vxori eius quatuor pecias terre in Holkham quarum vna pecia iacet
apud Wadelond iuxta terram quondam Martini Goldwyne ex parte australi et
terram prioris de Walsingham ex parte boriali. Et vna pecia que vocatur
Wellelond que iacet iuxta terram Matildis Choud' ex parte occidentali cuius
caput australe abbuttat super terram Iohannis Carpentarij. Et tercia pecia iacet
apud Cathil cuius caput orientale abbuttat super terram Willelmi Asty et
caput occidentale super predictam peciam que vocatur Wellelond. Et quarta
pecia iacet in eadem quarentena cuius caput orientale abbuttat super terram
predicti Willelmi Asty et caput occidentale super predictam terram que
vocatur Wellelond et iacet inter terras Thome Idessone ex vtraque parte. Dat'
apud Holkham die Martis proxima ante festum Sancti Gregorij pape anno
regni regis Edwardi filij regis Edwardi nono.

> NOTE: Lucas allotted no number. Cross-reference in Lucas's Gazetteer no. 260 Fo. 50.

226   *William Silk of Holkham grants Richard Neel of Burnham and*
Caterine his wife 3 plots.   9 March 1316

<Holkham Estgate, Scrulescroft, Bruera, drawing of an index finger>
Ex feoffamento Willelmi Silke de Holkham facto Ricardo Neel de Brunham
et Caterine vxori eius tres pecias terre mee cum pertinenciis in Holkham
quarum vna pecia terre iacet in Holkham Estgate que vocatur Scrulescroft et
iacet iuxta terram Iohannis le Bret cuius caput australe abbuttat super terram
Thome Chartre. Et altera pecia iuxta terram Iohannis Godwyne ex parte
boriali cuius caput australe abbuttat super Brueram.[a] Et tercia pecia iacet ad

caput predicte pecie. Dat' apud Holkham die Martis proxima ante festum Sancti Gregorij pape anno regni regis Edwardi filij regis Edwardi nono.

NOTE: Lucas 71. Cross-reference in Lucas's Gazetteer no. 260 Fos. 43, 41v. Geoffrey le Bret's grant to William Silk called Scrulescroft is no. 3 (damaged by damp) and 62. His grant of land next to John Go[l]dwyne's land is described as *at Wadlonde* in no. 63 and possibly in no. 58.

227   John le Bret of Holkham grants Richard Neel of Burnham and Katerine his wife 1 rood.   **15 May 1321**

Ex feoffamento Iohannis le Bret de Holkham facto Ricardo Neel de Brunham et Katerine vxori eius vnam rodam terre in camp' de Holkham iacet prope terram antedicti Ricardi per partem occidentalem cuius caput aquilon*ale* abbuttat super terram prioris et conuentus de Petra et caput australe abbuttat super terram heredum Rogeri Chele. Dat' apud Holkham die Veneris proxima ante festum Sancti Dunstani anno regni regis Edwardi*ᵃ* quartodecimo.

NOTE: Lucas 72. In no. 95 land abuts on land of Ralph Chele towards the south but it was granted to Simon Hammond not to John le Bret, the grantor in no. 227. It lay in Sladaker.

VARIANT: *ᵃ* filij Edwardi probably omitted in Ms. after Edwardi.

228   Roger Everard of Holkham grants Katerine, widow of Richard Neel, 2d. rent of Alice, daughter of Osbert Longe of Holkham, for 1 plot of 3/4 acre.   **16 Feb. 1335**

<ij d. annui redditus>
Ex feoffamento Rogeri Euerard de Holkham facto Katerine relicte Ricardi Neel de eadem duas denariatas annui redditus quos percipio de Alicia filia Osberti Long*e* de eadem vicelicet pro vna pecia terre iacentis in camp' de Holkham in Dalegate iuxta terram prioris et conuentus de Wals*ingham* ex vna parte et continet in se tres rodas terre. Dat' apud Holkham in festo Iuliane Martiris anno regni regis Edwardi tercij post conquestum nono.

NOTE: Lucas 73. Land which once belonged to Roger Everard, the grantor, who is mentioned at Neel manor court on 8 Oct. 1449 as in Saltergate at Brymbyldykes. William Newgate was distrained to show what title he had (HD 194a) but in no. 228 the land is in Dalegate.

229 *Release and quitclaim from Peter le Bret of Holkham to Richard Neel of Burnham and Katerine his wife of lands, tenements, villeins, villeinages and 1 fold, with all liberties which they had by gift of Adam, son of Simon Hammond, by lease from John, son of Harvey Underburgh and Cecily his wife.* 5 April 1315

<Quietaclamacio Dominij le Bret et seruiciorum villanorum et vnius Falde cum libertatibus>
Ex relaxacione et quietaclamacione Petri le Bret de Holkham facto Ricardo Neel de Brunham et Katerine vxori eius totum us et clameum quod habui vel aliquo modo habere potero in omnibus terris et tenementis villanis et eorum villenagiis et in vna falda cum omnibus libertatibus ad predictam faldam pertinentibus in villa de Holkham que predictus Ricardus et Katerina habent de dono Ade filij Simonis Hammond ex dimissione Iohannis filij Heruici Vnderburgh et Cecilie vxoris sue. Dat' apud Holkham die Sabbati proxima post festum Sancti Ambrosij episcopi anno regni regis Edwardi filij regis Edwardi octauo.

NOTE: No Lucas number. Nos. 190 and 191 are closely related but do not mention the fold.

230 *Release and quitclaim from Adam, son of Simon Hammond of Holkham, to Richard Neel of Burnham and Katerine his wife of all rights in 7 acres 1 1/2 roods and 33 acres, 1 fold and 2 villeins etc.* 3 April 1315

Fo. 21v <Quietaclamacio xl acrarum 1 rode et dimidie et natiuorum et eorum sequelarum et de falda cum libertatibus eius>
Ex relaxacione et quietaclamacione Ade filij Simonis Hammond de Holkham facto Ricardo Neel de Brunham et Katerine vxori eius totum ius et clameum que habuit vel aliquo modo habere poterit in septem acris et vna roda et dimidia terre cum pertinenciis in villa de Holkham quas predictus Ricardus et Katerina habent et tenent ex dono et feoffamento meo ac eciam in triginta et tribus acris terre cum libertate vnius falde et cum omnibus aliis pertinenciis et in Gilberto Gurle et Eluiua Daleman villanis cum omnibus eorum villenagiis seruiciis consuetudinibus et in eorum catallis sequelis omnibus procreatis et procreandis que predicti Ricardus et Caterina habent et tenent in predicta villa de Holkham ex dono et feoffamento Iohannis filij Heruici de Burgh' et Cecilie vxoris sue qui predicta tenementa et villanos tenuerunt de hereditate mea in predicta villa nomine dotis seu alio quoquomodo. Dat' apud Brunham die Iouis proxima ante festum Sancti Ambrosij episcopi anno regni regis Edwardi filij regis Edwardi octauo.

NOTE: Lucas 74. The survey of folds of 16 May 1306 mentions one let to John Hammond by Geoffrey le Bret (no. 1). John son of Geoffrey le Bret granted the two villeins in 1296 to Simon Hammond and Cecily his wife (no. 104). This may be the fold which Richard and Katerine Neel had from Adam son of Simon Hammond on 8 April 1316 (no. 230) and which Peter le Bret released to them on 10 April (no. 229).

231 *Ralph le Deye and Agnes his wife of Holkham grant Katerine, widow of Richard Neel, 1 rood.* 20 April 1336

Original: HP 1088

<Hugge>
Ex feoffamento Radulfi Deye et Agnetis vxoris eius de Holkham facto Katerine que fuit vxori Ricardi Neel vnam peciam terre continentem vnam rodam cum pertinenciis in Holkham iacentem apud Le Hugge inter terram predicte Katerine ex parte occidentali et terram Heilote le Meir' ex parte orientali cuius caput boriale abbuttat super terram predicte Katerine. Dat' apud Holkham vicesimo die Aprilis anno regni regis Edwardi tercij post conquestum decimo.

> NOTE: Lucas 75. Cross-reference in Lucas's Gazetteer no. 260 Fo. 44v. This plot of land adjoined that of Katerine Neel both in the west and in the north near Le Hugge. It was rounding off the precinct of Neel manor house which is marked on the 1590 map as to the south-east of the Howe. Cf. no. 242.

232 *Simon Mous of Kettlestone and Cecily his wife of Holkham grants Katerine, widow of Richard Neel of Burnham, 1 acre.* 9 Feb. 1336

Original: HP 1082

<Scamelond>
Ex feoffamento Simonis Mous de Ketelston' et Cecilie vxoris sue de Holkham facto Katerine que fuit vxor Ricardi Neel de Brunham vnam acram terre iacentem in camp' de Holkham apud Schamelond iuxta terram eiusdem Katerine ex parte boriali et est forera cuius caput occidentale abbuttat super terram Iohannis Mey et caput orientale abbuttat partim super terram Andree sub le Klynt. Dat' apud Holkham nono die Februarij anno regni regis Edwardi tercij post conquestum decimo.

> NOTE: Lucas 76. Cross-reference in Lucas's Gazetteer no. 260 Fo. 49v. No. 174 between the same parties on the same date has quite different abuttals. Nos. 5 and 9 are grants of 28 Nov. 1329 from Ralph son of William a le Gateshende de Brisley to Simon and Cecily Mous in Scamelond.

233   *William Wake of Holkham grants Thomas, son of Richard Neel of Burnham, 2s. rent with homages and services for a messuage and croft of 33/4 acres and 1/2 rood, a plot of 1 acre, 3 other plots and 6d. rent for a portion of a messuage at the Stathe.*   28 July 1347

<[i]j, s. annui redditus cum falda, S. Elverych, Johan. Weylond [struck off], Thomas Grygge, Johan. Buntyng, Elen. Elevrych>
Ex feoffamento Willelmi Wake de Holkham facto Thome filio Ricardi Neel de Brunham duas solidatas annui redditus cum homagiis et omnibus seruiciis prouenientibus de omnibus terris et tenementis que Cecilia Erneys tenuit de me in predicta villa de Holkham in dominico et in seruicio videlicet de mesuagio predicte Cecilie et crufta continente tres acras terre et de tribus rodis et dimidia roda terre iacent' apud Schortadowe iuxta terram Katerine Neel cum falda. Et de vna acra terre quam Willelmus Curchon' tenet in dominico iacent' apud Longeadowe. Et de tribus peciis terre quas Iohannes filius Rogeri Eluerich' tenet in predicta villa de feodo meo quarum due pecie iacent apud Longeadowe et tercia pecia iacet apud Thorpegate subtus Sexakerhil. Ac eciam concessi et dedi etc. eidem Thome sex denar' redditus cum homagio et seruicio Iohannis Ayneld percipiend' de parcella mesuagij apud le Stathe. Dat' apud Holkham die Sabbati proxima post festum Sancti Iacobi apostoli anno regni regis Edwardi tercij post conquestum vicesimo primo.

NOTE: Lucas 77. The same hand has struck out *Iohannes Weylond* written above *Thomas Grygges* <*ij annui redditus*>. Added about 1500: <Robert Koo>. John Weylond held 3 acres, John Buntyng 31/2 roods and Simon Elferych has three plots at Neel court of 22 April 1449, first court of Yelverton. On 1 July 1449 Henry Silk held John Aynild's empty messuage at le Stathe (HD 194a). In 1550 at Neel's first court of John Pepys and subsequently there are repeated precepts to distrain on these lands once of John Weylond, John Buntyng, William Mere and Simon Elveryche (HD 473). William Wake bought a fold described in survey of 13 May 1306 (no. 1). See also no. 74. John Aynild's empty messuage at Le Stathe, later held by Henry Silk, is mentioned at Neel court of 1 July 1449 (HD 194a).

234   *Roger, son of Everard of Holkham, grants Katerine, widow of Richard Neel, 31/2 rent once received of Richard Neel for 4 plots acquired by him and 21/2d. rent received of Richard Speller for 3 plots.*   2 Dec. 1334

Fo. 22   <Relaxacio redditus iij d., perquisicio, Edmundus Elferych' modo tenet>
Ex feoffamento Rogeri filij Eborardi de Holkham facto Katerine vxori quondam Ricardi Neel de eadem tres denariatas annui redditus et oboli quas percipere annuatim solebam de Ricardo Neel marito predicte Katerine in Holkham pro quibusdem terris quas idem Ricardus adquisiuit in camp' de eadem. Quarum vna pecia iacet sub mesuagio Iohannis Vnderclynt. Alia

pecia iacet apud Cleylond. Alia pecia iacet apud Steynhil. Alia pecia iacet
apud Hugge. Et duas denariatas et obolum annui redditus quas percipere
solebam de Ricardo Spellere de Holkham pro tribus peciis terre iacentibus in
camp' de Holkham quarum vna pecia iacet ad caput crofte Matild' Donge
iuxta terram Roberti Henry ex parte orientali. Alia pecia iacet ex parte
occidentali ecclesie collateraliter et semita que ducit de ecclesia versus le
Dale abbuttat super caput orientale pecie predicte et vtraque pecia dat
denarium per annum. Tercia pecia iacet ex parte orientali ecclesie inter
terram Heruei Stoward versus occidentem et ista pecia dat vnum obolum per
annum. Dat' apud Holkham die Veneris proxima post festum Sancte Katerine
virginis anno regni regis Edwardi tercij post conquestum octauo.

NOTE: Lucas 78. The grantor is called Roger Everard in 1335, no. 28 (see note). On 8
Oct. 1449 Edmund Edrych was distrained to show title and did fealty, HD 194a.

235   *William the smith of Holkham and Emma Curson his wife grant*
Richard Neel of Burnham and Caterine his wife 1/2 acre and reversion of
1/2 acre which Agnes, widow of William Curson, holds in dower.

7 May 1321

<Lambulhil, Gibbesgate>
Ex feoffamento Willelmi Fabri de Holkham et Emme Curson vxoris sue facto
Ricardo Neel de Brunham et Caterine vxori eius vnam dimidiam acram terre
cum pertinenciis suis et reuersionem vnius dimidie acre terre quam Agneta
vxor quondam Willelmi Curson tenet in dote ex assignacione nostra iacentes
inuicem in camp' de Holkham super Langebuthelhil inter terram Iohannis filij
Fratters ex parte australi et terram Gilberti Mayn ex parte aquilonali et caput
orientale abbuttat super Gibbesgate et caput occidentale abbuttat super terram
prioris et conuentus de Petriston. Dat' apud Holkham die Iouis proxima post
festum Sancti Iohannis ante portam Latinam anno regni regis Edwardi[a] xiiij°.

NOTE: Lucas 79. Cross-reference in Lucas's Gazetteer no. 260 Fo. 46 which reads
Edwardi Secundi 14 (half acre abutting east on Gibbesgate not one acre as in no. 235).
William *Faber* of Holkham is evidently the same as William *Faber* of Gresham and
grants another rood to Richard and Caterine Neel in 1321 in no. 203 with Emma his
wife. Agnes Curthun grants the 3 acres in no. 218 which William de Gresham quitclaims
to them. In no. 86 William son of Gilbert Curthun received a plot of land abutting north
on Gibbesgate.

VARIANT: [a] filij Edwardi omitted.

236   *Mariot Edwy of Holkham grants Richard Neel and Caterine his wife a part of a messuage with a house.*   6 July 1323

<examinatur, De domo apud le Steithe>
Ex feoffamento Mariote Edwy de Holkham facto Ricardo Neel et Caterine vxori eius vnam porcionem mesuagij iacentis in Holkham iuxta mesuagium predicte Mariote ex parte orientali et mesuagium quondam Iohannis Ayneld ex parte occidentali cum quadam domo in eadem sita cuius caput australe abbuttat super cruftam predicte Mariote et caput aquilonale abbuttat super le Stathegate. Dat' apud Holkham die Mercurij proxima ante translacionem Sancti Thome Cantuariensis archiepiscopi anno regni regis Edwardi filij regis Edwardi sextodecimo.

> NOTE: Lucas 80. W.G. Hoskins wrongly stated that Holkham village used to be near the church and was moved to the Stathe when the Park was created in the nineteenth century. The 1590 map shows a village already at the Stathe and no. 236 is one of many documents testifying to its earlier existence.

237   *John Aynild of Holkham grants Gilbert Neel of Burnham 3/4 acres.*
13 Sept. 1345

<inquiratur, Scothowgate>
Ex feoffamento Iohannis Aynyld*e* de Holkham facto Gilberto Neel de Brunham tres rodas terre in camp' de Holkham apud Scothowgate inter terram predicti Iohannis ex parte orientali et terram Cecilie Sweyn ex parte occidentali et caput boriale abbuttat super Scothowgate. Dat' apud Holkham die Martis proxima post festum Natiuitatis beate Marie virginis anno regni regis Edwardi tercij post conquestum nonodecimo. Et sequitur antiqua carta eiusdem terre etc.

> NOTE: Lucas 81. Cross-reference in Lucas's Gazetteer no. 260 Fo. 50. John acquired this plot of land at Scothowgate early the same year, according to his *antiqua carta.*

238   *Simon Mous of Holkham grants Richard Neel and Katerine his wife 1 plot.*   1 March 1330

Fo. 22v   <examinatur, Brunhamgate>
Ex feoffamento Simonis Mous de Holkham facto Ricardo Neel et Katerine vxori eius vnam peciam terre iacentem in campis occidentalibus de Holkham inter terram prioris et conuentus de Petirston ex parte orientali et terram rectoris medietatis ecclesie de Holkham ex parte occidentali cuius caput boriale abbuttat super Brunhamgate. Dat' apud Holkham kalend' Martij anno regni regis Edwardi tercij a conquestu quarto.

> NOTE: Lucas 82. Cross-reference in Lucas's Gazetteer no. 260 Fo. 41v. This land is granted to Simon Ide of Kettlestone by Margery Craske in no. 76. The grant to Neel Manor is dated a few months before the grant to Ide.

239   *Simon, son of William Eyr of Morston, grants Katerine, widow of Richard Neel of Burnham 1 plot of 3 acres.*   **11 July 1335**

Original: HP 1083

<Wyghtoungate>
Ex feoffamento Simonis filij Willelmi Eyr de Mershton' facto Katerine que fuit vxor Ricardi Neel de Brunham pro seruicio suo et pro fidelitate quam michi fecit pre manibus vnam peciam trium acrarum terre iacentem apud Aldelose cum pertinenciis in Holkham iuxta terram abbatis de Creyk ex parte occidentali et caput australe abbuttat super Brueram de Holkham siue viam que ducit versus Wyghtone habend' et tenend' predicte Katerine heredibus et assignatis suis de me et heredibus meis: reddendo inde annuatim mihi et heredibus meis quinque denarios ad duos anni terminos scilicet ad festum Sancti Andree duos denarios et ad festum natiuitatis Sancti Iohannis Baptiste tres denarios pro omni seruicio. Et ego predictus Simon et heredes mei predictam peciam trium acrarum terre siue in ea plus habeatur siue minus cum suis pertinenciis predicte Katerine heredibus et assignatis suis per seruicia predicta pro omni seruicio contra omnes homines acquietabimus imperpetuum. In cuius rei testimonium etc. Hiis testibus etc. Dat' apud Holkham die Martis proxima post festum translacionis Sancti Thome martiris anno regni regis Edwardi tercij post conquestum nono.

NOTE: Lucas 83.Cross-reference in Lucas's Gazetteer no. 260 Fo. 41.

240   *Gilbert, son of John le Bret of Holkham, grants Richard Neel of Burnham and Katerine his wife 1 plot with a house thereon.*   **16 Aug. 1322**

<de pecia terre cum quadam domo>
\Iacet in Southgate/ Ex feoffamento Gilberti filij Iohannis Bret de Holkham facto Ricardo Neel de Brunham et Katerine vxori eius vnam peciam terre cum quadam domo insuper sita prout iacet intra duas diuisas in villa de Holkham iuxta mesuagium et cruftam Iohannis Eylot per partem orientem et tenementum domini Eymerici de Valencia ex parte occidentali cuius caput australe abbuttat super regalem viam et caput aquilonale abbuttat super terram Heruei Buleman. Dat' apud Holkham die Lune proxima post assumpcionem beate Marie virginis anno regni regis Edwardi sextodecimo.

NOTE: Lucas 84.

241 *John Huberd of Holkham grants Richard Neel of Burnham and Katerine his wife 1 plot of 1¹/₄ acres.* 20 Dec. 1328

<Wyghtoungate>
Ex feoffamento Iohannis Huberd de Holkham facto Ricardo Neel de Brunham et Katerine vxori eius vnam peciam terre continentem in se vnam acram et vnam rodam cum pertinenciis in Holkham iacentem iuxta terram Bartholomei Calewere ex parte orientali et caput australe abbuttat super viam ducentem de Holkham versus Wyghton'. Dat' apud Holkham xx° die Decembris anno regni regis Edwardi tercij post conquestum secundo.

NOTE: Lucas 85. Cross-reference in Lucas's Gazetteer no. 260 Fo. 50v. Cf. no. 72 of 22 Dec. 1298.

242 *Ralph le Deye and Agnes his wife of Holkham grant Caterine, widow of Richard Neel, 1 plot of ¹/₂ acre.* 20 Nov. 1335

Original: HP 1086

<apud le Clynt iac' apud Scamelond>
Ex feoffamento Radulfi Deye et Agnet*is* vxoris sue de Holkham facto Caterine que fuit vxor Ricardi Neel vnam peciam terre continentem dimidiam acram cum pertinenciis in Holkham iacentem inter terram predicte Katerine ex parte boriali et terram Simonis Mous ex parte australi. Et caput orientale abbuttat super terram Andree Ad Le Clynt. Dat' apud Holkham xx° die Nouembris anno regni regis Edwardi tercij post conquestum nono.

NOTE: Lucas 86. Cross-reference in Lucas's Gazetteer no. 260 Fo. 42. The grantors gave another rood the following year in no. 231.

243 *John le Bret of Holkham grants Richard Neel of Burnham and Katerine his wife 1 plot.* 15 May 1321

Fo. 23 <memorandum, Wadelond alias Podelond>
Ex feoffamento Iohannis le Bret de Holkham facto Ricardo Neel de Brunham et Katerine vxori eius vnam peciam terre \prior de Petyrston iniuste ocupat/ iacentem in camp' de Holkham in vna quarentena que vocatur Wadelonds prope tenementum domini Eymerici de Valencia per partem borialem et terram Iohannis Charle versus austrum cuius caput occidentale abbuttat super terram Iohannis Charle predicti et caput orientale abbuttat super terram heredis Roberti Ayneld. Dat' apud Holkham die Veneris proxima ante festum Sancti Dunstani archiepiscopi anno regni regis Edwardi xiiij°.

NOTE: Lucas 87 Cross-reference in Lucas's Gazetteer no. 260 Fo. 50v. The tenement of Aymer de Valence (heir of Montchesney) may be the lost manor house of Burghall. He succeeded Denise de Montchesney in 1304, Farrer, p. 108.

244   *Geoffrey de Sharrington of Holkham grants Richard Neel of Burnham*
and Katerine his wife all the land in his croft.   6 Dec. 1323

<terra in crofta Nicol>.
Ex feoffamento Galfridi de Scharneton' de Holkham facto Ricardo Neel de
Brunham et Katerine vxori eius totam terram meam in illa crofta mea que
fuit quondam Gilberti Nicol cum pertinenciis in Holkham et iacet inter terras
domini Adomari de Valencia ex vtraque parte et caput eius australe abbuttat
super terram ecclesie de Petirston et caput boriale super mesuagium predicti
Galfridi. Dat' apud Holkham vj^{to} die Decembris anno regni regis Edwardi
filij Edwardi septimodecimo.

          NOTE: Lucas 88.

245   *Adam, son of William Craske of Holkham, grants Richard Neel of*
Burnham and Caterine his wife 4 acres in 2 plots, each of 2 acres
          13 Dec. 1318

          Original: HP 1063

<examinatur, Steynhil, Marledlond>
Ex feoffamento Ade filij Willelmi Craske de Holkham facto Ricardo Neel de
Brunham et Caterine vxori eius quatuor acras terre iacentes in camp' de
Holkham quarum vna pecia iacet apud Steynhil inter terram predicti Ade ex
parte orientali et terram Roberti de Gristone et Mariote matris dicti Ade ex
parte occidentali et continet in se duas acras terre. Alia pecia vocatur
Marledlond et iacet inter terram Roberti de Gristone et Mariote matris
predicti Ade ex parte boriali et terram predicti Ricardi et Katerine ex parte
australi et continet in se duas acras terre. Dat' apud Holkham in die Sancte
Lucie virginis anno regni regis Edwardi filij regis Edwardi duodecimo.

          NOTE: Lucas 89. Cross-reference in Lucas's Gazetteer no. 260 Fos. 46v, 49v. For marled
          land, cf. no. 189.

246   *Gilbert le Calewere of Holkham grants Katerine Neel of Holkham*
23/4 roods.   [c. 1338–9]

<inquiratur, Dedquenepit, Elsiscote>
Ex feoffamento Gilberti le Calewere de Holkham facto Katerine Neel de
eadem duas rodas et dimidiam et quartam partem vnius rode terre iacentis in
campis de Holkham in quarentena vocata Dedquenespit inter terram quondam
Willelmi Haye ex parte australi et terram predicte Katerine ex parte
aquilonali et caput orientale abbuttat super Elsiscot' habend' et tenend' etc.
cum clausula warantie etc. Hiis testibus etc. Nulla data.

NOTE: Lucas 90. Cross-reference in Gazetteer, no. 260 Fo. 42v, under Dedquenepit dates this 12 Edward III (1338–9). As the Gazetteer gives a date but the cartulary says 'nulla data' the Gazetteer must have been compiled from original deeds but the cartulary may have been copied from some previous summary. In no. 25 Walter de Calthorpe grants this land to Bartholomew le Calwere in *quarantena vocata Dedquenepit*. On 22 April 1449, at the Neel court, there was an inquiry with distraint on the Prior of Walsingham about the 2³/4 roods in Dedquenepit abutting on Elsyescoote.

247 *William de Hindringham grants Richard Neel of Burnham 1 'place'*
with house and 3 ft. of land to the east and 4 ft. of land to the south .
28 Jan. 1320

<inquiratur, 1 placea cum domo in Holkham Estgate>
Ex feoffamento Willelmi de Hindringham facto Ricardo Neel de Brunham vnam placeam cum quadam domo desuper sitam et cum tribus pedibus terre ex parte orientali et cum quatuor pedibus terre ex parte australi et dicta placea iacet in Holkham videlicet in Estgate inter regiam viam et mesuagium Gilberti Mayn. Dat' apud Holkham die Lune proxima ante festum purificacionem beate Marie anno regni regis Edwardi filij regis Edwardi terciodecimo. [Et modo iacet inter ortum prioris de Walsyngham ex parte orientali et terram hered' Willelmi Waylond ex parte occidentali.]*ᵃ*

NOTE: Lucas 91. Cross-reference in Lucas's Gazetteer no. 260 Fo. 43. There were no houses shown in Eastgate in the 1590 map, but the crofts which adjoined them still remained as late as 1778 (Fiche 3: D2).

VARIANT: *ᵃ* added in dark ink.

248 *John Hoddes of Holkham grants Gilbert, son of late Richard Neel, 5s.*
rent at All Saints.
9 Dec. 1347

<perquisicio v s. redditus>
Ex feoffamento Iohannis Hoddes de Holkham facto Gilberto filio quondam Ricardi Neel quemdam annuum redditum quinque solidorum percipiendum illi et heredibus suis de omnibus terris et tenementis predicti Iohannis in villa et campis de Holkham annuatim ad festa Omnium Sanctorum. Et si contingat quod predictus annuus redditus in parte vel in toto a retro fuerit aliquo anno ad terminum predictum concedo quod predictus Gilbertus et heredes sui extunc distringant in omnibus terris et tenementis meis predictis et in qualibet particula eorumdem et districciones retineant quousque de arreragiis predicti annui redditus plenarie deuenerint persolut' ad quoscumque manus predicte terre et tenementa in posterum deuenerint. In cuius rei testimonium present' sigillum meum apposui. Hiis testibus etc. Dat' apud Holkham die Dominica proxima post festum conceptionis Beate Marie anno regni regis Edwardi tercij a conquestu vicesimo primo.

NOTE: Lucas 92.

249　*Gilbert Calwere of Holkham grants Thomas Neel of Holkham 31/4 acres in 5 plots, and their release.*　　　**26 and 27 July 1345**

Fo. 23v　<Wyghtongate, inquiratur, Schortlond, Scothowgate, Skamlond, Longfurlong', inquiratur, Wellegate> [left margin]
<Iohannes Andrewe tenet j acram ibidem vt dicitur vel Willelmus Newgate> [right margin]

Ex feoffamento Gilberti Calewere de Holkham facto Thome Neel de eadem tres acras terre et vnam rodam iacentem in campis de Holkham in diuersis peciis quarum vna pecia quinque rodarum iacet apud Le Lyng' iuxta terram quondam Ricardi Neel ex parte orientali et caput australe abbuttat super regiam viam que ducit de Holkham apud Wyghton'. Alia pecia^a vnius acre iacet apud Schortlond iuxta terram Iohannis Andrew ex parte orientali et caput australe abbuttat super Scothowgate. Alia pecia^a dimidie acre et dimidie rode iacet apud Skamlond iuxta terram Rogeri Kroude ex parte orientali et caput boriale abbuttat super Scothowgate. Alia pecia^a vnius rode iacet apud Longfurlong iuxta terram Iohannis Andreu ex parte orientali et caput boriale abbuttat super Skothowgate. Et alia pecia^a dimidie rode iacet apud Wellegate iuxta terram abbatis et conuentus de Creyk' ex parte orientali et caput boriale abbuttat super Wellegate quas Sayeva vxor quondam Bartholomei Calewere tenet in dotem de Hereditate mea et que post mortem dicte Sayeue mihi et heredibus meis reuerti debeant. Remaneant dicto Thome heredibus et assignatis suis imperpetuum tenend' de capitalibus dominis feodi per seruicia debita et consueta. Dat' apud Holkham die Martis proxima post festum Sancti Iacobi apostoli anno regni regis Edwardi tercij post conquestum nonodecimo. Et sequitur relaxacio et quietaclamacio predicti Gilberti Calewere facto predicto Thome Neel et heredibus suis totum us et clameum quod habuit vel aliquo modo habere potuit in predictis tribus acris et vna roda terre cum pertinenciis in Holkham quas Sayeua quondam vxor Bartholomei Calewere tenuit in dote de hereditate predicti Gilberti. Dat' apud Holkham die Mercurii proxima post festum Sancti Iacobi apostoli anno regni regis Edwardi tercij post conquestum nonodecimo.

NOTE: Lucas 93. Cross-reference in Lucas's Gazetteer no. 260 fos 46, 49v, 50v where the date is wrongly given as *Edwardi tercij 10* (1336–7). Everard *sub Hoga* granted 3/4 rood on Wellegate to Roger Calwere on 1 Dec. 1291 in HD 9.

VARIANT: ^{a} Inquiratur interlineated.

250   *Gilbert Neel of Holkham grants Thomas his son and Margaret his*
daughter all lands and tenements which Gilbert Neel or Caterine his mother
ever had from John Craske.   11 May 1364

   Original: HP 1108 (not printed)

<Alienacio terrarum per Gilbertum Neel>
Sciant presentes et futuri quod ego Gilbertus Neel de Holkham dedi et hac
presenti carta mea confirmaui Thome filio meo et Margarete filie mee et
heredibus dicti Thome omnes terras et tenementa quas ego Gilbertus Neel vel
Caterina mater mea vnquam perquisiuimus de Iohanne Craske in villa et in
Campis de Holkham: habend' et tenend' dictas terras et tenementa dicto
Thome et Margarete et heredibus dicti Thome de capitalibus dominis feodi
per seruicia debita et consueta. Et ego predictus Gilbertus et heredes mei
predictas terras et tenementa predictis Thome et Margarete et heredibus
Thome contra omnes gentes warantizabimus imperpetuum. In cuius rei
testimonium huic presenti carte sigillum meum apposui. Hiis testibus.
Waltero Souter' . Waltero Bettis . Rogero Herueye et aliis. Dat' apud
Holkham die Sabbati in vigilia Pentecosten anno regni regis Edwardi tercij
post conquestum tricesimo octauo.

   NOTE: No Lucas number. The original deed HP 1108 is badly faded. No grant from
   John Craske is in the cartulary.

251   *Brother Warin, Prior of Peterstone, and brethren release to Richard*
Neel of Burnham and Katerine his wife all claims on 4d. rent for 2 plots in
Holkham Fields.   5 June 1318

Ex relaxacione fratris Warini prioris de Petreston et confratres eiudem domus
facta Ricardo Neel de Brunham et Katerine vxori eius totum us et clameum
quod habuerunt seu aliquo modo habere potuerunt in quatuor denariis
redditus quas idem Ricardus solebat nobis reddere per annum cum wardis
releuiis maritagiis et escaetis pro duabus peciis terre iacentes in campis de
Holkham videlicet apud Scothowgate et apud Duuesty. Dat' apud Holkham
die Lune proxima post festum ascencionis domini anno regni regis Edwardi
xj°.

   NOTE: No Lucas number. For Richard Neel's relation with Peterstone Priory see also no.
   252.

252   *Agreement of Warin, Prior of Peterstone, and brethren with Richard Neel of Burnham and Katerine his wife, who grant the Priory of Peterstone 13 acres in 5 plots and an annual rent of 23d.*   5 June 1318

Fo. 24   <preceptum seisire quia>
<**Petyrston**, preceptum seisire quia nullus prior neque confratres ibidem existunt> [left margin]
<xxiii d.> [right margin]
Die Lune proxima post festum assencionis domini anno regni regis Edwardi vndecimo conuenit inter fratrem Warinum priorem de Petriston et eiusdem domus confratres ex parte vna et Ricardum Neel de Brunham et Katerinam vxorem eius ex altera. Ita videlicet quod predicti Ricardus et Katerina concesserunt predictis priori et confratribus et eorum successoribus tresdecim acras terre iacentes in campis de Holkham in diuersis peciis videlicet apud Bramlond quinque acras apud Lethrgraues tres acras apud Dalegate duas acras et dimidiam apud Chelegate vnam acram et apud Longehaddehowe vnam acram et dimidiam habend' et tenend' de nobis et heredibus nostris per homagium et fidelitatem et per seruicia viginti trium denariorum per annum ad duos terminos reddend' videlicet ad festum Sancti Michaelis vndecim denarios et obolum et ad pascha vndecim denarios et obolum. Et ad scutagium domini regis quando venerit in sokna domini Audomari de Valencia in Holkham ad viginti solidos sex denarios ad plus plus et ad minus minus. Et nos predicti Ricardus et Katerina et heredes nostri predictos priorem et confratres et eorum successores acquietabimus erga dominum Audomari de Valencia pro predictis seruiciis sicut Martinum Goldewenum feoffatorem predictorum prioris et confratrum actenus acquietauimus et non amplius pro predictis seruiciis. In cuius rei testimonium sigillum comune predictorum prioris et fratrum vni parti huius indenture est appensum et remanet penes predictum Ricardum et Katerinam. Dat' apud Petriston die et anno supradictis.

Fos. 24v–26v   [rare blanks]

Fos. 27–29v

FEODARY OF HOLKHAM

NOTE: There are various versions of this Feodary as the facts concerned any of the many lords and important tenants in medieval Holkham. The title in HD 5a, 5b and 71 is the same, but adds *'transcriptum per Iohannem Waylond de eadem de capitalibus dominis ibidem anno Edwardi primi [or primo?]'*. One version is added at the beginning of the Dereham Cartulary, BL Ms. Add. 46352 Fos. 3v–4v. This has no title. It was probably known to Edmund Lucas who appears from Burghall court rolls to have been the bailiff of the Abbot of West Dereham at Holkham. It lacks all sub-titles and the spaces between the paragraphs devoted to the different tenants by Edmund Lucas. Lucas appears to have made a conscious effort at producing a text that would be easy to consult. He precedes every chapter and paragraph with a large or small paragraph mark. Among many divergencies noted below, the Dereham Cartulary habitually calls de Dakeney de Hakeney, as does HD 55, and spells *Feodum Feudum*. It is likely that the thirteenth-century original was the return to the *Hundred rolls inquiry* of 1279–80.
Cf. Appendix III for Commentaries.

(Quire 3) **Fo. 27**

253 FEODARIUM DE DOMINIIS IN HOLKHAM ET DE EORUM TENENTIBUS TRANSCRIPTUM PER EDMUNDUM LUCAS DE EST DERHAM

[c. 1279–80]

DE CAPITALIBUS DOMINIS IBIDEM

<Feodum^{1a} de Wyghton>^{1b} [*left margin*]

Galfridus Lyseny^{1c} qui est in custodia Iohannis Harcourt^{1d} tenet de domino rege in capite sex sokemannos qui tenent de domino Galfrido octo acras terre cum mesuagiis suis de inferiori tenura pertinentibus ad manerium de Wygthton^{1e} et visus francipleg'^{1f} cum suis libertatibus et Wreccum^{1g} maris et tolnetum portus^{1h} de Holkham.

DE FEODO NOIOUN

<Prior de Pe[terston] tenet>^{2a} [*right margin*]^{1}

Radulfus Noioun^{2b2} de Salle tenet in Holkham de dicto Galfrido Lyseny^{2c} . et. Galfridus de domino Rege in capite. xxiij . sokemannos^{2d} qui tenent in villenagio^{2e} vj^{xx} . acras et xij acras cum suis mesuagiis et idem tenet iij coterellos qui tenent in villenagio^{2e} . iiij . acras terre cum suis cotagiis. Et^{2f} dictus Radulfus tenet predict' per seruicium dimidij militis de dicto Galfrido Lyseny

---

1   See Commentary III for a terrier and rental of Peterstone's *Feodum Noion*.
2   See Commentary III. For Ralph Nuggun, 1279, 1290, see Moor, *Knights*, vol. 1, p. 279. Ralph, lord of Batheley, son of Richard and Joan, was alive in 1303; see Blomefield, *Norfolk*, 1775, vol. iv, p. 421 on Manor of Salle and the de Nugouns. The Noyons are mentioned in the cartularies of Creake and West Dereham. A mid 15th century list of Peterstone's bond tenants late of John Nogeons in HD 300 (no. 23) contains nine names.

Iohannes Goldewyne^{2g} tenet de dicto Radulfo de eodem feodo vnum mesuagium^{2h} xl. acras terre et vnam faldam^3 et reddit ei per annum v s. iiij d.

Iohannes Silk^{2i} tenet de eodem^{2j} Radulfo . iij acras et j rodam et reddit per annum j d.^{2k}

De Feodo Dakeney^{3a}

<Feodum Radulfi Tony> [*left margin*]

<Gregorius Hol[kham] . tenet . et vocatur Hilhalle> [*right margin*]

Thomas Dakeney$^{3a\,4}$ in Holkham de Iohanne de Dakeney^{3b} et reddit ei unum turettum$^{3c\,5}$ argenteum ad unum speruerum et Iohannes de Dakeney de Radulfo Tony^6 et Radulfus de domino Rege in capite vnum mesuagium^{3d} et xiiij acras terre unum forum^7 et vnum molendinum. Item dictus Thomas tenet xxxvj . sokem*annos* qui tenent in villenagio vj^{xx} . acras terre et x acras cum suis mesuagiis de dicto feodo. Item^{3d} idem Thomas tenet . iij . coterellos qui tenent . iij . acras^{3e} cum suis cotagiis^{3f} in villenagio.

Prior de Petirston$^{3g\,8}$ tenet de eodem feodo xl acras terre et j faldam^9 et reddit dicto Thome per annum iiij s. x d. ob.

Idem^{3h} prior tenet de eodem feodo duos coterellos^{3i} qui tenent in villenagio^{3j} ij acras terre cum suis cotagiis^{3k} vt patet per cirograffum leuatum^{3l}

Abbas de Creyk$^{3m\,10}$ tenet de dicto Thoma^{3n} de eodem feodo^{3o} xl acras terre et vnam faldam^{11} et reddit per annum ix s.^{3p} . vj d. et j^{3q} buss. et dimid. frumenti

Idem Abbas tenet iij sokemannos qui tenent in villenagio viij acras terre cum mesuagiis^{3r} suis et ij coterellos qui tenent j acram et dimidiam de dicto feodo cum cotagiis suis per predictum seruicium

---

3   The fold is mentioned in no. 1.

4   See Commentary IV.

5   See Commentary V.

6   See Commentary VI.

7   See Commentary VII.

8   For the lands of Peterstone see above (Noion) and no. 53, HD 114 (1427-8), HD 205 and HD 300. Peterstone obtained land on the south side of Holkham in Quarles from William Bulman of Holkham and Cecily his wife (1318). See Appendix 5, no. 31. Peterstone lands passed to Walsingham priory in 1449. This 40 acre estate of Tosny fee is described as Walsingham's in the Hillhall Book HD 75 Fo. 15 where it includes Goldwynscrofte in Stathe Field. In a rental of 25 July 1428, HD 115 Peterstone's total rent is '*per annum 5s. et ad scutagium aduen*'.

9   The fold is one of nine listed in no. 1. Its location, between Haddehowe and Thorpemere, was in the direction of Peterstone Priory on the west side of Holkham parish.

10   For Creake, see Commentary VIII.

11   This fold is among the nine listed in no. 1.

<Dyvers Persons>[3s]

Robertus le Heyre[12] tenet de eodem[3t] feodo de eodem Thoma vnum mesuagium xl. acras terre et reddit ei per annum xx d.[3u] et dimidium quarterium frumenti

Iohannes Silk[3v] tenet de eodem Roberto le Heyre de eodem feodo iiij acras terre[3w] et j rodam et reddit per annum ij s.

Heruueus[3x] Bulleman[3y][13] tenet de \Bartholomeo / Burgate[3z] xiiij . acras terre de eodem feodo et reddit ei per annum xxj d. et j libram cimini[3aa] dictus Bartholomeus tenet predicta de predicto Thoma de Dakeney.[3bb]

Fo. 27v Iohannes[3cc] Silk tenet de Radulfo Hacoun[3dd] xxiiij acras terre et vnam faldam[14] cum quodam[3ee] marisco de eodem feodo et reddit ei per annum iiij[3ff] d. et vnam libram cimini.[3gg] Et Radulfus[3ee] Hacoun tenet predictas xxiiij acras terre de Thoma[3ee] de Dakeney et reddit ei ij d. et . j . libram cimini[3ee] . Idem Iohannes Silk[3cc] tenet de eodem feodo[3gg] de Galfrido le Bret[3hh] de Warham[3ii] in Holkham iiij acras terre et reddit ei per annum iiij d. et Idem Galfridus tenet de Abbate de Creyk[3jj]

DE FEODO DOMINE DE MONTE CANISI <ARUNDEL>I[4a]

<Feodum Roberti de Tatessale> [*left margin*]
<Dominus de Holkham tenet et vocatur Burhall> [*right margin*][4a]

Domina Dionisia de Monte Canisi[4b] tenet in Holkham[4c] vnum messuagium[4d] vj[xx] . [4e] acras terre arabilis[4f] et vj[xx] . acras de marisco et viij . acras de prato et vnam faldam et j letam[4g] et visum franciplegij et tomerell[4h]et Wreccum[4i] maris et molendinum et warennum[4j] per medietatem feodi[4k] militis de Willelmo de Monte Caniso et[4l] Willelmus de Roberto de Tatishale[4m] et Robertus de domino rege in capite. Eadem[4n] domina tenet in eadem villa de eodem xxxvj villanos qui tenent in villenagio[4o] xij[xx] . acras terre et xij acras cum mesuagiis suis. Idem domina tenet iij coterellos qui tenent in villenagio . iij . acras[4p] terre cum suis cotagiis

Prior de Petirston[4q][15] tenet de dicta domina[4r] xv acras terre et reddit ei per annum iiij d. et ad scutagium xxiij d. et ad plus plus et c*etera*

DE FEODO GALFRIDI LE BRET[5a]

<Edmundus Lucas et parcenarij eius tenent et vocatur Neles> [*right margin*]

Galfridus le Bret tenet de dicta Domina de eodem feodo vnum

---

12   16 acres of Tosny's fee once held by Robert le Heyr is later Tenementum Balteys (HD 75 Fo. 17) fragmented by 1428 (HD 115). All plots described lay in NE quarter of parish.

13   See Commentary IX.

14   In no. 1, William Silk's fold is said to have been let by Payn Wolleman. For Silk's tenement see Commentary X.

15   See Commentary XI.

mesuagium^{5b} et vj^{xx5c} acras terre et vnam faldam^{16} per seruicium vnius quarterij feodi^{5d} militis.^{17} Idem^{5e} Galfridus tenet lx acras terre quas villani sui . de eo tenent in villenagio per seruicium predictum faciend' eidem ij^{5f} sectas curie per annum et vnam sectam ad hundredum de Northgrenowe^{5g} de tribus septimanis in tres septimanas [et ad ij tornas generales. Et reddit per annum dicte domine ij d. et j libram piperis]^{5h}. Idem Galfridus tenet de^{5i} dicta domina dimidiam acram terre [quam Willanus suus de eodem tenet et mesuagium suum] et reddit^{5h} per annum ij d.^{5j}

LIBERE TENENTES GALFRIDI LE BRET^{6a}

<G. Porter> [*left margin*]^{6b} [18]

Bartholomeus de Burgate tenet de predicto^{6c} Galfrido^{6d} j acram terre et^{6e} reddit ei per^{6f} annum^{6g} j d.^{6g}

Radulfus Mariot^{6h} tenet de eodem^{6i} j acram terre et reddit per annum vj d. et j caponem^{6j}

<Rob. Fuller> [19] [*left margin*]

<T. Gonthorp> [*left margin*]

Willelmus le Meir^{6k} [20] tenet de eodem Galfrido j acram terre et reddit ei per annum . vj d.

<G. Porter> [*left margin*]

Adam Carpenter tenet j mesuagium^{6l} et vj acras^{6m} terre et reddit ei per annum . xxv d.

Radulfus le^{6n} Rymour tenet de eodem^{6o} vnum cotagium^{6p} et reddit ei^{6q} per annum vj d.

Iohannes Silke^{6r} tenet de eodem^{6s} iiij acras terre et dimidiam . et reddit iiij d. et ad scutagium xxj d. ob. ad plus et *cetera*.^{6t}

Iohannes Goldewyne^{6u} tenet de eodem^{6v} xvj acras terre et [per annum xvi d.] reddit et *cetera*^{6w}

Isabella^{6x} Goldewyne tenet de eodem feodo^{6y} j acram terre et reddit per annum j d.

---

16 For Bret pedigree, see Appendix II. Lucas included the later accessions of the Neel family which he had inherited giving a larger acreage than the other versions; significantly only the Neel Cartulary mentions the fold. In 1306 nine common folds included one held by Geoffrey's successor John and another was leased to John Hammond by Geoffrey le Bret. Cf. Fo. 1, no. 1.

17 Richard Neel or 'the heirs of Peter le Bret' held 1/4 knight's fee in Holkham and Swainsthorpe in 1324 on the death of Aymer de Valence of the barony of Montchesney and in 1327 on the death of David de Strabolgy, Earl of Atholl, *Cal. IPM*, vi, no. 518, p. 333 and no. 759, p. 482. This is the quarter of a knight's fee held by Eustace le Bret of Holkham in *Feudal Aids 1284–1431*, iii, 420.

18 Porter was a considerable tenant of various lords, 1456–75.

19 See Commentary XIV.

20 In 1439-40 Thomas Gonthorp's holdings of Burghall included *terram quondam Meyre*. He held of other manors. Several generations were called Thomas.

DE FEODO RADULFI HAKOUN[7a][21]

Radulfus \Hakoun/ tenet de predicta[7b] domina[7c] vnum mesuagium et xxx[ta] acras cum j[7d] falda per seruicium xvj partis vnius[7e] feodi militis et[7f] viij d.[7g] redditus vnam libram cumini[7h][22] par cirotecarum[7i] precij ob. Idem[7j] tenet de eadem[7k] xx acras terre quas villani sui de eo tenent in villenagio[7l] cum suis mesuagiis.[7m]

LIBERE TENENTES RADULFI HAKOUN[8a]

Iohannes Silk[23] tenet de eo[8b] v acras terre et reddit ei[8c] per annum. ix d.

<vocatur Skullflett> [*right margin*]

Prior de Wals*ingham* tenet de eo[8d] vnum[8e]mariscum continentem xlj acras[24] et reddit ei per annum iij d.[8f]

Fo. 28 Rogerus Osmund tenet de eo[8g] j acram terre et reddit per annum j d. ob[8h] et ad scutagium xx s. quadr' et ad plus et *cetera*

Simon filius Hamonis[8i] tenet de eo[8j] dimidiam acram et reddit ei per annum. Et ad scutagium xx s. quadr' et ad plus plus et *cetera*

Willelmus Speller' tenet de eo[8l] dimidiam acram[8m] et reddit ei vnam libram cumini

Robertus[8n] Belneye[8o] tenet de eo dimidiam acram et reddit ei per annum ob.

Rogerus le Carpenter[8p] tenet de eo iiij acras terre et reddit ei iiij d. Idem Rogerus tenet de eo dimidiam acram et reddit ij d. ob. Et ad scutagium xx s. quad. et ad plus plus et *cetera*

Iohannes de Bintre[8r] tenet de eo ij acras terre et reddit ei ij d.[8s]

Willelmus de Freburs[8t] tenet de eo[8q] j rodam terre et reddit ei per annum j d.

Prior de Petirston tenet de eo[8u] xiij acras terre in liberam puram et perpetuam elemosinam

DE FEODO BARTHOLOMEI DE BURGATE[9a][25]

<Sewallus Jonesson tenet apud Burgate> [*right margin*][26]

Bartholomeus de Burgate tenet de dicta domina . xl acras terre et vnum

---

21   See Commentary XII.

22   In no. 1, one of nine common folds was let by Walter Hakun to John Aynild. There was also a 'Cotesfold' which William Wake bought of the fee of Hakon between the hall of Montchesney and Creyksty.

23   John Silk, see Commentary XIII.

24   The map of 1590 shows the marsh said to be Walsingham's. Sculesflet is also named in the Cart. of Walsingham, no. cxxii.

25   A Bartholomew de Burgate was Abbot of Creake. Was he the same as the Bartholomew de Burgate who was prominent at Holkham, apparently in his own right and not as Abbot of Creake? He was reputed to reign between 1285 and 1303, *Cart of Creake*, p. xxiii.

26   Jonesson died seised of 20½ 'native' acres and his son John paid Burghall 2s. 8d. heriot 27 January 1424, HD 194.

mesuagium quod fuit Bertrami[27] et vnam faldam et reddit ei[9b] per annum xij d. et j precari*am* cum caruca sua ad cibum domine Et ad scutagium ad xxv d. ad plus et[9c] *cetera* et faciet vnam sectam curie[9d] et j sectam ad hundredum[9e] de Northgrenehowe de iij septimanis in tres septimanas et bis in anno ad comitatum[9f] Norwyci. Idem Bartholomeus tenet iiij acras quas villani sui tenent de eo.

LIBERE TENENTES BARTHOLOMEI DE BURGATE[10a]

Willelmus filius Reginaldi tenet de eo j acram terre et reddit ei per annum . viij d.

Herueus Buleman[10b] tenet de eo . ij acras terre et reddit ei per annum. iiij d.

<H. Elueryche> [*left margin*]

Thomas Lamekyn[10c] tenet de eo[10d] j mesuagium . j acram terre et reddit[10e] ij capones.[10f]

Galfridus Gudwyne[10g] tenet de dicta domina[10h] vj acras terre[10i] et reddit ei[10j] per annum xiij d. et facit j precari*am* cum caruca sua ad cibum domini et falcabit per tres dies in autumpno ad[10k] cibum domini et dabit ij gallinas

DE FEODO IOHANNIS BRET[11a]

<Feod' Roberti [de] Tatessale, Feodum Arundell, Hillhall>[28] [*left margin*]
<Gregorius Holkham tenet et vocatur Tubers> [*right margin*]

Iohannes le Bret[11b] tenet in Holkham de Rogero Broun[11c] et Rogerus[11d] de Roberto de Tateshale et Robertus de domino rege . lx acras terre[11e] et j faldam per seruicium tercie partis vnius feodi militis.[11f]

Idem Iohannes tenet quinque villanos qui tenent de eo xxxij acras terre cum mesuagiis suis in villenagio.[11g]

LIBERE TENENTES IOHANNES LE BRET[12a]

Isabella Fraunceys[12b] tenet de eo[12c] vnum mesuagium et vij[12d] acras terre et reddit ei[12e] per annum ij s. et ad scutagium xxxv d. et ad plus plus et *cetera*[12f]

27　　i.e. Bertram Verdoun. Cf. Bertram de Holcham v. Robert son of Hugh and Thomas son of Peter in Holkham, 1227–8, Appendix 5, nos. 12, 13. In an extent of 1241–2 Bertram le Verdoun held 52 acres of Warin de Montchesney for 5s. 2d. p.a. Cf. Fo. 29v. An earlier Bertram de Verdun held Farnham Royal Manor in Bucks. by the service of supporting the King's right hand which held the sceptre at his coronation; he was given four knight's fees by Robert de Ferrers with his daughter Matilda. He was Justiciar in Ireland. See letters from G. Wrottesley to J.H. Round in London University Library, Institute of Historical Research Ms. 694.

28　　See Commentary XV and XVI.

Willelmus Cursoun$^{12g\,29}$ tenet de eo^{12h} vj acras terre et reddit ei^{12i} per annum xviij d.^{12j} Et ad Scutagium xx quadr'. et ad plus et *cetera*^{12f}

Iohannes Silk^{12k} tenet de eo^{12l} vij acras terre et dimidiam et reddit per annum xiiij d.

Prior de Walsyngham$^{12m\,30}$ tenet de eo^{12n} xlvj^{12o} . acras terre et j faldam$^{12p\,31}$

DE FEODO GALFRIDI DE HINDRINGHAM^{13a}

Fo. 28v <Feod' Marie de Neuile> [*left margin*]

Galfridus de Hindringham^{13b} tenet in Holkham de Humfredo de Wyghton^{13c} et^{13d} Humfredus de Maria de Neuile^{32} et Maria de domino rege in capite tres villanos^{13e} qui tenent in villenagio xviij . acras terre cum suis mesuagiis

LIBERE TENENTES GALFRIDI DE HINDRINGHAM^{33}

<Robt. Fuller> [*right margin*]

Galfridus Gudwyne^{14a} tenet de eo^{14b} vnum^{14c} mesuagium xij acras terre et j faldam et reddit ei^{14d}per annum v s. et ad scutagium xxx d. ad plus et^{14e} *cetera* ad Schirrenesshoc^{14f} et Wodewellehat^{14g} iij d. et ad curiam^{14h} de Wyghton' vj s.^{14i}

Iohannes Cursoun^{14j} tenet de eo vnum mesuagium et quatuor acras terre et dimidiam et reddit ei^{14k} per annum ij s. j d. et j skeppe^{14l} pisarum^{14m}

Iohannes Roberd^{14n} tenet de eo^{14o} dimidiam acram terre et reddit ei^{14p} iij d.

DE FEODO TATESSALE$^{15a\,34}$

<Feod' Roberti de Tatessale> [*left margin*]

Petrus le Vewtre$^{15b\,35}$ tenet in^{15c} Holkham de Roberto de Tatessale$^{15d\,36}$ et Robertus^{15e} de domino Rege in capite xvj^{15f} acras terre quas villani sui tenent de eo in villenagio cum suis mesuagiis.^{15g}

DE FEODO DE CLARE$^{16a\,37}$

<Feod' Gilberti de Clare> [*left margin*]　　<W. Waylond> [*right margin*]

Fratres Sancti Lazarij tenent in Holkham in liberam puram et perpetuam elemosinam^{16b} xxxj acras de Gilberto de Clare^{16c} de domino rege in capite^{16d}

29　William le Curzon or Curszoun held 1/2 fee in Besthorpe and 'Hokham' of Robert de Tattershall in 1303, *Cal. IPM*, iv, no. 163, p. 105.

30　See Commentary XVI.

31　See Commentary XVII.

32　See Commentary XIX.

33　See Commentaries XIV, XVIII, XX.

34　See Commentary XV.

35　See Commentary XXI.

36　For Robert de Tattershall's Honor of Buckenham see Commentary XV, note on fee of John le Bret whose manor of Tobers was also held of him.

37　See Commentary XXII.

LIBERE TENENTES SANCTI LAZARIJ[17a]

<falda>

Thomas Leffe tenet vnum mesuagium et octo acras terre et reddit eis viij d.

Prior de Petirston tenet de dicto Thoma medietatem vnius falde[17b]

Gilbertus Souter'[17c] et Humfredus Dauy tenent de dictis fratribus xij acras terre cum mesuagiis suis et medietatem vnius falde in comuni et reddit eis xij d.

Bartholomeus Faber et Lucie Lange tenent vnum mesuagium et v acras terre et reddent dictis fratribus viij d.

Mariota Bendyng[17d] tenet vnum mesuagium et vj acras terre et reddit per annum viij d.

DE FEODO BARDOLF ET EPISCOPI N[ORWYCENSIS[18a 38]

<Feod' Episcopi Norwycen'> [*left margin*]   <Robert Gunors> [*right margin*]

Rogerus Bakoun[18b] tenet in[18c] Holkham de Willelmo Bardolf[18d] xv acras terre quas villani sui tenent[18e] de eo cum mesuagiis suis pro dimidio feodo militis[18f] quod tenet[18g] in Cokethorp'[18h] et in[24i] Holkham Et Willelmus[18j] Bardolf tenet de Episcopo Norwycensi[18k] et Episcopus de domino Rege in capite

LIBERE TENENTES ROGERI BAKOUN[19a]

<falda> [*left margin*]

Bartholomeus de Burgate tenet de eo[19b] de eodem feodo[19c] xv acras terre et[19d] vnam[19d] faldam[19d] et[19d] reddit per annum ij s. vj d. et ad scutagium[19e] ad xx s. ij s. vj d. et ad plus et c*etera*

Prior de Petirston tenet de dicto Bartholomeo viij acras terre de[19f] eodem[19f] feodo[19f] et reddit ei[19g] xiij d. ob. et ad scutagium ad[19g] xx s. vij d.[19g] ad[19h] plus[19h] et c*etera*[19h]

DE FEODO HUBERTI DE WYGHTON[20a 39]

Fo. 29 <Feod' de Wyghton> [*left margin*]

Hubertus de Wyghton[20b] tenet in Holkham de Galfrido de Lyseny[20c] et Galfridus de domino Rege in capite . xv . acras terre quas villani[20d] sui tenent de eo in villenagio

LIBERE TENENTES DICTI HUBERTI

Matilda Quint[21a] tenet de eo ij acras terre de eodem feodo et reddit per annum[21b] xv d.

Iohannes Roberd[21c] tenet de eo ij acras terre de eodem feodo et reddit ei per annum[21b] iiij d.

---

38   See Commentary XXIII.
39   See Commentary XXIV.

Bartholomeus de Burgate tenet de eo xij . acras terre et j faldam et reddit ei per annum^{21b} . ij s.

Iohannes Silk^{21d} tenet de eo iij rodas^{21e} terre et reddit ei per annum ij d.

DE FEODO DE KERBROK^{22a} [40]

<Feod' de Kerbrok'> [*left margin*]

Fratres Hospitalis de Kerbrok^{22b} tenent in Holkham de sua capitali domo et illa domus de domino rege in capite^{22c}

Bartholomeus Vnderclynt tenet de eis vnum mesuagium et dimidiam acram terre et reddit eis j . d.

Bartholomeus de Burgate tenet de eis^{22d} vnum mesuagium et xij acras de marisco et reddit eis^{22e} per annum . vj s.

Prior de Walsyngham^{22f} tenet de dicto Bartholomeo^{22g} dictum^{22h} mariscum et reddit ei per annum^{22i} . xij d.

DE FEODO WARENIE^{23a} [41]

<Feod' comitis Warenne falda> [*left margin*]　　<Prior de Walsingham> [*right margin*]

Eborardus Cayly et Humfredus Dauy^{23b} tenent in Holkham^{23c} de Iacobo Thorp'^{23d} et Iacobus^{23e} e comite^{23f} Warenne et comes de domino rege in capite^{23g} xxiiij^{23h} acras terre cum mesuagiis suis et j faldam et reddunt priori de Walsyngham . xx d.^{23i} per annum et ad scutagium ad xx s. vj d. ad plus et cetera.^{23j}

Et tenent vnum villanum qui tenet de eis vnum mesuagium et vj acras^{23k} terre de eodem feodo in villenagio et ij . cotagia que duo coterelli tenent in villenagio de eodem feodo^{23l}

Bartholomeus de Burgate tenet vnum messuagium^{23m} de eodem feodo et reddit per annum j d.

Idem Bartholomeus tenet^{23n} ij villanos qui tenent de eodem feodo xij acras terre^{23o} cum mesuagiis suis

Iohannes Silk^{23p} tenet de dicto Eborardo iij rodas terre et reddit ei per annum j d.

DE ADUOCACIONE ECCLESIE DE HOLKHAM^{24a} [42]

<Feodum de Wyghtone (struck off)> [*left margin*]

Dicunt quod dominus Iohannes Rex Anglie dedit Abbati Viterbie medietatem ecclesie de Holkham in proprios vsus cum xx acras terre et vno mesuagio de quibus dicta medietas dotata est libere Et ix . acras terre quas villani dicte ecclesie tenent de dicta ecclesia cum suis mesuagiis in villenagio^{24b} Et vnum coterellum qui tenet vnum cotagium in villenagio de dicta ecclesia

---

40　See Commentary XXV.
41　See Commentary XXVI.
42　See Commentary XXVII.

DE ADUOCATIONE DICTE ECCLESIE[25a]

<Feod' Roberti Tatessale> [*left margin*]

Willelmus de Montecanisi dedit ecclesie de Derham medietatem ecclesie de Holkham in proprios vsus Et xx acras terre de quibus dicta medietas dotata est libere Et[25b] memorandum quod tenent in comuni ix acras terre quas villani sui tenent in villenagio de dicta ecclesia vt supradictum est etc.[25b]

HUNDREDUM DE HOLT[43]

Fo. 29v Memorandum quod in quodam veteri rotulo in manu Prioris de Norwyco scribitur in forma que sequitur

Willelmus de Roos tenet in Holt et Cleye de hereditate Matilde vxoris eius in feodo et dominico vnum feodum militis et dimidium et j quarterium. De comite Aubermarlie et idem Comes de Rege in capite

Petronilla de Nerforde tenet vnum feodum militis et dimidium et j quarterium in dictis villis de dicto comite et idem comes de Rege in capite

Rogerus de Perers et tenentes sui tenent de eadem Petronilla et eadem Petronilla de dicto comite et Idem comes de Rege in capite

Agneta que fuit vxor Petri de Leryngsete et tenentes sui tenent de dictis Willelmo et Petronilla in Holt Leryngsete Scharneton'. Bayfeld . Kellyngge . Glaunford et Bodham ij . feodo militis et ijdem de dicto comite et idem comes de Rege in capite

Item in Feodario comitisse de Norf' scribitur sic. Thomas Bakon de Leryngsete tenet de domino de Nevile j quarterium et dimidium feodi militis in Leryngsete et idem dominus de . comitissa Norf.'

Item scribitur in eodem Feodario. Dominus Thomas de Leryngsete tenet in Leryngsete j feodum et dimidium militis et idem dominus Thomas de Comitissa Norff.'

Memorandum quod Bertramus Le Verdoun tenuit in capite in villa de Holkham lij acras terre de domino Warino le[26a] Mounchensy pro quo tenemento reddit annuatim v s. ij denarios et ad scutagium ad xx s. vjd. Ad plus plus quod compertum est per dominum Hugonem de Veer per quamdam extentam factam tempore dicti domini Anno regni Regis Henrici xxvj[to] [1241–2]

VARIANTS: [1a] Titles only in HD 22a. [1b] Wython written in left margin, HD 71, 120. [1c] Capitalis dominus de Holkham Galfridus de Lisini, D, HD 6 (see Commentary I). [1d] Harcurt, D, HD 5a, 5b, 6, 71, 120, qui tenent, HD 71. [1e] Wython, HD 5b; Wythun, HD 5a, 71, 120; Wittone, D, HD 6. [1f] francipleg', HD 5a; frauncipleg', HD 5b; visufrancipleg', HD 71; visu franci plegi, HD 120; cum visu franciplegij, D, HD 6. [1g] Wrect', HD 5b; Wrectum, HD 5a, HD 71. [1h] in foro, D. [2a] Feod' Noion Peterston in right margin, HD 71, 120. [2b] Nogoun, HD 55; Noiun, HD 71; le Nuugun, D, HD 6. [2c] Lisini, D, HD 6, Leseyney, HD 5; Lesyny, HD 5a, 120;

---

43   Absent from the other copies of the Feodary.

Lesyney, HD 55. [2d] xxiiij[ti], HD 120; Sokem, HD 5a, 5b. [2e] velinagio, HD 5b; villenagio, HD 5a, 5b, 71, 120. [2f] dictus ... Lyseny omitted, D, HD 6; Leseny per annum xix d. ob., HD 5, 120. [2g] Peterston in margin, HD 5a, 5b; HD 120; Peterstone miscopied Palston, HD 71. [2h] et xl, D, HD 6, 120. [2i] Selk, HD 5a, 5b; 71; 120; Sylk, HD 55. [2j] dicto, D. [2k] vj d. HD 71, 120.

[3a] Feoda Dakeney Hylhall Thomas Grigg', HD 5b; Gryggs in margin, HD 5a. Feod' Dakeney Hylhall' Greggs', Hd 120; Feod' Dakeney Hylhall Thomas Greggs in margin, HD 71. [3b] de Hakeney, D, HD 6, HD 55; Dakeney, HD 71, 120. [3c] Turret' argenti, D; Turellam argenti, HD 5b; terellam argenti, HD 55. First word left blank, HD 5a, 6, 71, 120; tectum elsewhere. [3d] omitted, HD 71, 120. [3e] acras terre, D. [3f] mesuagiis suis, D. [3g] Petraston, D1; Peterston', HD 6. [3h] Et idem, D. No et, HD 6. [3i] cotag', HD 5b, 71, 120; ij coterrellos, HD 55. [3j] will', HD 120; vilenagio, D; vellinagio, HD 6. [3k] cum cotagiis suis, D, HD 6. [3l] in curia domini Regis, D, HD 6. [3m] Petraston, D; Cryeke, HD 5a, 5b; Creke, HD 120; Kreyke, HD 5b. [3n] Thoma Dakeney, HD 5a, 71, 120. [3o] de eodem feodo in Holkham, HD 71; in Holkeham, HD 120. [3p] x s. vj d., HD 5a, 5b, HD 71; xi s. vj d., HD 120; x s. x d., HD 55. [3q] iiij buss., HD 5a, 5b, 71, 120; dimidium quarterium, HD 55. [3r] viij acras cum vil' messuagiis suis, D, HD6; octo acras terre cum sokemannis in villenagio et messuagiis, HD 5a, 71, 120; vellinagio, HD 5b; iij sokemannos omitted, HD 71, 120. [3s] HD 5b. [3t] de dicto feudo de Thoma de Hakeney in Holkham, D; de dicto feodo de Thoma Dakeney in Holkham, HD 5a, 5b, 71; do. Holkeham, HD 120. [3u] xv s. xj d., HD 5a, 5b, 120; x s. et v denarios, D. [3v] Sylke, HD 71, 120; Silke, D. [3w] reddit ei, D, HD 6, 120. [3x] Henricus, HD 5a, 5b, HD 71, 120 [3y] Bolleman, D, HD 6; Bulleman, HD 55; Bulman, HD 5a, 5b, 71, 120. [3z] Burhgate, D; Burgate, HD 6; eodem Roberto, HD 5a, 5b, 71, 120. [3aa] cumini, HD 5a, 5b, 120. [3bb] et dictus Bartholomeus tenet predictam terram de Thoma de Hakeney', HD 55; omitted, HD 71, 120. [3cc] Sylk, HD 5a, 5b, 71, 120; Silke, D; Sylke, HD 6. [3dd] Hakon, HD 5b; Hacun, HD 5b, D; Hacon, HD 71; Hacoun, HD 120. [3ee] quodam and Radulfus ... acras de Thoma omitted, HD 5a, 71, 120; et reddit ei ij denarios et j libram cimini, D. [3ff] xiij d., HD 5a, 120; xij d., HD 5b; xxj d., HD 71. [3gg] cumini, HD 5a, 71, 120; comini, HD 5b; cumyni, HD 120; tenet predicta xxiiij acras de Thoma de Hakenet et reddit ei ij den. ei j. lb. cimini, HD 55. [3hh] Silke, D; Sylke, HD 6; Galfrido le Bret de Warham in Holkham, HD 55, D, HD 6. [3ii] Galbret, HD 5b; Gabrett, HD 5a, 71, 120; Gabret de Hokam, HD 5a, 5b, 71; de Hokam, HD 5a, 71, 120; Warram, D, HD 6. [3jj] et reddit per annum j d. added, HD 5a, 71; Crec', D; Creyke, HD 6; Kreyke, HD 71; Kreyke ij acras et reddit per annum j d.

[4a] Full title only in HD 22a. Arundell, HD 5a, HD 71, 120; Feod' de Monte Caniso Borowhall in margin, HD 71, 120. [4b] Caniso, HD 5a, 5b, HD 71, 120; Dyonisia de Montecanisio, D. [4c] Holkeham, HD 120. [4d] j mesuagium, D; j messuagium, HD 6; et, HD 71. [4e] vij[xx] acras in PROIMP C 134/35 (1). [4f] arrabilis, HD 71, 120. [4g] letum, HD 71; cum suis libertatibus pro eruicio feodi militis omitting details, HD 5a, 5b, 71, 120. [4h] tunerell', D; tunnerell', HD 6. [4i] wrecum, HD 55. [4j] warennam, HD 55, D, HD 6. [4k] cum medietate feodi, D. [4l] Willelmo ... et omitted, HD 5a, 5b, 71, 120; Canisio, HD 55, D. [4m] Tattishall et Robertus de domino, D, HD 6; Tatesale, D, HD 55; Tattysall', HD 6; Tatyssale de feodo Arundell et dictus Robertus de rege, HD 71; Tatyesale ... et dictus Robertus de rege in capite, HD 120. [4n] But predicta domina tenet de eodem feodo cc xij acras terre quas villani sui de eodem tenent in villenagiis suis et messuagiis, HD 5b (tenet de dicto Roberto ... et ... willani), HD 71, 120. [4o] vilenagio,

D; villenagio, HD 6.   [4p] iij acras terre quas cotarij sui de eo tenent cum cotagijs suis, HD 71; quas cotagij sui de eodem tenent, HD 120.   [4q] Peterstone, HD 5a, 5b; Petra, HD 71, 120.   [4r] de eodem feodo follows domina, HD 5a, 5b, 71, 120.

[5a] The title and marginal note are peculiar to HD 22a, no. 253. Neales, Nellis in left margin, HD 5a, 5b; Nelys, Nelis do., HD 71 and 120.   [5b] de eadem domina, D; messuagium, HD 5a, 5b, 6, 120.   [5c] c acras, HD 5a, 5b, 71 and 120.   [5d] omitted, HD 5b; militis feodi, HD 6, 71, 120; feudi, D; vnius militis, HD 120.   [5e] Idem ... ii omitted, HD 5a, 6, 71 and 120.   [5f] ad ij curias generales dicte Domine et ad Hundredum, et ij sectas ad ij curias generales, HD 120; j sectam, HD 71.   [5g] abbreviated, HD 5b, 71, 120; Northgranehoo, HD 5a; Northgrenhowe, D; omitted in Neel Cart.; et bis in anno ad comitatum Norwicensem, D.   [5h] eodem feodo, HD 5a, 5b, 71, 120.   [5i] HD 71, 120 (not in cartulary); willani, HD 5a.   [5j] acras terre quas villani sui de eodem tenent. Summa de eodem tenemento et messuagio ij d., HD 5b.

[6a] title only in HD 22a; John Goldewyne between the above and the fee of Ralph Hakoun, D.   [6b] HD 5b, 22a.   [6c] dicto, HD 5a, 5b, 71, 120.   [6d] Galfrido de eodem feodo, HD 5a, 5b, 71, 120.   [6e] omitted, HD 5a, 5b, 71, 120.   [6f] omitted, HD 5a, 5b, 71.   [6g] omitted, HD 71, 120; reddit vj d. et j capon', HD 71, 120.   [6h] Mariot, HD 5a; Mariott, HD 5b, 71, 120.   [6i] de eodem Galfrido de eodem Feodo, HD 5a, 5b, 71, 120.   [6j] omitted, HD 5a, 5b, 71, 120.   [6k] Willelmus Mayre, HD 5a; Meyre, HD 5b, 71, 120; T. Gonthorp in left margin, HD 5a, 5b, 22a.   [6l] messuagium, HD 5b.   [6m] acras terre et vnum messuagium, HD 5a, 5b, 71, 120; interlineated above vj, HD 22a.   [6n] le omitted, HD 5a, 5b, 71, 120; Rymar, HD 5b.   [6o] Feodo de eodem Galfrido, HD 5a, 5b, 71, 120; Galfrido de eodem Feodo, HD 71.   [6p] mesuagium, HD 5a, 71, 120; messuagium, HD 5b; j cotagium de eodem, D.   [6q] omitted, HD 5a, 5b, 71, 120.   [6r] Sylke, HD 71, 120.   [6s] de eodem feodo de eodem Galfrido, HD 120.   [6t] per annum iij d., HD 120.   [6u] Goldwyne, HD 5a, 5b; none of the other 8 free tenants specified, D.   [6v] de eodem feodo de eodem Galfrido, HD 5a, 5b, 71, 120.   [6w] reddit per annum xvj d., HD 5a, 71; j d., HD 120; terre redd' per annum xvj d., HD 5b.   [6x] item added later by Edmund Lucas; item included in HD 71, but omitted in HD 120 and D.   [6y] de eodem Feodo de eodem Galfrido, HD 71.

[7a] Only HD 22a has this title.   [7b] <Libere tenentes Radulfi Hacun>, D.   [7c] De dicta domina Deonisia, HD 5a, 5b; de dicta domina Dionisia, HD 71, 120.   [7d] cum falda, HD 5a, 5b.   [7e] xvj partis unius omitted, HD 5a, 5b, 71, 120.   [7f] et reddit per annum xiij d. et lib., HD 5a, 5b, 71, 120.   [7g] perhaps viij is scribal error for xiij, unnoticed and uncorrected, as it did not concern the Neels.   [7h] et j lib' cumini, HD 5a, 5b, 120; et lib', HD 71; et vnius libre cumine, D.   [7i] careticarum, HD 5a, 5b; ceretecarum, HD 5b; cerotecarum, HD 71, 120.   [7j] Et debet [ij] sectas ad ij curias generales de dicta domina, HD 5a, 5b, 71, 120; Item idem tenet, D, HD 6; Idem Radulfus tenet de dicta domina de eodem feodo xx acras, HD 71.   [7k] de dicta domina, HD 5a, 5b, 71, 120.   [7l] villenagij sui cum mesuagijs suis, HD 5a, 5b, 71, 120.

[8a] The title is omitted in HD 5a, 5b; it is entered in the margin of D with spelling Hacun.   [8b] de eodem feodo de Radulfo Hakun, HD 5a, 5b, 71, 120; in the mss. eodem is sometimes omitted and sometimes read eo, passim.   [8c] omitted in HD 5a, 5b, 120.   [8d] de dicta domina, HD 5a, 5b, 71, 120.   [8e] xlj acras marisci salsi, HD 5a, 5b, 71, 120.   [8f] vj d. not iij d., HD 5a, 5b, 71, 120; ix d., D; iij d., HD 6.   [8g] Hosmundus, D, HD 6; de dicto Radulfo, HD 5a, 71, 120; de Radulfo, HD 5b.   [8h] ij d., D; j d. et j ob., HD 6.   [8i] minus minus, HD 5a, 71, 120; Simon Hamond, HD 5a, 5b, 120.   [8j] de eodem

Radulfo, HD 5a, 71, 120; de Radulfo, HD 5b; this follows William Speller, HD 71; in D the order is the same as in HD 22a. [8k] de eodem Radulfo, HD 5a, 71, 120; de Radulfo, HD 5b. [8l] et dimidiam rodam, HD 5a, 5b, 71. Evidently HD 22a is right to omit the dimidiam rodam, as in HD 120 it is entered but struck out; et j rodam, D, HD 6. [8m] Robertus, HD 22a; not elsewhere. [8n] Rogerus Bynney, HD 5b; Bysney, HD 5a; Rogerus Byney, HD 71, 120. [8o] Rogerus Carpentarius, HD 5a, 5b, 6, 71; Carpenter', HD 120; reddit per annum iv d., HD 120. [8p] Et idem Rogerus, D; de eodem Radulfo, HD 5b, 71, 120, D; j d. et ob., D. [8q] Byntree, HD 5a; Byntre, HD 5b, 71, 120; Beyntrius, D; Beynter, HD 6. [8r] reddit per annum ij d., HD 5a, 5b, 120. [8s] Frebras, HD 5a, 71, 120; Frebrus, HD 5b; de omitted, D, HD 6; per annum omitted, D, HD 6. [8t] de dono Ricardi Hakun xiij acras, HD 5a, 5b, 71, 120. [8u] in liberam et puram elemosinam following Radulfo, HD 51, 5b, 71, 120.

[9a] Title and marginal note, HD 22a only; Geoffrey Goodwyn's holding precedes this, HD 5a, 5b, 71, 120. [9b] omitted, HD 5a, 5b, 71, 120; j faldagium, HD 71; cibum domini, D. [9c] minus minus, HD 5a, 5b, 71. [9d] et ad curiam dicte domine j sectam et, HD 5a, 5b, 71, 120. [9e] ad hundredum Northgreneho[e] j sectam, HD 5a, 5b, 71, 120. [9f] et ad tornum generalem ij sectas pro se et tenetibus suis, HD 5a, 71, 120; de eodem feudo de eodem, D.

[10a] only HD 22a has this title; in HD 71 the next item follows on the same line; in HD 120 it runs on after villani sui. [10b] de eodem Bartholomeo de eodem feodo, HD 120; de eodem feodo de Bartholomeo, HD 5a, 5b, 71; Harvey Bulman, HD 120; Bolman, D, HD 6; et reddit ij capones ad cibum domini, D. [10c] Lamken, Lamkin, HD 5a, 5b, 71, 120. [10d] eodem feodo de Bartholomeo struck out, dicta domina substituted, HD 71. [10e] reddit per annum, HD 5a, 5b, 71, 120. [10f] capones et iiij dies in autumpno ij d. ob., HD 5a, 5b, 71, 120. [10g] This item, unlike others in HD 22a, has no title; in HD 22a and D it comes between the free tenants of Bartholomew de Burgate and the fee of John Bret; but it comes between the free tenants of Ralph Hakun and the fee of Bartholomew de Burgate on HD 5a, 5b, 71 and 120; in HD 71 and 120 Galfridus is followed by Godeknapp' before Godewyn, struck out in HD 71 but not in HD 120; in a corresponding entry in the extent of Burghall, Geoffrey Godwyne's liabilities also include payment towards scutage; <Robertus Fuller>, HD 5a. [10h] Dionisia added, HD 5a, 5b, 71, 120. [10i] de eodem feodo, HD 5a, 5b, 71, 120; reddit per annum, D, HD 6, 120. [10j] omitted, HD 5a, 5b, 71, 120. [10k] ad ... domini struck out. HD 120.

[11a] Title only in HD 22a; <Feodum Roberti Tatessale> and <Grigges. Gregorius Holkham tenet et vocatur Tubers> <Feod' Arundell>, HD 5a, 5b, 71, 120; <Hilhall>, HD 5b, 120; Hillhall, HD 71; Greggs, HD 5b. [11b] feodum Ade Brett, HD 5a, 5b, 71, 120. [11c] de Brown[e], HD 5a, 5b, 71; de Brun, Feudal Aids 1284–1431, vol. iii, p. 420, de Browne, HD 120. [11d] Rogerus ... nege omitted in HD 5a, 5b, 71, 120; in capite follows rege, D, HD 6. [11e] add et j messuagium, HD 5a, 5b, 71, 120. [11f] et faciet vnam sectam ad hundredum Northgreenho de iij septimanis in tres septimanas et ad ij comitatus generales ij sectas et ad auxilium vicecomitis Wudewellhuc et placita renouata, HD 5a, 5b; Wadewelle hoc, HD 71; Wudewell followed by space, 120; Dictus Rogerus Browne tenet de Roberto de Tattsall et Robertus rege in capite, HD 5a, 71, 120; HD 5b ends at Robertus. [11g] tenet de dicto Rogero Brown de eodem feodo xxxij acras terre quas villani sui de eo tenent in villenagio suis et messuagiis, HD 5a, 5b, 71, 120; vilenagio, D; in vellinagio, HD 6.

[12a] Title only in HD 22a. [12b] le Frauceys, HD 5a, 5b. [12c] de dicto Iohanne, HD 5a,

5b, 71, 120. ^{12d} viij, HD 5a, 5b, 71, 120, D, HD 6. ^{12e} omitted, HD 5a, 5b, 71, 120. ^{12f} plus plus minus minus, HD 5a, 5b, 71; etc., HD 120. ^{12g} le Churchun, HD 5a, 5b, 71, 120; Curson, D; Cursun, HD 6. ^{12h} de eodem Iohanne, HD 5a, 5b, 71; de dicto Iohanne, HD 120. ¹²ⁱ eidem, HD 5a, 71, 120. ^{12j} only xj d., HD 5a, 5b, 71, 120; illegible, D; sum left blank, HD 6. ^{12k} Sylk', HD 71; Sylke, HD 120; Silke, D; reddit ei xiij d., D, HD 6. ^{12l} de eodem feodo, HD 5a, 5b, 71, 120. ^{12m} Walsingham, D, HD 5a, 5b; Walsynham, HD 71, 120. ¹²ⁿ de eodem Iohanne de eodem feodo, HD 5a, 71, 120; de eodem feodo, HD 5a. ^{12o} xl acras, HD 5a, 5b, 71, 120; xlvj acras, D, HD 6. ^{12p} faldagium et reddit eidem per annum ij s. ij d., HD 120; in HD 71 this item is followed immediately by Peter de Vewter's land (12 acres); in HD 22a his land (16 acres held of Robert de Tattershall) follows Geoffrey of Hindringham.

^{13a} Title only in HD 22a; <Feodum Marie de Neuille>, HD 22a; <Feodum Richmond>, HD 5a, 5b; <Richemond>, HD 71, 120; this item follows Veutre and Clare (or St. Lasarus), HD 5a, 5b, 71, 120. ^{13b} Hyndringham, HD 5a, 5b; Hyndryngham, HD 71, 120. ^{13c} Wythun, HD 5a, 5b; Wythun, HD 71, 120; Vutone, D; wittune, HD 6. ^{13d} for et ... capite substitute de feodo de Richemond. HD 5a; de feodo de Wythun de feodo Rychemond, HD 120; Rechemond, HD 5b; Richemonde, HD 71; item ends: et dictus Humfridus tenet de Maria Nevill et Maria de domino rege, HD 71. ^{13e} for tres villanos ... mesuagiis substitute xviij acras terre quas villani sui de eodem tenent in villenagiis suis [et] messuagiis per seruicium vj d. et, HD 5a, 5b, 71, 120; vilenagio ... cum mesuagiis suis, D; villenagio, HD 6.

^{14a} Goodwyn, HD 5a, 5b, 71, 120; Goodwyne, HD 6; <Robert Fuller>, HD 22a. ^{14b} de dicto Galfrido de Hindringham, HD 5a; do. Hyndryngham, HD 71, 120; Hindryngham, HD 5a. ^{14c} for vnum mesuagium ... faldam substitute ixij acras terre et j mes[s]uagium, HD 5a, 5b, 71, 120; i mesuagium et xij acras, D. ^{14d} eidem v s., HD 5a, 5b, 71, 120. ^{14e} plus plus minus minus, HD 5a, 5b, 71, 120; ad xx s. v d. scutagium x d., D, HD 6. ^{14f} auxilium vicecomitis, HD 5a, 5b, 71, 120; scirenisstoytus, D, HD 6. ^{14g} Wodewelhoc, HD 5a; Wodwellhoc, HD 5b, HD 71, 120; Wodeuellehoyt, D, HD 6. ^{14h} manerium, HD 5a, 5b, 71, 120; Wythun, HD 5a; Wython, HD 5b, 71, 120. ¹⁴ⁱ vj d. not vj s., HD 5a, 5b, 71, 120. ^{14j} Curchon, HD 5a, 5b, 71, 120; de dicto Galfrido, HD 71; messuagium, HD 120; iij not quatuor, HD 71. ^{14k} eidem HD 5a, 5b, 71; eidem per annum, HD 120. ^{14l} ij buss', HD 5a, 5b, 71, 120. ^{14m} de feodo de Mettun', HD 5a, 5b, 71, 120. ¹⁴ⁿ Robert', HD 5a, 5b, 120. ^{14o} dicto Galfrido, HD 5a, 5b, 71, 120. ^{14p} eidem, HD 5a, 5b, 71, 120; per annum, HD 120.

^{15a} Title only in HD 22a; <Feodum Roberti de Tatessale>, HD 22a. ^{15b} Veutre, HD 5b, 71, HD 6; Vewtre, HD 120; Veutre (followed by Clare) precedes Hindringham, HD 5a; it follows Walsingham's 40 acres, HD 5a, 5b. ^{15c} omitted, HD 5a, 5b, 71, 120. ^{15d} Tatissale, HD 5a, 5b, 71, 120; de eo cum mesuagiis suis in villinagio, D. ^{15e} omitted, HD 5a, 5b, 71, 120. ^{15f} xij acras, HD 5a, 5b, 71, 120. ^{15g} messuagiis pertinentibus as [blank in Ms.] de Burnham per seruicium j militis in terra sua de Burnham prescripta, HD 5a, 5b, 71, 120.

^{16a} Title in HD 22a only; <Feodum Gilberti de Clare> <W. Waylond>, HD 22a; <Feod'> HD 1a Lazari, D; for in Holkham substitute de feodo de Clare. ^{16b} For liberam elemosinam substitute de terris Iordani de Benney in Libera et pura elemosina, HD 5a, 5b, 71, 120. ^{16c} For domino ... capite substitute de Gilberto ...; Clare omitted in HD 51, 5b, 71, 120. ^{16d} xxxj acras terre quas villani sui de eodem tenent in villenagio cum suis messuagiis et debent vnam sectam hundredi de Northgrenhowe de iij septimanis in iij

septimanas et ad auxilium vicecomitis ad Woodewelhoc et ad renouanda, HD 5a; do. Woddewelhoc et ad plus renouandum, HD 5b, 71, 120.

[17a] Title and details of five free tenants omitted in HD 5a, 5b, 71, 120. The tenants are included in D, HD 6. [17b] <falda> added later, HD 22a. [17c] Sutor, D; Sutter, HD 6. [17d] Item omitted, D; Bendinge, HD 6.

[18a] Titles only in HD 22a; <Feodum Episcopi Norwycensis>, <Rob. Gunnor>, HD 22a; Feodo de Bardolff et episcopi Norwic', HD 5a, 5b, 71, 120; this follows Richmond fee in Hd 5a, 5b, 71, 122. [18b] Bakun, HD 5a, 5b, 71, 120. [18c] omitted, HD 5a, 5b, 71, 120. [18d] de Willelmo Barlof follows xv acras terre, HD 5a, 5b, 71, 120; Bardolfes de feodo episcopi, HD 5a, 5b, 120. [18e] tenent ... eo follows de eodem tenemento in villenagiis suis, HD 71, 120. [18f] pro seruicio dimidii feodi vnius militis, HD 5a, 5b, 71, 120. [18g] continetur, HD 5a, 5b, 71, 120. [18h] Cokethorpp, HD 5a, 71, 120; Cockethorpe, HD 5b. [18i] omitted, HD 71, 120; et Holkham, HD 5a, 5b. [18j] dictus Willelmus tenet, HD 5a, 5b. [18k] omitted, HD 5a, 5b

[19a] Full title only in HD 22a. [19b] tenet de eodem feodo, HD 5a, 5b, 71, 120. [19c] de Rogero Bakun, HD 5a, 5b, 71, 120. [19d] omitted, HD 5a, 5b, 71, 120; <falda>, HD 22a; minus minus et j faldam follows plus, HD 71. [19e] scutagium domini regis. HD 5a, 5b, 120; plus plus minus et j faldagium, HD 120. [19f] precedes viij, HD 5a, 5b, 71, 120. [19g] viij d. ob., HD 5a, 5b, 71, 120. [19h] omitted, HD 71, 120; et Holkham, HD 5a, 5b.

[20a] Titles omitted except in HD 22a; <Feodum de Wyghton<, HD 22a; HD 5a, 5b, 71 and 120 omit this item altogether; HD 55 includes it, but omits Clare, Richmond and Warenne; D has it in the same place as HD 22a; <Libere tenentes de Huberto>, D; HD 71 has fee of Warenne here. [20b] Wittone, D, HD 6. [20c] Leseni, D; Lesyny, HD 6. [20d] xv ... villani omitted, D, HD 6.

[21a] The name appears to be Dunt in D. [21b] de ... feodo, per annum omitted, HD 55. [21c] Robert, D, HD 6. [21d] Sylk, HD 55; Silke, D; Sylke, HD 6. [21e] dimidiam acram et j rodam, D; j rodam et dimidiam rodam, HD 6.

[22a] Title only in HD 22a; <Feodum de Kerbrok>, HD 22a; <Feodum de Kerebrok>, HD 5a, 5b, 71; <Feodum de Kerebroke>, HD 120; this section follows Warenne fee, HD 5a, 5b, 71, 120. [22b] Kerebroc, HD 5a, 5b, 71, 120; Fratris Ospital' de Kerebroc, HD 5b; item about Bartholomeus Vnderclynt omitted, HD 71, 120. [22c] de sua ... in capite omitted, HD 5a, 5b, 71, 120; in elemosina, HD 5a, 5b, 71, 120. [22d] de dictis fratribus, HD 5a, 5b, 71, 120. [22e] eisdem, HD 5a, 5b, 71, 120; eis, D, HD 6. [22f] Walsingham, HD 5a, 5b, D, HD 6. [22g] eodem Bartholomeo de eodem feodo, HD 5a, 5b, 71, 120; dicto, D, HD 6. [22h] j mariscum, HD 5a, 5b, 71; dictum, HD 120. [22i] eidem. Dictus mariscus continet x acras iuxta ibidem le Dyff'hyrne, HD 5a, 5b, 71, 120.

[23a] Title only in HD 22a; <Feodum comitis Warenne>, <Falda> and <Prior de Walsingham>, HD 22a. [23b] Cayly and Dauy follow fee of Bradolph and Bishop of Norwich, HD 5a, 5b, 71, 120; <Feodum Warenie de Walsyngham>, HD 71, 120; Cali, D; Eborardus le Kalye et parcenarij sui tenent, HD 71, 120; et Humfredus Daui, D; Dauy, HD 6. [23c] omitted, HD 5a, 5b. [23d] de Iacobo de Thorpp', HD 6, 71, 120, D. [23e] omitted, HD 5a, 5b. [23f] de feodo Warennie, HD 71; de feodo Warenie, HD 120; de comite de Warenne, D, HD 6. [23g] de domino ... capite omitted, HD 71, 120. [23h] xxiv acras terre follows tenent, omitting fold, HD 71, 120. [23i] et j feodo de Wython de dono Antecessor' Philippi de Narrygge in elemosina xx d. de dicto Iacobo, HD 71, 120. [23j] iij d., D; plus plus minus minus, HD 71, 120. [23k] iij acras, D. [23l] Idem Eborardus tenet de dicto Iacobo vj acras terre de eodem feodo quas villani sui de eodem tenent cum

mesuagiis, HD 71, 120; D, HD 6 read as HD 22a. [23m] de eodem Eborardo de eodem
feodo vnum mesuagium, HD 71, 120; D, HD 6 read as HD 22a.

[23n] tenet de eodem Eborardo de eodem feodo, HD 71, 120; D, HD 6 read as HD 22a.

[23o] quas villani sui de eodem tenent cum suis messuagiis Et reddit per annum xij d., HD
71, 120; D reads as HD 22a; Matilda le Marshall tenet de dicto Eborardo de eodem
feodo medietatem vnius messuagij et iiij acr' terre et reddit per annum j d. Idem Matilda
tenet parcenariis suis de dicto Eborardo de eodem feodo xij acras terre et medietatem
vnius messuagij et reddit per annum j d., HD 5a, 5b, 71, 120; omitted in HD 22a and D.

[23p] Sylk, HD 71; Syke, HD 6, 120; Silke, D.

[24a] This paragraph is also in D and HD 6; <Feodum de Wyghton> struck out, D; in HF
71 and 120 the Feodary ends: Warham Prior de Petraston tenet de Humfrido de Wythun
quondam Bartholomei Orchyerd xiij acras terre. Et reddit dicto Humfrido xvj d. et iac' in
Warham. [24b] vilenagio, D; vellinagio, HD 6.

[25a] de Holkham, D, HD 6. [25b] Et dicta medietas quidem ... et superius dictum est, D.

[26a] Ms. reads le, not de.

Fo. 30

THE NEEL PEDIGREE

254 PETEGR. RICARDUS NEEL DE BRUNHAM ET KATERINA
UXOR EIUS [c. 1430–5]

Fiche 1: B12

Thomas Neel primogenitus predictorum Ricardi et Katerine et obiit sine herede de corpore suo.

Gilbertus Neel frater predicti Thome secundus filius predictorum Ricardi et Katerine habuit vxorem nomine Isabellam et ex ea genuit Thomam primogenitum et duas filias filia prima Margareta et secunda filia Maria.

Thomas primogenitus predicti Gilberti obiit sine herede de corpore suo et Margareta prima filia predicti Gilberti habuit virum nomine Iohannem Qwarles qui habuerunt inter se Stephanum primogenitum qui quidem Stephanus duxit in vxorem [*space in Ms.*] filiam Thome Gurnay de Wesenham et habuerunt inter se filiam nomine [*space in Ms.*] qui^a obiit apud Lynniam episcopi et sic defecit exitus predictorum Iohannis Qwarles et Margareta vxoris et sic hereditas apud Holkham et Kipton' descendebat ad Mariam sororem predicte Margarete.

Maria secunda filia predicti Gilberti Neel habuit virum nomine Edmundum Lucas filium Rollandi Lucas de Estderham qui habuerunt inter se Thomam primogenitum Stephanum secundum filium et Ricardum tercium filium et Margaretam quartam filiam et primogenitam.

Thomas primogenitus predictorum Edmundi Lucas et Marie duxit in vxorem Etheldredam filiam Nicholai de Castello et habuerunt inter se Thomam primogenitum Ricardum^b secundum.

VARIANTS: ^{a} *sic* in Ms. ^{b} Recordum, Ms.

NOTE: The sons of Edmund Lucas, Thomas and Stephen Lucas, and perhaps also their younger brother Richard Lucas, rector of Horningtoft, were students in Cambridge. Thomas Lucas, the elder son of Edmund Lucas, was admitted to King's Hall, Cambridge, on 7 July 1409, and Stephen Lucas, the second son, was admitted to King's Hall, Cambridge, on 25 August 1415, after his brother had resigned in his favour; B.A. by 1420, he had left Cambridge by 1441 and died in 1469. Richard Lucas, their uncle, was a fellow of Pembroke Hall, Cambridge, in 1388 and still in 1390, by which time he was Lic. A.; M.A. and B.Th. by 1399. Thomas and Stephen Lucas were cousins of another Cambridge *alumnus*, Richard Dereham (1367–1417), warden of King's Hall (1399–1413 and 1415–17); M.A. by 1391; B.Th. by 1399; Lic.Th. in 1401; D.Th., Notary Public by pontifical authority by 1410. In 1407 he was a candidate for the See of Norwich. J.P. in Cambridge in 1404 and 1407, he held several prebends in London, Chichester and Salisbury. King's Clerk and Chaplain by 1400, he represented the University of

Cambridge at the Councils of Pisa (1408–9) and of Constance (1415–16). In fact, Richard Dereham and Richard Lucas, brother of Edmund Lucas, may have been the same person. Cf. J. and J.A. Venn, *Alumni Cantabrigienses*, pt. 1, 1924 and A.B. Emden, *A biographical Register of the University of Cambridge to 1500*, 1963.

Fo. 30v   Feodum Domine Dionisie de Monte Canisi modo

NOTE: Pinned onto Fo. 30v (blank) is a small piece of paper, with the following:

<Edmundus Lucas et parcennarij eius tenent et vocatur Neles> [*right margin*]
Galfridus Bret tenet in Holkham de domina Dionisia de Monte Canisi vnum mesuagium vi^{xx} acr. terre et vnam faldam pro seruicio vnius quarterij feodi militis. Idem Galfridus tenet clx acr. terre quas villani sui de eo tenent in villenagio per seruicium predictum faciend' eidem ij sectas curie per annum et vnam sectam ad hundredum de Northgrenowe de tribus septimanis in tres septimanas. Idem Galfridus tenet de dicta domina dimidiam acram terre et reddit per annum ij d.

Fos. 31–34v

BURGHALL RENTAL

Fo. 31   RENTALE DE BURGHALL' IN HOLKHAM[a]

255 ROTULUS[b] DE TENEMENTO QUOD FUIT DOMINI WARINI DE MONTE CANISO[c] DE REDDITIBUS[d] ET CONSUETUDINIBUS TAM LIBERORUM QUAM VILLANORUM IN HOLKHAM   7 Dec. 1303

> Fiche 1: B13
>
> NOTE: HD 4 and HD 4a are original parchment rolls of 1272–3 and 1303, 93/4 and 7 3/8 in. wide. Fiche 1: A5 and 6. HD 4a has paragraph marks and some initial capitals rubricated. This copy of the Burghall rental by Edmund Lucas was made after HD 4a dated 7 Dec. 1303.

Radulfus Hakon[e] tenet xl. acras pro xvj[a] parte de feodo militari[f] et quinque acras[g] de Bruera pro vno pari cirotecarum prec' ob.

Idem tenet \in manu domine/ iiij acras terre iuxta cruftam Rogeri Wynter et abbuttant[h] super Brunhamgate pro j libra cimini prec' iij ob.

Idem tenet \Iohannes Silk tenet/[i] iij acras terre que vocantur Goldwynescroft[j] pro vj d. de censa ad quatuor terminos[k]

Idem tenet dimidiam acram de Henrico capellano[l] pro ij d. de censa ad iiij terminos

Summa xij d.

Willelmus Presbiter tenet j. acram terre pro xj d. de censa

Summa xj d.

<Lucas>

Petrus le Bret tenet centum acras terre in Holkham et in Sueynesthorp et in Surlyngham pro vno quarterio Militis et quando scutagium aduenerit ad xl . s.[m] x . s. ad plus plus[n]

Idem soluet pro vna roda terre de terra Tonestel[o] de censa ij d. et Rogerus Eluerich' tenet eam

Summa ij d.

Thomas Frater eius[p]

Adam le Bret \Iohannes Silk/ tenet j rodam terre pro ij d[q] de censa

Summa ij d.[q]

Bertramus Verdoun[r] tenuit xl acras terre pro v. s. de Censa ad iiij[or] terminos ad comune auxilium xx s. de scutagio v d. et pro j roda terre ij d.

Prior[s] de Petra Reginaldus filius Willelmi et plures alij tenent de domina

Summa v s. ij d.

Bartholomeus de Burgate[t] Willelmus Mariot tenent xl acras terre pro ix s. x d. de censa ad iiij[or] terminos et ad commune auxilium domini dabunt x d. ad xx s.[u] et facient vj precar' in autumpno ad cibum domini pret. vj d. et facient ij precar' cum caruca licet habeant equos vel non[v] pret' xij d. pro qualibet caruca vj d. \ad cibum domini/ Et pro Brimilescruft[w] j d. et iiij altilia pret' vj d.

Summa xij s.xj d.

Henricus filius Galfridi tenuit[x] dimidiam acram terre pro ij d. de censa Et Willelmus Crask tenet

Summa ij d.

Radulfus Colt[y] tenet j acram terre cum soc*agio*[z] suo pro x d. pro omnibus consuetudinibus et Bartholomeus[aa] molendinarius et Willelmus[aa] clericus tenent

Summa x d.

Willelmus filius Iohannis tenet ij acras terre et iij perticatas pro xvj d. \de censa/ ad cibum domini pret' iij d. et ad commune auxilium ad xx s. j d.[bb] ad plus plus[cc]

Summa xvj d.

Galfridus Godwyne tenet vj acras terre pro xiij d. de censa et ij gallinis pret' ij d. et faciet j precar' cum caruca licet habeat equum vel[dd] non pret' iij d. in autumpno[ee] et ad comune auxilium[ee] ad xx s. j d.

Summa ij s.

Iohannes filius Roberti tenet dimidiam acram terre et faciet j precar' cum caruca ad cibum domini licet habeat equum vel[ff] non pret' vj d.

Summa vj d.

Henricus[gg] de Monte et parcenarij[hh] sui tenent xviij acras terre pro xxij d. de censa ad iiij[or] terminos et iiij[or] gallinis pret' iiij d. et facient iij dimidias[ii] dies[ii] ad sarcland' pret' iij ob. et vj[jj] precar' in autumpno ad cibum domini pret' vj d. et facient j precar' cum caruca si habeat equum pret' vj d. ad cibum domini et dabit pro Wodelode ij d. et portabit breue vel den. per ij vices in anno pret' iiij d. Et quando[kk] dominus venerit in villa ad exitum eius accomodabit domino equum suum si habeat ad portandum panes[ll] per xij leucas et ibit ad stagnum domini scilicet molendinum per ij dies pret' j d. et ad Wardese ob. et cariabit bladum domini in autumpno per j diem pret' ij d. si habeat equum

Summa iiij s. j d.

Fo. 31v Godmannus le Burgoyne*a* tenet xij. acras terre pro xiiij d. de censa ad ad iiij*or* terminos et ad Wardese ob. ij gallinis pret' . ij d.*b* pro Wodelode ij d.*b* vj precar' in autumpno pret' vj d. ad cibum domini j precar' cum caruca ad cibum domini pret' vj d. si habeat equum cariabit bladum domini in autumpno per j diem pret' ij d. et sarclabit iiij dimidias dies pret' iiij ob. Ire*c* ad stagnum per ij dies pret' j d. et portabit breue vel denar, per ij vices pret' iiij d. et si dominus venerit in villa ad exitum eius accomodabit domino equum suum si habeat per xij leucas Rogerus Simon et Iohannes Burgoyne nunc tenent*d*

Summa iij s. iij d.

<manus domini>

Godwinus paruus*e* et parcenar'*f* eius tenent xij acras terre pro xiiij d. de censa ad faldagium iiij d. ad Wardese ob. pro Wodelode ij d. ij gallinis pret' ij d. vj precar' in autumpno pret' vj d. ad cibum domini*h* j precar' cum caruca ad cibum domini si habeat \equum/ pret' vj d. sarclabit per iiij. dimidias dies pret' iiij ob. Ire*i* ad stagnum per ij dies pret' j d. et portabit breue*j* vel den. per ij vices*k* pret' iiij d. et inueniet*l* equum suum si habeat ad exitum domini*m* per xij leucas et cariabit bladum domini in autumpno si habeat equum per j diem*n* pret'*o* ij d. et Robertus Hade*p* nunc tenet

Summa iiij s. vij d.

Herueus Guthild et parcenar*ij* eius tenent xij acras terre pro xvj d. de censa ad faldagium domini viij d. et ad Wardese ob. et facient omnia*q* sic*ut* predictus Godwynus et Iohannes*r* Fayrman*s* nunc tenet*t*

Summa vs. j d.

Thomas de la Dale et parcenar*ij* eius*s* tenent xij acras terre pro xiiij d. de censa ad faldagium iiij d. ad Wardese ob. et omnia alia*t* sic*ut* predictus Godwynus et Iohannes de la Dale nunc tenet

Summa iiij s. vij d.

Thurbern*u* et Willelmus Herbelot tenent v rodas terre pro xij d. vj precariis in autumpno pret' vj d. ad cibum domini Et*v* Rogerus Speller et Cecilia filia Galfridi*w* Thurbern nunc tenent

Summa xviij d.

Terra Talbot xviij acr' terre*x* pro ij s. viij d. iiij gallinis pret' iiij d. ix precariis in autumpno pret' ix d. et ij quarteriis auene pret' ij s. Scarlunderys*y* solebat reddere\vj d.*z*/ que nunc est in dominico

Summa v s. ix d.

Rogerus Rauen et Herueus Carpe tenent xxij acras terre pro xxvj d. ad^{aa} faldagium ix d. ij summas auene pret' ij s. et facient ij quarteria brasei ad cibum domini pret' iij d. et cariabunt dimidium Rengnum^{bb} fimorum pret' iiij d. ob. et xvj opera in autumpno et iij precar' pret' xix d. et flagellabunt per xxxij dies pret' xvj d. et ij precar' cum caruca si habeat equos pret' xij d.^{cc} ad cibum domini et sarclabit^{dd} per iij dimid' dies pret' iij ob. et facient aueragia pret' iij d. et ibunt ad stagnum operand'^{ee} iiij^{or} dies pret' ij d. iiij gallin' pret' iiij d. et cariabunt in autumpno ad cibum domini per j diem^{ff} si habeant equum pret' vj d.

Summa x s. x d.

Galfridus Payn et fratres eius tenuerunt xij acras terre pro xiiij d. ad^{gg} faldagium iiij d. ob. ij gallin' pret' ij d. et facient ij summas^{hh} brasei ad cibum domini pret'^{ii} iij d. et dabunt vnam summam^{jj} auene pret' xij d. et facient xviij dies in autumpno pret' xviij d. et dimid' diem in autumpno sine cibo domini nullo pretio et ducent dimidium Rengnum^{kk} fimorum pret' iiij d. ob. ad cibum domini et facient j precar' cum caruca si habeant equum pret' vj d. et flagellabunt per xxxij dies pret' xvj d. et sarclabunt^{ll} iij dimid' dies pret' iij ob. et ibunt ad stagnum per ij vices pret' j d. cariabunt in autumpno per j diem ad cibum domini^{mm} pret' iij d. et facient aueragia pret' iij de et Reginaldus Euerard^{nn} et parcenarij nunc tenent

Summa vij s. iiij d. ob.

Fo. 32 Herueus Sturstan^{a} et parcenarij eius tenent xij acras terre et facient omnia sicut predictus Galfridus et Rogerus Slopere^{b} et Willelmus Cupere^{b} et Rogerus Aleyn nunc tenent

Summa vij s. iiij d. ob.

Iohannes Leuere et parcenarij eius tenent xij acras terre pro xv d. ad Wardese quadr' ad faldagium iiij d. ob. et omnia alia sicut dictus Galfridus pret' j diem^{c} et Galfridus Thurbern^{d} et Matilda Wlmerus^{d} nunc tenent

Summa vij s. v d. ob. qua.

Idem^{e} Iohannes tenet j acram terre pro xij d. j gallinam pret' j d. iiij precar' in autumpno pret' iij d. Et Robertus^{f} et Oliua Leuere^{f} nunc tenent

Summa xvj d.

<Terra Biscop.^{g}>

Radulfus Wlrun tenuit xiiij acras terre pro xvij d. ad Wardese quadr. iij galin' pret' iij d. et cetera^{h} omnia sicut dictus^{i} Galfridus et domina^{j} tenet^{j}

Summa vij s. viij d. ob. qua.

Miriild^{k} Kygemond' tenet xij acras terre et fac' omnia sicut^{l} dictus Galfridus Et Hugo Molendinarius^{m} tenet

Summa vij s. iiij d. ob.

<Terra Dusyng.>^{m}

Bartholomeus filius Rogeri tenet xij acras terre et facient omnia sicut^l dictus Galfridus. Et domina^n tenet inde vij acras^n

Summa vij s. iiij d. ob.

Rogerus de Campo tenet xij acras terre et facit omnia sicut^o dictus Galfridus et Margareta^p nunc tenet Et Domina^p tenet inde^q ij acras terre

Summa vij s. iiij d. ob.

Euerardus^r et parcenar' eius tenent xij acras terre et fac' omnia sicut^o dictus Galfridus . Et Edmundus filius Willelmi^q tenet

Summa vij s. iiij d. ob.

Hugo Elsi^s et parcenar' eius tenent xviij acras terre pro xxviij d.^{t} ad Wardese ob. ad Faldagium vj d. v scepp'^{u} auene pret' xv. d.^{v} et ducent ij partes Rengni fimorum pret' vj d. ob. quad. et cetera^w omnia sicut dictus^x Galfridus et Martinus Rust^q Ricardus Schipman^q et Galfridus Austyn^q nunc tenent

Summa viij s. j d. ob. qua.

Thoue Fouel^y et parcenar' eius tenent xij acr' terre pro ix d. quad. et ad Wardese^z quad. et cetera^{aa} omnia sicut dictus Galfridus et Gilbertus Chosse^{bb} nunc tenet

Summa vij s.

Galfridus filius Heruei le^{cc} Grene tenet xxiiij^{or} acras terre pro xxviij d.^{dd} et pro marisco vj acr' ij d. ad^{ee} faldagium vj d. ob. ad^{ee} Wardese ob. iiij^{ff} gallin' pret' iiij d. Item^{gg} vnam summam et iij schepp'^{hh} auene pret' xxj d. Et fac' ij summas^{ii} brasij pret' iij d. et habebit cibum et^{ij} xxiiij^{or} opera in autumpno et iij precar' in autumpno pret'^{kk} ij s. iij d. ad cibum domini et ducet dimidium Regnum fimorum pret' iiij d. ob. ad cibum domini et flagellabit xxxij dies pret' xvj d. et faciet j precar' cum caruca^{ll} si habeat equum pret' vj d. et sarclabit per iij dimid' dies pret' iij ob. et faciet auerag' pret' iij d. et ibit ad stagnum per ij dies pret' j d. et cariabit in autumpno per j diem ad cibum domini pret' iij d.

Summa x s. vij d.^{mm}

Matilda Coppyng^{nn} tenet iij perticatas terre pro vj d. j gallina pret' j d. iij precar' in autumpno pret' iij d.

Summa x d.

Ricardus filius Gilberti Hagne^{oo} tenet vj acras terre pro x d. j gallina Pret' j d. ad^{pp} Wardese ob. vj precar' in autumpno pret' vj d. ad cibum domini et portabit breue vel den per ij vices pret' iiij d. et sarclabit per iij dimid' dies pret' iij ob. et ibit ad stagnum per ij vices^{qq} pret' j d. Et Iohannes Maynard^{rr} nunc tenet

Summa ij s

Fo. 32v Willelmus filius Rogeri et socius eius^a tenet vj acras pro viij d. ad faldagium iij d. quadr. j gallina pret' j d. et dimidiam summam^a auene pret' vj d. et facient j summam bras' pret' iij ob.^{b} ad cibum domini et xvj opera in autumpno ad cibum domini pret' xvj d. et spargent dimidium Rengnum^c fimorum ad cibum domini pret' ob. et facient j precar' cum caruca si habeant equum pret' vj d. et sarclabunt per iij dimid' dies pret' iij ob. et ibunt ad stagnum per ij dies pret' j d. et facient auerag' pret' iij d. et flagellabunt per xvj dies pret' viij d. et cariabunt per j diem ad cibum domini pret' iij d. Et Helewys' Dersy^d tenet

Summa iiij s. x d. ob. quadr.

Herueus Dersy tenet vj acras terre pro viij d. ad^d faldagium ij d. quadr. et cetera^e omnia sicut dictus^f Willelmus Et Isabella de la Droue et Iohannes Dersy nunc tenent

Summa iiij s. ix d. ob. qudr.

Thurstan et parcenar' eius tenent vj acras terre pro viij d. ad faldagium ij d. quadr. et cetera^e omnia sicut predictus Willelmus Et Rogerus Coleman et Sarra Deusacre nunc tenent

Summa iiij s. ix d. ob. quadr.

Semannus Asketell' tenet vj acras pro viij d. ad faldagium iij d. et cetera^e omnia sicut predictus Willelmus set non facit bras'. Et Iohannes Fayrman^d et Iohannes Peper^g nunc tenent

Summa iiij s. ix d. ob. quadr.

Radulfus super montem tenet vj acras terre pro viij d. ad faldagium iij d. quadr. et cetera^e omnia sicut predictus Willelmus

Summa iiij s. ix d. ob. quadr.

Willelmus Walterus tenet vj acras terre pro viij d. ad faldagium ij d. quadr. et cetera^h omnia sicut predictus Willelmus

Summa iiij s. ix d. ob. quadr.

Willelmus Thurild tenet vj acras terre pro viij d. ad faldagium ij d. quadr. et cetera^h omnia sic*ut* predictus Willelmus Et domina tenet inde ij acras j rodam et dimidiam

Summa iiij s. ix d. ob. quadr.

Radulfus Peter tenet vj acras terre pro viij d. ad faldagium ij d. quadr. et
cetera omnia sicut predictus Willelmus

Summa iiij s. ix d. ob. quadr.

Warinus Bedel tenet vj acras terre pro viij d. faldagium*[i]* j d. j gallin' pret'
j d. vj precar' in autumpno ad cibum domini pret' vj d. et portabit Breue vel
den. per ij vices pret' iiij d. et sarclabit*[j]* iiij dimid' dies pret' iiij ob.*[k]* Ibit ad
stagnum per ii dies pret' j d. et j precar' cum caruca ad cibum domini si
habeat equum pret' vj d. et cariabit in autumpno per j diem pret' iiij d. Et
Thomas Waryn tenet*[l]*

Summa ij s. v d. ob.

Willelmus Faber tenet vj acras terre pro viij d. faldagium*[m]* ij d. quadr. et
cetera*[h]* omnia sicut predictus Willelmus filius Rogeri fecit et Willelmus de
Hindringham*[n]* et W*illelmus* Huberd*[n]* nunc tenent

Summa iiij s. ix d. ob. quadr.

Iohannes Stute tenet vj acras terre pro viij d. ad faldagium iiij d. quadr. et
cetera*[h]* omnia sicut predictus Willelmus filius Rogeri Et domina*[o]* tenet
inde*[p]* iiij acras et dimidiam et dimidiam rodam

Summa iiij s. ix d. ob. quadr.

Robertus Kitte*[q]* et socius eius tenent vj acras terre pro viij d. et de istis
den. Thomas de Burgate soluet iiij d. et Bartholomeus Carpentar' j d. fil*ia*
Bete ij d. Et dictus*[r]* Robertus j d. et ad Wardese*[s]* quadr. ad faldagium ij d.
quadr. j gallin' pret' j d. dimidiam summam auene pret' vj d. et xiiij opera in
autumpno ad cibum domini pret' xiiij d. et flagellabunt per xiij dies pret' vj
d. ob. et facient aueragia pret' ij d. et sarclabunt per iiij dimid' dies pret' iiij
ob. et ibit ad stagnum per ij dies pret' j d. et spargent dimidium Rengnum*[t]*
fimorum pret' ob. Et Galfridus Scot*[u]* et Oliua Sutor*[w]* nunc tenent

Summa iij s. vij d.

Fo. 33 Henricus*[a]* Grigge tenuit vj acras terre pro viij d. ad faldagium ij d.
quadr. facit omnia alia sicut sepe nominatus*[b]* predictus Willelmus

Summa iij s. vij d.

Willelmus Asketel tenuit*[c]* tres acras terre pro iiij d. ad faldagium j d. ad
Wardese ob. viij opera in autumpno pret' viij d. ad cibum domini j. gallin'
pret' j d. vj precar' in autumpno ad cibum domini pret' vj d.*[d]* et sparget
dimidium Rengnum*[e]* fimorum pret' ob. et cariabit in autumpno per j diem
pret' vj d. et j precar' cum caruca pret' iiij d. ad cibum domini et flagellabit
viij dies pret' iiij d. et sarclabit iiij dimid' dies pret' iiij ob. et faciet aueragia
pret' ij d. Ibit ad stagnum per.ij dies pret' j d.

Summa iij s. ij d. ob.

Willelmus Wytbret^f \ten' iij acras terre/ pro vij d. quadr. j gallin' pret' j d. ad Wardese^g quadr. xiiij opera in autumpno ad cibum domini pret' xiiij d. et flagellabit viij dies pret' iiij d. et cetera^h omnia sic*ut* predictus Willelmus set non sparget fimum Et Willelmus Asty Cecilia Adam et Radulfus Asty nunc tenent

Summa iij s. iiij d. ob. quad.

Willelmus Colyn^i tenet iij acras terre pro iiij d. ad faldagium j d. ad Wardese^g quadr. et cetera^h omnia sicut predictus Willelmus

Summa iij s. ij d. quadr.

Willelmus Alberd^j \ten' iij acras terre/ pro iiij d. ad faldagium j d. ad Wardese^g quadr. et cetera^h omnia sicut predictus Willelmus

Summa iij s. ij d. quadr.

Lerwyf^i ad caput ville tenet \iij acras terre pro viij d.^{k}/ ad faldagium j d. ad Wardese quadr. et cetera^l omnia sicut dictus^m Willelmus et Emma Godman^n et parcenar' eius nunc tenent

Summa iij s. vj d. quadr.

Ricardus Carpe de terra Bruuger ij d. ad faldagium j d. j gallin' pret' j d. vj precar' in autumpno pret' vj d. et fac' aueragia pret' ij d. Et Matilda^n Chosse^o Bert' Wynter^n et Christiana Wynter^n nunc tenent

Summa xij d.

Mabilia vxor Vlphi^p tenet^n iij acras terre pro iiij d. ad faldagium j d. j gallin' pret' j d. xj opera in autumpno ad cibum domini pret' xj d. et^n cetera^l omnia sic*ut* predictus Willelmus Asketell^n Et Rogerus et *Willelmus* de Stiberde tenent

Summa ij s. xj d. ob.

Godmannus filius Bartholomei^q tenet iij acras pro iiij d. ad Wardese quadr. ad faldagium j d. j gallin' pret' j d.^{r} et cariabit in autumpno per j diem pret' iij d. et cetera^l omnia fac' sic*ut* predictus Willelmus et Radulfus Coltyng^s nunc tenet

Summa iij s. iiij d. quadr.

Dauyd Knyt^t tenet iij acras pro iiij d. ad Wardese quadr. ad faldagium j d. j gallin' pret' j d. et cetera^l omnia sicut dictus^m Willelmus et Radulfus Coltyng^s nunc tenet

Summa iij s. ij d. quadr.

Cecilia de Hogate^u tenet iij acras terre et facit omnia sicud predictus^s Dauyd facit

Summa iij s. ij d. quadr.

Dilegrim^v tenet iij acras terre pro iiij d. gallin' pret' i d. ad faldagium j d. et cetera omnia^w sic*ud* dictus Willelmus Et Robertus Emelot tenet

Summa iij s. ij d.

Rogerus Wyit^x tenet ij acras terre pro vj d. j gallin' pret' j d. iij precar' in autumpno pret' iij d. et ibit ad stagnum per ij dies pret' j d. et sarclabit per iij dimid' dies pret' iij ob. et Ricardus Stirtup^y nunc tenet

Summa xij d. ob.

Fo. 33v Gregorius filius Iohannis tenet ij acras terre pro vj d. j gallin' pret' j d. viij opera in autumpno pret' viij d. et flagellabit per viij dies pret' iiij d. et sarclabit per iij dimid' dies pret' iij ob. et ibit ad stagnum per ij dies pret' j d.

Summa xxj d.

Thurbern tenet ij acras terre pro vj d. et cetera^a omnia sicut predictus Gregorius set non flagellabit

Summa xvij d. ob.

Dauyd Knyt^b tenet j acram et dimidiam terre pro iiij d. j gallin' pret' j d. vj precar' in autumpno pret' vj d. et sarclabit per iij dimid' dies pret' iij ob. et ibit ad stagnum per ij dies pret' j d. Et Radulfus Coltyng'^{c} et Iohanna Thurbern^c tenent

Summa xiij d. quad.

Rogerus Edwy^d tenet vj acras pro xx d. de censa ad Wardese ob. ij gallin' pret' ij d. et pro Wodelode ij d. viij opera in autumpno pret' viij d. et iij precar' in autumpno pret' xj d. et j precar' cum caruca ad cibum domini pret' vj d. si habeat equum ad cibum domini et cariabit in autumpno per j diem ad cibum domini pret' iij d. et sarclabit iij dimidiis diebus pret' iij ob. et ibit ad stagnum per ij dies pret' j d. et inueniet domino equum si habeat quando ibit extra villam per xij leucas Et Adam Trowman^c et Thomas nunc tenent

Summa iij s. xj d.

Rogerus Philippe et parcenar' eius tenent ij acras et dimidiam terre pro xiij d. j gallin' pret' j d. iiij precar' in autumpno pret' iiij d. j precar' cum caruca^e pret' vj d. si habeat equum et cariabit in autumpno per j diem pret' iij d. si habeat equum et sarclabit per iij dimid' dies pret' iij ob. et ibunt ad stagnum per ij dies pret' j d. Idem^f Rogerus per parcenar' eius tenent j acram terre pro iiij d. pro omni seruicio Et Agn*eta* Edwyne^g et Thomas Waryn^g nunc tenent

Summa ij s. ix d. ob.

Iohannes Hingenald*[h]* tenet dimidiam acram pro ob.*[i]* ad Wardese quadr.*[j]* Et Iohannes Fayrman et Iohannes Peper*[g]* nunc tenent

Summa j d.

Vxor Henrici Coket tenet j mesuagium pro ij d. j gallin' pret' j d. iij precar' in autumpno pret' iiij d. Et domina*[g]* tenet

Summa vj d.

Ricardus Dersy tenet dimid' acram pro viij d. et vj precar' in autumpno pret' vj d. Et Adam Dersy*[g]* nunc tenet

Summa xiiij d.

Radulfus Stirt*[k]* tenet ij acras pro iiij d. j gallin' pret' j d. vj precar' in autumpno pret' vj d. Et Willelmus de Hindringham*[g]*

Summa xj d.

Galfridus filius Wyd tenet j acram pro v d. et j gallin' pret' j d. iiij precar' in autumpno pret' iiij d. Et Matilda Noteman*[g]* tenet

Summa ix d.

Rogerus Wynter tenet j acram pro v d. j gallin' pret' j d. iiij precar' in autumpno pret' iiij d. Et Bert' Wynter*[g]* nunc tenet

Summa ix d.

Geruasius Sutor tenet j rodam terre ante pratum domini pro ij d. Et *Willelmus[l]* Church*[g]* iunior nunc tenet

Summa ij d.

Hubertus filius *Galfridi[i]* et parcenar' eius tenent dimidiam acram terre pro x d.

Summa x d.

Iohannes*[m]* Ouerman reddit de censa iiij d.

Willelmus*[m]* Nicol de censa j d. et Gilbertus*[m]* filius eius tenet

Radulfus*[m]* de Hil*[n]* tenet iij acras de terra *Galfridi* prepositi pro vj d.*[o]*

Summa xj d.

Cheuagium ij s. aliquando plus aliquando minus

Summa ij s.

Fo. 34 Rogerus de Thorp*[a]* de incremento ad festum*[b]* Sancti Iohannis*[c]*

Iohannes de Foxele*[a]* tenet j peciam terre de terra Iohannis Wlrun*[d]* et*[f]* reddit j ob. pro omni seruicio Et Rogerus Slopere nunc tenet Et Martinus Rust ad terminum Sancti Iohannis ob.

Summa

<Summa^f Arur'>

xlvj Caruc' quarum iiij^{or} si fuerit equus vel non

<Summa^f cariag'>

xlj cariag'

<Summa^f faldag'>

ix s. vj d.

<Summa^f cariag' fimorum>

v et dimid' et ij partes cuiuslibet ix d.

<Summa^f Sparsion' fimorum>

x regn' pret' cuiuslibet ob.

<Summa sarclac'>

vij^{xx} et j operac' de consuetud' pret' cuiuslibet ob.

<Summa Bras' faciend'>

xxxiiij quarter' pret' quarter' iij ob.

<Summa denar' reddit' et consuetud'>

xiij li. iiij s. j d. ob. quadr.

<Summa dicti redditus in denar'>

lxxj s. iiij d. quadr.

<Faldag'>

x s. ob. qua.

<Wardese>

ix d. ob.

<Summa de Wodelode>.

xij d.

<1 par cirotecarum>

<j lib. cimini>

<j lib. piperis>

<Summa Auerag'>

lix auerag' Inde in decasu super terram in manu domine pro particulis iij auerag'. Item super terram Iohannis Aleyn j auerag' et dimid' Anno xxiij^o Item super terram Hugonis molendinarij Anno xxiiij^o j auerag' et dimidium Item super terram Iohanne Thurbern ij aueragia

<Summa^g consuetud' in autumpno>
pret' quam de terra Wlrun xviij opera que est in manu domine et pret' x opera de iij acris et iij rodis de terra Thurgild que est in manu domine et pret' xiij opera de terra Bartholomei scilicet ix acr' in manu domine ix^{xx} et j homines quilibet per j diem et valet quilibet j d. qui habebunt cibum et ccc v^{xx} viij opera maiore numero quorum quilibet valet j d. qui habebunt cibum et ix homines per dimid' diem sine cibo set inde allocat' super W. prepositum viij opera autumpnalia. Et sic sunt inde de claro in toto ad cibum anno xxj^o Dxlj homines quilibet per j diem et ix homines per dimid' diem sine cibo pret' cuiuslibet j d. Vnde Anno xxj^o expend' in toto iiij^i xxij ad cibum jt sic restant in toto vj^{xx} pret' j diem

<Summa opera yemalia>
Dlxxij pret' cuiuslibet ob. Vnde indecasu super terram Biscop et Wlrun xxxij opera. Item super terram Thurgihild x opera. Item super terram Bartholomei xxiiij opera. Item super prepositum et super messorem

De xiij acris terre Biscop^j et Wlrun Iohannes Holigod tenet iij rodas et dimidiam Willelmus Asty^i iij rodas et dimidiam Helewys Wulkyns^j j acram terre Rogerus Slopere^k Radulfus Herward^l Simon Faber Matilda Chosse^m et Ricardus Schipman^n tenent j rodam. Et domina tenet x acras

De vj acris terre Thurgild^o Gilbertus Grigge j acram dimidiam Willelmus Huberd^p iij rodas dimidiam Willelmus Asty^q j rodam et dimidiam Margareta in^r Campo j acram terre. Et domina tenet ij acras j rodam

De vj acris terre Blome Gilbertus Nicol^s j rodam Stephanus de Hyndryngham^t j rodam et dimidiam Willelmus Putbred^u iunior j rodam et dimidiam Willelmus Cupere j rodam et dimidiam. Et domina tenet in toto v acras j rodam et dimidiam

De tenemento Kekes^v domina tenet iij acras^w terre

De tenemento Iohannis^x Aleyn domina tenet vj acras^y scilicet totum^y

De tenemento Hugonis molendinarij domina tenet xij acras^{aa} scilicet totum^{aa}

Fo. 34v Summa Acrarum de tenementis villanorum xx^{xx} et ij acr' [403 acres] vnde sunt in manu domine Anno regni regis Edwardi xxxij^o in crastino Sancti Nicholai [Saturday 7 December 1303] cum tenementis Iohannis Aleyn et Hugonis molendinarij xlij acr' et dimid' et dimid' rod'. Et sic restant in tenura villanorum predicto die xvij^{xx} xix acr' j roda et dimidia^a [359 acres 1 rood 1/2 rood]

[*the rest of the page is blank*]

VARIANTS: **Fo. 31** [a] E. primo, HD 4. [b] <Burhowhall> added later. [c] Canisio, HD 4. [d] tam de liberis quam de seruilibus redditibus et consuetudinibus Holcham, HD 4a. [e] Hakun, HD4. [f] feodi militis, *ib.* [g] vnam faldam ad Bruar', *ib.* [h] abuttant, *ib.* [i] omitted, *ib.* [j] Perhaps scribal error for Goldwynescroft, Gobwynescroft, HD 4. [k] terminos annuales, *ib.* [l] de feodo Henrici Capellani, HD 4. [m] dabit, HD 4. [n] et ad minus minus, *ib.*; <nel>, HD 4. [o] omitted, *ib.* [p] tenet ij acras pro j libra piperis, HD 4. [q] iij d., HD 4. [r] Verdun tenuit, HD 4; tenet, HD 4 of sums. [s] Prior ... domini omitted, HD 4. [t] <Wake>, HD 4. [u] order reversed, HD 4. [v] annon, HD 4. [w] omitted, HD 4; Brunlescruft, HD 4a. [x] tenet, HD 4. [y] Hakun, HD 4. [z] cum crofto suo, HD 4. [aa] omitted, HD 4. [bb] order reversed, HD 4. [cc] et ad minus minus, HD 4. [dd] an non, HD 4. [ee] omitted, HD 4. [ff] an non, HD 4. [gg] Herueus, HD 4. [hh] participes, HD 4 (here and below). [ii] reversed, HD 4. [jj] tria, HD 4. [kk] si, HD 4. [ll] panem, HD 4.

Fo. 31v [a] Godmannus Burgoine, HD 4. [b] et, HD 4. [c] et ibit, HD 4. [d] Rogerus ... tenent, omitted <Walsoken>, HD 4. [e] omitted, HD 4a. [f] et j quarterio auene pretij xij d. et, HD 4; do. (omitting auene), HD 4a. [g] j d. ob. HD 4. [h] et ibit, HD 4. [i] vices, HD 4. [j] breue domini, HD 4, 4a. [k] dies expunged, HD 4. [l] inueniet domino, HD 4, 4a. [m] exitum suum, HD 4. [n] order reversed, HD 4. [o] ad cibum domini, *ib.* [p] not in HD 4; Haddock, HD 4a. [q] omnia seruicia, HD 4. [r] Iohannes ... tenet omitted, HD 4. [r] Fayeriman, HD 4a. [s] et, HD 4. [t] seruicia, HD 4. [u] Thurben, HD 4. [v] Et ... tenent omitted, HD 4. [w] Turbern, HD 4a. [x] in duabus pecijs vnum mesuagium et duas acras, HD 4a. [y] Stondelmersh, HD 4. [z] vj s., HD 4a. [aa] quarteria, HD4; Carpenter, HD 4, 4a. [bb] regnum, HD 4. [cc] Caruca ... xij d., order reversed, HD 4; carruca, HD 4a. [dd] sarclabunt, HD 4. [ee] stagnum per iijor vices, HD 4, 4a. [ff] per ... diem omitted, HD 4, 4a. [gg] tenent, HD 4. [hh] et, HD 4. [ii] quart, HD 4. [jj] order reversed, HD 4.* [kk] quart., HD 4. [ll] regnum, HD 4. [mm] Abbas de Dereham added in margin, HD 4. [nn] order reversed, HD 4.* [oo] not in HD 4.*

Fo. 32 [a] Thurstan, HD 4, 4a. [b] omitted, HD 4. [c] diem tria precar', HD 4. [d] not in HD 4.* [e] Preterea idem, HD 4. [f] not in HD 4.* [g] biscopi, HD 4. [h] seruicia, HD 4. [i] predict', HD 4. [j] not in HD 4.* [k] Muriella, HD 4, 4a. [l] prout, HD 4. [m] not in HD 4.* [n] domina ... acras omitted, HD 4; Inde omitted HD 4a. [o] seruicia sicud predictus, HD 4. [p] omitted, HD 4. [q] omitted, HD 4a. [r] Eborardus Debet, HD 4. [s] Elsy et participes, HD 4; Elsi, HD 4a. [t] xvj, HD 4. [u] et ad faldagium vj d. quad. ij buss. auene, HD 4; v scepp., HD 4a. [v] iih d., HD 4; xv d., HD 4a. [w] seruicia, HD 4. [x] predictus, HD 4. [y] Thomas Fuel, HD 4; fouel, HD 4a. [z] omitted, HD 4a. [aa] seruicia, HD 4. [bb] omitted HD 4; Choste, HD 4a. [cc] atte, HD 4. [dd] ij s. iiijor d., HD 4a. [ee] et ad., HD 4. [ff] quatuor, HD 4. [gg] omitted, HD 4. [hh] sex buss., HD 4. [ii] vnum quarterium, HD 4. [jj] ad, HD 4. [kk] repeated, Ms. [ll] carruca, HD 4. [mm] x s. viij d., HD 4. [nn] omitted, HD 4; Coppingg', HD 4a. [oo] Haigne, HD 4; Agne, HD 4a. [pp] et ad Wardse, HD 4; Wardese, HD 4a. [qq] dies, HD 4. [rr] omitted, HD 4; Manard, HD 4a.

Fo. 32v [a] quatuor buss., HD 4. [b] iij d., HD 4. [c] regnum fimi, HD 4. [d] omitted, HD 4. [e] predictus, HD 4. [f] seruicia, HD 4. [g] Iohannes Peper Iohannes Fayerman, HD 4a. [h] seruicia, HD 4. [i] et ad faldagium, HD 4. [j] in autumpno, HD 4; omitted, HD 4a. [k] j d. ob., HD 4. [l] omitted, HD 4. [m] ad, HD 4. [n] omitted, HD 4; Willelmus written in full, terram Blome added, HD 4a. [o] omitted, HD 4. [p] omitted, HD 4a. [q] Kytte, HD4, 4a. [r] predictus, HD 4. [s] Wardse, HD 4; Wardese, HD 4a. [t] regnum fimi, HD 4. [u] omitted, HD 4.

Fo. 33 [a] Herueus Crude, HD 4; Grigge, HD 4a. [b] omitted, HD 4. [c] tenet, HD 4. [d] order reversed, HD 4. [e] regnum fimi, HD 4. [f] Wytbred, HD 4; Whitbred, HD 4a. [g] Warse, HD 4. [h] seruicia, HD 4. [i] order reversed, HD 4, 4a. [j] Helewysia, HD 4. [k] iij d., HD 4; viij, HD 4a. [l] seruicia, HD 4. [m] predictus, HD 4. [n] omitted, HD 4. [o] Cosse, HD 4a. [p] Willelmi, HD 4; Vlphi, HD 4a. [q] preceded by seven items (terra Bisschop' to tenementum Iakes) in HD 4. [r] seruicia precedes cariabit, HD 4. [s] omitted, HD 4. [t] Nun, HD 4; Knut, HD 4a. [u] Hougate, HD 4; Hogate, HD 4a. [v] Pilgrum, HD 4; Delgogrun ?, HD 4a. [w] seruicia, HD 4. [x] Yrik, HD 4; Wtr, HD 4a. [y] omitted, HD 4; this item is followed by Rogerus Edwyht in HD 4a.

Fo. 33v [a] seruicia, HD 4. [b] Dauit Kyng, HD 4. [c] omitted, HD 4. [d] Edwyht (following Rogerus Wyit), HD 4. [e] carruca, HD 4. [f] Item dictus, HD 4a. [g] omitted, HD 4. [h] Ygnald, HD 4; Hingenald, HD 4a. [i] de redditu, HD 4. [j] ob., HD 4. [k] Styrke, HD 4. [l] not abbreviated, HD 4a. [m] bracketed together, Ms., HD 4. [n] Monte, HD 4; Hil, HD 4a. [o] de censa pro omni seruicio, HD 4.

Fo. 34 [a] order reversed, HD 4, 4a. [b] terminum, HD 4. [c] Iohannis extended, HD 4, 4a. [d] Wlron, HD 4; Wlrun, HD 4a. [e] Summa denar' de Reddit. et de consuet. in Holkham xiiij libr. iijor s. j den. ob. quadr. added, HD 4. [f] <Ciiij.xliij opera xijxx precaria in autumpno> followed by bracket, HD 4. [g] thus with variants, HD 4a. [h] follows Mabilie vxor Vlphi preceding Godmannus filius Bartholomei, HD 4. [i] Esty, HD 4a. [j] Helewis, HD 4a. [k] followed by Rogerus de Steynton, HD 4. [l] Messor, HD 4. [m] Cosshe, HD 4; Cosse, HD 4a. [n] Chapman, HD 4; Scapman, HD 4a. [o] Thurild, HD 4; Thurchild, HD 4a. [p] Hubert, HD 4, 4a. [q] Asti, HD4; Hasty, HD 4a. [r] in, HD 4a. [s] Nichol, HD 4; Nicol, HD 4a. [t] Hindringham, HD 4, 4a. [u] Qwytbret, HD 4; Withbred, HD 4a. [v] Iakes, HD 4; Kekes, Hd 4a; follows Hugo molendinarius, HD 4, 4a. [w] omitted, HD 4, 4a. [x] extended, HD 4. [y] order reversed, HD 4, Ha.

Fos. 35–35v

256 TERRE DOMINI WILLELMI DE CALTHORPE IN CAMPIS DE HOLKHAM [c.1449]

Not printed
Fiche 1: B14

NOTE: William de Calthorpe's lands lay in south-western precinct of parish near to his manor of Burnham Thorpe.

Fos. 36–37

257 TERRE PRIORIS DE WALSINGHAM IN HOLKHAM DIMISSE EDMUNDO LUCAS 1414–15

Not printed
Cf. BD O
Fiche 1: C1

NOTE: Lands let by the Prior of Walsingham to Edmund Lucas. These Walsingham lands also lay in the South Field. They excluded Walsingham Grange and were concentrated on the western side of the parish.

Fo. 37v   Presentation of Letheringsett

258 COPIA VLTIME PRESENTACIONIS ECCLESIE DE LERNYNGSET 23 April 1430

Fiche 1: C2

Reuerendo in Christo patri ac *domin*o Willelmo dei gratia Norwycen' episcopo. Vestri humiles et deuoti in Christo Edmundus Lucas domicellus de Estderham, Maria vxor mea et Margareta Waylond alias Neel filie et heredes legitime Gilberti Neel de Holkham defuncti vestre Norwycensis diocesis omnimodas reuerencias ac obediencias tanto patri debitas cum honore. Ad vnam medietatem ecclesie parrochialis de Lernyngset per liberam resignacionem domini Iohannis Estker' capellani vltimi rectoris eiusdem vacantem et ad nostram presentacionem spectantem dilectum nobis in Christo dominum Iohannem Caprowun capellanum dicte vestre diocesis paternitati vestri reuerende *prese*ntamus. Deuotissime supplicantes quatinus dictum dominum Iohannem Caprowun ad dictam medietatem ecclesie de Lernyngset predictam admittere ipsumque rectorem cum suis iuribus et pertinenciis vniuersis canonice instituere in eadem ceteraque que vestro incumbunt officio pastorali in hac parte peragere dignemini gratiose intuitu caritatis. Ad ecclesie sue sancte et gregis vobis commissi regimen conseruet in prosperis clemencia deitatis. In cuius rei testimonium presentes sigillis nostris apposuimus. Dat' apud Estderham predict' vicesimo tercio die Aprilis anno domini millesimo quadragentesimo tricesimo.

> NOTE: Letheringsett is a mile west by north of Holt. The patron-saint of its church was St. Andrew. Lists of the rectors and patrons are printed in Basil Cozens-Hardy, *The History of Letheringsett*, Norwich, 1957, and C.L.S. Linnell, *Letheringsett and Bayfield Church and Farm*, 8th impression, 1975.

Fos. 38–39v

259 FEODARIUM TERRARUM HEREDUM GILBERTI NEEL PER INFORMACIONEM WILLELMI SOUTERE, JOHANIS TOLLYS ET ALIORUM FIDELIUM ANNO REGNI REGIS RICARDI SECUNDI POST CONQUESTUM XII   1388–9

> Not printed
> Fiche 1: C3

Fos. 40–40v   [blank]

Fos. 41–50v

EDMUND LUCAS'S GAZETTEER

260　*An alphabetical index of lands acquired by the Neel family*

PURCHESE LONDYS

(Quire 4) **Fo. 41　A. ADELOSE & ADOWEBOTME**
<Edwardi secundi viij°>.
Carta Simonis Hammond facta Ricardi Neel et Katerine de v acris terre in diuersis peciis videlicet apud **Steynhil, Adelose, Hadowebotme et apud Dalegate** [= *no. 156* = *HP 1051: 1 Nov. 1314*]
<Edwardi secundi xx, habet>
j roda terre iacente apud **Adowe** iuxta terram Ricardi Nel ex parte boriali cuius caput occidentale abbuttat super regalem viam apud Douuecrundel perquisita de Matilda Peper quondam vxore Ed*mund*i Keteleston' per R*icardum* et K*aterinam*. [= *no. 159: 30 Oct. 1326*]
<Edwardi tercij primo, inquiratur>
Dimidia acra terre iacente apud Adowe iuxta terram Rogeri le Wryghte ex parte australi et caput occidentale abbuttat super Hadowgate perquisita de Margeria quondam vxore **Willelmi Craske** per R. et K. [= *no. 158* = *HD 33: 20 Dec. 1327*]
<Edwardi secundi 20>
j acra iij rodis terre iacentibus apud **Adowe** inter terram Ricardi Nel ex parte australi et terram Iohannis Rutele ex parte aquilonali et abbuttat versus occidentem super Adowgate perquisitis de Ada filio Willelmi Craske [= *no. 154* = *HP 1075: 29 Oct. 1326*]
<Edwardi tercij 10, Willelmus Newgate>
iiij rodis iacentibus apud **Algerescrofteshende** et caput occidentale abbuttat super viam que ducit versus Statham.
iiij rodis iacentibus per eamdem viam ex parte orientali et caput orientale abbuttat super viam predictam. Perquisitis de Thoma Northerne. [= *no. 187: 30 April 1336*]
<Edwardi tercij 9, h*abet*>.
iij acris terre iacentibus apud **Adelose** iuxta terram abbatis de Creyk ex parte occidentali et caput australe abbuttat super Bruaram siue viam que ducit versus **Wighton'** reddendo v denarios Simoni filio Willelmi Eyr de Merston. Et perquisitis de eodem Simone per K*aterinam*. [= *no. 239* = *HP 1083: 11 July 1335*]

<Edwardi tercij 19, h*abet*>.

j roda et dimidia iac' apud **Adowgate** inter terram Iohannis Grenpage ex parte australi et terram Thome Nel ex parte boriali et capud orientale abbuttat super comunem viam que ducit de Holkham vsque Qwarles. Perquisitis de Ricardo filio Simonis Fabri per Thomam Nel. [= *no. 153: 15 March 1336*]

Fo. 41v   B. BRAMLOND

<Edwardi secundi xj>

j pecia terre iacente apud **Bramlond** inter terram Roberti atte Grenge et terram Rogeri Kayshe et caput occidentale abbuttat super terram Roberti **Marchal** perquisita de Ada filio Willelmi Sylk' per R. et K. [= *no. 182: 22. April 1318*]

<Edwardi secundi ix, Bruara>

j pecia terre iacente iuxta terram Iohannis **Goldewyne** ex parte **boriali** et caput australe abbuttat super **Bruara**m.

Alia pecia iacet ad capud predicte pecie. Perquis' de **W. Sylk per R. et K.** [*no. 226: 9 March 1316*]

<Edwardi tercij 4, Brunhamgate>

j pecia terre iacente in campis occidentalibus inter terram prioris de Petirston ex parte orientali et terram rectoris medietatis ecclesie de Holkham ex parte occidentali. **Caput boriale** abbuttat super **Brunhamgate**. Perquisita de **Simone Mous.** [= *no. 238: 1 March 1330*]

<Edwardi secundi ix, Billesmere>

j pecia terre iacente apud **Billesmer**e inter terram quondam Hunfredi Dauy ex parte aquilonari et caput orientale abbuttat super Qwarlesgate et caput occidentale super terram prioris de Walsingham perquisita de Bartholomeo Pay. [= no. 27: 1295–6 and no. 180: 12 Jan. 1316]

<Edwardi secundi 12, Bondescroft>

iij acris terre iacentibus apud **Bondescroft** inter terram Iohannis **Wryghte** ex parte australi et caput occidentale abbuttat super regiam viam et caput orientale super terram **Ricardi Sylke et Cicilie** vxoris sue perquisitis de eisdem Ricardo et Cicilia per Ricardum et Katerinam. [= *no. 165: 14 Dec. 1318*]

<Edwardi tercij 6>

v acris terre apud **Bondescroft** inter terram Agnetis **Bulwer'** ex parte orientali et pars occidentalis est quoddam forarium quarum caput australe abbuttat super terram **Willelmi Wake** perquisitis de **Ada Craske.** [= *no. 184: 13 Oct. 1332*]

<Edwardi secundi 17>
j pecia dimidie acre iacente apud **Baconescrundell'** iuxta terram **Iohannis Bulwere** perquisita de **Willelmo Roteney**.
Alia pecia j rode et dimidie iacet apud **Blakelond** iuxta terram Hugonis Otes perquisita de eodem. [= *no. 186: 4 Nov. 1323*]
<Edwardi secundi 13>
j acra terre apud **Billesmere** iacente inter terram Ricardi Nel et Elueue **Daleman** et caput occidentale abbuttat super **Qwarlesgate** perquisita de **Ada Crask'**. [= *no. 169: 4 Oct. 1319*]
<Edwardi secundi 10>
j pecia terre iacente apud **Billesmere** inter terram **abbatis de Creyk** ex parte boriali et terram Ricardi Nel ex parte australi et caput occidentale abbuttat super **Qwarlesgate** perquisita de **Rogero Hewerard**. [= *no. 175: 17 May 1317*]
<Edwardi secundi 13>
j crofta iacente in **Burgate** inter terram quondam Alexandri de Burgate versus occidentem et terram abbatis de Creyk versus orientem et caput aquilonale abbuttat super mesuagium Gilberti filij Willelmi Silk perquisita de eodem Gilberto. [= *no. 209 = HP 1064: 25 Feb. 1319*]
<Edwardi tercij 9>
j pecia terre iacente in **Burgate** iuxta terram abbatis de Creyk' ex parte orientali et terram Agate Brythe ex parte occidentali cuius caput australe abbuttat super terram Ricardi Nel et caput aquilonale super viam regiam que ducit de Welles versus Holkham perquisita de **Thoma Northerne**. [= *no. 212 = HP 1085: 11 Nov. 1335*]
<Edwardi tercij 10>
j acra et j roda iac*entibus* apud **Bramlond** iuxta terram prioris de Petra*ston* versus occidentem perquisitis de **eodem Thoma**. [= *no. 161 = HP 1091: 20 July 1336*]
<Edwardi tercij 10>
v rodis iacentibus apud **Bramlond** iuxta terram prioris de Petra*ston* ex parte orientali et caput boriale abbut*tat* super terram Ricardi Nel perquisitis de Thoma filio Ricardi Northerne. [= *no. 187: 30 April 1336*]

Fo. 42 C. CREYKGATE

<Edwardi secundi xj>

j pecia terre iacente apud Ringwareslond abbuttat super **Creykgate**. Require in R. Anno Edwardi secundi xj. [= *no. 219: 20 Jan. 1318*]

<Edwardi tercij vj, Collesmere>

j pecia terre iacente apud **Collemer'** inter terram Ricardi Nel ex parte aquilonari et terram **Willelmi Gres** ex parte australi et caput occidentale abbuttat super **Caldhowegate** perquisita de **Ada Crask' per R. et K.** [= *no. 171: 13 Nov. 1332*]

<Edwardi tercij 7>

ij acris terre iacentibus apud Caldowegate inter terram Iohannis Tuber ex vna parte et terram Walteri Bulwere ex alia parte et caput occidentale abbuttat super Caldhowgate perquisitis de Ada Crask' per R. et K. [= *no. 168: 13 July 1333*]

<Edwardi tercij 6>

v rodis terre iacentibus apud Collemere inter terram rectoris de Holkham ex parte australi et terram Heylote le Meire ex parte boriali et abbuttantibus super **Caldowegate** perquisitis de **Ada Craske' per R. et K.** [= *no. 183: 9 May 1332*]

<Edwardi secundi ix>

j roda terre iacente inter terram Roberti Marschall' ex parte aquilonali et terram Willelmi Fabri ex parte australi cuius caput occidentale abbuttat super **Caldowegate** perquisita de Bartholomeo le Muner per R. et K. [= *no. 188: 12 April 1316*]

ij acris terre iacent' inter Abbatis de Derham ex parte australi et terram de Burghalle ex parte boreali et apud orientale abuttat super Dalegate [struck off].

<Edwardi secundi 20>

Dimidia acra terre iacente apud Hungerhil cuius caput orientale abbuttat super Caldowgate cum medietate vnius faldesokne perquisita de Ada filio Willelmi Crask' per R. et K. **Require in H.** [= *no. 185: 14 Oct. 1326*]

<Edwardi secundi 9>

iij rodis terre iacentibus apud Schortlond cuius caput orientale abbuttat super Caldowgate. Require in S. Perquisitis [de] Bartholomeo Molendinario. [= *no. 188: 12 April 1316*]

<Edwardi tercij xj, Cleylond>

j roda et dimidia iac' apud **Cleylond** iuxta terram Katerine Nel ex parte occidentali et caput australe abbuttat super **Grenegate** perquisit' de Simone atte Cros per **Katerinam.** [= *no. 160: 29 Nov. 1337*]

<Edwardi tercij 9, Northfeld, per Katerinam>
iij acris et dimidia iacentibus apud Cleylond inter terram quondam Iohannis
Ayneld ex parte occidentali et terram Gilberti Calwere ex parte orientali cuius
caput boriale abbuttat super terram quondam Iohannis Charle.

Alia pecia vij rodarum iac*ent*' ad caput **australe** earu*n*dem inter terram
Radulfi Grigge ex parte occidentali et terram Clericie de Howgate ex parte
orientali et caput boriale abbuttat super predictas tres acras et dimidiam.

Alia pecia vij rodarum terre iac' fere ibidem inter terram Thome Escher ex
parte occidentali et terram heredum Willelmi Cat ex parte orientali cuius
caput australe abbuttat **super terram abbatis de Creyk***e*.

Alia pecia j acre iac' fere ibidem inter terram Iohannis Spellere ex parte
orientali et terram Iohannis Daukyn ex parte occidentali cuius caput boriale
abbuttat super **Wellegate**.

Alia pecia j acre et dimidie inter terram Roberti Andrew ex parte orientali et
terram quondam Roberti Mayn ex parte occidentali cuius caput boriale
abbuttat super **Wellegate**. Istae*ᵃ* v pecie perquisite erant de Thoma Northerne
per K. [= *no. 162* = *HP 1087: 18 Jan. 1336*]

<Edwardi tercij 10>
Item j acra iij rode terre quas Willelmus Wake tenet **ex dimissione Ele que
fuit vxor Bartholomei de Burgate** ad terminum [vitae] eiusdem Ele et quas
Ela prius tenuit in dotem de hereditate Thome filij Ricardi Northerne
perquisit' de eodem Thoma per **Katerinam**. [= *no. 161: 20 July 1336*]

<Edwardi tercij 10, per Katerinam, perquisit' de Thoma Northerne>
j acra et j roda iac' apud **Caldowe** iuxta terram prioris de Petra*ston* versus
borialem: alia pecia dimidie acre iac' fere ibidem iuxta terram Walteri Osbern
versus borialem: perquisit' de Thoma Northerne per K. [= *no. 187: 30 April
1336*]

Dimidia acra iac' apud le **Cheker** inter terram Iohannis Bilneye ex parte
australi et terram Iohannis Charle ex parte boriali.

Alia pecia j rode et dimidie iac' in eadem quarentena et caput orientale
abbuttat super Herueum Buleman. [= *no. 187: 30 April 1336*]

Alia pecia j rode iac' ibidem inter terram prioris et conuentus de Petra*ston* ex
parte australi et terram abbatis de Creyk*e* ex parte boriali perquisit' de
Thoma filio Ricardi Northerne. [= *no. 187: 30 April 1336*]

Alia pecia j acre et dimidie iac' apud **Estcleylond** et caput australe abbuttat
super croftam Katerine relicte Ricardi Nel.

Alia pecia j rode iac' fere ibidem inter terram quondam Iohannis Charle ex
parte occidentali et terram quondam Roberti Mayn ex parte orientali. [= *no.
187: 30 April 1336*]

Alia pecia j rode et dimidie iac' ibidem iuxta terram Thome Cowper' ex
parte orientali et caput boriale abbuttat super terram Rogeri Ioundy.

Alia pecia dimidie acre iac' apud le **Clynt** inter terram Willelmi **Randolf** et

abbutt' super mariscum, perquisit de Thoma Northerne. Alia pecia dimidie acre dimidie rode iac' fere ibidem et est forera perquisit' de Thoma Northerne. [= *no. 187: 30 April 1336*]

Alia pecia v rodarum iac' apud **Caldehowe** iuxta terram prioris de Petra*ston*: de Thoma Northerne. [= *no. 187, 30 April 1336*]

Alia pecia dimidie acre iac' ibidem iuxta terram **Walteri Osbern** ex parte boriali et caput occidentale super **Caldehowgate**. [= *no. 187: 30 April 1336*]

<Edwardi tercij 9>

Dimidia acra terre iac' apud **le Clynt** inter terram Simonis Mous ex parte australi et caput orientale abbuttat super terram Andree ad le Clynt perquisit' de **Radulfo le Deye per Katerinam**. [= *no. 242 = HP 1086: 20 Nov. 1335*]

VARIANT: *a* Ista for iste, Ms.

Fo. 42v   D. DALEGATE

<Edwardi tercij 4to>

j pecia terre iacente inter terram prioris et conuentus de **Petirston** ex parte boriali et terram quondam Ed*mundi* Atelwald ex parte australi et capud occidentali abbuttat super **Dalegate**. [= *no. 215: 17 April 1331*]

j roda terre iac' inter terram Thome Northerne ex parte australi et terram Rogeri Ode ex parte boriali et caput occidentale abbuttat super **Dalegate**.

<j roda et dimidia>

j pecia j rode et dimidie terre iac' inter terram Ricardi Bulwere ex parte boriali que continet in se j rodam terre et dimidiam abbuttat super Dalegate perquisit' de **Edmundo filio Hugonis Hotes de Holkham** per R. et Kat. [= *no. 215: 17 April 1331*]

<Edwardi tercij 3°>

j pecia terre iacent*e* apud **Dalegate** inter terram Ricardi et Katerine Nel ex parte australi.

Item alia pecia iac' iuxta eamdem terram eoru*m*dem Ricardi et Katerinam. [= *no. 167: 6 June 1329*]

<Edwardi tercij primo>

j pecia terre vocate **Marlond** iac' inter terram prioris de Petirston ex parte boriali et terram Ricardi Nel ex parte australi. Capud orientale abbuttat super Dalegate. Perquisit' de Ada filio Willelmi Crask' [*per*] Ricardum. [= *no. 189: 27 Feb. 1327*]

<Edwardi tercij 7>

j acra terre et plus iacente apud **Dalegate** inter terram Iohannis Tuber ex parte vna et terram prioris de Walsingham ex parte altera et caput occidentale abbuttat super **Dalegate** perquis' de Ada Crask'. [= *no. 168 (first piece): 3 July 1333*]

<Edwardi secundi 20>

ij acris iac' inter terram **abbatis de Derham** ex parte australi et terram de Burghalle ex parte aquilonali et caput orientale abbuttat super **Dalegate** perquisit' de **Ada filio Willelmi Crask**e per R. et K. [= *no. 185: 14 Oct. 1326*]

<Edwardi secundi 17, perquisit' de Willelmo Roteney per Ricardum et Katerinam>

iiij acris et dimidia iac' apud **Duuspet** iuxta terram Iohannis Tydy perquisit' de **Willelmo Roteney** per R. et K.

j pecia dimidie acre et dimidie rode iac' apud **Duuescrundel** iuxta terram Bartholomei le Soutere perquisit' de Willelmo Roteney. [= *no. 186: 4 Nov. 1323*]

j pecia j acre jacent' apud **Dalegate** iuxta terram Gilberti Puyson, perquisita de eodem Willelmo Roteney.

Alia pecia j acre iij rodarum iac' apud **Dalegate** iuxta terram Rogeri Ioudy. Alia pecia j rode iac' fere ibidem iuxta terram Ade Craske [= *no. 186: 4 Nov. 1323*]

<Edwardi tercij 6>

iij rodis terre iacentibus apud **Dalegate** inter terram Ricardi Nel ex parte boriali et terram prioris de Petirston ex parte australi cuius caput occidentale abbuttat super **Dalegate** perquisit' de Waltero de Mundene vicarij de Holkham. [= *no. 197: 10 Feb. 1332*]

<Edwardi secundi 13>

iij rodis et dimidia iac' apud **Douwesty** inter terram Ricardi Nel ex parte australi et terram quondam Iohannis Hayneld ex parte boriali perquisit' de Galfrido filio Iuliane. [= *no. 201: 22 Oct. 1319*]

<Edwardi tercij 6, Don*um* Thome filij Ricardi le Northerne>

ij rodis terre iacentibus apud **Dalegate** iuxta terram Ricardi Nel **perquisit' de Thoma filio Ricardi le Northerne**. Item perquisit' de eodem Thoma per ea*n*dem cartam omnia terras et tenementa que **Iohannes le Wryghte, Willelmus Goldewyne, Cicilia atte Hil, Berta vxor Iohannis Speller' et Amisius filius Willelmi filii Radulfi de Walsingham** coniunctim et diuisim tenuerunt de predicto Thoma Northerne ad voluntatem suam per virgam. Et etiam perquisit' de predicto Thoma Northerne per eamdem cartam **Agnetam et Helwysiam filias Thome filij Iohannis Ide, Amisiam et Ciciliam filias Ricardi filij Iohannis Ide natiuas dicti Thome Northerne** cum omnibus sectis et sequelis terris et tenementis bonis et catallis eorum. [= *nos. 221 and 222: 6 April 1332*]

<Edwardi secundi 9>

j acra terre iac' iuxta terram prioris de Petra*ston* et Roberti Swanton' ex parte australi et caput occidentale abbuttat super Dalegate et caput orientale super Caldowegate perquisit' de **Willelmo de Hindringham**. [= *no. 196: 1 Aug. 1315*]

<Edwardi tercij 10>

ij acris et dimidia iacentibus apud **Dalegate** iuxta terram quondam Iohannis Tuber versus borialem et caput occidentale abbuttat super **Dalegate** perquisit' de Thoma filio Ricardi Northerne. [= *no. 187 and no. 161: 30 April and 20 July 1336*]

<Edwardi tercij 10>

iij acris apud **Dalegate** inter terram prioris de Walsingham ex parte australi et terram prioris de Petra*ston* ex parte boriali et caput occidentale abbuttat super terras predicte Katerine perquisitas de **Iohanna que fuit vxor Ade Craske per Katerinam**. [= *no. 170: 20 Nov. 1336*]

<Edwardi tercij 12>

ij rodis et dimidia et quarter' vnius rode iac' apud **Dedquenepit'** inter terram quondam Willelmi Haye ex parte australi et terram Katerine Nel ex parte boriali et caput orientale abbuttat super Elsiscote perquisit' de **Gilberto le Calwere per Katerinam**. [= *no. 246: c. 1338–9*]

Fo. 43   E. ESTGATE

<Edwardi secundi 13>

j placea cum quodam domo iac' in **Estgate** cum tribus pedibus ex parte orientali et quatuor pedibus ex parte australi iuxta regiam viam et mesuagium Gilberti Mayn perquisit' de Willelmo de Hindringham per Ricardum in feodo simpl. [= *no. 247: 28 Jan. 1320*]

<Edwardi secundi ix>

j pecia iac' in **Holkham Estgate** et vocatur **Scrulescroft** et iac' inter terram **Iohannis Bret**. Capud australe abbuttat super terram Thome **Chartre** perquisit' de Willelmo Silk. [= *no. 226: 9 March 1316*]

<Edwardi secundi 17>

j pecia dimidie acre iac' apud **Endaker** iuxta terram abbatis de Derham perquisit' de Willelmo Roteney. [= *no. 186: 4 Nov. 1323*]

<Edwardi tercij 10>

iij rod' iac' apud **Estgatecroft** iuxta terram **Willelmi Wake** et caput australe abbuttat super Regiam viam que ducit apud **Wygton'**. [= *no. 187: 30 April 1336*]

Alia pecia j acre et dimidie iac' apud **Estclylond**. Queritur in C. Perquis' de Thoma Northerne. [= *no. 187: 30 April 1336*]

Fo. 43v   F. [FULMERESGATE]

<Edwardi secundi xx, medietas>
[medietas] vnius **faldesokne** perquisite de **Ada filio Willelmi Craske** cum terris apud **Dalegate** et **Hungirhil**. [= *no. 185: 14 Oct.* 1326]
<Edwardi secundi 17>
j pecia j acre iac' apud **Fulmeresgate** iuxta terram Simonis Fabri perquisit' de Willelmo **Roteney**. [= *no. 186: 4 Nov. 1323*]
<Edwardi secundi 9>
Feoffamentum de mesuagio j tofto et xxiiij acris terre quondam Iohannis filii Heruici Vnderburghe. [= *no. 190: Jan. 1316*]
<Edwardi tercij 10>
j roda et dimidia iac' apud **Fulmerescrofteshende** et abbutt' super Fulmerescroft versus austrum. [= *no. 187: 30 April 1336*]
Alia pecia j rode et quarter' part' vnius rode iac' fere ibidem et abbuttat super eamdem croftam versus austrum. [= *no. 187: 30 April 1336*]
Alia pecia iij rodarum iac' in eadem **quarentena** inter terram Iohannis Tuber ex parte occidentali et terram Iohannis Bilneye ex parte orientali cuius caput boriale abbuttat super terram*a* Ricardi Calwer' perquisit' de Thoma Northerne. [= *no. 187: 30 April 1336*]

VARIANT: *a* super terram repeated in error, M*s*.

Fo. 44   G. GOLDEWYNE

<Nulla data>
j pecia terre que est vna **forera** et iac' iuxta terram Iohannis **Goldewyne** ex parte orientali et v*erificatur* per cartam Goldew[yne]. [= *no. 75: c. 1276-82*]
<Edwardi secundi xj. Gibesgate>
j pecia terre jacente inter terram prioris de **Petirston** et caput occidentale abbutat super viam vocatam **Gibbesgate**.

Alia pecia iac' inter terram prioris de **Petirston** ex parte boriali et terram Iohannis Bret ex parte australi et caput occidentale abbuttat super viam vocatem **Gibbesgate**. [= *no. 220: 22 Nov. 1317*]

<Edwardi secundi 10>

iij rod' et dimidia terre iac' inter terram quondam Gilberti **Edwyth** ex parte australi et terram Henrici Anger' ex parte boriali et caput occidentale abbuttat super croftam Martini Goldewyne perquisit' de **Gilberto Silk**. [= *no. 172: 31 March 1317*]

<Edwardi secundi xj>

j roda et dimidia terre iacent' iuxta terram **Ricardi Nel** et caput occidentale super croftam quondam **Martini Goldewyne** perquisit' [de] Henrico Anger de Holkham et Isabella vxore sua.

<Edwardi tercij 6>

iij rod' et dimidia terre iac' apud Greyston iuxta terram dicti **Ricardi Nel** ex parte aquilonari et terram **Rogeri le Reue** ex parte australi cuius caput occidentale abbuttat super **Thorpegate** perquisit' de Simone atte chruche et Cicilia vxore eius. [= *no. 157: 21 Dec. 1332*]

<Edwardi secundi xj>

ix acr' terre iac' apud **Gonyeswong'** inter terram domini **Heymeri le Walawnc** ex parte australi et terram prioris de Walsingham ex parte aquilonari et caput occidentale abbuttat super terram prioris de Petirston et caput orientale super terram quondam **Galfridi le Bret** perquisit' **Ada filio Willelmi Crask'**. [= *no. 164: 6 May 1318*]

<Edwardi secundi 14>

j roda terre iac' apud **Gonyeswong** inter terras Ricardi Nel ex vtraque parte et caput orientale abbuttat super terram prioris de Walsingham et caput occidentale abbuttat super terram **Willelmi Wake** perquisit' de **Thoma filio Iohannis de Holkham**. [= *no. 204: 16 March 1321*]

<Edwardi tercij 10>

j pecia v rodarum iac' iuxta terram Willelmi Eyres ex parte australi et vocatur **Gondesheftlond** perquisit' de **Thoma Northerne**. [= *no. 187: 30 April 1336*]

Alia pecia i rode et dimidie acre jacet in eadem quarentena et caput orientale abuttat super **Henricum Buleman**. [struck out]

Alia pecia i rode jacet fere ibidem inter terram prioris et conventus de Petraston ex parte australi et terram **Abbatis de Creyk** ex parte boriali perquisite de Thomas filii Ricardi Northerne per K. [struck out]

'Iste due pecie scribuntur in alio loco'.

<Edwardi tercij 10>

Dimidia acra iac' collateraliter ex parte boriali de Grenegate et caput orientale abbuttat super terram **Katerine Nel perquisit' de Simone atte Cros per Katerinam**. [= *no. 216 = HD 38: 20 Nov. 1336*]

Fo. 44v H. HOSOLESTUNGE

<Edwardi secundi viij>
j pecia terre iac' aput **Hosolestunge** iacent' iuxta terram Hunfredi Dauy. Et alia pecia abbuttat super **Thorpegate** perquisit' de Ada filio Simonis Hammond per R. et Katerinam. Require in T. [= *no. 206: 29 March 1315*]

<Edwardi secundi 20>
Dimidia acra iac' apud **Hungirhil** inter terram **Ricardi Nel ex parte boriali** et terram Iohannis Ayneld ex parte australi et caput orientale abbuttat super **Caldehowegate** cum medietate **j faldesoke perquisit' de Ada filio Willelmi Craske.** [= no. 185: 14 Oct. 1326]

<Edwardi secundi 17>
j pecia dimidie acre iac' apud ad*^a* portam quondam **Hardy** iuxta terram Reginaldi Hougate perquisitam de Willelmo **Roteney.** [= *no. 186: 4 Nov. 1323*]

<Edwardi tercij 6>
iij rodis terre iac' apud **Hangandehadowe** inter terram Simonis atte Cros ex parte orientali et terram **Ricardi Nel** ex parte occidentali et caput boriale abbuttat super terram predicti Ricardi perquisit' de Cicilia Hammond. [= *no. 155: 25 Aug. 1332*]

<Edwardi tercij 6>
iij rodis terre iac' apud **Hangandehadowe** inter terram **Ricardi Nel** ex parte occidentali et terram Rogeri le Reue perquisit' de Simon atte Cros. [= *no. 157: 21 Dec. 1332*]

<Edwardi tercij 10>
j roda terre iac' apud **le Hugge** inter terram Katerine Nel ex parte occidentali et terram Heylote Meyre ex parte orientali cuius caput boriale abbuttat super terram predicte Katerine perquisit' de Radulfo Deye et Agnet*a* vxore eius per **Katerinam.** [= *no. 231: 20 April 1336*]

[*Later interpolation on blank space (No. 260 resumes after no. 262, on Fo. 46.)*]

VARIANT: *^a* *sic* in Ms.

261　*Land held for cash rent by bondmen in hand of Gilbert Neel and his heirs*[44]

TERRA SOLIDATA PER NATIUOS IN MANUS GILBERTI NEEL ET HEREDUM SUORUM.　　　　　　　　　　　　　　　　[c. 1370–90]

Cf. Terrier of Gilbert Neel, no. 259 Fos. 38–39v (not printed).
Fiche 1: C5

Agnes Ernalde tenet per antiquam perquisicionem j acram iacentem in iij peciis videlicet in crofta apud Burgate inter croftam Ricardi Broun et croftam Rogeri de Erpingham. Et alia pecia iacet aput Kokeflet inter terram Willelmi Stewy et terram Bartholomei de Burghgate. Et tercia pecia iacet apud Wellegate inter terram Willelmi Soutere et terram Ade Craske et facit aliis dominis seruicia videlicet viij d. per annum et de incremento quadr. et pertinet ad feodum Dakeney vt patet plenius per cartam antiquam.

Iohannes Thurbern tenet j acram et dimidiam in tribus peciis videlicet apud Schortlond iij rodas inter terram abbatis de Derham et terram domini Adomari de Valencia. Et alia pecia iacet inter terram Ricardi Broun et terram Thome Northerne et continet j rodam et dimidiam. Tercia pecia iacet inter terram Iohannis Goodwyne et terram Rose Buleman et continet j rodam et dimidiam et reddit aliis dominis feodi per annum viij d. et de incremento quadrantem.

Clericia de Hougate tenet apud Bondescroft de terris Emme de Campo dimidiam rodam terre et reddit per annum obolum.

Iohannes Cat et Oliua vxor eius tenet de terra libera de Burghalle apud Mersshgrene dimidiam acram terre [et] reddit domino de Burghalle iiij d. et de incremento obolum.

Item idem tenet apud Schortlond de feodo prioris de Petraston iij rodas terre [et] reddit pro domino dicto priori iij d. et eidem domino de incremento quadrantem per annum.

Item idem tenet apud Wellegate ex transuerso vie ibidem de feodo Dakeny j rodam et dimidiam et apud Hegmere j rodam et dimidiam [et] reddit pro domino v d. et vlterius eidem domino de incremento quadrantem.

Item memorandum quod omnes predicte terre furate sunt extra manus dicti Gilberti Neel et heredum suorum.

---

[44]　The *Revised Medieval Latin Word-list* (R.E. Latham, 1965) proposes a different interpretation: '*terra solidata*, 1400, "soiled" land, former freehold land purchased by bondman (Norfolk and Suffolk)', p. 443.

Fo. 45

The page is headed 'I' for the index of Neel acquisitions but the blank paper has been used thus:

262 *Land of bond tenants of the Manor of Gilbert Neel*

TERRE NATIUORUM TENENCIUM IN MANUS DOMINI DE FEODO
GILBERTI NEEL IN HOLKHAM.   [c. 1370–90]

Fiche 1: C5

Mesuagia cum croftis contenentia in toto prout iacent in diuersis peciis ij acras et dimidiam in tribus peciis vnde j acra in Rutelescroft, dimidia acra fere ibidem et j acra in Hougatecroft.

Apud Chirchecros in diuersis peciis	v rode.
Apud Howgate dimidia roda terre abuttans super Byrgate	j roda.ᵃ
Apud Wongeshende	j roda.
Item fere ibidem ex parte boriali	dimidia roda.
Apud Wychecroft	ij rode et j quarterium vnius rode.
Apud Kirkedele de terra Idessone	iij rode.
Apud Kirkefeld	dimidia roda.
Apud Kirkegate	j roda.
Apud portam Hardy	j roda.
Ad caput occidentale de Burghallecroft	dimidia roda de tenemento Dallyng' item j acra dimidia ibidem ex parte occidentali de Burghall' quondam Rogeri de Berneye et Thome Alberd.
Ex parte australi de Burghalle subtus curiam	j roda dimidia.
Ex parte australi pecie predicte	iij rode.
Supra Burghalle	dimidia roda. Item j acra ibidem.
Apud Bondescroft	j roda. Et j acra terre Alicie Speller' iacet inter eas que tenet de feodo Gilberti Neel.

[*A later hand has added*: Galfridus Bocher vel vicarius tenet vt dicitur et iacet inter terram Alicie Speller ex parte

occidentali. Memorandum quod vicarius habet
istam acram libere vt dicitur et est
terra natiua idem[b] numquam.]

Item fere ibidem	Dimidia acra.
Apud Estbondescroft	j acra j quarterium vnius rode.
Apud Westbondescroft	ij acre dimidia roda.
Apud Sexacres	j roda.
Apud Sexakerhil	j roda.
Ad eius caput occidentale	dimidia roda.
Apud Scukelif	ij acre.
Apud Warldousty	v rode.
Apud Cleylond	j roda j quarterium vnius rode.
	Item j roda et dimidia roda.
	Item dimidia roda.
Item apud Cleylond	dimidia roda iuxta terram domine ex parte occidentali.[c]
Apud Warldehow	j roda dimidia.
Item supra caput Cleylond	
ex parte aquilonali et est forera.	j roda et dimidia.
	Item dimidia ro[da] in Cleylond.

Plus de alia parte de terris nativorum tenentium.

VARIANTS: [a] added by later hand [b] Perhaps error in Ms. [c] Added by later hand.

Fo. 45v

The page is headed 'K' for the index of Neel acquisitions

AD HUC DE TERRIS NATIUORUM TENENCIUM IN MANUS DOMINI.

Item apud Nunnesdore	j roda et dimidia.
Apud portam Willelmi filij Alicie	
versus boriam	j roda.
Ad caput occidentale ville	j roda et abbuttat super Brunhamgate versus aquilonem.
Ad eius caput australe et est forera	j roda.
Apud Lethirpittes	dimidia acra.

Item ibidem	j roda dimidia.
Item ibidem	iij rode.
Apud Longadowe	j roda. Item j roda.
Ex parte boriali ecclesie	iij pecie
	Item j roda ad portas
ecclesie.	
Ex orientali ecclesie	j roda et dimidia.
Item ex orientali ecclesie	j roda.
Item in Burgate	j crofta.*a*
Aput Cathil	iij rode.
Apud Saltmershgrene in croftis	
et abbuttat super Salsum Mariscum	iij rode cont'..
et fuit mesuagium Ide natiui domini	Item dimidia roda.
iuxta terram prioris de Walsingham	
ex transuerso semite ecclesie per partem	
borialem dicte ecclesie	
Apud Gibbesgate	j acra. Item j acra.
Apud Dalehil	j acra.
Apud Dalebrest	iij rode.
	Item iij rode ibidem.*a*
Apud Wytherwong'	j roda terre abbuttans
	super Gybbesgate.*a*

VARIANT: *a* added by later hand.

Fo. 46   L. LITELHOWE

260, continued from Fo. 44v

<Edwardi tercij Vto>
j pecia terre iacent' apud **Lytelhowe** inter terram quondam Rogeri Cheles ex parte australi et terram Simonis Fabri ex parte boriali et capud occidentale abbuttat super terram Ricardi Nel perquisit' de Edmundo filio Hugonis Hotes per R. et K. [= *no. 215: 17 April 1331*]
<Edwardi secundi 14, Lambulhil>
j acra terre iacent' apud **Langebuthelhil** inter terram Iohannis filio Fratris ex parte australi et terram Gilberti Mayn ex parte aquilonali et caput orientale abbuttat super **Gibbesgates** et caput occidentale super terram prioris de Petirston perquisit' de Willelmo Fabro et Emma Curson per R. et K. [= *no. 235: 8 May 1320*]

<Edwardi secundi 17, perquisit' de Willelmo Roteney>

j pecia dimidie acre iac' apud **Larkescote** iuxta terram Ricardi Nel.

Alia pecia dimidie acre iac' fere ibidem iuxta terram abbatis de Derham.

Alia pecia dimidie acre et dimidie rode iac' apud **Leyrgraues** iuxta terram domini comitis de Penebrok.

Alia pecia j rode et dimidie iac' fere ibidem iuxta terram Simonis Fabri perquisit' de eodem. [= *no. 186: 4 Nov. 1323*]

<Edwardi tercij 7>

j acra iij rod' terre iac' apud **Lambulbotme** inter terram Petri Cowper' ex parte australi et terram Gilberti Poysoun ex parte aquilonari cuius caput orientale abbuttat super Gibbesgate perquisit' de Ada Craske. [= *no. 200: 10 April 1333*]

<Edwardi tercij 19>

j pecia v rodarum iac' apud **le Lyng** iuxta terram Ricardi Nel ex parte orientali et caput australe abbuttat super viam regiam que ducit de Holkham apud Wyghton' perquisit' de Gilberto **Calwere** per **Thomam Nel.** [= *no. 249: 26 July 1345*]

Fo. 46v   M. MARLLOND

<Edwardi tercij primo>

j pecia terre vocata Marlond abbutt' super **Dalegate**. Require in **Dalegate**. Perquisit' (de) **Ada filio Willelmi Craske** per R. et K. anno Edwardi tercij primo. [= *no. 189: 25 Sept. 1327*]

<Edwardi secundi 17>

j pecia j rode et dimidie iac' apud **Millestede** ex transuerso semite ibidem perquis' de **Willelmo Roteney.** [= *no. 186: 4 Nov. 1323*]

<Edwardi secundi 12>

ij acre vocate le **Marllond** et iac' inter terram **Roberti de Griston'** ex parte boriali et terram Ricardi Nel ex parte australi perquis' de **Willelmo Crask'.** [= *no. 245: 13 Dec. 1318*]

<Edwardi tercij 10>

j acra j roda iac' apud **Mundiesaker** et sic vocatur cuius caput occidentale abbuttat super terram quondam Iohannis Leuere perquisit' de **Thoma Northerne.** [= *no. 187: 30 April 1336*]

Fo. 47 N. [NORTH PILMAN]

<Edwardi secundi 16>
j roda terre **iac' apud Northpilman** iuxta Ricardum Nel ex parte orientali perquis' de **Ada filio Willelmi Craske**. [= *no. 207 = HP 1072: 1 May 1323*]
<Edwardi tercij 6>
Natiui tenentes et natiui de sanguine perquisiti de **Thoma filio Ricardi Northerne**. Require in D littera fere in fine. [= *no. 221: 6 April 1332*]

263 *Dominium of Peter le Bret*

<Lucas>
<Edwardi secundi 8, **Dominium Petri le Bret, Lucas**>
Carta de dimidia acra terre et cum crofta perquisita de **Petro le Bret** una cum Henrico Vnderhowe et Cristiana Vnderhowe natiuis et villanis predicti Petri cum totis sectis et sequelis seruiciis bonis et catallis eorum. Et seruicia et homagia omnium libere tenencium videlicet homagia et seruicia **Iohannis Bilneye, Willelmi Cursoun, Gilberti Elueriche, Martini Goldewyne, Willelmi le Meyre, Radulfi Mariot, Willelmi Alissessione, Gilbert Edwy, Roberti filij Emme, Ricardi Spellere, Willelmi Wake, Iohannis Dauy, Rogeri filij Emme, Ade Craske, Henrici Aungere, Hugonis Otes, Iohannis le Bret, Reginaldi le Bercher, Radulfi Paye et Radulfi Holneye** et cum omnibus wardis maritagiis releuiis excaetis omnibus etc. perquisit' per **Ricardum Nel**. [= *no. 191: 19 Aug. 1314*]
<Edwardi secundi 8>
Carta Petri le Bret perquisita per **Ricardum Nel** de j pecia terre iac*ent*' in crofta predicti Petri cuius capud occidentale abbuttat super mesuagium predicti Ricardi et continet in latitudine tres perticatas et dimidiam et in longitudine xxv perticatas vnacum Iohanne Thurbern et Reginaldo Thurbern et cum Matilda et Mabilia Ernald natiuis predicti Petri cum totis sectis et sequelis bonis et catallis eorum.
<Edwardi secundi 8>
Carta Petri le Bret de j mesuagio quondam Galfridi le Bret patris predicti Petri cum iij peciis terre. [= *no. 194: 18 Aug. 1315*]

Fo. 47v   O.   [blank]

260   *continued*

Fo. 48   P. PILMAN

<Edwardi tercij 4to>

j acra terre iacent' apud **Pilman** inter terras Ricardi Nel ex vtraque parte capud occidentale abbuttat super Qwarlesgate perquisit' de Edmundo filio Hugonis Otes. [= *no. 214: 16 March 1330*]

<Edwardi secundi 17>

j acra et j roda iac' apud **Pilman** iuxta terram Hugonis Otes perquis' de Willelmo Roteney. [= *no. 186: 4 Nov. 1323*]

<Edwardi secundi 16>

j roda terre iac' apud Nortpilman iuxta terram Ricardi Nel **perquis' de Ada filio Willelmi Crask**e. **Require in N.** [= *no. 186: 4 Nov. 1323*]

Fo. 48v   Q. QWARLESGATE

<Edwardi secundi ix>

j pecia terre iacent' apud Billesmer*e* abbuttant' super **Qwarlesgate**. Require in B. perquisita per Ricardum et Katerinam de **Bartholomeo Pay**. [= *no. 180: 12 Jan. 1316*]

<Edwardi secundi 13>

j acra terre iac' apud Billesmere abbutt' super **Qwarlesgate**. Require in B. **perquisita de Ada Crask***e*. [= *no. 169: 4 Oct. 1319*]

<Edwardi [*blank*] 10>

j pecia terre iac' apud Billesmere abbutt' super **Qwarlesgate**. Require in B. **perquisita de Rogero Hewerard**. [= *no. 175: 17 May 1317*]

<Edwardi tercij xj^{o}>

Dimidia acra terre iac' apud **Qwytewong'** cuius caput orientale abbuttat super Regiam viam que ducit apud **Qwarles** et iacet inter terram Willelmi Wake ex parte australi et terram Katerine Nel ex parte boriali perquisita de Simone atte Cros per Katerinam. [= *no. 179: 12 March 1337*]

[A later addition on lower half of page]

<Ed. Eluerych>

Londs holden of the manor of Foxle sumtyme John Waylond & after Edmund Eluerych.

Iohannes Waylond tenet in Holkham mesuagium in Southgate cont' ij^as acras et dimidiam quondam Walterus Tolly inter mesuagium Thome Wailond nuper Iohannis Wailond ex parte orientali et terram dicti Iohannis Wailond vocatam Saffrengardeyne ex occidente et abbuttat versus aquilonem super regiam viam de tenemento Foxle.

<Robertus Holkham tenet>

Idem tenet ij acris apud Bondescroft et est forera inter terram domini de Burghall ex occidente et abbuttat versus austrum [super] terram T. Morse quondam Goodwyn Wake, ex aquilone abbuttat super terram de Hillhall de tenemento Foxle.

<Tenet Edmundus Eluerych>

Idem tenet j acram apud Scotbarbyllhill ex austro inter terram T. Morse nuper Roberti Gonnor ex austro et terram dicti Iohannis Waylond ex aquilone et abbuttat super regiam viam vocatam Adowgate versus occidentem et orientem abbuttat super abbatem de Derham.

<in manu W. Calthorp militis>

Idem tenet v rodas apud Northgate que vocatur Cokthorpis croft iacentes inter terram domini de Burghall ex parte orientali et terram nuper Henrici Sylk ex occidente et abbuttat super Saltemerse seperrab' domini de Burghall. Feod' de Foxle.

Summa vj acre iij rode de Foxle.

NOTE: Interpolation of about 1449, on the lower half of Fo. 48v, concerning lands in Holkham held of the manor of Foxley. Foxley is situated to the south east of Holkham, on the road from Fakenham to Norwich.

Fo. 49   R. RINGWARESLOND

260 continued

<Edwardi secundi xj>

j pecia terre iacent' apud **Ringwareslond** iuxta terram quondam Willelmi Chollyng ex parte aquilonali et caput orientale abbuttat super **Creykgate**.

Alia pecia iac' iuxta terram quondam Matilde Godkoc ex parte australi et capud occidentale abbuttat super terram quondam Rogeri Eluerich'.

Alia pecia iac' iuxta terram quondam Hunfredi Dauyd ex parte aquilonali et caput occidentale abbuttat super terram prior de Walsyngham. [= *no. 219: 20 Jan. 1318*]

Istae tres pecie perquisite erant de Bartholomeo filio Willelmi Marchale per R. et K.

<Edwardi secundi 17>

j pecia j acre et dimidie rode iac' apud **Ringwareslond** iuxta terram Ricardi Nel perquisit' de **Willelmo Roteney**. [= *no. 186: 4 Nov. 1323*]

<Edwardi tercij xj>

Dimidia roda iacent' apud **Rusteshowe** iuxta terram Katerine Nel ex parte occidentali et caput boriale abbutt' super **Marketsty atte Howe** perquisit' de **Simone atte Cros** per Katerinam. [= *no. 160: 29 Nov. 1337*]

Fo. 49v   S. STEYNHILL

<Edwardi [secundi] 16>

j pecia terre iacent' apud Steynhil inter terras Ricardi et Katerine Nel et caput aquilonale abbuttat super terram domini Adomari de Valencia perquisit' de Bartholomeo filio **Roberti de Holkham**. [= *no. 177: 20 Aug. 1322*]

<Edwardi secundi 8>

j pecia terre contin' iiij acras terre iac' apud **Scotbarbles** iuxta terram Willelmi Crask' ex parte australi perquisit' de vxore quondam Henrici Hammond de Nortbarsham. [= *no. 205: 1 July 1315*]

<Edwardi secundi 17, perquisit' de Willelmo Roteney>

iiij acre iac' apud **Scuckelif** iuxta terram Willelmi filij Alicie perquisit' de Willelmo Roteney. [= *no. 186: 4 Nov. 1323*]

Alia pecia j acre iac' fere ibidem iuxta terram prioris de Walsingham.

Alia pecia i acre fere ibidem iuxta terram Iohannis de Hougate.

Alia pecia j rode et dimidie iac' fere ibidem iuxta terram Iohannis Bulwere.

Alia pecia j acre et j rode iac' apud Slyngeshowe iuxta terram Hugonis Otes.

Alia pecia iac' apud **Sladacr'** ij acr' iuxta terram Rogeri Ode.

Alia pecia j rode iac' fere ibidem iuxta terram Iohannis Deye.

Alia pecia j rode iac' fere ibidem iuxta terram abbatis de Dereham.

Alia pecia j rode iac' fere ibidem iuxta terram Gilberti Puysoun. [= *no. 186: 4 Nov. 1323*]

<Edwardi secundi 9>

j pecia iij rodarum iac' apud Schortlond inter terram Iohannis Aynild ex parte aquilonari et terram Galfridi Sutoris ex parte australi et caput orientale abbuttat super Caldowegate perquis' de Bartholomeo Molendinario. [= *no. 188: 12 April 1316*]

<Edwardi secundi 12>

ij acr. terre iac' apud **Steynhil** inter terram Willelmi Craske ex parte orientali et terram Roberti de Griston' ex parte occidentali perquis' de **Willelmo Craske.** [= *no. 245: 13 Dec. 1318*]

<Edwardi secundi 16>

v rod' iac' apud **Scotbarbles** iuxta terram Ricardi Nel ex parte australi perquisit' de Ada filio Willelmi Craske. [= *no. 207: 1 May 1323*]

<Edwardi secundi 13>

ij acr' et dimidia terre iac' apud **Steynhil** iuxta terram Bartholomei filij Maddy de Campo ex parte occidente et est vna forera perquisit' de Ada Craske. [= *no. 169 = HP 1065: 4 Oct. 1319*]

<Edwardi tercij 10, per Katerinam, perquisit' de Thoma filio Ricardi le Northerne>

j acra iac' apud **Salteresgate** et capud boriale abbuttat super Wellegate.

Alia pecia dimidie rode et quarte partis vnius rode iac' ad caput eiusdem acre inter [terram] quondam Willelmi Dersy ex parte occidentali et regalem viam que ducit apud Estgronge ex parte orientali perquisit' de Thoma Northerne.

Alia pecia dimidie acre apud **Scothowgate** iuxta terram Walteri Osbern ex parte occidentali.

Alia pecia j rode et dimidie iac' fere ibidem iuxta terram Iohannis Speller' ex parte occidentali et caput boriale abbuttat super Scothowgate.

Alia dimidia acra et dimidia roda iac' apud **Langfurlong** iuxta terram Thome filij Gilberti le Northerne ex parte occidentali et caput boriale abbuttat super eamdem viam videlicet **Scothowgate.**

Alia pecia j rode et dimidie iac' ibidem iuxta terram Thome Broun ex parte occidentali et caput boriale abbuttat super eamdem viam.

Alia pecia dimidie acre iac' ibidem iuxta terram Willelmi Eyre ex parte orientali et caput boriale abbuttat super eamdem viam.

Alia pecia j rode et dimidie iac' ibidem iuxta terram Thome filij Gilberti Northerne ex parte occidentali et caput boriale abbuttat super eamdem viam.

Alia pecia iij rodarum iac' ibidem iuxta terram Willelmi Dollon ex parte orientali et caput boriale abbuttat super eamdem viam.

Alia pecia dimidie acre dimidie rode iac' apud **Scamlond** et caput boriale abbuttat super terram Radulfi Grigge.

Alia pecia j rode et dimidie iac' apud **Schortlond** iuxta terram Henrici Camplyny ex parte orientali et caput australe abbuttat super **Scothowgate.**

Alia pecia j acre et dimidie iac' ibidem iuxta terram Rogeri Esser ex parte orientali et caput australe abbuttat super eamdem viam.

Alia pecia j acre et j rode iac' ibidem iuxta terram Willelmi Eyr' ex parte orientali et caput australe abbuttat super eamdem viam.

Alia pecia j rode iac' fere ibidem iuxta [terram] heredum Gilberti Crane ex parte occidentali.

Alia pecia iij rodarum iac' fere ibidem iuxta terram Ricardi Daukyn capellani ex parte occidentali.

Alia pecia dimidie acre iac' fere ibidem terram Thome Ester ex parte orientali perquisit' de Thoma Northerne.

Alia pecia j rode et dimidie iac' fere apud **Scothowgate** iuxta terram Seman ex parte occidentali et caput australe abbuttat super **Scothowgate**.

Alia pecia j rode iac' ibidem iuxta terram Iohannis Calwere et caput australe super eamdem viam.

Alia pecia dimidie acre dimidie rode iacet apud **Langfurlong** iuxta terram Gilberti Chapman ex parte orientali et caput boriale abbuttat super **Scothowgate**. [= *no. 187: 30 April 1336*]

<Edwardi tercij 10>

Dimidia acra terre iac' apud **Scamlond** inter terram Rogeri Carpenter ex parte occidentali et terram Iohannis May ex parte orientali cuius caput australe abbuttat super terram Willelmi filij Alicie perquisit' de **Simone Mous de Keteleston' per Katerinam**. [= *no. 174 = HP 1084: 9 Feb. 1336*]

<Edwardi tercij 10>

j acra terre iac' apud **Scamlond** iuxta terram Katerine Nel ex parte boriali et est forera cuius caput occidentale abbuttat super terram Iohannis Meye et caput orientale abbuttat super terram Andree sub le Klynt perquisit' de eodem Simone per Katerinam. [= *no. 232 = HP 1082: 9 Feb. 1336*]

<Edwardi tercij 19>

Dimidia acra dimidia roda iac' apud **Skamlond** iuxta terram Rogeri Crowde ex parte orientali et caput boriale abbuttat super **Scothowgate** perquis' [*space in Ms.*].

Alia pecia j rode iac' apud **Langfurlong'** iuxta terram Iohannis Andrew ex parte orientali et caput boriale abbuttat [super Scothowgate] perquisit' de **Gilberto Calwer per Thomam Nel**. [= *no. 249: 26 July 1345*]

[*Continued at foot of Fo. 50*]

<Edwardi tercij 19>

iij rode iac' apud **Scothowgate** inter terram Iohannis Ayneld ex parte orientali et terram Cicilie Swey[n] ex parte occidentis et caput boriale abbuttat super Scothowgate perquisit' de Iohanne Ayneld per Gilbertum [Nel]. [= *no. 237: 13 Sept. 1345*]

Fo. 50   T. THORPEMERE

<Nulla data>

j pecia terre iacent' inter terram Reginaldi Osmod et terram Gilberti Sutoris de **Westgate** et vnum capud super terram prioris de Walsingham et aliud capud super **Thorpemere** perquis' de Willelmo Clerke per Ricardum et Katerinam. [= *no. 199: c. 1300*]

<Edwardi secundi viij, Thorpegate et Hendaker>

j pecia terre abbutt' super **Thorpegate**.

Alia pecia iacent' apud **Hendaker** inter terram Ricardi Nel ex parte boriali et terram abbatis de Derham ex parte australi et capud orientale abbuttat super **Lethirpitgate** perquisit' de Ada filio Simonis Hammond per R. [= *no. 206: 29 March 1315*]

<Edwardi tercij 6>

iij rode et dimidia iac' apud **Greyston** cuius caput occidentale abbuttat super Thorpgate perquisit' de Simone atte Cruche. **Require in G**. [= *no. 157: 21 Dec. 1332*]

<[Edwardi tercii 42]>

Sciant presentes et futuri quod nos He[yle]wys la Marchalle Robertus Hore de Wyghton' et Matilda vxor mea concessimus dedimus et hac presenti carta nostra confirmauimus Iohanni Bryce de Holkham et assignatis suis septem rodas terre nostre iacentes in quatuour peciis in campis orientalibus dicte ville de Holkham cum omnibus suis pertinenciis quorum vna pecia ij rode et dimidia iacet inter terram Gilberti Nel ex parte orientali et terram dicti Iohannis Ide et vxoris eius ex parte occidentali et abbuttat versus aquilonem super Skothowgate alia vero pecia etc. Dat' die dominica proxima post festum Sancti Iohannis Baptiste anno regni regis Edwardi tercij post conquestum quadragesimo secundo. Hiis testibus. Roberto Galon' . Iohanne Andreu . Gilberto Neel etc. [*25 June 1368*]

Fo. 50v   W. [WADELOND]

<Edwardi secundi 14>

j pecia terre vocata **Wadelond** prope tenementum domini Eymerici de Valencia per partem borialem et terram Iohannis Charle versus australem et capud occidentale abbuttat super terram dicti Iohannis Charle et capud orientale abbuttat super terram hered*um* Roberti Ayneld perquisit' de Iohanne le Bret per R. et K. [= *no. 243: 15 May 1321*]

<Edwardi secundi ix>

j pecia terre iacentis apud **Wadelond** iuxta terram Martini Goldewyne cuius caput orientale abbuttat super **Bruaram** et caput occidentale super terram prioris de Walsingham.

j pecia v rodarum iac' apud **Wellelond** et iac' inter terram Matild*e* Choud ex parte occidentali cuius caput australe abbuttat super terram Iohannis Carpentarii.

Alia pecia iac' apud **Cathil** cuius caput orientale abbuttat super terram **Willelmi Asty** et caput occidentale super predictam peciam que vocatur **Wellelond**.

Alia pecia iac' in eadem quarentena cuius capud orientale abbuttat super terram predicti **Willelmi Asty** et caput occidentale super predictam peciam que vocatur **Wellelond** et iacet inter terras Thome Idessone perquis' de Willelmo Silk' per R. et K. [= *no. 223: 30 Dec. 1315*]

<Edwardi primi xj>

iij acre terre iac' apud **Wodegate** inter terram **abbatis de Creyk perquisit' de Willelmo Athewald de Southcreyk.** [= *no. 181: 25 March 1318*]

<Edwardi secundi 17>

j pecia j rode iac' apud **Warldhousty** iuxta terram Bartholomei le Soutere [perquisit' de] **Willelmo Roteney.** [= *no. 186: 4 Nov. 1323*]

<Edwardi tercij 1>

j acra j roda iac' iuxta terram **Bartholomei Calwere** ex parte orientali et [caput] australe abbuttat super viam ducentem de Holkham versus Wightone vocatam **Wyghtonegate** perquisit' de Iohanne Huberd. [= *no. 241: 21 Dec. 1328*]

<Edwardi secundi xj>

vj acr' terre iac' apud **Wodegate** iij acr' et apud **Wardehowh'** iij acr' perquisit de **Ada filio Willelmi Crask'** de Holkham. [= *no. 166: 12 April 1318*]

<Edwardi tercij 10, perquisit' de Thoma filio Ricardi Northerne per Katerinam>

j acra iac' apud [*Wellesgate, hole in Ms.*] iuxta terram **Ade Ayneld** ex parte occidentali et caput australe abbuttat super **Wellegate**.

Alia pecia j rode et dimidie iac' [ibidem] iuxta terram Gilberti Chapman ex parte occidentali et caput australe abbuttat super eamdem viam.

Alia pecia j acre [similiter ibidem iuxta] terram Bartholomei le Millere ex parte orientali et caput australe abbuttat super eamdem viam.

Alia pecia j rode et dimidie [apud *hole in Ms.*, Popi]wong' iuxta terram Thome filij Gilberti le Northerne ex parte orientali et caput abbuttat [super eamdem] viam.

Alia pecia dimidie acre iac' [*Ms. destroyed*] fere ibidem iuxta terram Iohannis Daukyn ex parte orientali et caput boriale abbuttat super eamdem viam. [= *no. 187: 30 April 1336*]

<Edwardi tercij 19>

Alia pecia dimidie rode iac' apud **Wellegate** iuxta terram abbatis de Creyke ex parte orientali et caput boriale abbuttat super **Wellegate** perquisit' de **Gilberto Calwere per Thomam Nel.** [= *no. 249: 26 July 1345*]

xxij^{xx} **acre j acra j roda et dimidia roda** [441 acres 1 rood and 1/2 rood]

Fos. 51–52v

264 TERRARIUM DE TERRIS PRIORIS DE WALSINGHAM IN HOLKHAM RENOVATUM PER MANUS JOHANNIS WEYLOND ANNO REGNI REGIS HENRICI VI^{to} XXXV° 1456–7

Not printed
Fiche 1: C7

Fos. 53–54

265 TERRARIUM DE DOMO DE PETERSTON ANNO REGNI REGIS H. VI^{to} XXXV° 1456–7

Not printed
Fiche 1: C8

Fos. 54v–55v

266   RENTALE DE PETERSTONE TERR. NATIV. *[n.d.]*

Not printed
Fiche 1: C9

Fo. 55

267   PETERSTONE FEODUM NOION *[n.d.]*

Not printed
Fiche 1: C10

HOLKHAM DOCUMENTS: HD 22b – HD 205

c. 1291–1352

HD 22b

Grant from John, son of Geoffrey le Bret of Holkham, to Simon, son of Hamo of Holkham of 1 plot of 4 acres and 1 other plot.   24 Dec. 1293

Cf. HD 22a, Fo. 10 no. 121
Fiche 1: C11

Sciant presentes et futuri quod Ego Iohannes filius Galfridi Le Bret de Holcham Concessi dedi et hac presenti Carta mea Confirmaui Simoni filio Hamonis eiusdem Wille et Heredibus suis . pro . quadam summa pecunie quam . mihi . dedit premanibus . duas pecias terre mee cum pertinenciis Iacent' in Campis de Holcham . quarum . Prima pecia in se Continens quatuor Acras terre Iacet apud Duuespit inter terram Henrici Dauyd ex parte Australi et terram Iohannis filij Rogeri Belneye ex parte aquilon' . et Capud orient' abuttat super terram que fuit Radulfi Hakun et Capud occidentale abuttat super Gunyeswong Et . Alia pecia Iacet inter terram Prioris de Walsingham ex parte occidentali . et terram meam ex parte orientali . et Capud aquilonale abuttat super terram predicti Simonis . et Capud Australe abuttat super terram Rogeri filij Berte . Habend' et tenend' de Capitalibus . Dominis feodi illius . illi et heredibus suis . Libere . quiete . Bene . in pace . Iure . et Hereditarie . Cuicumque vel . quandocumque predictas pecias terre . cum pertinenciis . dare . vendere . vel assignare voluerint exceptis domibus Religionis . faciend' inde Annuatim pro . me et Heredibus meis Capitalibus Dominis feodi illius . vnum quadrantem ad Natiuitatem Sancti Iohannis . Baptiste . pro omni seruicio . Consuetudine . Exaccione . Secta Cur*ie* et secular*i* demand*a* . Et Ego . predictus Iohannes et heredes mei . Warantizabimus . predictas pecias terre cum pertinenciis predicto Simoni et heredibus suis contra omnes Homines inperpetuum. In Cuius rei testimonium Huic Carte sigillum meum Apposui . Dat' Apud Holkham . die Iouis proxima Ante Natiuitatem domini . Anno Regni Regis Eadwardi. vicessimo . Secundo . Hiis testibus . Bartholomeo de Burgate . Iohanne filio Ada Le Bret . Iohanne Sylke . Willelmo Silke . Martino Goldwyne . Galfrido Godwyne . Willelmo Crask*e* . Iohanne Aynild . Waltero Hakun . Ricardo Le Northerne . Iohanne Rutur . Roberto Le Marshall et aliis Multis.

Seal: white, vesica shaped, varnished with reddish paint. A bird with a long tail facing towards the sinister side within inscription *Iohannis le Bret* 13/8 x 11/4 in.
Hand: See note on HD 10.

HD 23

Grant from Godeman Sutor of Holkham to Margery, widow of William
Craske of Holkham of 1/2 acre of land.   21 Feb. 1309

Cf. HD 22a, Fo. 11v no. 145
Fiche 1: C12

Sciant presentes et futuri quod ego Godemannus Sutor de Holcham . concessi
. Dedi et hac presenti carta mea confirmaui Margerie quondam vxori
Willelmi Craske de eadem pro quadam summa pecunie quam mihi dedit
premanibus vnam dimidiam acram terre mee Iacent' in campo de Holcham in
quadam Quarentena que vocatur Hadowe . inter terram Thome Craske ex
parte Aquilon' et terram Henrici Dauyd ex parte Austral' . Et Capud
Orientale abuttat super terram que quondam fuit Simonis Charle et Capud
Occidentale abuttat super Hadowgat' Habendam et Tenendam illi et heredibus
suis aut suis Assignatis . de Capitalibus Dominis feodi illius . Libere . quiete
. bene . in pace . Iur' et hereditarie faciend' inde Annuatim Dominis
Capitalibus eiusdem feodi . seruic' inde debit' et consuet'. Et ego predictus
Godemanus et heredes mei Warantizabimus predictam dimidiam acram terre
cum pertinenc' siue maius aut minus infra Bundas prescriptas Continetur .
predicte Margerie et heredibus suis siue suis assignatis contra omnes homines
inperpetuum . In Cuius Rei Testimonium huic presente carte sigillum meum
Apposui . Hiis Testibus . Willelmo Silke . Willelmo Wake . Roberto de
Griston . Martino Goldwyne . Iohanne Aynild . Ricardo le Northerne .
Iohanne Godwyne . Humfrido Dauyd et aliis . Datum apud Holcham Die
veneris proxima ante festum sancti Mathie apostoli . Anno Regni Regis
Edwardi Secundo.

Seal: missing.
Hand: HP 1002, 1003, 1078. This scribe always omits *filij Edwardi* in the regnal year.

NOTE: William Craske's widow Margery is a grantor in 1327, HD 33–4. Presumably the
second year of Edward II not Edward I since witnesses occur together in HD 24.

HD 24

Grant from Helewise, widow of John le Bret of Holkham, to Gilbert her son of 6 acres in 6 plots.   4 May 1309

Fiche 1: C13 and 3: G1 (seal)

Sciant presentes et futuri quod ego Helwysia quondam vxor Iohannis le Bret de Holcham in pura viduitate mea concessi. Dedi et hac p[re]senti carta mea confirmaui . Gilberto filio meo sex acras terre mee . cum pertinenciis . Iacent' in Campis de Holcham. Quasquidem acras terre habui ex dono Gilberti Payn Quarum vna acra Iacet in campo australi in quodem loco qui nuncupatur Langgebulebotme iuxta terram Gilberti Poysoun versus Aquilonem Cuius Capud orientale abbutat super Gibbesgate. Et vna acra et vna roda Iacent collateraliter in vna Cultura que vocatur Langgebulehil iuxta terram Isabelle Le Bret quam tenet in Dote ex parte aquilonali. Et vna dimidia acra Iacet iuxta terram Prioris de Walsigham versus austrum et illa vocatur Seyntemari aluaker. Et due acre et vna dimidia acra simul iacent apud Larkscote inter terram Iohannis filij mei ex parte boriali et terram Matilde Silk' quam tenet in dote ex parte Australi Quarum capita Orientalia abuttant super Gibbesgate. Et vna dimidia acra Iacet apud Wellegate inter terram Iohannis Le Eyre de Merstone versus Occidentem et Terram Ricardi Le Northern versus Orientem cuius capud Australe abuttat super Regiam viam. Et vna Roda et dimidia Iacent apud Scothowegate iuxta terram Radulfi Daulyn versus Orientem et Capud Australe abuttat super terram Gilberti Silke et capud Boriale abuttat super Viam Regalem que vocatur Scothowegate. Habendas et Tenendas illi et heredibus suis de capitalibus dominis feodorum illorum libere . quiete . Bene . in pace . Iure et hereditarie . faciendo inde Annuatim Capitalibus Dominis feodorum illorum Seruicia de iure debita et consueta. Et michi annuatim in tota vita mea . iij . quarter' ordei. Et ego predicta Helwysia et Heredes mei warantizabimus predictas pecias terre pro vt in Campis iacentes siue maius siue minus infra eas Continentur . Predicto Gilberto filio meo et heredibus suis Contra omnes homines inperpetuum . In Cuius rei testimonium huic presenti carte Sigillum meum apposui . Testibus . Willelmo Silke . Willelmo Wake . Martino Goldwyne Willelmo Buleman . Iohanne Ayneld . Ricardo Le Northerne . Johanne Goldwyne . Humphrido Dauyd et multis aliis. Datum apud Holcham die dominica post festum sancte crucis anno Regni Regis Edwardi filij Edwardi secundo.

Seal: Circular seal of brown wax, 3/4 in. diam. A stag's head cabossed, a cross between its antlers, within an inscription. 1 x 3/4 in. Cf. HP 1044 of 1302.
Endorsement: *Carta Helwys' quondam vxoris Johannes le Bret de vj acris terre seynt Mar' halfacre* 'Memorandum off' seynt mari half acr' in ye Walsingham Evydenses'.

HD 25

Grant from Roger Chele of Holkham to William of Walsingham of 1 rood in exchange for another rood.   6 Dec. 1315

> Cf. HD 22a, Fos. 3 no. 26 and 7v no. 96
> Fiche 1: C14

Sciant presentes et futuri quod Ego Rogerus Chele de Holkham concessi dedi et hac presenti carta mea confirmaui Willelmo de Walsingham vnam rodam terre arabilis iacent' in Campo de Holkham iuxta terram predicti Willelmi ex parte aquilon' et terram Iohannis Charle ex parte Australi et iacet predicta terra apud Sladeaker . Videlicet in puram et perpetuum excambeum pro vna roda terre iacent' in eodem Campo iuxta terram meam ex parte aquilonali et terram Roberti de Gristone que sibi cecidit per exkaetam de terra Thome Briche ex parte australi cum omnibus suis pertinenciis habend' et tenend' de Capitalibus Dominis feodi predicto Willelmo heredibus suis et suis assingnatis Libere quiete bene et in pace in feodo inperpetuum per seruic' inde debita et consueta. Et ego predictus Rogerus et heredes mei predictam rodam terre siue plus siue minus Habeatur warantizabimus predicto Willelmo heredibus suis et suis assignatis contra omnes gentes inperpetuum. In cuius rei testimonium Huic carte sigillum meum apposui Hiis testibus Willelmo Wake . Willelmo Silke . Iohanne Bret . Ricardo le Norierne . Thoma filio suo . Roberto de Gristone et aliis . Dat' apud Holkham die sabati in festo Sancti Nicholai Episcopi . Anno Regni Regis Edwardi filij regis Edwardi nono.

> Seal: missing.
> Hand: HD 26, HP 1051, 1053, 1054, 1055.
> Endorsement: *Vetus Carta de Sladaker.*

HD 26

Grant from William Silke of Holkham to Richard Neel of Burnham and Caterine his wife of 1 plot of 11/4 acres and 3 other plots.   23 Dec. 1315

> Cf. HD 22a, Fo. 20v no. 223 (Lucas no. 69)
> Fiche 1: D1

Sciant presentes et futuri quod ego Willelmus Silke de Holkham concessi dedi et hac presenti carta mea confirmaui Ricardo Nel de Brunham et Catherine vxori sue quatuor pecias terre mee in villa de Holkham quarum vna pecia iacet apud Wadlond iuxta terram Martini Goldwyne cuius caput orientale abbuttat super Bruaram et capud occidentale super terram Prioris de Walsyngham et vna pecia que vocatur Wellelond et iacet iuxta terram Matill' Choud ex parte occidentali et continet in se quinque Rodas terre cuius capud Australe super terram Iohannis Carpentar' et tercia pecia iacet apud Cathil cuius capud orientale abbuttat super terram Willelmi Asti et capud occidentale super predictam peciam que vocatur Wellelond et quarta pecia iacet in eadem quarentena cuius capud orientale abbuttat super terram predicti Asti et capud occidentale super predictam terram que vocatur Wellelond et iacet inter terras Thome Idessone Habend' et tenend' predictas pecias terre cum omnibus suis pertinenciis predicto Ricardo et Caterine et heredibus de eorumdem corporibus legitime procreatis ac Rectis heredibus predicti Ricardi si predicti Ricardus et Caterina sine heredibus de eorumdem corporibus legitime procreatis obierint de capitalibus dominis feodorum libere et quiete faciend' inde predictis capitalibus dominis feodorum seruicia debita et consueta Et ego predictus Willelmus et heredes mei totam predictam terram cum omnibus suis pertinenciis prout iacet in predictis peciis predictis Ricardo et Caterine et heredibus de eorumdem corporibus legitime procreatis vt predictum est ac rectis heredibus predicti Ricardi si predicti Ricardus et Caterina absque hered' de eorumdem corporibus legitime procreatis obierint . vt predictum est contra omnes gentes inperpetuum Warantizabimus In cuius rei testimonium huic carte sigillum meum aposui Dat' apud Brunham die martis proxima post festum Sancti Thome apostoli anno Regni Regis Edwardi filij regis Edwardi nono. Hiis testibus Roberto de Burgh de Brunham . Roberto del Hil de eadem . Willelmo le chapeleyn de eadem . Iohanne filio Radulfi de eadem . Willelmo Wake de Holkham . Roberto de Griston de eadem . Iohanne le Bret de eadem apud Burnham.

Seal: Circular seal of white wax, 7/16 in. diam. a man's hand within inscription 'S. WILL SILK'.
Hand: See note on HD 25.
Endorsement: *Carta Willelmi Sylk de iij peciis terre in diuersis locis, 69.* In later hand *Ricardo Nel Cathill' et Wellond.*

HD 27

Grant from Roger Hewerard of Holkham to Richard Neel of Burnham and Katerine his wife of 1 plot.   17 May 1317

Cf. HD 22a, Fo. 15 no. 175 (Lucas no. 24)
Fiche 1: D2

Sciant presentes et futuri quod ego Rogerus Hewerard de Holkam concessi dedi et hac presenti carta mea confirmaui Ricardo Neel de Brunham et

Katerine vxori eius et heredibus de corporibus eorumdem legitime procreatis .
et rectis heredibus dicti Ricardi si predicti Ricardus et Katerina absque
heredibus de corporibus eorumdem legitime procreatis obierint vnam peciam
terre mee iacentis in campo de Holkam apud Byllesmere inter terram abbatis
de Crek ex parte boriali et terram predictorum Ricardi et Katerine ex parte
australi . et caput occidentale abuttat super Quarlesgate cum suis pertinenciis
habend' et tenend' predictis Ricardo et Katerine et heredibus de corporibus
eorumdem legitime procreatis . et rectis heredibus dicti Ricardi si predicti
Ricardus et Katerina absque heredibus de eorumdem corporibus legitime
procreatis obierint de capitali domino feodi libere quiete bene et in pace
Reddendo inde annuatim seruicia debita et consueta . et Ego predictus
Rogerus et heredes mei predictam peciam terram cum pertinenciis . predictis
Ricardo et Katerina vxori eius et heredibus de eorumdem corporibus legitime
procreatis . et rectis heredibus dicti Ricardi. Si predicti Ricardus et Katerina
absque heredibus de eorumdem corporibus legitime procreatis obierint contra
omnes gentes Warantizabimus imperpetuum . In Cuius rei testimonium huic
presenti carte sigillum meum apposui . Hiis testibus . Willelmo Wake .
Ricardi le Northerne . Thoma filio suo . Iohanne Bulwere . Roberto de
Grystone . Martino Goldewyne . et Aliis. Dat' apud Holkam die martis
proxima post festum assensionis Anno regni regis Edwardi filio Regis
Edwardi decimo.

Seal: Round seal, white wax, hunting horn inside beaded circle, diam. 3/4 in.
Hand: HP 1059.
Endorsement: *carta Rogeri Hewrard de j pecia terre abutt' super Quarlesgate et iacet apud Billesmere.*

HD 28

Grant from Henry Anger of Holkham and Isabel his wife to Richard Neel of Burnham and Katerine his wife of 11/2 roods.   22 Mar. 1318

Cf. HD 22a, Fo. 18v no. 202 (Lucas no. 50)
Fiche 1: D3

Sciant presentes et futuri quod Nos Henricus Anger de Holkam et Ysabella
vxor mea dedimus concessimus et hac presenti carta nostra confirmauimus
Ricardo Nel de Brunham et Katerine vxori eius et heredibus de eorum
legitime procreatis corporibus ac eciam rectis heredibus predicti Ricardi si
predicti Ricardus et Katerina absque heredibus de eorum corporibus legitime
procreatis obierint vnam rodam terre et dimidiam iacent' in Camp' de
Holkam iuxta terram predicti Ricardi et Katerine ex parte Aquilonali et capud

occidentale abuttat super Cruftam que quondam fuit Martini Goldewyne et Capud orientale abuttat super Cruftam Iohannis Sylke. Habendum et tenendum de Capitalibus domini feodi predicto Ricardo et Katerine et heredibus de eorum corporibus legitime procreatis ac etiam rectis heredibus Ricardi si predicti Ricardus et Katerina absque heredibus de eorum corporibus legitime procreatis obierint libere quiete per seruicia inde debita et consueta pro porcione tenementi . Et nos predicti Henricus et Ysabella vxor mea et heredes nostri predictam rodam terre et dimidiam predictis Ricardo et Katerine et heredibus de eorum corporibus legitime procreatis ac etiam rectis heredibus predicti Ricardi si predicti Ricardus et Katerina absque heredibus de eorum corporibus legitime procreatis obierint contra omnes gentes Warantizabimus in perpetuum. In cuius rei testimonium huic presenti carte sigilla nostra apposuimui . Hiis testibus Thoma Northerne . Roberto de Gristone . Bartholomeo Kalwer . Iohanne Bulwere et aliis. Dat' apud Holkam die mercurij proxima ante festum annunciacionis beate Marie anno regni regis Edwardi filij Edwardi undecimo.

Seals: Two seals, one imperfect, white wax, circular. 16 and 20 mm. 3/4 and 15/16 in. diam., on one, a hare.
Endorsement: *Carta Henrici Aunger de j roda et dimidia abutante super croftam nuper Martini Goldewyn'.*

HD 29

Letter of Attorney from Adam, son of William Craske of Holkham, to Thomas, son of William Grene, chaplain of South Creake to give seisin ro Richard Neel of Burnham and Caterine his wife of 1 plot. 25 Sept. 1327

Cf. HD 22a, Fo. 17v no. 189 (Lucas no. 38)
Fiche 1: D4

Pateat vniuersis per presentes quod Ego Adam filius Willelmi Craske de Holkham ordinaui feci et constitui . dilectum mihi in christo Thomam filium Willelmi Grene de Suthcreyk Capellanum fidelem atornatum meum ad imponendum et introducendum Ricardum Neel de Brunham et Caterinam vxorem suam in plenam et pacificam Seysinam vnius pecie terre cum pertinenciis in Holkham que vocatur Le Marledelond et Iacet iuxta terram Prioris et conuentus de Petraston ex parte boriali et terra predicti Ricardi habuttat super partem australem et capud orientale habuttat super Dalegate prout in carta feoffamenti inde confectam plenius continetur. Ratum et gratum habiturus quicquid Idem Thomas nomine meo duxerit faciend' . In Cuius rei testimonium presenti scripto sigillum meum apposui Data apud Holkham die veneris proxima post festum Sancti Mathei Apostoli et evangeliste Anno regni regis Edwardi [tertij a conquestu primo].

Seal: missing.
Hand: HD 33, 34, HP 1071, 1073, 1074, 1075.

HD 30

Grant from Rose, widow of Elias Crane of Holkham, to Richard Neel and Katerine his wife of Burnham of 11/2 roods and the reversion of 11/2 roods, dower of Sibyl Buleman.　　　　　　　　　　　　　　11 May 1322

Cf. HD 22a, Fo. 15 no. 176 (Lucas no. 25)
Fiche 1: D5 and 3: G8 (seal)

Sciant presentes et futuri quod ego Rosa vxor quondam Helie Crane de Holcham in pura viduitate mea concessi dedi et hac presenti carta mea confirmaui Ricardo Neel et Katerine vxori sue de Brunham et heredibus de corporibus eorumdem legitime procreatis vnam rodam terre et dimidiam cum reuersione vnius rode terre et dimidiam quam mater mea Sibilla Buleman tenet de me nomine dotis cum pertinenciis iacentem in camp' de Holkam inter terram predicti Ricardi ex parte orientali et terram quondam Heruei Buleman ex parte occidentali . et caput Australe abuttat super regiam viam que ducit de Witton' versus Brunham . habend' et tenend' de capitali domino feodi predictis Ricardo et Katerine vxori sue et hered' de corporibus eorumdem procreatis. et si contingat quod predictus Ricardus et Katerina vxor sua sine heredibus de corporibus eorumdem procreatis legitime obierint tum predicta terra heredibus predicti Ricardi remaneat . libere . quiete bene et in pace . Faciendo inde annuatim capitali domino feodi seruic' inde debit' et consuet' Et ego predicta Rosa et heredes mei et assignati mei predict' rodam terre et dimidiam cum pertinenciis cum reuersione vnius rode terre et dimidie quam Sibilla predicta mater mea tenet nomine dotis cum pertinenciis predicto Ricardo et Katerine et heredibus de corporibus eorumdem legitime procreatis . et heredibus predicti Ricardi sicut predictum est contra omnes gentes Warantizabimus imperpetuum . In Cuius rei testimonium huic presenti carte sigillum meum apposui . Hiis testibus . Iohanne le Bret . Iohanne Godewine . Martino Rust . et multis aliis . Dat' apud Holkam die Martis proxima post festum sancti Iohannis ante portam Latinam . Anno regni regis edwardi filij regis edwardi quintodecimo.

Seal: Circular, brown wax. Squirrel within inscription 1 in.
Endorsement: *Carta Rose Buleman de j roda et dimidia terre cum reversione 1 rode et dimidie terre abb' super Wightongate versus austrum.*

HD 31

Grant from John, son of Thomas Leffe of Holkham, to John son of William Renaud of Burnham of the homage and 1d. annual rent of the Prior of Peterstone for a plot and half a fold. 21 Aug. 1323

Not in Neel Cartulary.
Fiche 1: D6

Sciant presentes et futuri quod ego Iohannes filius Thome Leffe de Holkham concessi et hac presenti carta mea confirmaui Iohanni filio Willelmi Renaud de Brunham . Homagium Prioris ecclesie Sancti Petri de Peterston in Brunham et successorum suorum et seruicium vnius denarij annui redditus . quod michi . fieri solebat ad festum Sancti Michaelis . pro vna pecia terre apud Depcrundel cum pertinenciis in Holkham . iacente inter terram eiusdem Prioris ex parte australi . et terram Bartholomei sutoris ex parte boreali . et caput occidentale abuttat super terram de Burghhalle . et caput orientale super terram quondam Willelmi Crask' . Et pro libertate medietatis vnius faldesoke ad predictam terram pertinente . et in campis de Holkham currente . simul cum wardis . releuiis . maritagiis . Eschaetis . scutagiis . et omnibus aliis proficuis et auantagiis . predicta homagium . et seruicia qualitercumque contingentibus. Habend' et tenend' eidem Iohanni . heredibus . et assignatis suis de capitali domino feodi illius per seruicia inde ei debita et consueta. Et ego et heredes mei predictum annuum redditum cum suis proficuis et appruamentis omnibus cum suis pertinenciis predicto Iohanni Renaud . heredibus. et assignatis . suis warantizabimus contra omnes homines imperpetuum. In cuius rei testimonium huic presenti carte sigillum meum apposui. Hiis testibus. Willelmo Wake . Hugone Otes . Iohanne de Bilneye . Iohanne le Bulwere . Ricardo le Northerne . Thoma filio eius . Willelmo Roteney et aliis . Dat' apud Brunham. xxj . die Augusti . anno regni regis Edwardi filij Regis septimodecimo.

Seal: Circular seal of yellow-brown wax. a device within an eight pointed star formed by intersecting squares. Straw is tied round the parchment strip by which the seal is attached to the deed. 1 1/8 in.
Hand: HD 32, 35, 38, HP 1071, 1073, 1076, 1100.
Endorsement: *Carta contra priorem de Petra [medieval hand]; one pece of londe in Holkham et dimid. Foldecourse et redd' per annum j d.* [Tudor hand]

HD 32

Letter of Attorney from William Roteney of Walsingham to Martin Rust of Holkham to give seisin to Richard Neel and Caterine his wife of Burnham of all his lands and holdings in Holkham.   4 Nov. 1323

> Cf. HD 22a, Fos. 16–16v no. 186
> Fiche 1: D7

Pateat vniuersis per presentes quod ego Willelmus Roteney de Walsingham constitui et feci Martinum Rust de Holkham Attornatum meum ad Liberandum Ricardo Nel et Caterine vxori eius de Brunham plenariam seisinam . de omnibus et singulis terris et tenementis cum pertinenciis in Holkham . de quibus ipsos iam per carta meam feoffaui . Ratum habiturus et gratum quicquid idem Martinus nomine meo fecerit in premissis . iuxta formam feoffamenti predicti . In cuius rei testimonium . has litteras meas inde fieri feci patentes sigillo meo signatas . Dat' apud Holkham quarto die Nouembris . Anno . regni . regis . Edwardi . filij . regis Edwardi decimo septimo.

> Seal: missing.
> Hand: See note on HD 31.

HD 33

Grant from Margery, widow of William Craske of Holkham, to Richard Neel of Burnham and Caterine his wife of 1/2 acre of land.   20 Dec. 1327

> Cf. HD 22a, Fo. 13v no. 158 (Lucas no. 7)
> Fiche 1: D8 and G10 (seal)

Sciant presentes futuri quod Ego Margeries quondam vxor Willelmi Craske de Holkham concessi dedi et hac presenti carta mea confirmaui Ricardo Neel de Brunham et Caterine vxori eius vnam dimidiam acram terre mee cum pertinenciis in Holkham et Iacet apud Hadowe iuxta terram Rogeri Le Wryte ex parte Australi. et Capud occidentale abuttat super Hadowegate Habend' et Tenend' prefat' Ricardo et Caterine et heredibus suis de corporibus eorum exeuntibus de Capitali domino feodi per seruicia que ad illa tenementa pertinent . Et si contigat quod predicti Ricardus et Caterina sine heredibus huiusmodi de se exeuntibus infata decedant . tunc terra predicta cum suis pertinenciis rectis heredibus predicti Ricardi quiete et integre remaneat. Habend' et tenend' de Capitali domino feodi per Seruicia que ad illa tenementa pertinent imperpetuum. Et ego predicta Margeries et heredes mei predictam dimidiam acram terre cum omnibus pertinenciis suis prefato Ricardo et Caterine et heredibus suis de se exeuntibus. Ac eciam rectis heredibus eiusdem Ricardi et suis assignatis. Si contingat predictos Ricardum et Caterinam sine huiusmodi heredibus de se exeuntibus infata decedere . contra omnes homines imperpetuum Warantizabimus. In cuius rei testimonium Huic presenti carte sigillum meum apposui . Hiis testibus Iohanne Le Bret . Iohanne Bulwere . Willelmo Wake . Hugone Otes . Iohanne Belneye . Ricardo Speller' . Willelmo filio Alicie et aliis. Dat' apud Holkham vigilia Sancti Thome Apostoli . anno regni regis Edwardi tercij post conquestum. primo.

> Seal: Circular white seal, 3/4 in. diam. An animal passant in front of a fleur-de-lys within an inscription. Same seal used in HP 1077 by Margery and her next husband William a le Gateshende, 1329.
> Endorsement: *Carta Willelmi Craske de dimidia acra terre apud Adow* T[ranscriptum] 4 in hand of Edmund Lucas.

HD 34

Letter of Attorney from Margery, widow of William Craske of Holkham, to Adam her son to give seisin to Richard Neel of Burnham and Caterine his wife of 1/2 acre of land.   20 Dec. 1327

> Cf. HD 22a, Fo. 13v no. 158
> Fiche 1: D9

Pateat vniuersis per presentes quod Ego Margeries quondam vxor Willelmi Craske ordinaui feci et constitui dilectum mihi in Christo Adam filium meum fidelem attornatum meum ad imponendum et introducendum Ricardum Neel de Brunham et Caterinam vxorem suam in plenam et pacificam seysinam vnius dimidie acre cum pertinenciis in Holkham apud Hadhowe prout in quadam carta feofamenti inde confecta plenius continetur . Ratum et gratum habiturus quicquid idem Adam nom[ine] meo in premissis duxerit faciendum . In cuius rei testimonium huic Scripto sigillum meum apposui . Dat' apud Holkham vigilia Sancti Thome apostoli anno regni r[egis] Edwardi tercij post conquestum primo.

> Seal: missing.
> Hand: HD 29, 33, HP 1074, 1075.

HD 35

Confirmation from John le Bret of Holkham to Walter de Mundene, vicar of half Holkham church, of his brother Gilbert's grant of 1 plot.   6 May 1328

Cf. HD 22a, Fos. 3 no. 22 and 4v no. 50
Fiche 1: D10

Omnibus Christi fidelibus ad quos hoc presens scriptum peruenerit Iohannes le Bret de Holcham salutem in Domino . Nouerit vniuersitas vestra mea inspecsisse*a* Donacionem et concessionem quam Gilbertus frater meus fecit domino Waltero de Mundene vicario medietatis ecclesie de Holcham et Alicie sorori sue de vna pecia terra cum pertinenciis Iacent' in campo de Holcham que est de feodo meo in quadam quarentena que nuncupatur Lumbulebotme prout carta quam predictus dominus Walterus et Alicia Habuit de donacione prefate pecie terre melius et plenius testatur . Quamquid Donacionem et concessionem antedicte pecie terre per seruicium de iure debit*um* ratam et integram habeo . Et illam Prenominatis domino Waltero et Alicie Confirmo. Reddendo inde annuatim Michi et Heredibus meis vnum denarium ad festum Sancti Michaelis . Et ego dictus Iohannes et Heredes mei predictam peciam terre cum pertinenciis. Antedictis . Domino Waltero et Alicie Sorori eius contra omnes gentes confirmauimus . Pro hac autem confirmacione predicte pecie terre Dedit mihi dominus Walterus quandam vrbanitatem pre manibus . In cuius Rei Testimonium huic scripto Confirmacionis Sigillum meum apposui apud Holcham Die Veneris in festo Sancti Iohannis ante portam Latinam Anno Regni Regis Edwardi filij regis . Edwardi . Secundi . Secundo.

VARIANT: *a* Written as two words.

HD 36

Grant from William Curthun of Holkham to William Craske of Holkham of 1 plot of 13/4 acres.   [c. 1291–8]

Cf. HD 22a, Fo. 3 no. 20
Fiche 1: D11

Sciant presentes et futuri quod ego Willelmus Curthun de Holkham Concessi Dedi et hac presenti Carta mea Confirmaui Willelmo Craske de eadem et heredibus suis . pro homagio et seruicio et pro triginta solidis Argenti quos mihi dedit in gersumam . vnam peciam terre mee continentem septem rodas terre et Iacet dicta pecia in Camp' de Holkham Apud Caldhowesty inter terram Iohannis Le Bret ex parte Aquilonari et terram Cristiane Talbot ex parte Australi et capud Orientale Abuttat super terram Gilberti Aynild et capud occidentale Abuttat super Caldhowesty. Habend' et tenend' de me et heredibus meis vel meis Assignatis . illi et heredibus suis vel suis assignatis libere . quiete . bene. in pace . iure . et hereditarie . Cuicumque . et quantumcumque dictam peciam terre . dare . legare . vendere . vel assignare voluerit exceptis domibus Religionis . Reddendo inde Annuatim mihi et heredibus meis vel meis Assignatis vnum denarium ad pasch' pro omni seruicio . Consuetudine . Exaccione. secta Curie . et demanda. Et ego predictus Willelmus Curthun et heredes mei vel mei Assignati warantizabimus et adquietabimus et omnino defendemus predictam peciam terre predicto Willelmo et heredibus suis vel suis Assignatis pro predicto seruicio Contra omnes homines inperpetuum. In cuius rei testimonium huic Carte sigillum meum apposui Hiis testibus. Bartholomeo de Burgate .[1] Galfrido le Bret . Iohanne filio suo . Iohanne Le Bret . Iohanne Silke . Willelmo filio suo . Galfrido Godwyne . Martino Goldwyne . Gilberto Aynild . Simone Hamund . Iohanne Rutur . Humfrido Dauid et aliis.

Seal: missing.
Hand of a later William Curchoun when *messor* of John Andrew 1351 occurs in HD 47; HP 1026, HP 1033 and HD 36 are all in the same hand.
Endorsement: by Edmund Lucas, T[ranscriptum].

HD 37

Grant from Walter de Mundene, vicar of half Holkham church, and Alice his sister to William of Heveringlond, rector of Holkham, and Robert of Knapton, chaplain, of 3 acres in 2 plots. 23 Oct. 1330

Cf. HD 22a, Fo. 2v no. 19
Fiche 1: D12

Sciant presentes et futuri quod Nos Walterus de Mundene perpetuus vicarius medietatis ecclesie de Holcham et Alicia soror eiusdem vnanimi assensu concessimus dedimus et hac presenti carta mea confirmauimus domino Willelmo de Heueringlond Rectori medietatis ecclesie de Holcham et domino Roberto de Cnapetone capellano tres acras terre nostre cum pertinenciis iacentes in duabus peciis in campo australi de Holcham . quarum vna acra et

---

[1] These six witnesses occur in 1303 together. The latest occurrence of Humphrey David is noted in 1302 and of Simon Hamund in 1298. John Silk occurs in 1291–1337 and William Silk in 1276–1316. Simon Hamund occurs in 1276–1298.

dimidia iacent in vna quarentena que vocatur Wytheriswong' iuxta terram
Iohannis le Bret versus aquilonem cuius capud orientale abuttat super
Gybbesgate et alia acra et dimidia iacent super vnam culturam que
nuncupatur Lambolebotme iuxta terram que quondam fuit Edmundi
Athelwald per partem australem et capud orientale abuttat super communem
viam ducentem de Holcham erga Egemere . Habendas et tenendas predictas
duas pecias terre cum pertinenciis prefatis dominis . Willelmo et Roberto .
Heredibus suis et eorum assignatis de capitalibus dominis feodorum illorum
per seruicia inde de iure debita et consueta . libere . integre . et in feodo
imperpetuum. Et nos vero antedicti Walterus et Alilicia*a* et heredes nostri
warantizabimus prefatas pecias terre cum pertinenciis . predictis Willelmo et
Roberto . Heredibus eorum et eorum assignatis contra omnes gentes
imperpetuum. In cuius rei testimonium Huic carte sigilla nostra apposuimus
Dat' apud Holcham die Martis proxima ante festum apostolorum Simonis et
Iude Anno regni regis Edwardi tercij post conquestum quarto . Hiis testibus.
Ricardo Nel . Willelmo Wake . Thome le Northerne . Iohanne Bilneye .
Iohanne Bret . Adam Craske . Iohanne Silk et multis aliis.

Seals: fragments of circular seals of pinkish white wax had disintegrated by Aug. 1982.
Hand: See note on HD 31.
Endorsement: by Edmund Lucas, *Carta domini. Walteri de Mundene vicarij medietatis ecclesie de Holcham et Alicie sororis eiusdem . de tribus acris terre iacent' versus Egmere.* T[ranscriptum].

VARIANT: *a* *sic* in Ms.

HD 38

Grant from Simon atte Cros of Holkham to Katerine, widow of Richard Neel of 1/2 acre of land.　　　　　20 Nov. 1336

Cf. HD 22a, Fo. 29 no. 216 (Lucas no. 63)
Fiche 1: D13

Sciant presentes et futuri quod Ego Simon Atte Cros de Holkham concessi .
dedi . et hac presenti carta mea confirmaui Katerine que fuit vxor Ricardi
Neel . dimidiam acram terre mee iacentem collateraliter ex parte boreali . de
Grenegate cum pertinenciis in Holkham cuius caput orientale abuttat super
terram predicte Katerine . Habend' et tenend' eidem Katerine . heredibus . et
assignatis suis de capitali domini feodi illius per seruicia que ad illam terram
pertinent imperpetuum . Et ego predictus Simon et heredes mei predictam*a*
peciam terre siue in ea plus habeatur siue minus cum suis pertinenciis .
prefate Katerine . heredibus . et assignatis suis . Warantizabimus contra

omnes homines imperpetuum . In cuius rei testimonium presenti carte
sigillum meum apposui . Hiis testibus Willelmo Wake . Thoma le Northerne
. Iohanne de Belneye . Ricardo le Spellere . Iohanne le Wrighte . Iohanne
Hoddes . Iohanne le Meire et aliis . Dat' apud Holkham vicesimo die
Nouembris . Anno regni regis Edwardi tercij post conquestum Decimo.

Seal: missing.
Hand: See note on HD 31.
Endorsement: by Edmund Lucas, *Carta Simonis atte Cros de quandam pecia apud
Grenegate videlicet de dimidia acra terre* 63. T[ranscriptum].

VARIANT: *a* Repeated in Ms.

HD 39

HD 39 is wrongly catalogued and relates to Burghwood Hall in Mileham not to Burghall.

HD 40

*Certificate from John de Cromhale, subescheator, that the manor of Hillhall
is not held in chief, but of the heirs of Robert de Tony for the 20th part of a
knight's fee. John D'Akeny granted it to Thomas de Lacy.*   10 Mar. 1338

Fiche 1: D14

Omnibus ad quos presentes littere peruenerint Iohannes de Cromhale
subescaetor domini Regis in comitatibus Norf' et Suff' salutem in domino.
Noueritis me recepisse mandatum domini mei Willelmi Trussel eschaetoris
domini regis citra Trentam in hec verba recepi.*a* Willelmus Trussel escaetor
domini regis citra Trentam Iohannis de Cromhale subescaetori suo in
comitatu Norf' salutem in domino. Mandatum domini Regis vobis in hec
verba mittimus exequendum. Edwardus etc. dilecto et fideli suo Willelmo
Trussel escaetori suo citra Trentam salutem. Cum nuper volentes certiorari
super causam capcionis terrarum et tenementorum Thome de Lacy in
Holcham in Comitatu Norf' per vos vt dicebatur in manum nostrum vobis
mandauerimus quod vos de causa predicta sub sigillo etc. redderetis certiores
ac vos nobis significaueritis quod vos cepistis tenementa predicta in manum
nostram pro eo quod Iohannes Dakeny qui ea de nobis tenuit in capite eadem
tenementa prefato Thome licencia nostra super hoc non optenta alienauit et
postmodum ad prosecucionem prefati Thome nobis suggerentis prefata
tenementa non de nobis teneri in capite nec ipsum Iohannem aut antecessores

suos nec aliquos alios tenementa predicta actenus tenentes ea de nobis aut progenitoribus nostris aliquo tempore tenuisse vobis mandauerimus quod per sacramentum etc. si tenementa predicta teneantur de nobis in capite an de alio et si de nobis tunc per quod seruicium et qualiter et quomodo et si de alio tunc de quo vel de quibus et per quod seruicium etc. et que huiusmodi tenementa illa sint et quantum valeant per annum etc. Ac per inquisicionem super premissis per vos de mandato nostro sic factam et in Cancellaria nostra retornatam compertum sit. Idem predictus Thomas tenet vnum mesuagium [c]um molendino ventritico duas acras terre et sexaginta solidos redditus cum pertinenciis in eadem villa et mercatu ibidem per quemlibet diem Lune per annum de heredibus Roberti de Tony per seruicium . xx . partis feodi militis et reddendo inde annuatim . duos denarios et obolum ad Hundredum de Northgreneho per manus balliui eiusdem hundredi qui pro tempore fuerit pro Warepund' pro omni seruicio et quod predictus Thomas et antecessores sui tenuerunt tenementa predicta de antecessoribus prefati heredis et de nullo alio. a tempore cuius contrarij memoria non existit. Vobis mandamus quod de terra et tenementis predictis si occasione premissa et non alia de causa in manu nostra existant vos vlterius non intromittatis . Exitus si quod inde perceperitis prefato Thome liberantes. Teste me ipso apud Wodestok . xviij . die Septembris anno regni nostri xj°. Virtute cuiusdam breuis terram et tenementa in breui contenta liberaui Iohanni de Shortegraue attornato dicti Thome. In cuius rei testimonium presentibus sigillum meum apposui. Dat' apud Peterston' . x . die Martij anno regni regis Edwardi tercii post conquestum xij°.

Seal: missing.
Endorsed: *Inquisicio Hillhall non tenetur in capite sed per xx partis vnius feodi militis* (sixteenth century).

VARIANT: *^a* *sic* in Ms.

HD 41

Final Concord, John Sage and his wife Joan to Thomas de Lacy of one messuage, 2 acres of land, a mill, 60s. rent and 2 quarters and 3 bushels of corn.						9 Feb. 1341

Cf. PRO CP 25(1) case 165 file 154 no. 539, Appendix 5, no. 37
Fiche 1: E1

Hec est finalis concordia facta in curia domini Regis apud Westmonasterium in octabis Purificacionis beate Marie Anno regni Edwardi regis Anglie tercij a conquestu quinto decimo et regni eiusdem Regis Francie secundo Coram Rogero Hillary Willelmo Basset et Thoma de Heppescotes Iustic' et aliis domini Regis fidelibus tunc ibi presentibus . Inter Thomam de Lacy querentem et Iohannem Sage et Iohannam vxorem eius deforciant*es* de vno mesuagio et duabus acris terre vno molendino sexaginta solidatis redditus et redditu duorum quarteriorum et trium bussellorum frumenti cum pertinenciis in Holkham . Vnde placitum conuencionis summonitum fuit inter eos in eadem Curia . Scilicet quod predicti Iohannes et Iohanna recog*nouerunt* predicta tenementa cum pertinenciis esse Ius ipsius Thome. Vt illa que idem Thomas habet de dono predictorum Iohannis et Iohanne . Habend' et tenend' eidem Thome et heredibus suis de capitalibus dominis feodi illius per seruicia que ad predicta tenementa pertinent imperpetuum . Et preterea iidem Iohannes et Iohanna concesserunt pro se et heredibus ipsius Iohanne quod ipsi Warantizabimus predicto Thome et heredibus suis predicta tenementa cum pertinenciis contra omnes homines imperpetuum . Et pro hac recognicione Warantizacione fine et concordia idem Thomas dedit predictis Iohanni et Iohanne quadraginta marcas argenti.

NOTE: The two principal parties were both included in the list of the lords of Hillhall. John Sage of Walford acquired the lordship through marriage to Joan who was the sister and heir of John d'Akeny (Hillhall Book, HD 75 and 155). This is the only original Final Concord to survive at Holkham earlier than 1350, for HD 3 and HD 22a, nos. 109 and 190 are only transcripts. Cf. Appendix 5, Final Concords (1198–1406).

HD 42

Grant from William, son of John Godwyne of Holkham, to Walter Osbern of Holkham and Juliana his wife of the reversion of 3/4 acres and of an 'itinerant' foldcourse.   30 May 1342

Fiche 1: E2

Sciant presentes et futuri quod ego Willelmus filius Godwyne de Holcham concessi et dedi et hac presenti carta mea confirmaui Waltero Osbern de Holcham Iuliane vxori sue heredibus et assignatis predicti Walteri reuersionem trium rodarum terre mee iacencium in campis de Holcham apud Briarium iuxta terram Iohannis Elwan ex parte boreali et capud orientale abuttat super bruar*ium* et vnius falde itinerantis annuatim per totum annum in perpetuum michi hereditarie succedencium iure hereditarie quas Ida mater mea tenet ad terminum vite sue habend' et tenend' predictis Waltero . Iuliane . heredibus et assignatis predicti Walteri predictas tres rodas terre et faldam cum libertate sua de capitalibus dominis feodi illius libere iure et hereditarie imperpetuum per seruicia inde debita et de iure consueta . Et ego predictus

Willelmus et heredes mei predictis Waltero . Iuliane heredibus et assignatis predicti Walteri predictas tres rodas terre et faldam cum libertate sua per predicta seruicia in perpetuum Warantizabimus contra omnes gentes . In cuius rei testimonium huic presenti carte sigillum meum apposui die Iouis proxima post festum Sancti Augustini Anglorum episcopi anno regni Regis Edwardi tertij post conquestum Sextodecimo . Hiis testibus Willelmo Wake . Thoma Northerne . Iohanne Andreu . Iohanne Wrighte . Iohanne Buleman . Thoma filio Willelmi . Iohanne Silk et multis aliis.

Seal: missing.
Hand: HP 1108.
Endorsement: *Carta Willelmi Godwyni. Carta vnius falde itinerantis annuatim per annum.*

HD 43

HD 43 is copy of grant of church and vicarage from the Bishop of Norwich to the abbey of West Dereham (transferred to church records). See HD 22a no. 253 (at end) and note from Dereham Cartulary in the version of the Feodary in HD 6. Fiche 1: A9.

HD 44

Acquittance by the Official of the Archdeacon of Norwich of administration of the will of Thomas Neel of Burnham.   1 Mar. 1350

Cf. HP 3808
Fiche 1: E3

Nouerint vniuersi quod audito a nobis . Offic*iali* domini Archidiaconi Norwyc' finali compoto Administracionis executorum testamenti Thome Neel de Brunham defuncti in Holkham defuncti in bonis eiusdem defuncti habite . Inuenientes quod dictos executores in bonis dicti defuncti fideliter administrasse eosdem executores ab onere administracionis sue . et vltimi compotus reddicione absoluimus et quietos dimittimus per presentes In cuius rei testimonium sigillum officij nostri presentibus apposuimus Dat' apud Well' Kalend' Martij . anno . domini . millessimo . ccc^{mo} . xl^{mo} . nono .

NOTE: The reckoning here is from the Incarnation with the feast of the Annunciation on 25 March as starting point for the year. Thomas Neel's will, dated 20 Feb. 1350, proved at Wells 1 March 1350 is HP 3808. It made bequests to churches of Holkham and Weasenhamthorpe and to his sister Agnes. His executors were his brother Gilbert Neel, his sister Helen and Roger Stalworth. The latter occurs in many Weasenham deeds. Thomas was called *Dom* in HP 2477 and of Weasenham in HP 2463. He was the maternal great-uncle of Thomas Lucas, whose will (1447. NCC, Fo. 133 Wilbey) is printed in Appendix 2.

HD 45

Hillhall Manor hayward's account.   29 Sept. 1349–29 Sept. 1350

Cf. HD 82 for the account of Richard Blakeman collector (1332) which is the earliest account. This is the earliest account for Hillhall.
Fiche 1: E4

HOLKHAM HILHALL'.[2] COMPOTUS THOME CLERK' MESSORIS IBIDEM A FESTO SANCTI MICHAELIS ANNO XXIIJ VSQUE IDEM FESTUM ANNO VICESIMO QUARTO.

<Redditus ass'>

Idem respondet de lxx s. ij d. de redditibus ass' tam liber' quam villan' percipiendis ad festum Sancti Andree, Annunciacionis Beate Marie et Natiuitatis Sancti Baptiste per equales porciones. Et de j d. de incremento redditus de Willelmo Atteston.

Summa lxx s. iij d.

<Perquis' fori>

Idem respondet de xij d. de tolneto fori hoc anno.

Summa xij d.

<Perquis' curie>

Idem respondet de lxxix s. ix d. de perquis' curiarum hoc anno tentarum quarum vltima tenta fuit die Lune prox' post festum Sancte Wytburge virginis.

Summa lxxix s. ix d.

Summa totalis recept' vij li xj s

<Allocaciones reddit'>

Idem computat in allocac' diuersorum tenementorum causa pestis iij s. vj d. quadr. et dimid. In allocac' reddit' Prior' de Petra*ston* eo quod predictus redditus implacitatur et nescitur vtrum dominus debet percipere necne v s.

<Denar' liber'>

Idem computat liber' domino. lxxix s. j d. pro j tall'.

<Summa alloc' et liber' iiij li vij s. quadr. et dimid>

Et debet lxiij s. iiij d. ob. quadr. dimid. quadr. De quibus allocantur eidem de quodam amerciamento Thome Calwere capellani iij s. iiij d. Et sic debentur domino lx s. ob. quadr. De quibus postea allocantur eidem de reddit' et de diuersis amerciamentis et condonac' que sibi superius non allocantur per sacramentum messoris. Eo quod dominus prius dixit predictos denarios talliasse et idem messor iurauit super sacramentum suum quod numquam de dictis denariis sibi talli*ari* fecit. Et pro omnibus aliis calumpniis

---

2   Presumably a building near or on the site of the old manor house which stood S.W. of family wing to which it was linked by a corridor while the present Holkham was being built. The site was landscaped in 1764 by Capability Brown.

et peticionibus suis xxix s. ij d. Et sic debentur domino de claro xxx s. x d. ob. quadr. – que onerantur in compoto Heruei Pope in anno sequenti.

Dorse
<Frumentum>
De reddit' ij quarter. iiij buss. et dimid. De quibus liber' ad hospicium' domini j quarter. vij buss. iiij pec. et dimid. Et remanent iiij buss. pec. et dimid. In allocac. pro tenemento Iohannis de le Dale in manu domini j pec. In manu custodis a retro.

<Cymini>
De redditu' ij lib. De quibus liberatur ad hospicium domini j lib. Et remanet j lib. super tenementum quondam Iohannis Sylk.

HD 46

Hillhall Manor hayward's account.   29 Sept. 1350–29 Sept. 1351

Fiche 1: E5

HOLKHAM HILHALLE. COMPOTUS HERUEI POPE MESSORIS IBIDEM A FESTO SANCTI MICHAELIS ANNO VICESIMO QUARTO VSQUE IDEM FESTUM VICESIMO QUINTO.

<Arreragia>
Idem respondet de xxx s. x d. ob. quadr. de arreragiis Thome Clerk' messoris in anno precedenti.
<Redditus Assise>
Idem respondet de lxx s. ij d. de redd. assise tam liberorum . quem villanorum . percipiend ad fest. Sancti Andree Annunciat. Beate Marie et Nativitatis Sancti Johannis Baptiste per equales porciones. Et de j d. de incremento redditus de Willelmo Atteston
                    Summa lxx s. iii d.
<Perquis' fori>
Idem respondet de v d. quadr. de tolneto fori hoc anno.
                    Summa v d. quadr.

<Perquis' curie>

Idem respondet de xiij s. x d. ob. de curia tenta die Lune proxima post festum Concepcionis Beate Marie.[3] Et de xij s. iij d. de curia tenta die Sabbati in festo Georgij martiris.[4] Et de xv s. xj d. de curia tenta die martis proxima ante festum Sancte Margarete.[5]

Summa xlij s. ob.

Summa totalis recept' cum arreragiis vij li. iij s. vij d. ob.

<Allocaciones reddit'>

Idem computat in allocacione diuersorum tenementorum in manu domini causa pestilentie iij s. vij d. ob. quadr.

Summa iij s. vij d. ob. quadr.

<Denar' liber'>

Idem computat liber' domino lxix s. iij d. pro j tall'. Item eidem xj s. vij d. sine tall'. Item v d. quadr.

Summa iiij li xv d. quadr.

<Summa omnium expens' et liber' iiij li iiij s. ij d.>

Et debentur domino tam de arreragiis anni instantis quam de arreragiis computi precedentis lviij s. viij d. ob. De quibus allocantur Herueo Pope messori huius anni de redditu tenementi quondam Iohannis Sylk iij d. Et sic debentur domino lviij s. v d. ob. de quibus alloc' eidem ex gratia domini pro omnibus calumpniis et peticionibus suis vna cum fine maritagij Alicie Mayn v s. Et sic debentur domino liij s. v d. ob. Debentur item xij d. de quadam fine Heruei Pope pro custodia habenda Alicie filie predicti Heruei vsque etatem predicte Alicie de onere dicti Heruei messoris nunc superius non oneratur. Et sic est summa totius debiti liiij s. v d. ob. De quibus ponitur in respectu de redditu prioris de Peterston eo quod dictus redditus implacitatur et nescitur vtrum dominus percipere debet necne v s. Et sic debentur domino de claro xl s. v d. ob. Vnde super Thomam Clerk messorem in anno precedenti xxx x d. ob. quadr. Et super Heruum Pope messorem nunc xviij s. vj d. ob. quadr.

Dorse

<Frumentum>

De rem' iij buss. pec. et dimid. in manu custodis

De reddit' ij quarter. iij buss. et dimid.

Summa ij quarter. vj buss. iij pec. et dimid.

De quibus in allocacione pro tenemento Iohannis Attedale quia in manu domini hoc anno pec. Liber' ad hospicium domini j quarter. vij buss iij pec. Et reman' vj buss. iij pec. et dimid. frumenti a retro et in custodia vnde de tempore Thome Clerk' messoris iij buss. pec. et dimid. de tempore Heruei Pope messoris nunc iij buss. et dimid.

---

3   13 Dec. 1350
4   23 April 1351
5   19 July 1351

<Cyminum>

De rem' j li. De reddit' ij li. Summa iiij li. De quibus liber' ad hospicium domini li. Et reman' ij li. cymini super tenementum Sylk' vnde super messorem precedentem j li. super messorem nunc j li.

HD 47

Hillhall Manor hayward's account (fragment).   29 Sept. 1351–29 Sept. 1352

> Cf. HD 36 a grant in hand of William Curthun
> Fiche 1: E6

HOLKHAM HILLHALLE. COMPOTUS WILLELMI CURCHOUN MESSORIS IOHANNIS ANDREW IBIDEM A FESTO SANCTI MICHAELIS ARCHIANGELI ANNO XXV VSQUE IDEM FESTUM ANNO XXVJ.

<Arrerag'>

Idem respondet de xlix s. v d. ob. de arreragiis computi precedentis vnde super Thomam Clerk nuper messorem xxx s. x d. ob. quadr. Et super Herueum Pope messorem in anno precedenti xviij s. vj d.

Summa xlix s. v d. ob.

<Redditus ass'>

Idem respondet de lxx s. ij d. de reddit' assis' tam liber' quam villan' percipiend' ad festa Sancti Andree, Annunciacionis beate Marie et Natiuitatis Sancti Iohannis Baptiste per equales porciones. Et de j d. de incremento redditus Willelmi Atteston. Et de xj d. ob. quadr. de redditu' non perquisito de Herueo Bulman. Et de iiij d. de redditu non perquisito de Iohanne Sylk'. Et de ob. de incremento redditus Iohannis Daulyn per annum.

Summa lxxj s. vj d. quadr.

<Perquis' fori>

Idem respondet de v d. de tolneto fori ... [*The rest of the roll is missing*]

Dorse

<Frumentum>

De rem. vij buss. iiij peces et dimid. De redditu hoc anno ij quarter. iiij buss. et dimid. Summa iiij quarter. ij buss. pec. et dimid. De quibus liber' ad hospicium domini vt idem testat' iiij quarter. j buss et dimid. Et rem. iiij pec. et dimid. in manus Andree Atte Chirch' vt creditur de tempore Thome Clerc et Heruei Pope messor' *etc.* Preceptum est solvere per preceptum domini.

<Cyminum>

De rem' ij li. De redditu ij li. Summa iiii li. De quibus liber' ad hospicium domini ut idem testatur j li. Item in allocacione pro tenemento Thome Northern eo quod oneratur vt dicitur quousque videat eius cartam j li. Et rem' ij li. super messores precedentes.

HD 75 Fo. 2v

Lords of the manor of Hillhall and of Bret-Tobers in Holkham from Hillhall Book.

Fiche 1: E10 and F12

NOTE: there are two copies of the Hillhall Book. See HD 155, Fo. 1v for the text.

HD 79

Richard Neel's court rolls.   1322–9

NOTE: The roll consists of one membrane 8 in. wide.
Cf. HD 20 for courts of 1314 and 1321
Fiche1: E11

CURIA RICARDI NEEL TENTA APUD HOLCHAM DIE MERCURIJ PROXIMA POST FESTUM SANCTI THOME APOSTOLI ANNO REGNI REGIS EDWARDI FILIJ REGIS SEXTODECIMO.   22 Dec. 1322

<Finis . iiij . sol'>

Ricardus Yttekil reddit in manu domini vnam acram terre ad opus Iohannis Thorbern et Reginaldi Thorbern illis et eorum heredibus tenend' in villenagio per seruicia debita saluo iure cuiuslibet.

Et predicti Iohannes et Reginaldus dant domino pro ingressu habendo . iiij sol'.

Helwysia Le Meyre perquisiuit de feodo domini libere vnum mesuagium et tres rodas terre iacentes inter terram Ricardi Lamkin et terram Mariote Leman . per seruicia et fecit fidelitatem . liberam.

<Preceptum est>

Iurati dicunt quod Abbas de Crek tenet de vilnagio domini dimidiam acram terre apud Billesmere de \terra quondam Gilberti Gurle/ et ideo preceptum est distringere predictum abbatem qualiter etc.

<\Simon Elreche tenet/>*a*

<Preceptum est>

Preceptum est distringere Halkynum de Olney in vna acra et vna roda terre apud Adehowe . ad ostendendum et faciendum quod etc.

<Inquiratur>

Agn*eta* Ernald tenet per antiqu*am* perquisicionem vnam acram terre iacentem in tribus peciis videlicet \Iohannes Geyton/ tenet in crofta apud Burgate inter croftam Ricardi Broun et croftam Rogeri de Erpingham et alia pecia iacet apud Kokeflet inter terram Willelmi Otewy et terram Bartholomei de Burgate qui fuit et tercia pecia iacet apud Wellegate inter terram Willelmi Sutere et terram Ade Crask*e* et terra predicta capta in manu domini et Agnes facit aliis dominis feodi seruicia debita . videlicet . viij . d. per annum.

<j . quadr'. per annum . de incremento>

Et de incremento reddit domino . j . quadr . per annum ad festum Sancti Michaelis.

<Perquisicio, inquiratur>

Iohannes Thorbern et Reginaldus Thorbern tenent per antiqu*am* perquisicionem vnam acram et dimidiam terre iacentem in tribus peciis . videlicet apud Shortlond . tres rodas inter terram abbatis de Derham et terram Adomari de Valencia . et alia pecia iacet inter terram Ricardi Broun et terram Thome Northerne et continet . j . Rodam et dimidiam . et tercia pecia Iacet inter terram Iohannis Godwyne et terram Rose Buleman et continet j. Rodam et dimidiam terre et predicti Iohannes et Reginaldus faciunt dominis feodi per annum viij . d.

<j . quadr'. per annum de incremento>

Et de incremento domino . j . quadr. per annum ad festum Sancti Michaelis.

Prima curia anni

CURIA IBIDEM DIE LUNE PROXIMA ANTE FESTUM SANCTI THOME APOSTOLI ANNO REGNI REGIS EDWARDI XIX.[6]   16 Dec. 1325

<Misericordia iiij d.>

De Iohanne Thurberd querente versus Willelmum filium Alicie in placito debiti vnde recuperauit . versus . eum . xix . d.

<Preceptum est>

Et dampna taxata ad . iij . d. quos preceptum est Leuare . pleg'. Reginald' Thurberd. \sine die per mortem querentis/

<Preceptum est>

Iohannes Thurberd queritur de Willelmo filio Alicie de placito debiti.

---

6   The order of the membranes is not chronological as it should be. Some membranes are interspersed with ones on HD 83.

<Preceptum est>

Iohannes Thurberd queritur de Willelmo filio Alicie de placito transgressionis. pleg' de prosequendo Reginald' Thurberd . et preceptum est distringere.

<Finis . xij . d. \soluit domino/>

De Ricardo Yidekil pro firma sua habenda de . iij . rodis et dimidia terre tota vita Cecilie Ruddon ex concessione eiusdem Cecilie. Fac' etc. saluo iure etc.

<Memorandum>

Idemque Ricardus soluet per annum tota vita predicte Cecilie pro eadem Cecilia \quolibet anno ad gulam Augusti domino[b]/ Ade de Saxlingham capellano. vj . d. quousque eidem domino Ade satisfiat de . j . marca argenti ex debito in quo eadem Cecilia eidem domino Ade tenetur.

<Misericordia . xij . d.>

De Mabillia Ernald pro licencia Matill*dam* filiam suam maritandi. Pleg' . Thom' de Dallyng' et Iohann' Cat.

<Preceptum est>

Preceptum est facere venire Agne*tam* Gurle . ad recipiend' dimidiam rodam terre per virgam quam tenet de villenagio domini vel scire. \Predicta venit et recepit eam per virgam./

<Preceptum est>

Preceptum est venire duas filias Gilberti Eluerich ad ostendendum qualiter ingresse sunt feodum . domini . etc.

<Preceptum est>

Preceptum est facere venire \duas filias Bartholomei[c]/ le Sutere ad ostendendum quomodo ingressus est feodum domini etc.

<Preceptum est>

Preceptum est capere in manu domini . dimidiam . rodam terre quam Reginaldus de Berneye tenet de villenagio domini pro seruicio aretro etc.

Summa xij d.[d]

Prima curia anni.

CURIA IBIDEM DIE IOUIS PROXIMA POST FESTUM SANCTE CATERINE VIRGINIS ANNO VICESIMO.   27 Nov. 1324

<ij . s. iij . d.>

De tota curia pro respectu curie habendo. Et videtur quod sit quasi ex consuetudine . quia alibi inuenitur in diuersis curiis tenta de domino Eustacio le Bret.

<Preceptum est, Misericordia, Contempt'>

Preceptum est sicut alias exequi plura precepta curie predecentis non dum executa. Et quia Reginaldus de Hogate cui preceptum fuit illa exequi vt messori . nichil inde fecit . Ideo ipse in graui misericordia pro contemptu.

<Finis xij d.>

De Iohanne Cat pro ingressu habendo sibi et sequele sue in vno Cotagio quondam Matild'*e* Ernald ex concessione et reddicione Mabill*ie* Ernald. Fac' etc. saluo iure etc. Pleg' Reginald' de Hogate . et Thom' Dallinge.

<Finis xij d. Dominus recepit. W. Neugate>

De Rogero de Erpyngham \et Agnet*a* vxore/ eius pro ingressu habendo sibi et sequele sue in vno mesuagio et crufta continenti dimidiam acram terre quondam Ricardi Mariot . ex concess' et reddic' Iohannis Cat \et Oliue vxoris eius/. Fac. etc. saluo iure. Pleg' . Reginald' de Hogate et Thom' de Dallyngg'.

<Finis iij s. vj d., Modo Ioh' soluit domino ij s. vj d. et debet xij d.>

De Iohanne Cat et Oliua vxore eius pro Herieto . j . mesuagii et . j . acre et trium rodarum terre . post mortem Matill*de* Ernald matris predicte Oliue cuius heres ipsa est . et que inde obiit seisita etc. Pleg' Reginald' de Hogate et Thom' Dallyngg'.

<Preceptum est>

Preceptum est distringere Reginaldum le Shepperde in duabus peciis vna dimidie . rode apud Cleylond et vna rode et dimidie apud Westkotcroft . pro arreragiis seruic*iorum* et ad ostendendum qualiter ingressus est etc.

<Preceptum est>

Preceptum est distringere Rogerum carpentarium in dimidia. roda terre apud Nunnesdore ad ostendendum qualiter ingressus est et pro seruic*iis* aretro.

<'vacat quia infra'> [*entry cancelled*]

Agnes que fuit uxor Johannis Thurbern pro custodia habenda de uno mesuagio cum quatuor acris et dimida roda terre quondam predicti viri sui per minorem etatem Bartholomei filii sui qui nunc est etatis vii annorum. Et memorandum quod Clere que fuit uxor Rogeri Thurbern tenet in dotem et predicta Agnes similiter. Ita quod ad presens remanet preter dotes predictas . j acram j rodam . pleg. Rogerum de Hogate et Thomam de Dallyngg.

<Finis v s. Dominus recepit>

De Bartholomeo filio Iohannis Thurbern pro herieto . j . mesuagij cum quatuor acris et iij quateriis vnius rode terre post mortem predicti Iohannis cuius heres etc. Pleg' vt supra.

<Memorandum. Abbas de Derham>

Helwis*ia* et Cecilia filie Bartholomei Sutoris exhibuerunt quamdam cartam predicti Bartholomei per quam adquisierunt de predicto patre earum . \et de feodo domini/ . dimidiam . acram terre apud Scuklyf cuius caput occidentale abuttat super viam ducentem apud Leyrpittes anno regni . regis . nunc xix . habend' et tenend' prefatis sororibus et heredibus suis de corporibus earum procreatis de capitali domino feodi . per seruicia inde debita reseruata reuersione . etc. Reddendo . j . d. per annum. Et fecerunt fidelitatem.

<Thomas Aylesham tenet>

Item Agnes filia predicti Bartholomei . exhibuit cartam per quam predictus Bartholomeus dedit ei . j . rodam terre de feodo domini apud Warledhousty . habend' . sibi et heredi de se procreato de capitali domini feodi per seruicia etc. reseruata reuersione etc. tempore predicto . etc. Reddendo . ob. per annum. Et fecerunt fidelitatem.

<Finis xj s.>

De toto homagio pro arreragiis officij prepositi per . viij . annos allocato cuilibet eorum pro suo turno . de tempore predicto [cum] sibi \allocatis/ allocandis videlicet omnibus consuetudinibus . suis . et allocatis pro hoc anno iam instante pro terra in manu domini . sicut . fieri debet quolibet tercio anno ex consuetudine.

<Memorandum>

Ita quod in anno iam proximo futuro videlicet ad festum Sancti Michaelis recuperand' erit ad homagium predictum etc. et hoc ex conuencione coram domino prelocuta. etc.

<Offic'>

Reginaldus Thurbern electus ad officium messoris hoc anno. Et iuratus est.

Dorse

Prima curia anni.

CURIA IBIDEM DIE MERCURIJ PROXIMA POST FESTUM SANCTI ANDREE APOSTOLI ANNO REGNI REGIS EDWARDI TERCIJ POST CONQUESTUM PRIMO . 3 Dec. 1327

<Finis dimidia marca>

De Iohanne filio Reginaldi Thurberd pro herieto vnius mesuagij quatuor acrarum et dimidie terre post mortem predicti Reginaldi cuius heres etc. Et qui de parte obiit seisitus et cui de parte spectabat reuersio. Pleg' Thoma de Dallyngges et Iohanne Cat.

<Preceptum est>

Preceptum est sicut pluraliter distringere duas filias Gilberti Eluerich' ad ostendendum qualiter ingresse sunt feod' domini.

<Preceptum est>

Preceptum est sicut pluraliter capere et retinere in manu domini dimidiam rodam terre ad caput de Robbescroft quam Reginaldus de Berneye \tenet etc./

<Officium>

Presentant quod Agnes Hoddes debet officium messoris hoc anno. Et iurata est ad officium faciendum.

Presentant quod Ricardus Yudekil \et parcenarij sui/ debent officium prepositi hoc anno. Et fecit finem etc.

<Fines . iij s. ij . d.>

<Anlepimman>
 Agnes Gurle.
 Matill*da* Ernald.
<Finis ij s.>
 De Heruico Scoward pro terra sua habenda extra custod*iam* domini. et pro
maritagio suo. Pleg'. Thoma de Dallyngg' et Iohanne Cat. Et fecit domino
fidelitatem.

                                                      Prima curia anni.

[CURIA] IBIDEM DIE LUNE PROXIMA POST FESTUM
CONUERSIONEM SANCTI PAULI ANNO REGNI REGIS EDWARDI
TERCIJ POST CONQUESTUM TERCIO.   31 Jan. 1329

<Preceptum est>
 Preceptum est capere in manu domini . ij . pecias terre continentes j
rodam terre quas Mabillia ad caput ville dimisit Willelmo filio Alicie sine
licencia et iudicantur domino de exitibus.
<Finis vj d.>
 Postea fecit \finem/ domino de vj d. vt dominus cognouit etc. Ideo etc.
<Inquiratur>
 Emma que fuit vxor Reginaldi Osebern \exhibuit duas cartas per quas*f*/
Reginaldus de Berneye feoffauit Reginaldum Osebern et predictam Emmam
vxorem eius de duabus peciis terre de feodo domini . quarum vna iacet apud
West Cleylond et continet dimidiam rodam terre et iacet inter terram Claricie
de Hogate et terram Walteri Hamond [aquil'] et alia pecia j rode et dimidie .
apud Bondescroft . inter terram Claricie de Hogate et terram Abbatis de
Derham : habend' et tenend' predictis Reginaldo Osebern et Emma et
heredibus de corpore suo exeuntibus etc. capitali domino etc. Et si contingat
quod predicti Reginaldus et Emme obierint sine hered*ibus* de corpore suo
exeunt*ibus* tunc terra predicta hered*i* eiusdem Reginaldi remaneat. Et eadem
Emma admittitur vt tenens et fecit domino fidelitatem. Et recognouit se tenere
per seruicium j d. ob. per annum etc. pleg' Agn*eta* Hoddes. Presentant quod
Johannes Cat et Oliva uxor ejus debuerunt officium messoris hoc anno. De
omnibus de homagio quia contempserit eligere prepositum hoc anno.
<Abbas de Creyk>
 Preceptum est distringere abbatem de Creyk in dimidia acra terre apud
Billesmere quondam de villenagio domini de terra videlicet que fuit Gilberti
Gurle natiui etc. ad ostendendum qualiter ingressus est etc. et de quo et
qualiter tenere debet.
 De tota curia pro dispectu curiarum. [*Rest of line erased*]

[Memorandum] . quod recepit dominus hac die de Agne*ta* Hoddes messore de anno preterito . viij s. v d. ob.

Prima curia anni.

CURIA IBIDEM DIE IOUIS PROXIMA POST FESTUM SANCTE LUCIE VIRGINIS ANNO REGNI REGIS EDWARDI SUPRADICTI TERCIO.

14 Dec. 1329

<Inquiratur>

Iurat' de curia presentant quod Iohannes le Bulwere nuper obiit et tenuit de domino . iij . rodas terre in vna pecia vocata Mariotescroft . pro homagio fidelitate et seruicio . vj . d. et vnius caponis per annum . Et ad scutagium etc. Herede . predicti Iohannis plene etatis. Et preceptum est distringere pro homagio . fidelitate . Releuio . scutagio et aliis seruiciis aretro.

Presentant quod Thomas Dallyngge debet officium messoris Hoc anno. Et iuratus est.

<ij s.>

Presentant quod tenentes terre quondam Thurbern debent officium prepositi hoc anno.

Presentant quod . dimidia roda terre abuttans super viam que ducit de domo Willelmi filij Alicie vsque ecclesiam vnde Agne*ta* Gurle obiit seisita . remanere debet in manu domini vt eschaeta sua imperpetuum. Ideo preceptum est . etc.

De Ricardo Yudekyl pro defectu.

De Claricia de Hougate, Custancia Charles et Agne*ta* Hoddes pro defectu vnius precarie in autumpno.

[Entry about Thomas Aylesham erased]

Memorandum quod Hugo Otes nuper obiit et tenuit de domino mesuagium et cruftam quondam Petri filij Ade le Bret per seruicium militare. Et obijt in homagio domini. Edmundo filio suo et herede infra etatem cuius custodia et maritagium ad dominum pertinet etc. Et venit idem Edmundus et satisfecit domino de eisdem etc. per finem dimidie . marce etc.

Et memorandum quod dominus recepit hac die de Iohanne Cat messore anni precedentis de arreragiis [computi] sui . onerand' eum de curia tenta die Iouis proxima post festum conuersionis Sancti [Pauli] anno. Regni Regis Edwardi nunc tercio et deinceps vsque ad hanc curiam ix s. ix d.

[The last seventeen lines of the roll and the marginalia of the last thirty lines of the roll are too rubbed to be legible.]

VARIANTS: [a] Added later (22 Dec. 1322). [b] Ad festam Sancti Michaelis domini struck out (16 Dec. 1325). [c] Willelmi struck out (16 Dec. 1325., end.). [d] ij s. iij d. struck out (16 Dec. 1325, end.). [e] Mabilie struck out (27 Nov. 1324). [f] Cartam per quam struck out (31 Jan. 1329).

HD 81

Agenda arising from Neel manor court.   1329

NOTE: Parchment roll of 4 membranes of widely varying widths. Mem. 1 is 8½ in. wide.

HOLKHAM PRECEPTA CURIE IBIDEM EXEQUENDA ANNO REGNI REGIS EDWARDI TERCIJ POST CONQUESTUM TERCIO.

Preceptum est distringere Iohannem Wrighte in tenementis subscriptis que quondam fuerunt Rogeri Belneye ad ostendendum quem statum inde habet et videndum per que seruicia tenere debet de domino etc. videlicet in dimidia . acra ex parte orientali ecclesie quondam Iohannis de Dallyngge in quatuor acris apud Billesmere . et in vna acra apud Scuklif quondam Warini de [Whorles].*a*

Preceptum est distringere hered' Reginaldi le Shepperde in tenementis que quondam fuerunt Emme de Campo ad ostendendum per que seruicia [teneri debent]*a* rentale dicit de iiij . d. Et inquirere que quantum et vbi etc.

Preceptum est distringere hered' Rogeri filij Emme et inquiratur que tenementa \predictus Rogerus tenuit/ de feodo domini et per que seruicia quia dicit per seruicium iij d. per annum.

Preceptum est distringere Willelmum Craske et inquirere que tenementa tenet de domino et per que seruicia quia dicitur per . seruicium . iiij . d. quadr. sicut in tenemento.

Preceptum est distringere Thomam le Northerne et inquirere que tenementa tenet de domino post mortem Ricardi patris sui de tenemento quondam Iohannis Ide et similiter de terra Rutele quondam Natiui pro quibus redditibus. j. d. Et distringere pro homagio releuio et arreragiis redditus.

Preceptum est diligenter inquirere que tenementa Willelmus Silke quondam tenuit de feodo Bret et per que seruicia et qui modo sunt inde tenentes et eos distringere pro arreragiis eorumdem seruiciorum.

Preceptum est inquirere quid et quantum Willelmus Douk quondam tenuit de feodo le Bret et per que seruicia et qui modo sunt inde modo tenentes. Et distringere pro seruiciis aretro etc.

Preceptum est inquirere quid et quantum Willelmus Digge quondam tenuit de eodem feodo per que seruicia et qui modo sunt tenentes. Et distringere etc.

Preceptum est inquirere quid et quantum Heruicus Bolleman tenuit aliquando de eodem feodo per quod seruicium qui modo sunt tenentes et distringere etc.

Preceptum est inquirere quid et quantum Simon Charles tenuit aliquando de eodem feodo per quod seruicium. Et tenen*tes* distringere . etc.

Preceptum est inquirere quid et quantum . Iohannes filius Aǂe Bret tenuit aliquando de terra quondam Eborardi sub Monte natiui etc. et . per que seruicia. Et distringere.

Preceptum est inquirere de . iij . rodis terre dificientibus in terra quondam Roberti Ape eo quod vetus rentale mencionem facit de . v . acris et nouum rentale facit de [iiij]*b* acris j roda etc. et qui sunt modo inde tenentes per que seruicia et distringantur.

Preceptum est inquirere de . iij . rodis terre deficientibus in terra quondam Ernaldi sub Monte eo quod vetus rentale facit de iiij acris et nouum rentale de iij acris et j roda. Et qui sunt inde modo tenentes per que seruicia et distringantur.

Preceptum est inquirere de ij acris deficientibus de terra quondam Gilberti Gurle quia vetus rentale facit de iiij acris vbi nouum rentale nil de ij acris. Et qui inde modo sunt tenentes per que seruicia et distringantur.

<Bete>

Memorandum quod . j . mesuagium et [v] acre terre que Willelmus filius Bete aliquando tenuit in villenagio alienata sunt in diuersas manus. De quibus Mariota que fuit vxor Gilberti filij Radulfi tenet de mesuagio et crufta. dimidiam . acram in Hougate inter mesuagium quondam Gilberti Gurle et cruftam que fuit Willelmi Bete et caput orientale abbuttat super Hougate. Et debet inde reddere per annum vt dicit . j . d. \per annum/ Matil*da* Peper tenet inde . j . rodam apud Kirkecros . pro qua reddere debet vt dicit ob. per annum. Set quia terra predicta aliquando prius fuit Iohannis Broun qui soluit inde per annum ij d. ideo preceptum est distringere etc. Heruicus Scoward tenet inde de mesuagio et crufta dimidiam acram apud Kirkecros iacent' ex parte orientali ecclesie . j . rodam . apud Cleylond . dimidiam . rodam que tenementa quondam fuerit Rogeri filij Emme Reddendo per annum iij d. prout in veteri rentali. Et preceptum est eum distringere in tenementis predictis ad ostendendum qualiter ingressus est etc.

<Vicarius tenet>

Ricardus le Spellere tenet inde apud Westbondescroft . j . acram Reddendo . ij . d. ad pasch'. et ad festum Sancti . Michaelis . qualiter tamen inquirendum. Et preceptum est distringere.

<Preceptum est>

Emma que fuit [vxor] Reginaldi le Schepperde tenet ex parte occidentali ecclesie j . rodam terre . que est forrerra set per quod seruicium inquirendum. Et preceptum est distringere.

<Preceptum est>

Iuliana Le Sutere tenet inde apud [Scuk]lyf iuxta terram domini versus boriam dimidiam acram apud Wardelhousty . j . rodam. Reddendo vt dicit . j . d. ob. set qualiter inquirendum. Et preceptum est distringere etc.

<Preceptum est>

In manu domini Apud Scuklif quondam Roteney . j . acra et apud Wardelhousty . j . roda.

<Eborard'>

De iiij acris terre quondam Eborardi sub monte . Willelmus filius Alicie tenet apud Crucem . j . rodam Apud portam eius dimidiam rodam Apud West Cleylond dimidiam rodam In crofta quondam dicti Eborardi . dimidiam . acram . apud Estbondescroft j . rodam . Apud Scuklif . dimidiam . acram apud Wardelhousty j rodam ex parte australi de Burghhalle[7] j rodam que quondam fuerit Iohannis filij Ade le Bret. Reddendo . j . d. ob. prout in Rentali. Qualiter tamen inquirendum. Predictus Eborardus fuit natiuus et tenuit in villenagio.

<Preceptum est>

Et preceptum est distringere. Agneta que fuit vxor Gilberti le Smyth' tenuit apud West [Bondescroft] dimidiam acram . Reddendo j . d. quadr. que quidem terra quondam fuit Rogeri Eluerich'. Set tamen qualiter inquirendum.

<Preceptum est>

Et preceptum est distringere. In manu domini Apud Hardiesgate . j . roda Apud Billesmere dimidiam acram^c apud Steynhil . j roda . apud Wardelhousty j roda.

<Memorandum, inquiratur De Campo>

<Johannes Grygges>

De . iij . acris . j . roda terre quondam Rogeri de Campo . Dominus de Burghhalle tenet in mesuagio suo . versus . austrum j . rodam . dimidiam set qualiter inquirendum est per quod. Et preceptum est distringere.

Heredes Reginaldi le Schepperde tenent inde Apud Westbondescroft . j . rodam . et dimidiam et Apud Claylond [dimidiam rodam Reddendo] . j . d. ob. Set tamen quia prius fuit villenagium . Inquirendum est de modo ingressus. Et preceptum est distringere.

Bartholomeus et Iohannes de Hougate [tenent] inde Apud Scuklif . j . rodam . dimidiam Apud Cleylond . dimidiam . rodam . et . Apud Wichescroft . dimidiam rodam. Et inquirendum per quod seruicium qualiter [et quo modo]. Et preceptum est distringere . etc. Et in manu domini Apud Billesmere . dimidiam . acram Apud Steynhil . j . rodam dimidiam. Summa huius ij acre [j roda dimidia]. Et sic deficiunt iiij rod. dim. Et preceptum est inquirere qui sunt inde tenentes per que seruicia. Et distringantur.

De xij acris terre quondam Rogeri Ernald' Natiui. Inquirendum qui sunt modo tenentes per que seruicia et distringantur.

---

7   An indication that the Burghall manor house lay to the southwest of Holkham Town.

Willelmus Calthorp armiger tenet[d] De j [acra] terre quondam Ricardi Norne quam Margar*eta* Haukyn tenet in Nornescroft' reddendo j d. set dicitur quod plus reddere [consueuit].

Et de terra quondam Rutele quam predictus Ricardus Norne tenuit reddendo j d. inquirendum quantum et per quod seruicium [et qualiter] Et preceptum est distringere.

De vj acris terre quondam Thome Waryn. Inquirendum qui sunt inde modo tenentes per que seruicia. Et distringantur.

De vj acris terre quondam Iohannis filij Ade . Inquirendum qui sunt inde modo tenentes per que seruicia et distringantur.

De j roda terre quondam Ade Dersy. Inquirendum quis modo tenet et qualiter. Et distringatur.

De iiij acris terre quondam Hawisie Rutele dicitur quod Bartholomeus Margery tenet inde in crufta quondam predicte Hawisie . j . acram terre reddendo [*illegible*].

Set qualiter et quod modo inquirendum. Et distringatur. Et de residuo [inquirendum].

De j acra terre quondam Gillberti Gant Robertus Mayn nunc est tenens vt dicitur. Et est mesuagium et crufta quondam Willelmi [de Hindringham] reddendo per annum . ij . d. Set tamen qualiter ingressum habuit inquirendum. Et distringatur.

De iiij . acris terre quondam Rogeri molendinarii . Hugo Otes tenet mesuagium et cruftam continent' [*illegible*] debet inquirendum. Et distringatur.

Et de residuo inquirendum et tenentes inde distringantur.

Memorandum quod in nouo rentali dicitur quod tenentes terre quondam Ernaldi Vnderhou iiij d. reddent per annum ... [*The last five lines of the membrane are too damaged by damp to be legible.*]

VARIANTS: [a] The ends of lines are badly rubbed.   [b] The acreage is supplied from mem. 4.   [c] j rodam struck out.   [d] Inserted later.

Tenements acquired from William Roteney in Holkham [1329]

NOTE: Mem. 2, 75/8 in. wide x 43/4
Fiche 1: E13

TENEMENTA QUE RICARDUS NEL ET CATERINA VXOR EIUS ADQUISIERUNT DE WILLELMO ROTENEY IN HOLKHAM.[8]

Apud Duuspet iiij acre et dimidia.	De feodo quondam Bret.[9]
Apud Scucklyf. iiij. acre.	De eodem feodo.
Fere ibidem . j . acra.	De eodem feodo.
Fere ibidem . j . acra.	De eodem feodo.
Fere ibidem . j . roda dimid.	De eodem feodo.
Apud Baconescrondel di. acr.	De eodem feodo.
Apud Enedacre . di. acr.	De
Apud Slyngeshou . j . acr. j . rod.	De
Apud Ryngwareslond . j . acr. di . rod.	De feodo Bret.
Ad portam quondam Hardy . di . acr.	De Rogero Euerard' per obolum.
Apud Sladacre . ij . acr.	De Levegold[a] Payn per iiij . d.
Fere ibidem . j . rod.	De feodo Bret.
Item fere ibidem j. rod.	De eodem feodo.
Item fere ibidem . j. rod.	De eodem feodo.
Apud Larkescote . dim. acra.	De Wightone per iij d.
Fere ibidem . dim. acra.	De
Apud Duuescrondel di. acr. di . rod .	De Emma Humfrey per iij d.
Apud Pilleman . j . acra . j roda.[b]	De Wightone.
Apud Dalegate[c] j . acra.	De Bret.
Apud \Lethrgraues/[c] dimidia . acra dimidia . roda.	De Bret.
Apud \Lethrgraues/ . j . roda dimidia.	De Bret.
Apud Warldhousty . j . roda.	De
Apud Dallegate . j . acra iij . rode.	De feodo Dakeny.[b]
Ibidem . j . roda.	De eodem feodo.
Apud Fulmeresgate . j . acra.	De Priore de Petraston per obolum.
Apud Millested . j . roda . dimidia.	De Bret.
Apud Blakelond . j . roda . dimidia.	De Bret.

VARIANTS: [a] Possibly Leuegold in Ms. [b] This and the following lines are written in a third column in Ms. [c] Dalegraues struck out.

---

[8]   See HD 22a, Fo. 16 no. 186 and HD 32.
[9]   John le Bret's manor of Tobers became part of Hillhall, but the land of John son of Geoffrey le Bret went to the Neels.

Schedule of original lords of Neel lands   [1329]

NOTE: Mem. 3, 4¹/₂ in. wide

[1]   *Feodum W. Hak[oun].*

> iij Rode apud Stynhil.
> In eadem quarentena vij . rode.
> Apud Lithrpit . vij . rode.

<Walt'. Mes' de I . Silk'>

> Apud Wlfcrundel . v . rode.
> Apud Hadhowe . v . rode.
> In eadem quarentena . j . acra . ij . rode.
> Apud Ringwalelond . j . roda et dimidia.
> Apud Bondecruft . ij . rode.
> In eadem quarentena . vij . rode.
> In eadem quarentena . v . rode.
> Ad capud crufte Hardy . iij . rode et dimidia. Adam.
> In quarentena Lewerich' ij . rode.
> Apud Dale . j . roda et dimidia . terre . j . E . \Edrich'/. aquil.
> Apud Ringwalelond de h *er ed'*. C. j. roda et dimidia. M. Hardy
>
> aquil'.
>
> Apud Duuecrundel . ij . rode . ex parte orientali. W .
> In Hadhowebotme . v . rode . inter terram . Al. Brun aquil.
> In eadem quarentena . ij . rode . inter . R. Eluerich . aquil.

Summa . xvj . acre et dimidia.

[2]   *Feodum G[alfridi] le Bret.*

<G>

> Apud Hadhowe . vj . acre.
> In eadem quarentena . iij . acre.   }
> In eadem quarentena . ij . acre.   } Adam.
> Apud Osolfistung' . iij . acre.   }
> Apud Shortlond . j . acra.
> Apud Hangelond . iiij . acre.
> Apud Scutkelif . iij . rode j dimidia.   }
> In eadem quarentena . j . acra.   } Willelmus.
> In eadem quarentena . iiij . acre.   }
> Apud Hendaker . vij . rode. Adam.
> Apud Greyston vij rode. Hered'
> Apud Duuespeit iiij acre. Adam.
> Apud Bakunescrundel ij rode. Terr' I. } W[illelmus]
> Scil' austral'.

Apud Leirgraues ij rode.   }

        Terr' I. Bel austral'.

Apud Grenegate . j . acra.   }

Ad capud dicte pecie iij rode   } Hered'

In eadem quarentena . j . roda.   }

[Next column] [10]

De eodem feodo.

Ad Millestede . j . roda et dimidia. }

Ad portam Hardy . ij . rode.   }

Ad Warldhowesti . j . roda.   } W[illelmus].

Apud Feildhus . ij . rode.   }

De Roberto filio Emme . j . acra. }

        Summa xxxviij acre . j . roda.

Dorse

[3]   *Feodum Caly.*

Ex parte orientali ecclesie . iij rode . et dimidia.

Apud Cleylond . ij . rode.

Apud Bondescruft . ij . rode.

j roda abuttat super Osolfistung.

Apud Estadehowe . dimidia . roda.

        Summa ij acra . j . roda et dimidia.

[4]   *Feodum B[artholomei] de Burgate.*

Apud Wytewong' v . rode.

Apud Hadehowe . v . rode.

Apud Wandelond . v . rode.

Ad capud Crufte G. Godwynn . j . acra et dimidia.

Ad portam predicti G. v rode.

Apud Brueram . ij . acre et dimidia.

        Summa . ix . acre

[5]   *Feodum W. Curthon senioris.*

Apud Hadehowebotme . iij . rode et dimidia.

Apud Sladaker . j . roda.

Apud Kappescrundel . j . roda.

        Summa . v . rode et dimidia.

---

10   Written parallel to Feodum W. Hakun. This evidently continues Feodum G. le Bret which would otherwise lack a summa.

[6] *Feodum W. [Curthun] iunioris.*

Apud Dalegate . j . acra.   }
Apud Pileman . v . rode.   }
Apud Larkescote . ij . rode.   } W[illelmus]
In eadem quarentena . j .   }
roda et dimidia.
Apud Litelhowe j . rode   }
Apud Sladacr' . ij rode.   }

Summa . iiij . acre et dimidia roda.

[7] De . I . Charles . j . acra et dimidia.

[8] De Stephano Ossebern iij rode.

Summa ij acre et j roda.

Other agenda arising from Neel manor court

NOTE: This schedule of agenda on mem. 4 is written in the same hand as mem. 1 but on
a shorter piece of parchment 6½ in. wide.

HOLKHAM ROTULUS PRECEPTORUM CURIE RICARDI NEL IBIDEM
DE ANNO REGNI REGIS . EDWARDI . TERCIJ POST CONQUESTUM
TERCIO.   1329

Preceptum est distringere Johannem le Wrighte in tenementis que
quondam fuerunt Rogeri Belneye videlicet j dimidia acram terre ex parte
orientali ecclesie quondam Johannis de Dallyngge. In quatuor acris terre apud
Billesmere et in j acra terre apud Scuklif que quondam fuit Martini de
Wharles ad ostendendum per que servicia clamat etc.

Preceptum est distringere heredem Reginaldi le Shepperde et inquirere que
tenementa tenet que quondam fuerunt Emme de campo et per que servicia.

Distringantur heredes Rogeri filii Emme et inquirere tenementa tenuit de
domino et per que servicia.

Inquiratur quid et quantum Willelmus Craske tenuit de domino et per que
servicia et distringatur.

Inquiratur quid et quantum Thomas le Northerne tenet de domino/ post
mortem patris sui de tenemento quondam Johannis Ide . et similiter de terra
Rutele et distringere pro homagio et fidelitate et relevio et arreragiis redditus.

Inquiratur quid et quantum Willelmus Silke quondam tenuit de domino et per que servicia et qui sunt modo tenentes inde. Et distringantur.

Inquiratur quid et quantum Willelmus Douk quondam tenuit de domino per que servicia et qui nunc tenent. Et distringantur.

Inquiratur quid et quantum Willelmus Digge quondam tenuit de domino per que servicia et qui nunc tenent. Et distringantur.

Inquiratur quid et quantum Hervicus Bulleman aliquando tenet de domino per que servicia et qui nunc tenent. Et distringantur.

Inquiratur quid et quantum Simon Charles aliquando tenet de domino per que servicia et qui nunc tenent. Et distringantur.

Inquiratur quid et quantum Johannes filius Ade Bret aliquo tenet de domino de terra que quondam Eboradi sub Monte per que servicia. Et distringantur.

Inquiratur de iij rodis terre deficientibus de v acris/ in terra quondam Robert Ape. Et tenentes inde distringantur.

Inquiratur similiter de iij rodis terre deficientibus de iiij acris terre quondam Ernaldi sub monte. Et tenentes inde distringantur.

Inquiratur de ij acris terre deficientibus de iiij acris terre quondam Gilberti Gurle. Et tenentes inde distringantur.

Preceptum est distringere tenentes j mesuagii et v acrarum terre que Willelmus filius Bete aliquando tenuit in villenagio pro serviciis a retro videlicet Mariota que fuit uxor Gilberti filii Radulfi que tenet de mesuagio et crufta dimidiam acram in Hougate Matilda Peper que tenet inde j rodam apud Kirkecros Hervicus Scoward qui tenet inde de mesuagio et crufta dimidiam acram. Apud Kirkecros j rodam. Ex parte orientale ecclesie j rodam et Apud Cleylond dimidiam rodam que quondam fuerunt Rogeri filii Emme Ricardus le Spellere tenet inde apud Westbondescroft j acram Emma que fuit uxor Reginaldi le Schepperde tenet inde ex parte occidentale ecclesie j rodam et est forrera Juliana le Sutere tenet inde apud Scuklif juxta terram domini versus borealem dimidiam acram. Et preceptum est omnes distringere ad ostendendum per que servicia tenere clamant.

Preceptum est distringere tenentes iiijor acrarum terre quondam Eborardi sub monte videlicet Willelmum filium Alicie qui tenet inde apud Crucem j rodam. Apud Westclaylond dimidiam rodam. In Crufta quondam dicti – Eborardi dimidiam acram. Apud Estlondescroft i rodam. Apud Scuklif dimidiam acram. Apud Wardelhousty j rodam. Ex parte australi de Burghhalle j rodam Agnes que fuit uxor Gilberti le Smith tenet inde apud Westbondescroft dimidiam acram quondam Rogeri Eluerich. Et preceptum est pro arreragiis redditus.

Preceptum est distringere tenentes iij acrarum et j rodam terre quondam Rogeri de Campo unde dominus de Burghhalle tenet in mesuagio suo versus australem j rodam et dimidiam.

Heredes Reginaldi le Scheppere tenent apud Westlondescroft j rodam et dimidiam et Apud Claylond dimidiam rodam. Bartholomeus et Johannes de Hougate tenent inde Apud Skuklif j rodam et dimidiam. Apud Clailond dimidiam rodam et apud Wichescroft dimidiam rodam . Et preceptum est eos distringere pro arreragiis serviciorum. Et quia deficiunt de terra predicta iij rode et dimidia praeter iij rodas et dimidiam que sunt in manu domini supra non nominate Ideo preceptum est inquirere qui sunt inde tenentes et distringere.

De xij acris terre quondam Rogeri Ernald nativi. Inquirendum qui sunt tenentes et per que servicia, Et distringantur.

Preceptum est distringere Margaretam Haukyn in vna acra terre in Nornescroft quondam Ricardi Norne qui tenuit in villenagio pro serviciis a retro.

Inquiratur de terra quondam Rutele quam Ricardus Norne aliquando tenuit qui sunt modo tenentes . Et distringantur.

De vj acris terre quondam Thome Waryni. Inquirendum qui sunt inde modo tenentes et distringantur.

De vj acris terre quondam Johannis filii Ade. Inquirendum qui sunt inde modo tenentes. Et distringantur.

De j roda terre quondam Ade Dersy . Inquirendum quis modo tenet. Et distringatur.

Adhuc de eodem

Dorse

De iij acris terre quondam Hawisie Rutele. Inquirendum qui sunt inde modo tenentes. Et distringantur pro serviciis a retro.

Preceptum est distringere vel facere venire Robertum Mayn, vel tenentes mesuagii et cruftae quondam Willelmi de Hindringham.

Preceptum est distringere Heredes Hugonis Otes et alios tenentes trium acrarum terre quondam Reginaldi Molendinarii pro servicio a retro.

Inquirendum de j acra terre quam heredes Johannis Aynild tenent vel tenuerunt pro qua reddent iij ob. ubi jacet. Et distringantur pro arreragiis serviciorum.

Dower of Katerine Neel in Burnham [1329]

REDDITUS QUOS KATERINA NEEL DEBET SOLVERE PER ANNUM
PRO DOTE SUA IN BRUNHAM

Pro terra apud le Chryne ij s. d. ob.
ad duos terminos et ij d. ad wardam douveri
Pro vii peciis per cartam Radulfi de
Hernenhalle ij d.
Pro tertia parte j acre apud Redlond qa.
Pro feodo Ade de Brankestre de quo
tenet tertiam et de aliquibus.med. vj d.
ad Fest. Sancti Michaelis.
Pro tertia parte v rodarum apud
Bustardhyl ad S. Sanct. Mich. ob.
Pro medietate j rode et dimidie apud
Stupemars ob.
Pro tertia parte dimidie acre apud
Bustardeswong qa.
Pro medietate tenementi Abbatis de
Ramesey et ad
Schyrenechot j d. qa.
Pro diversis peciis apud Redlond ob.

Pro tertia parte dimidie acre in Suttone ob.
Pro tertia parte iij peciarum j d.
Pro tertia parte iij acrarum apud
Stanhowesty j d. qa.
Pro medietate xj rodarum super
Brungeshowe qa.
Pro tertia parte magne pecie ibidem j d.
Pro tertia parte Longelond ob.
Pro tertia parte ij acrarum
apud Lamkotswong ob.
Pro tertia parte Dunkesdelehyl qa.
Pro tertia parte/ Chortlond et
aliarum peciarum j d.
Pro tertia parte Longebusk ob.
Pro tertia parte de Berkelesdale qa.
Pro iij rodis et dimidie ibidem qa.
Pro tertia parte de Friserildesty qa.

Pro Dunkesdeleshyl iij qa.

Pro tertia parte
de Berdemere iij d.
Pro tertia parte de Scephouse j d.
Pro v rodis ad Ryberesty ob.
Pro ij peciis ad Superdewong
et sub Holdhowe j d. o. qa.
Pro j pecia ad veterem
crucem qa.
Pro fourtene acre j d.
Pro le Hewemere et turnefers ob.
Pro sede Saliati j d. qa.
et ad Chyrehenechot j d.
Pro ij acris apud
Fourteneacres j d.

Pro feodo ecclesie
Sancte Margarete iiij d.
Pro Garbrodlondes ob.
Pro Millecroft j d.
Pro Cleylond qa.

Pro parte de Kalkhyl vj d.

Pro parte j rode in Depesdale qa.

Summa ix s. xj d. qa. de quibus v s. xj d. qa. soluti sunt
ad festum Sancti Michaelis et iiij s. ad Pascham.

HD 82

First Court after lease by Earl of Atholl to Richard Neel, Henry and Gilbert Burgeys and William of Waterden.   3 July 1332

NOTE: Parchment 95/8 in. wide on which is sewn a small piece 21/2 in. long, containing the collector's account of Richard Blakeman (1332).
Fiche 1: E14

HOLKHAM. CURIA RICARDI NEEL, HENRICI BURGEYS, GILBERTI BURGEYS ET WILLELMI DE WATERDEN' TENTA DIE VENERIS PROXIMA POST FESTUM SANCTORUM PETRI ET PAULI APOSTOLORUM ANNO REGNI REGIS EDWARDI TERTIJ POST CONQUESTUM [SEXTO].

Prima curia post dimissionem domini comitis. etc.[11]

<Aff>

Thomas Storm \quer'./ versus Simonem Mous preceptum est distringere de placito debiti per Iohannem Mey . pleg' . Ricardo Spellere . et Willelmo Buleman.

<Aff>

Iohannes le Smith senior \quer'./ versus . Ricardum de Steynton et Ceciliam vxorem eius de placito transgressionis per Iohannem le Wryghte pleg' Bartholomeo Miller*e* et Rogero Ode.

<Aff>

Iohannes le Smith senior \quer'./ versus . Roeseam le Bulwere de placito transgressionis . per Ricardum Blakeman pl. Iohanne Wrighte et Iohanne Mey.

<Finis. vj . d.>

De Simone Mous pro licencia concordandi cum Willelmo filio Alicie de placito transgressionis . pleg' . Ricardo Blakeman et Iohanne Mey.

<Finis. iij . d.>

De Iohanne le Smyth' iuniore pro . licencia . concordandi . cum Iohanne Daulyn in placito transgressionis . pleg' . Iohanne Mey.

<Finis j . d.>

De Iohanne le Smith' iuniore . pro . licencia . concordandi . cum Iohanne le Mey in placito transgressionis . pleg' Iohanne Mey.

<Finis ij . s. vj . d.>

De Alicia le Wrighte pro ingressu habendo sibi et sequele sue in dimidia . acra et dimidia . roda terre apud Nighenacres \et Claylond./ ex concessione et reddicione Alicie Hamond. Facit etc. saluo iure etc. Pleg' Ioh' Wrighte . et messor.

---

11   The lease indenture is printed infra, HP 1080, 30 May 1332.

<Finis xviij . d.>

De Alicia filia Bartholomei Calwere pro ingressu . habendo . sibi et sequele sue in . j . roda et dimidia . apud Wellegate . ex concessione et reddicione Heruici Vallet et Sayue vxoris eius facta extra Curia. Facit etc. saluo iure etc. Pleg' . messore. Et fecit fidelitatem.

<Finis ix . d.>

De Rychemaya Broun pro ingressu habendo sibi et sequele sue in tria quarteria vnius rode terre . apud Schipmancros . ex concessione et reddicione Sayue filie Rogeri le Chapman . facta extra Curiam Facit etc. saluo iure etc. Pleg' . messor.^a

<Finis ij . d.>

De Ricardo Blakeman pro licencia concord' cum Reginaldo Crane in placito debiti. Pleg' messor.^a

<Finis vj . d.>

De Willelmo Curthoun pro ingressu habendo sibi et sequele sue in . j . roda terre . apud Lambulhil ex concessione et reddicione Agnete Reynald. Facit etc. saluo iure etc. Pleg' messore.^a

<Finis ix . d.>

De Willelmo Curthoun pro ingressu habendo sibi et sequele sue in . iij . quarter' vnius rode terre apud Schipman cros ex concessione et reddicione Agnete Rauen. Facit . etc. saluo iure . etc. Et ista reddicio . facta fuit extra curiam Pleg'. messore.

<Finis xij . d.>

De Galfrido Balteyn^b et Agneta vxore eius pro ingressu Habendo sibi et sequele sue in vno Cotagio cum vna crufta continentibus j . rodam terre ex concessione et reddicione Bartholomei Colyn . extra curiam Facit . etc. saluo iure etc. pleg' Ioh. Mey . et messor.

<Finis iij . d.>

De Amicia de Burgate pro ingressu habendo . sibi et sequele sue in . j . roda terre apud Wadlondes . ex concessione et reddicione Matillde vxoris Bartholomei Carpe. Facit . etc. saluo iure etc. Pleg' . messore

<Finis iij . d.>

De Agneta Le Bulwere pro licencia . concordandi cum Alicia Otes . in placito capcionis vnius vacce. Pleg'. messor.

<Finis xx . s. Fidelitatem>

De Roberto de Cetlestone et Helewisiam vxorem eius pro ingressu Habendo sibi et sequele sue in . vno mesuagio cum crufta continentibus . vnam rodam terre et dimidiam in Northgate . ex concessione et reddicione Iohannis le Wrighte. Facit etc. saluo iure etc. pleg' Iohanne Mey . et messore.

<Misericordia ij . d. Preceptum est>

De Rosea le Bulwere pro defalta. Et preceptum est retinere districciones factas super eam per duos bidentes et . ij . porcos et capere plures . quousque iusticiauerit se ad respondendum Simon Mous de placito . debiti.

<Preceptum est>

De sex acris terre quas Ida Godwyne . clamat tenere libere in exheredacione. eo quod tenere debet in villenagio etc. vt dicitur. Preceptum est vt prius retinere etc.

<Misericordia. Con'>

De Willelmo^c Huberd pro defalta Et preceptum est sicut pluries ponere eum per meliores plegios . ad respondendum . Ricardo Spellere de placito detencionis catall'. \Non prosequitur/.

<Preceptum est>

Preceptum est sicut plur' distringere Thomam filium Miriele Cosche pro fidelitate.

<Misericordia. Condonatur.>

De Rosea le Bulwere pro defalta. Et preceptum est retinere districciones super eam^d factas vt supra et plur' capere etc. ad . respondendum . Galfrido Crome de placito debiti.

<Preceptum est>

De Adam Charle \iuniore/ pro defalta et preceptum est retinere vnam tunicam albam pret'. vj . d. Et vnum Barmskyn pretij . xij . d. et plures capere etc. quousque etc. ad respondendum Simoni Burgonye de placito debiti.

<Preceptum est>

Preceptum est sicut plur' retinere in manu domini . j . rodam terre quam Rogerus Attehil tenet \exitus . dimidium quarterium . ordei precij ij . s./ Et . j . rodam terre quam Andreas Vnderclynt tenet \exitus ij buss. pisarum precij x d./ pro eo quod se maritauerit sine licencia.

<Misericordia xij . d.>

De Iohanne Attedale quia maritauit filiam suam sine licencia. pleg. Willelmo Buleman . Et habet diem vsque ad festum Sancti Michaelis prox' futur'.

<Misericordia. Condonatur>

De Willelmo Gunnok' pro defalta

<Misericordia j . d.>

De Thoma Northerne et plegiis suis quia non est prosequens . versus . Willelmum Gunnok' in placito debiti.

<Misericordia j . d.>

De Simone Mous pro eodem.

<Misericordia j . d.>

De Ricardo Blakeman pro eodem.

<Misericordia j . d.>

De Iohanne le Wrighte pro eodem.

<Misericordia j . d.>

De Iohanne de Warham pro defalta. Et preceptum est retinere per meliores plegios . ad respondendum . Iacobo Bettes de placito debiti. Postea predictus Iacobus ponit . se.

<Preceptum est>

Preceptum est sicut alias leuare de Ricardo le Bulwer ad opus Roberti atte Esh et Aliciam vxorem eius iij . s.

<Misericordia. Pauperi>

De Ricardo le Deye . et Iohanne Craske pro defalta. Et preceptum est facere venire ad . respondendum . Simonem Burgonye de placito debiti.

<Pleg' Preceptum est>

Preceptum est sicut alias capere in man' domini iij quarteria vnius rode terre quam Seyua filia Godmanni Chapman vendidit Iohanni Meyre sine licencia.

<Recogn' . xl . d.>

De toto homagio pro recognicione . pleg' quilibet alterius.

<Misericordia . iiij . d.>

De Rosea Bulwere pro pluribus defaltis. Et preceptum est ipsam distringere ad respondendum Simoni Mous et ad respondendum Galfrido Crome \non prosequitur/ vtrique de placito debiti.

<Preceptum est>

Preceptum est distringere Ricardum le Bulwere ad respondendum Thome le Northerne de placito debiti.

<Misericordia ij . d.>

De Ricardo Steyntone et Cecilia vxore eius pro defalta. Et preceptum retinere . ij . bidentes super eos capt' . et capere plures. ad . respondendum Iohanni le Smith seniori de placito transgressionis.

<Misericordia ij . d.>

De Edmundo Tebbe et plegiis suis videlicet Iacobo Bette . et Messore quia non est prosequens versus . Agnetam Troweman in placito debiti.

<Preceptum est>

Preceptum est distringere Simonem Mous . ad . respondendum Thome Storm de placito debiti.

<Misericordia ij d.>

De Roberto Elyot pro defalta. Et preceptum est ipsos facere venire ad . respondendum . Simoni Mous de placito detencionis vnius Stremere.

<Preceptum . est >

Mirielda Cosche optulit se versus Iohannem le Smithe in . placito terre et petit . versus . eum vnam acram et tres rodas terre cum pertinenciis in Holkham vt ius suum etc. Et predictus Iohannes non venit. Et diem sibi alias

sibi datum per essoniam non obseruauit. Ideo terra predicta capiatur in man'
domini. Et preceptum est summon*ire* predictum Iohannem quod sit ad
proximam curiam . ad . respondendum de eadem defalta.
<Preceptum est>

Mirielda Cossche . \optulit . se ./ versus . Iohannam filiam Ricardi
Blakeman \optulit se/ de placito terre. Et petit . versus eum. vnam rodam et
dimidiam terre cum pertinenciis in Holkham vt ius suum etc. Et predicta
Iohanna non venit. Et diem alias sibi datum per essoniam non obseruauit.
Ideo terra predicta capiatur in manu domini. Et Preceptum est summonire
predictam Iohannam quod sit ad proximam curiam ad respondendum de
eadem defalta.
<Misericordia ij . d.>

De Iohanne Charle pro defalta
<Misericordia ij . d.>

De Helwisia Carpe pro eodem.
<Misericordia ij . d.>

De Ricardo Bulwere pro eodem.
<Misericordia j . d.>

De Heruicio Vallet pro eodem.
<*Misericordia*. iij d.>

De Iohanne Spellere pro eodem.
<Non sum'>

De Adam Silke pro eodem.
<. ij d.>

De Beatrice Otes pro eodem.
<ij d.>

De domino Willelmo persona ecclesie de Holkham . pro eodem.
<ij d.>

De Ed*mund*o Praywen pro eodem.
<Pauper>

De Rogero del Hil pro eodem.
<Preceptum est>

Preceptum est distringere dominum Willelmum de Calethorp' . dominum
priorem de Petra*ston* . Iohannem Charle . Willelmum Godwyne . Helwisiam
Carpe . Ricardum Bulwere . Heruicum Vallet . Iohannem Spellere .
Gilbertum Crane . Henricum Camplyoun . Henricum Chapman . Matilldam
Sweyn . Willelmum Edwy . Willelmum Acke . Rogerum Carpentarium .
Adam Sylke . Iohannem Iernemuth . Laurencium Crumme . Alexandrum de
Oxle . Bartholomeum filium Cecilie . Agnetam Whitbred . Beatricem Otes .
Galfridum de Scharneton . Willelmum Huberd . Iohannem de Hapesburghe .
Iohannem Maynard . dominum Willelmum personam ecclesie de Holkham .
Rogerum Broun . Bartholomeum Carpe . Ed*mundu*m Praywen . Rogerum

Colyn . Iohannem Asty . Willelmum Bere . Ceciliam Northerne . Iohannam filiam Ricardi Blakeman . Walterum Derse . Heruicum Yudekyl . Iohannem de Grace . Iohannem Lomb . Bartholomeum del Hil . Thomam del Hil . Rogerum del Hil . et omnes alios tenentes manerij qui nondum fecerunt fidelitatem etc . ad faciendum fidelitatem.

Pro summa xxxv s. viij d. et exitus.

Iohannes Mey

Afferatores   Ricardus Blakeman   Iurat'

VARIANTS: *a* The nominative, not the ablative, are used equally. *b* Balteys is the normal form of this name. *c* An interlineated word might be iunore or seniore. *d* eum in Ms.

Burghall Manor collector's account, 24 June–29 Sept. 1332

NOTE: Sewn on to this membrane at the level of the leet court, 22 July 1332

VISUS COMPOTI[12] RICARDI BLAKEMAN COLLECTORIS . A FESTO NATIUITATIS SANCTI IOHANNIS BAPTISTE . ANNO REGNI REGIS . EDWARDI TERCIJ POST CONQUESTUM SEXTO VSQUE AD FESTUM SANCTI MICHAELIS PROXIME SEQUENTIS ETC.

<Recepta>

Idem respondet de xviij . s. redditus de termino Sancti Iohannis Baptiste . De . vj . d. ob. de Wardese pro termino Pentecost'. de . iiij . li . x . s. ij . d. de placitis et perquisicionibus Curiarum et Lete. De . ij . s. x . d. de exitibus terrarum captarum in manu domini etc. Et de vij . s. ij d. de iiij^{xx}. vj . precariis autumpnalibus venditis.

Summa receptorum . cxviij . s. viij . d. ob.

<Inde>

Liberat' domino per diuersas parcellas per indenturam . lxxiij . s. iiij . d. Allocat' ei in manu predicti domini . fratri Ade de Hundecrundel de quodam amerciamento Lete . vj . d. Pro Ricardo Bulwere quia non leuari potuit . ij d. Pro Iohanne Charle . iij . d. Pro Roberto Elyot . ij . d. Pro Ricardo de Steyntone' . ij . d. Pro . Rosea Bulwere . ij . d. Pro Alicia de Olneye \j . d./ Pro Thoma Northerne . j . d. Pro Iohanne Silk j d. Pro capitalibus plegiis de concelamento . ij . s. Allocat' ei pro quadam Gersuma de Helwisia Carpe quia domina recepit . xxxij . d. Item allocat' ei pro officio suo . pro . xxx

---

12   This Burghall collector's account is earlier than HD 84 of 1333–4 or those in PRO SC 6/937/16 (1363–77).

precariis autumpnalibus . ij . s. vj . d. Pro Iohanne le Smith'. j . d. Pro Simone Mous . j . d.

Summa huius solucionum et allocacionum iiij . li . ij . s. iiij . d. sic reman' xxxvj . s. iiij . d. ob. postea allocatur ei pro Benebred . xxijs. x d. videlicet pro . cccc . lxviij . precariis autumpnalibus receptis pro qualibet die ob. Et sic reman' . xiij . s. vj . d. ob. Postea vt supra. Postea allocatum ei de quibusdam exitibus terrarum vt supra quia dominus partem recepit et partem perdonauit . ij . s. In manu predicti domini Ade Crask' de quodam amerciamento. j . d. Et soluit xj s. j . d. Item . iiij d. ob. Et sic eque.

Burghall Leet Court

22 July 1332

LETA ET CURIA TENTA IBIDEM DIE MERCUIJ IN FESTO SANCTE MARIE MAGDALENE ANNO REGNI REGIS SUPRADICTI SEXTO

<Afferatur>

Ricardus de Steynton versus Johannem le Smith quer. op. se de placito trespassus per Johannem Mey pleg. Ricard. Blakeman et Ricard. Coupere.

<Afferatur>

Cecilia uxor ejus de eodem pleg. Will. filius Alicie.

<Finis . ij. d.>

De Rosea le Bulwere versus Johannem le Smith quer. op. se de placito trespassus per Simonem Mous pleg. Joh. Mey et Messor.

<Finis . ij. d.>

De Rosea Bulwere pro licentia concordand cum Simone Mous in placito debiti pleg. Ricard. Blakeman.

<Finis . ij. d.>

De Thoma Storm et plegiis suis videlicet Ricardo Spellere et Willelmo Buleman quia non est prosecutus versus Simonem Mous in placito debiti.

<Finis . ij. d.>

De Ricardo Spellere et plegiis suis videlicet messore quia non est prosecutus versus Willelmum Huberd de placito detentionis catallorum.

<Finis . xij. d.>

De Luca filio Johannis Parmelay pro ingressu habendo sibi et sequele sue in vno cotagio apud Crosgate ex concessione et redditione predicti Johannis facta vt salvo jure. Et pro ista redditione predictus Luca reconcessit eidem Johanni predictum cotagium tenendum in tota vita sua salva reversione pleg. Jacobo Betes et Johanni Parmelay.

<Finis . ij. d.>

De Johanne de Jerum pro despectu curie per annum integrum integrum pleg. messore.

<Finis . ij. d.>

De Bartholomeo Coltyng pro licentia concord. cum Thome filio Willelmi in placito trespassus pleg. Joh. Mey.

<Misericordia . j. d.>

De eodem Bartholomeo et plegiis suis videlicet Johanne Mey et Johanne Belneye quia non est prosecutus versus Thomam filium Willelmi in placito trespassus.

<Misericordia . j. d.>

De Elena Cat quia reponit blada sua extra villenagium domini.

<Misericordia . j. d.>

De Bartholomeo Atte Hil pro eodem.

<Misericordia . j. d.>

De Simone le Coupere pro eodem.

<Misericordia . j. d.>

De Alicia filia Johannis le Wrighte pro eodem

<Misericordia . j. d.>

De Beatricia Huberd pro eodem.

<Misericordia . j. d.>

De Willelmo Crane pro eodem.

<Misericordia . j. d.>

De Henrico Camplioun pro eodem.

<Misericordia . j. d.>

De Henrico Chapman pro eodem.

<Misericordia . j. d.>

De Thomas Astier pro eodem.

<Misericordia . j. d.>

De hered. Johannis Cappe pro eodem.

<Misericordia . j. d.>

De Simone Mous pro eodem.

<Misericordia . j. d.>

De Agnes Aleyn pro eodem.

<Misericordia . ij. d.>

De Johanne le Wrighte pro eodem.

<Misericordia . j. d.>

De Johanne Parmelay pro eodem.

<Misericordia . j. d.>

De hered. Ricardi Tryntenale pro eodem.

<Misericordia . j. d.>

De Johanne atte Dale pro eodem.

<Misericordia . j. d.>
  De Margareta Godecok pro eodem.
<Misericordia . j. d.>
  De Cecilia Godecok pro eodem.
<Misericordia . j. d.>
  De Hugone le Sutere pro eodem.
<Misericordia . j. d.>
  De Mirielda Cosche pro eodem.
<Misericordia . iij. d.>
  De Galfrido le Heyward pro eodem.
<Misericordia . j. d.>
  De her. Thome Sweyn pro eodem.
<Misericordia . j. d.>
  De Gilberto le Chapman pro eodem.
<Misericordia . j. d.>
  De Johanne le Spellere pro eodem.
<Condonatur>
  De Simone Bulwere pro eodem.
<Misericordia . j. d.>
  De Ricardo Asner pro eodem.
<Misericordia . j. d.>
  De Ricardo Blakeman pro eodem.
<Misericordia . j. d.>
  De Agneta Bryche pro eodem.
<Misericordia . j. d.>
  De Simone le Smith ad molendinum pro eodem.
<Misericordia . j. d.>
  De Rogero de Reppes pro eodem.
<Misericordia . j. d.>
  De Custancia Charles pro eodem.
<Misericordia . j. d.>
  De Helwysia Whynne pro eodem.
<Misericordia . j. d.>
  De Johanne Tardy pro eodem.
<Misericordia . j. d.>
  De Helwysia Jay pro eodem.
<Misericordia . j. d.>
  De Matilda Freshbred pro eodem.
<Misericordia . j. d.>
  De Ricardo Wrighte pro eodem.
<Misericordia . ij. d.>
  De Helwysia le Meyrè pro eodem.

<Misericordia . j. d.>

De Johanne Meynard pro eodem.

<Misericordia . j. d.>

De Rosea Bulwere pro eodem.

Preceptum est capere . j. rodam dim. terre juxta Wardehousty quam Sibilla Debeth dimisit Gilberto de Folsham sine licencia.

P.e. capere . iij. rodas terre apud Stafgatemere quam Johan. Asty dimisit Johani Beneyt sine licencia.

Terra quondam Galfridy le Gynun pro . xij. acris debet officium prepositi hoc anno . postea tota curia elegit . xij. acras terre quod Godman Burgoine debet idem officium a festo Sancti Michaelis proximo futuro.

Terra quondam Johannis Dersy et parcenarius ejus debet officium messoris pro . vj. acris terre hoc anno a festo Sancti Michaelis prox. futur.

<Finis . iij. d.>

De Domino Waltero le Bulwere capellano pro ingressu habendo sibi et sequele sue in duabus acris et dimidie terre ex concessione er redditione Ricardi le Bulwere facta coram quibusdam de homagio extra curiam nomine pignoris sub hac forma videlicet quod predictus Ricardus solvat predicto domino Waltero ad festum Sancti Michaelis prox. futur. . xiiij. quarter. ordei tunc terra predicta predicto Ricardo quiete et integre revertatur sin autem terra predicta predicto Waltero quiete et integre remaneat inperpetuum per finem de novo tunc faciend.

<Capitales Plegii>

    Johan. le Wrighte.

    Johan. le Mey.

    Johan. le Smith.

    Reginald Crane.

    Roger Odes.   <Jurati>

    Johan. Crane.

    Godmannus Burgonye.

    Willelmus filius Alicie.

    Simon Burgonye.

    Johan. Tordy.

    Willelmus Whyte.

    Rogerus de Reppes.

<Afferatores>

    Johan. Mey.

    Ricardus Blakeman.

<Probatores>

    Johan. Mey.

    Gervasius de Ryburg.

De Capitalibus Plegiis ne evasion ... quilibet eorum alterius. Et hoc ex annua consuetudine.

<Misericordia . j. d.>

Presentant quod Bartholomeus Coltyng traxit sanguinem de Thoma filio Willelmi maliciose. Ideo in misericordia pleg. Johan. Mey.

Dorse

Adhuc

<Misericordia . xij. d.>

Capitales plegii presentant quod Abbas de Derham leuavit quamdam faldam injuste et ante tempus.

<Misericordia . iij. d.>

Capitales plegii presentant quod Thomas filius Willelmi traxit sanguinem de Bartholomeo Coltyng maliciose pleg. Simon . Burgoine.

<Misericordia . ij. d.>

Presentant quod Berta atte Drone fecit hamsoken Alicia Digge. Ideo in misericordia.

<Misericordia . iij. d.>

Presentant quod Edmundus Haldeyn fecit hamsoken Rogero de Monte.

<Misericordia . ij. d.>

Presentant quod Willelmus de Warham manucaptor Helwysie le Mayre fecit rescussum Reginaldo de Thorpe de bidentibus captis in dampno suo.

<Misericordia . ij. d.>

Presentant quod Heruicus Lode fecit rescussum Ricardo Blakeman de una districcione facta pro executione debiti.

<Misericordia . vj. d.>

Presentant quod Margareta Otes et Alicia Otes . fregerunt parcum domini de quatuor porcis captis pro debito domini et executione judicii curie.

<Misericordia . iij. d.>

Presentant quod Alicia Otes fecit rescussum Ballivo domini de quodam velo capto pro executione judicii curie domini.

<Misericordia . iij. d.>

Presentant quod Agnes Bulwere fecit rescussum Ballivo domini de vna vacca capta pro eo ad quer. Alicie Otes.

<Misericordia . iij. d.>

Presentant quod Mariota manucaptor Henrici Spellere fecit rescussum Willelmo filio Thome de . ij. equis captis pro servicio sibi debitis.

<Misericordia . vij. d.>

Presentant quod Johannes le Wrighte et Andreas Underclynt Frater Adam de Derham Edmundus Haldeyn Johannes Silke Johannes Spellere Adam Craske fecerunt injustam semitam ultra terram domini apud le Clynt.

<Misericordia . iiij. d.>

Presentant quod Frater Adam de Derham fecit injustam semitam ultra terram domini ad caput occidentale ville de Holkham.

<Misericordia . j. d.>

Presentant quod Margareta vxor Ricardi Marchal fecit injustam semitam ultra terram Margarete Godecok apud Crosgate.

<Misericordia . iij. d.>

Presentant quod Willelmus manucaptor Matilde Charle fecit injustam semitam ultra terram domini apud Walsinghamgate cum caretta.

<Misericordia . iiij. d.>

Presentant quod Willelmus Curzoun fecit injustam semitam ultra terram Ricardi Blakeman apud Algeres.

<Misericordia . iiij. d.>

Presentant quod Henricus Buleman i d. Johannes Acke i d. Galfridus Casche . j. d. Benedictus Cappe j d. fecerunt injustam semitam apud Algeres ultra terram Ricardi Blakeman.

<Misericordia . j. d.>

Presentant quod Sewallus manucaptor Rogeri de Reppes fecit injustam semitam ultra cruftam Willelmi Amour cum caruca.

<Misericordia . ij. d.>

Presentant quod Ricardus Blakeman fregit sequestrum domini.

<Misericordia . ij. d.>

Presentant quod Johannes Mey leuavit quamdam faldam injuste et ante tempus.

<Misericordia . xij. d.>

Presentant quod Rogerus de Reppes est pistor et vendidit panem contra assisam.

<Misericordia . ij. s.>

Presentant quod Cecilia Mous braciavit et vendidit contra assisam.

<Misericordia . ij. s.>

Presentant quod Mariota Leman fecit similiter.

<Misericordia . xij. d.>

Presentant quod Matilda White fecit similiter.

<Misericordia . j. d.>

Presentant quod Alicia Slopere fecit similiter et non tulit mensuram.

<Misericordia . ij. s.>

Presentant quod Matilda Burgonye fecit similiter.

<Misericordia . xij. d.>

Presentant quod Thomas Prestessone est regrator panis et ceruisie.

<Misericordia . iij. d.>

Presentant quod Agnes Broun est similiter.

<Misericordia . j. d.>

Presentant quod Johanna Cheseman est similiter.

<Misericordia . j. d.>

Presentant quod Ricardus Blakeman est braciator contra assisam.

<Misericordia . xij. d.>

Presentant quod Ricardus Spellere fecit similiter.

<Misericordia . vj. d.>

Presentant quod Ricardus Marchal fecit similiter.

<Misericordia . vj. d.>

Presentant quod Willelmus Huberd fecit similiter.

<Misericordia . ij. s.>

Presentant quod Helwisia le Meyre fecit similiter.

<Misericordia . ij. d.>

Presentant quod Berta atte Drone est regrator panis.

<Misericordia . ij. d.>

Presentant quod Margareta Crome est similiter.

<Misericordia . j. d.>

Presentant quod Alicia Wrighte est braciator contra assisam.

<Misericordia . ij. d.>

Presentant quod Alicia Otes est similiter.

<Misericordia . iij. d.>

Presentant quod Johannes Mey et Gervasius de Ryburgh probatores ceruisie non fecerunt officium suum.

<Misericordia . iij. d.>

De Johanne le Bret et plegiis suis videlicet Willelmo Buleman et Heruico Buleman quia non est prosecutus versus Johannem Mey in placito captionis averorum.

<Misericordia . iij. d.>

De Rogero Otes querente versus Galfridum de Hindringham per cognatum suum unde recuperavit . iiij. bus. ordei pretio . iij. s. et dampnum taxatum per curiam ad . x. d. quos p.e. leuare pleg. Joh. le Wrighte et Reginald. Crane.

P.e. sic. pluries distringere Thom. filium Mirielde Cosche pro fidelitate.

Exitus sex acrar. terre capte in m. domini quod ..... Golwyn eas clamat tenere libere in exheredatione in manu domini. Et respondeat de exitis. P.e. sic. alias retinere districciones factas super Roseam Bulwere et capere plur. quousque attach se ad respond. Simoni Burgonye de placito debiti.

P.e. sic. pluries leuare de Ricardo Bulwere ad opus Roberti atte Esh et Alicie vxoris ejus . iij. s.

P.e. sic. alias facere venire Ricardum le Deye et Johannem Crakestheld ad respondendum Simoni Burgonye de placito debiti. . Et postea venit Ricardus Deye.

<Misericordia . ij. d.>

Sicut alias distringere Ricardum le Bulwere ad respondendum Thome le Northerne de placito debiti . postea districtus est per . iij. rodas frumenti et p.e. retinere et capere plura.

Sic. alias distr. Simonem Mous ad respondendum Thome Storm de placito debiti . postea invenit plegios Will. fil. Alicie et Joh. le Smith senior.

Sic. alias facere venire Robertum Elyot ad respond. Simoni Mous de placito detentionis unius strepe . postea attach est per Joh. Wrighte et Johan. Mey.

<Placitum>

Mirielda Cosche optulit se versus Johan. le Smith in placito terre . et petit recognitionem fieri si Willelmus frater predicti Mirielde fuit seisitus in dominico suo vt feodo per virgam et die quo obiit de vna acra et tribus rodis terre in Holcham et si ipsa propinquior heres nunc sit. Et si obiit postea terminum exitus. Et predictus Johannes venit et nichil dicit quare ass. remanere debet. Ideo capiatur ass. . Et sunt nomina juratorum Rogerus Odes Joh. le Wrighte Galf. Heyward Godmannus Burgonye Reginald Crane Rogerus de Reppes et Johannes Mey. Et dicunt quod non dum habuerunt visum. Et petunt diem. Ideo habeant inde visum citra proximam curiam.

<Placitum>

Mirielda Cosche op. se versus Joh. filiam Ricardi Blakeman in placito terre. Et petit recognitionem fieri si Willelmus frater predicte Mirielde fuit seisitus in dominico suo vt de feodo per virgam de vna roda et dimidia terre in Holkham die quo obiit Et si ipsa est propinquior heres et si obiit. . Et predicta Johanna venit. Et nichil dicit quare assensum inter eos inde fieri non debet. Ideo capit assensum per juratos supradictos. et inde petit visum citra prox. curiam.

Preceptum est sicut alias facere venire dominum Willelmum de Calethorp Willelmum Godwyne Helwysia Cappe Ricardum Bulwere Henricum Vallet Joh. Mey Willelmum Crane Henricum Camplyoun Heruicum Chapman Willelmum Acke Laurencium Crome Bartholomeum filium Cecilie Agnes Whitbred Johannem de Happesburgh Johannem Maynald Dominum Willelmum personam de Holkham Rogerum Broun Bartholomeum Carpe Rogerum Colyn Walterum Dersy Hervicum Yudekil Johannem de Grace Johannem Lomb Bartholomeum del Hil Rogerum del Hil. Et omnes alios tenentes hujus manerii qui nondum fecerunt fidelitatem ad faciendum fidelitatem.

<Attornatus>

Sewallus Herward quer. de Simone Mous de placitu debiti pleg. de prosequendo Ricardus Blakeman. Et p.e. . Et Sewallus ponit loco suo Johannem Mey.

\<Attornatus\>

Robertus medicus manens in Brunham Ulp. quer. de Johanne Belneye de placito debiti pl. de ps. Joh. Mey et Ricardus Blakeman. Et Robertus ponit loco suo Joh. Mey.

Johannes Crane quer. de Ric. Marchal et Margareta vxore ejus de placito trespassus pleg. de ps. Joh. Mey et messor. Et p.e.

\<Misericordia . iij. d.\>

De Rogero le Reue pro licentia concord. cum Thoma Lyffald in placito conventionis pleg. Joh. Mey.

\<Misericordia . j. d.\>

De messore videlicet Ricardo Blakeman quia non est executus precepta curie.

\<Misericordia . j. d.\>

De Willelmo Charle juniore quia non est in decena.

\<Misericordia . ij. d.\>

De Ricardo Wake pro eodem.

\<Misericordia . j. d.\>

De Johanne Mous pro eodem.

\<Misericordia . j. d.\>

De Johanne Bere pro eodem.

\<Misericordia . j. d.\>

De Ricardo filio Willelmi de Hindringham.

\<Misericordia . j. d.\>

De Thoma filio Godmanni Burgonye.

\<Misericordia . ij. d.\>

De Hervico Haldeyn qui non est in decena.

\<Misericordia . j. d.\>

De Ricardo filio Willelmi Huberd pro eodem.

\<Misericordia . j. d.\>

De Ricardo filio Rogeri clerici pro eodem.

\<alibi\>

De Willelmo filio Johannis Churche pro eodem.

\<Misericordia . j. d.\>

De Roberto le Skynnere pro eodem.

\<Misericordia . j. d.\>

De Johanne de Happesburgh pro eodem.

\<Misericordia . iij. d.\>

De Johanne Spellere pro defalta.

\<Misericordia . j. d.\>

De Gilberto Crane pro eodem.

<Misericordia . j. d.>
    De Henrico Camplyoun pro eodem.
<Misericordia . j. d.>
    De Henrico Chapman pro eodem.
<Misericordia . iij. d.>
    De tenentibus terre quondam Mariot pro eodem.
<Condonatur>
    De Adam Charle pro eodem.
<Misericordia . j. d.>
    De Willelmo Randolf pro eodem.
<Misericordia . j. d.>
    De Johanne Lomb pro eodem.
<Misericordia . j. d.>
    De Reginaldo Botsweyn pro eodem.
<Misericordia . j. d.>
    De Rogero filio Johannis le Smith pro eodem.
<Misericordia . j. d.>
    De Hervico Hodenild pro eodem.
<Misericordia . j. d.>
    De Reginaldo Colyn pro defalta.
<Condonatur>
    De Waltero Asty pro eodem.
<Misericordia . j. d.>
    De Adam Spryngdale pro eodem.
<Misericordia . j. d.>
    De Rogero Attehil pro eodem.
<Misericordia . iij. d.>
    De Ricardo Marchal pro eodem.
<Misericordia . iij. d.>
    De Willelmo Acke pro eodem.
<Misericordia . iij. d.>
    De Hervico Lode pro eodem.
<Misericordia . j. d.>
    De Laurencio Cromme pro eodem.
<Misericordia . j. d.>
    De Henrico Spellere pro eodem.
<Misericordia . j. d.>
    De Hervico Rolond pro eodem.
<Misericordia . j. d.>
    De Simone Atte Cros pro eodem.

\<Misericordia . j. d.\>

De Johanne filio Ade Silk pro eodem.

\<Misericordia . j. d.\>

De Rogero Digge pro eodem.

\<Condonatur\>

De Bartholomeo le Millere pro eodem.

\<Misericordia . ix. d.\>

De omnibus Braciat. quia vendiderunt sine mesuris sigillatis videlicet . iij. d. Cecilia Mous . iij. d. Mariota Leman . iij. d. Matilda Whyte . iij d. Matilda Burgonye et . j. d. Alicia Otes.

\<Misericordia . x. d.\>

De predictis Braciat. quia non miserunt pro probatoribus et vendiderunt ante tempus.

\<Misericordia . ij. s.\>

De omnibus capitalibus plegiis pro plur. concelamentis maxime de faldis injuste levatis et pro hutesio per Willelmum filio Alicie levato.

De Matilda Cheyle quer. de Adam Craske de placito trespassus pl. de ps. Roger Renne et messor.

Joh. Trebbe quer. de Agn. Treweman de placito debiti pleg. de proseq. Jacob. Bete et messor.

| \<Afferatores\> | Johannes le Mey } | \<jur\> |
| | Ricardus Blakeman } | |

Summa . xliii. s. . ix. d.

exit.

Agnes que fuit vxor Johannis Thurbern pro custodia habenda de vno mesuagio cum quatuor acris et dimidia roda terre quondam predicti viri sui per minorem etatem Bartholomei filii sui qui nunc est etatis vii annorum. Et memorandum quod Clere que fuit vxor Rogeri Thurbern tenet in dotem et predicta Agnes similiter. Ita quod ad presens remanet preter dotes predictas . j acram j rodam . pleg. Rogerum de Hogate et Thomam de Dallyngg.

Presentant quod Johannes Cat et Oliva vxor ejus debuit officium messoris hoc anno.

HD 98

Letter of Attorney from Richard Payn of Holkham to Martin Rust of Holkham to give Richard Neel of Burnham and Katerine his wife seisin of 1 plot.
[c. 1318]

NOTE: This document is wrongly dated by H.A. Davidson c. 1400. The corresponding grant is HD 19 witnessed by Martin Rust, three of the same witnesses and the holder of adjoining land. Both are in the same hand. This document is the top left corner of a rectangular piece of parchment from which a large circular piece had been cut, leaving an almost triangular piece 5 in. wide. The seal was attached to the bottom corner 6 inches down the left hand side. This is a very rare example of a legal document being written on what might be called a 'flanky bit'.

Pateat vniuersis per presentes quod ego Ricardus Payn de Holkham posui et loco meo constitui attornatum meum Martinum Rust de Holcham ad deliberandum Ricardo Neel de Brunham et Katerine vxori eius plenarie et pacifice seysinam in vna pecia terre que de me adquisierunt in Holcham prout carta feoffamenti mei testatur. In cuius Reij testimonium huic presenti scripto sigillum meum apposui. Iohanne Bret Hugone Otes Thoma Large de Creyk et aliis testibus.

Seal: missing, was attached to bottom corner of deed at the lower end of the left-hand margin.
Hand: See note on HD 19. Not same as HP 1057.

HD 155 Fo. 1v

Lords of the manor of Hillhall and of Bret-Tobers in Holkham from Hillhall Book.

NOTE: Similar statement of Thomas d'Akeny's holding followed by similar list of lords of Hillhall occur in rentals of Hillhall, HD 118 and 175. HD 118 differs in reading Sage de Wethesford *not* Waleford. Though it is entitled the terrier of John Foster, bailiff (1436–7), it is "coppyed and examined the 29th Jan., 1600 by me William Armiger, Robert Segon" and it continues the list of lords up to Meriel Wheatley the heiress who married John Coke, son of Chief Justice Coke, and lord of Neel Manor which thus became united with Hillhall.
Fiche 1: E10

Thomas*ᵃ* de Dakeney Miles tenuit c et x acras terre [*corner of Ms. missing*] [quas Sokemanni sui tenent de eo] cum mesuagiis de eodem feodo quibus [*Ms. torn*] [contulit vna carta] vt illi seu ille filij eorum et filie si [*Ms. torn*] [debeant allegian' extra] homagium dabunt x s. et si infra homagium et pet[ant licenciam] dabunt v s. et si non dabunt . x . s. et vnam bursam dict' argent' imponere. Et predicti dabunt ad Wardse ij d. ob. vt patet per antiquas evidencias in tempore Regis Edwardi filij Regis Edwardi etc cuius carta remanet in custodia Iohannis Waylond.

<Nomina dominorum manerij de Hillehalle in Holkham>

Baudewinus Thouny

Baldewynus de Akeny Miles

Thomas de Akeny Miles^b filius dicti Baudewini Anno regni regis Edwardi filij Regis Henrici viij° [1279–80]

Radulfus de Akeny Miles

Iohannes de Akeny et Alicia vxor eius

Bawdewinus de Akeny Miles filius et heres dictorum Iohannis et Alicie vt patet in Anno Regis Edwardi Primi xxxv^{to} et etatis xxiiij Annorum [1306–7]

Thomas de Akeny Miles filius dicti Bawdewini

Iohannes de Akeny Miles frater dicti Thome

Iohannes de Akeny filius dicti Iohannis de Akeny Militis Anno regni Regis Edwardi tercij primo [1327–8]

<Washefford>

Iohannes Sage de Waleford et Iohanna vxor eius soror et heres Iohannis de Akeny

Thomas de Lacy de Hersham^c Anno regis Edwardi tercij xiiij° [1340–1]

Iohannes Andrew de Welles postea manens in Holkham Anno regis Edwardi tercij xv° [1341–2].

<Nomina dominorum Manerij de Brett et postea vocati Tobers in Holkham>

Adam le Brett filius Ade [le B]ret^d

Iohannes le Bret filius dicti Ade

Iohannes le Bret filius dicti Iohannis [le] Bret anno regni regis Edwardi tercij quinto [1331–2]

Iohannes Tober' de Wyueton et fert in Armis suis j bend inter duos vrsos[13]

Iohannes Tober' filius et heres dicti Iohannis Anno Regis Edwardi tercij viij° [1334–5]

Iohannes de Kirkham Armiger Anno regis Edwardi tercij x° [1336–7]

Robertus de Kirkham filius et heres dicti Iohannis

Iohannes Andreu predictus de Holkham Anno Regis Edwardi tercij xliij° [1369–70].

---

13   *duo ursi* allude cantingly to the Two Bears suggested by the surname Tobers.

<Nomina dominorum vtrumque maneriorum modo sub nomine vnius Manerij vocati Hillehall in Holkham>

Iohannes Andreu predictus de Welles et postea de Holkham
Iohannes de Holkham filius et heres dicti Iohannis Andreu de Holkham ...

VARIANTS: [a] First word of HD 153 Fo. 2v. [b] Thomas de Akenny Miles is repeated in corner in Ms.; it is omitted in HD 118 and 155. [c] HD 175, Fo. 1v reads [Domina Matilda de Lacy struck out] Thomas de Lacy [filius eius struck out]. [d] Added with remainder of page in darker ink.

HD 205 no. VIIa Fo. 15–15v

Terrier of Peterstone Priory Lands in Holkham.   16 or 23 Jan. 1315

NOTE: A copy in a book of Peterstone and Walsingham terriers and rentals, a copy in a similar book referenced BD Fo. 16v and a translation into English in HD 300, all lack a reference to the feast of SS. Fabian and Sebastian, but indicate the regnal year 8 Edward II (1314–15). The original BD 28 is badly damaged by damp at the top. It is a parchment roll 6 3/8 in. wide. It is impossible to read whether it is dated Thursday before or after the feast. HD 300 Fo. 25v omits the regnal year. The following text is taken from BD 28. This alone gives details of what crop is sown or whether a piece of land lies fallow. For convenience variants of spelling etc. are noted after each item instead of at the foot of the page or at the end of the document. H.A. Davidson miscatalogued it as a Burnham 15th century court roll. This terrier is the only evidence for the use before 1350 of no fewer than twenty-seven toponyms.
Fiche 3: F11 and F12

VISUS TERRARUM PRIORATUS DE PETERSTON[a] DIE IOUIS [ANTE?] FESTUM SANCTORUM FABIANI ET SEBASTIANI [ANNO] REGNI REGIS EDWARDI VIIJ[uo]

<Holcham>

(1)   Apud Boweslothes vij acre terre[14]

(2)   Hamestale . j . acra et j . roda et seminat' cum ordeo eodem anno
        [*Hamestalle, HD 300*]

(3)   Holcham Tounesende iij acre terre seminat' cum auena [*HD 205 and
        BD 0 insert* Apud *in (3) and (4). HD 300 inserts* At *in both. HD
        205 omits* terre. *BD 0 often retains* terre *and HD 300 often
        translates* of land. *Examples are not noted below.* Thownesend, HD
        205, Holkhamtownesende, BD 0, Townesend, HD 300]

---

14   Boweslothes at the north-east corner of the South Field is the first piece named in terriers
      of 1452-3 and 1456-7, HD 129 and HD 22a, Fo. 53 no. 265. Peterstone had a warren in
      adjoining land beyond Burnham Thorpe boundary near the Priory on the opposite side of
      the road from Holkham to Burnham.

(4)   Millecroft . iij Pecie continent v . acras terre. Et seminat' cum auena
        [*in tres pec'*, *HD 205, BD 0. In thre peces, HD 300. Millescroft, HD
        205, Myllecroft, BD 0, Myll croft, HD 300*]

(5)   Vna [pecia] est ibidem prope Walsinghamsti et contin' v acr' terre
        Et seminat' cum auena [*vna pecia, HD 205, BD 0. One pece there,
        HD 300. They leave area blank, suggesting it was already rotted
        away in BD 28 when transcribed.*]

(6)   Apud Chelescroftisende j . roda Et seminat' cum ordeo
        [*Chelescroftisende, HD 205, Chelescroftsend, BD 0, Chelescrofts
        end, HD 300. terre added, BD 0. j rod of land, HD 300*]

(7)   Item iuxta Chelsgate dimidia acra terre et iacet eodem anno
        [*Chelesgate, BD 0, Chellesgate, HD 300*]

(8)   Item ad capud eiusdem versus austrum iuxta Chelesgate iij rode terre
        et iacet [*caput, HD 205, capud, BD 0*]

(9)   Item ibidem iuxta eandem peciam terre dimidia acra et dimidia rode
        terre Et Iacet [*This item is omitted, HD 205*]

(10)   Item ibidem iuxta eandem peciam terre ex parte orientali j acra terre
        et Iacet

(11)   Item alia pecia iuxta Chelesgate que vocatur Dankenysconiger . j .
        acra et j . roda et iacet [*Dankesconingger, HD 205,
        Dankenesconyngger, BD 0, Dankenesconyngger, HD 300*]

(12)   Item vna pecia abuttat super Chelesgate versus orientem et continet .
        iij . rodas Et Iacet [*Chellesgate, HD 300*]

(13)   Item j . acra terre iacet ad capud orientale predictarum rodarum
        versus austrum et borealem. et Iacet [*N and S ignored, HD 205, BD
        0 and HD 300*]

(14)   Item . vna . pecia abuttat ad Chelesgate ad capud occidentale . et .
        continet j rodam . et dimidiam . et Iacet

(15)   Item ibidem ex parte Austr*ali* . dimidia . roda Et Iacet

(16)   Item est ibidem ex parte occident*ali* predicte vie . dimidia . roda .
        cuius capud orientale abuttat super predictam viam [*illegible note in
        left margin of Ms.*]

(17)   Item Tokeshalfaker continet dimidiam acram terre Et semin' cum mixtilione [*Cookes halfe acre, HD 205, Tokes halfacre, BD 0, Tokes half acre, HD 300*]

(18)   Item apud Collesmere vij . rode terre et abuttat super Caldehougate . et seminat' cum ordeo [*Collesmer, HD 300. Caldowgate, HD 205, BD 0, HD 300*]

(19)   Moltysaker . j . acra terre . et abuttat super Caldehougate Et seminat' cum frumento [*Moltesacre, HD 205, BD 0, HD 300. Caldowgate, HD 205, BD 0, HD 300*]

(20)   Blakelond prope ibidem . abuttat super predictam viam Et seminat' cum ordeo [*Blaklond, HD 205, Blakelond, BD 0, Blake land, HD 300*]

(21)   Hungerhil . j . acra . et . j . roda terre . abuttat super Caldehougate versus occidentem . et seminat' cum ordeo [*Hungerhill', HD 205, BD 0, HD 300. Caldowgate, HD 205, BD 0, Caldowe gate, HD 300*]

(22)   Item apud Stryecrundel ex parte orient*ali* predicte vie . dimidia acra et seminat' cum frumento [*Screyncrundell, HD 205, Streyecrundell', BD 0, Streycrundell, HD 300. Inserted later in Ms. between (22) and (23) in BD 28: vna pecia roda terre apud ... houey inter terram Burhalle*]

(23)   Item apud Stryecrundel ex parte orient*ali* predicte vie . iiij . acre. Et Iacet [*ibidem, HD 205, BD 0, Also ther, HD 300*]

(24)   Item apud Suthbondyswong' vij . rode terre. Et seminat' cum frumento [*Southbondswong, HD 205, Southbondeswong, BD 0, Southbondswonge, HD 300. Inserted later in Ms. between (24) and (25): Item vna pecia iac' inter terras predicti prioris quondam Thome de Akeney*]

(25)   Item apud Bondeswong' . iiij^{or}. acre et dimidia . terre. Et seminat' cum pisiis

(26)   Item apud Northbondyswong' ij . rode terre Et seminat' cum frumento [*Northbondswong', HD 205, Northbondeswong, BD 0, North bondeswonge, HD 300*]

(27)   Item apud Cotecroft vij . acre terre. vnde pars iacet. Et pars seminat' cum ordeo [*Cootecroft, HD 205, Cotecrofte BD 0, Cote Crofte, HD 300*]

(28) Item apud Fulmere iuxta Estgronge ij . acre et dimidia. Et seminat' cum ordeo [*Fulmere, HD 205, BD 0, Fullmere, HD 300. <R.Dockyng> BD 28 (mid fifteenth century)*]

(29) Item . j . roda et dimidia . iacent vltra Gibbysgate in duabus pecijs Et Iacet. [*Gibbesgate, HD 205, Gybbesgate, BD 0, HD 300*]

(30) Item alia pecia est ibidem que continet . j . acram et j . rodam terre et abuttat super Gibbysgate versus [occid]entem que vocatur Branchescrundel [*Faded interlineation not in transcripts. Braunchcrundell, HD 205, Braunchecrundell', BD 0, Branchecrundell, HD 300*]

(31) Item . iij . rode terre abuttant super Gibbysgate ad caput occidentale Et Iacent [*Gibbesgate, HD 205, Gybbesgate, BD 0, Gybbesgate and Gybbsgate, HD 300*]

(32) Item prope ibidem . j . acra terre. Et Iacet.

(33) Item ad capud orientale predicte pecie terre . j . acra terre Et Iacet.

(34) Item iuxta Croftam Gilberti Payn vltra Gibbesgate j . roda terre Et Iacet. [*Gybbesgate, BD 0, HD 300*]

(35) Item Burgate Croftes . ij . acre terre Iacent in . iiij^{or} partibus. Et seminat' cum ordeo

(36) Item iuxta forum de Holcham . j . mesuagium cum . j . roda terre [*Holkham, HD 205, BD 0, HD 300 . forne, HD 300*]

(37) Item Alberdshil . iij . acre terre Et seminat' cum ordeo [*Alberdhill, HD 205, BD 0, Albete hill, HD 300*]

(38) Item apud Dalgate ex parte orient*ali* predicte vie . j . roda et dimidia . terre Et seminat' cum ordeo [*Dalegate, HD 205, BD 0, HD 300*]

(39) Item apud Dalgate ex illa parte. dimidia acra terre Et seminat' cum ordeo [*Dalegate, HD 205, BD 0, HD 300*]

(40) Item apud Dalgate ex parte occident*ali* . dimidia . acra terre . Et Iacet. [*Dalegate, HD 205, BD 0, HD 300*]

(41) Item apud Dalgate ex parte occident*ali* iij . acre et dimidia terre Et Iacent. [*Dalegate, HD 205, BD 0, HD 300*]

(42) Item apud Dalgate ex parte occid*entali* . j acra et j roda terre. Et Iacent [*Dalegate, HD 205, BD 0, HD 300*]

(43)   Item alia pecia est ibidem iuxta Dalgate ex parte orientis et continet
       . iiij^{or}. acras. Et Iacet. [*Dalegate, HD 205, BD 0, HD 300*]

(44)   Item alia pecia est ibidem que est de Excambio

(45)   Item . j . acra est ibidem iuxta Dalgate ex parte orient*ali* Et Iacet.
       [*Dalegate, HD 205, BD 0, HD 300*]

(46)   Item apud Billismere . j . acra et j . roda terre. Et Iacet. [*Billesmere,
       HD 205, Byllesmere, BD 0, HD 300*]

(47)   Item Longelond iuxta terram Abbatis de Crek' ex parte boreali iiij^{or}.
       acre Et Iacent [*Longlond, HD 205, BD 0, HD 300. Creike, HD 205,
       Creyke, BD 0, HD 300.*]

(48)   (*Inserted later in Ms. after (47)*) Item iij rode apud Longlond que
       vocatur Depcrundel quondam Thome Lefe cum medietate vnius falde
       [*Depecrundell', HD 205, BD 0, HD 300. Thomas Lefe only in BD
       28*]

(49)   Item alia pecia que vocatur Longelond . continet . iij . acras et
       dimidiam . terre. Et Iacet [*Longland, HD 205, Longlond, BD 0, HD
       300*]

(50)   Warldogh . j . acra et . j . roda terre. Et seminat' cum siligine
       [*Wardhough, HD 205, Wardehough', BD 0, HD 300*]

(51)   Gunnynggiswongh vj . acre terre. Et seminat' cum siligine
       [*Gonninggeswong, HD 205, Gunnynggeswong, BD 0, HD 300*]

(52)   Item Iuxta Wlsiscrundel . j . acra . et . j . roda terre Et seminat' cum
       ordeo [*Wolsyescrundell', HD 205, Wulsyescrundell' HD 0,
       Wulsyescrundell HD 300*]

(53)   Item apud Thorphil . j . acra et . j . roda terre Et seminat' cum
       ordeo [*Thorpehill', HD 205, BD 0, Thorphill, HD 300*] [*Inserted
       later in Ms. between (53) and (54) ... duas acras quondam Eborardi
       le Kalie apud Thorphil*]

(54)   Item Calislond iuxta viam ex parte orient*ali* vij . rode terre Et Iacet
       [*Calieslond, HD 205, Calyeslonde, BD 0, Calyes lond, HD 300*]

Summa iiij^{xx} . xix . acre . dimidia.

NOTE: Only BD 28 gives this total. BD 0 continues in a rather larger and slightly later
hand in a different format. Separate lines are no longer devoted to separate items and the
lines have much narrower blank margins each side of the parchment. Areas are stated at
the beginning instead of the end of each item. In (55) BD 28 does not name John Silk,
who occurs in the transcripts. This suggests that they are derived from some other, lost,
original.

(55)   ix acras et j rodam in cruft' [*Item vna crofta continet ix acras et j rodam terre iuxta messuagium Iohannis Silke in Holkham, HD 205. Sylke, BD 0, HD 300*]

(56)   et ij acras in Estgacroft [*Estgate crofte, HD 205, BD 0, HD 300*]

(57)   et vna roda terre apud Payniscroftisende [*Painescroftes ende, HD 205, Paynescroft' eend, BD 0, Paynescroftes end, HD 300*]

(58)   et xij acr' terre apud Shepehousecrofte [*Shepehouscroft, HD 205, Shepehouscrofte, BD 0, HD 300*]

(59)   vnam rodam apud Bondys Wonggate [*Bowden Wonggate, HD 205, Bondeswonggate, BD 0. Item omitted, HD 300*]

(60)   1 acr' et j rod' apud Bonddyswong

(61)   et j acr' et j rod' in . iij peciis in eadem quarentena. [*Between (59) and (60) HD 300 leaves a blank as if the translator could not read (or understand) quarentena, cf. (65)*]

(62)   et iij acr' apud Caldhowhill' [*Caldowehill', HD 205, Caldowhill', BD 0, Caldowehill, HD 300*]

(63)   iij acre apud Lethrgraues [*Leighes, HD 205 (a spelling which suggests unfamiliarity with Holkham toponyms), Leygraues, BD 0, HD 300*]

(64)   et ij acr' apud Longlond [*Longlond, HD 205, BD 0, Long londe, HD 300*]

(65)   et ij acr' apud Dedquenespyt [*Dedqueanes pitt, HD 205, Dedquenespitte, BD 0, Dedquenes pitt', HD 300*]

(66)   vnam rodam et dimidiam in eadem quarentena [*as in (61) HD 300 leaves a blank as if the translator could not read (or understand) quarentena*]

(67)   dimidiam acram et dimidiam rodam apud Colysmer' [*Colysmere, HD 205, BD 0, HD 300*]

(68)   dimidiam acram et dimidiam rodam apud Egmeryschote. [*Egmershote, HD 205, BD 0, HD 300*]

(69)   v acr' apud Bramlond [*Brantelond, HD 205, Bramlond, BD 0, HD 300*]

(70)   dimidiam acram et dimidiam rodam ad caput orientale de Bramlond
          [*Bramlond, HD 205, BD 0, Bramlonde, HD 300*]

(71)   vna roda super Bondyswonggat' [*Bondeswonggate, HD 205, BD 0,
          HD 300*]

(72)   et iij acr' apud Hadhowe in ij peciis

(73)   vnam acram et iij rodas apud Thorphyl in iiij peciis [*Thorpehill, HD
          205, Thorphill', BD 0, Thorpehill, HD 300*]

(74)   et ij acras in vj peciis apud Kyrlond' [*Kirklondes, HD 205,
          Kyrkelond, BD 0, Kyrklond, HD 300*]

Summa totalis vij^{xx} acre et dimidia terre.[15]

NOTE: Shortly after 1315 Peterstone acquired the estate described in items 55–74 of the
Peterstone terrier of land in Holkham. These lands were probably the estate which
Peterstone acquired in Holkham from the Abbot of Creake in exchange for land at
Quarles according to a memorandum entered after a terrier of Peterstone's original
holding at Quarles, of 1315, BD 0 no. 19, Fo. 18v, BD 28, HD 205 Fo. 16 and HD 300
Fo. 27v. A terrier of Peterstone's land in Quarles of 1317–8 describes 553/4 acres in
Quarles, once of William Bulman. It is preceded by another memorandum which states
that Peterstone has all the lands of Creake abbey in Holkham Fields in exchange for all
the lands of Peterstone in Quarles, BD 0, Fo. 18, BD 28, HD 205, Fo. 17, HD 300, Fo.
38. This estate could not have been correctly described as comprising all the land in
Holkham of Creake as the Abbey still had 40 acres, a fold and bond land with two
cottages in 1428 for which it paid Hillhall 9s. 6d. and 1 1/2 bushels of wheat, HD 115.
The name of William Bulman recurs in the next century. A bondman of that name
maliciously caused William Gloye, *messor* of Wighton, to seal the doors of his cottage at
the Stathe so that the Prior of Peterstone, his steward and tenants could not hold their
court there, 26 June 1439 (HD 194).

VARIANT: *ᵃ* Petyrston, BD 0, Fo. 16v

---

15   Total omitted here in BD 28, but given in HD 205, BD 0 and HD 300.

HD 205 no. XIII Fo. 18v

Rental of Peterstone in Holkham.   [c. 1337]

NOTE: Extract from the Walsingham Book with former Peterstone lands; this document is part of a survey which describes Peterstone rents in 21 other parishes of which there is a Tudor English translation in HD 300 no. 21, Fiche 1: G2. These tenants are described as free in HD 205 no. XV Fo. 24. These holdings lie in Westgate. Another version of this rental is in a paper Peterstone book of 31 leaves referenced Burnham Deed O. Fiche 1: F13

(1)   Walterus Vicarius de Holkham tenet vnum messuagium cum croft' continente j acram quondam Iohannis Byntre[16] et reddit per annum viij d.

(2)   Idem tenet j messuagium cum dimidia acra terre in croftes[a] quondam Iohannis Somerding et reddit per annum iiij d.

(3)   Heredes Iohannis Somerding tenet j acram terre apud Griggeshow[b] et reddit per annum ij d.

(4)   Iohannes de Kyrkham tenet quoddam Curtilage quondam Walteri[c] Hamonde iacens iuxta messuagium Rogeri Hevd[d] et reddit xiij d. ob.

(5)   Simon ad crucem de Warham et Radulfus Dey pro messuagio et croftes quondam Simonis Hamond et quodam Curtilage vocato Pidelyarde[e] et reddit iiij s. iiij d.

(6)   Stephanus Vicarius de Holkham tenet vnum messuagium quondam Roberti Mershall[f] iacens apud le Skote et reddit per annum iiij d. qua.

(7)   Isabella Pey pro tercia parte dicti messuagij reddit per annum j d.

(8)   Willelmus[g] filius Vicarij pro messuagio suo reddit per annum j d.

(9)   Willelmus Curcham[h] pro messuagio et croftes[a] quondam Iohannis et Radulfi Curcham iac' iuxta messuagium et croftes[a] quondam Simonis Hamond ex parte orientali et pro j cotagio cum croftes[a] iac' in Estgate iuxta messuagium Iohannis Chastle[i] ex parte orientali et reddit per annum xxij d.

---

16   John de Bintry's messuage and croft were granted by William son of Simon son of Hamon in 1313 to Walter de Helweton, perpetual vicar of Holkham, HD 22a no. 105. All these Peterstone tenants holdings were concentrated along the south side of Holkham Westgate, the part of the old road from Burnham to Wighton which lay under Coke of Norfolk's southern extension of Thomas Coke's artificial lake. They lay on ground, which rises towards the south and where fragments of medieval pottery remain.

(10)   Ricardus de Snoring pro messuagio cum croftes^j quondam Iohannis Dey ex parte occident*ali* messuagij Prioris de Peterston apud forum^k de Holkham reddit vj d .

(11)   Matilda neptis Walteri vicarij pro quodam messuagio vocato Vardon croftes^l et reddit per annum iij d .

(12)   Iohannes at Dale reddit per annum ij d. pro quadam terra iacente in le Gong et continet j acram et dimidiam et pro vna pecia^m apud Letherpitts^n cont' j acram et reddit per annum j d .

        <De tenentibus>^{o}

(13)   Thomas le Northerne^p pro quadam pecia quondam Ricardi Wat'^{q} reddit per annum iiij d. ob .

(14)   Galfridus filius Iuliani reddit per annum iiij d .

(15)   Heredes Willelmi Craske reddunt per annum j d. ob .

(16)   Rogerus Bright^r reddit per annum iij d .

(17)   Heredes Vnfridi Davy viz. Alicia Davy reddit per annum j d. ob .

(18)   De quondam messuagio cum croftes^j Bertolomei Curchiun^s vnde Thome Wiseman et reddit per annum ij d .

(19)   Et Matilda neptis Walteri Vicarij reddit per annum ob.

(20)   Iohannes Rust reddit per annum ob. et dictus Curthun ij d. ob.

(21)   Heredes Iohannis Oddes^t et Reginaldus^u de Barney videlicet Rust pro quadam parte messuagij dicti Reginaldi de Berney et dimid' acre terre ex parte orient' messuagij sui reddit per annum ij d. ob.

(22)   Heredes Matilde Ernald^v reddunt ij d.

(23)   Heredes^w Rogeri de Howgate redd' iij d.

(24)   Tenentes apud^x Estgate Croftes viz. Baron' Sundcus^y Tappe Matilda Pepir^z et Sibilla Crofte^{aa} viij d. per annum similiter eorum^{bb} pro se ij d.

(25)   Robertus Bullman^{cc} tenet j acram iacentem in le Gonge et reddit per annum j d.

(26)   Iohannes frater eius reddit pro dicta acre terre in le Gong j d.

(27)   Heredes Edmundi Athewald reddunt j d.

(28)   Robertus Herward tenet j acram apud Grigg Howe et reddit per
        annum ij d.

NOTE: HD 300 nos. 17–21 are translations of Peterstone terriers and may be taken from
the 'olde booke' of Peterstone which is cited in HD 129 p. 27. This is the earliest
surviving original book of Peterstone and is the original from which HD 300 no. 4 is a
translation. HD 205 contains Latin transcripts evidently taken from BD 0. The earliest
dated document found, translated in HD 300 no. 20, deals with 553/4 acres in Quarles
bought by William Bulleman in 1312–13. Of persons mentioned in the rental, Simon at
Cross occurs in 1326–7 and Thomas Northerne occurs often between 1321 and 1347.
John de Kirkham esq. is lord of Tobers in 1337–8 after John Tobers II who was lord in
1334–5 according to the list of lords of Hillhall and Tobers in the Hillhall Book, (HD
155, Fo. 1v). Though many of the surnames of tenants are familiar, most of those tenants
of Peterstone in 1337 are absent from the court rolls; but Tappe may be Tebbe mentioned
in 1322 (HD 82), Robert Bulman occurs in 1337 (HD 86) and John Bulman in 1347 (HD
85a).

VARIANTS: ^a a crofte, HD 300.   ^b Gryggeshowe, *ib.*.   ^c William, *ib.*.   ^d Woods, *ib.*.
^e Pidelesyerd, *ib.*.   ^f Marshalls, *ib.*.   ^g at Crosse, *ib.*.   ^h Curchun, *ib.*.   ⁱ Charle, *ib.*.   ^j a
croft, HD 300.   ^k The market place, HD 300.   ^l Verdonescrofts, HD 300.   ^m Pece of
land, HD 300.   ⁿ Lether Pytts, HD 300, 'y' represents 'th'.   ^o Title added in margin in
hand that could be that of Chief Justice Coke.   ^p Thomas of Northerne, HD 300.
^q Richard Waters, HD 300.   ^r Roger Wright, HD 300.   ^s Bartholomew Curchun, HD
300.   ^t Follows next item, HD 300.   ^u Reynold Berney, HD 300.   ^v Heirs of Maud
Ernalde precede last item, HD 300.   ^w The heir of Roger Howgate payeth, HD 300.
^x Tenants of Estgate Crofte, HD 300.   ^y Barett Buders, apparently, HD 300.   ^z Mawd
Petyr, apparently, HD 300.   ^{aa} Sybill Cosshe, apparently, HD 300.   ^{bb} Every of them for
himself, HD 300.   ^{cc} Bulman, HD 300.

HOLKHAM PAPERS:
HP 995 – HP 1103, HP 3808

c. 1270–1350

HP 995

Grant from Geoffrey son of Peter le Bret of Holkham to Simon son of Hamo of Holkham of 1 plot of 3 acres. [c. 1294–6]

Cf. HD 22a, Fos. 3v no. 37; 10 no. 120
Fiche 1: G3

Notum sit omnibus hoc scriptum visuris vel audituris quod ego Galfridus filius Petri le Bret de Holkham concessi dedi et presenti scripto confirmauy Symoni filio Hamonis eiusdem ville vnam peciam terre mee iacentem in camp' de Holcham que continet in se tres Acras terre et Iacent inter terram Ade Carpentarij ex parte australi et terram meam ex parte aquilonari et capud occidentale abuttat super terram dicti Symonis et capud orientale abuttat super viam Regalem que ducit de Holcham apud Warles habend' et tenend' predictam peciam terre de capitalibus dominis feodi per seruicia inde debita et consueta. Reddendo inde annuatim vt patet in carta feoffamenti sui quam habet ex dono Iohannis filij mey pro omnibus seruiciis et consuetudinibus exaccionibus curie sectis et omnibus secularibus demandis. Et ego predictus Galfridus et heredes mey vel mei assignati Warantizabimus adquietabimus et defendemus predictam peciam terre cum pertinenciis predicto Symoni et heredibus suis vel suis assignatis contra omnes in perpetuum. In cuius rey testimonium Huic scripto sigillum meum apposui . Hiis testibus . Iohanne le Bret . Bartholomeo de Burgate . Willelmo Crask . Iohanne Sylk . Willelmo filio suo. Waltero Hacon . Martino Goldewyn . Galfrido Godwyn . Humfrido Davy et Aliis multis.

Seal: Fragment of seal of which complete specimen is on 996.
Endorsement: *iij acre apud Hadhoue.* T[ranscriptum] (in ink), 2, 995 and 1292 (in pencil).

NOTE: William Silk witnessed HP 1012 and 1014 with his father, John Silk, 5 June and 13 July 1295.

HP 996

Grant from Geoffrey son of Peter le Bret of Holkham to Simon son of Hamo of Holkham of 1 plot of 1 rood. [c. 1294-6]

Cf. HD 22a, Fo. 2v no. 13
Fiche 1: G4

Sciant presentes et futuri quod Ego Galfridus filius Petri le Bret de Holcham Concessi dedi et hac presenti carta mea confirmaui Simoni filio Hamonis de eadem et heredibus suis pro homagio et seruicio suo et pro duabus marcis argenti quas mihi dedit premanibus . vnam peciam terre continentem in se unam rodam terre Iacentem in camp' de Holcham silicet inter terram Rogeri Eluerich ex parte orientali . et terram Willelmi Grige ex parte occidentali . et caput australe abuttat super terram Gilberti Nicol et caput Aquilon' abuttat super semitam que tendit de horreo Abbatis de Derham in Holcham ad ecclesiam de Holcham . Habend' et tenend' predictam peciam terre de me et heredibus meis vel meis assignat' illi et heredibus suis vel suis assignatis . libere . quiete . bene . et in pace jure et hereditarie . Et cuicumque vel quandocumque predictam peciam terre . Dare . legare . vendere . vel assignare voluerit . in quo statu fuerit. Reddendo Inde annuatim mihi et heredibus meis vel meis assignatis vnum ob. silicet ad festum Sancti Michaelis pro omnibus seruiciis consuetudinibus exaccionibus sectis Curie et secularibus demandis. Et ego vero predictus Galfridus et heredes mei vel mei assignati . Warantizabimus et adquietabimus et omnino defendemus predictam peciam terre pro vt iacet inter dictas terras siue sit ibi plus vel minus . predicto Simoni filio Hamonis et heredibus suis vel assingnatis suis per predictum seruicium contra omnes in perpetuum. In huius Rei testimonium presenti carte sigillum meum apposui . Hiis testibus . Radulfo Hacun . Iohanne le Bret . Bartolomeo de Burgate . Iohanne Silke . Willelmo Silke . Galfrido Godwine . Radulfo Mariot . Eborard Cali et aliis.

Seal: in exceptionally good condition: White wax painted red, Fleur-de-Lys within inscription S. GALFRIDI FIL PETR[I] 1³/₄ in. diam.

Hand: see note on HD 12.

Endorsement: *j rod' terre abbut' super semitam que ducit de Horreo Abbatis de Derham ad ecclesiam de Holkham vsque aquilonem* (in ink), 3, 996 and 1406 (in pencil).

HP 997

Grant from Gilbert son of John Brun of Holkham to Simon son of Hamo of Holkham of 1 plot of 1 acre. [c. 1283-93]

Cf. HD 22a, Fo. 8 no. 99
Fiche 1: G5

Sciant presentes et futuri Quod Ego Gilbertus filius Iohannis Brun de Holcham concessi dedi et hac presenti carta mea confirmaui . Symoni filio Hamonis de eadem pro homagio et seruicio suo et pro . xxij . solidis argenti quos . mihi dedit premanibus . vnam peciam terre mee cum pertinenciis Iacentem inter terram dicti Symonis versus occidentem . et terram Iohannis Asty versus orientem. Et Capud Aquilonare abuttat super le Grenegate . Illi et heredibus suis Habendam Tenendam de me et heredibus meis . libere . quiete . Bene . In pace . Iure et hereditarie . cuicumque et quando eam . dare . legare . vendere . vel assignare . voluerit . Reddendo inde annuatim mihi et heredibus meis duos . denarios . scilicet ad festum Andree . unum. obolum et ad Pascha . unum obolum . et ad Nativitatem Sancti Iohannis Baptiste . unum obolum . et ad festum Sancti Michaelis . unum obolum et ad commune auxilium quando euenerit in forinseca sokna de Wytton . scilicet ad . XX . solid' . vnum obolum . ad plus . plus . et ad minus minus. pro omni seruicio consuetudine exaccione secta Curie et seculari demanda. Ego vero predictus Gilbertus et heredes mei Warantizabimus acquietabimus et omnino defendemus prefatam peciam terre cum pertinenciis predicto Symoni et Heredibus suis vel eius assignatis sicut predictum est per predictum seruicium contra omnes inperpetuum. In huius Rey testimonium presenti carte sigillum meum apposui . Hiis testibus . Petro Le Bret . Rad*ulfo* Hacun . Roberto filio suo . Barth*olomeo* de Burgate . Ada le Bret . Iohanne Goldwyn . Galfrido Godwyn . Rad*ulfo* Mariot . David Man . Thomas Leffe et aliis.

Seal: missing
Hand: see note on HD 18.
Endorsement: 105 (in russet), T[ranscriptum] *abbutt' super Grenegate versus aquilonem et continet j acram. In carta ista continetur j acram* (in ink), 4, 360 and 997 (in pencil).

HP 998

Grant from John son of Gilbert of Bintry to Simon son of Hamo of Holkham of 1 plot.   [c. 1283-93]

cf. HD 22a, Fo. 3v no. 32
Fiche 1: G6

Sciant presentes et futuri quod Ego Iohannes filius Gilberti de Bynetre concessi dedi et hac presenti carta mea confirmaui Symoni filio Hamonis pro Homagio et seruicio suo et pro vndecim . solidis argenti quos mihi dedit In gersumam . Vnam . peciam terre mee cum pertinenciis Iacentem in campis de Holcham inter terram Willelmi Osebern versus orientem et terram Symonis Charle versus occidentem . Et capud australe abuttat super terram Prioris de Peterston illi et heredibus suis cuicumque et quando eam dare legare vendere vel assingnare voluerit . Habendam et tenendam de me et heredibus meis . libere . quiete . Bene . In pace . Iure . et hereditarie. Reddendo inde annuatim mihi et heredibus meis . vnum . obolum . scilicet ad festum Sancti Michaelis. Et ad commune auxilium quando evenerit in forinseca soca de Wyttone scilicet ad viginti soluendo . unum . obolum . ad plus plus . et ad minus . minus . Pro omnibus seruiciis consuetudinibus exaccionibus et omnibus aliis secularibus demandis: Ego . vero . predictus Iohannes et heredes mei . Warantizabinus. acaquietabimus.ᵃ et Omnino defendemus predictam peciam Terre cum pertinenciis prenominato Symoni et Heredibus suis vel suis assignatis sicut predeterminatum est per predictum seruicium contra omnes in perpetuum. In huius autem Rey Testimonium presenti carte pro me et heredibus meis sigillum meum apposui . Hiis testibus . Petro le Bret . Radulfo Hacun . Ada le Bret . Bartholomei de Burgate . Iohanne Goldwyne . Galfrido Godwyne . Radulpho Mariot . Iohanne filio Reginaldi de Norgate . Ada filio Bartholomei Carpentar' et Aliis.

Seal: missing
Hand: see note on HD 18
Endorsement: 164 (in russet ink), T[ranscriptum] (in ink), 5, 358 and 998 (in ink).

VARIANT: ᵃ *sic*.

HP 999

Grant from Richard son of Ralph Goldwyne of Holkham to William son of Geoffrey Silk of 3 plots. [c. 1270]

Cf. HD 22a, Fo. 6v no. 77
Fiche 1: G7

Sciant presentes et futuri quod ego Ricardus filius Radulfi Goldwyne de Holcham concessi Dedi Et hac presenti carta mea confirmaui Willelmo filio Galfridi Silke pro homagio et seruicio suo et cum Iuliana filia nostra tres pecias terre mee in Camp' de Holcham . silicet quarum vna Iacet apud Duuesti^a inter terram Reginaldi filij Gilberti . ex vna parte . et terram Iohannis Ossemod ex altera parte . Et altera pecia Iacet ad Wellegate inter terram Thome de Burgate ex orientali . et terram Ricardi Northerne ex occidentali . et Tercia pecia iacet inter terram Eborardi filij Pagani ex orientali . et terram Thome de Burgate ex occidentali. Habendas et tenendas de me et heredibus meis illi et heredibus de se et de predicta Iuliana venientibus. Libere quiete bene et in pace Iure et Hereditarie . Reddendo Inde annuatim mihi et heredibus . Octo denarios . Ad . iiii^{or}. Terminos . Anni . Silicet ad Natal' domini . ii . denarios Et ad Pascha . ii . denarios . et ad festum Sancti Iohannis Baptiste . ii denarios . et ad festum Sancti Michaelis . ii . denarios . et ad commune Auxilium in Forinseca sochna de Wyttune . ad xx^{ti}. solidos . j . denarium . ad . plus . plus . et ad minus . minus . pro omni seruicio consuetudine exaccione . et secta cur' seculari demanda. Et Ego vero predictus Ricardus et heredes mei Warantizabimus et acquietabimus deffendemus predictas pecias terre cum pertinenciis . predicto Willelmo et predicte Iuliane et heredibus et heredibus suis vel eorum assignatorum predictum seruicium contra omnes homines et feminas inperpetuum. Et si ita contingat quod predicta Iuliana sine herede de se et de predicto Willelmo obierit quod Willelmus in vita sua abebit medietatem predictarum peciarum et post obitum suum quod predicte pecie reuertantur predicto Ricardo et heredibus suis sine aliqua contradiccione alicuius . In huius autem rei testimonium presenti carte pro me et heredibus meis sigillum meum apposui . Hiis Testibus . Petro le Bret . Ada le Bret . Radulfo Hakun . Thoma de Burgate . Eborado Le Cally . Galfrido Godwyn . David Man . Herueo Leffe . Radulfo Clerico . Willelmo Mariot . et multis aliis.

Seal: Circular white, flower with four petals and four sepals inside inscription. 1½ in. diam.
Hand: see note on HD 8.
Endorsement: T[ranscriptum] 28 (in ink), 6, 999 and 1336 (in pencil).

VARIANT: ^a The third letter is 'u', not 'n', as the place is spelt Le Dowesty in HD 197d; cf. Douwesty in HD 22a, no. 201.

HP 1000

Grant from Thomas son of Harvey Leffe of Holkham to William the clerk of Holkham of 1 plot. [c. 1283–93]

Cf. HD 22a, Fos. 12 no. 149; 18v no. 199
Fiche 1: G8

Sciant presentes et futuri quod Ego Thomas filius Heruei Leffe de Holcham concessi dedi et hac presenti Carta mea confirmaui Willelmo clerico de Holcham pro homagio suo et seruicio et pro vna Marca argenti quam michi dedit pre manibus in Gersumam Vnam peciam terre arrabilis cum pertinenciis iacentem . In camp' de Holcham Inter terram Reginaldi Osmod ex parte australi et terram Gilberti Sutoris de Westgate ex parte aquilonari . et habutat super terram domini prioris de Wausigham versus orientem et super Thorpe mere versus occidentem . Tenendam et Habendam de me et Heredibus meis Illi et heredibus suis libere . quiete . Hereditarie . bene et in pace . vel cuicumque dare . legare . vendere assignare voluerit . Reddendo Inde annuatim mihi et heredibus meis vnum denarium ad duos anni terminos . scilicet ad festum Sancti Michaelis vnum obolum et ad Pascha vnum obolum pro omnibus seruiciis . consuetudibus . exactionibus et . secularibus demandis . Et Ego predictus Thomas Leffe et Heredes mei Warantizabimus adquietabimus et vbique defendemus totam predictam terram cum pertinenciis predicto Willelmo clerico et Heredibus suis vel suis assignatis per predictum seruicium contra omnes gentes inperpetuum . In huius rei testimonium huic scripto sigillum meum appossui . Hiis Testibus . Petro le Bret . Radulfo Hacun . Adam le Bret . Bartholomeo de Burgate . Iohanne Golwine . Radulfo Mariot . Galfrido Godwine . David Man[a] et Aliis.

Seal: missing.
Hand: Cf. HP 1001.
Endorsement: 102 Leff, T[ranscriptum] *Memorandum quis tenet de Holkham* (in ink), 7, 252 and 1000 (in pencil).

VARIANT: [a] 'm' is small compared with 'M' of Mariot.

HP 1001

Grant from Thomas son of David Man of Holkham to Henry his brother of
1 plot. [c. 1272-5]

Not in HD 22a
Fiche 1: G9

Sciant presentes et futuri quod Ego Thomas filius David Man de Holcham
concessi dedi et hac presenti carta mea confirmaui Henrico fratri meo pro
homagio et seruicio suo et pro sex solidis argenti quos mihi dedit in
Gersumam unam peciam terre mee cum pertinenciis Iacentem in Camp' de
Holcham apud Witewong' inter terram Custe de Prato ex parte australi et
terram dicti Henrici fratris mei ex parte aquilon' et abuttat super Haddoghgat'
versus occident' Habendam et tenendam de me et heredibus meis sibi et
heredibus suis seu assignatis et cuicumque dare vendere . legare . vel
assignare voluerit Libere . quiete . Iure et hereditarie. Reddendo inde
annuatim mihi et heredibus meis seu assignatis duos denarios . scilicet ad
festum Sancti Michaelis vnum denarium et ad Pascha vnum denarium . pro
omni seruicio consuetudine et seculari demanda. Et ego prefatus Thomas et
heredes mei Warantizabimus acquietabimus et defendemus predicto Henrico
et heredibus suis seu assignatis predictam peciam terre cum pertinenciis per
predictum seruicium contra omnes homines in perpetuum. In huius rei
testimonium huic scripto sigillum meum apposui . Hiis testibus . Radulfo
Hakun . Petro le Bret . Bartholomeo de Burgat' . Iohanne Goldwyn' .
Galfrido filio Godwyne . Eborardo Kaly . Adam Carpenter' . Thoma Leffe .
Gilberto Sutore . et multis aliis.

Seal: White vesica shaped seal (illegible) with inscription 1¼ x ¾ in.
Hand: HP 1000.
Endorsement: 8, 1001 and 1450 (in pencil).

HP 1002

Confirmation from Peter son of Geoffrey le Bret of Holkham of grant of 5 acres to Robert son of Emma of Holkham. 5 Dec. 1311

Not in HD 22a
Fiche 1: G10

Omnibus Christi fidelibus ad quos presens scriptum peruenerit Petrus filius Galfridi le Bret de Holcham Salutem in domino Sempiternam Nouerit Vniuersitas vestra me inspecsisse Donaciones et Concessiones quas Galfridus pater meus . Et Iohannes frater meus fecerunt Roberto filio Emme de Holcham De quincque acris Terre cum pertinenciis Iacent' in Camp' et in Villa de Holcham que sunt de feodo meo Cartas quidem donacionis et concessionis tocius predicte terre ratam et integram habeo. Et illas Bartholomeo filio predicti Roberti et heredibus suis aut suis Assignatis pro me et heredibus meis in perpetuum et in omnibus confirmo prout carte quas prenominatus Robertus Pater suus habuit de Donacionibus dictarum quincque acrarum Terre cum pertinenciis plenius et melius testantur Reddendo inde Annuatim . michi et heredibus meis vel meis Assignatis omnia seruicia de iure debita et consueta Et ego predictus Petrus et heredes mei Warantizabimus et adquietabimus predictas quincque acras terre cum pertinenciis . Prefato Bartholomeo et heredibus suis vel suis assignatis . contra omnes homines in perpetuum. Pro hac autem confirmacione et Warantia tocius predicte terre Predictus Bartholomeus dedit michi vnam summam pecunie pre manibus. In cuius rei Testimonium huic presenti scripto confirmacionis sigillum meum apposui . Hiis testibus . Willelmo Silk' . Willelmo Wake . Martino Goldwyne . Roberto de Griston . Gilberto le Bret . Ada filio Simonis Hamund . Iohanne Belneye . Iohanne filio Iohannis Le Bret et Aliis Confirmat' apud Holcham in vigilia sancti Nicholai episcopi Anno Regni Regis Edwardj Quinto.

Seal: missing but dark brown seal bag remains.
Hand: See note on HD 23.
Endorsement: 9, 1002 and 1264 (in pencil).

HP 1003

Grant from Thomas Likesalt and Caterine his wife of Holkham to Bartholomew Calwer of Holkham of 1 acre.   31 Oct. 1312

Cf. HD 22a, Fo. 2 no. 7
Fiche 1: G11

Sciant presentes et futuri quod Nos Thomas Likesalt' et Caterina vxor mea de Holcham concessimus Dedimus et hac presenti carta nostra confirmauimus Bartholomeo Calwer de Eadem pro quadam summa pecunia quam nobis dedit pre manibus . vnam acram terre nostre cum pertinenciis Iacent' in campo orientali eiusdem ville inter terram Iohannis Godwine versus Orientem et terram Gilberti Huberd versus occidentem cuius caput Australe abuttat super brueram . Et capud Aquilon' abuttat super terram Iohannis Aynild Habendam et tenendam illi et heredibus suis Libere Quiete Bene in pace Iure et hereditarie De capitali domino illius feodi pro seruic' inde de Iure debit' et consuet' Et nos vero supradicti Thomas et Katerina Warantizabimus predictam Acram terre siue sit maius aut minus antedicto Bartholomeo et heredibus suis siue suis assignatis contra Omnes gentes in perpetuum In cuius Rei Testimonium huic presenti carte sigilla nostra vnanimiter apposuimus . Hiis testibus . Willelmo Silke . Willelmo Wake . Martino Goldwyne . Roberto de Griston . Iohanne Aynild . Ricardo Le Northerne . Thoma filio suo . Iohanne Godwyne . Et multis aliis Dat' apud Holcham in vigilia Omnium Sanctorum anno Regni Regis Edwardi*ᵃ* Sexto.

Seal: Two seals missing.
Hand: See note on HD 23.
Endorsement: 53 T[ranscriptum] (in ink), 10, 1003 and 1506 (in pencil).

VARIANT: *ᵃ* filij Edwardi omitted.

HP 1004

Grant from Adam son of William Craske of Holkham to Richard Neel of Burnham and Caterine his wife of 6 acres in 2 plots.   12 Apr. 1318

Cf. HD 22a, Fo. 14v no. 166 (Lucas no. 15)
Fiche 1: G12

Sciant presentes et futuri quod ego Adam filius Willelmi Crask de Holcham concessi dedi et hac presenti carta mea confirmaui Ricardo Neel de Brunham et Caterine vxori sue et heredibus de eorumdem corporibus legitime procreatis ac rectis heredibus dicti Ricardi si predicti Ricardus et Katerina sine heredibus de eorum corporibus legitime procreatis obierint . sex acras terre mee Iacent' in camp' de Holcham videlicet . apud Wodegate tres acras terre et apud Warldhowh' tres acras terre tenend' et habend' dictas sex acras terre cum pertinenciis predicto Ricardo et Katerine et heredibus de eorumdem corporibus legitime procreatis ac rectis heredibus dicti Ricardi si predicti Ricardus et Katerina sine heredibus de eorumdem corporibus legitime procreatis obierint de Capitalibus dominis feodi per seruic' inde debit' et consuet' libere quiete bene et in pace in feod' et hereditarie. Et ego predictus Adam et heredes mei procreatis ac rectis heredibus dicti Ricardi si predictis Ricardo et Katerine et heredibus de eorumdem corporibus legitime predicti Ricardus et Katerina sine herede de eorumdem corporibus legitime procreatis obierint Warrantizabimus imperpetuum contra omnes gentes . In cuius Rei testimonium Huic presenti carte sigillum meum apposui . Hiis testibus . Willelmo Wake . Willelmo Roteney . Galfrido Gylion . Hugone Otes . Iohanne Belneye et aliis dat' apud Holcham die mercurij proxima ante dominicam Ramorum Palmarum anno regni Regis Edwardi[a] undecimo.

> Seal: Small black circular seal: Deer's head with cross between horns in inscription 3/4 in diam.
> Hand: See note on HD 23.
> Endorsement: *Carta Ade filii W Craske de VI acris terre apud Wodegate et Warledehow 19. de Holkham.* T[ranscriptum] on seal tag (in ink) 11, 1004 and 1556 (in pencil).

VARIANT: [a] filij Edwardi omitted

HP 1005

Grant from Bartholomew son of Robert of Holkham to Richard Neel and Katerine his wife of 1 plot.   20 Aug. 1322

> Cf. HD 22a, Fo. 15v no. 177 (Lucas no. 26)
> Fiche 1: G13 and 3: G12 (seal)

Sciant presentes et futuri quod Ego Bartholomeus filius Roberti de Holcham concessi dedi . et hac presenti carta mea confirmaui Ricardo Neel de eadem et Katerine vxori sue vnam peciam terre mee iacent' apud Steynhyl inter terras predictorum Ricardi et Katerine et Capud aquilonare abuttat super terram Domini Adomari de Valencia. Habend' et tenend' predictis Ricardo et Katerine et heredibus de corporibus eorum prouenientibus et suis assignatis predictam peciam terre libere quiete . bene et in pace iure et hereditarie de Capitalibus dominis feodi imperpetuum per seruicia inde de iure debita et consueta. Et Ego predictus Bartholomeus heredes mei et mei assignati prefatis Ricardo et Katerine heredibus de corporibus eorum legitime prouenientibus ac eorum assignatis predictam peciam terre cum pertinenciis per predicta seruicia imperpetuum Warantizabimus contra omnes. Si autem predicti Ricardus et Katerina sine heredibus obierint de corporibus suis legitime procreatis predicta pecia terre cum pertinenciis heredibus predicti Ricardi quiete et solute comititur.[a] In cuius rei testimonium huic carte sigillum meum apposui die Veneris proxima post festum assumpcionis Beate marie Anno regni regis Edwardi [filij Edwardi][b] sextodecimo. Testibus Iohanne Bret . Willelmo Wake . Ricardo Northerne . Thoma filio suo . Roberto de Gristone . Bartholomeo Calwere . Iohanne de Bylneye et aliis.

Seal: Small dark circular seal, Man's bearded profile facing left in hat, inside inscription 1/2 in. diam.

Hand: see note on HD 19.

Endorsement: *Carta Bartholomei filij Roberti de Holcham de j pecia terre apud Steynhyl abut' super terram domini Adomari de Valentia.* 26 (in black ink), T[ranscriptum] (on seal tag) 12, 507 and 1005 (in pencil).

VARIANTS: [a] *sic.* [b] filij Edwardi omitted in Ms.

HP 1006

Grant from John son of Geoffrey le Bret of Holkham to Richard of Barking rector of half Egmere church of 1 plot.   5 Sept. 1293

Cf. HD 22a, Fos. 7 no. 85; 11 no. 138
Fiche 1: G14

Sciant presentes et futuri quod Ego Iohannes filius Galfridi Le Bret de Holkham dedi concessi et hac presenti carta mea confirmaui . Ricardo de Berking Rectori medietatis ecclesie de Egemere . pro homagio et seruicio suo vnam peciam terre mee in villa de Holkham que vocatur Gunyeswong . Iacentem inter terram Dionisie de Munchansi ex parte australi et terram prioris de Walsyngham ex parte aquilonari et abuttat ad vnum capud super terram prioris de Petreston versus occidentem . et aliud capud super terram meam versus orientem. Habend' et Tenend' de me et heredibus meis sibi et heredibus suis vel suis assignatis libere quiete bene et in pace in feodo et hereditarie aut cuicumque aut quandocumque dare vendere legare vel assiignare[a] voluerit . Reddendo inde annuatim capitali domino feodi illius seruicium inde debitum. Et ego predictus Iohannes et heredes mei vel mei assignati . Warantizabimus defendemus predictam peciam terre cum pertinenciis predicto Ricardo et heredibus suis vel suis assignatis pro omni exaccione sectis Curiarum et Demanda contra omnes homines in perpetuum. In cuius rei testimonium huic presenti carte sigillum meum apposui . Hiis Testibus . Domino Radulfo le Nuggun . Domino Edmundo de Kokefeld .

Domino Iohanne de Walsygham milites[b] . Gydone de Mortuo Mari . Roberto Angri de Egemere . Radulfo Lark . Radulfo de Redham de Warfles . Thoma de Birston*e* . Iohanne Sylk de Holkham. Dat' die Sabati proxima ante Nativitatem Beate Marie Virginis anno regni regis Edwardi Vicesimo primo.

Seal: missing.
Endorsement: 4 and T[ranscriptum] (in ink), 13, 337 and 1006 (in pencil).

VARIANTS: [a] *sic* in M*s*. [b] nominative in M*s*.

HP 1007

Grant from Walter Hakun of Holkham to Simon Hamund of Holkham of 1 plot of 13/4 acres and 2 other plots. 17 Mar. 1294

Cf. HD 22a, Fo. 8 no. 100
Fiche 2: A2

Sciant presentes et futuri quod Ego Walterus Hakun de Holkham concessi dedi et hac presenti carta mea confirmaui Simoni Hamund eiusdem Wille et heredibus suis pro quadam summa pecunie quam Mihi dedit premanibus. Tres pecias terre mee Iacent' in Campis de Holcham quarum prima pecia terre continens in se septem Rodas terre Iacet inter terram prioris de Walsingham ex parte Aquilon' et terram que fuit Martini Rust ex parte Australi . Secunda pecia terre Iacet inter terram Domini Willelmi de Calethorp ex parte occident' . et terram que fuit Galfridi Golde ex parte orient' et Tercia pecia terre Iacet ad Caput australe predicte terre inter terram Domini Willelmi de Caletorp ex parte occidentali et terram Iohannis Le Burgonye ex parte orientali. Habend' et tenend' de capitalibus Dominis feodi illius per seruicia Inde debita et Consueta Libere . Iure . et Hereditarie. Et ego predictus Walterus et Heredes mei Warantizabimus predictas pecias terre predicto Simoni et Heredibus suis contra omnes homines in perpetuum. In Cuius Rei testimonium Huic Carte sigillum meum Apposui . Hiis testibus . Bartholomeo de Burgate . Iohanne filio Ade le Bret . Martino Goldwyne . Galfrido Godwyne . Waltero Hakun . Willelmo Craske . Iohanne Aynild . Ricardo le Northerne . Iohanne Rutur . Roberto Le Marschall . Gilberto Le Bret . Humfrido Dauyd et aliis. Dat' apud Holkham. die Mercurij proxim' post festum Sancti Gregorij pape. Anno Regni Regis Edwardi vicessimo secundo.

Seal: Fragment of white seal, star(?) inside inscription (H)AKU(N), 1/2 in. diam.
Hand: See note on HD 12.
Endorsement: 40, T[ranscriptum] Hakun and Steynhill' (in ink), 14, 1007 and 1417 (in pencil).

HP 1008

Grant from John son of Geoffrey le Bret of Holkham to Simon Hamund of Holkham of 9 acres in 2 plots and 1 other plot.   17 Mar. 1294

    Cf. HD 22a, Fo. 10 no. 126
    Fiche 2: A3

Sciant presentes et futuri quod Ego Iohannes filius Galfridi Le Bret de Holcham concessi . dedi . et hac presenti carta mea confirmaui Simoni Hamund eiusdem Wille et heredibus suis pro quadam summa pecunie quam mihi dedit premanibus . Tres pecias terre mee Iacent' in Campis de Holcham . quarum Prima pecia continens in se quatuor acras terre Iacet apud Duuespit inter terram Henrici Dauid ex parte australi et terram Iohannis filij Rogeri Belneye ex parte Aquilon' et Capud orientale abuttat super terram que fuit Radulfi Hakun. Secunda pecia terre iacet inter terram Prioris et Conuentus de Walsingham ex parte occidentali et terram meam ex parte orientali et capud Aquilon' abuttat super terram predicti Simonis. Et Tercia pecia terre Iacet inter terram meam ex parte Aquilon' . et terram Ade Carpentarij ex parte Australi et capud orientale abuttat super Hadhowegate et continet in se quinque acras terre . Habend' et tenend' de Capitalibus Dominis feodi illius per seruic' inde debit' et consuet' . Libere . quiete . Bene . Iure . et Hereditarie. Et Ego predictus Iohannes et Heredes mei Warantizabimus predictas pecias terre predicto Simoni et Heredibus suis Contra omnes Homines in perpetuum. In Cuius Rei testimonium Huic carte sigillum meum apposui . Hiis testibus . Bartholomeo de Burgate . Iohanne filio Ade Le Bret . Martino Goldwyne . Galfrido Godwyne . Willelmo Craske . Iohanne Aynild . Ricardo Le Northerne . Waltero Hakun . Roberto Le Marschall . Iohanne Rutur . Humfrido Dauyd et aliis. Dat' apud Holcham die Mercurij proxim' post festum Sancti Gregorij pape Anno Regni Regis Edwardi vicesimo secundo.

    Seal: missing.
    Hand: See note on HD 12.
    Endorsement: 7 T[ranscriptum] *Carta Iohannis Le Bret de nouo facta secundum Statutum nuper Editum* (in ink), 15, 848 and 1008 (in pencil).

HP 1009

Quitclaim from Geoffrey Le Bret of Holkham to Simon Hamund of Holkham
of 1 plot of 4 acres.   24 Dec. 1293

Cf. HD 22a, Fo. 4 no. 45
Fiche 2: A4

Sciant presentes et futuri quod Ego Galfridus le Bret de Holkham concessi
Remisi et presenti scripto confirmaui Simoni Hamund eiusdem Wille et
heredibus suis vnam peciam terre que in se continet quatuor acras terre
iacent' in vna Cultura in Campis de Holkham inter terram Henrici Dauid ex
parte Australi et terram Iohannis filij Rogeri De Belneye ex parte aquilon' .
et Capud orient' abuttat super terram que fuit Radulfi Hakun . et Capud
occident' abuttat super Gunniswong. Et totum Ius et clamium quod in
predicta pecia terre cum omnibus aliis pertinenciis quibuscumque habui vel
habere potui, eidem Simoni et heredibus suis . de me et heredibus meis
Remisi et quietum Clamaui in perpetuum Habend' et tenend' de Capitalibus
dominis feodi . illi et heredibus suis . libere . quiete Iure . et hereditarie
faciend' inde Annuatim dictis dominis prout plenius continetur in Carta
feoffamenti sui. Et istam concessionem et confirmacionem feci Ego Galfridus
predicto Simoni et heredibus suis in seisina ipsius Simonis de toto tenemento
predicto quod quidem tenementum predictus Simon adquisiuit de Iohanne
filio meo et herede. Et ego predictus Galfridus et heredes mei vel mei
assignati Warantizabimus adquietabimus et omnino defendemus predictam
peciam terre cum pertinenciis predicto Simoni et heredibus suis Contra omnes
homines inperpetuum. In Cuius Rei testimonium huic scripto sigillum meum
apposui . Hiis testibus Bartholomeo de Burgate . Iohanne filio Adam le Bret .
Iohanne Silke . Willelmo Silke . Galfrido Godwyne . Martino Goldwyne .
Waltero Hakun . Gilberto Le Bret . Willelmo Crask . Ricardo le Northerne .
Iohanne Rutur . Humfrido David et Aliis multis. Dat Apud Holkham die
Iouis proxima ante Natiuitatem domini Anno Regni Regis Eadwardi vicesimo
secundo.

Seal: Circular white seal painted red, broken, Fleur-de-lys inside inscription S.
GALFRIDI FIL. PETR. 2 in diam.
Hand: see note on HD 10.
Endorsement: 94 (in russet ink) and T[ranscriptum] (in ink), 16, 1009 and 1524 (in
pencil).

HP 1010

Quitclaim from John son of Geoffrey le Bret of Holkham to Simon son of Hamo of Holkham of 51/4 acres in 3 plots.   18 Dec. 1294

Cf. HD 22a, Fo. 10 no. 123
Fiche 2: A5

Sciant presentes et futuri quod Ego Iohannes filius Galfridi le Bret de Holkham in plena Etate mea et legitima scilicet viginti et vnius Anni concessi dedi et omnino pro me et heredibus meis in perpetuum quietum clamaui Simoni filio Hamonis eiusdem Wille et heredibus suis totum Ius et Clamium meum quod habui vel aliquo modo Habere potui in tribus peciis terre iacentibus in Camp' de Holkham quarum Prima pecia in se Continens tres acras terre iacet apud Hadhowebreyst et Secunda pecia terre in se Continens septem rodas terre iacet apud Ringwaleslond et Tercia pecia in se Continens duas Rodas terre iacet apud Schuckelif quas quidem Tres pecias terre predictus Simon adquisiuit de me infra annos Mee Etatis legitime. Ita quod nec Ego Iohannes nec Heredes mei nec assignati mei nec aliquis nomine meo nec heredum meorum aliquid Iuris vel Clamij in predictis tribus peciis terre cum pertinenciis de Cetero exigere vel vendicare poterimus. Istam autem Concessionem et quietam Clamacionem feci Ego Iohannes predicto Simoni et heredibus suis in seysina ipsius Simonis de toto tenemento predicto pro viginti solidis argenti quos mihi dedit premanibus.^a Et Ego predictus Iohannes et heredes mei vel mei assignati . Warantizabimus et omnino defendemus totum tenementum predictum cum pertinenciis predicto Simoni et heredibus suis vel suis assignatis Contra omnes homines inperpetuum. In Cuius Rei testimonium Huic Carte Sigillum meum apposui . Dat' apud Holkham Die Sabat' proxima ante festum Sancti Thome apostoli. Anno Regni Regis Eadwardi Vicessimo Tercio . Hiis testibus . Bartholomeo de Burgate . Iohanne filio Ade le Bret . Iohanne Sylke . Willelmo Sylke . Martino Goldwyne . Galfrido Godwyne . Willelmo Craske . Iohanne Aynild . Waltero Hakun . Ricardo le Northerne . Roberto Le Marshall . Humfrido Dauyd et aliis multis.

Seal: Circular while seal painted red: 2 rays of pointed star (with knobs) inside inscription: GALFRIDI... only 1/4 in. left.
Hand: see Note on HD 10.
Endorsement: G. le Brett. 9, T[ranscriptum], 17, 728 and 1010 (in pencil).

VARIANT: ^a written as one word in Ms.

HP 1011

Grant from John son of Geoffrey le Bret of Holkham to Simon son of Hamo
of Holkham of 153/4 acres in 8 plots.   30 Apr. 1295

     Cf. HD 22a, Fo. 4 no. 46
     Fiche 2: A6

Sciant presentes et futuri quod Ego Iohannes filius Galfridi Le Bret de
Holcham in plena Etate mea et legitima concessi et Hac presenti Carta mea
Confirmaui Simoni filio Hamonis eiusdem Wille et heredibus suis pro
Quadraginta et sex solidis Argenti quos mihi dedit pre manibus. Quindecim
Acras et tres Rodas terre cum pertinenciis Iacen' in Campis de Holcham in
Octo peciis terre quas de me adquisiuit infra Etatem meam Legitimam.
Quarum . Prima pecia in se continens septem Rodas terre Iacet apud
Greyston . Secunda pecia in se continens quatuor Acras terre Iacet apud
Duuespyt . Tertia pecia in se continens vnam acram terre Iacet apud
Grenegate . Quarta pecia in se continens tres Rodas terre Iacet ad Caput
orientale predicte pecie terre que vocatur Grenegate . Quinta pecia in se
Continens tres Acras terre Iacet apud Hadhowebreyst . Sexta pecia in se
continens septem Rodas terre iacet apud Ryngwaleslond . Septima pecia in se
continens duas Rodas terre Iacet apud Schuckelif . Et Octaua pecia in se
continens tres acras terre Iacet apud Hadhowe inter terram meam ex parte
Aquilonar' et Capud occidentale abuttat super terram predicti Simonis et
Capud Orientale abuttat super Hadhowegate. Habend' et tenend' predictas
pecias terre cum omnibus suis pertinenciis per seruicia debita et Consueta
sicut Carte sui feoffamenti testantur. illi et heredibus suis . Libere . quiete .
Bene . in pace . Iure . et Hereditarie. Cuicumque vel quandocumque predictas
pecias terre cum omnibus suis pertinenciis . dare vendere vel assignare
voluerit exceptis domibus Religionis . Istam autem Concessionem et
Confirmacionem feci Ego Iohannes predicto Simoni et heredibus suis in
seysina ipsius Simonis de toto tenemento predicto. Et Ego predictus Iohannes
et heredes mei vel mei assignati Warantizabimus et omnino defendemus
totum tenementum predictum cum omnibus suis pertinenciis predicto Simoni
et heredibus suis vel suis assignatis Contra omnes homines in perpetuum. In
Cuius Rei testimonium Huic Carte sigillum meum apposui. Dat' apud
Holcham die Sabat' proxima post festum Sancti Marci Ewangeliste . Anno
Regni Regis Eadwardi vicessimo Tertio . Hiis testibus . Bartholomeo de
Burgate . Iohanne filio Ade Le Bret . Iohanne Silke . Willelmo Silke .
Martino Goldwyne . Galfrido Godwyne . Willelmo Craske . Iohanne Aynild .

Waltero Hakun . Ricardo Le Northerne . Roberto Le Marschall . Gilberto Le
Bret et aliis multis .

Seal: Circular white seal, 8 pointed star with knobs on ends of rays within (illegible)
inscription 1¹/₂ in. diam.
Hand: see note on HD 12.
Endorsement: 13, T[ranscriptum], G. le Brett (in ink), 18, 901 and 1011 (in pencil).

HP 1012

*Quitclaim from John son of Geoffrey le Bret of Holkham to Humphrey David
of Holkham of a rent of 2d. for a messuage with a croft.*   5 June 1295

Not in HD 22a
Fiche 2: A7

Notum sit omnibus hoc scriptum visuris vel Audituris quod Ego Iohannes
filius Galfridi Le Bret de Holcham in plena Etate mea et Legitima Concessi
remisi et omnino pro me et heredibus meis in perpetuum quietum Clamaui
Humfrido Dauyd eiusdem Wille et Heredibus suis vel eius assignatis Totum
Ius et Clamium quod habui vel aliquo modo habere potui In duobus denariis
Annui Redditus quos percipere solebam de Willelmo Ducke de Holcham pro
quodam mesuagio cum Crufta quod tenuit de Mariota Relicta quondam
Willelmi Bending de Holcham quem quidem Redditum Antecessores patris
mei adquisiuerunt de predicta Mariota . et de Galfrido patre meo predictum
redditum adquisiui. Ita quod nec ego Iohannes nec Heredes mei nec aliquis
ex nomine Heredum meorum [Nihil] de Cetero ad dictum Mesuagium cum
Crufta vendicare nec exigere poterimus nomine redditus nec aliter eschaet'
pro hac au[tem remi]ssione et quieta Clamacione dedit mihi predictus
Humfridus quandam summam pecunie premanibus. In C[uius Rei
testim]onium Huic Scripto pro me et Heredibus meis sigillum meum
Apposui. Dat' apud Holcham die Dominica proxima [post festum S]ancte
Trinitatis. Anno Regni Regis Edwardi vicessimo tertio . Hiis testibus .
Bartholomeo de Burgate . [Iohanne] filio Ade Le Bret . Iohanne Sylke .
Willelmo filio suo . Martino Goldwyne . Galfrido Godwyne . Willelmo
Craske . Simone Hamund . Iohanne Aynild . Waltero Hakun . Iohanne Rutur
. Roberto Le Marshall et aliis multis.

Seal: missing.
Hand: see note on HD 12.
Endorsement: No T[ranscriptum] or other ink endorsement, perhaps comes from an
archive other than that of the Neels. 19, 790 and 1012 are pencil endorsements.

HP 1013

Grant from Roger Le Norne of Holkham to Simon son of Hamo of Holkham of 11/2 roods.   27 June 1295

Cf. HD 22a, Fo. 2v no. 18
Fiche 2: A8

Sciant presentes et futuri quod Ego Rogerus Le Norne de Holcham concessi dedi et hac presenti Carta mea confirmaui Symoni filio Hamonis de eadem et heredibus pro quadam summa pecunie quam mihi dedit premanibus*a* vnam Rodam et dimidiam terre Iacent' in villa de Holcham inter terram Iohannis Edryche ex parte Aquilonari et terram Thome filij Iohannis ex parte australi et capud occidentale abuttat super viam que ducit de La Dale apud Thorp. Habendam et tenendam dictam peciam terre cum pertinenciis de capitalibus dominis feodi . pro seruic' inde debit' et consuet' . Libere quiete bene et in pace Iure et hereditarie. Faciend' inde . annuatim dictis capitalibus dominis feodi . vnum ob. ad Pascha . pro omnibus seruiciis consuetudinibus exaccionibus . Cur' sectis et omnibus aliis . secularibus demandis. Et Ego Rogerus predictus et heredes [m]ey Warantizabimus et omnino defendemus dictam peciam terre cum omnibus pertinenciis predicto Symoni et heredibus suis vel suis assingnatis . per predictum seruicium contra omnes homines inperpetuum. In Huius Rey Testimonium . Huic scripto sigillum meum apposuy . Hiis testibus . Iohanne filio Ade Le Bret . Bartho*lomeo* de Burgate . Willelmo Crask . Waltero Hacon . Martino Goldewyne . Ricardo Le Northerne . Gilbertus Le Bret . Rogero Elveryche . Herueo Wytebred . Hunfrido Dauy et Aliis. Dat' apud Holcham die Lune proxima ante festum . Apostolorum . Petri et Pauli. Anno. Regni Regis Edwardi . vicesimo tercio.

Seal: missing.
Hand: HP 1018, 1025.
Endorsement: *1 roda et dimid' terre et abbutat super viam que ducit de la Dale apud Thorp versus occidentem.* T[ranscriptum] . *Socag'* (in ink), 20, 1099. 1013 (in pencil).

VARIANT: *a* written as one word in Ms.

HP 1014

Grant from Everard Underhowe of Holkham to Bartholomew le Muner of Holkham of 1 rood. **20 July 1295**

Cf. HD 22a, Fo. 11 no. 133
Fiche 2: A9

Sciant presentes et futuri quod Ego Eborardus UnderHowe de Holcham concessi dedi et Hac presenti Carta mea Confirmaui Bartholomeo Le Muner eiusdem Wille et heredibus suis pro sex solid' Argenti quos mihi dedit premanibus vnam Rodam terre mee cum pertinenciis iacent' in Campis de Holcham inter terram Robert Le Marschall' ex parte Aquilon'. et terram que fuit Willelmi Curthun ex parte australi Cuius capud occidentale abuttat super Caldhowegate. Habend' ettenend' de Capitalibus Dominis feodi illius illi et Heredibus suis Libere quiete . Bene . in pace . Iure et Hereditarie . Cuicumque vel quandocumque eam . dare . vendere vel assignare voluerit . Faciend' Inde Annuatim pro me et heredibus meis Capitalibus Dominis feodi illius vnum obolum ad Natiuitatem Sancti Iohannis Baptiste et ad Comune Auxilium quando Euenerit in forinseca Sokna de Wyttone ad viginti solid' vnum quadrantem ad plus plus . et ad minus minus . pro omni seruicio . Consuetudine . Exaccione . Sect' Curie . et Secular' demand' . Et Ego predictus Eborardus et Heredes mei vel mei assignati Warantizabimus predictam Rodam terre cum pertinenciis predicto Bartholomeo . et heredibus suis vel suis assignatis Contra omnes homines in perpetuum. In Cuius Rei testimonium Huic Carte Sigillum meum Apposui. Dat' apud Holcham Die Sancte Margarete Anno Regni Regis Edwardi vicesimo Tertio . Hiis testibus . Bartholomeo de Burgate . Iohanne filio Ade Le Bret . Iohanne Sylke . Willelmo filio suo . Martino Goldwyne . Galfrido Godwyne . Willelmo Craske . Simone Hamund . Iohanne Aynild . Iohanne Rutur . Waltero Hakun . Ricardo Le Northerne et aliis.

Seal: missing.
Hand: see note on HD 12.
Endorsement: T[ranscriptum] (in ink, russet and black), 21, 849 and 1014 (in pencil).

HP 1015

Quitclaim from John son of Geoffrey le Bret of Holkham to Simon Hamund of Holkham of 8¹/₂d. rent.   15 Oct. 1295

Cf. HD 22a, Fo. 6v no. 81
Fiche 2: A10

Notum sit omnibus hoc scriptum visuris vel audituris quod Ego Iohannes filius Galfridi Le Bret de Holcham Concessi . Remisi . et omnino pro me et heredibus meis in perpetuum quietum Clamaui . Simoni Hamund eiusdem Wille et Heredibus suis . octo denarios et obolum annui Redditus quos percipere solebam de predicto Simone pro tenemento quod predictus Simon adquisiuit de Galfrido patre meo et de me. Ita quod nec Iohannes nec heredes mei nec aliquo nomine Heredum meorum in predictis octo denariis et obolo Annui Redditus de Cetero aliquid Iuris vel Clamij Exigere vel vendicare poterimus Pro Hac autem Concessione et Iuris mei Relaxacione dedit Mihi predictus Simon . quinque Solidos premanibus.ᵃ In Cuius Rei testimonium Huic presenti scripto Sigillum meum Apposui . Hiis testibus . Bartholomeo de Burgate . Iohanne filio Ade Le Bret . Iohanne Sylke . Willelmo Sylke . Martino Goldwyne . Galfrido Godwyn . Willelmo Crask . Iohanne Aynild . Waltero Hakun . Ricardo Le Northerne . Iohanne Rutur . Humfrido Dauyd et Aliis multis. Dat' apud Holkham die Sabati proxima ante festum Sancti Luce Ewangeliste. Anno Regni Regis Edwardi vicessimo Tercio.

Seal: White vesica shaped seal bird (facing right) on column, inside inscription. Broken.
Hand: see note on HD 12.
Endorsement: T[ranscriptum] 87 (in ink), (T as ususal is black, 87 russet coloured), 22, 847 and 1015 (in pencil).

VARIANT: ᵃwritten as one word in Ms.

HP 1016

Grant from John son of Geoffrey le Bret of Holkham to Simon Hamund of Holkham of 1 acre.   12 Dec. 1295

Cf. HD 22a, Fo. 10 no. 118
Fiche 2: A11

Sciant presentes et futuri quod Ego Iohannes filius Galfridi Le Bret de Holcham Concessi . dedi et hac presenti Carta mea Confirmaui Simoni Hamund eiusdem Wille et heredibus suis pro quadam summa pecunie quam mihi dedit premanibus*a* vnam Acram terre mee Iacent' in Campis de Holcham inter terram meam ex parte Aquilon' et terram predicti Simonis ex parte Australi . Cuius Capud orientale abuttat super Hadhowegate . et Capud occidentale abuttat super terram predicti Simonis . Habend' et tenend' de Capitalibus Dominis feodi illius. illi et heredibus suis Libere . Quiete . Bene . in pace . Iure . et Hereditarie . Cuicumque vel quandocumque . eam . dare . vendere . vel assignare voluerit exceptis domibus Religionis Faciend' Inde Annuatim pro me et heredibus meis . Capitalibus Dominis feodi illius . vnum Clauum Garophili ad Natiuitatem Sancti Iohannis Baptiste pro omni seruicio . Consuetudine Exaccione . Sect' Cur' . et secular' demand'. Et Ego predictus Iohannes et heredes mei Warantizabimus predictam Acram terre predicto Simoni et Heredibus suis contra omnes Homines inperpetuum. In Cuius Rei testimonium Huic Carte sigillum meum apposui. Dat' apud Holcham vigil' sancte Lucie Virginis. Anno Regni Regis Edwardi vicessimo Quarto . Hiis testibus . Bartholomeo de Burgate . Iohanne filio Ade Le Bret . Willelmo Silke . Martino Goldwyne . Galfrido Godwyne . Willelmo Craske . Iohanne Aynild . Waltero Hakun . Ricardo Le Northerne . Roberto Le Marschall . Iohanne Rutur .*b* Humfrido Dauyd et aliis Multis .

Seal: missing.
Hand: see note on HD 12.
Endorsement: T[ranscriptum] (in ink), 23, 685 and 1016 (in pencil).

VARIANTS: *a*written as one word in Ms. *b* Iohanne Rutur repeated in Ms.

HP 1017

Quitclaim from John son of Adam le Bret of Holkham to Simon Hamund of Holkham of 2 plots.   24 Dec. 1295

Cf. HD 22a, Fo. 4 no. 43
Fiche 2: A12 and 3: G3 (seal)

Notum sit omnibus Hoc scriptum visuris vel Audituris quod Ego Iohannes filius Ade le Bret de Holcham . Concessi . Remisi . et omnino pro me et heredibus meis in perpetuum quietum . Clamaui . Simoni Hamund et heredibus suis eiusdem Wille . Totum Ius et Clamium meum . quod Habui vel aliquo modo Habere potui in duabus peciis terre iacent in Campis de Holcham . que . mihi contingebant . per . descentum hereditatis quondam Simonis consanguinei mei filij Issabell' Franceys . in quas predictus Simon non habuit ingressum nisi per Stephanum Ossebern et Herueum Fabrum Ita quod nec Ego Iohannes nec heredes mei nec aliquis nomine heredum meorum in predictis peciis terre aliquid Iuris vel clamij de Cetero exigere vel vendicare potuerimus . saluo seruicio Domini Regis videlicet ad Schyreuesscot et Wodewellekot secundum exigenciam predictarum peciarum terre et Mihi et Heredibus meis singulis annis . denarium et quadrantem . ad duos anni terminos videlicet ad Natiuitatem Domini . tres quadrantes et ad Annunciacionem Beate Marie Virginis vnum obolum pro omnimodis seruiciis . Istam autem concessionem et quietam Clamacionem feci Ego Iohannes . predicto Simoni et Heredibus suis in seysina ipsius Simonis de predictis peciis terre pro quadam summa pecunie quam mihi dedit premanibus. In cuius Rei testimonium huic scripto sigillum meum Apposui. Dat' Apud Holcham die Sabati proxima ante Natiuitatem Domini Anno Regni Regis Edwardi vicessimo Quarto . Hiis testibus . Bartholomeo de Burgate . Galfrido Le Bret . Iohanne filio suo . Martino Goldwyne . Willelmo Sylke . Galfrido Godwyne . Willelmo Craske . Iohanne Aynild . Waltero Hakun . Ricardo Le Northerne . Iohanne Rutur . Roberto Le Marschall et aliis.

Seal: Vesica shaped brown seal cross potence on which smaller St. Andrew's cross is superimposed within inscriptions... IOH LE BRET 3/4 in. diam.
Hand: See note on HD 12.
Endorsement: 91 in customary red ink but no T[ranscriptum] i.e. not transcribed for the Cartulary. 24, 113 and 1117 (in pencil).

HP 1018

Grant from John son of Geoffrey le Bret of Holkham to Simon son of Hamo of Holkham of 1/2 acre.   16 Feb. 1296

Cf. HD 22a, Fo. 10 no. 122
Fiche 2: A13 and 3: G4 (seal)

Sciant presentes et futuri quod Ego Iohannes filius Galfridi Le Bret de Holcham Concessi dedi et hac presenti Carta mea confirmaui Symoni filio Hamonis eiusdem ville et heredibus suis vnam dimidiam acram terre Iacent'[a] in Camp' de Holcham inter terram dicti Symonis ex parte australi et terram meam ex parte aquilonar' et capud occidentale abuttat super terram dicti Symonis et capud orientale abuttat super viam que vocatur Hadougat' Habend' et tenend' predictam dimidiam acre terre de capitalibus dominis feodi per servic' inde debit' et consuet'. faciend' inde annuatim. dictis capitalibus dominis feodi pro predicta dimidia acra terre . Vnum Clauum Gariofili pro omnibus seruiciis consuetudinibus exaccionibus Cur' Sectis et omnibus secularibus demandis. Et . Ego Iohannes predictus et heredes mey Warantizabimus et omnino defendemus predictam dimidiam acram terre predicto Symoni et heredibus suis vel suis assingnatis per seruicium predictum contra omnes homines In perpetuum. In Huius Rey testimonium Huic Carte Sigillum meum est appensum. Dat' apud Holcham die Veneris proxim' post festum Sancti Valentini . Anno Regni Regis Edwardi . vicesimo quarto . Hiis testibus . Iohanne Le Bret . Galfrido Le Bret . Bartholomeo de Burgate . Willelmo Sylk . Martino Goldewyn . Waltero Hacon . Willelmo Crask . Ricardo Le Northerne . Iohanne Aynild . Iohanne Parson' . Gilberto Le Bret . Humfrido Dauy et Aliis multis.

Seal: Fragment of white seal painted red, vesica, a bird facing right (left destroyed) in inscription (better specimen on HD 22b)
Hand: see note on HD 1013.
Endorsement: T[ranscriptum] (in ink), 25, 168 and 1018 (in pencil).

VARIANT: *a* Iacentent', M*s*.

HP 1019

Grant from John son of Geoffrey le Bret of Holkham to Simon Hamund of Holkham of 1/2 acre.   14 Mar. 1296

Cf. HD 22a, Fo. 9v no. 117
Fiche 2: A14

Sciant presentes et futuri quod Ego Iohannes filius Galfridi Le Bret de Holcham Concessi dedi et hac presenti Carta mea Confirmaui Simoni Hamund eiusdem*a* et heredibus suis pro quadam summa pecunie . quam mihi . dedit premanibus vnam dimidiam acram terre mee Iacent' in Campis de Holcham inter terram meam ex parte aquilon' . et terram predicti Simonis ex parte Australi . Cuius Capud orientale abuttat super Hadhowegate . Habend' et tenend' de Capitalibus Dominis feodi illius . illi et heredibus suis . Libere . quiete . Bene . in pace . Iure . et hereditarie. Cuicu*m*que vel quandocu*m*que . eam . dare . vendere . vel assignare voluerit exceptis domibus Religionis faciend' Inde Annuatim pro me et Heredibus meis . Capitalibus Dominis feodi illius seruicia debita et Consueta que ad predictam peciam terre pertinent. Et Ego predictus Iohannes et Heredes mei Warantizabimus predictam dimidiam acram terre predicto Simoni et Heredibus suis Contra omnes . Homines inperpetuum . In Cuius Rei testimonium Huic Carte sigillum meum Apposui . Hiis testibus . Bartholomeo de Burgate . Iohanne filio Ade Le Bret . Martino Goldwyne . Galfrido Godwyne . Willelmo Silke . Willelmo Craske . Iohanne Aynild . Ricardo Le Northerne . Waltero Hakun . Iohanne Rutur . Roberto Le Marschall . Humfrido Dauid et aliis. Dat' apud

Holcham . die Mercurij prox' post festum sancti Gregorij Pape . Anno Regni Regis Edwardi vicessimo Quarto .

Seal: Circular white seal. Four petalled flower with four small sepals in inscription. 1¹/8 in. diam.
Hand: see note on HD 12.
Endorsement: 99 T[ranscriptum] *Galfridus le Brett De Holkham* (in ink), 26, 247 and 1019 (in pencil).

VARIANT: *ª* ville omitted, M*s*.

HP 1020

Grant from John son of Geoffrey le Bret of Holkham to Bartholomew son of
William le Marschall of Holkham of 1 plot.   29 Nov. 1294

Cf. HD 22a, Fo. 5 no. 55
Fiche 2: B1

Sciant presentes et futuri quod Ego Iohannes filius Galfridi le Bret de Holkham in plena Etate mea et legitima scilicet viginti et vnius Anni Concessi . dedi et hac presenti Carta mea Confirmaui . Bartholomeo filio Willelmi le Marschall et heredibus suis eiusdem Wille pro quadam summa pecunie . quam mihi . dedit In gersumam vnam peciam terre mee cum pertinenciis Iacent' in Camp' de Holkham inter terram Ricardi Trippe ex parte aquilon' . et terram que fuit Matild' Godkoc ex parte australi et Capud occidentale abuttat super terram Rogeri Elweriche . Habend' et tenend' de Capitalibus Dominis feodi illius . illi et heredibus suis vel suis assignatis . libere . quiete . bene . et in pace . Iure . et hereditarie . Cuicum*q*ue vel quandocum*q*ue dictam peciam terre cum pertinenciis . dare . vendere . vel assignare voluerit exceptis domibus Religionis faciend' . Inde Annuatim Capitalibus Dominis feodi illius seruic' debit' et Consuet' que ad dictam peciam terre pertinent videlicet ad festum sancti Michaelis vnum obolum pro omni seruicio . Consuetudine . Exaccione secta Cur*i*e et seculari demanda . Et Ego predictus Iohannes et heredes mei vel mei Assignati Warantizabimus et omnino defendemus predictam peciam terre predicto Bartholomeo et heredibus suis vel suis assignatis Contra omnes homines inperpetuum In Cuius Rei testimonium Huic Carte Sigillum meum apposui . Dat' apud Holkham die lune proxima ante festum Sancte Katerine Virginis Anno Regni Regis Edwardi vicessimo tertio . Hiis testibus . Bartholomeo de Burgate . Iohanne filio Ade le Bret . Iohanne Sylke . Willelmo Sylke . Martino Goldwyne . Galfrido Godwyne . Iohanne Aynild . Willelmo Craske . Simone

Hamund . Waltero Hakun . Ricardo le Northerne . Humfrido Dauid et . aliis multis.

> Seal: Circular white seal. Star with 8 rounded points in inscription S. JOHANNIS F]IL GALFRIDI 2 ins. diam.
> Hand: HD 13.
> Endorsement: *Exact' liij* T[ranscriptum] 98 (in ink), 27, 878 and 1020 (in pencil).

HP 1021

Quitclaim from John son of Geoffrey le Bret of Holkham to Nicholas son of Aveline of Little Witchingham of 1 plot of 9 acres.   25 July 1298

> Not in HD 22a
> Fiche 2: B2

Notum sit omnibus hominibus hoc scriptum visuris vel audituris . quod Ego Iohannes filius Galfridi le Bret de Holcam concessi remisi et omnino quietum clamaui pro me et heredibus meis Nicholao filio Aueline de Parua Wichyngham et heredibus suis totum Ius et clamium quod habui vel aliquo modo habere potui In vna pecia terre Iacente In Campis de Holcam apud Gunnyeswongg' et continet in se nouem acras terre . Ita quod nec ego predictus Iohannes nec heredes mei nec aliquis ex parte mea vel nomine meo aliquid Iuris vel clamij in dicta pecia terre prout Iacet inter bundas siue habeatur plus siue minus de cetero exigere vel vendicare potero in perpetuum Pro hac autem Concessione remisione et quietaclamacione dedit michi predictus Nicholaus quadraginta solid' premanibus . In cuius rei testimonium huic presenti scripto sigillum meum apposui . Hiis Testibus . Domino Ricardo de Walsingham milite . Radulfo de Redham . Ranulpho de Burgate . Radu*lfo* filio Roberti de Quarlees . Iohanne le Bret de Holcam . Willelmo Silke . Simone Hamund . Waltero Hakun . Gilberto le Bret . Ricardo le Northerne . Willelmo Craske et aliis. Dat' apud Holcam die Veneris in festo sancti Iacobi apostoli anno regni regis Edwardi filij Regis Henrici Vicesimo sexto.

> Seal: White circular seal varnished yellow. Flower with four petals and four small sepals within inscription S. IOHANNIS BRET 1¹/₈ in. diam.
> Hand: HD 1022.
> Endorsement: 28, 744 and 1021 (in pencil). No medieval endorsement. The absence of T[ranscriptum] perhaps suggests that this land did not become part of the Neel estate.
>
> NOTE: This land had been granted to Nicholas by Richard de Barking, rector of half Egmere church on 15 Dec. 1296, HD 22a, no. 139. Richard had been enfeoffed by John son of Geoffrey le Bret on 5 Sept. 1293, HD 22a, no. 85.

HP 1022

Grant from Bartholomew of Burgate of Holkham to Simon Hamund of Holkham of 1 plot of 2¹/₂ acres.   27 Oct. 1299

Cf. HD 22a, Fo. 7 no. 88
Fiche 2: B3 and 3: G7 (seal)

Sciant presentes et futuri quod ego Bartholomeus de Burgate de Holcham concessi dedi et hac presenti carta mea confirmaui Simoni Hamund de eadem et heredibus suis pro duabus marcis et dimidiam quas mihi dedit . vnam peciam terre mee continentem in se duas acras et dimidiam terre et Iacet in campis de Holcham inter terram Galfridi Godwine ex parte orientali . et terram Galfridi Carpenter ex parte occid' . et capud australe abuttat super regalem viam que ducit de Holcham apud Wictone . et capud aquilon' abuttat super terram Iohannis Balteys . Illi et heredibus suis et suis assingnatis . habend' et tenend' dictam peciam terre cum pertinenciis de capitalibus dominis feodi . Libere . quiete . bene . et in pace . Iure et hereditarie et cuicu*m*que et quandocu*m*que dictam peciam terre dare . legare . vendere . vel assingnare voluerit . Faciend' inde annuatim capitalibus dominis feodi seruicium debitum et consuetum videlicet vnum ob*olu*m ad festum sancti Michaelis pro omni seruicio . consuetudine exaccione secta Curie . et seculari demanda . Et ego dictus Bartholomeus . et heredes mei . et mei assingnati Warantizabimus . et defendemus dictam peciam terre cum pertinenciis predicto Simoni et heredibus suis et suis assingnatis contra omnes inperpetuum . In cuius rei testimonium huic scripto sigillum meum apposui . Hiis testibus . Iohanne le Bret . Iohanne filio Galfridi Le Bret . Willelmo Silke . Ada Silke . Gilberto Silke . Martino Goldewine . Galfrido Godwine . Waltero Hacun . Willelmo Buleman et Aliis. Dat' apud Holcham in vigilia apostolorum Simonis et Iud' Anno regni Regis Edwardi Vicesimo septimo.

Seal: White circular seal with six pointed star inside inscription BARTHOL DE BVRGATE 1¹/₂ in. diam.
Hand: HD 1021.
Endorsement: *Carta Bartolomei de Burgat' . Socag' de ij acris terre apud cotecroft.* T[ranscriptum] (in ink), 29 Holkham 1022 and 8216 (in pencil).

HP 1023

Grant from William Bulleman of Holkham to Simon Hamund of Holkham of
1¹/₂ acres and ¹/₂ rood in 4 plots.   [c. 1291-3]

Cf. HD 22a, Fo. 8 no. 98
Fiche 2: B4

Sciant presentes et futuri quod Ego Willelmus Bulleman de Holkham
Concessi Dedi et hac presenti Carta mea confirmaui Simoni Hamund de
Holkham pro homagio et seruicio suo et pro tribus decim solidis Argent'
quos mihi dedit in gersumam quatuor Pecias terre mee in se Continentes
vnam Acram et dimidiam acram et dimidiam Rodam terre iacent' in Camp'
de Holcham quarum vna pecia iacet apud Hungerehil inter terram Willelmi
Cursun ex parte australi . et terram quam Elwisa vxor quondam Gilberti Payn
tenet in dote ex parte aquilon' et Capud orient' abuttat super Caldhowegate et
secunda pecia terre iacet apud Dallegate inter terram prioris de Walsingham
ex parte australi et terram que fuit Iohannis Bissop' et Capud Occiden*tale*
abuttat super Dallegate et Tercia pecia terre iacet inter terram Roberti le
Marschal ex parte orien*tali* et terram quam Elwisa vxor quondam Gilberti
Payn tenet in dote ex parte occiden*tali* et Quarta pecia iacet apud Dallegate
inter terram Willelmi Craske ex parte australi et terram quam dicta Elwisa
tenet in dote ex parte Aquilon' . et Capud orientale abuttat Dallegate Habend'
et tenend' de me et heredibus meis vel meis assignatis illi et heredibus suis
vel suis assignatis libere quiete bene et in pace Iure et hereditarie Cuicumque
vel quandocumque eas dare legare vendere vel assignare voluerit exceptis
domibus Religiosis Reddendo inde Annuatim mihi et heredibus meis vel meis
assignatis . vnum denarium ad Annunciacionem Beate Marie pro omni
seruicio Consuetudine . Exaccione . secta Cur' et seculari demanda Et Ego
predictus Willelmus et heredes mei vel mei assignati Warantizabimus et
adquietabimus et omnino defendemus predictas quatuor pecias terre prout
Iacent in Camp' de Holkam predicto Simoni et heredibus suis vel suis
assignatis pro predicto seruicio Contra Omnes homines inperpetuum . In
Cuius Rei Testimonium Huic Carte sigillum meum apposui . Hiis Testibus .
Bartholomeo de Burgate . Iohanne le Bret . Iohanne Silke . Willelmo filio
suo . Willelmo Craske . Gilberto Aynild . Galfrido Godwyn . Martino
Goldwin'. Ricardo le Northerne . Roberto le Marschal . Humfrido David et
Iohanne Rutur et Multis Aliis.

Seal: missing.
Endorsement: *Memorandum quod tenet peciam terre apud Hungyrhyll.* T[ranscriptum] 43
(in ink), 30, 1023 and 1606 (in pencil).

HP 1024

*Grant from John son of Warin of Walsingham to Bartholomew son of
William le Marschall of Holkham of 1/2 acre.*   2 Oct. 1294

Cf. HD 22a, Fo. 4v no. 54
Fiche 2: B5

Sciant presentes et futuri quod Ego Iohannes filius Warini de Walsingham
Concessi dedi et hac presenti Carta mea Confirmaui Bartholomeo filio
Willelmi le Marschall' de Holkham vnam dimidiam Acram terre mee cum
pertinenciis iacent' in Camp' de Holkham apud Ringwaleslond inter terram
Roberti le Leuere ex parte australi et terram Willelmi Cholling ex parte
Aquilon' et Capud orientale abuttat super Crekgate et capud occidentale
abuttat super terram Bartholomei de Burgate Habend' et tenend' de
Capitalibus Dominis feodi illius illi et heredibus suis vel suis assignatis libere
quiete . bene . In pace . Iure . et hereditarie . Cuicumque vel quandocumque
dictam peciam terre . dare . vendere . vel assignare voluerit exceptis domibus
religiosis faciend' inde Annuatim Capitalibus Dominis feodi illius seruicia
debita et Consueta' que ad dictam peciam terre pertinent videlicet ad Pasch'
vnum denarium pro omnibus seruiciis . Consuetudinibus . Exaccionibus .
Sectis Cur' et secularibus demandis . Et Ego predictus Iohannes et heredes
mei vel mei assignati Warantizabimus et omnino defendemus dictam peciam
terre predicto Bartholomeo et heredibus suis vel suis assignatis Contra omnes
homines inperpetuum In Cuius Rei testimonium Huic Carte sigillum meum
apposui . Dat' apud Holkham die Sabat' proxim' post festum Sancti
Michaelis Anno Regni Regis Edwardi vicessimo secundo . Hiis testibus .
Bartholomeo de Burgate . Iohanne filio Ade le Bret . Iohanne Silke .
Willelmo Silke . Iohanne Aynild . Willelmo Craske . Martino Godwyne .
Galfrido Godwyne . Simone Hamund . Gilberto le Bret . Roberto Le
Marscall' . Humfrido Dauid et Aliis multis.

Seal: missing.
Hand: see note on HD 22B.
Endorsement: *lij*, T[ranscriptum] 83 (in ink), 31, 1024 and 1664 (in pencil).

HP 1025

Grant from Geoffrey son of Peter le Bret of Holkham to John son of Geoffrey Silk of Holkham of 1 plot. [c. 1284]

Cf. HD 22a, Fo. 5v no. 63
Fiche 2: B6

Sciant presentes et futuri quod Ego Galfridus filius Petri le Bret de Holcham concessi dedi et hac presenti Carta mea confirmaui Iohanni filio Galfridi Selke de Eadem pro homagio et seruicio suo et pro septem Libris argenti quas mihi dedit premanibus vnam peciam terre mee Iacentem in camp' de Holcham apud Wadlondes inter terram que fuit Iohannis Goldewine ex parte Australi . et terram predicti Iohannis Silke ex parte Aquilon' . et capud Orientale abuttat super Brueram . capud Occidentale abuttat super terram prioris de Walsingham . Habend' et tenend' predictam peciam terre cum pertinenciis de me et heredibus meis vel meis assingnatis . illi et heredibus suis vel suis assingnatis . Libere quiete bene . et in pace Iure et hereditarie et cuicumque et quandocumque eam . dare . Legare . vendere . vel assingnare voluerit inquocumque statu fuerit Reddendo inde annuatim mihi et heredibus meis vel meis assingatis . duos denarios silicet ad Annunciacionem beate Marie . vnum denarium et ad Pascha vnum denarium . pro omnibus seruiciis . consuetudinibus . exaccionibus sectis Cur' . et secular' demand' . et Ego predictus Galfridus et heredes mei vel mei assingnati . Warantizabimus . et adquietabimus . et defendemus . totam predictam peciam terre cum pertinenciis . predicto Iohanni Silke et heredibus suis vel suis assingnatis pro predicto seruicio contra omnes inperpetuum . In cuius rei testimonium huic carte sigillum meum apposui . Hiis testibus . Radulfo Hacun . Iohanne le Bret . Bartholomeo de Burgate . Galfrido Godwine . Eborardo Cali . Willelmo Craske . Iohanne Rutur . Simone filio Hamonis et Aliis.

Seal: Broken circular white seal, fleur-de-lys in inscription S. GALFRIDI FIL PETRI.
Hand: HP 1031, 1038 and ? 1029 and ? 1036.
Endorsement: T[ranscriptum] (in ink), 32, 1025 and 1404 (in pencil).

HP 1026

Grant from Thomas son of John of Holkham to Bartholomew son of Stephen of Holkham of 1 plot.   [c. 1291-1300]

Cf. HD 22a, Fo. 11 no. 136
Fiche 2: B7

Sciant presentes et futuri quod Ego Thomas filius Iohannis de Holcham Concessi dedi . et hac presenti Carta mea confirmaui Bartholomeo filio Stephani eiusdem wylle . pro homagio et seruicio suo et pro quatuor solidis argenti quos mihi dedit in gersumam vnam peciam terre mee Iacent' in Camp' de Holcham inter terram Guylde . Copenote versus austrum et terram Roberti Fulmere versus aquilonar' et Capud orient' abuttat super Regalem viam Habend' et tenend' de me et heredibus meis vel meis Assignatis illi et heredibus suis vel suis assignatis libere quiete bene et in pace Iure et hereditarie Cuicumque vel quandocumque . eam . dare . legare vendere vel assignare voluerit exceptis domibus Religiosis . Reddend' inde Annuatim mihi et heredibus meis vel meis assignatis vnum obolum ad Natiuitatem Sancti Iohannis Baptiste et ad scutagium. domini Regis quando Euenerit in Sokna de Wyctone . ad viginti solidos vnum quadrantem ad plus plus et ad minus minus pro omni seruicio Consuetudine Exaccione . Secta Cur' et seculari demanda Et ego predictus Thomas et heredes mei vel mei Assignati Warantizabimus et adquietabimus et Omnino defendemus predictam peciam terre predicto Bartholomeo et heredibus suis vel suis Assignatis pro predicto seruicio contra omnes homines inperpetuum . In . Cuius Rei Testimonium huic Carte pro me et heredibus meis sigillum meum Apposui . Hiis Testibus . Bartholomeo de Burgate . Iohanne Le Bret . Iohanne Silke . Gilberto Aynild . Willelmo Craske . Martino Goldwyne . Simone Hamund . Ricardo Northerne . Iohanne Rutur . Galfrido Godwyne . Roberto le Marschal . Humfrido Dauid et aliis.

Seal: Circular white seal: fleur-de-lys in inscription SIGILLUM TOMA FILIJ IOHANNIS 2 in. diam.
Hand: see note on HD 36.
Endorsement: T[ranscriptum] 10 (in ink), 27, 32 and 1026 (in pencil).

HP 1027

Grant from Geoffrey son of Peter le Bret of Holkham to Simon son of Hamo of Holkham of 13/4 acres in 2 plots. [c. 1294-6]

Cf. HD 22a, Fo. 4 no. 41
Fiche 2: B8

Sciant presentes et futuri quod ego Galfridus filius Petri Le Bret de Holcham concessi dedi et hac presenti carta mea confirmaui Simoni filio Hamonis de Eadem pro homagio et seruicio suo . et pro tribus marcis et dimidia argenti quas mihi dedit premanibus. duas pecias terre mee continentes in se septem rodas terre et Iacent' in camp' de Holcham quarum vna pecia Iacet inter terram Radulfi de Ladale ex parte aquilon' . et viam que vocatur Grenegate ex parte australi et capud occident' abuttat super terram Bartholomei Hunder Clint . Et alia pecia que vocatur Heuedlond lond Iacet inter terram que fuit Simonis peper ex parte oriental' . et capud aquilon' abuttat super terram que fuit Iohannis filij Hide . et capud australe abuttat super viam que vocatur Grenegate. Habend' et Tenend' predictas duas pecias terre de me et heredibus meis vel meis assingnatis illi et heredibus suis vel suis assingnatis Libere quiete bene et in Pace Iure . et hereditarie . Et cuicumque et quandocumque predictas duas pecias terre cum pertinenciis dare Legare vendere vel assingnare voluerit . Reddendo inde annuatim pro me et heredibus meis capitalibus dominis feodi quindecim denarios ad duos anni terminos videlicet ad festum Sancti Michaelis septem denarios et ad pasch' septem denarios . et ob. et mihi et heredibus meis per annum vnum clauum Gariofil' ad Natal' domini pro omni seruicio . consuetudine. exaccione . Secta cur' et seculari demanda . et ego predictus Galfridus et heredes mei vel mei assingnati Warantizabimus et adquietabimus et defendemus predictas duas pecias terre cum pertinenciis predicto Simoni et heredibus suis vel suis assignatis pro predictis seruiciis contra omnes inperpetuum In cuius rei testimonium huic carte sigillum meum apposui . Hiis testibus . Iohanne filio Ade Le Bret . Bartholomeo de Burgate . Hamone de Tatersete tunc Baliuo . Iohanne Silke . Willelmo filio suo . Galfrido Godwine . Martino Goldewine . Humfrido Daui et Aliis.

Seal: Fragment of white seal. Fleur-de-lys inside inscription GALFRIDI FILIJ PETRI 1 in. diam.
Hand: HP 1043.
Endorsement: *Galfrydus de Brett de Holkham,* T[ranscriptum] 90 (in ink), 33 and 1027 (in pencil).

HP 1028

Confirmation from Geoffrey son of Peter le Bret of Holkham to Simon son of Hamo of Holkham of 1 plot. [c. 1294-6]

Cf. HD 22a, Fo. 4 no. 42
Fiche 2: B9

Sciant presentes et futuri quod Ego Galfridus filius Petri le Bret de Holcham concessi et hac presenti carta mea confirmaui Simoni filio Hamonis de eadem villa Donum Iohannis filij mey primogeniti videlicet vnam peciam terre Iacentis in campis de Holcham inter terram Iohannis Fabri ex parte Australi et terram que quondam fuit Nicholai in camp' ex parte aquilonari . et abuttat versus occidentem super viam que ducit de Holcham versus quaruel*es*. habend' et tenend' de dicto Iohanne filio meo primogenito et Heredibus suis . dicto Simoni et heredibus suis vel suis asingnatis libere . quiete . bene . et in pace . et hereditarie . Reddendo inde annuatim dicto Iohanni et heredibus suis vnum quadrantem ad festum Sancti Michaelis prout testatur in carta sua feofamenti quam habet de dicto Iohanne filio meo primogenito pro omnibus seruiciis consuetudinibus . cur' sectis et demandis . predictus vero Iohannes et heredes sui warantizabunt acquietabunt et defendent predictam peciam terre siue in ea sit maius vel minus per predictum seruicium contra omnes inperpetuum . Et vt ista mea confirmacio firma et stabilis permaneat inperpetuum . In huius Rey testimonium huic presenti scripto sigillum meum apposui . Hiis testibus . Iohanne le Bret . Bartholomeo de Burgate . Iohanne Silke . Willelmo filio suo . Gilberto Aynild . Willelmo Craske . Galfrido Godwin . Roberto Maresscallo . Rogero Belney . Willelmo de Hilling*ton* clerico et Aliis.

Seal: White Circular seal. Fleur-de-lys within inscription SIGILLUM GALFRIDI FILIJ PETRI 1³/₈ in. diam.
Endorsement: T[ranscriptum] 92 (in ink), 34, 1028 and 1526 (in pencil).

HP 1029

Grant from Geoffrey le Bret of Holkham to Simon son of Hamo of Holkham of 13/4 acres. [c. 1283-93]

Cf. HD 22a, Fo. 11v no. 147
Fiche 2: B10

Sciant presentes et futuri quod ego Galfridus le Bret de Holcham concessi dedi et hac presenti carta mea confirmaui Simoni filio Hamonis de eadem pro homagio et seruicio suo . et pro quinque marcis argenti quas mihi dedit premanibus vnam peciam terre mee que vocatur Endaker continentem in se vnam acram et dimidiam et vnam rodam terre Iacentem in camp' de Holcham inter terram Abbatis de Derham ex parte australi et terram prioris de Walsingham ex parte aquilon' et capud orientale abuttat super viam que vocatur Crek'gate . et . capud occidentale abuttat super terram prioris de Walsingham . Habend' et tenend' predictam peciam terre de me et heredibus meis vel meis assingnatis . illi et heredibus suis vel suis assingnatis. Libere . quiete . bene . et in pace . Iure et hereditarie et Cuicumque et quandocumque predictam peciam terre . dare . legare . vendere . vel assingnare voluerit . In quocumque statu fuerit . Reddendo inde annuatim mihi et heredibus meis vel meis assingnatis vnum denarium . ad festum sancti Michaelis et ad scutagium domini Regis quando venerit ad viginti solid' vnum quadrantem ad plus plus et ad minus minus pro omnibus seruiciis . consuetudinibus . exaccionibus sect' Cur' et secularibus demandis et ego predictus Galfridus et heredes mei et mei assingnati Warrantizabimus . et adquietabimus . et defendemus predictam peciam terre siue in ea sit magis vel minus predicto Simoni et heredibus suis vel suis assignatis pro predicto seruicio contra omnes inperpetuum In Cuius rei Testimonium huic carte sigillum meum apposui . Hiis testibus. Rad*ulfo* Hacun . Iohanne Le Bret . Bartholomeo de Burgate . Galfrido Godwine . Willelmo Craske . Eborardo Caly . Humfrido Daui . Iohanne Rutur et aliis.

Seal: Fragment of white circular seal. Fleur-de-lys within inscription.
Hand: see note on HP 1031.
Endorsement: T[ranscriptum] *Antiqua Carta de pecia Endaker* (in ink), 35. 742, 1029 (in pencil).

NOTE: Usually Humphrey David is the last witness.

HP 1030

Grant from Geoffrey son of Peter le Bret of Holkham to Simon Hamund of Holkham and Cecily his wife of 1 plot of 6 acres. [c. 1294]

Cf. HD 22a, Fo. 9v no. 116 and HP 1032
Fiche 2: B11

Sciant presentes et futuri quod Ego Galfridus filius Petri le Bret de Holcham concessi et hac presenti carta mea confirmaui Simoni Hamund eiusdem ville et Cecilie vxori sue et eorum heredibus pro quadam summa pecunie quam michi dederunt premanibus sex acras terre mee cum pertinenciis Iacentes in camp' de Holcham in vna pecia aput Hadowe inter terram Ade carpentar' ex parte australi et terram Iohannis Godman ex parte aquilonal' et caput occidentale abuttat super Ryngwarislond et caput orientale super Hadowegate illis et heredibus eorum tenendas et habendas de Capitalibus dominis feodi illius libere quiete bene et in pace Iure et hereditarie et cuicumque vel quandocumque predictas sex acras terre cum pertinenciis dare vendere legare vel assignare voluerit exceptis domibus religiosis faciend' Inde anuatim*a* capitalibus dominis feodi illius seruicia debita et consueta pro omni seruicio Consuetud' Exaccione sectis cur' et secularibus demandis. Et Ego predictus Galfridus et heredes mei warantizabimus predictas sex acras terre cum pertinentiis predictis Simoni et Cecilie et eorum heredibus contra omnes gentes inperpetuum. In cuius rei testimonium Huic presenti carte sigillum meum apposui . Hiis testibus . Bartholomeo de Burgate . Iohanne filio Ade le Bret . Willelmo Silke . Martino Goldwine . Galfrido Godvine*b* . Willelmo Crask . Iohanne Aynild et aliis.

Seal: Quarter of white seal. Fleur-de-lys within inscription.
Endorsement: T[ranscriptum] 36, 320 and 1030 (in pencil).

NOTE: This land is included with two others in a grant of 17 Mar. 1294, HD 22a, no. 126 (HP 1008). The same land is gift of John son of Geoffrey le Bret in HP 1032. William Silk's father John, who is often a witness with him, is absent in HP 1030 and 1032. In HP 1033 John occurs without William. HP 1032 is almost identical, but grantor is John son of Geoffrey le Bret whose grants get confirmed by his father Geoffrey son of Peter.

VARIANTS: *a* written as one word in Ms. *b* Contrary to usual practice the form 'v' is used, not 'u'.

HP 1031

Grant from Geoffrey son of Peter le Bret of Holkham to Simon son of Hamo of Holkham of 1 plot of 13/4 acres.   [c. 1294-5]

Cf. HD 22a, Fo. 3v no. 31
Fiche 2: B12

Sciant presentes et futuri quod Ego Galfridus filius Petri le Bret de Holcham concessi dedi et hac presenti Carta mea confirmaui Simoni filio Hamonis de eadem pro homagio et seruicio suo et pro quatuor marcis argenti quas mihi dedit premanibus vnam peciam terre mee continentem in se septem rodas terre et Iacet in camp' de Holcham apud Greyston inter terram que fuit Rogeri super campum ex parte australi et terram Iohanne Thurbern ex parte aquilon' et capud occident' abuttat super terram prioris de Peterston . Habend' et Tenend' predictam peciam terre cum pertinenciis de me et heredibus meis vel meis assingnatis illi et heredibus suis vel suis assingnatis . libere . quiete bene et in pace . Iure . et hereditarie . Et cuicumque et quandocumque predictam peciam terre dare . legare . vendere . vel assingnare voluerit Reddendo inde annuatim mihi et heredibus meis vel meis assingnatis vnum obolum ad Natiuitatem Sancti Iohannis Baptiste pro omni seruicio . consuetudine . exaccione secta Curie et Seculari demanda . Et ego predictus Galfridus et heredes mei vel mei assingnati Warantizabimus . et adquietabimus . et defendemus predictam peciam terre cum pertinenciis predicto Simoni et heredibus suis vel suis assingnatis per predictum seruicium contra omnes inperpetuum . In cuius rei testimonium huic carte sigillum meum apposui . Hiis testibus . Iohanne filio Ade le Bret . Bartholomeo de Burgate . Iohanne Silke . Willelmo filio suo . Galfrido Godwine . Martino Goldewine . Hamone de Tatersete tunc baliuo . Humfrido Daui et aliis.

Seal: missing.
Hand: see note on 1031.
Endorsement: T[ranscriptum] 101 (in ink), 37, 1031 and 1068 (in pencil).

NOTE: The date is earlier than HP 1011.

HP 1032

Grant from John son of Geoffrey le Bret of Holkham to Simon Hamund of Holkham and Cecily his wife of 1 plot of 6 acres.   [c. 1294-6]

Cf. HP 1030
Fiche 2: B13

Sciant presentes futuri quod Ego Iohannes filius Galfridi le Bret de Holcham . concessi dedi et hac presenti carta mea confirmaui Simoni Hamund eiusdem ville et Cecilie vxori sue et eorum heredibus pro quadam summa pecunie quam michi dederunt pre manibus . sex acras terre mee cum pertinent' Iacent' in vna pecia in camp' de Holcham apud Hadowe inter terram Ade carpentar' ex parte Australi et terram Iohannis Godman' ex parte aquilonal'. Et caput occidentale abuttat super Ryngwareslond et caput orientale super Hadowegate . illi et heredibus eorum tenend' et habend' de capitalibus dominis feodi illius libere . quiete Bene . in pace . iure hereditarie . Et Cuicumque vel quandocumque predictas sex acras terre cum pertinenciis dare . legare . vendere . vel assignare voluerint . exceptis domibus religiosis . faciend' Inde annuatim Capitalibus dominis illius feodi seruicia debita et consueta . pro omni seruicio Consuetudine . Exaccione . Cur' sect' et seculari demanda . Et Ego predictus Iohannes et heredes mei warantizabimus predictas sex acras terre cum pertinenciis predictis . Simoni et Cecilie et eorum heredibus contra omnes gentes imperpetuum . In Cuius rei testimonium huic presenti carte sigillum meum apposui . Hiis testibus . Bartholomeo de Burgate . Iohanne filio Ade le Bret . Willelmo Silke . Martino Goldewine . Galfrido Godwine . Willelmo Craske . Iohanne Aynild . Waltero Hacun . Ricardo le Northyerne . Roberto le Mar.all' . Humfrido Dauid . et multis aliis.

Seal: White circular seal. Flower with four pointed petals and four minute sepals within inscription. 12/5 in. diam.
Endorsement: T[ranscriptum] *de Hadhowe*. Schortadow 49 (in ink), 38, 1032 and 1069 (in pencil).

NOTE: HP 1030 is almost identical but grantor is Geoffrey son of Peter le Bret.

HP 1033

Confirmation from John son of Geoffrey le Bret of Holkham to Simon Hamund of Holkham of 1 plot.   [c. 1291-3]

Cf. HD 22a, Fo. 10 no. 119
Fiche 2: B14 and 3: G5 (seal)

Notum sit Omnibus hoc presens scriptum visuris vel audituris quod Ego Iohannes filius Galfridi Le Bret de Holcham Concessi et presenti scripto meo Confirmaui . Simoni Hamund de Eadem pro quadam summa pecunie quam mihi dedi premanibus . vnam peciam terre Iacent' in Campo de Holcham inter . terram Prioris de Walsingham versus austrum et terram Marior' in Camp' versus Aquilonar' et Capud Orient' abuttat super terram dicti Galfridi et Capud occident' Abuttat super Krecgate . quam quidem peciam terre adquisiuit de Galfrido patre meo . Habend' et tenend' de dicto Galfrido et de me herede suo et nostrorum heredibus vel Assignatis . Cuicumque vel quandocumque . eam . dare . legare . vendere . vel Assignare voluerit . libere . quiete . bene . et in pace . faciend' pro predicta pecia terre sicut Continetur in Carta feoffamenti quam dictus Simon habet de Galfrido patre meo . Et Ego Iohannes et heredes mei vel mei Assignati Warantizabimus et adquietabimus et omnino defendemus predictam peciam terre . predicto Simoni et heredibus suis . vel suis Assignatis pro predicto seruicio contra omnes homines inperpetuum . In Cuius Rei testimonium . Huic scripto pro me et heredibus meis sigillum meum Apposui . Hiis Testibus . Bartholomeo de Burgate . Iohanne filio Ade le Bret . Iohanne Silke . Gilberto Aynild . Willelmo Craske . Galfrido Godwyne . Martino Goldwyne . Ricardo le Northerne . John Rutur . Hunfrido Dauid et Aliis.

Seal: Round circular seal on tag cut from 14th century deed. Star or flower with eight points terminating in small circular head within inscription [SIGILLUM IOHANNIS FILIJ] GALFRIDI.
Hand: see note on HD 36.
Endorsement: T[ranscriptum] 8 (in ink), 39, 512 and 1033 (in ink).

HP 1034

*Confirmation from John son of Geoffrey le Bret of Holkham to Simon
Hamund of Holkham of 1 plot of 3 acres.*   [c. 1294-6]

Cf. HD 22a, Fo. 10 no. 124
Fiche 2: C1

Nouerint vnuiersi et singuli quod Ego Iohannes filius Galfridi Le Bret de
Holcham Concessi et presenti Scripto meo confirmaui Simoni Hamund de
eadem pro homagio et seruicio suo et pro quadam summa pecunie quam mihi
dedit premanibus tres acras terre iacent' in vna Cultura in Campis de
Holcham inter terram Prioris de Walsingham ex parte occident' et terram
meam ex parte orient' et Capud' aquilon' abutat super terram dicti Simonis et
Capud australe super terram Rogeri filij Berte quas dictus Simon adquisiuit
de Galfrido patre meo . Habend' et tenend' de dicto Galfrido et de me
Iohanne filio et herede suo et heredibus nostris vel nostris assignatis libere .
quiete . bene . et in pace . in feodo et hereditarie . Cuicumque vel
quandocumque . eas . dare . legare . vendere . vel assignare voluerit exceptis
domibus Relig' . faciend' inde Annuatim sicut continetur in Carta feoffamenti
quam dictus Simon Habet de Galfrido patre meo . Et Ego predictus Iohannes
et heredes mei vel mei assignati Warantizabimus et omnino defendemus
predictas tres acras terre . predicto Simoni et heredibus suis vel suis
assignatis pro predicto seruicio quod continetur in Carta sua contra omnes
Homines inperpetuum . In Cuius Rei . testimonium huic scripto sigillum
meum apposui . Hiis testibus . Bartholomeo de Burgate . Iohanne filio Ade le
Bret . Iohanne Silke . Willelmo filio^a suo . Galfrido Godwyne . Martino
Goldwyn . Gilberto Aynild . Willelmo Craske . Ricardo Northerne .
Humfrido Dauid et aliis multis .

Seal: missing.
Endorsement: T[ranscriptum] 32 (in ink), 40, 1034 and 1654 (in pencil).

VARIANT: ^{a} omitted.

HP 1035

Confirmation from John son of Adam le Bret of Holkham to Bartholomew the miller of Holkham of 1 rood. [c. 1294-6]

Cf. HD 22a, Fo. 11 no. 134
Fiche 2: C2

Sciant presentes et futuri quod Ego Iohannes filius Ade le Bret de Holkham Concessi et Hac presenti Carta mea confirmaui. Bartholomeo Molendinario eiusdem wille et heredibus suis pro quadam summa pecunie quam mihi dedit premanibus . vnam Rodam terre . quam adquisiuit de Roberto Fulmer*e* Natiuo meo . et Iacet in Campis de Holkham aput Schortlond*a* inter terram predicti Bartholomei ex parte australi . et terram Iohannis Aynild ex parte aquilonali . et Caput occidentale abuttat super terram que fuit Iohannis Curthun . et Caput orientale abuttat super Caldhowegate . Habend' et tenend' secundum tenorem statuti de Emptoribus terrarum nuper Editi . Libere . quiete . Bene . et in pace . Iure . et hereditarie . Reddend' Inde annuatim michi Domino feodi illius et heredibus meis vnum obolum ad festum Sancti Michaelis pro omni seruicio . Consuetudine . Exactione . sect' Cur*ie* . et secular*ibus* demand*is* . Et Ego predictus Iohannes et heredes mei Warantizabimus predictam Rodam terre predicto Bartholomeo et heredibus suis Contra omnes Homines inperpetuum . In Cuius Rei testimonium Huic Carte sigillum meum Apposui . Hiis testibus . Bartholo*meo* de Burgate . Martino Goldwyne . Galfrido Godwyne . Willelmo Craske . Simone Hamund . Iohanne Aynild . Ricardo Le Northerne . Gilberto Le Bret . Waltero Hakun . Robert le Marschalle . Iohanne Rutur . Humfrido Dauy et aliis.

Seal: Small circular seal. Device: Creature curled up within inscription. 7/8 in. diam.
Hand: see note on HD 12.
Endorsement: Ad. le Brett T[ranscriptum] 14 (in ink), 41, 75 and 1035 (in pencil).

VARIANT: *a* 'ch' is represented by 'y' in Ms.

HP 1036

Grant from Isabel daughter of Ralph le Bret of Holkham in her widowhood to William Craske of Holkham of 1 plot of 1/2 acre. [c. 1284]

Cf. HD 22a, Fo. 2v no. 15
Fiche 2: C3 and 3: G2 (seal)

Sciant presentes futuri quod Ego Isabella filia Radulfi le Bret de Holcham per assensum et voluntatem Thome filij mei in legitima viduitate mea . concessi dedi et hac presenti carta mea confirmaui. Willelmo Craske de eadem et heredibus suis pro homagio et seruicio suo . et pro sex solidis argenti quos mihi dedit premanibus vnam peciam terre mee continent' in se dimidiam acram terre Iacentem in campo de Holcham . inter terram Gilberti filij Matild' ex parte australi . et terram Willelmi Pippinger ex parte aquilon' . et capud orientale abuttat super Caldowgate . et capud occidentale abuttat super terram Gilberti Haynild . Habend' et tenend' predictam peciam terre de me et heredibus meis vel meis assingnatis illi et heredibus suis vel suis assingnatis . libere quiete . bene . et in pace Iure . et hereditarie. et Cuicumque vel quan documque predictam peciam terre . dare . legare . vendere . vel assingnare . voluerit In quocumque statu fuerit . Reddendo inde annuatim mihi et heredibus meis vel meis assingnatis Tres ob. ad festum sancti Michaelis vnum denarium et ad Purificacionem beate Marie . vnum ob. pro omnibus seruiciis consuetudinibus . exaccionibus . sectis cur' et omnibus aliis secularibus demandis. Et ego predicta Isabella et heredes mei vel mei assingnati . Warantizabimus et adquietabimus et omnino defendemus predictam peciam terre predicto Willelmo Crask' et heredibus suis vel suis assingnatis pro predicto seruicio contra omnes Inperpetuum. In Cuius rei testimonium ego predicta Isabella et Thomas filius meus huic carte sigilla nostra apposuimus . Hiis testibus . Radulfo Hacun . Galfrido le Bret . Iohanne le Bret . Bartholomeo de Burgate . Iohanne Silke . Galfrido Godwine . Eborardo Cali . Hunfrido Daui et Aliis.

Seal: Broken white seal. Fleur-de-lys within inscription SIGILLUM ISABELE FILIE RADVL. 1 in. diam.
Hand: see note on HP 1025.
Endorsement: T[ranscriptum] *Carta Isabelle filie Radulfi le Bret De dimidia acra terre abbutt' super Caldougat' versus orientem* (in ink), 42, 434 and 1036 (in pencil).

HP 1037

Confirmation from Thomas son of Isabel daughter of Ralph le Bret of Holkham to William Craske of Holkham of 1/2 acre of land.   [c. 1284]

Cf. HD 22a, Fo. 2v no. 16
Fiche 2: C4

Sciant presentes et futuri Quod Ego Thomas filius Isabelle filie Radulfi le Bret De Holcham . Concessi et Confirmaui Willelmo Crask de eadem et heredibus suis vnam dimidiam acram terre quam predicta Isabella mater mea vendidit predicto Willelmo Craske pro Nouem solidis argenti et duobus denariis. Que dicta dimidia acra terre Iacet in camp' de Holcham ad Colismere inter terram Willelmi Cursun ex parte aquilonari . et terram predicti Thome filij Isabelle ex parte Australi Et capud occidentale abuttat super regalem viam que tendit de Holcham ad Egemere . Habend' et tenend' predictam dimidiam Acram terre post obitum matris mee De me et heredibus meis . illi et heredibus suis vel suis assingnatis . libere . quiete . bene . et In pace . Iure . et hereditarie et Cuicumque vel quandocumque predictam dimidiam acram terre Dare legare vendere vel assingnare voluerit Reddendo Inde Annuatim mihi et heredibus meis vel meis assingnatis post obitum Isabelle matris mee vnum denarium et vnum ob. silicet ad festum sancti Michaelis vnum ob. et ad natale domini vnum ob. et ad pascha vnum ob. pro omnibus seruiciis consuetudinibus exaccionibus sect' Cur' et demandis. Et ego predictus Thomas et heredes mei post obitum Isabelle Matris mee warantizabimus et acquietabimus et defendemus predictam dimidiam acram terre . predicto Willelmo Craske et heredibus suis vel suis assingnatis per predictum seruicium contra omnes gentes Inperpetuum In cuius Rei testimonium huic carte sigillum meum apposui . Hiis testibus . Radulfo Hacun . Galfrido le Bret . Iohanne le Bret . Bartolomeo De Burgate . Iohanne Silke . Galfrido Godwyne . Radulfo Mariot . Eborardo Cali . Humfrido Dauid et aliis.

Seal: missing. Strips of parchment with text about *viam que vocatur [S]chothowgatte. Memorandum quod Willelmus Crask debuit Iohanni filio Ade le Bret per annum de redditu assis' viij den' et obolum ad duos anni terminos ad festum Sancti Michaelis. Et ad festum Pasch' pro equalibus porcionibus.*
Endorsement: *dimidia acra apud Collesmer* T[ranscriptum] (in ink), 43, 433 and 1037 (in pencil).

HP 1038

Grant from Everard son of Everard le Caly of Holkham to William Craske of Holkham of 1 plot and half a fold. [c. 1284]

Cf. HD 22a, Fo. 5v no. 66
Fiche 2: C5

Sciant presentes et futuri quod Ego Eborardus filius Eborardi Le Caly de Holcham Concessi dedi et hac presenti carta mea confirmaui Willelmo Crask' de eadem pro homagio et seruicio suo et pro viginti et sex solid' argenti quos mihi dedit premanibus vnam peciam terre mee cum pertinenciis Iacentem in camp' de Holcham inter terram predicti Willelmi ex parte Australi . et terram que fuit quondam Warini de montekanisio ex parte aquilon' et capud Orientale abuttat super Dalgate gate. Preterea concessi dedi et hac presenti carta mea confirmaui predicto Willelmo pro homagio et seruicio suo medietatem vnius falde quam habui cum Rad*ulfo* capellano currentem in villa et in campis de Holcham cum omnibus libertatibus ad medietatem dicte falde pertinentibus . habend' et tenend' predictam peciam terre et predictam medietatem dicte falde . de me et heredibus meis assingnatis illi et heredibus suis vel suis assingnatis . Libere . quiete bene . et in pace . Iure et hereditarie et Cuicumque et quantumcumque eas . dare legare vendere . vel assingnare . voluerit . Reddendo inde Annuatim mihi et heredibus meis vel meis assingnatis vnum ob' ad festum Sancti Michaelis . et ad scutagium domini Regis quando Euenerit ad viginti sol' vnum quant' tantum . pro omnibus seruiciis consuetudinibus . exaccionibus . sectis curie . et secularibus demandis . Et ego predictus Eborardus et heredes mei vel mei assingnati Warantizabimus et adquietabimus . Et defendemus predictam peciam terre et medietatem dicte falde cum omnibus libertatibus ad dictam medietatem falde pertinentibus predicto Willelmo et heredibus suis vel suis assingnatis pro predicto seruicio contra omnes inperpetuum. In cuius rei testimonium huic carte sigillum meum apposui . Hiis testibus . Radulfo Hacun . Galfrido le Bret . Iohanne le Bret . Bartholomeo de Burgate . Galfrido Godwine . Iohanne Rutur . Simone filio Hamonis et Aliis.

Seal: missing from tag which is made from strip of 13th century deed.
Hand: see note on HP 1025.
Endorsement: *Carta Eborardi filij Eborardi Kaly. Medietat*em *falda*m *in Holkham.*
T[ranscriptum] 109 (in ink), 44, 893, 1038 (in pencil).

HP 1039

Grant from Robert le Heire of Morston to William Cursun and Agnes le Heire his daughter of 3 acres of land in Holkham as dowry.   [c. 1284]

Cf. HD 22a, Fo. 6 no. 70
Fiche 2: C6

Sciant presentes et futuri quod Ego Robertus le Heire de Meristune Concessi dedi et hac presenti Carta mea Confirmaui Willelmo Cursun et Angneti filie mee In maritagio*a*. Tres acras terre mee iacentes in campo de Holkham . silicet inter terram abbatis de creic ex parte occidentali et terram que quondam fuit Ade gilion ex parte orientali . et capud australe abuttat super viam que*b* tendit de Holkham ad varam*c* . et capud boriale super terram Iohannis le Bret Habend' et tenend' de me et heredibus meis . illi et heredibus eius . libere . quiete . bene . et in pace . Reddendo inde annuatim mihi et heredibus meis . tres denarios et dimidiam sceppam frumenti . pro omni seruicio Consuetudine secta curie et demanda . Ego predictus Robertus et heredes mei Varantizabimus et defendemus predictam terram predicto Willelmo et Angneti filie mee . et heredibus suis . propter predictum seruici*um* contra omnes gentes . et si ita contingat quod predicta Angnes filia mea sine herede moriatur . predicta terra remanebit cum Willelmo dum vitam habeat et post obitum predicti Willelmi . ad me et ad heredes meos omni impedimento postposito reuertetur . In cuius rei testimonium pro me et heredibus meis sigillum meum Apposui . Hiis testibus . Radulfo Hacun . Galfrido le Bret . Iohanne le Bret . Bartolomeo de Burgate . Iohanne Silke . Galfrido Godwine . Thoma Leffe et multis aliis.

Seal: Broken circular green seal. Flower with four petals and four sepals within inscription SIG ROBERTI. 1¼ in. diam.

Hand: The hand and the witnesses suggest a date near to that of HP1103

Endorsement: T[ransciptum] 1039 (in pencil), xx d., 45, 222 and 34 (in ink).

NOTE: Morston is a small coastal village between Stiffkey and Blakeney.

VARIANTS: *a* written as one word in Ms. *b* Ms. reads in this order. *c* i.e. Warham.

HP 1040

Grant from William son of Bartholomew Mariot of Holkham to Richard his brother of 3 plots.   [c. 1284]

Obliterated in HD 22a, Fo. 2 no. 2
Fiche 2: C7

Sciant presentes et futuri quod Ego Willelmus filius Bartholomey Mariot de Holcham concessi dedi et hac presenti carta mea confirmaui Ricardo fratri meo filio dicti Bartholomey pro homagio et seruicio suo tres pecias terre mee Iacentes in camp' de Holcham quorum vna pecia que est medietas crufte mee Iacet Inter terram meam ex parte orient' et terram Iohannis mariot ex parte occident' et abuttat versus aquilonem super terram Iohannis Asty . et versus Austrum super Regalem viam que vocatur Burgate . et alia pecia Iacet Inter terram Gilberti Sutoris ex parte orient' . et terram Willelmi Craske ex parte occident' et abuttat versus aquilonem super Wellegate . et tercia pecia Iacet Iuxta kokeflet Inter terram Bartholomei de Burgate ex parte orient' et terram Willelmi Otewy de Welles ex parte occident' . et abuttat versus aquilonem super mershgate . et versus austrum super semitam que ducit de Ripa de Holcham apud Welles. Habend' . et tenend' de me et heredibus meis sibi et heredibus suis vel suis asingnatis vel cuicumque aut quandocumque . dare . legare . vendere . vel asingnare voluerit In quocumque statu fuerit preter quam in Religionem . libere . quiete . bene . et in pace Iur' . et hereditar' . Reddendo Inde annuatim mihi et heredibus meis octo denarios videlicet ad pascha duos denarios et ad Natiuitatem sancti Iohannis baptiste . duos denarios et ad festum sancti Michaelis . duos denarios . et ad festum sancti Andree . apostoli . duos denarios . et ad . xx^{ti} . solidos de scutagio domini Regis quando venerit . vnum denarium . ad plus . plus . et ad minus . minus . pro omnibus seruiciis . consuetudinibus . curiarum sectis . et secularibus demandis . saluo seruicio forinseco . silicet ad viginti solid'. de comuni ausilio In sokna domini Baldewini de Hakeny . vnum quadrantem . et ad plus . plus . et ad minus . minus . Et Ego predictus Willelmus et heredes mey Warantizabimus aquietabimus . et defendemus predictas tres pecias terre predicto Ricardo et heredibus suis vel suis asingnatis per predictum seruicium contra omnes homines et feminas In perpetuum . In cuius Rey testimonium huic presenti scripto sigillum meum apposui . Hiis testibus . Radulfo Hakun . Iohanne le Bret . Bartholomeo de Burgate . Iohanne Silke . Gilberto Aynild . Willelmo Craske . Simone Hamund . Rogero Belney . Galfrido Godwin . Iohanne persone . Vmfrido Dauy et Aliis.

Seal: missing.
Endorsement: T[ranscriptum] 45 (in ink), 46, 591 (in pencil).

HP 1041

Grant from Gilbert son of William Nichol of Holkham to Simon son of Hamo of Holkham of 1/2 rood.   [c. 1294-6]

Cf. HD 22a, Fo. 6v no. 79
Fiche 2: C8

Sciant presentes et futuri quod Ego Gilbertus filius Willelmi Nichol de Holcham concessi dedi et hac presenti confirmaui Simoni filio Hamonis de Eadem villa pro homagio et seruicio suo et pro decem solidis argenti quos michi dedit in gersumam vnam dimidiam Rodam terre mee Iacentem*a* in Campis de Holcham super Cleylond inter terram Rogeri Thurbern ex parte orient' . et terram dicti Simonis filij Hamonis ex parte occident' . et capud aquilon*ale* abuttat super terram Iohanne Thurbern . et capud australe abuttat super cruftam Iohannis Aleyn . Habend' et tenend' de me et heredibus meis et heredibus suis sibi suis asingnatis . vel cuicumque aut quandocumque dare . legare . vendere . vel asingnare . voluerit . libere . quiete . bene . et in pace . in feodo . et hereditarie . Reddendo inde annuatim michi et heredibus meis . vnum obolum . ad festum sancti Andree apostoly . pro omnibus seruiciis . consuetudinibus et secularibus demandis . Et Ego predictus Gilbertus et heredes mey vel mey asingnati . warantizabimus . aquietabimus . et defendemus predictam dimidiam Rodam terre cum pertinenciis predicto Simoni et heredibus suis vel suis asingnatis per predictum seruicium contra omnes homines et feminas Inperpetuum . In Cuius Rey testimonium huic presenti scripto sigillum meum apposui . Hiis testibus . Iohanne filio Ade le Bret . Bartholomeo de Burgate . Hamone de Tatersete . Iohanne Silke . Willelmo . Ada . et Gilberto filiis suis . Gilberto Aynilde . Willelmo Craske . Gilberto le Bret . Galfrido Godwine . Martino Goldwine . Vmfrido Dauy*b* et aliis .

Seal: Brown seal painted green, broken, circular. Star (eight pointed) within inscription SIGILLUM GILBERTI FILIJ WILLELMI NICHOL 2 in. diam.
Endorsement: T[ranscriptum], 49, 752 and 1041 (in pencil)

NOTE: Perhaps in hand of Humphrey David, although many letters differ from those in HP 1040.

VARIANTS: *a* Iacentem repeated in Ms. *b* Dauy has small d.

HP 1042

Grant from Ralph son of Thouey Powel of Holkham to Simon son of Charles del Hil of Holkham 1 plot of 1/2 rood. [c. 1270]

Cf. HD 22a, Fo. 9v no. 110 (almost obliterated)
Fiche 2: C9

Sciant presentes et futuri Quod Ego Radulfus filius Thouey Powel de Holcham concessi dedi et hac presenti Carta mea confirmaui Symoni filio Karoli del Hil eiusdem ville pro homagio et seruicio suo et pro duobus solidis argenti quos michi dedit Ingersumam*ᵃ* . vnam peciam terre mee scilicet que iacet Incampis*ᵇ* de Holcham et continet In se vnam dimidiam rodam terre . siue habeatur plus vel minus . Et Iacet Inter terram Eborard' Thurbern versus austrum. Et terram predicti Symonis versus aquilonem . Et capud occidentale Abbuttat super Warledouhesty . illi et heredibus suis cuicumque et Quandocu*m*que illam dare legare vendere vel assingnare voluerit siue inegritudine*ᶜ* constitutus siue extra . Habendam et Tenend*am* de me et heredibus meis libere . quiete . Bene . In pace . Iure . et Hereditarie . Reddendo Inde annuatim mihi et heredibus meis . vnum . obolum . scilicet . ad Pascha . Pro omni seruicio consuetudine sect' Cur' et exaccione et omn' secular' demand'. Et Ego vero prefatus Radulfus et heredes mei Warantizabimus . acquietabimus . et omnino deffendemus predictam peciam Terre cum pertinenciis prenominato Symoni et heredibus suis vel suis assingnatis sicut predictum est per predictum seruicium contra omnes Christianos et Iudeos Inperpetuum . In huius rei Testimonium presenti carte pro me et heredibus meis sigillum meum appossui*ᵈ* . Hiis Testibus . Petro le Bret . Radulfo Hacun . Adam Le Bret . Thoma de Burgate . Galfrido Godwyne . Radulfo Mariot . Ricardo Goldwyne . Iohanne filio suo . Eborardo Le Kayilly . Herueo Leffe . Dauid Man . Willelmo Hayie et aliis.

Seal: Circular dark green seal. Flower with eight petals and eight sepals within inscription: SIGILLUM RADULFI FIL. TOVE. 1 in. diam.

VARIANTS: *ᵃ sic. ᵇ sic. ᶜ sic. ᵈ sic.*

HP 1043

Confirmation from John son of Geoffrey le Bret of Holkham to Simon son of Hamo of Holkham of 3 plots.   [c. 1294-6]

Cf. HD 22a, Fo. 2 no. 8
Fiche 2: C10

Sciant presentes et futuri quod Ego Iohannes filius Galfridi le Bret de Holcham concessi et hac presenti carta confirmaui Simoni filio Hamonis de eadem pro homagio et seruicio suo . tres pecias terre quas habet ex dono Galfridi patris mei et Iacent in camp' de Holcham quarum una pecia apud Greyston . inter terram que fuit Rogeri super campum ex parte australi . et terram Iohanne Thurbern ex parte aquilon' . et capud occident' abuttat super terram prioris de Peterston . et alia pecia Iacet inter terram Radulfi de Ladale ex parte aquilon' et viam que vocatur Grenegate ex parte australi . et capud occident' abuttat super terram Bartholomei Hunderclint . Et tercia pecia que vocatur Heuedlondlond Iac' inter terram que fuit Simonis peper ex parte orientali . et capud aquilon' abuttat super terram que fuit Iohannis filij Hide et capud australe abuttat super viam que vocatur Grenegate . Habend' et tenend' predictas tres pecias terre cum pertinenciis de me et heredibus meis vel meis assingnatis . illi et heredibus suis vel suis assignatis . Libere . quiete . bene . et in pace . Iure . et hereditarie . et cuicumque et quandocumque predictas tres pecias terre cum pertinenciis dare . legare . vendere vel assingnare voluerit . faciend' Inde annuatim post discessum Galfridi patris mei mihi et heredibus meis seruicia debita vt carte feofamenti sui testantur . pro omni seruicio . consuetudine . exaccione . secta curie et seculari demanda . Et ego predictus Iohannes et heredes mei vel mei assingnati warantizabimus . et adquietabimus . et defendemus . predictas tres pecias terre cum pertinenciis predicto Simoni et heredibus suis vel suis assignatis per predictum Seruicium sicut predictum est contra omnes imperpetuum . In cuius rei testimonium huic carte sigillum meum apposui . Hiis testibus . Iohanne filio Ade le Bret . Bartholomeo de Burgate . Hamone de Tatersete . tunc baliuo . Galfrido Godwine . Martino Goldewine . Iohanne Silke . Willelmo filio suo . Humfrido Daui et aliis.

Seal: missing.
Hand: HP 1027.
Endorsement: T[ranscriptum], 49 and 1519 (in pencil).

HP 1044

*Quitclaim from Helewise widow of Geoffrey le Bret of Holkham to John de
Fallegate of Burnham and Cecily his wife of Holkham of her dower of 1/3 in
3 plots.*　　　　　　　　　　　　　　　　　　　　　　　　　　21 Nov. 1302

> Cf. HD 22a, Fo. 4 no. 44
> Fiche 2: C11

Notum sit omnibus hoc scriptum visuris vel audituris quod Ego Helwysa
vxor quondam Galfridi le Bret de Holcham in pura viduitate mea concessi
remisi et omnino inperpetuum quietum clamaui Iohanni de Fallegate de
Brunham et Cecilie vxori sue de Holcham Totum Ius et clamium meum quod
habui vel aliquo modo habere potui nomine dotis michi contingent' de libero
tenemento predicti Galfridi quondam viri mei videlicet in tercia parte trium
Peciarum terre prout Iacent in Campis de Holcham in diuersis culturis et
quarentenis . scilicet apud HadHoweBreist'. Schortlond et Greiston . Ita quod
nec Ego Helwys' nec aliqui nomine meo aliquid Iuris vel clam[ium] de
Cetero In predictis Peciis Exigere vel vendicare potuerimus . In Cuius rei
testimonium Huic Scripto Sigillum meum apposui . Hiis testibus .
Bartholomeo de Burgate . Iohanne filio Ade le Bret . Willelmo Silke .
Martino Goldwine . Willelmo Craske . Iohanne Aynild . Ricardo Le
Northerne . Waltero Hakun . Galfrido Godwyne . Iohanne filio eius .
Humfrido Dauyd . Roberto Charles clerico et multis aliis . Dat' apud
Holcham die mercurij proxima ante festum Sancte Katerine Virginis . Anno
Regni Regis Edwardi filij Regis Henrici Tricessimo Primo.

> Seal: White circular seal in good condition. Agnus dei inside inscription S. ELWYSE -
> 1¹/₂ in. diam.
> Endorsement: T[ranscriptum] (in black ink), 93 (in russet ink), 50, 1044, 1525 (in pencil).

HP 1045

*Quitclaim from Bartholomew de Burgate of Holkham to Richard le Northerne
of Holkham of 1 plot with his sheep-house, the saltmarsh, and a fold with all
its liberties in the fields and heaths of Holkham.*　　　　　　13 Sept. 1303

> Not in HD 22a
> Fiche 2: C12

Notum sit omnibus hoc scriptum visuris vel Audituris quod Ego
Bartholomeus de Burgate de Holcham Concessi et quietum Clamaui Ricardo
Le Northerne de eadem villa et Heredibus suis vnam Peciam terre cum domo

Bercarie mee sita in Capite Aquilon' predicte pecie terre . vna cum Toto
marisco salefico et Libertat' vnius falde videlicet . pascuis . pasturis . viis .
semitis . fugacionibus . in Campis et Brueris predicte ville . et omnibus aliis
Asiamentis tam innominatis quam nominatis ad predicta tenementa et fald'
spectantibus quibuscumque . Et Totum Ius et Clamium quod in predictis
pecia terre . marisco . fald' . et Libertate predictis . ad predicta tenementa et
fald' spectantibus Habui vel habere potui eidem Ricardo et heredibus suis vel
suis assignatis de me et heredibus meis remisi et quietum Clamaui
inperpetuum. Istam autem concessionem et quietam Clamacionem feci Ego
Bartholomeus predicto Ricardo et Heredibus suis in seisina ipsius Ricardi de
tenementis predictis . Et Ego predictus Bartholomeus et Heredes mei Omnia
predicta tenementa et fald' cum omnibus suis Libertatibus tam innominatis
quam nominatis ad predicta tenementa et fald' spectant' vt predictum est .
predicto Ricardo et heredibus suis vel suis assignatis contra omnes homines
inperpetuum Warantizabimus et defendemus . In Cuius rei testimonium Huic
scripto sigillum meum Apposui Dat' apud Holcham die veneris proxim' post
Nativitatem Beate Marie . Virginis . Anno Regni Regis Edwardi filij Regis
Henrici Tricesimo Primo . Hiis testibus . Iohanne filio Ade le Bret . Willelmo
Silke . Ada . et Gilberto fratribus suis . Martino Goldwyne . Waltero Hakun .
Willelmo Craske . Iohanne Aynild . Ada . et Gilberto Fratribus eius . Thoma
Le Northerne . Roberto Charles clerico et multis Aliis .

Seal: missing. Tag is strip from conveyance to grantee.
Endorsement: *Bartholomeus de Burgate Concess. Ricardo Le Northerne vnam peciam*
terre cum domo cum toto marisco et Libertate Falde. (in russet 17th cent. ink), 51, 95
and 1045 (in pencil). No T[ranscriptum].

NOTE: From the Newgate archive, a property which included marsh and fold at the
Stathe, acquired through marriage in 15th century from the Northernes and bought by
John Coke in 17th century.

HP 1046

Grant from Thomas Seloue of Wells-next-the-Sea and Matilda his wife to
Bartholomew Calwere of Holkham of 1 plot.   9 May 1304

Cf. HD 22a, Fo. 6v no. 82
Fiche 2: C13

Sciant presentes et futuri quod Ego Thomas Seloue de Welles et Matilda
vxor mea concessimus dedimus et hac presenti carta nostra confirmauimus
Bartholomeo Caluere de Holkham pro seruicio suo et pro quadam summa
pecunie quam nobis dedit premanibus vnam peciam terre nostre cum
pertinenciis in Campis de Holkham prout iacet siue sit plus siue minus . inter

terram Iohannis Eyr que quondam fuit Bartholomei de Burgate ex parte orientis et terram Gilberti Silk' ex parte occidentis . Et Abuttat versus austrum super viam que vocatur Scothoghgate Illi et Heredibus suis vel suis assignatis de nobis et heredibus nostris Habend' et tenend' de Capitali domino feodi ill*ius* per seruicia inde debita et consueta Et Nos vero predicti Thomas et Matilda Warantizabimus et defendemus predictam peciam terre cum pertinenciis predicto Bartholomeo et heredibus suis vel suis assignatis contra omnes homines et feminas inperpetuum . In cuius Rei testimonium huic presenti scripto sigilla nostra apposuimus . Hiis Testibus . Willelmo Craske . Ricardo Northerne . Iohanne Aynild . Waltero Hacon . Willelmo Silke . Adam Silk*e* de Holkham . Iohanne Norman . Andrea de Stiuck' . Hamone Ernys de Welles et multis aliis. Dat' apud Holkham die sabbati proxima post festum sancti Iohannis ante portam Latinam Anno . regni . Regis . Edwardi filij Regis Henrici xxx^{mo}. secundo.

Seal: Two illegible white vesica shaped seals, broken.
Endorsement: Holkham T[ranscriptum] Scothougate (in black ink), 38 (in russet ink), 52 and 1046 (in pencil).

HP 1047

Grant from Adam Hamund of Holkham to William son of Robert de Dunwich of Walsingham 21/4 acres, which is half of the plot called Duuessped.

1 Feb. 1314

Cf. HD 22a, Fo. 9v no. 112
Fiche 2: C14

Sciant presentes et futuri quod Ego Adam Hamund de Holkham dedi concessi hac presenti carta mea confirmaui Willelmo filio Roberti de Dunewich*e* de Walsingham medietatem vnius pecie terre mee *que* vocatur Duuessped et continet in se dicta medietas duas acras et vnam rodam terre et Iacet Iuxta terram Henrici Daui ex parte australi . et Capud occidentale abbuttat super semitam que vocatur Lethrpittesheuedes et capud orientale super terram Ade Crask' siue in dicta medietate habeatur plus siue minus . Habend*am* et tenendam illi et heredibus suis siue assignatis predictam medietatem pecie terre cum suis pertinenciis de Capitalibus dominis feodi per seruicia inde debita libere quiete bene et in pace Et ego predictus Adam et heredes mei Warantizabimus et defendemus predictam medietatem dicte pecie cum omnibus suis pertinenciis dicto Willelmo et heredibus suis ac assignatis prout predictum est contra omnes gentes in perpetuum In cuius rei testimonium Huic presenti carte mee sigillum meum apposui . Hiis testibus . Willelmo

Silke . Willelmo Wake . Roberto de Gristone . Iohanne le Bret . Martino Goldwyne . Iohanne Haynild . Bartholomeo Kalwere et aliis. Dat' apud Holcham . die veneris proxima an*te* Purificacionem Beate Marie Anno Regni Regis Edwardi filij Regis Edwardi Septimo.

> Seal: Small circular white seal. Squirrel inside inscription. Thick parchment. 7/8 in. diam. cf. HP 1050.
>
> Endorsement: T[ranscriptum] (in black ink), 53 (in russet ink), 53, 1047 and 1760 (in pencil).

HP 1048

Grant from John atte Falgate of Burnham and Cecily his wife to William son of Robert de Dunwich of Walsingham 21/4 acres, which is half of the plot called Duuesped.   13 Apr. 1314

> Cf. HD 22a, Fo. 7v no. 47
> Fiche 2: D1

Sciant presentes et futuri quod Ego Iohannes Attefalgate de Brunham et Cecilia Vxor mea dedimus concessimus et Hac presenti carta nostra confirmauimus Willelmo filio Roberti de Walsingham et Heredibus suis siue Assignatis medietatem vnius pecie terre nostre iacent' in Campo de Holcham . que quedam pecia vocatur Duusped . et continet in se dicta medietas duas acras et vnam rodam . et iacet iuxta terram predicti Willelmi ex parte australi . et capud occiden*tale* abbuttat super semitam que vocatur Lethpittesheuedes . et Capud orientale super terram Ade Crasky . siue in dicta medietate Habeatur plus siue minus . Habend' et tenend' illi et heredibus suis siue assignatis predict' medietatem predicte pecie cum suis pertinenciis de Capitalibus Dominis feodi Libere quiete bene et in pace . Reddendo inde annuatim capitalibus dominis feodi Seruicia inde debita et consueta . Et ego predictus Iohannes et Cecilia vxor mea et heredes . nostri Warantizabimus et defendemus predictam medietatem dicte pecie que vocate Duusped cum omnibus suis pertinenciis dicto Willelmo et heredibus suis ac assignatis contra omnes gentes inperpetuum . In cuius rei Testimonium Huic presenti carte sigilla nostra apposuimus . Hiis testibus . Domino Waltero de Calthorp . Thoma de Snitterthoun . et Ricardo de Walsingham militibus . Willelmo Silke . Willelmo Wake . Iohanne Ayneld . Roberto de Gyrsthon*e* . Iohanne Bret et aliis. Dat' apud Brunham die sabbati in septimana Pasch*e* . anno . regni . regis . Edwardi . filij Regis . *Edwardi* . septimo .

> Seal: 1 seal missing. 1 seal, shield, black. Perhaps a bird. No inscription. 1 x 3/4 in.
> Hand: HP 1049.
> Endorsement: T[ranscriptum] (in black ink), 60 (in russet ink), 54, 1048 and 1452 (in pencil).

HP 1049

Quitclaim from Adam son of Simon Hamond of Holkham to William son of Robert de Dunwich of Walsingham of half the plot called Duusped.

14 Apr. 1314

Cf. HD 22a, Fo. 9v no. 112 and HP 1047
Fiche 2: D2

Sciant presentes et futuri quod Ego Ada filius Simonis Hamond de Holkham concessi Remisi de me et Heredibus meis imperpetuum quiet' clamaui Willelmo filio Roberti de Walsingham totum ius et clamium quod habui vel habere potui in medietate cuiusdam pecie terre que vocatur Duusped . que quedam medietas iacet ex parte boriali \dicte pecie/ que Cecilia mater mea tenuit nomine dotis . Ita Videlicet quod nec Ego predictus Ada nec Heredes mei nec assignati . nec aliquis nomine meo aliquid ius vel clamium in predicta boriali medietate dicte pecie terre que vocatur Duusped de cetero exigere nec vendicare potero vel poterimus imperpetuum Et Ego predictus Ada et Heredes mei et assignati mei Warrantizabimus et defendemus predictam medietatem predicte pecie predicto Willelmo et heredibus suis ac assignatis contra omnes gentes imperpetuum . In cuius rei testimonium Huic scripto sigillum meum apposui . Hiis Testibus . Domino Waltero de Calthorp . Thoma de Snitterthoun . et Ricardo de Walsingham militibus . Willelmo Sylke . Willelmo Wake . Iohanne Aynild . Roberto de Gyrston . Iohanne Le Bret et aliis. Dat' apud Holkham die dominica in octabas pasch' Anno . regni . regis . Edwardi . filij . Regis Edwardi . Septimo .

Seal: Broken white seal. ?Bird's head with curved beak, or head facing right in inscription. 1¼ in. diam.
Hand: HP 1048.
Endorsement: T[ranscriptum] (in ink), 55, 1049 and 1605 (in pencil).

HP 1050

Grant from Adam Hamond of Holkham to William son of Robert de Dunwich of Walsingham of 1 acre ½ rood.

24 June 1314

Cf. HD 22a, Fo. 9v no. 111
Fiche 2: D3

Sciant presentes et futuri quod ego Adam Hamond de Holcham dedi concessi et Hac presenti Carta mea confirmaui Willelmo filio Roberti Donewych de Walsigham^a vnam Acram terre mee et dimidiam Rod' Iacent' in campis de Holcham apud Ringwareslond Iuxta terram Cicilie matris mee ex parte Boriali et Capud Occidental' abbuttat super viam que vocatur Lethrpitgate et capud Orientale abbuttat super terram predic*te* Cicilie quod tenet nomine dotis . Habend' et Tenend' dicta pecia terre illi et Heredibus suis cum omnibus suis pertinenciis de Capitalibus dominis feodi illius . libere . quiete . bene . et in pace . Reddendo inde Annuatim capitalibus dominis feodi illius seruicia debita et consueta Ego predictus Ad*am* et Heredes mei et Asignati . Warantizabimus et defendemus predictam peciam terre cum suis pertinenciis siue in dicta pecia habeatur plus siue minus predicto Willelmo et Heredibus suis et Assignatis Contra omnes gentes inperpetuum. In Cuius Rei testimonium Huic presenti carte mee sigillum meum apposui . Hiis testibus . Willelmo Silk*e* . Willelmo Wake . Iohanne Le Bret . Roberto de Gristone . Martino Goldewyne . Iohanne Belneye . Gilberto Le Bret et Aliis. Dat' apud Holcham die Nativitatis sancti Iohannis Babtiste . Anno Regni . Regis Edwardi . filij . Regis . Edwardi . Septimo .

Seal: Small white circular seal. Squirrel inside inscription. 1¹/₄ in. diam. cf. HP 1047.

Hand: see note on HD 25.

Endorsement: *Testamentum 1 acra et dimidia acra Ryngwarislond* (in black ink), 56 and 1050 (in pencil).

VARIANT: *a* *sic.*

HP 1051

Grant from Adam son of Simon Hamond of Holkham to Richard Neel of Burnham and Caterine his wife of 5 acres in 4 plots. 5 Nov. 1314

Cf. HD 22a, Fo. 13v no. 156 (Lucas no. 5)

Fiche 2: D4

Sciant presentes et futuri quod ego Adam filius Simonis Hamond de Holkham concessi dedi et hac presenti carta mea confirmaui Ricardo Nel de Brunham et Caterine vxori eius quinque acras terre cum pertinenciis in Holkham prout iacent in diuersis peciis videlicet apud Steynhul Aldelose . Haddohouebotme et apud Dalgate . habend' et tenend' predictas quinque acras terre cum pertin*enciis* predictis Ricardo et Caterine et heredibus de corporibus eorum legitime procreatis de me et heredibus meis faciend' inde annuatim pro me et heredibus meis capitalibus dominis feodorum seruicia inde debita et consueta' . Et si predictus Ricardus et Caterina sine herede de eorum corporibus legitime procreatis obierint volo perpresentes*a* quod predicte quinque acre terre cum pertinenciis integre rectis heredibus ipsius Ricardi Nel remaneant Habend' et tenend' de capitalibus dominis feodorum per seruicia inde debita et consueta inperpetuum Et ego predictus Adam et heredes mei predictas quinque acras terre cum pertinenciis predicto Ricardo et Caterine et heredibus de eorumdem corporibus legitime procreatis vt predictum est et Rectis Heredibus predicti Ricardi si exitus deficiat contra omnes gentes Inperpetuum Warantizabimus . In cuius Rei testimonium huic carte Sigillum meum apossui hiis testibus Willelmo Sylke de Holkham . Willelmo Wake de eadem . Ricardo Northerne de eadem . Iohanne Aynild de eadem . Iohanne le Bret de eadem . Thoma Large de Creike . Henrico le Mayster de Bretham. Dat' apud Brunham die martis proxima post festum Omnium Sanctorum . Anno Regni Regis Edwardi filij Regis Edwardi octavo .

> Seal: missing.
> Hand: same hand as HP 1053, 1054, 1056.
> Endorsement: *Carta Ade fil' Simon Hamond de v acr' terr' apud steynhil . Adelose Adowebotme et Dalegate Examinatur.* T[ranscriptum], (in black ink), 39 (in russet ink), 57, 1051 and 1112 (in pencil).
>
> VARIANT: *a* perpresentes written as one word.

HP 1052

Grant from Martin Goldwyne of Holkham to William son of Robert de Dunwich of Walsingham of 1 acre.   3 May 1315

> Cf. HD 22a, Fo. 2v no. 17
> Fiche 2: D5

Sciant presentes et futuri quod Ego Martinus Goldwyne de Holcham concessi dedi et hac presenti carta mea confirmaui . Willelmo filio Roberti de Donewych de Walsingham vnam acram terre mee arabilis cum omnibus pertinenciis suis . Iacent' in camp' de Holcham apud Fulmerisgate . iuxta terram Iohannis le Bret ex vna parte . et terram Alicie Tutte . ex altera parte . et Habuttant' super Regeam viam . siue in dicta*a* pecia terre cum pertinenciis suis plus siue minus habeatur . Habend' et tenend' . predictam peciam terre cum omnibus pertinenciis suis . de capitalibus dominis feodi . predicto Willelmo et Heredibus suis vel suis assignatis per Seruicia Inde debita de iure et consueta . libere . quiete . bene in pace in feodo et in hereditate perpetua . Et ego predictus Martinus . et Heredes mei . predictam . acram terre cum omnibus pertinenciis suis . predicto Willelmo et heredibus suis vel suis assignatis . contra omnes gentes Warantizabimus inperpetuum . In cuius Rey testimonium . Huic presenti carte Sigillum meum apposui . Dat' apud Holcham predictam die Sabbati in festo Inuencionis Sancte Crucis . Anno . regni. regis Edwardi filij regis Edwardi . octavo . Hiis testibus . Willelmo Wake . Willelmo Silke . Ricardo Le Northerne . Thoma filio suo .

Roberto de Gristone . Iohanne Belneye . Gilberto Le Bret . Iohanne Le Bret .
Iohanne Godwyne et aliis.

Seal: missing.
Hand: see note on HD 25.
Endorsement: *Fulmeresgate 1 acra* T[ranscriptum], 46 (in russet ink).

VARIANT: *a* in dicta written as one word

HP 1053

*Grant from Joan widow of Henry Hamond of North Barsham to Richard
Neel of Burnham and Caterine his wife of 1 plot of 3 acres.*   1 July 1315

Cf. HD 22a, Fo. 19 no. 205 (Lucas no. 53)
Fiche 2: D6

Sciant presentes et futuri quod ego Iohanna quondam vxor Henrici Hamond
de Northbarsham concessi dedi et hac presenti carta mea confirmaui Ricardo
Nel de Brunham et Caterine vxori sue et heredibus de eorum*dem* corporibus
legitime procreatis vnam peciam terre mee in campis de Holkham iacentem
apud Schotbarbles que continet in se tres acras terre et iacet iuxta terram
Willelmi Cras*k*e ex parte Australi habend' et tenend' predictam peciam terre
cum pertinenciis predictis Ricardo et Caterine et Heredibus de [eorumdem]
corporibus legitime procreatis ac rectis heredibus predicti Ricardi Si predictus
Ricardus et Caterina sine heredibus de eorumdem corporibus legitime
procreatis obierint de capitalibus dominis feodi libere et quiete . faciend*o*
inde predictis [capitalibus] dominis feodi seruicia debita consueta . Et ego
predicta Iohanna heredes et assignati mei predictam peciam terre cum
pertinenciis predictis Ricardo et Caterine et heredibus eorumdem corporibus .
legitime procreatis ac Rectis heredibus ipsius Ricardi si predicti Ricardus et
Caterine obierint absque heredibus de eorum*dem* corporibus legitime
procreatis vt predictum est contra omnes gentes inperpetuum Warantizabimus
. In cuius rei testimonium huic carte sigillum meum apposui . Hiis testibus .
Roberto de Burgh de Brunham . Willelmo chapelein de eadem . Roberto del
Hil de eadem . Willelmo Wake de Holkham . Willelmo Silke de eadem .
Iohanne Le Bret de eadem . Ricardo le Northerne . Thoma le Northerne et
aliis. Dat' apud Brunham die Martis proxima post festum apostolorum Petri
et Pauli anno Regni Regis Edwardi filij regis Edwardi octauo finiente.

Seal: Small yellowish gray seal in good condition but not legible, in garter. 7/8 in. (cf.
HP 1051, 1054, 1056).
Hand: see note on HP 1051.
Endorsement: *Skotbarbl* and longer endorsement (obscured by white stain) ... *defunct'* ...
(in ink), 59, 1053 and 1709 (in pencil). There is no T[ranscriptum] visible though this is
a Neel deed.

HP 1054

Quitclaim from William and Hamo sons of Henry Hamond of North Barsham to Richard Neel of Burnham and Caterine his wife of 3 acres granted by Joan Hammond, their mother.   **15 July 1315**

Cf. HD 22a, Fo. 19 no. 208 (Lucas no. 56)
Fiche 2: D7

Vniuersis pateat per presentes quod nos Willelmus et Hamo filij Henrici Hamond de Northbarsham Remisimus et omnino quietum clamauimus pro nobis et heredibus nostris Ricardo Nel de Brunham et Caterine vxori sue et heredibus de eorumdem corporibus legitime procreatis ac Rectis Hered' ipsius Ricardi si predicti Ricardus et Caterina absque heredibus de eorumdem corporibus legitime procreatis obierint totum ius et clameum quod habuimus vel aliquo modo habere potuerimus in tribus acris terre cum pertinenciis in villa de Holkham quas habuimus ex dono et feoffamento Iohanne matris nostre Ita quod nos nec heredes nostri nec aliquis nomine nostro in predictis terris et tenementis nichil iuris seu clamei de cetero exigere vel vendicare potuerimus imperpetuum . Preterea Nos predicti Willelmus et Hamo predictas tres acras terre cum pertinenciis heredes et assignati nostri predictis Ricardo et Caterine et heredibus de eorumdem corporibus legitime procreatis ac Rectis Heredibus predicti Ricardi Si predicti Ricardus et Caterine absque heredibus eorumdem corporibus legitime procreatis obierint contra omnes gentes Warantizabimus imperpetuum . Hiis testibus . Roberto de Burgh de Brunham . Willelmo Chapeleyn de eadem . Roberto Attehil de eadem . Willelmo Wake de Holkham . Willelmo Silke de eadem . Iohanne le Bret de eadem . Ricardo le Northerne de eadem et aliis. Dat' apud Brunham die Martis proxima ante Festum Sancte Margarete Virginis anno Regni Regis Edwardi filij Regis Edwardi Nono incipiente.

Seal: Dark yellowish green oval seal in good condition, but not deciphered. Second seal missing. 7/8 x 5/8 in.
Hand: see note on HP 1051.
Endorsement: T[ranscriptum] (in ink), 60, 219 and 1054 (in pencil).

HP 1055

Grant from Bartholomew le Muner of Holkham to Richard Neel of Burnham and Caterine his wife of 1 rood with its crop. 1 Aug. 1315

Cf. HD 22a, Fo. 18v no. 198 (Lucas no. 46)
Fiche 2: D8

Sciant presentes et futuri quod Ego Bartholomeus le muner de Holkham concessi dedi et hac presenti carta mea confirmaui Ricardo Nel de Brunham et Caterine vxori sue et heredibus de eorumdem Corporibus Legitime procreatis ac eciam rectis heredibus predicti Ricardi si predicti Ricardus et Caterina absque heredibus de eorumdem corporibus legitime procreatis obierint vnam rodam terre Cum tota vestura et omnibus pertinenciis Iacent' in Campis de Holcham inter terram Roberti le Marschall' ex parte aquilon' et . terram Willelmi Fabr' ex parte australi Cuius capud occidental' abuttat super CaldeHowgate . Habend' et tenend' predictam Rodam terre . Cum Vestura et omnibus pertinenciis predictis Ricardo et Caterine et eorumdem heredibus de Eorumdem corporibus legitime procreatis at eciam Rectis Heredibus predicti Ricardi si predicti Ricardus et Caterina absque Heredibus de eorumdem corporibus Legitime procreatis obierint de Capitalibus dominis feod' Libere et quiete bene et in pace faciend' inde predicto Capitali domino seruicia inde debita et consueta et Ego predictus Bartholomeus et heredes mei predictam Rodam terre vt predictum est predictis Ricardo et Caterine et heredibus de eorumdem corporibus legitime procreatis ac etiam rectis heredibus predicti Ricardi si predicti Ricardus et Caterina absque Heredibus de eorum corporibus legitime procreat' obierint contra omnes gentes in perpetuum Warantizabimus . In cuius Rei testimonium Huic Carte sigillum meum aposui . Hiis Testibus . Willelmo Wake . Willelmo Silke . Willelmo Rotuney . Iohanne Le Bret . Martino Goldewyne et aliis. Dat' apud Holcham die veneris proxima post festum Sancti Iacobi apostoli Anno Regni Regis Edwardi filij Regis Edwardi nono.

Seal: Circular white seal, flower with four petals and four sepals within inscription. Broken. 1¹/₄ in. diam. 'S...ROARD' in inscription suggest the use of Eborard's seal, but on HD 9 Eborard sub Hoga uses a seal with a fleur-de-lys.
Hand: HP 996.
Endorsement: *Carta Bartholomei le Munier de Caldhowe 1 roda terre abutt' super Caldhowe.* 46 T[ranscriptum] (in black ink), 6 (in russet ink), 61, 850 and 1055 (in pencil).

HP 1056

*Quitclaim from William Silk of Holkham to Richard Neel of Burnham and
Caterine his wife of 4 plots.*   9 Mar. 1316

Cf. HD 22a, Fo. 20v no. 223 and HD 26
Fiche 2: D9

Vniuersis pateat per presentes quod ego Willelmus Silke de Holkham
Relaxaui et omnino quietum clamaui Ricardo Nel de Brunham et Caterine
vxori sue et here*dibus* de eorumdem corporibus legitime procreatis ac Rectis
heredibus predicti Ricardi si predicti Ricardus et Caterina sine heredibus de
eoru*m*dem corporibus legitime procreatis obierint . totum ius et clameum
quod habui vel aliquo modo habere potui in quatuor peciis terre cum
pertinenciis in villa de Holkham . quarum vna pecia iacet apud le Wadlond
iuxta terram quondam Martini Goldwyne ex parte australi et terram Prioris de
Walsingham ex parte boriali Et vna pecia que vocatur Wellelond que iacet
iuxta terram Matill' Choud ex parte occidentali cuius capud australe super
terram Iohannis Carpentarii abbuttat . Et tercia pecia iacet apud Cathil cuius
capud orientale super terram Willelmi Asti Abbuttat et capud occidentale
super predictam peciam que vocatur le Wellelond et quarta pecia iacet in
eadem Quarentena cuius capud orientale super terram predicti Willelmi Asti
abbuttat et capud occidentale super predictam terram que vocatur le
Wellelond et iacet inter terras Thome Idessone extraque*a* parte . Ita quod nec
ego predictus Willelmus Silke nec heredes mei nec aliquis nomine nostro in
predictis peciis nichil iuris seu clamei de cetero exigere vel vendicare
poterimus inperpetuum In cuius Rei testimonium presentibus sigillum meum
aposui . Hiis testibus . Roberto de Burgh de Brunham . Roberto del Hil de
eadem . Willelmo Chapeleyn de eadem . Iohanne filio Radulfi de eadem .
Willelmo Wake de Holkham . Roberto de Griston de eadem . Iohanne le Bret
de eadem et aliis. Dat' apud Holkham die Martis proxima ante festum Sancti
Gregorij Pape Anno regni regis Edwardi filij Regis Edwardi Nono.

Seal: Broken seal, amorphous.
Hand: see note on HP 1051.
Endorsement: *Relaxacio W. Silk de iiij peciis terre Wellond.* T[ranscriptum] (in black
ink), 62 (in russet ink) (62 does not correspond with deed numbered 62 on 19v of HD
22a), 62, 1056 and 1369 (in pencil).

VARIANT: *a* extraque written as one word.

HP 1057

Letter of Attorney from Bartholomew the miller of Holkham to Martin Rust of Holkham to give seisin to Richard Neel of Burnham and Caterine his wife of 1 plot. 12 Apr. 1316

Cf. HD 22a, Fo. 17v no. 188 (Lucas no. 37)
Fiche 2: D10

Pateat vniuersis per presentes quod Ego Bartholomeus molendinarius de Holcham attornaui et in loco meo posui Martinum Rust de Holcham ad deliberand' Ricardo Nel de Brunham et Caterine vxori sue plenariam seisinam de vna pecia . terre mee cum pertinenciis in Holcham prout in carta mea feoffamenti quam predictus Ricardus et Caterina habent de me plenius nominatur habitur' firmum et stabile quicquid predictus Martinus in premissis duxerit faciend' In cuius rei testimonium predicto Martino has literas meas sigillo meo*ᵃ* signatas feci patentes Dat' apud Holcham die Lune proxima post passca Anno regni Regis Edwardi filij Regis Edwardi Nono .

Seal: missing.
Endorsement: by Edmund Lucas but as he did not transcribe letters of attorney into the cartulary, there is no T[ranscriptum]. 17 (in russet ink). 63, 886 and 1057 (in pencil).

NOTE: HD 22a, Fo. 17v no. 188 shows that this land was at Schortlond.

VARIANT: *ᵃ* mei, Ms.

HP 1058

Grant from William Silk of Holkham to Gilbert Silk his son of 1 messuage and croft. 3 Oct. 1316

Cf. HD 22a, Fo. 6 no. 73
Fiche 2: D11

Sciant presentes et futuri quod ego Willelmus Silke de Holkham dedi concessi et hac presenti carta mea confirmaui Gilberto filio meo vnum mesuagium et Cruftam super eandem abbuttant' cum pertinenciis suis in Holkham Iacent' inter terram Abbatis et conuentus de Crek' ex parte orientis et terram Angnet' Bryche ex parte occident' et abbutt' versus aquilonem super Regalem viam que vocat' Burgate et versus Austrum super terram Ade Aynild . Habend' et Tenend' illi predicto Gilberto et heredibus suis et assingatis suis de capitalli domino feodi illius per seruicia inde debita et consueta . Et ego dictus Willelmus et Heredes mei Warrantizabimus et

defendemus totum predictum mesuagium et Croftam cum pertinentiis suis
predicto Gilberto et heredibus suis et assignatis suis per predictum seruicium
contra omnes gentes Inperpetuum In cuius rei testimonium presenti carte
sigillum meum aposui . Dat' apud Holkam die dominica proxima post festum
Sancti Michaelis . Anno . regni regis . Edwardi filij Regis . Edwardi Decimo
. Hiis testibus. Willelmo Wake . Roberto de Grestone . Ricardo Northerne .
Thoma filio suo . Iohanne Aynild . Ada fratre eius . Iohanne Goldwyne .
Iohanne Belneye et Aliis.

> Seal: Small circular dark green shield. Profile facing left with small nose and large beard
> perhaps from ancient gem inside S. WILLELMI SILK. 4/5 in. diam.
> Endorsement: T[ranscriptum] on seal tag.

HP 1059

*Grant from William the Smith of Gresham and Emma his wife to Richard
Neel of Burnham and Katerine his wife of 1 rood.*   7 July 1317

> Cf. HD 22a, Fo. 18v no. 203 (Lucas no. 51)
> Fiche 2: D12

Sciant presentes et futuri quod nos Willelmus Faber de Gressham et Emma
vxor mea dedim*us* concessimus et hac presenti carta nostra confirmauimus
Ricardo Neel de Brunham et Katerine vxori eius . et heredibus de eorumdem
corporibus legitime . procreatis. Ac rectis heredibus dicti Ricardi . si predicti
Ricardus et Katerina Sine heredibus de eoru*m*dem corporibus legitime
procreatis obierint vnam rodam terre nostre iacent*em*' in Camp' de Holkam
inter terram Willelmi de Walsigham ex parte australi . et terram predictam
Ricardi ex parte aquilonari cum pertinenciis . Habend' et tenend' de capitali
domino feodi predictis Ricardo et Katerina et heredibus de eoru*m*dem
corporibus legitime procreatis . ac rectis heredibus dicti Ricardi . si . predicti
Ricardus et Katerina sine heredibus de eorumdem corporibus legitime
procreatis obierint libere quiete bene et in pace in feodo et imperpetuum .
Reddendo inde annuatim seruicia debita et consueta . Et nos predicti
Willelmus et Emma vxor mea et heredes nostri predictam rodam terre cum
pertinenciis predictis Ricardo et Katerine et heredibus de eoru*m*dem
corporibus legitime procreatis ac predictis heredibus dicti Ricardi si predicti
Ricardus et Katerina sine heredibus de eoru*m*dem corporibus legitime
procreatis obierint contra omnes gentes Warantizabimus imperpetuum . In
Cuius rei Testimonium huic presenti carte sigilla nostra apposuimus . Hiis
Testibus . Willelmo de Walsingham . Willelmo Hotynel . Willelmo Wake .

Roberto de Gristen . Gylberto Burgeys et Aliis. Dat' apud Holkam in Translatione Sancti Thome Martiris . Anno Regni Regis Edwardi filij Regis Edwardi decimo.

Seal: Thick parchment. Fragment of dark green seal.
Hand: HD 27.
Endorsement: *Carta Willelmi Fabr' de Gresham de rod' terre iuxta terram Ricardi Nel. ex aquil' et terram Willelmi de Walt' ex austr'* [in hand of Edmund Lucas]. 51 T[ranscriptum] on seal tag. 69 (in russet ink).

HP 1060

Grant from John son of William Silk of Holkham to Richard Neel of Burnham and Katerine his wife of 2 plots.   22 Nov. 1317

Cf. HD 22a, Fo. 20v no. 220 (Lucas no. 67)
Fiche 2: D13

Sciant presentes et futuri quod . Ego Iohannes filius Willelmi Sylke de Holkam dedi concessi et hac presenti carta mea confirmaui Ricardo Nel de Brunham et Katerine vxoris sue et heredibus de eorum corporibus legitime procreatis ac eciam rectis heredibus predicti Ricardi si predictus Ricardus et Katerina absque heredibus de eorum corporibus legitime procreatis obierint duas pecias terre mee cum pertinenciis iacent' in Camp' de Holkham quarum vna pecia iacet iuxta terram prioris et conuentus de Peterston et Capud occidentale abuttat super viam que vocatur Gibbesgate . altera pecia iacet inter terram prioris et Conuentus de Peterston ex parte boreali et terram Iohannis Breth ex parte australi et capud occidentale abuttat super viam que vocatur Gibbesgate . Habend' et tenend' predictas pecias terre cum pertinenciis predictis Ricardo et Katerine et heredibus de eorum corporibus legitime procreatis ac eciam rectis heredibus predictis Ricardo et predictis Ricardo et Katerine absque heredibus de eorum corporibus legitime procreatis obierint de Capitalibus dominis feodi libere et quiete . faciend' inde annuatim predictis Capitalibus dominis feodi seruicia debita consueta pro porcione tenementi . et Ego predictus Iohannes et heredes mei predictas pecias terre cum pertinenciis predictis Ricardo et Katerine et heredibus de eorum corporibus legitime procreatis ac eciam rectis heredibus predicti Ricardi si predictus Ricardus et Katerina absque herede obierint de eorum corporibus legitime procreatis contra omnes gentes in perpetuum Warantizabimus . In cuius rei testimonium huic carte sigillum meum apposui . Hiis Testibus . Roberto de Gristone . Willelmo Wake . Iohanne le Bret . Ricardo le

Northerne . Martino Goldewyne . Rogero de Orlions et aliis. Dat' apud Holkham die Martis proxima ante festum Sancti Clementis . Anno regni regis Edwardi filij regis Edwardi vndecimo.

Seal: Small grey circular seal, remains of fleur-de-lys? 1¹/₂ in. diam.
Endorsement: *Carta Iohannis fil' Willelmi Sylk . de ij pec' terr' ab' super. Gybbesgate.* 67. The endorsement and the number 67 is in the same hand as the cartulary where 67 is written in the margin.

HP 1061

HP 1061 does not exist. Number vacant in the catalogue.

HP 1062

Grant from Bartholomew son of William le Marchale of Holkham to Richard Neel of Burnham and Katerine his wife of 3 plots.   20 Jan. 1318

Cf. HD 22a, Fo. 20v no. 219 (Lucas no. 66)
Fiche 2: D14

Sciant presentes et futuri quod Ego Bartholomeus filius Willelmi le Marchale de Holkam concessi et hac presentes carta mea confirmaui Ricardo Nel de Brunham et Katerine vxori eius et heredibus de Corporibus eorum legitime procreatis ac eciam rectis heredibus predictis Ricardi si predicti Ricardus et Katerina absque heredibus de eorum corporibus legitime procreatis obierint tres pecias terre mee iacentes in Camp' de Holkam quarum vna iacet apud Ringge Waleslond iuxta terram que quondam fuit Willelmi Chelling ex parte aquilonali et capud orientale abuttat super Crekgate . altera iacet iuxta terram que quondam fuit Matild' Godkoc ex parte australi et capud occidentale abuttat super terram que quondam fuit Rogeri Elwerich' . tercia iacet iuxta terram que quondam fuit Humfridi Dauid ex parte aquilonali et Capud Occidentale abbutat super terram Prioris et Conuentus de Walsingham habend' et tenend' predictas tres pecias cum pertinenciis predictis Ricardo et Katerine et heredibus de eorum Corporibus legitime procreatis ac etiam rectis heredibus predictis Ricardi si predicti Ricardus et Katerina absque heredibus de corporibus eorum legitime procreatis obierint de Capitalibus dominis feodi libere quiete faciend' inde Capitalibus dominis feodi seruicia debita et consueta pro porcione tenement' Et Ego predictus Bartholomeus et heredes mei predictas tres pecias terre cum pertinenciis predicti Ricardo et Katerina et heredibus de eorum corporibus legitime procreatis Ac eciam rectis heredibus predictis Ricardo si predictus Ricardus et Katerina absque heredibus de eorum Corporibus legitime procreatis obierint contra omnes gentes Warantizabimus in perpetuum . In huius rei testimonium huic presenti sigillum meum apposui carte . Hiis testibus . Iohanne le Bret de Holkam . Ricardo le Northerne . Thoma filio eius . Willelmo Wake . Willelmo de Walsigham*a* . Roberto le Marchale . Martino Rust et aliis. Dat' apud Holkam die veneris in festo sancti Fabiani et Sebastiani . Anno regni regis Edwardi filij regis Edwardi vndecimo.

> Seal: Circular grey seal complete. Device: two-legged creature looking over shoulder within inscription 'confirmaui Ricardi Nel de Brunham et Kater[ine] ... Ricard .. altera' 1 in. diam. Seal tag is fragment of deed.
>
> Endorsement: by Edmund Lucas, *Carta Bartholomei Marchale iij pec' terr' apud Ryngwareslond et alibi 66 Examinatur* T[ranscriptum] on seal tag. (Later) in Holkham (in russet ink), 84 (in pencil) 68, 545 and 1060.
>
> VARIANT: *a* Walsigham no abbreviation mark for 'n'.

HP 1063

Grant from Adam son of William Craske of Holkham to Richard Neel of Burnham and Katerine his wife of 2 plots each of 2 acres. 13 Dec. 1318

> Cf. HD 22a, Fo. 23 no. 245 (Lucas no. 89)
> Fiche 2: E1

Sciant presentes et futuri quod Ego Adam filius Willelmi Craske de Holcham dedi concessi et hac presenti carta mea confirmaui Ricardo Nel de Brunham et Katerine vxori sue et heredibus de eorumdem corporibus legitime procreatis ac rectis heredibus dicti Ricardi si predicti Ricardus et Katerina sine heredibus de eorumdem corporibus legitime procreatis obierint quatuor acras terre mee Iacentes in Campis de Holcham quarum una pecia iacet apud steynil inter terram meam ex parte orientis et terram Roberti de Gristone et Mariore matris mee . ex parte occident' et continet in se duas acras terre et alia pecia vocatur Le Marledelond . Iacet inter terram Roberti de Gristone et Mariore matris mee ex parte boriali et terram predicti Ricardi et Katerine ex parte australi et continet in se duas acras terre . Tenend' et abend' dictas quatuor acras terre cum pertinenciis . Predictis Ricardo et Katerine et heredibus de eorumdem corporibus legitime procreatis ac rectis heredibus dicti Ricardi . si predicti Ricardus et Katerina sine heredibus de eorumdem corporibus legitime procreatis obierint de capitalibus dominis feodi per seruicia Inde debita et consueta . Libere quiete bene et in pace in feodo et hereditarie si Ego predictus Adam et heredes mei predictis . Ricardo et

Katerine et heredibus de eoru*m*dem corporibus legitime procreatis ac rectis heredibus dicti Ricardi . Si predicti Ricardus et Katerina sine heredibus de eoru*m*dem corporibus legitime procreatis obierint contra omnes gentes Warantizabimus In perpetuum . In cuius rei tesstimonium huic presenti carte sigillum meum apposui . Hiis testibus Willelmo Wake . Roberto de Gristone . Martino Rust et multis Alliis[7a]. Dat' apud Holcham in die sancte Lucie Virginis . Anno Regni regis edwardi filij regis edwardi duodecimo.

Hand: HP 1064.

Endorsement: *Carta Ade filij Willelmi Craske de iiij acr' terre apud Stey[n]hyll et Marledelond* 89 T[ranscriptum] *examinatur*; (in russet ink), 58; (in pencil) 69, 249, 1063.

VARIANT: [7a] alliis, Ms.

HP 1064

Grant from Gilbert son of William Silk of Holkham to Richard Neel of Burnham of his croft in Burgate.   25 Feb. 1320

Cf. HD 22a, Fo. 19 no. 209 (Lucas no. 57)
Fiche 2: E2

Sciant presentes et futuri quod Ego Gilbertus filius Willelmi Silk*e* de Holkham . dedi concessi et hac presenti carta mea confirmaui Ricardo Nel de Brunham . et heredibus suis et suis assignatis . Totam Croftam meam cum pertinenciis Iacent*em* in Burgate . inter terram quondam Alexandri de Burgate versus occidentem et terram domini abatis et conuentus de creek*e* versus orientem et capud aquilonare abuttat super mesuagium meum habend' et tenend' dictam croftam dicto Ricardo et heredibus suis et suis assignatis in feodo et hereditate de capitali domino per seruicia inde debita et consueta . Et ego predictus Gilbertus et heredes mei Warantizabimus et defendemus dictam croftam terre cum pertinenciis predicto Ricardo et heredibus suis et suis assignatis contra omnes gentes in perpetuum . In Cuius Rei testimonium Huic presenti carte sigillum meum aposui. Hiis testibus . Willelmo Wake . Roberto de Gristone . Martino Rust . Iohanne Silk*e* et multis aliis. Dat' apud Holcham die Lune proxima post festum Sancti Mathei Anno Regni regis edwardi filij regis edwardi tercio decimo.

Seal: Circular seal complete. White wax. Device in inscription. An animal? 1 in. diam.

Hand: HP 1063.

Endorsement: *Carte Gilberti Silk de Crofta in Burgate.* 57 T[ranscriptum] (in pencil) Burgate 1228, 694, 1064.

HP 1065

Grant from Adam Craske of Holkham to Richard Neel of Burnham and Katerine his wife of a headland of 2½ acres and a plot of 1 acre.

5 Oct. 1319

Cf. HD 22a, Fo. 14v no. 169 (Lucas no. 18)
Fiche 2: E3

Sciant presentes et futuri quod ego Adam Crask*e* de Holcham dedi concessi et hac presenti carta mea confirmaui Ricardo Neel de Brunham et Katerine vxori eius et heredibus de eoru*m*dem corporibus legitime procreatis ac rectis heredibus dicti Ricardi si predicti Ricardus et Katerina sine heredibus de eoru*m*dem corporibus legitime procreatis obierint tres acras terre mee et dimidiam . iacent' in Holcham in diuersis peciis videlicet apud Steynhil . duas acras et dimidiam terre iuxta terram Bartholomei filij Maddi de Campo ex parte occident' et est vna forera . et apud Billesmere vnam acram terre inter terram predicti Ricardi et terram Elueue Dalman et capud occident' abuttat super Quarlesgate Tenend' et habend' predictas tres acras et dimidiam terre cum pertinenciis predictis Ricardo et Katerine et heredibus de eoru*m*dem corporibus legitime procreatis . Ac rectis heredibus dicti Ricardi si predicti Ricardus et Katerina sine heredibus de eoru*m*dem corporibus legitime procreatis obierint de capitali domino feodi per seruicia debita et consueta in feodo et hereditate . Et ego predicti Adam et heredes mei predictas tres acras et dimidiam terre predictis Ricardo et Katerine et heredibus de eoru*m*dem corporibus legitime procreatis ac Rectis heredibus dicti Ricardi siue predicti Ricardus et Katerina siue heredes de eoru*m*dem corporibus legitime procreatis obierint . contra omnes gentes imperpetuum Warantizabimus . In cuius Reij testimonium Huic presenti carte sigillum meum apposui . Hiis testibus . Willelmo Wake . Ricardo Northerne . Roberto de Gristone . Iohanne Bret . Iohanne Belneye et aliis. Dat' apud Holcham die Veneris proxima post festum sancti Michaelis Archangeli anno regni Regis Edwardi filij Regis Edwardi tercio decimo.

Seal: White seal. Broken, but good impression. ?Fish inside inscription. Better example on HP 1062.
Hand: see note on HD 19.
Endorsement: *Carta Ade Craske de iij . acr' et dimid' terr' apud Steynhill et Byllesmere* .
18. T[ranscriptum], [Later] Holkham. (in russet ink), 27; (in pencil) 70, 650 and 1065.

HP 1066

Grant from Humphrey son of David and Amice his wife of Holkham to
William Craske of Holkham of 2 plots.   [c. 1284]

Cf. HD 22a, Fo. 11v no. 146
Fiche 2: E4

Sciant presentes et futuri quod Nos Humfridus filius Dauid et Amicia vxor
mea de Holkham concessimus dedimus et hac presenti carta nostra
Confirmauimus Willelmo Craske de Eadem villa pro homagio et seruicio suo
et pro quinquaginta sex solidis quos nobis dedit in gersumam duas Pecias
terre nostre Iacentes in Camp' de Holkham . quarum vna pecia terre Iacet
inter terram domini Prioris de Walsingham ex parte Australi et terram
Gilberti Aynild ex parte Aquilonali et abuttat versus orientem super Dalegate
. Et alia pecia Iacet apud Hadehowe inter Terram Bartholomey de Burgate ex
parte Australi et terram Iohannis Rutele ex parte aquilon' et abuttat versus
occidentem super HadeHogate Habend' et Tenend' de nobis et heredibus
nostris sibi et heredibus suis vel suis assignatis libere quiete bene in pace
Iure et Hereditarie . Reddendo Inde annuatim nobis et heredibus nostris vel
nostris assignatis duos denarios ad Pascha. Et ad scutagium domini Regis
quando venerit ad . xx^{ti}. Solid' vnum denarium . ad plus . plus . et ad minus
. minus . pro omnibus seruiciis consuetudinibus curiarum Sectis et secularibus
demandis . Et Nos predicti . Humfridus et Amicia Vxor mea et heredes nostri
Warantizabimus acquietabimus et defendemus predictas duas pecias terre cum
pertinenciis predicto Willelmo et heredibus vel assignatis suis contra omnes
imperpetuum . In Cuius rei testimonium Huic presenti Scripto Sigilla nostra
apposuimus . Hiis testibus . Radulfo Hakun . Rogero Belneye . Iohanne Le
Bret . Bartholomeo de [Bur]gate . Iohanne Silke . Gilberto Aynild . Simone
Hamund et aliis.

Seal: missing.
Endorsement: by Edmund Lucas, T[ranscriptum], (in russet ink), 35; (in pencil) 71, 1066
and 1236.

HP 1067

Quitclaim from William de Gresham to Richard Neel of Burnham and Katerine his wife of 3 acres. [c. 1300]

Cf. HD 22a, no. 218 (Lucas no. 65)
Fiche 2: E5

Pateat vniuersis per presentes quod Ego Willelmus de Gressam Remisi Relaxaui et penitus quietum clamaui Ricardo Nel de Brunham et Katerine vxori eius et heredibus de corporibus eorum legitime procreatis hac Rectis heredibus predicti Ricardi si predicti Ricardus et Katerina sine heredibus de corporibus eorumdem legitime procreatis obbierint*a* Totum Ius et clameum quod habui vel aliquo modo habere potui in tribus acris terre cum pertinenciis in Holcham prout Iacent inter terram Abbatis de Creyke et terram Ade Gillyon que fuit Ita quod nec Ego predictus Willelmus nec heredes meij nec aliquis per me seu nomine meo aliquid in predictis tribus acris terre exigere vendicare nec habere poterimus Et Ego predictus Willelmus et heredes meii predictas acras terre tres cum pertinenciis predictis Ricardo et Katerine et heredibus eorumdem legitime procreatis hac Rectis heredibus predicti Ricardi si predicti Ricardi et Katerine sine heredibus de corporibus eorumdem legitime procreatis obierint Contra omnes gentes imperpetuum Warantizabimus . In cuius Reij Testimonium huic presenti scripto sigillum meum apposui.

Seal: White, circular, flower within two interlacing squares which form eight-pointed star, 3/4 in. diam.
Endorsement: by Edmund Lucas, *Relaxac' Willelmi de Gresham de iij acr' terr'* T[ranscriptum] on seal tag (in russet ink) 79, (in pencil) 72, 500 and 1067.

VARIANT: *a* *sic* in Ms.

HP 1068

Grant from Roger Marchal of Holkham to Richard Neel of Burnham and Katerine his wife of 3 acres. [c. 1319]

Cf. HD 22a, Fo. 20 no. 217 (Lucas no. 64)
Fiche 2: E6

Sciant presentes et futuri quod Ego Rogerus Marchal de Holcham concessi dedi et hac presenti carta mea confirmaui Ricardo Neel de Brunham et Katerine vxori eius et heredibus de corporibus eorum legitime procreatis . hac

Rectis heredibus predicti Ricardi si Ricardus et Katerina sine heredibus corporibus eorum legitime procreatis obierint . tres acras terre mee Iacent' in Holcham inter terram abbatis de Crek et terram que fuit Ade gylyon et capud austrum abbuttat super viam que ducit de Holcham ad Warram et capud boriale abbutat super terram Iohannis Le Bret . Habend' et tenend' predictas tres acras terre cum pertinenciis predictis Ricardo et Katerine et heredibus de corporibus eorum Legitime procreatis . Hac rectis heredibus predicti Ricardus si Ricardus et Katerina sine heredibus de corporibus eorum Legitime procreatis obierint de capitalibus dominis feodi per seruicia debita et consueta . Et ego predictus Rogerus Et heredes mei Warrantizabimus predictis Ricardo et Katerine et heredibus de corporibus eorum legitime procreatis . Hac rectis heredibus predicti Ricardi . si predicti Ricardus et Katerina sine heredibus de corporibus eorum legitime procreatis obierint predictas tres acras terre cum pertinenciis imperpetuum . In cuius Rei testimonium presenti carte sigillum meum apposui . Hiis testibus . Willelmo Wake . Iohanne Bret . Iohanne Belneye . Hugone Otes . Ricardo Northerne . Thoma le Northerne . Roberto de Gristone et aliis.

> Seal: White circular seal; 2 interlacing squares. 8 in. diam.
> Hand: see note on HD 19.
> Endorsement: by Edmund Lucas, *Carta Rogeri Marchal de iij acr' terr' iacent' in Holkham*. 64 (in russet ink), 80 (in pencil) 73, 499, 1068.
> Orthography: Ac aspirated consistently.

HP 1069

Letter of Attorney from Roger Marchal of Holkham to Thomas Large of South Creake to give seisin to Richard Neel of Burnham and Katerine his wife of 3 acres. [c. 1319]

> Not in HD 22a
> Fiche 2: E7

Pateat vniuersis per presentes quod Ego Rogerus Marchal de Holcham attornaui et in loco meo posui Thomam Large de Suthcreyk atornatum meum ad deliberand' Ricardo Nel de Brunham et Katerine vxori eius seysynam de tribus acris terre cum pertinenciis in Holcham que perquiserunt de me prout in carta feofamenti meij testatur . In cuius Reij Testimonium hiis literis patentibus sigillum meum aposui.

> Seal: missing.
> Endorsement: by Edmund Lucas, *Litera attornatus Rogeri Marchall de seisina libera de iij acr' terre R. Neel:* (in russet ink), 100; (in pencil) 74, 1069 and 1440.

HP 1070

Grant from Gilbert son of John Silk of Holkham to Richard Neel of Burnham of a rent of 13d. on his messuage of 9 perches long and 6½ perches wide.

3 March 1320

Cf. HD 22a, Fo. 19v no. 211 (Lucas no. 58)
Fiche 2: E8

Sciant presentes et futuri quod ego Gilbertus filius Iohannis Silk de Holcham dedi concessi et hac presenti carta mea confirmaui Ricardo Neel de Brunham heredibus et assignatis suis Tresdecim denarios annuatim imperpetuum percipiend' Videlicet de mesuagio meo[1] in Holcham inter mesuagium quondam Alexandri de Burgate et terram Abbatis et conuentus de Creyk et capud Boriale abbutat super Burgate et capud australe abbuttat super terram predicti Ricardi et continet in se dictum mesuagium in Longitudine nouem perticatas terre et in latitudine sex perticatas et dimidiam terre . Habend' et tenend' predicto Ricardo heredibus et assignatis Habend' predictos tresdecim denarios in feodo et hereditate de dominis feodi per seruicia debita et consueta Et ego predictus Gilbertus et heredes mei Warrantizabimus et defendemus predictos tresdecim denarios annuatim percipiend' de mesuagio predicto vt predictum est . predicto Ricardo heredibus et assignatis suis imperpetuum . In cuius Reij testimonium Huic scripto sigillum meum apposui . Hiis testibus . Willelmo Wake . Iohanne Bret . Roberto de Gristone . Iohanne Belneye . Ricardo Northerne . Thoma Northerne . Martino Rust et aliis dat' apud Holcham die Lune proxima post festum Sancti Mathie apostoli anno Regni Regis Edwardi filij Regis Edwardi terciodecimo.

Seal: White seal complete. Device in inscription. 1 in. diam.
Hand: see note on HD 19.
Endorsement: by Edmund Lucas, *Cart' Gilberti Sylk' de xiij d. redd.* 78 T[ranscriptum] (in russet ink), 44 (in pencil), 75, 170 and 1070.

---

1   A note in cartulary says Gilbert Silk's messuage 'modo non edificat'.

HP 1071

Grant from Gilbert Silk of Holkham to Thomas Le Northerne of Holkham
1 messuage with a house.   22 Oct. 1321

   Not in HD 22a but cf. nos. 73 and 212
   Fiche 2: E9 and 3: G13 (seal)

Sciant presentes et futuri quod Ego Gilbertus Silk de Holcham concessi dedi
et hac presenti carta mea confirmaui Thome le Northerne de eadem
mesuagium meum cum pertinenciis et cum quadam domo insita iacens inter
terram Abbatis de Cre*k*e ex parte orientali et mesuagium Agnet' Briche ex
parte occidentali et capud australe abuttat super terram Ricardi Nel et capud
aquilonare abuttat in parte versus orientem super Regalem viam et in parte
occidentali super porcionem quam dedi Iohanni de Walsingham et Berte
vxori sue in eodem mesuagio Habend' et tenend' dictum mes*suagium* cum
pertinenciis et cum dicta domo . predicto Thome heredibus et suis assignatis
de Capitalibus dominis feodi libere quiete bene et in pace iure et hereditarie
imperpetuum per seruicia inde de iure debita et consueta . Et Ego predictus
Gilbertus heredes et assignati mei predictum mesuagium cum pertinenciis et
predictam domum vt predictum est prefato Thome heredibus et assignatis suis
per predicta seruicia Warantizabimus imperpetuum contra omnes . In cuius
rei testimonium Huic presenti Carte sigillum meum apposui Testibus .
Willelmo Wake . Ricardo Nel . Ricardo le Northerne . Roberto de Gristone .
Iohanne Bret . Bartholomeo Calwere . Willelmo Buleman et Alijs . Dat' apud
Holcham die Iouis proxima post festum sancti Luce Ewangeliste Anno regni
Regis Edwardi Quintodecimo.

   Seal: Black, a one masted ship within inscription. 1 in. diam.
   Hand: see note on HD 31.
   Endorsement: (in pencil) 76, 474 and 1071.

HP 1072

Grant from Adam son of William Craske of Holkham to Richard Neel and
Katerine his wife of Burnham Norton of 11/2 acres in 2 plots.   1 May 1323

   Cf. HD 22a, Fo. 19 no. 207 (Lucas no. 55)
   Fiche 2: E10

Sciant presentes et futuri quod ego Adam filius Willelmi Crasc de Holcham
concessi dedi et hac presenti carta mea confirmaui Ricardo Neel et Katerine
Vxori eius de Brunham Nortone et heredibus de corporibus eorumdem
legitime procreatis ac rectis heredibus dicti Ricardi . si predictus Ricardus et

Katerina sine heredibus de eorumdem corporibus legitime procreatis obierint .
duas pecias terre mee iacent' in camp' de Holcham . quarum vna pecia iacet
apud Scotbarbles iuxta terram predictorum Ricardi et Katerine ex parte
australi . et continet in se quinque rodas terre cum pertinenciis . Alia pecia
terre iacet apud Nortpilman . iuxta terram predicti Ricardi et Katerine ex
parte orientali . et continet in se vnam rodam terre cum pertinenciis .
Habend' et tenend' de capitalibus dominis feodorum predictorum Ricardo et
Katerine vxori eius et heredibus de corporibus eorumdem legitime procreatis
ac rectis heredibus dicti Ricardi . Si predict' Ricardus et Katerina sine
heredibus de corporibus eorumdem legitime procreatis obierint . libere. quiete
. bene et in pace . Faciendo inde annuatim capitalibus dominis feodorum
seruicia inde debita et consueta . Et ego predictus Adam et heredes mei
predicti duas pecias terre cum pertinenciis predictis Ricardo et Katerine Vxori
eius . et heredibus de corporibus eorumdem legitime procreatis . Ac rectis
heredibus dicti Ricardi si predictus Ricardus et Katerina sine heredibus de
corporibus eorumdem legitime procreatis . obierint . contra omnes gentes
Warantizabimus imperpetuum In cuius rei testimonium Huic presenti carte
sigillum meum Apposui . Hiis testibus . Willelmo de Walsingham . Martino
Rust et Aliis. Dat' apud Holcham in festo Apostolorum Philippi et Iacobi .
Anno regni regis Edwardi filij regis Edwardi sextodecimo .

Seal: missing.
Hand: HD 30.
Endorsement: by Edmund Lucas, *Carta Ade Craske de terra apud Scotbarbele 1 acr et.*
dimid. 55. T[ranscriptum] (in russet ink), 15 (in pencil), 77, 1072 and 1708.

HP 1073

Quitclaim from Margery Craske of Holkham to her son Adam Craske of
Holkham of 1 plot.　　　　　　　　　　　　28 Sept. 1326

Cf. HD 22a, Fo. 5v no. 67
Fiche 2: E11

Pateat vniversis per presentes quod ego Margeria Craske de Holkham
concessi Ade . filio meo . et in manus eius reddidi vnam peciam terre quam
tenui nomine dotis . siue ad terminum vite mee de hereditate predicti Ade .
apud Dalegate cum pertinenciis in Holkham . et iacet inter terram predicti
Ade ex parte australi . et terram de Burghhalle ex parte boreali . cuius caput
orientale abbuttat super Dalegate . Et totum ius meum et clameum quod
umquam habui vel aliquo modo habere potui in terram predictam cum suis
pertinenciis eidem Ade . heredibus . et assignatis suis . de me et heredibus

meis . penitus remisi et quietum clamaui . Ita videlicet quod nec ego . nec heredes mei nec aliquis nomine nostro . aliquid iuris vel clamei . in terram predictam cum suis pertinenciis . exigere . capere . vel habere de cetero valeamus imperpetuum . In cuius rei testimonium presenti scripto sigillum meum apposui . Hiis testibus . Iohanne le Bret de Holkham . Iohanne Le Buluwere de eadem . Iohanne de Belneye de eadem . Hugone Otes de eadem . Ricardo le Spellere de eadem et aliis. Dat' apud Holkham die dominica proxima ante festum Sancti Michaelis Archangeli . Anno . regni . regis . Edwardi . filij Regis . Edwardi . Vicesimo .

Seal: White. Device on shield three heads of barley, unidentified charges in chief. 1¹/₄ x 1 in.

Hand: se note on HD 31.

Endorsement: T[ranscriptum] (in russet ink), 107 (in pencil), 78, 894 and 1073.

NOTE: All the witnesses (except le Buluwere) and the grantee were among the freeholders whose homage and services were granted by Peter le Bret to Richard and Caterine Neel in 1314 (HD 22a, Fo. 12v no. 191).

HP 1074

Letter of Attorney from Adam son of William Craske of Holkham to Thomas son of William Grene of South Creake, chaplain, to give seisin to Richard Neel of Burnham and Caterine his wife of 2 plots, together with half a foldcourse. 14 Oct. 1326

Cf. HD 22a, Fo. 16 no. 185
Fiche 2: E12

Pateat vninersis per presentes quod Ego Adam filius Willelmi Craske de Holkham ordinaui feci et constitui dilectum in Christo Thomam filium Willelmi Grene de Suthcreyke Capellanum fidelem atornatum meum ad ponendum et introducendum Ricardum Neel de Brunham et Caterinam vxorem eius in plenam et pacificam Seysinam duarum peciarum terre Iacent' in Camp' de Holkham cum omnibus pertinenciis . Vna cum medietate vnius Faldesok' currentis in camp' de Holkham et omnibus libertatibus ad predictam medietatem faldesoke spectantibus . prout in quadam carta feofamenti inde eis confecti plenius continetur in Ratum et gratum habiturus quicquid Idem Thomas nomine meo in deliberacione dicte seysine duxerit faciend' in Cuius rei testimonium Huic presenti scripto sigillum meum apposui . Hiis testibus . Iohanne le Bret . Willelmo Wake . Hugone Otes et aliis. Dat' apud Holkham . xiiij die Octobris . Anno regni regis Edwardi filij regis Edwardi vicesimo.

Seal: White, broken, a ship, with cross on mast painted red (better specimen on HP 1081).
Hand: see note on HD 29.
Endorsement: (in russet ink), 108 (in pencil), 79, 895 and 1074.

HP 1075

Grant from Adam son of William Craske of Holkham to Richard Neel of Burnham and Caterine his wife of 1 plot of 13/4 acres.   29 Oct. 1326

Cf. HD 22a, Fo. 13 no. 154 (Lucas no. 3)
Fiche 2: E13

Sciant presentes et futuri quod Ego Adam filius Willelmi Craske de Holkham concessi dedi et hac presenti carta mea confirmaui Ricardo Neel de Brunham et Caterine vxori eius Vnam peciam terre mee cum pertinenciis in Holkham que continet in se Vnam acram et tres rodas terre et Iacet apud Hadehowe inter terram predicti Ricardi ex parte australi . et terram Iohannis Rutele ex parte aquilonali . et abuttat versus occidentem super Hadehogate Habend' et Tenend' prefatis Ricardo et Caterine et heredibus suis de corporibus eorum simul exeuntibus de capitali domino feodi per seruicia que ad illa tenementa pertinent . Et si contingat quod predicti Ricardus et Caterina sine huiusmodi heredibus de se exeuntibus infata*ᵃ* decedent . tunc terra predicta cum suis pertinenciis rectis heredibus predicti Ricardi quiete et integre remaneat habend' et tenend' de capitali domino feodi illius per seruicia que ad illa tenementa pertinent imperpetuum . Et Ego predictus Adam et heredes mei predictam peciam terre cum suis pertinenciis continent' vnam acram et tres rodas terre prefato Ricardo et Caterine et heredibus suis de se exeuntibus . Ac eciam rectis heredibus eiusdem Ricardi et suis assignatis si contingat predictos Ricardum et Caterinam sine huiusmodi heredibus de se exeuntibus infata*ᵃ* decedere . Warantizabimus contra omnes homines imperpetuum . In Cuius rei testimonium presenti carte sigillum meum apposui . Hiis testibus . Iohanne le Bret . Iohanne le Bulwere . Willelmo Wake . Hugone Otes . Iohanne de Belneye . Ricardo Speller' . Willelmo filio Alicie de Holkham et aliis. Dat' apud Holkham die Mercurij proxima post festum Apostolorum Symonis et Iude . Anno Regni Regis Edwardi filij Regis Edwardi vicesimo.

Seal: White, painted red, broken. Ship with cross on mast (better specimen on HP 1081).
Hand: see note on HD 33.
Endorsement: *Carta de vna pecia terre contin' j acr. iij. rod. apud Adowe - ex feoffamento Ade filij Willelmi Craske* 3 T[ranscriptum] (in russet ink), 36.

VARIANT: *ᵃ* in fata written as one word, twice.

HP 1076

*Grant from Adam Craske of Holkham to Richard Neel of Burnham and
Caterine his wife of 2 plots.*   6 June 1329

Cf. HD 22a, Fo. 14v no. 167 (Lucas no. 16)
Fiche 2: E14

Sciant presentes et futuri quod ego Adam Craske de Holkham concessi . dedi
. et hac presenti carta mea confirmaui Ricardo Neel de Brunham et Caterine
vxori eius . duas pecias terre mee . iacentes apud Dalegate cum pertinenciis
de Holkham . quarum vna . iacet iuxta terram predictorum Ricardi et
Caterine ex parte australi . et alia iuxta eamdem terram eorum . ex parte
boreali . Habend' et tendend' eisdem Ricardo et Caterine . et heredibus de
corporibus eorum legitime exeuntibus . Et si eos contingat sine huiusmodi
heredibus de se exeuntibus in fata decedere . tunc tota terra predicta rectis
Heredibus . prefati Ricardi . quiete et integre remaneat cum suis pertinenciis .
Habend' et tenend' eisdem heredibus et suis assignatis . de capitalibus
dominis feodi illius per seruicia que ad illa tenementa pertinent inperpetuum .
Et ego predictus Adam et heredes mei predictas duas pecias terre siue in eis
plus habeatur siue minus cum suis pertinenciis . predictis Ricardo et Caterine
et heredibus de corporibus eorum legitime exeuntibus . Ac eciam rectis
Heredibus ipsius Ricardi et suis assignatis . si ipsos Ricardum et Caterinam
sine Heredibus de se exeuntibus . decedere contingat . Warantizabimus contra
omnes imperpetuum . In cuius rei testimonium presenti carte sigillum meum
apposui . Hiis testibus . Willelmo Wake . Thoma le Northerne . Iohanne le
Bulwere . Iohanne le Bret . Willelmo filio Alicie . Iohanne Belneye .
Willelmo Buleman . et aliis. Dat' apud Holkham . sexto die Iunii . Anno
regni . regis . Edwardi . tercij post conquestum . tercio .

Seal: White, fragment but good impression - interlace. But A. Craske uses ship on HP
1077.
Hand: see note on HD 31.
Endorsement: *Examinatur. Dalegate Carte Ade Craske de ij peciis terre ibidem.* 16 .
T[ranscriptum] (in russet ink).

HP 1077

Grant from Ralph son of William a le Gateshende of Brisley and Margaret his wife to Simon Mous of Kettlestone and Cecily his wife of 1/2 acre.
27 Nov. 1329

Cf. HD 22a, Fo. 2 no. 5
Fiche 2: F1

Sciant presentes et futuri quod Nos Radulfus filius Willelmi a Le Gateshende de Brisele et Margareta vxor mea vnanimi assensu nostro dedimus bona voluntate concessimus et hac presenti carta nostra confirmauimus Simoni Mus de Ketelesthone et Cicilie vxori sue pro quadam summa peccunie quam nobis pre Manibus dederunt dimidiam acram terre nostre arabilis cum pertinenciis suis iacent' in campo occidentali de Holcham Loco Vocato Schamelond inter terram Rogeri Carpentar' ex parte occidentali et terram Iohannis Meye ex parte orientali cuius capud Australe abuttat super terram Willelmi filij Alicie et capud Boriale abuttat super terram dicti Radulfi . Habend' et tenend' totam dictam dimidiam acram terre cum pertinenciis suis de capitali domino feodi illius dictis Simoni et Cicilie et heredibus hac assignatis suis . libere . quiete . bene . et in pace in feodo et hereditate imperpetuum . per seruicia inde de iure debita et consueta pro omnibus aliis seruiciis consuetudinibus . et secularibus demandis Vniuersis Et Nos predicti Radulfus et Margareta et heredes nostri predictam dimidiam acram terre cum pertinenciis suis . predictis Simoni et Cicilie et heredibus dicte Cicilie contra omnes gentes Warantizabimus imperpetuum In cuius rei testimonium dicti Radulfus et Margareta huic presenti carte sigilla sue apposuerunt Dat' apud Holkham die Lune proxima post festum sancte Katerine Virginis Anno regni regis Edwardi tercij post conquestum tercio Hiis testibus . Ricardo Nel . Thoma Northerne . Willelmo Wake . Iohanne Belneye . Ada Craske . Iohanne Bret . Iohanne Silke et aliis.

Seal: The seal tags are cut from contemporary deeds. White wax painted red. Two seals, good impressions. Devices: Fleur-de-lys above lion within inscription. Both 3/4 in. diam.
Endorsement: *Carta Ranulphi filij Willelmi atte Gatesende de Brisele de dimidia acra terre apud Stanielond* (in darker ink), *Examinatur iij.*

HP 1078

Grant from Lovegold and Alice daughters of Gilbert son of Richard Payn of Holkham to William Roteney of Holkham of 1¹/₂ acres.   29 May 1317

Cf. HD 22a, Fo. 7v no. 93
Fiche 2: F2

Sciant presentes et futuri quod Nos Louegolda et Alicia quondam filie Gilberti filij Ricardi Payn de Holcham concessimus et hac presenti carta nostra confirmauimus Willelmo Reteney de eadem et heredibus suis vnam acram et dimidiam terre Iacent' collateraliter in campo de Holcham apud Sladaker inter terram dicti Willelmi versus austrum et terram Rogeri Ode per partem borealem Cuius capud orientale abuttat super terram Prioris et conuentus de Petraston . Habendam et tenendam totam Predictam terram cum pertinenciis . illi et heredibus suis et suis assignatis . De Nobis et Heredibus nostris seu nostris Assignatis . Libere . quiete . bene in pace Iuris et in feodo Reddendo inde Annuatim Nobis et heredibus nostris vel nostris assignatis . quatuor denarios et obolum . Ad Natale sancti Iohannis Baptiste pro omni seruicio consuetudine secta curia cuiuscumque et omni seculari demanda. Et Nos Predicte Louegolda et Alicia Et heredes nostri . siue Assignati Acquietabimus et Defendemus totam terram predictam Antedicto Willelmo et Heredibus suis aut suis Assignatis . Per predictum seruicium contra omnes Homines inperpetuum In Cuius Rei testimonium Huic presenti carte Adquietancie . Sigilla nostra apposuimus Die Dominica in festo sancte Trinitatis Anno Regni Regis Edwardi*ᵃ* Decimo . Hiis testibus . Willelmo Wake . Roberto de Gristone . Thome Le Northerne . Bartholomeo Calwer . Iohanno Belneye . Willelmo filio Alicie Iohanne Le Bret . Gilberto fratre suo. Et multis Aliis.

Seal: Two seals, one missing. White circular seal: device (a plant?) within inscription. ⁷/₈ in. diam.
Hand: see note on HP 1002.
Endorsement: *Vetus cart' de Sladaker* T[ranscriptum] (in pencil), 83, 1078, 1572.

VARIANT: *ᵃ* filij Edwardi probably omitted.

HP 1079

Grant from John son of John Bret of Holkham to William of Heveringlond and Robert of Knapton, chaplains of 1 plot of 13/4 acres. 6 Feb. 1330

Cf. HD 22a, Fo. 2 no. 6
Fiche 2: F3

Sciant presentes et futuri quod ego Iohannes filius Iohannis Bret de Holcham concessi dedi et hac presenti carta mea confirmaui dominis Willelmo de Heueringlond et Roberto de Knapetone capellanis . vnam peciam terre . iacentem apud Collesmere continentem in se septem rodas terre videlicet inter terram Ade Craske ex parte aquilonari et terram . Willelmi Grys ex parte australi . cuius capud occidentale . abuttat . super Caldhowegate . Habend' et tendend' . predictam peciam terre predictis dominis Willelmo et Roberto . illis . heredibus . eorum ac eorum assignatis . libere . quiete . bene et in pace . iure et in feodo de capitalibus dominis feodi illius per seruicia inde debita . et de iure consueta . Et ego predictus Iohannes . et heredes mei . predictam peciam terre . Warantizabimus et acquietabimus contra omnes gentes . imperpetuum . Dat' apud . Holcham die Martis proxima post Festum Purificacionis beate Marie Virginis . Anno regni Regis Edwardi . tercij . a conquestu quarto . Hiis testibus . Ricardo Nel . Willelmo Wake . Thoma le Northerne . Willelmo Bulman . Iohanne Bylneye . Adam Crask et aliis.

Seal: Grey, broken, 1/2 in. diam.
Hand: 14th century hand, not Lucas.
Endorsement: T[ranscriptum] 57 (rather red ink), *Carta . Iohannis Bret de vij rodis terre apud Collesmere* (in pencil), 84, 318, 1079.

HP 1080

Indenture between David de Strabolgy Earl of Atholl and Richard Neel of Burnham Gilbert Burgeys of Titchwell Henry Burgeys of same and William of Waterden. 30 May 1332

Not in HD 22a
Fiche 2: F4 and 3: G14 (seal)

Hec indentura facta apud Holkham tricesimo die Maij anno regni Regis Edwardi tercij post conquestum sexto . inter dominum David de Strabolgi Comitem Athol' ex parte vna et Ricardum Neel de Brunham Gilbertum Burgeys de Tichewell Henricum Burgeys de eadem et Willelmum de Waterden de altera testatur quod predicti Ricardus Gilbertus Henricus et

Willelmus cognoscunt se teneri predicto domino Comiti in quatuor libris sterlingorum soluend' eidem domino Comiti vel eius assignatis apud Holkham in festo Sancti Michaelis Arcangeli in fine quinque annorum proximo sequenti post diem confeccionis presencium nisi predicti Ricardus Gilbertus Henricus et Willelmus citra festum sancti Michaelis predictam quandam bercariam de nouo reparauerint ad valenciam quatuor librarum in manerio quod idem Ricardus Gilbertus Henricus et Willelmus super habuerunt ex dimissione predicti domini comitis ad terminum vite eor*um*dem Ricardi Gilberti Henrici et Willelmi cum pertinenciis in Holkham iuxta bruar*am* eiusdem ville . Et ad predictam bercariam faciend' vel predictum debitum soluendum in forma predicta predicti Ricardus Gilbertus Henricus et Willelmus se et quemlibet eorum in solid' heredes et executores suos specialiter obligauit per presentes . In cuius rei testimonium partes predicte sigilla sua presentibus indentat' alternatim apposuerunt . Dat' anno die et loco supradictis pro Ricardo Neel et al'[a]

Seal: scarlet wax. Armorial within inscription. Heater shaped. three pales. 1 in. diam. The superior quality of the engraving of the seal contrasts with that of the others.
Endorsement: (in pencil) 85, 1076, 1080.

NOTE: Augustus Jessopp remarks that 'No. 1080 is a bond from Richard Neel and others to repair the sheep-house in the manor of Holkham which the lessees held in lease of David de Strabolgy Earl of Atholl. This bond is dated 30 May, 1332, at which time Earl David had revolted from Edward III and had joined Edward I Balliol, titular King of Scots. The Earl had become possessed of the manor in right of his wife, Joan, co-heiress of Aymer de Valence Earl of Pembroke.' HMC, *Various Collections*, iv, 315. The extent of the manor (Burghall) is given in PRO C. Edw. III, File 45 (24), cited in *Cal. IPM*, vol. vii, no. 713, pp. 502-4. In 1337 on Strabolgy's death his son and heir, David, was aged 3. The manor was held of the king for 1/2 knight's fee. The lessees' first court is HD 82. The lease by David de Strabolgy to Richard Neel and his associates was confirmed on 11 June 1332 at Woodstock: 'Ratification of a demise by David de Strobolgi, earl of Athole (*sic*) to Richard Neel of Burnham, Gilbert Burgeis of Titchwell, Henry Burgeis of Titchwell and William de Waterden of the manor of Holkham, Co. Norfolk (advowsons of churches and foreign knight's fees without the town of Holkham, pertaining to the manor, excepted) to hold for their lives by the rent of 1d. at Midsummer for five years from Michaelmas next, and then of £100, payable at All Saints and Easter', *Cal. Patent* 1330-1334, p. 306.

VARIANT: [a] A fold at bottom of the parchment conceals this line.

HP 1081

*Letter of Attorney from Adam Craske of Holkham to John Mey of Holkham
to give seisin to Richard Neel of Burnham and Katerine his wife of 2 plots.*
18 June 1333

Cf. HD 22a, no. 168
Fiche 2: F5 and 3: G9 (seal)

Pateat vniuersis per presentes quod ego Adam Crask de Holkham ordinaui et
feci Iohannem Mey de eadem fidelem attorn[atum] meum ad imponendum et
introducendum Ricardum Neel de Brunham et Katerinam vxorem eius in
plenam et pacificam seisinam duarum peciarum terre mee iacent' in camp' de
Holcham . vna apud Dalgate . Altera apud Caldehowegate prout in carta
feofamenti quam predicti Ricardus et Katerina Habent ex dono meo plenius
specificatur. Ratum et gratum Habiturus quicquid predictis Iohannes nomine
meo in premisis duxerit faciend' . In cuius rei testimonium Huic presentes
litere sigillum meum apposui . Hiis testibus . Willelmo Wake . Ricardo filio
suo . Toma Le Northerne . Willelmo Buleman . Iohanne Sylk et aliis. Dat'
apud Holcham . xiiij . Kalend' Iulij . Anno regni regis Edwardi tercij post
conquestum Septimo.

Seal: Round white seal. 5/8 in. diam. One masted ship in inscription, mast surmounted by
cross.
Hand: HP 1082–92 (1335–36), feoffments to Richard's widow, Katerine, possibly in her
own hand.
Endorsement: by Edmund Lucas, *Litera attorn' Ade Craske de terra apud Caldowe et
Dalegate* (in russet ink), 21 (in pencil), 86, 1414.

HP 1082

*Grant from Simon Mous of Kettlestone and Cecily his wife to Caterine widow
of Richard Neel of Burnham a headland of 1 acre.* 9 Feb. 1336

Cf. HD 22a, Fo. 21v no. 232 (Lucas no. 76) and HP 1084
Fiche 2: F6

Sciant presentes et futuri quod nos Simon Mous de Ketelestone et Cicilia
vxor mea manentes in villa de Holkham concessimus . dedimus hac presenti
carta nostra confirmauimus Caterine que fuit vxor Ricardi Neel de Brunham .
vnam acram terre nostre iacent' in camp' de Holcham apud Schamelonde
iuxta terram eiusdem Caterine ex parte boreali . et est forera . Cuius caput
occidentale abuttat super terram Iohannis Mey . et caput orientale abuttat

super terram Iohannis Mey . et caput orient*ale* abuttat partim super terram
Andrei sub le Klynt . siue in predictis peciis terre Habeatur plus siue minus .
Habend' et tenend' predicte Caterine . Heredibus et Assignatis suis de
capitali domino feodi per seruicia que ad illam peciam terre pertinent
imperpetuum . Et nos predicti Simon et Cecilia et heredes nostri predictam
acram terre cum suis pertinenciis predicte Caterine. Heredibus et Assignatis
suis Warantizabimus contra omnes gentes imperpetuum . In cuius rei
testimonium huic presenti carte sigilla nostra aposuimus . Hiis testibus .
Willelmo Wake . Ricardo filio suo . Thoma le Northerne . Iohanne Bylneye .
Iohanne le Wrighte . Iohanne Sylk . Iohanne Mey et aliis. Dat' apud
Holcham nono die Februarij . Anno regni Regis Edwardi tercij post
conquestum . decimo.

> Seal: Two white seals. Good impressions. A bundle (?) between two arrow heads
> pointing outwards, 3/4 in. diam.
> Hand: see note on HP 1081.
> Endorsement: by Edmund Lucas, *Carta Simonis Mous de j acra terre apud Scamelond* 76
> (in russet ink), 67 (in pencil), 87, 1082 and 1492.

> NOTE: HP 1084 (HD 22a, Fo. 15 no. 174, 9 Feb. 1336) of same date between same
> parties gives different abuttals.

HP 1083

*Grant from Simon son of William Eyr of Morston to Katerine widow of
Richard Neel of Burnham of a plot of 3 acres.*   11 July 1335

> Cf. HD 22a, Fo. 22v no. 239 (Lucas no. 83)
> Fiche 2: F7

Sciant presentes et futuri quod Ego Simon filius Willelmi Eyr de Mershton*e*
concessi et hac presenti carta mea confirmaui Katerine que fuit vxor Ricardi
Neel de Brunham pro seruicio suo . et pro fidelitate quam mihi fecit pre
manibus vnam peciam trium acrarum terre que iacent apud Aldelose cum
pertinenciis in Holcham . iuxta terram Abbatis de Creyk*e* ex parte occid*ent*' .
et caput Australi abuttat super brueram de Holcham siue viam que ducit
versus Wyghton*e* . Habend' et tenend' predicte Katerine . heredibus . et
assignatis suis de me et heredibus meis . Reddendo inde annuatim mihi et
heredibus meis quinque denarios ad duos anni terminos . scilicet . ad festum
Sancti Andree . duos den' et ad festum nativitatis beate Iohannis Baptiste .
tres den' pro omni seruicio . Et ego predictus Simon . et heredes mei
predictas pecias trium acr' terre siue in ea plus habeatur siue minus cum suis
pertinenciis predicte Katerine . heredibus et assignatis suis per seruicia
predicta pro omni seruicio contra omnes homines acquietabimus imperpetuum
. In cuius rei testimonium huic presenti carte sigillum meum apposui . Hiis

testibus . Willelmo Wake de Holcham . Thoma le Northerne de eadem .
Iohanne Bylneie . Ricardo le Spellere . Iohanne le Wryghte . Iohanne Sylk .
Gilberto Calwere de eadem et aliis. Dat' apud Holcham die Martis proxima
post festum translacionis sancti Thome martiris . Anno regni Regis Edwardi
tertij post conquestum nono.

> Seal: Armorial white seal, vairy. diam. x 1 3/16 in.
> Hand: see note on HP 1081.
> Endorsement: by Edmund Lucas, *Carta Simonis filij Willelmi Eyr de iij acris terre apud Adelose redditus v d . 83* . T[ranscriptum] (in russet ink), 33 (in pencil), 88, 221, 1083.
>
> NOTE: Cf. HD 22a, Fo. 41 no. 260, Adelose.

HP 1084

Grant from Simon Mous of Kettlestone and Cecily his wife to Caterine widow of Richard Neel of Burnham of 1/2 acre.   9 Feb. 1336

> Cf. HD 22a, Fo. 15 no. 174 (Lucas no. 23) and HP 1082
> Fiche 2: F8 and 3: G11 (seal)

Sciant presentes et futuri quod nos Simon Mous de Ketelestone et Cicilia
vxor mea manentes in Holcham concessimus dedimus et hac presenti carta
nostra confirmauimus . Caterine que fuit vxor Ricardi Neel de Brunham .
vnam dimidiam acram terre nostre cum pertinenciis iacent' in Camp' de
Holcham apud Schamelond inter terram Rogeri carpentarij ex parte
occiden*tali* . et terram Iohannis Mey . ex parte orien*tali* . cuius caput australe
abuttat super terram Willelmi filij Alicie siue in predicta pecia terre Habeatur
plus siue minus Habend' et tenend' predicte Caterine . Heredibus . et
Assignatis suis de capitali domino feodi illius per seruicia que ad illam
peciam terre pertinent imperpetuum . Et nos predicti Simon et Cicilia et
heredes nostri predictam dimidiam acram terre cum suis pertinenciis predicte
Caterine . Heredibus et Assignatis suis Warantizabimus contra omnes gentes
imperpetuum In cuius rei testimonium huic presenti carte sigilla nostra
apposuimus. Hiis testibus . Willelmo Wake . Ricardo filio suo . Thoma le
Northerne . Iohanne Bylneie . Ricardo le Spellere . Iohanne le Wryghte .
Iohanne Sylk . Iohanne Mey et aliis. Dat' apud Holcham . Nono die
Februarij . Anno regni Regis Edwardi tercij post conquestum decimo.

> Seal: Two seals. One missing, one good impression. St. Andrew within inscription, oval. 1 x 3/4 in.
> Hand: see note on HP 1081.
> Endorsement: by Edmund Lucas, *Carta Simonis Mous et Cecilie vxoris de terra apud Stainlond 23* T[ranscriptum] (later) Holkham (in russet ink), 68 (in pencil), 89, 1495.

HP 1085

Grant from Thomas Le Northerne of Holkham to Katerine widow of Richard Neel of Holkham of a 'place of land'.　　　　11 Nov. 1335

Cf. HD 22a, Fo. 19v no. 212 (Lucas no. 59)
Fiche 2: F9

Sciant presentes et futuri quod Ego Thomas le Northerne de Holcham concessi dedi et hac presenti carta mea confirmaui Katerine que fuit vxor Ricardi Neel de eadem . vnam placeam terre mee iacent' in camp' de eadem apud Burgate . iuxta terram Abbatis de Crek ex parte orient*ali* et terram Agnet' Brithe ex parte occident*ali* . Cuius caput Australe abuttat super terra predicte Katerine . et caput aquilonare abuttat super viam regiam que ducit de villa de Welles . versus Holcham . Habend' et tenend' predicte Katerine et heredibus suis et assignatis suis de capitali domino feodi illius . libere . quiete . bene et in pace in feodo et imperpetuum per seruicia inde debita et consueta . Et ego predictus Thomas et heredes mei predictam placeam terre cum pertinenciis predicte Katerine et heredibus suis et suis assignatis contra omnes gentes Warantizabimus imperpetuum . In cuius rei testimonium huic presenti carte sigillum meum apposui . Hiis testibus . Willelmo Wake . Ricardo filio eiusdem . Iohanne Bylneie . Iohanne Sylk . Iohanne Le Wrycte . Iohanne Mey . Iohanne Le Meyre et aliis. Dat' apud Holcham in festo Sancti Martini confessoris . Anno regni regis Edwardi tercij post conquestum nono.

Seal: White circular seal, figures within engrailed circle and inscription. 1³/4 in. diam.
Hand: see note on HP 1081.
Endorsement: by Edmund Lucas, *Carta Thome le Northerne de terra apud Burgate* 59
T[ranscriptum] (in pencil), 90, 226, 1085.

HP 1086

Grant from Ralph le Deye and Agnes his wife of Holkham to Caterine widow of Richard Neel of 1 plot of ¹/2 acre.　　　　20 Nov. 1335

Cf. HD 22a, Fo. 27v no. 242 (Lucas no. 86)
Fiche 2: F10

Sciant presentes et futuri quod nos Radulfus le Deye et Agnes vxor mea de Holcham concessimus dedimus et hac presenti carta nostra confirmauimus Caterine que fuit vxor Ricardi Neel vnam peciam terre nostre continentem dimidiam acram cum pertinenciis in Holcham iacent' inter terram predicte Caterine ex parte boriali et terram Simonis Mous ex parte australi . Et caput orient' abuttat super terram Andree ad le Clynt . siue in predicta pecia plus habeatur siue minus . Habend' et tenend' predicte Caterine . Heredibus . et assignatis suis de capitali domino feodi illius per seruicia que ad illam terram pertinent imperpetuum . Et nos predicti Radu*lfus* et Agnes vxor mea predictam peciam terre cum suis pertinenciis predicte Caterine heredibus . et assignatis suis Warantizabimus contra omnes homines imperpetuum . In cuius rei testimonium presenti carte sigilla nostra apposuimus . Hiis testibus . Willelmo Wake . Iohanne de Bylneie . Thoma le Northerne . Iohanne le Wryghte . Iohanne Sylk et aliis. Dat' apud Holcham vicesimo \die/ Nouembris . anno regni regis Edwardi tercij post conquestum . Nono .

Seal: Two seals missing.
Hand: see note on HD 1081.
Endorsement: [Two different medieval hands], [? Nel] *Carta Radulfi le Deye et Agn'
vxoris sue*; by Edmund Lucas, *Carta Radulfi le Deye de dimidia acra terra apud le Clynt
. 86 .* T[ranscriptum] (in russet ink), 66 (in pencil), 91 and 1086.

HP 1087

*Grant from Thomas son of Richard le Northerne of Holkham to Caterine
widow of Richard Neel of Burnham of 9½ acres in 5 plots.*   18 Jan. 1336

Cf. HD 22a, Fo. 14 no. 162 (Lucas no. 11)
Fiche 2: F11

Sciant presentes et futuri quod Ego Thomas filius Ricardi le Northerne de Holcham concessi dedi et hac presenti carta mea confirmaui Caterine que fuit vxor Ricardi Neel de Brunham . quinque pecias terre mee iacentes in camp' de Holcham apud le Cleyelond .quarum vna pecia que continet . iij . acras terre et dimidiam iacet inter terram quondam Iohannis Ayneld ex parte occide*ntali* et terram Gilberti Caluere ex parte orientali cuius caput Bor*eale* Abuttat super terram quondam Iohannis Charle . Alia pecia terre iacet ad caput australe earu*m*dem . inter terram Radulfi . Grygge ex parte occidentali et terram Cleric*ie* de Howegate ex parte or*ientali*. Et caput bor*eale* abuttat super terram eiusdem Thome et continet in se septem rodas terre . Tercia pecia iacet fere ibidem . inter terram Thome Escher ex parte occide*ntali* et terram Hered*um* Willelmi Kat ex parte or*ientali* . Cuius caput australe abuttat super terram abbatis et conuentus de Creyk . et continet in se Septem rodas terre . quarta pecia continens vnam acram terre . iacet ibidem prope inter terram Iohannis Spellere ex parte or*ientali* et terram Iohannis Daulyn ex parte occide*ntali* . Cuius caput boreale abuttat super Wellesgat*e* . Quinta pecia iacet ibidem inter terram Roberti Andrehu ex parte orientali terram quondam

Roberti Mayn . ex parte occidentali . Cuius caput boreale abuttat super
Wellegate et continet in se vnam acram terre et dimidiam siue in predictis
peciis terre habeatur plus siue minus . Habend' et tenend' predicte Caterine .
Heredibus . et assignatis suis . de capitalibus dominis feodorum illorum per
seruicia que ad illas pecias terre pertinent imperpetuum . Et ego predictus
Thomas et heredes mei predictas pecias terre cum suis pertinenciis predicte
Caterine . Heredibus et assignatis suis Warantizabimus contra omnes gentes
imperpetuum . In cuius rei testimonium presenti carte sigillum meum apposui
. Hiis testibus . Willelmo Wake . Iohanne de Bylneye . Iohanne Le Wryghte .
Iohanne Sylk . Iohanne Mey et aliis. Dat' apud Holcham . xv . Kalendas
februar' . Anno Regni Regis Edwardi tercij post conquestum . Nono.

> Seal: missing. Medieval copper wire twisted round seal tag.
> Hand: see note on HP 1081.
> Endorsement: by Edmund Lucas, *Carta Thome filij R. de Northerne de v pec' terre apud
> Cleylond quinque ix acr' et dimid* . 11 . (in russet ink), 51 (17th century) Holkham (in
> pencil), 92 and 400.
>
> NOTE: Several of the grants from Thomas, son of Richard le Northerne occurred
> between 1332–6. See HD 22a, Fos. 14 no. 163; 16 no. 187; 20v nos. 221 and 222

HP 1088

*Grant from Ralph le Deye and Agnes his wife of Holkham to Caterine widow
of Richard Neel 1 plot of 1 rood.*   20 Apr. 1336

> Cf. HD 22a, Fo. 21v no. 231 (Lucas no. 75)
> Fiche 2: F12

Sciant presentes et futuri quod nos Radulfus Le Deye et Agnes vxor mea de
Holcham concessimus dedimus et hac presenti carta nostra confirmauimus
Caterine que fuit vxor Ricardi Neel . vnam peciam terre nostre continentem
vnam Rodam cum pertinenciis in Holcham iacentem apud Hugge inter terram
predicte Caterine ex parte occidentali et terram Heilote Meyre ex parte
orientali . cuius caput boriale \abuttat/ super terram predicte Caterine . siue in
predicta pecia habeatur plus siue minus . Habend' et tenend' predicte
Caterine Heredibus et Assignatis suis de capitali domino feodi illius per
seruicia que ad illam terram pertinent imperpetuum . et Nos predicti Radulfus
et Agnes vxor mea predictam peciam terre cum suis pertinenciis predicte
Caterine Heredibus et Assignatis suis Warantizabimus contra omnes homines
imperpetuum In cuius rei testimonium presenti carte sigilla nostra
Apposuimus . Hiis testibus . Willelmo Wake . Ricardo filio suo . Iohanne
Bylneie . Thoma le Northerne . Iohanne Le Wryghte . Iohanne Mey .

Iohanne Oddes et aliis. Dat' apud Holkam vicesimo die Aprilis . anno regni Regis Edwardi tercij post conquestum . decimo .

Seal: Two seals. Right hand one missing. White circular seal, broken but legible. 1/2 in. diam. A bundle (?) between two arrowheads pointing outwards.
Hand: see note on HP 1081.
Endorsement: by Edmund Lucas, *Carta Ricardi Deye de roda terre apud le Hugge* 45 (in russet ink), 95 (in pencil), 93, 1088 and 1457.

HP 1089

Quitclaim from Simon atte Cros and Cecily his wife of Holkham to Caterine widow of Richard Neel of Holkham of 1 rood.   20 Apr. 1336

Cf. HD 22a, Fos. 13v no. 160; 15v no. 179; 20 no. 216
Fiche 2: F13

Pateat vninersis per presentes quod nos Simon at ye Cros et Cicilia vxor mea de Holcham . remisimus relaxauimus et omnino de nobis et heredibus nostris quiet*am* clamauimus Caterine que fuit vxor Ricardi Neel de eadem . Heredibus . et Assignatis eiusdem Caterine imperpetuum . totum ius nostrum et clameum quod vuncquam habuimus . vel aliquo modo habere poterimus in vna roda terre iacent' in camp' de Holkham apud Hugge inter terram Caterine parte occidentali et terram Heylie Meyre ex parte o*rientali* . Et abuttat ad capud boreale super terram eiusdem Caterine cum pertinenciis in Holcham quam quidem rod*am* terre dicta Caterina nuper habuit de dono et feofamento Radulfi Le Deye . et Agnet*e* vxoris sue . Ita videlicet quod nec Nos nec heredes nostri nec aliquis nomine nostro aliquid iuris vel clamei in terra predicta . exigere . capere . vel habere de cetero valeamus imperpetuum . In cuius rei testimonium presenti sigilla nostra apposuimus . Hiis testibus . Willelmo Wake . Ricardo filio suo . Iohanne Bylneie . Thoma Le Northerne . Iohanne Le Wryghte . Iohanne Mey . Iohanne Oddes et aliis. Dat' apud Holcham . vicesimo die Aprilis . anno regni Regis Edwardi tercij post conquestum . decimo .

Seal: Two white seals, circular (as on HP 1093). Both 1/2 in. diam. One a bundle between two arrowheads pointing outwards. The other a fleur-de-lys.
Hand: see note on HP 1081.
Endorsement: by Edmund Lucas, *Relaxacio Simonis atte Cros de j pecia terre apud le Hughe* (in russet ink), 96 (in pencil), 94, 1089, 1456.

HP 1090

Letter of Attorney from Thomas son of Richard le Northerne of Holkham to Peter Longe of Burnham, chaplain, to give seisin to Caterine widow of Richard Neel of Burnham of 30 1/2 acres.   30 Apr. 1336

Cf. HD 22a, Fo. 16 no. 187.
Fiche 2: F14

Pateat vninersis per presentes quod ego Thomas filius Ricardi le Northerne de Holcham constitui et feci Petrum Longe de Brunham Capellanum atornatum meum ad liberandum Caterine que fuit vxor Ricardi Neel de Brunham plenariam seysinam de triginta acris et dimid' terre . de quibus ipsam feofaui cum pertinenciis in Holcham iuxta formam feofamenti mei predicti . Ratum habiturus et gratum quicquid predictus Petrus nomine meo fecerit in forma predicta . In cuius rei testimonium presenti sigillo mea apposui Dat' apud Holcham vltimo die Aprilis anno regni Regis Edwardi tertij post conquestum decimo.

Seal: White circular seals complete, Virgin (?)3/4 in. diam.
Hand: see note on HP 1081.
Endorsement: (in pencil) 95, 817 and 1090.

HP 1091

Confirmation from Thomas son of Richard le Northerne of Holkham to Caterine widow of Richard Neel of Burnham of 7 1/4 acres in 5 plots.
20 July 1336

Cf. HP 1092 and HD 22a, Fo. 13v no. 161 (Lucas no. 10)
Fiche 2: G1

Sciant presentes et futuri quod ego Thomas filius Ricardi le Northerne de Holcham concessi et hac presenti carta mea confirmaui Caterine que fuit vxor Ricardi Neel de Brunham . quod vna acra et tres rode terre quas Willelmus Wake de Holkham tenet ex dimissione Ele que fuit vxor Bartholomei de Burgate ad terminum vite eiusdem Ele . et quas eadem Ela prius tenuit in dote de Hereditate mea apud Claylond cum pertinenciis in Holcham . et que post decessum eiusdem Ele ad me ad heredes meos reuerti debuerunt . Post mortem eiusdem Ele prefate Caterine quiete et integre remaneant . Concessi etiam . et hac presenti carta mea confirmaui eidem Caterine quinque acras et dimidiam terre . iacentes in quatuor peciis . et in seysina eiusdem Caterine adhuc existentes vt illas quas prius habuit de dono in feofamento meo cum pertinenciis in Holcham . quarum vna pecia duarum acrarum et dimidie iacet apud Dalegate iuxta terram quondam Iohannis Tuber versus boream . Alia pecia vnius acre et vnius rode iacet apud Caldhowe iuxta terram domini prioris de Petr[aston] versus boream . Tercia pecia dimidie acre iacet similiter ibidem . iuxta terram Walteri Osbern versus boream . quarta pecia vnius acre et vnius rode iacet apud Bramlond iuxta terram domini prioris predicti versus occidentem . Habend' et tenend' eidem Caterine heredibus et assignatis suis de capitalibus domini feodorum illorum per seruicia que ad illa tenementa pertinent imperpetuum . Et ego predictus Thomas et heredes mei omnia tenementa supradicta cum suis pertinenciis predicte Caterine heredibus et assignatis suis Warantizabimus contra omnes homines imperpetuum . In cuius rei testimonium presenti carte sigillum meum apposui . Hiis testibus . Henrico Neel . Willelmo Wake . Iohanne Bylneie . Iohanne Le Wryghte . Iohanne Spellere . Willelmo filio Alicie . Ricardo de Redham . Willelmo de Waterdene et aliis. Dat' apud Holcham die sabati in festo sancte Margarete Virginis . Anno regni Regis Edwardi tercij post conquestum . decimo .

> Seal: White. Virgin and child (?) within engrailed pentagon. Good specimen also on HP 1090 and 1095.
>
> Hand: see note on HP 1081.
>
> Endorsement: in contemporary ink, *examinatur*; by Edmund Lucas, *Carta Thome le Northerne de diuersis peciis in Cleylond, Dalegate . Caldhowe et Bramlond contin . vij acr' et 1 rod* T[ranscriptum] (in pencil), 96, 820 and 109.
>
> NOTE: This deed is called the Great Charter of Thomas Northerne in HP 1092 in endorsement. The initial S in HP 1091 is exceptionally large and handsome. The cartulary differs in spelling Caterine with a K, but there are no variants in the field names. See also HD 22a, Fos. 14 nos. 162, 163; 16 no. 187; 20v nos. 221, 222.

HP 1092

Confirmation from William Wake of Holkham to Caterine widow of Richard Neel of Burnham of 13/4 acres. 22 July 1336

> Cf. HP 1091 and HD 22a, Fo. 14 no. 163 (Lucas no. 12)
> Fiche 2: G2

Vniuersis presens scriptum visuris vel audituris . Willelmus Wake de Holcham salutem in domino . Cum Thomas filius Ricardi le Northerne de Holcham nuper per cartam suam concesserit Caterine que fuit vxor Ricardi Neel de Brunham quod vna acra et tres rode terre quas ego teneo ad totam vitam Ele que fuit vxor Bartholomei de Burgate . ex dimissione eiusdem Ele . et quas eadem Ela prius tenuit de hereditate predicti Thome in dotem apud le Cleylond . cum pertinenciis in Holcham . et que post decessum eiusdem

Ele ad prefatum Thomam et heredes suos reuerti debuerunt post mortem eiusdem Ele prefate Caterine quiete et integre remaneant . Habend' et tenend' eidem Caterine heredibus et assignatis suis imperpetuum . Noueritis quod ego virtute concessionis predicti Thome predicte Caterine me atornaui . et ei feci fidelitatem de essendo eidem Caterine heredibus . et assignatis suis decetero intendens vt eorum tenens de tenemento predicto in forma predicta . In cuius rei testimonium presentibus sigillum meum apposui . Dat' apud Holcham die Lune in festo Sancte Marie Magdall' Anno regni regis . Edwardi . tercij post conquestum . decimo . presentibus tunc ibidem . domino Roberto de Cane clerico . Petro le Longe capellano . Willelmo de Waterdene et aliis.

> Seal: missing.
> Hand: see note on HP 1081.
> Endorsement: (contemporary) *examinatur*, by Edmund Lucas, *Feoffamentum Willelmi Wake de reuersione j. acr' 3 rod . terre in Cleylond ut patet in magna Carta Thome Northerne continet xxx acras et dimidiam acram et iij rodas in Cleylond* 12 T[ranscriptum] Homag (in pencil), 97, 821 and 1092.

> NOTE: Perhaps the pedigree was:
>
> Richard le Northerne
> |
> Thomas le Northerne
> |
> (1) Bartholomew of Burgate   – Ela –   (2) William Wake of Holkham

HP 1093

Quitclaim from Simon atte Cros and Cecily his wife of Holkham to Katerine Neel of Holkham of 1/2 acre of land.   12 Mar. 1337

> Cf. HD 22a, Fo. 15v no. 179 (Lucas no. 28) and HP 1094.
> Fiche 2: G3

Sciant presentes et futuri quod nos Simon ate Cros et Cecilia vxor mea de Holkam concessimus et hac presenti Carta nostra confirmauimus et omnino de nobis et heredibus nostris quietum clamauimus Katerine Neel de eadem heredibus et assignatis eiusdem Katerine imperpetuum totum ius et clameum quod habuimus vel aliquo modo habere poterimus in vna dimidia acra terre iacenti apud qwythewonge cuius capud orientale abbuttat super Regiam viam que ducit apud Qwarles et iacet inter terram Willelmi Wake ex parte australi et terram dicte Katerine ex parte boriali pro quadam summa pecunie quam nobis dedit premanibus nostris Habend' et tenend' dictam dimidiam acram terre prout iacet in villa de Holkam siue habeatur magis siue minus dicte Katerine heredibus et assignatis suis de Capitali domino feodi per seruicia inde debita et consueta ita quod nec Nos nec heredes nostri nec aliquis nomine nostro aliquid iuris Vel clam*eum* in terra predicta exigere vel vendicare poterimus Imperpetuum In cuius rei testimonium huic carte sigilla nostra apposuimus . Hiis testibus . Willelmo Wake . Thoma le Northerne . Iohanne Belneye . Iohanne Silke . Iohanne Wrygthe et aliis. Dat' apud Holkam In die Sancti Gregorij Pape Anno regni Regis Edwardi tercij a Conquestu Vndecimo.

> Seal: Two seals (as on HP 1089), one seal missing; the other is a fleur-de-lys, 1/2 in diam. Old deed used for seal tag.
>
> Hand: HP 1094.
>
> Endorsement: by Edmund Lucas, *Carta Simonis atte Cros et Cecilie vxoris eius de quadam pecia apud Whithwong de dimidia acra etc* . 28 T[ranscriptum] (in russet ink), 89 (in pencil), 98, 142, 1093.

HP 1094

Letter of Attorney from Simon atte Cros and Cecily his wife of Holkham for Thomas Wake, chaplain, to give seisin to Caterine widow of Richard Neel of 1/2 acre of land.   2 June 1337

> Fiche 2: G4

Pateat vniversis per presentes quod Nos Simon attecros et Cecilia vxor mea de Holkam constituimus et fecimus Thomam Wake cappelanum fidelem atornatum nostrum ad liberand' Caterinam que fuit vxor Ricardi Neel . plenariam seisinam de Vna dimidia acra terre abuttante*m* super terram eius Caterine iacentem apud Hugge iuxta Mesuagium Simonis Fabri cum pertinenciis vt patet in carta feofamenti quam nuper inde fecimus in cuius rei Testimonium presenti litere sigilla nostra apposuimus Dat' apud Holkam Secundo die Iunij Anno Regni Regis Edwardi tercij post conquestum xi.

> Seal: Two white seals, broken. One is possibly shield within inscription.
>
> Hand: HP 1093.
>
> Endorsement: by Edmund Lucas, *Littere attornatus Simonis Crucis pro seisina respect' terram apud le Hogge lib' K[aterine] Neel* (in russet ink), 97 (in pencil), 94, 1458 and 1094.
>
> NOTE: See HD 22a, Fo. 15v no. 179 of 12 March 1337. In Aug. 1982 we were told there had been anciently a smithy west of the kitchen garden (which is on the southwest of Howe Hill), for numerous nails were found on the site.

HP 1095

Bond from Thomas son of Richard le Northerne of Holkham to Katerine widow of Richard Neel for £20.   **19 July 1337**

Cf. HP 1096
Fiche 2: G5

Pateat vniuersis per presentes quod ego Thomas filius Ricardi le Northerne de Holkham teneor Katerine vxori quondam Ricardi Neel in viginti libras Starlingorum soluendas eidem vel attornato suo apud Holkam ad festum sancti Michaelis proximo sequens ad quam quidem solucionem fideliter faciendam tempore et loco supradictas . obligo me heredes et executores meos . prefate Katerine \heredibus/ et executoribus suis per presentes In cuius rei testimonium huic obligacioni sigillum meum apposui . Dat' apud Holkam die sabati ante festum sancte Margarete anno regni . regis . Edwardi tercio post conquestum vndecimo.

Seal: White, the Virgin and child within engrailed circle, ³/₄ in. diam. Better example on HP 1090.
Hand: rather rough and idiosyncratic as in HP 1096, perhaps written by le Northerne himself.
Endorsement: *obligacio Thome filij Ricardi le Northerne* (in russet ink), 56 (in pencil), 100, 95, and 1095.
Orthography: Starlingorum . Abbreviations: *tpre* with stroke for tempore (as in HP 1096).

HP 1096

Defeasance of bond between Thomas son of Richard le Northerne and Katerine widow of Richard Neel (£20), Indenture.   **19 July 1337**

Cf. HP 1095
Fiche 2: G6

Die Sabati proxima ante Festum Sancte Margarete anno regni regis Edwardi tercij post conquestum vndecimo apud Holkam ita conuenit inter Thomam filium Ricardi le Northerne ex vna parte et Katerinam vxorem quondam Ricardi Neel ex altera videlicet quod si predicta Katerina vel heredes sui placitentur . seu aliquo modo grauentur per predictum Thomam vel heredes suos vel aliquem ex consensu eorum . occasione cuiusdam donacionis de diuersis tenementis in Holkham dudum prefate Katerine . facte . per ipsum Thomam vel alicuius contractus inter ipsos Thomam et Katerinam prehabiti a principio mundi vsque in diem confeccionis presentis quod tunc quoddam scriptum obligatorium viginti librarum Starlingorum quod predicta Katerina habet penes se ex confeccione ipsius Thome stet in Robore suo . Et quam diu*ᵃ* prefata Katerina seu heredes sui per predictum Thomam vel heredes suos vel per aliquem ex consensu eorum non placitentur nec in aliquo grauentur quod dummodo predictum scriptum obligatorium nullius sit vigoris . ad quas quidem conuenciones tenendas partes predicte obligant se et heredes suos alternatim . Et presentibus sigilla sua apposuerunt . Hiis testibus . Willelmo Wake . Iohanne de Bylneye . Iohanne Hoddes . Iohanne Mey et aliis. Dat' loco et tempore supradictis.

> Seal: missing.
> Hand: see note on HP 1095.
> Endorsement: conuencio obliga*toria* . (in russet ink), 57 (in pencil), 101, 1096, 1679.
> Orthography: Starlingorum (cf. HP 1095).
>
> VARIANT: *ᵃ* written as two words.

HP 1097

Grant from Lawrence Bending of Holkham to Lawrence Skinner of Holkham of 1 plot.   28 Apr. 1339

> Cf. HD 22a, Fo. 10v no. 128
> Fiche 2: G7

Sciant presentes et futuri quod Ego Laurencius Bending de Holcham concessi dedi et hac presenti carta mea confirmaui Laurencio Skynnere de eadem vnam peciam terre mee iacent' in villa de Holcham inter terram Matild' Charle ex parte Australi et terram Willelmi Craske ex parte aquilon' et capud orientale abuttat super Cruftam predicti Laurencij et capud occidentale abuttat super placeam terre Matild' Charle Habend' et tenend' predicto Laurencio heredibus suis et assignatis predictam peciam terre siue in ea continetur magis seu minus de capitalibus dominis feodi illius libere iure hereditarie in perpetuum per seruicia inde debita et de iure consueta . Et Ego predictus Laurencius et heredes mei predicti Laurencij Heredibus suis et assignatis predictam peciam terre sicud predictum est per predicta seruicia imperpetuum Warantizabimus contra omnes In cuius rei testimonium Huic presenti carte sigillum meum apposui . Hiis testibus . Willelmo Wake . Thoma Northerne . Iohanne de Bilneye . Iohanne Wrighte . Iohanne Aynild et aliis. Dat' apud Holcham die mercurij proxima post festum Sancti Marcij euuangeliste anno regni Regis Edwardi tercij post conquestum terciodecimo.

> Seal: Black seal, shield inside inscription in pentagon, 1¼ in. diam. Seal Tag: strip of old deed in similar hand.
> Endorsement: (medieval) .. *Inquiratur* (?); by Edmund Lucas, T[ranscriptum] (in russet ink), 55 (in pencil), 102, 302, 1097.

HP 1098

Grant from Caterine widow of Richard Neel of Burnham to Thomas Neel her son of an annual rent of 10 marks, payable on the feast of All Saints.

26 Sept. 1339

Fiche 2: G8

Pateat vniuersis per presentes quod Ego Caterina quondam vxor . Ricardi Nel . de Brunham dedi et concessi Thome Nel filio meo et heredibus suis . decem marcas argenti de annuo redditu Habendas et percipiendas annuatim ad . festum omnium sanctorum apud Holkam . de omnibus terris et tenementis meis in Holkam ad quam quidem solucionem dicto die et loco fideliter faciendam obligo me et omnes terras et tenementa mea in Holkam districcioni predicti Thome vel eius attornat' . In cuius rei testimonium huic presenti scripto sigillum meum apposui Data apud Holkam die dominica proxima ante festum . sancti . Michaelis archangeli anno regni Regis Edwardi tercij post conquestum terciodecimo .

Seal: Black. Agnus dei inside inscription, 3/4 in. diam.
Hand: possibly that of Thomas Neel, but resembles HP 1095
Endorsement: (in russet ink) 81, (in pencil) 103, 1098, 1249.

HP 1099

Grant from Lawrence Skinner of Holkham to Gilbert Neel of Burnham of 1 plot.

9 Aug. 1344

Cf. HD 22a, Fo. 15v no. 178 (Lucas no. 27)
Fiche 2: G9

Sciant presentes et futuri quod ego Laurencius Skynnere de Holkham concessi dedi et hac presenti carta mea confirmaui Gilberto Neel de Brunham vnam peciam terre meo iacent' in villa de Holkham inter terram Matild' Charle ex parte australi et terram Willelmi Craske ex parte Aquilon' . Et caput orientale abuttat super croftam Laurencij Bending'. et caput . Occident' abuttat super quandam placeam terre Matild' Charle . Habend' et tenend' predictam peciam terre predicto Gilberto et heredibus suis et suis assignatis de capitalibus dominis feodi per seruicia inde debita et consueta . Et ego predictus Laurencius et heredes mei predicto Gilberto et suis heredibus et assignatis predictam peciam terre cum omnibus suis pertinenciis Warantizabimus contra omnes gentes imperpetuum . In cuius rei testimonium Huic presenti carte sigillum meum apposui . Hiis testibus . Thoma Vicari . Roberto Erneys . Iohanne Wrygte . Willelmo Curthun . Iohanne Aynyld et

Aliis. Dat' apud Holkham die lune in Vigilia Sancti Laurencij anno regni regis Edwardi tercij post conquestum octauo decimo.

Seal: missing.
Hand: Decorative line ending: four fish. Self-confident script perhaps of the aggressive Gilbert Neel.
Endorsement: by Edmund Lucas, *Carta Laurencij Skynner de j pec . terre iuxta terram Matild' Clarke* 27 T[ranscriptum], (in russet ink), 54 (in pencil), 104, 301, 1099.

HP 1100

Bond from William de Barney dwelling in Holkham to Gilbert Neel of Burnham for 20s. sterling.   2 Oct. 1345

Cf. HP 1101
Fiche 2: G10

Pateat vniuersis per presentes quod ego Willelmus de Berneye manens in villa de Holkham recepi apud Holcham die confeccionis presencium de Gilberto Neel de Brunham viginti solidos sterlingorum ad marcantizandum et approuandum ad opus dicti Gilberti et de approuamentis inde prouenientibus dicto Gilberto Neel compotum reddendo . Ad quod quidem compotum fideliter facien*dum* et denarios predictos simul cum approuamentis inde prouenientibus dicto Gilberto fideliter soluend*is* ad festum Sancti Michaelis proxim' sequens obligo me per presentes . In cuius rei testimonium huic presenti scripto sigillum meum apposui . Dat' apud Holcham die dominica post festum Sancti Michaelis Archangeli . Anno regni regis Edwardi tercij post conquestum nonodecimo .

Seal: missing.
Endorsement: (in russet ink) 42, (in pencil) 105, 495, 1100.

NOTE: There are numerous cases of debt in the court rolls. HP 1100 and 1101 seem to record transactions whereby Gilbert Neel advanced credit to a merchant who had moved into Holkham. Augustus Jessopp noted that Nos. 1100 and 1101 are among the evidences, so rarely to be met with, of money-lenders having plied their trade in the villages during the 14th century. HMC, *Various Collections*, iv, p. 315.

HP 1101

Bond from Benedict Scot of Horning dwelling in Holkham to Gilbert Neel of Burnham for £ 3 sterling. 17 Aug. 1347

Cf. HP 1100
Fiche 2: G11

Pateat vniuersis per presentes quod ego Benedictus Scot de Horninge manens in Holcham recepi ibidem de Gilberto Nel de Brunham die confeccionis presencium tres libras starlingorum ad marcandizand' et approuand' ad opus dicti Gilberti et de approuamentis inde prouenientibus fidelem compotum ad festum Sancti Petri ad vincula proxima sequens . Ad quod quidem compotum fideliter faciendum et denarios predictos simul cum omnibus approuamentis inde prouenientibus fideliter soluendis dicto Gilberto Nel vel suo certo attornato ad terminum predictum obligo me per presentes . In cuius rei testimonium huic presenti scripto sigillum meum apposui Dat' apud Holcham die Veneris proxima post festum asumcionis beate marie Anno regni regis Edwardi tercio post conquestum vicesimo Primo.

Seal: missing.
Endorsement: (in russet ink) 48, (in pencil) 106, 1680 and 1101.
Orthography: starlingorum, asumcionis.

HP 1102

Quitclaim from Gilbert Calwere of Holkham to John Calwere his brother of 1³/4 acres. 13 June 1347

Fiche 2: G12

Omnibus christi Fidelibus ad quos presens scriptum peruenerit Gilbertus Calwere de Holcham salutem in domino . Noueritis me relaxasse et omnino de me et heredibus meis in perpetuum quietum clamasse Iohanni Calwere fratri meo heredibus suis et assignatis totum ius et clameum quod habui habere potui et potero habere*ᵃ* et in una pecia terre septem rodas terre in se continente quod*ᵇ* mesuagium et cruftam Thome Northerne et placeam terre Benedicti de Hornigge ex parte orientali et mesuagium et cruftam Iohannis Shepherde ex parte occidentali et abuttat versus boream super viam que ducit ad ripam de Holcham et predicta pecia terre siue in ea sit magis se minus iacet in stathe cum seld' inter terram Iohannis de Hapesburgh ex parte orientali et terram Iohannis Spellere ex parte occidentali et capud australe abuttat super Scothowegate ita quod nec ego predictus Gilbertus nec heredes mei nec aliquis nomine nostro aliquod ius vel clameum in^c crufta nec in predicta pecia terre decetero exigere clamare habere nec vendicare poterimus in perpetuum set ego predictus Gilbertus et heredes mei predicta^d et peciam terre predicto Iohanni heredibus suis et assignatis imperpetuum Warantizabimus contra omnes gentes . In cuius rei testimonium huic presenti scripto iuris relaxacionis sigillum meum apposui . Hiis testibus . Iohanni Andreu . Willelmo Wake . Thoma Northerne . Iohanne Aynild . Iohanne Wright et aliis. Dat' apud Holcham die Mercurij in crastino sancti Barnabe apostoli anno regni Regis Edwardi tercij post conquestum vicesimo primo.

Seal: Vesica shaped. Broken but good impression, cross of Lorraine within inscription.
Endorsement: (in pencil) 107, 1102 and 1489.
Orthography: relaxasse, clamasse, capud.

VARIANTS: ^{a} followed by *in uno cotagio edificato cum crufta adiacenti* struck out.
^{b} followed by *cotagium iacet inter* struck out. ^{c} followed by *predictis cotagiis* struck out. ^{d} followed by *cotagia croftam* struck out.

HP 1103

Grant from Ralph Colt of Holkham to John son of Richard the smith of 1 plot.   [c. 1284]

Cf. HD 22a, Fo. 3v no. 38
Fiche 2: G13

Sciant presentes et futuri quod ego Radulfus Colt de Holcham concessi dedi et hac presenti carta mea confirmaui Iohanni filio Ricardi Fabri pro homagio et seruicio suo et pro octodecim solidis argenti quos mihi dedit in gersumam vnam peciam terre cum pertinenciis Iacentem in camp' de Holcham apud Cleygraues . videlicet inter terram Godmanni Delfen ex parte australi . et terram Iohannis filij Emme ex parte Aquilon' et abuttat super Regiam viam que ducit se versus quarveles ad capud occidentale . Habendam et tenendam de me et heredibus meis sibi et heredibus suis vel cuicumque et quibscumque illam peciam terre dare vendere legare vel assignare volerint libere quiete Iure et hereditarie . Reddendo inde Annuatim mihi et heredibus meis vel assignatis vnum obolum ad festum sancti Michaelis . pro omni seruicio consuetudine et seculari demanda. Et ego prefatus Radulfus et heredes mei Warantizabimus acquietabimus et defendemus predicto Iohanni et heredibus suis seu assignatis predictam peciam terre cum pertinenciis per predictum seruicium contra omnes homines inperpetuum . In huius rei testimonium huic presenti carte mee sigillum meum apposui . Hiis testibus . Radulfo Hakun . Petro le Bret . Bartholomeo de Burgate . Gilberto Payn . Iohanne Goldwine . Galfrido Godwine . Eborardo Kaly . Thoma Leffe et multis aliis.

Seal: missing.
Endorsement: by Edmund Lucas, T[ranscriptum] (in pencil), 108, 357 and 1103.

NOTE: Bartholomew de Burgate and Geoffrey Godwin are together in 1294-6 but Peter le Bret occurs in 1329. Ralph Hacun, Bartholomew de Burgate, Geoffrey Godwine and Thomas Leffe witness HP 1039 (HD 22a, Fo. 6 no. 70).

HP 3808

Will of Thomas Neel of Burnham.   20 Feb. 1350, 1 Mar. 1350

Cf. HD 44
Fiche 2: G14

In dei nomine amen Ego Thomas Neel de Brunham die sabati proxima ante festum Sancti Mathei Apostoli Anno domini m^o. ccc^{mo} xl^{mo} nono condo testimonium meum in hunc modum In Primis lego deo et beate Marie animam meam et corpus meum ad sepeliendum in cimiterio ecclesie Sancte Wytburge de Holkham. Item lego summo altari dicte ecclesie pro transgressionibus decimarum x . solidos Item lego ad emendacionem dicte ecclesie de Wesenham Thorp' ecclesie . x . solidos Item lego ad emendacionem . dimidiam marcam. Item lego Agnete sorori mee . xl . solidos. Item do et lego omnia bona et catalla mea vbicumque fuerint inuenta non legata executoribus meis ad faciendum pro anima mea secundum disposicionem eorum per visum domini Iohannis Leche de Eggemer' Et constituo executores meos Gilbertum Neel fratrem meum . Elenam sororem meam et Rogerum Stalworth et *sic* est clausum die et anno supradictis.
[*On dorse:*]
Istud testamentum fuit probatum coram nobis Official' domini Archidiaconi Norwyc' Kal' Martij Anno domini m^o ccc^{mo}[XL^{mo}] . nono. Et comyss' administracio omnium bonorum dictum testimonium conting*ent*' Gilberto Neel^a executoribus in eodem testamento nominatis in forma iuris . In cuius rei testimonium sigillum Offic*ij* nostri present' Apposuimus. Dat' apud

Wellys die et Anno domini supradictis . Reseruamus insuper nobis potestatem ... eius administracionis in eisdem bonis Elene et Rogero cum venerint et omnis administracionis seruire voluerint.

Endorsement: formerly numbered 47 (in ink), 38 and 737 (in pencil).

VARIANT: ^a *Elene Neel, Rogero Stalworth* struck out.

NOTE: The reckoning here is from the Incarnation with the feast of the Annunciation on 25 March as starting point for the year. The will-maker, Thomas Neel, son of the late Richard Neel, was mentioned with his mother Katerine, as to their Weasenham and Raynham possessions, in an inquisition of 1346: '*Hundredum de Brothercross ..., Thomas Neel et Katerina mater eius tenent tenementa sua in Kypton et Reynham per seruicium dimidii feodi militis de heredibus Roberti de Tateshale, que Hugo de Sprouston quondam tenuit*', cf. *Feudal Aids*, 1284–1431, vol. 3, p. 515. This Thomas Neel was the uncle of the Thomas Neel (son of his brother Gilbert Neel), who died on 24 July 1376, and upon whom there was an inquisition *post mortem* (indented 24 Oct. 1376; Writ, 28 Sept. 1376).

Holkham

'A messuage, 80 a. land and 5s. rent, held of the heiresses of the Earl of Atholl, minors in the King's wardship, as of the manor of Holkham, by service of half a knight's fee and 4s. rent; and 40 a. land, held of John Duke of Lancaster, as of his manor of Wighton, of the priors of Walsingham and Peterston, of the Abbot of Creake, of John Andrew, of John de Holkham and of Robert Galoun, by a yearly rent of 5s. 8¹/₂d.'

Weasenham

'A messuage called Kypton, 80 a. land and 40s. rent, held of John, Duke of Brittany, by service of a quarter of a knight's fee and 5s. for ward of the castle; and 80 a. land, held of Edmund de Thorp, Roger Scales, and Hugh Hastyngges, knights, the Prioress of Blakeberwe (*sic*), and the heirs of Thomas Beaupré, knight, as of the manor of Wesenham, by a yearly rent of 7s. He died on Thursday the eve of St James last (24 July 1376). Margaret and Mary [Neel] his sisters, aged respectively 24 years and 12 years and more, are his heirs'. Cf. *Cal. IPM*, XIV, no. 273, pp. 274–5.

Writ to the Escheator to make a partition of the premises between the said heirs
Westminster, 7 Dec. 1376

'Order to John de Rokewode, Escheator in the County of Norfolk, – pursuant to an inquisition made by him, shewing that Thomas Neel did not hold any lands in chief in his demesne as of fee in the said county on the day of his death, but held in his demesne of as fee a messuage, 80 acres of land and 5s. of yearly rent in Holkham of the heirs of the Earl of Atholl, minors in the King's ward, by the service of a moiety of a knight's fee and 4s. rent yearly, and also held divers other lands in the county of others than the king, and that Margaret, one of his sisters, who is of full age, and Mary, his other sister, a minor, are his next heirs, – to make a partition of the premises held of the Earl's heirs into two equal parts, take the fealty of John Quarles, who has taken Margaret to wife, and deliver to him and Margaret their pourparty, retaining Mary's pourparty in the King's hand until further order; and to meddle no further with the lands not held of the said Earl's heirs, delivering any issues thereof taken since the death of Thomas to those to whom they belong'. Cf. *Calendar of Fine Rolls*, VIII, 1368–1377, p. 373.

PRO E 179 – PRO C 47

PRO E 179 – PRO C 47

PRO E 179/149/9

Rotulus taxacionis quinte decime et decime domini regis E. Tertio Concesse Anno Sexto per Anselmum Mareschal et Iohannem de Caly Taxatores et Collectores Decimarum XVme et Decime in Comite Norfolci   1332–3

Mem. 32   Tax Return for the Hundred of North Greenhoe, Holkham

Villata de Holkham

De Ricardo Nel	xii s.	
De Iohanne de Billeye	x s.	
De Iohanne Beneyt		xii d.
De Bartolomeo le Millere		xii d.
De Agneta Marchall		xii d.
De Bartholomeo ate Hil		viii d.
De Thomas Elyot	ij s.	viii d.
De Edmundo Haldeyn	ij s.	
De Waltero Osbern	iiij s.	
De Rogero Croudde		xviij d.
De Andrea Hokere		xij d.
De Gilberto Crane		viij d.
De Gilberto le Chapman	v s.	
De Iohanne Spellere	vj s.	viij d.
De Andrea Atechirche		viij d.
De Benedicto Scoth		viij d.
De Ada Aynyld		xvj d.
De Rogero Esser		viij d.
De Sayena Walet		viij d.
De Thoma Elwan		xij d.
De Bartholomeo Calwere	vij s.	viij d.
De Isabela de Barsam	iij s.	
De Mariota Gibbes		xviij d.
De Ricardo Broun		viij d.
De Willelmo Dollow	viij s.	
De Bartholomeo Greys	ij s.	

De Ricardo Blekeman	ij s.	
De Iohanne Fabro	ij s.	
De Symone Mowes		xvj d.
De Iohanne le Carpenter	ij s.	
De Thoma Esser	ij s.	iiij d.
De Ricardo Meydegong		viij d.
De Iohanne Silk		viij d.
De Clericia de la Dale		viij d.
De Willelmo Sake		viij d.
De Roberto Keynot		xxij d.
De Margareta Hawkyn		viij d.
De Roberto Carpenter	viij s.	
De Iohanne Mey		xvj d.
De Ricardo Spellere	iiij s.	
De Berta Lyne		xij d.
De Godman Burgonie		xxij d.
De Symone Burgoine	ij s.	
De Rogero Carpenter	iiij s.	
De Agnete Bulwer		xij d.
De Reginaldo Crane	iiij s.	
De Rogero Leman	iiij s.	j d.
De Iohanne Crane		xviij d.
De Petro de Langham	viij s.	
De Matilda Pell		viij d.
De [Mati]lda Charle	v s.	
De Thoma le Northerne	ij s.	
De Adam Crask		xviij d.

Summa vij li. xxj d. pb.

PRO C 47/2/25

No. 18   Masters of Fishing Vessels at Holkham and Wells-next-the-Sea
1336–7

Inquisicio capta apud Wells coram Willelmum de Wardale clerico assignato ad supervidendum omnes naves qui transire possunt ultra mare ab ore aque Taimis' versus partes boreales et ad alia facienda prout in commissione Regis content' per sacramentum Iohannis Bilneye de Holkham Thome le Northerne de eadem Radulfi Griggs de Wells Roberti Andreu de eadem Iohannis Andreu de eadem Thome Hardy de eadem Ade Broun de eadem Thome Balteys Willelmi Yudekil Hugonis Haltre Iohannis Hamond et Iohannis Grere qui dicunt quod sunt in Holkham ix naves piscatrices quarum una vocatur le Hayet de pondere xx doliorum cuius dominus est Iohannes de Belneyt et idem est magister. Et alia vocatur la Katerine de pondere xx doliorum cuius dominus est idem Iohannes Belneyt et magister similiter. Et alia navis vocatur la Plente de pondere xij doliorum cuius dominus et magister est idem Iohannes. Et alia vocatur la Katerine de pondere xij doliorum cuius dominus et magister est Walterus Osbern. Et alia vocatur Cogge de pondere xij doliorum cuius dominus et magister est Willelmus Dollon. Et alia vocatur St Christofer de pondere xx doliorum cuius dominus et magister est Iohannes Speller. Et alia vocatur la Welyfair de pondere xij doliorum cuius dominus et magister est Iohannes Speller. Et alia vocatur la Charité de pondere xij doliorum cuius dominus et magister est Ricardus Silk. Et alia vocatur le Nicolas cujus dominus et magister est Ricardus Speller. Et dicunt quod sunt in Wells xiij naves piscatrices quarum una vocatur la Katerine de pondere xx doliorum cuius dominus et magister est Thomas Hardy. Et alia vocatur le Edmond de pondere xij doliorum cuius dominus et magister est Robertus Andreu. Et alia vocatur la Katerine de pondere xij doliorum cuius dominus et magister est idem Robertus. Et alia vocatur la Jolye de pondere xij doliorum cuius dominus et magister est Radulfus Grigge. Et alia vocatur la Garlond de pondere xij doliorum cuius dominus et magister est idem Radulfus. Et alia vocatur la Grene de pondere xij doliorum cuius dominus et magister est Iohannes Andreu. Et alia vocatur la Seyntemariship de pondere xij doliorum cuius dominus et magister est idem Iohannes. Et alia vocatur la Welifair de pondere xij doliorum cuius dominus et magister est Adam Broun. Et alia vocatur Seintemariship de pondere x doliorum cuius dominus et magister est Radulfus Grigge. Et alia vocatur la Skardeyn de pondere xij doliorum cuius dominus et magister est Thomas Balteys. Et alia vocatur la Godyet de pondere xij doliorum cuius dominus et magister est Iohannes atte Mille. Et alia vocatur la Malekyn de pondere xij doliorum cuius dominus et magister est Willelmus Silk. Et alia vocatur la Godale de pondere xij doliorum cuius dominus et magister est Iohannes Nicol. Et dicunt quod nulla navis de portu predicto inter tempus mandati Regis de veniendo ad portus de ..[illegible] et ..[illegible] Sancti Andree nec ad alios portus exteros aliqui... In cuius rei testimonium juratores huic inquisitioni sigilla sua posuerunt.

NOTE: The owners and masters of the fishing vessels of Holkham and Wells-next-the-Sea owned land in both places, as the Silk, Andreu, Balteys, Grigge etc. Nine ships in Holkham and thirteen in Wells were the resources on which Edward III could count for his war needs. Apart from the profits derived from piracy and wrecks, to which many references occur, fish was a useful alternative source of food when harvests were poor and salt was produced. The Stathe had its 'fish-house' and there are even grounds to suspect the use of ice before the Jacobean ice-house was built. Tithe of fish caught and landed at Burnham and Holkham was the subject of an early agreement, cf. West Dereham Abbey Charters *supra*, HD 6, no. viii. In the sixteenth century, John Pepys, a prosperous merchant who farmed much of Holkham, had a ship which went as far as Dublin. The 'mariners of Holkham' are mentioned in the eighteenth century, but the construction of a sea wall for Thomas Coke in 1720 destroyed the use of the Stathe as a stathe or harbour, and the tenant of Stathe Farm had to keep his ship at Wells instead of Holkham. In the early nineteenth century, Coke of Norfolk and his chief local tenants had ships – one was called 'The Washington'.

APPENDICES

Prosopography of Holkham

1330–1350

This prosopography, based on all the available and unprinted court rolls of the Holkham manors between 1330 and 1350, illustrates the social context of the documents printed here. It sheds light on a number of the Holkham tenants mentioned in the charters, and on some others with whom they interacted essentially through debt litigation and land transfers in the manor court. As noted above in our introduction (IV), several aspects of the every day life of Holkham as a community of peasants, mariners and small merchants can be approached through these rolls. These court rolls all relate to the Burghall and Neel manors, except for a court of Holkham Noion of 23 May 1334 which probably belonged to Peterstone. There are none for Hillhall during these two decades. The handwritings and lay-outs of sample membranes from each bundle of rolls are shown on Fiche 1: F. Burghall is often called *Holkham comitis*: for Warin de Montchesney's daughter Denise married William de Valence, Earl of Pembroke (d. 1296), the father of Earl Aymer (d. 1324). Aymer's sister Joan (d. 1329) married 'The Red Comyn', whom Robert the Bruce stabbed at Dumfries in 1306. A co-heiress married David de Strabolgy, 9th Earl of Atholl (d. 1326). His namesake (1309–35) left an heir, another David, aged three.[1] On 3 July 1332, the first court was held of the celebrated Walter de Manny whom Edward III preferred to an Earl who adhered to Scottish rebels;[2] but it is not clear why John Andrew held the court on 8 April 1342 and why Cassander de Bramber held a first court, apparently in 1347 (presumably to farm it).[3] Courts of 1332, described by Davidson as Neel were really Burghall, farmed by Richard Neel and others from David de Strabolgy, Earl of Atholl,[4] but real Neel manor courts are well represented.[5] Based on the prosopography and all other available documents, sixteen main Holkham families (1250–1350) are presented at the end of this first appendix. Estimates of the population based on numbers named in the prosopography and index must allow for persons recorded in the lost rolls of Peterstone and Burghall. The following prosopography includes every person in the relevant rolls. It ignores references to pledging by persons who are amply recorded. It also ignores *sequele* to whom many references occur.

a) **Court Rolls preserved at Holkham Hall:** HD 82, 1 m., (Burghall-Neel), 3 July 1332, 22 July 1332. HD 83, 8 mm., (Neel), 24 April 1332, 31 March 1333, 12 Nov. 1333, 10 Nov. 1335, 3 Dec. 1335, 3 Dec. 1339, 1 Dec. 1340, 8 Dec. 1341, (undated) c. 1341–2 list of tenants, 4 Dec. 1342, 15 Nov. 1343, 16 Nov. 1344, 18 Nov. 1345,

---

1   G.E.C. *Peerage*, I, 306–7; *Scots Peerage*, I, 509; *Cal. IPM*, VI, no. 759, pp. 479, 489–3; *id.*, VII, no. 713, pp. 502–4; *id.* XII, no. 327, p. 312; *id.* XIV, no. 86, pp. 84–5.
2   *Cal. Close*, 1337–9, pp. 62–3, *Cal. Patent*, 1334–8, pp. 61, 176, 266.
3   HD 86.
4   HD 82.
5   HD 83.

20 Oct. 1347, 9 Dec. 1348, 15 Oct. 1349, 24 Nov. 1349, 7 July 1350. HD 84, 5 ms., (Burghall), 29 Sept. 1332, 22 July 1332, 6 May 1333, 1 July 1333, 29 Sept. 1333, 25 Jan. 1334, 3 March 1334, 23 May 1334, 22 June 1334, 22 July 1334, 29 Sept. 1333–4, 21 Oct. 1334, 1 Nov. 1334, 8 Dec. 1334, 28 March 1335. HD 85, 1 m., (Noion), 31 May 1334, 23 May 1334, 4 Nov. 1334, 18 Jan. 1335. HD 85a, 27 ms. (1335–72), (Burghall), 11 Dec. 1335, 8 Jan. 1336, 22 July 1347, 7 Jan. 1336, 22 July 1347, 7 Jan. 1348, 8 April 1348, 14 Oct. 1348, 10 Dec. 1348. HD 86, 8 ms., (Burghall-Manny, Gilb. Neel), 24 March 1337, 22 July 1337, 10 June 1346, 6 Jan. 1346, c. 1346–7, 6 Dec. 1346, 20 Jan. 1347. HD 87, 1 m., (not Holkham, wrong classification), 29 June 1339, 18 Oct. 1340. HD 87a, 1 m., (Burghall), 9 Aug. 1348, 22 July 1350, 26 Nov. 1350.

b) **Court Rolls preserved at the PRO:** SC 2 193/1, (Burghall), 13 Dec. 1336, 16 Feb. 1337, 11 Sept. 1337, 29 Sept. 1337, 6 April 1342 (John Andrew), 12 Oct. 1342 (Walter de Manny), 28 Dec. 1342, 17 Dec. 1343, 4 June 1344 (Walter de Manny), 15 April 1345, 31 March 1349 (Walter de Manny), 5 Oct. 1349, 28 May 1350.[6]

c) **HD 82–87a. Fiche 1: E14, F1–7:** Specimen extracts from unpublished rolls of proceedings of manor courts in HD 82–87a. HD 82, first court of Richard Neel and others after lease of Burghall by David de Strabolgy, Earl of Atholl, 13 July 1332, Fiche 1: E14; HD 83, court rolls of Richard and Gilbert Neel of Neel Manor in Holkham (1332–84), list of Neel Manor tenants on narrow strip, Fiche 1: F1; HD 84, Burghall accounts in court rolls of the manor of Holkham (1333–4), account of Ioh. Mey, collector, Fiche 1: F2; HD 85, court roll of Holkham Noyon (Peterstone), 23 May 1334, Fiche 1: F3; HD 85a, Walter de Manny's court leet (Burghall), 22 July 1348, Fiche 1: F4 and 5; HD 87 and 87a, Walter de Manny's court leet (Burghall), 1339–40, Fiche 1: F6 and 7.

---

6   The PRO holds the following Holkham documents: 1) 1336–64, 10,11, 16–19, 23, 24, 29, 31, 35–37 E.III (12 mem.), courts of John Andrewe, of Walter de Manny and of Elizabeth de Burgh, Lady de Clare and others, cf. SC 2/193/1. 2) 1363–77, 37–39 E.III, 42 E.III, 44–50 E.III, 'Holkham Burghalle, *messores et collectores, compoti*', cf. SC 6/937/16. 3) 1462–83, [2,3?], 4–7, 9–23 E.IV, 1 Ric. III, (16 mem., defective), cf. SC 2/193/2. 4) 1608–20, 6 Jas.I, 17 Jas.I, courts of William Read, cf. SC 2/193/3.

Abraham, Seman, default, 4 Nov. 1334, HD 83; paid rent of 5d., 1341–1342 *circa*, HD 83; held parcel in Ernald's *terra*, answered for office of *prepositus* with John Cat, 1 Dec. 1340, HD 83; default, withheld rent 2d., 6 April 1342, SC 2 193/1; withheld 1/2 *precaria* autumn, 4 Dec. 1342, HD 83; sold land 1/2 acre to Richard atte Bakhous, 15 Nov. 1343, HD 83; as *prepositus* fined for contempt of court with John Cat, 15 Nov. 1343, HD 83; withheld 1 day autumn, 20 Oct. 1347, HD 83; withheld 2 days autumn, 9 Dec. 1348, HD 83; withheld rent 5d., 9 Dec. 1348, HD 83.

Abraham, Matilda, wife of Seman, died, succession land 3 roods and 1/2, heir cousin, Thomas, relief 6d., 15 Oct. 1349, HD 83.

Acke (Ake), John, debtor v. Bartholomew le Miller, 6 April 1342, SC 2 193/1; plaint is not prosecuted by creditor Bartholomew le Miller, 28 Dec. 1342, SC 2 193/1; order to levy 11s. for 3 quarters of malt detained, 6 April 1342, 28 Dec. 1342, SC 2 193/1; default, withheld rent 6d., 6 April 1342, SC 2 1342; sold some land to Bartholomew le Miller, 28 Dec. 1342, SC 2 193/1.

Acke (Ake), Alice, wife of John, 28 Dec. 1342, SC 2 193/1.

Acke (Ake), William, default, 22 July 1332, HD 82; ordered to come for fealty, 22 July 1332, HD 82; default, 8 Dec. 1334, HD 84; default, 28 March 1335, HD 84; default, 22 July 1337, HD 85; default, 8 April 1348, HD 85a; oath of fealty, 31 March 1349, SC 2 193/1.

Acloner, John, capital pledge, fined 18d. in assize of ale, 22 July 1350, HD 87a.

Adwald, John, of Waterden, plea v. William Mariot, 31 March 1349, SC 2 193/1.

Albard (Albere), John, of Creake, creditor, debt agreement with John Mey and Bartholomew le Miller, 11 Sept. 1337, SC 2 193/1.

Albard (Albere), Thomas, default, 22 July 1337, HD 86; bought 1 acre 31/2 roods from Richeman Brown, 6 Dec. 1346, HD 86; oath of fealty, after 6 Dec. 1346, HD 86.

Aldefader, Gilbert, bought a cottage at the Stathe from John Asty, 24 March 1337, HD 86; regrater of bread and ale, 22 July 1337, HD 86; bought 1/2 acre in Adowgate from Isabel Peper, 20 Jan. 1347, HD 86; bought half a cottage with a *placea curtilagii* from Joan Cheseman, 22 July 1347, HD 85a; regrater of bread, 22 July 1347, HD 85a; essoin for Ralph Soper, 14 Oct. 1348, HD 85a; fined 2d. in assize of bread, 10 Dec. 1348, HD 85a; bought 1 acre in South Field from Isabel and Matilda Payn, 31 March 1349, SC 2 193/1.

Aldefader, Helewise, wife of Gilbert, 24 March 1337, HD 86.

Aleyn, Agnes, sold 1/2 rood in Northclynt to John Crane, 3 March 1334, HD 84; sold 1 rood, north of lord's mill, to Henry de Surlingham, 24 March 1337, HD 86.

Alger, Alice, not prosecuting her plaint v. Thomas Esser, sold 1/2 acre to Thomas Esser, 28 Dec. 1342, SC 2 193/1.

Alice, William son of, agreement with Simon Mous, 3 July 1332, HD 82; capital pledge, 22 July 1332, HD 82; failure of pledging, fined 4d. with John Smith because they did not have Simon Mous to answer Bartholomew le Miller, 11 Dec. 1335, HD 85a.

Amour, Nicholas, of Burnham, creditor v. John Asty, 4 June 1344, SC 2 193/1.

Andrew, Alice, married without lord's licence, order to seize her cottage which is dilapidated, 6 April 1342, SC 2 193/1.

Andrew, John, of Wells, trespass v. Adam Craske, 6 May 1333, HD 84; bought a
tenement from William Parson, order of distraint for fealty and arrears of
services, 6 May 1333, HD 84; for common suit, 3 March 1334, 23 May
1334, HD 84; default, 22 June 1334, HD 84; oath of fealty, 3 Dec. 1339,
HD 83; bought 3 roods from lord, order of distraint for fealty, 12 Oct. 1342,
17 Dec. 1343, SC 2 193/1; order to attach, with Robert Andrew and
pledges, for raising a fold, 15 April 1345, SC 2 193/1; trespass with pigs on
lord's land, 15 April 1345, SC 2 193/1.

Andrew, Nicholas, bought 1 rood from Bartholomew de Howgate, 6 Dec. 1346, HD
86; died, heir under age, 6 Dec. 1346, HD 86.

Andrew, Robert, creditor v. Agnes Bulwer, 36s., 6 May 1333, HD 84; creditor v.
Roger Odes, 11 Dec. 1335, 8 Jan. 1336, HD 85a; creditor v. John de
Bilney, 13 Dec. 1336, SC 2 193/1; creditor v. Cecily Erneys, 13 Dec. 1336,
SC 2 193/1; default, 12 Oct. 1342, SC 2 193/1; order to attach, with John
Andrew and pledges, for raising a fold, 15 April 1345, SC 2 193/1.

Angelond, Garin, oath of fealty, 31 March 1349, SC 2 193/1.

Arenburgh, Robert of, clerk of the steward, 9 Aug. 1348, HD 87; attorney with
Geoffrey Saundre for William le Somynour, 14 Oct. 1348, HD 85; attorney
for John Adwald, 31 March 1349, SC 2 193/1.

Ashwycken, John de, sold 1½ acres to William le Somynour, 9 Aug. 1348, HD 87a.

Asty, Emma, bought a cottage at the Stathe from her brother, Walter Asty, 25 May
1334, HD 84; creditor v. William Henry, 16 Feb. 1337, SC 2 193/1; creditor
v. William Henry, 10 June 1346, HD 86; *hamsoken* v. Mary Lorys, 22 July
1350, HD 87a; regrater of ale, 22 July 1350, HD 87a.

Asty, John, default, order of distraint, 3 July 1332, HD 82; sold without lord's
licence 3 roods at Stafformere, order of distraint, 22 July 1332, HD 82;
trespass v. Abbot of West Dereham, 1 July 1333, HD 84; debtor v. William
de Barney, 1 July 1333, HD 84; lessor of 5 roods, without lord's licence, to
Peter de Langham, order to seize, 1 July 1333, HD 84; lessor of 3 pieces of
land to Richard Blakeman, at Bondeswong and Nortclynt, 4 years term, 25
Jan. 1334, HD 84; lessor of 5 roods, at Dyklyng, to John Crane, 25 Jan.
1334, HD 84; heir of brother, Walter Asty, paid heriot 32d. for a messuage
and 6 acres land, 23 May 1334, HD 84; lessor of ½ acre, at Odesgate, to
John de Bilney, 23 May 1334, HD 84; default, 23 May 1334, 22 July 1334,
HD 84; lessor of 3 roods, at Stathegate, to William Dolon, 10 years term,
28 March 1335, HD 85; lessor of 1½ roods to Adam Aynild, 8 years term,
28 March 1335, HD 85; pledge for Richard Blakeman, 13 Dec. 1336, SC 2
193/1; pledge for Emma Asty, 16 Feb. 1337, SC 2 193/1; sold a cottage, at
the Stathe, to Gilbert and Helewise Aldefader, 24 March 1337, HD 86;
default, 22 July 1337, HD 86; default, did not perform labour services, 12
Oct. 1342, SC 2 193/1; debtor v. Nicholas Amour, 4 June 1344, SC 2
193/1; bought 1 rood from John de Conteshale, order to keep it in lord's
hands, 4 June 1344, 15 April 1345, SC 2 193/1; lessor of a messuage with
½ acre to Caterine Neel, without lord's licence, order to seize, 4 June 1344,
15 April 1345, SC 2 193/1; default, 27 March 1346, HD 86; debtor v.
Gilbert le Souter, 22 July 1347, HD 85a; debtor v. Richard Meydegong, 8
April 1348, HD 85; lessor of 1 acre to William le Somynour, 3 years term,

without lord's licence, order to seize land, 14 Oct. 1348, HD 85; sold 1/2 acre to John Aynild, without licence, order to seize land, 31 March 1349, SC 2 193/1.

Asty, Richard, default, 21 Oct. 1334, HD 84.

Asty, Thomas, default, 21 Oct. 1334, HD 84.

Asty, Walter, sold a cottage, at the Stathe, to Emma Asty, his sister, 23 May 1334, HD 84; lessor of 11/2 roods to Reynald Crane, at Hallemille, 6 years term, 23 May 1334, HD 84; died, John Asty his brother, inherited a messuage and 6 acres land, paid heriot 32d., 23 May 1334, HD 84.

Aveline, Matilda, paid an ale fine 1d., 22 July 1334, HD 84; paid an ale fine 18d., and a bread fine 2d., 22 July 1347, HD 85; paid an ale (18d.) and a bread fine (2d.), 10 Dec. 1348, HD 85a.

Aveline, Warin, default, 8 April 1348, 14 Oct. 1348, HD 85a.

Aynild, Adam, lessee of 11/2 roods from John Asty, 8 years term, 28 March 1335, HD 84.

Aynild, Alice and her daughter Matilda, bought 1 rood from Simon Coupere and 11/2 roods from John Statehoppe, 8 April 1348, HD 85a.

Aynild, John, paid rent 2d., 6 April 1342, SC 2 193/1; order of distraint for fealty, 1346, HD 86; sold a messuage with 1 acre land to William le Somynour, 6 Dec. 1346, HD 86; debtor v. John Speller, inquisition ordered, 22 July 1347, HD 85a, bought 1/2 acre from John Asty, without lord's licence, 31 March 1349, SC 2 193/1; order of distraint for fealty, 15 Oct. 1349, HD 85a; creditor v. Simon Silk but not prosecuting his plaint, 28 May 1350, SC 193/1; trespass v. Gilbert Neel, 22 July 1350, HD 87a; not prosecuting his plaint v. Gilbert Neel in trespass plea, 26 Nov. 1350.

Bakhous (atte), Richard, trespass v. John Crane, 12 Oct. 1342, SC 2 193/1; trespass v. Roger Crane, 12 Oct. 1342, SC 2 193/1; fined in agreement on trespass with John Crane, 17 Dec. 1343, SC 2 193/1; false claim of Roger Crane in trespass plea, 17 Dec. 1343, SC 2 193/1; bought 1/2 acre from Seman Abraham, 15 Nov. 1343, SC 2 193/1; bought 1 rood from Thomas atte Hil, 4 June 1344, SC 2 193/1; bought 1 rood from Lawrence Skinner, 4 June 1344, SC 2 193/1; bought 1 rood from Gilbert Edwy, 4 June 1344, SC 2 193/1; bought 1/2 rood from Matilda Dersy, 4 June 1344, SC 2 193/1; land plea v. Roger Crane, 15 April 1345, SC 2 193/1; order to retain 1 rood purchased, without lord's licence, from Lawrence Skinner, 15 April 1345, SC 2 193/1; trespass v. Richard Speller, 15 April 1345, SC 2 193/1; retained 1 day autumn, 20 Oct. 1347, HD 83; bought 1 acre and 1 rood in several pieces from Simon Eyr, 8 April 1348, HD 85a; for common suit, 14 Oct. 1348, HD 85a; trespass v. Gilbert Kittour, 31 March 1349, SC 2 193/1; died, seized of 2 roods of land held by the rod and no heir came forward: later the lord granted his holding to John and Margaret Bulwer and their heirs by the rod, 15 Oct. 1349, HD 83.

Bakhous (atte), Rose, wife of Richard, 4 June 1344, 15 April 1345, SC 2 193/1.

Balteyn, Geoffrey with wife Agnes, bought a cottage with croft 1 rood from Bartholomew Colyn, 3 July 1332, HD 82; contempt of court, 1 Nov. 1334, HD 84.

Balteys, John, essoin for Thomas Balteys, 15 April 1345, SC 2 193/1.

Balteys, Thomas, for common suit, 15 April 1345, SC 2 193/1; order to retain 1/2 acre leased, without lord's licence, from William Huberd, 12 years term, 15 April 1345, SC 2 193/1; bought 1/2 acre in Wellgate from William Huberd, 8 April 1348, HD 85a; bought 1/2 acre in Welleresthommestead from Matilda Coupere, 8 April 1348, HD 85a; for common suit, 14 Oct. 1348, HD 85a; for common suit, 28 May 1350, SC 2 193/1.

Barney, Roger de, paid rent 7d., 1341–42 *circa,* HD 83; bought 1/2 acre, above Berhalle, from John le Wrighte, 3 Dec. 1339, HD 83; sworn in for the office of messor with Cecily atte Hil, 8 Dec. 1341; held 1 acre and 1 rood in the tenement of the heirs of Northgate responsible for the office of messor, this year, 20 Oct. 1347, HD 83; fealty for 3 roods, and 2 roods held by the rod, 15 Oct. 1349, HD 83.

Barney, William de, paid rent 9d., 1341–42 *circa,* HD 83; creditor v. John Asty, 1 July 1333, HD 84; bought 1 acre 3 roods from Cecily, daughter of Richard de Northgate, 4 Dec. 1334, HD 83; took lease 1 acre 31/2 roods, for one year, from Cecily de Northgate, 4 Dec. 1342, HD 83; agreement in trespass plea v. Roger le Smith, 4 June 1344, SC 2 193/1; debtor v. Harvey Speller, 4 June 1344, SC 2 193/1; withheld 1 day autumn, 20 Oct. 1347, HD 83; for common suit, 22 July 1347, HD 85; not prosecuting debt plea v. Harvey Buleman, 22 July 1347, HD 85a; trespass v. Robert Keynot, order to attach William, 22 July 1347, HD 85a; held 3 roods in tenement of the heirs of Northgate responsible for the office of messor this year, 20 Oct. 1347, HD 83; granted lease of 11/2 acres to Richard Speller, 6 years term, 8 April 1348, HD 85a; granted lease of 3 roods to Richard Speller, 8 years term, 8 April 1348, HD 85a; debtor v. Richard Speller, 10 Dec. 1348, HD 85a, debtor v. Richard Speller, 31 March 1349, SC 2 192/1; impleaded out of Holkham manor court by John Speller, chaplain, 31 March 1349, SC 2 193/1; died, seized of 2 acres 3 roods, no heir came forward: his holding later granted by lord to Richeman Brown and brood, 15 Oct. 1349, HD 83.

Baron, John, default, 6 April 1342, 28 Dec. 1342, SC 2 193/1.

Barsham, Isabel de, widow of John de, not prosecuting her debt plea v. Beatrice Huberd, 6 May 1333, HD 84; debtor v. Agnes Bulwer, 6 May 1333, HD 84; dower plea agreement, quitclaimed to Matilda Dersy all her dower portion in all tenements of her deceased husband in Holkham, 6 May 1333, HD 84; creditor v. William Huberd and wife Alice, 23 May 1334, 22 June 1334, 21 Oct. 1334, HD 84.

Barsham, Nicholas de and wife Agnes, creditor v. John Pye, detaining 2 bushels of barley, 6 April 1342, SC 2 193/1.

Bartholomew, John son of, default, 22 July 1332, HD 82.

Bartholomew, Walter son of, minor, order to seize him with 2 acres land because he was under age, 1346, HD 86, 15 Oct. 1349, HD 83.

Baye, Thomas le, creditor v. Thomas Jagge, 8 April 1348, HD 85.

Becces, James, messor, pledge in debt plea Joan Tobers v. Agnes Treweman, and in land entry for Lucy Parmelay, 22 July 1332, HD 82; creditor v. Ralph Dikes fined for not appearing in court with pledges, 6 May 1333, HD 84; creditor v. Simon atte Cros, 1 July 1333, 25 May 1334, HD 84; Agreement with John Crane in debt and trespass plea, 25 Jan. 1334, HD 84; not prosecuting his debt plea v. Simon atte Cros, 22 June 1334, HD 84; default, 21 Oct. 1334, 8 Dec. 1334; contempt of court, 1 Nov. 1334, HD 84; debtor v. Roger de Berwick, 8 Dec. 1334, HD 84, 8 Jan. 1336, HD 85; bought 1 rood, next to Westhowe, from Thomas son of Alice, 24 March 1337, HD 86; sold 1 1/2 roods to Simon and Helewise Bulwer, order to retain this land in lord's hands because Cecily, wife of James Becces, did not come to know her right, 6 April 1342, SC 2 193/1; default, withheld rent 2d., 6 April 1342, SC 2 193/1; failed to perform labour services, 12 Oct. 1342, SC 2 193/1; default, 28 Dec. 1342, SC 2 193/1; order to retain in lord's hands 1 1/2 roods sold to Simon and Helewise Bulwer, 28 Dec. 1342, SC 2 193/1; order of distraint to answer Simon Bulwer in a plea of agreement, 28 Dec. 1342, SC 2 193/1; did not use the lord's mill, 4 June 1344, SC 2 193/1; creditor v. Reynald Crane, 4 June 1344, 15 April 1345, SC 2 193/1; default, 22 July 1350, HD 87a.

Becces, Cecily, wife of James, 6 April 1342, 28 Dec. 1342, SC 2 193/1.

Bek (atte), Peter and wife Lecia, sold 1 1/4 roods to Peter de Langham, 4 Nov. 1334, HD 85; let 1 1/2 roods, at Hillergatecroft, to John Maynard, 4 Nov. 1334, HD 85.

Belaugh, Lawrence de, his tenants fined, 28 Dec. 1342, SC 2 193/1.

Beneyt, John and wife Helen, order of distraint, bought land without licence from John Asty, 22 July 1332, HD 82; creditor v. Richard Blakeman, 6 May 1333, HD 84; trespass v. Richard Blakeman, 6 May 1333, 1 July 1333, HD 84; not prosecuting debt plea v. Richard Blakeman, 1 July 1333, HD 84; bought a cottage and 3 1/2 acres and 1/4 rood in 7 pieces from Agnes, daughter, and Cecily, widow, of Richard Bilte, 1 July 1333, HD 84; contempt of court, 1 Nov. 1334, HD 84; default, 29 Sept. 1337, SC 2 193/1; default, 6 April 1342, SC 2 193/1; bought 1/2 rood from Roger atte Hil, in Est feld, 17 Dec. 1343, SC 2 193/1; default, 10 June 1346, HD 86; default, 27 March 1346, HD 86.

Bengamyn, William, of Walsingham, took lease of 1 acre from Geoffrey and Alice Saundre, 8 April 1348, HD 85a.

Bercar, John, mainpast of the Abbot of West Dereham, made illegal path with sheep to the marsh, 22 July 1334, HD 84.

Bere, Beatrice, died seized of a cottage and 1 acre, had 2 sons, William and John who is absent, heriot 22d., 25 Jan. 1334, HD 84.

Bere, John, son and heir of Beatrice, absent, 25 Jan. 1334, HD 84; default, 22 July 1334, HD 84; default, 11 Dec. 1335, HD 85a; default, 22 July 1337, HD 86.

Bere, William, son and heir of Beatrice, paid heriot 22d. for a cottage and 1 acre, 25 Jan. 1334, HD 84; paid marriage fine, 24d., 25 Jan. 1334, HD 84; default, 21 Oct. 1334, HD 82; default, 10 June 1346, HD 86.

Bernard, Bartholomew, of Wighton, creditor v. Joan, widow of William de Hindringham, for contracts and merchandising, 5s. and damages 4d., inquisition ordered, 22 July 1347, HD 85a.

Bertere, Robert le, granted lease, without lord's licence, of 1 acre in several pieces to John Crane, 23 May 1334, HD 85.

Berwick, Roger de, creditor v. Simon and Cecily Mous, not in court to answer, 6 May 1333, HD 84; agreement in debt plea with Simon Mous, 1 July 1333, HD 84; debtor v. James Becces, 8 Dec. 1334, HD 84 and 8 Jan. 1336, HD 85a.

Beeston, Benedict de, bought 1 rood, headland at Wykenlond, from Adam Dering, 4
　　Nov. 1334, HD 85.
Beyson, Walter, order to come for fealty, 22 July 1332, HD 82.
Billington, parson of, default 6 May 1333, HD 84.
Bilney (Belney), Agnes de, order of distraint with co-parcener Robert Erneys to
　　swear fealty, 1346, HD 86; her servant, William Tobill, did trespass with
　　pigs on the lord's crops, 22 July 1350, HD 87a.
Bilney (Belney), Helewise de, debtor v. Richard Blakeman who is not prosecuting his
　　plaint, acquitted, 8 April 1348, HD 85a.
Bilney (Belney), John de, leased 1/2 acre, at Odesgate, from John Asty, 4 years term,
　　23 May 1334, HD 84; debtor, order of distraint to answer Henry le Longe,
　　chaplain, 11 Dec. 1335, HD 85a; bought 3 acres, without licence, from
　　Harvey Wytbred, order to retain land in lord's hands, 11 Dec. 1335, HD
　　85a; order of attachment for 1 cow, 8 Jan. 1336, HD 85a; debtor v. Robert
　　Andrew, 13 Dec. 1336, SC 2 193/1.
Bilney (Belney), Roger de, bought 11/2roods, lying at the head of Holkham
　　villeinage, from John Mey, 8 April 1348, HD 85a.
Bilney (Belney), Walter de, default, 10 June 1346, HD 86.
Bilney (Belney), William de, held 1 acre 2 roods yielding 31/2 bushels, 3 Dec. 1339,
　　HD 83.
Bilte, Cecily, widow of Richard, and Agnes her daughter, sold a cottage and 31/2
　　acres and 1/4 rood, in 7 pieces, to John and Helen Beneyt, 1 July 1333, HD
　　84.
Binham, Peter de, bought all lands and tenements, 7 acres, of Andrew le Heir and
　　Geoffrey de Walsingham,, paid 8s. entry fine, 28 May 1350, SC 2 193/1.
Blakeman, Agnes, wife of Richard Blakeman, see Agnes Bulwer.
Blakeman, Joan, daughter of Richard Blakeman, detained 11/2 roods, did not come to
　　answer Muriel Casche plaint: order to seize land, and summons, 3 July
　　1332, HD 82; default, order of distraint for fealty, 3 July 1332, HD 82; took
　　lease of 1 rood, at Dalebrest, from Gervase de Ryburgh, 4 years term, 28
　　March 1335, HD 84; default, 13 Dec. 1336, SC 2 193/1; paid heriot 32d.
　　for 2 acres and a messuage as closest heir of Richard the Chaplain, oath of
　　fealty, 16 Feb. 1337, SC 2 193/1; default, 4 June 1344, SC 2 193/1.
Blakeman, Richard, afferator, 3 July 1332, 22 July 1332, HD 82; agreement with
　　Reynald Crane in debt plea, 3 July 1332, HD 82; withheld grain 22 July
　　1332, HD 82; violated lord's orders of sequestration, 22 July 1332, HD 82;
　　sold ale, 22 July 1332, HD 82; held office of collector, 22 July 1332, HD
　　82; creditor v. John Beneyt, 6 May 1333, 1 July 1333, HD 84; defendant in
　　trespass v. John Beneyt, 6 May 1333, HD 84; took lease of 11/2 acres and
　　1/2 rood from Cecily atte Hil, 12 Nov. 1333, HD 83; creditor v. Peter and
　　Helewise de Langham, 6 May 1333, HD 84; held office of afferator, 6 May
　　1333, 1 July 1333, HD 84; marriage with Agnes Bulwer (widow, in first
　　marriage, of John Bulwer), marriage fine 1/2 mark, 25 Jan. 1334, HD 84;
　　took lease of 1 acre in 3 pieces from John Asty, 25 Jan. 1334, HD 84; took
　　lease of 11/2 roods in 2 pieces from Cecily atte Hil, minor, 4 years term, 25
　　Jan. 1334, HD 84; plea of novel disseisin v. Walter Bulwer, chaplain, 23
　　May 1334, HD 84; plaintiff in trespass v. Simon Mous, for 20 sheep, 23
　　May 1334, 21 Oct. 1334, HD 84; plaintiff in trespass v. Walter Bulwer,
　　chaplain, 22 June 1334, 22 July 1334, HD 84; plaintiff in trespass v. John le

Wrighte, 22 June 1334, 22 July 1334, HD 84; plaintiff in trespass v. Alice de Olney, 22 June 1334, 22 July 1334, HD 84; order to attach Walter Bulwer, chaplain, Simon Mous, John le Wrighte, Alice de Olney, to answer Richard Blakeman in pleas of trespass, 22 July 1334, 21 Oct. 1334, 1 Nov. 1334, HD 84; did *hamsoken* v. Alice de Olney, 22 July 1334, HD 84; creditor v. Simon Mous, 21 Oct. 1334, 1 Nov. 1334, HD 84; default, 4 Nov. 1334, HD 83; settlement about dower land of wife Agnes, 1 messuage and 20 acres granted to Agnes and Richard Blakeman by Richard Bulwer, which in case of death of Agnes would remain with husband Richard, 28 March 1335, 11 Dec. 1335, HD 84; took lease of 1 rood, at Lazareswong, from the Prior of Walsingham, 10 Nov. 1335, HD 83; debtor of 10s. v. John Crane, 11 Dec. 1335, HD 85a; did not use the lord's mill, 11 Dec. 1335, HD 85a; false claim in debt plea v. Edmund Milner, 11 Dec. 1335, 8 Jan. 1336, HD 85a; withheld all his services, order of distraint, 8 Jan. 1336, HD 85a; granted for life a messuage and 2 acres to Richard Blakeman, chaplain, 8 Jan. 1336, HD 85a; agreement in debt plea with Harvey Pope, 8 Jan. 1336, HD 85a; creditor v. Thomas Halman, 13 Dec. 1336, SC 2 193/1; agreement in debt plea with Walter Bulwer, chaplain, 13 Dec. 1336, SC 2 193/1; granted lease of 8$1/2$ acres to John Speller, 5 years term, 16 Feb. 1337, SC 2 193/1; debtor v. Walter Bulwer, chaplain, order to come to next court, 29 Sept. 1337, SC 2 193/1; default, 12 Oct. 1342, 4 June 1344, SC 2 193/1; debtor v. Mariota Crane, widow of John Crane, order to pay back, 20 Jan. 1347, HD 86; agreement with John Crane, 22 July 1347, HD 85a; ale fine, 22 July 1347, HD 85a; creditor but not prosecuting his plaint v. Helewise de Bilney, 8 April 1348, HD 85a; debtor v. Peter Ram of Stiffkey, chaplain, 14 Oct. 1348, HD 85a; default, 14 Oct. 1348, 10 Dec. 1348, HD 85a; ale fine, 10 Dec. 1348, HD 85a; for common suit, 31 March 1349, SC 2 193/1; agreement with Peter Ram, chaplain, about repayment of 8s., 31 March 1349, SC 2 193/1.

Blakeman, Richard, the chaplain, took for life a messuage and 2 acres, from Richard Blakeman, 8 Jan. 1336, HD 85a; died, his closest heir, Joan Blakeman, paid heriot of 2s. 6d. for the messuage and 2 acres, 16 Feb. 1337, SC 2 193/1.

Blewyrd, Roger, bought 1 rood, without licence, from John Burgoine, order to retain land in lord's hands, 11 Dec. 1335, HD 85a.

Boald, Richard, paid rent 2d. for his messuage, 6 April 1342, SC 2 193/1; debtor v. Matilda Joudy, order to distrain Matilda Joudy to answer Richard, 28 Dec. 1342, SC 2 193/1; debt plea v. John Skinner, SC 2 193/1.

Botsweyn, Roger, default, 22 July 1332, HD 82; default, 22 July 1334, HD 84.

Boulde, Simon, default, 22 July 1337, HD 86.

Brancaster, Richard de, creditor v. Rosa Bulwer, 25 Jan. 1334, HD 84.

Brekepotte, John, agreement in trespass v. Thomas Jagge, 28 May 1350, SC 2 193/1.

Briche, Agnes, agreement with Richold Dewaghe, 6 April 1342, 193/1; tenant of Cecily Parson, 6 April 1342, SC 2 193/1.

Brid, John, bought 1 acre by charter from John Mey, 10 Dec. 1348, HD 85a.

Brising, John, default, 6 April 1342, SC 2 193/1.

Brown (Broun), Agnes, ale fine, 22 July 1332, HD 82; ale fine, 22 July 1334, 22 July 1334, HD 84.

Brown, Alice, held land next to 1/2 acre sold by Beatrice le Slopere to Bartholomew
le Miller, at Langefurlong, 17 Dec. 1343, SC 2 193/1.

Brown, Bartholomew, son of Roger, succeeded to father's tenure, 7 roods, ward of
lord with land, 6 May 1333, HD 84.

Brown, Beatrice, ale fine, 22 July 1337, HD 86.

Brown, Cecily, executor of Roger Brown, claimed 18d. to Roger Crane, 1 July 1333,
HD 84.

Brown, heirs of Gilbert, default, 6 May 1333, HD 84.

Brown, John, fine 6d. for being able to remain out of lord's fief, 5 Oct. 1349, SC 2
193/1.

Brown, Richard, died, seized of 1 acre 1 rood, heir son Thomas, 4 Nov. 1334, HD
84.

Brown, Roger, order of distraint for fealty, 3 July 1332, 22 July 1332, HD 82; died,
seized of 7 roods, his minor son, Bartholomew, succeeded and Cecily
Brown. was executor, 6 May 1333, HD 84.

Brown, Thomas, son and heir of Thomas, succeeded to 1 acre 1 rood, 4 Nov. 1334,
HD 84.

Brown, Richemayn, bought 3/4 rood, at Schipmancross, from Sayene, daughter of
Roger le Chapman, 3 July 1332, HD 82; sold 1 acre 31/2 roods to Thomas
Albard, 6 Dec. 1346, HD 86; was granted 2 acres 3 roods by the rod after
death of William de Barney without heir, 15 Oct. 1349, HD 83.

Bulman, Cecily, order of distraint for fealty, 15 Oct. 1349, HD 83.

Bulman, Harvey, made illegal path, 22 July 1332, HD 82; default, 6 May 1333, HD
84; debtor v. Muriel Casche, 13 Dec. 1336, SC 2 193/1, 16 Feb. 1337, SC 2
193/1, 24 March 1337, SC 2 193/1; debtor, did not come to answer Muriel
Casche, better pledges, 11 Sept. 1337, SC 2 193/1; debtor, order of distraint
of 1 animal until answer at next court, 29 Sept. 1337, SC 2 193/1; order to
retain in lord's hands 11/2 roods held with Richard Hendry for withholding
of rents and services, 28 Dec. 1342, SC 2 193/1; debtor v. Richard Huberd,
12 Oct. 1342, 17 Dec. 1343, SC 2 193/1; debtor v. Geoffrey Dering, 12
Oct. 1342, 17 Dec. 1343, SC 2 193/1; debtor v. William de Barney, non
prosecution of plaint, acquitted, 22 July 1347, HD 85a.

Bulman, John, for common suit, 12 Oct. 1342, SC 2 193/1; prosecution pledge in
debt plea of Robert Hereward v. Margaret Dersy, 15 April 1344, SC 2
193/1; trespass with sheep in the lord's marsh, 22 July 1347, HD 85a;
essoin for Prior of Peterstone, 10 Dec. 1347, HD 85a.

Bulman, Robert, made illegal path, 22 July 1337, HD 86; debtor v. Thomas Jagge,
order to retain 2 sheep and more, 4 June 1344, SC 2 193/1.

Bulman, William, pledge for Thomas Storm in debt plea v. Simon Mous, 22 July
1332, HD 82; default, 6 May 1333, HD 84; contempt of court, 1 Nov. 1334,
HD 84; default, 11 Sept. 1337, 29 Sept. 1337, SC 2 193/1.

Bulwer, Agnes, wife of Richard Blakeman, agreement with Alice Otes, 3 July 1332,
HD 82; creditor v. Isabel de Barsham, 6 May 1333, HD 84; debtor v.
Robert Andrew: will pay back 36s. at next Martinmas, 6 May 1333, HD 84;
marriage with Richard Blakeman, marriage fine 1/2 mark, 25 Jan. 1334, HD
84; granted lease of 5 roods to John Crane up to Michaelmas, 25 Jan. 1334,
HD 84; plea of novel disseisin v. Walter Bulwer, chaplain, 22 June 1334,
HD 84; dower land granted by Richard Bulwer, 1/2 messuage and 20 acres,
after death of Agnes would remain with husband Richard Blakeman, 28
March 1335, HD 84.

Bulwer, John, detained chattels v. Simon Mous, 25 Jan. 1334, HD 84; not prosecuting plaint v. Simon Mous, 23 May 1334, HD 84; creditor v. John Daulin, 6 April 1342, SC 2 193/1; retained 1 *precaria* from a holding which belonged to Seman Abraham, did it with Thomas Cat, 1346, HD 86; with wife Margaret was granted tenure of Richard atte Bakhous who had died without heir, 2 roods by the rod, 15 Oct. 1349.

Bulwer, Richard, debtor, order to collect 36d. owed to Robert and Alice atte Esch, 3 July 1332, HD 82; order of distraint for fealty, 3 July 1332, HD 82; debtor, order of distraint to answer Thomas le Northerne, 22 July 1332, HD 82; granted dower land to Agnes Bulwer and husband Richard Blakeman, 28 March 1335, HD 84.

Bulwer, Roger, default, 3 July 1332, HD 82; debtor, order to retain 2 sheep and 2 hogs for answer to Simon Mous, 3 July 1332, HD 82; debtor, order to collect 2s. due to John Speller, chaplain, 10 Dec. 1348, HD 85a.

Bulwer, Margaret, daughter of John, marriage without licence, 8 Dec. 1334, HD 84.

Bulwer, Rose, debtor, order of distraint to answer Simon Mous and Geoffrey Crome, 3 July 1332, HD 82; trespass v. John le Smith senior, 3 July 1332, agreement in debt plea with Simon Mous, 22 July 1332, HD 82; withheld grain, 22 July 1332, HD 82; debtor v. Richard de Brancaster, order to pay back, 25 Jan. 1334, HD 84; ale fine, 22 July 1347, HD 85a; ale fine, 10 Dec. 1348, HD 85a.

Bulwer, Simon and wife Helewise, withheld grain, 22 July 1332, HD 82; took grain out of manor, 1 Nov. 1334, HD 84; bought 1½ roods from James Becces and Cecily, order to retain this land because Cecily did not come to know her right, 6 April 1342, 28 Dec. 1342, SC 2 193/1.

Bulwer, Walter, chaplain, was granted by Richard Bulwer 2½ acres, 22 July 1332, HD 82; took lease from lord 3 acres 1 rood in 3 pieces, 3 March 1334, HD 84; plea of novel disseisin v. Richard Blakeman, 23 May 1334, 22 June 1334, HD 84; plea of trespass v. Richard Blakeman, 22 June 1334, 22 July 1334, HD 84; order to attach to answer Richard Blakeman in plea of trespass, 21 Oct. 1334, HD 84; took grain out of manor, 1 Nov. 1334, HD 84; default, dispensed of suit of court for a year, 8 Dec. 1334, HD 84; agreement with Richard Blakeman and Agnes Bulwer, his wife, about dower land of Agnes, 11 Dec. 1335, HD 85; creditor v. Cecily Erneys and her son, Robert Erneys, 13 Dec. 1336, SC 2 193/1; debtor in association with Simon Mous of 17s. v. James of Northcreyk, chaplain, repayment scheduled over 2 years, 11 Sept. 1337, SC 2 193/1; his servant James, in debt plea agreement with William Huberd, 4 June 1344, SC 2 193/1; default, 4 June 1344, SC 2 193/1; default, 8 April 1348, HD 85a; dispensed of suit of court for a year, 14 Oct. 1348, HD 85a; default, 28 May 1350, SC 2 193/1, 22 July 1350, HD 85a.

Burgate, Amice de, bought 1 rood, at Wadlonds, from Matilda Carpe, wife of Bartholomew, 3 July 1332, HD 82.

Burgate, John de, did not perform labour services, 12 Oct. 1342, SC 2 193/1; for common suit, 17 Dec. 1343, 4 June 1344, SC 2 193/1; essoin for Simon Roke, 15 April 1345, SC 2 193/1; essoin for William de Barney, 22 July 1347, HD 87a; essoin for Peter Cory, 10 Dec. 1348, HD 85a; essoin for Robert de Kendale, 31 March 1349, SC 2 193/1; capital pledge, 22 July 1350, HD 87a.

Burgh, Ralph de, bought a messuage with 5 roods land from Margaret Dersy, 28 May 1350, SC 2 193/1; ale taster, 22 July 1350, HD 87a.

Burgoine, Godman, capital pledge, 22 July 1332, HD 82; capital pledge, 22 July 1337, HD 86; pledge in debt plea John Crane v. Simon Burgoine, 12 Oct. 1342, SC 2 193/1; essoin for William Huberd, 14 Oct. 1348, HD 85a; essoin for Adam Cage, 31 March 1349, SC 2 193/1.

Burgoine, Godman junior, essoin for John Margery, 31 March 1349, SC 2 193/1.

Burgoine, John, sold 1 rood, without licence, to Roger Blewyrd, order to retain land in lord's hands, 11 Dec. 1335, HD 85a.

Burgoine, Matilda, wife of Simon, ale fine, 22 July 1332; ale fine, 22 July 1337, HD 86; paid heriot 2s. 8d. after death of husband Simon, and held for life a messuage and 12 acres, 4 June 1344, SC 2 193/1; ale fines, 22 July 1347, 10 Dec. 1348, HD 85a; sold a messuage and 3 acres to Simon Silk, 5 Oct. 1349, SC 2 193/1.

Burgoine, Simon, creditor v. Richard le Deye, and Thomas Craske (pauper), 3 July 1332, HD 82; capital pledge, 22 July 1332, HD 82; capital pledge, 22 July 1334, HD 84; capital pledge, 22 July 1337, HD 86; debtor v. John Crane, 12 Oct. 1342, 17 Dec. 1343, SC 2 193/1; creditor v. Geoffrey Saundre, order to levy 1 bushel barley, 17 Dec. 1343, SC 2 193/1; died, held a messuage and 12 acres, his wife, Matilda paid heriot 2s. 8d. to hold land for life, 4 June 1344, SC 2 193/1.

Burgoine, Thomas, son of Godman, not in tithing, 22 July 1332; marriage, without licence, 20 Jan. 1347, HD 86.

Busche, William, held 1/2 acre and 1 rood, at Hougate, 3 Dec. 1339, HD 83.

Briche, Agnes, withheld grain, 22 July 1335, HD 82.

Cage, Adam and wife Alice, bought a messuage and 1/2 acre from Bartholomew le Miller, 13 Dec. 1336, SC 2 193/1; false quarrel v. Alice Crome, 17 Dec. 1342, SC 2 193/1; bought 1 rood, north of tenement of Ida Godwyne, from Matilda Coupere, 8 April 1348, HD 85a; for common suit, 31 March 1349, SC 2 193/1.

Caldwell, John de, granted lease, with his son Thomas, of 2½ acres taken at farm from John Mey to Harvey de Massingham, 5 years term, and also of 1½ acres taken at farm from Cecily Erneys, 5 years term, 17 Dec. 1343, SC 2 193/1.

Caldwell, Thomas de, son of John, debtor v. Hugh, parish chaplain of Holkham, summons, order to come to next court, 12 Oct. 1342; failed to perform labour services, 12 Oct. 1342, SC 2 193/1; in debt plea v. Hugh, parish chaplain of Holkham, non prosecution of plaint, 17 Dec. 1343, SC 2 193/1; with father, John, granted lease of 2½ acres taken at farm from John Mey to Harvey de Massingham, 5 years term, and also of 1½ acres taken at farm from Cecily Erneys, 17 Dec. 1343, SC 2 193/1.

Calthorpe, William de, knight, order of distraint for fealty, 3 July 1332, 22 July 1332, HD 82; default, 1 July 1333, HD 84.

Calwere, Adam, not in tithing, 22 July 1347, 10 Dec. 1348, HD 85a.

Calwere, Alice, daughter of Bartholomew, bought 1½ roods, at Wellgate, from Henry and Sayene Vallet, 3 July 1332, HD 82.

Calwere, Gilbert, default, 18 Jan. 1335, HD 85.

Calwere, Richard, pledge in several pleas, 23 May 1334, 22 June 1334, 21 Oct. 1334, HD 84.

Calwere, Sayene, wife of Bartholomew, co-parcener of Cecily Parson, 6 April 1342, SC 2 193/1; ale fine, 22 July 1347, HD 85a, ale fine, 10 Dec. 1348, HD 85a.

Calwere, Thomas, chaplain, trespass with pigs in lord's meadow, 26 Nov. 1350, HD 87a.

Calwere, William, default, 22 July 1350.

Camplioun, Henry, order of distraint for fealty, 3 July 1332, HD 82; dispensed with suit of court for 1 year, 11 Sept. 1337, SC 2 193/1; default, 4 June 1344, SC 2 193/1; for common suit, 15 April 1345, SC 2 193/1; for common suit, 31 March 1349, SC 2 193/1.

Carpe, Alice, daughter of John, for *gersuma* 32d., 25 Jan. 1334, HD 84; did *hamsoken* v. Helewise, 22 July 1334, HD 84; put corn outside villeinage, 1 Nov. 1334, HD 84; childwite fine 32d., for giving birth out of wedlock, 8 Jan. 1336, HD 85a; leyrwite fine 32d., 16 Feb. 1337, SC 2 193.

Carpe, Bartholomew, order of distraint for fealty, 3 July 1332, 22 July 1332, HD 82; trespass plea v. Peter Meyr, 11 Sept. 1337, SC 2 193/1; trespass plea v. Peter de Langham, 11 Sept. 1337, SC 2 193/1; no prosecution of plaint in trespass pleas, 11 Sept. 1337, SC 2 193/1; default, 10 June 1346, HD 86; default, 28 May 1350, SC 2 193/1.

Carpe, Benedict, made illegal path, 22 July 1332, HD 82; took lease of 1/2 rood from lord, 4 years term, 28 Dec. 1342, SC 2 193/1.

Carpe, Cecily, wife of John, pledge for Ralph Dikes in debt plea, 6 May 1333, HD 84; debtor v. Richard Blakeman, order to come for answer, 6 May 1333, HD 84; day given in debt plea v. Richard Blakeman, 1 July 1333, HD 84.

Carpe, Helewise, daughter of John, order of distraint for fealty, 3 July 1332, 22 July 1332, HD 82; put corn outside villeinage, 1334, HD 84; default, 10 June 1346, HD 86.

Carpe, John, withholding grain, 22 July 1332, HD 82.

Carpe, Matilda, wife of Bartholomew, sold 1 rood, at Wadlonds, to Amice de Burgate, 3 July 1332, HD 82.

Carpenter, John le, pledge in trespass plea Adam Craske v. Reynald Crane, 1 July 1333, HD 84.

Carpenter, Roger le, order of distraint for fealty, 3 July 1332, HD 82; defendant in trespass plea v. John Mey, 11 Sept, 1337, SC 2 193/1; agreement in trespass plea with John Mey, 11 Sept. 1337, SC 2 193/1.

Casche, Geoffrey, for common suit, 4 Nov. 1334, HD 85; pledge for Sibyl Fox in land entry plea, 18 Jan. 1335, HD 85.

Casche, John, order of distraint for fealty, 1346 HD 86.

Casche, Muriel, claimed 1 1/2 roods in land plea, 3 July 1332, HD 82; claimed 1 acre 3 roods from John le Smith, 3 July 1332, HD 82; land plea v. John son of Richard Blakeman, 22 July 1332, HD 82; creditor v. John Lomb, 25 Jan. 1334, HD 84; agreement in debt plea with Roger Ode, 3 March 1334, HD 84; creditor v. Harvey Buleman, 13 Dec. 1336, 11 Sept. 1337, SC 2 193/1; order to distrain 1 head of cattle for obliging Harvey Buleman to be at next court to answer Muriel Casche, 29 Sept. 1337, SC 2 193/1; creditor v. Margaret Peper, 12 Oct. 1342, SC 2 193/1; better pledges v. Harvey Buleman, 10 June 1346, HD 86.

Casche, Thomas, son of Muriel, order of distraint for fealty, 3 July 1332, 22 July 1332, HD 82; did not use lord's mill, 23 May 1334, HD 84.

Cat, Adam, fealty, 31 March 1349, default, 28 May 1350, SC 2 193/1.

Cat, Bartholomew, bought 1/2 rood from Adam Cat, 20 Jan. 1341, HD 86; messor, 22 July 1347, HD 85; dispensed with suit of court until Michaelmas, 14 Oct. 1348, HD 85a; made illegal rescue, 10 Dec. 1348, HD 85; default, 28 May 1350, SC 2 193/1; bought 1/2 plot of land, at the Staithe, from Bartholomew le Miller, 7 July 1350, HD 83.

Cat, Helen, put corn outside villeinage, 22 July 1332, HD 82; bought 2 roods from Helewise Qwyne, 4 June 1344, SC 2 193/1.

Cat, John, 1/2 office of prepositus, 24 April 1332, HD 83; collector from Sept. 1333 to Sept. 1334, 10 Nov. 1335, HD 83; messor, 3 Dec. 1339, HD 83; prepositus with Seman Abraham, 1 Dec. 1340, HD 83; paid 8d. rent, 1341–42 *circa*, HD 83; as messor paid 5s. for other tenants, 8 Dec. 1341; with his sheep in lord's fold, 15 Nov. 1343, HD 83.

Cat, Philip, died, seized of a messuage with 2 acres 31/2 roods held by the rod: his son, Thomas, as heir, paid 12d. fine, 15 Oct. 1349, HD 83.

Cat, Thomas, son and heir of Philip Cat, paid 12d. fine to succeed to a messuage with 2 acres 31/2 roods, 15 Oct. 1349, HD 83; for common suit, 24 Nov. 1349, HD 83.

Cecily, Bartholomew son of, order of distraint for fealty, 3 July 1332, 22 July 1332, HD 82.

Chaplain, Thomas son of, bread and ale fine, 22 July 1332, HD 82; creditor, with James Becces, not prosecuting his plaint v. Simon atte Cros, 22 June 1334, HD 84; regrator of bread and ale, 22 July 1334, HD 84.

Chapman, Gilbert le, withheld grain, 22 July 1332, HD 82; prosecution pledge in debt plea of Thomas Elwan creditor v. Harvey Lode, 4 June 1344, SC 2 193/1.

Chapman, Harvey le, order of distraint for fealty, 3 July 1332, 22 July 1332, HD 82; withheld grain, 22 July 1332, HD 82; essoin for Ralph Soper, 22 July 1347, HD 85a; default, 22 July 1350, HD 87a; for common suit, 26 Nov. 1350, HD 87a.

Chapman, Sayene, daughter of Godman le, sold, without licence, 3/4 rood to John (le) Meyre, order to seize land, 3 July 1332, HD 82.

Chapman, Sayene, daughter of Roger le, sold 3/4 rood, at Scipmancros, to Richemayn Brown, 3 July 1332, HD 82.

Charle, Adam, default, 22 July 1332, HD 82; debtor v. Simon Burgoine, order of distraint to answer creditor, 22 July 1332, HD 82; default, 22 July 1334, HD 84; sold 1 rood, at the mill of Burghalle, to Roger Crane, 28 March 1335, HD 84.

Charle, Beatrice, wife of William, debtor v. John Speller, chaplain, 4 June 1344, SC 2 193/1.

Charle, Constance, withheld grain, 22 July 1332, HD 82; did not perform 1 day in autumn, 3 Dec. 1339, HD 83; kept 1/2 *precaria* in autumn, 4 Dec. 1342, HD 83; trespass v. Robert and Agnes Keynot, 9 Dec. 1348, HD 83.

Charle, Gilbert, default, 22 July 1337, HD 86.

Charle, John, order of distraint for fealty, 3 July 1332, HD 82; default, 6 May 1333, HD 84; default, 11 Sept. 1337, SC 2 193/1; fealty, 31 March 1349, SC 2 193/1.

Charle, Matilda, trespass v. Thomas son of William, 6 May 1333, HD 84; trespass v. Robert Keynot, 1 July 1333, HD 84; her mainpast, Robert, made damages to the road from Hougate to the hill, 22 July 1334, HD 84.

Charle, heirs of Robert, default, 4 Nov. 1334, HD 85.

Charle, William son of John, not in tithing, 22 July 1332, HD 82; not in tithing, 22 July 1334, HD 84; default, 18 Jan. 1335, HD 85; debtor with wife Beatrice v. John Speller, chaplain, 4 June 1344, SC 2 193/1.

Chele, William, fealty, 31 March 1349, SC 2 193/1.

Church, Robert atte, made illegal path beyond land of Richard Neel, at Westfeld, 22 July 1334, HD 84.

Clerk, Harvey, essoin for John Bulwer, 3 March 1334, HD 84; essoin for John Buleman, 12 Oct. 1342, SC 2 193/1; essoin for John Mey, 15 April 1345, SC 2 193/1; attorney for Peter Ram, chaplain of Stiffkey, 9 Aug. 1348, HD 87a.

Clerk, John, son of Robert, default, 22 July 1337, HD 86.

Clerk, John, son of Roger, not in tithing, 22 July 1332, HD 85a; not in tithing, 22 July 1347, HD 85a.

Clerk, Richard, son of Roger, not in tithing, 22 July 1332, HD 82; not in tithing, 22 July 1334, HD 84.

Clerk, Sarah, quarrel v. William Hammond, 29 Sept. 1337, SC 2 193/1; failure to glean, 12 Oct. 1342, SC 2 193/1.

Clerk, Thomas, trespass with pigs in lord's meadow, 26 Nov. 1350, HD 87a.

Clerk, William, default, 1 Nov. 1334, HD 84.

Clynt, Andrew atte, sold 1/2 rood to William de Stodeye, 6 April 1342, SC 2 193/1; default, 6 April 1342, SC 2 193/1.

Colin, Adam, son of Agnes, heir of mother, a cottage and 1/2 acre of land, heriot 2s. 8d., order to seize until heir came, 4 June 1344, SC 2 193/1.

Colin, Agnes, granted lease of 1/2 acre, at Cathil, to Robert de Kettlestone, 4 years term, 25 Jan. 1344, HD 84; failed to glean, 12 Oct. 1342, SC 2 193/1; sold 1 rood to Robert de Kettlestone, 4 June 1344, SC 193/1; died, seized of a cottage with 1/2 acre, heriot 2s. 8d., heir Adam, her son did not come, 4 June 1344, SC 2 193/1; order to retain 1 rood sold to Robert de Kettlestone in lord's hands, 15 April 1345, SC 2 193/1.

Colin, Bartholomew, sold a cottage with a croft containing 1 rood to Geoffrey and Agnes Balteyn, 3 July 1332; HD 82; sold 3 roods, at Dalehil, to Clarice atte Dale, 25 Jan. 1334, HD 84; default, 22 July 1334, HD 84.

Colin, Reynald, default, 6 May 1333, HD 84.

Colin, Roger, order of distraint for fealty, 3 July 1332, 22 July 1332, HD 82.

Colle, James, default, condoned, 22 July 1334, HD 84.

Colting, Bartholomew, agreement in trespass plea with Thomas son of William, 22 July 1332, HD 82; malicious assault and bloodshed v. Thomas son of William, 22 July 1332, HD 82; granted lease of his land, without licence, to John le Wrighte, 21 Oct. 1334, HD 84; sold 1/2 rood to John Mey, 1 Nov. 1334, HD 84; default, 10 June 1346, HD 86; died, seized of 31/2 acres, no heir came, order to keep in lord's hands, 22 July 1347, HD 85a.

Comyns, John le, for common suit, 22 July 1347, HD 85a.

Conteshale, John de, sold 1 rood to John Asty who did not come, order to keep land in lord's hands, 4 June 1344, SC 2 193/1; order to keep in lord's hands 1 rood sold to John Asty, 15 April 1345, SC 2 193/1; default, 14 Oct. 1348, HD 85a.

Cony, Simon, creditor v. William Huberd, agreement, 13 Dec. 1336, SC 2 193/1; creditor v. Richard Speller, agreement, 4 June 1344, SC 2 193/1.

Corpusty, Sabina, ale fine, 22 July 1334, HD 84.

Cory, Peter, for common suit, 10 Dec. 1348, HD 85a; capital pledge, 22 July 1350, HD 87a; ale fine, 22 July 1350, HD 87a; sold 1/2 acre to John Wolner, 26 Nov. 1350, HD 87a.

Coteler, Alice, ale fine, 22 July 1337, HD 86.

Coteler, Geoffrey, ale fine, 22 July 1334, HD 84.

Coupere, Margaret, widow of Thomas, debtor v. John Mey: order to levy 18d., Margaret to pay John Mey, 8 April 1348, HD 85a.

Coupere, Matilda, daughter of Simon, sold 1/2 acre, at Welleresthommestead, to Thomas Balteyn, 8 April 1348, HD 85a; sold 1 rood to Adam Cage, 8 April 1348, HD 85a.

Coupere, Matilda, daughter and heir of Thomas, failure to glean, 12 Oct. 1342, SC 2 193/1; oath of fealty as tenant, paid 32d. as heriot for a messuage and 31/2 acres after death of father Thomas, 20 Jan. 1347, HD 86.

Coupere, Richard, essoin in trespass plea, 22 July 1332, HD 82.

Coupere, Simon, withheld grain, 22 July 1332, HD 82; default, 6 May 1333, HD 84; default, 23 May 1334, HD 84; default, 22 June 1334, HD 84; put corn out of villeinage, 1 Nov. 1334, HD 84; land dispute re. 1/2 rood v. Richard Blakeman, 11 Dec. 1335, HD 85a; sold 1 rood to Alice Aynild and Matilda her daughter, 8 April 1348, HD 85a.

Coupere, Thomas, default, 22 July 1334, HD 84; granted lease of 3 roods, without licence, order to seize land, 16 Feb. 1337, SC 2 193/1; default, 22 July 1337, HD 86; default, 1 autumn *precaria*, 11 Sept. 1337, SC 2 193/1; for common suit, 15 April 1345, SC 2 193/1; default, 10 June 1346, HD 86; died, seized of a messuage and 31/2 acres, heir daughter Matilda paid heriot 32d. and made fealty, 20 Jan. 1347, HD 86.

Crane, Berta, tenant of Cecily Parson, 6 April 1342, SC 2 193/1.

Crane, Eustace, son and heir of Gilbert, paid heriot 32d. for 3 acres after death of Gilbert, 23 May 1334, HD 84; sold with brother John 1 acre, at Wadlond, to Peter de Langham, 28 March 1335, HD 85; granted lease with brother John of 11/2 acres to John Speller, 16 Feb. 1337, SC 2 193/1; sold with brother John 1/2 rood, north of Wakescroft, to Hugh le Soper, 24 March 1337, HD 86.

Crane, Gilbert, order of distraint for fealty, 3 July 1332, HD 82; died, seized of 3 acres, sons and heirs John and Eustace paid jointly heriot 32d., 23 Jan. 1334, 23 May 1334, HD 84.

Crane, John, capital pledge, 22 July 1332, HD 82; trespass v. Richard Marchal, 22 July 1332, HD 82; debt and trespass agreement v. James Becces, 25 Jan. 1334, HD 84; took lease of 5 roods from Agnes Bulwer, 25 Jan. 1334, HD 84; took lease of 5 roods from John Asty, 4 years term, 25 Jan. 1334, HD 84; afferator, 25 Jan. 1334, HD 84; bought 1/2 rood, at Northclynt, from Agnes Aleyn, 3 March 1334, HD 84; bought 1 acre in several pieces, 23 May 1334, HD 84; paid heriot 32d. with brother Eustace for 3 acres, after death of Gilbert, their father, 23 May 1334, HD 84; in contempt of court took away by force barley crop of 11/4 roods let, without licence, by Roger Everard, 23 May 1334, HD 84; messor, took office and failed to perform, 1 Nov. 1334, HD 84; contempt of court, 1 Nov. 1334, HD 84; put corn out of villeinage, 1 Nov. 1334, HD 84; afferator, 1 Nov. 1334, 8 Dec. 1334, HD 84; sold without licence, 1 acre, at Wadlond, to Peter de Langham, 28 March 1335, HD 84; collector, 28 March 1335, HD 84; creditor v. Richard Blakeman, 11 Dec. 1335, HD 85; took a sheaf out of the manor, 11 Dec. 1335, HD 85; creditor, agreement in debt plea v. Cecily Erneys, 23 Dec. 1336, SC 2 193/1; granted lease of 1¹/₂ acres to John Speller, 5 years term, 16 Feb. 1337, SC 2 193/1; sold 1 rood, north of Wakescroft, to Hugh le Soper, 24 March 1336, HD 86; capital pledge, 22 July 1337, HD 86; trespass v. Bartholomew Carpe, 11 Sept. 1337, SC 2 193/1; default, withheld a *precaria* in autumn, 11 Sept. 1337, SC 2 193/1; creditor v. Thomas atte Hil, 29 Sept. 1337, SC 2 193/1; trespass v. Cecily Erneys, 29 Sept. 1337, SC 2 193/1; default, 6 April 1342, SC 2 193/1; trespass v. Richard atte Bakhous, 12 Oct. 1342, SC 2 193/1; creditor v. Simon Burgoine, 12 Oct. 1342, SC 2 193/1; trespass v. Richard atte Bakhous, 12 Oct. 1342, SC 2 193/1; afferator, 12 Oct. 1342, SC 2 193/1; creditor v. Simon Burgoine, order to levy 11d. and recover money owed for 3 years, 17 Dec. 1343, SC 2 193/1; creditor v. Agnes Pontaye, order to levy 12d., 4 June 1344, SC 2 193/1; fined 4d. for not attaching Margaret Dersy to answer Robert Herward, 15 April 1345, SC 2 193/1; granted 3 acres to Margaret (Burgoine), his wife for her life, she paid entry fine 6s. 8d., 22 July 1347, HD 87a; granted a cottage with 1 acre 1 rood, lying in Burgate, to Roger Crane, his son, who paid an entry fine 3s. 4d., 22 July 1347, HD 85a.

Crane, John, son of Thomas, grandson of John, was granted a cottage in Burgate from John Crane senior, 22 July 1347, HD 85a; did *hamsoken* and drew blood from John Shortebar, 22 July 1347, HD 85a; ale taster, failed to carry office, 22 July 1347, HD 85a; ale taster, failed to carry office, 10 Dec. 1348, HD 85a.

Crane, Lawrence, order for fealty, 22 July 1332, HD 82; for neglect of suit of court, 1 Nov. 1334, HD 84.

Crane, Margaret, tenant of ¹/₂ rood, marriage without licence, 1 Nov. 1334, HD 84; bought 6 *denariates* from Cecily Jay, 8 Jan. 1336, HD 85a.

Crane, Margaret (Mariota), widow of John Crane, creditor, as executor, v. John Blakeman, order to levy 5s., 20 Jan. 1347, HD 86; creditor, as executor of John Crane's will, v. Robert and John Erneys, order to levy 5s., 20 Jan. 1347; false quarrel v. Robert and John Erneys, 20 Jan. 1347, HD 86; victim of *hamsoken* by Thomas Crane, raised hue and cry justly, 22 July 1347, HD 85a.

Crane, Reynold and wife Christiana, agreement in debt plea, 3 July 1332, HD 82; capital pledge, 22 July 1332, HD 82; trespass v. Adam Craske, non prosecution of plaint by Adam Craske, 6 May 1333, 1 July 1333, HD 84; took lease of 1¹/₂ roods, at Hallemille, from Walter Asty, 6 years term, 23 May 1334, HD 84; default, 22 June 1334, HD 84; capital pledge, 22 July 1334, HD 84; bought 1 messuage, 2 acres 3 roods from John le Smith and regranted them to John le Smith with a reversion clause, 8 Jan. 1336, HD 85a; bought 1 rood from Margaret Slopere, 8 Jan. 1336, HD 86; capital pledge, 22 July 1337, HD 86; trespass v. Bartholomew le Miller, 11 Sept. 1337, SC 2 193/1; debtor v. James Becces, 4 June 1344, SC 2 193/1; creditor v. Roger le Smith, order to levy 12d., 4 June 1344, SC 2 193/1; for bad gesture in court in front of steward, fined 3s. 4d., 15 April 1345, SC 2 193/1; sold, without licence, 3 acres to Matilda Joudy, 9 Aug. 1346, HD 87a; was granted by the lord confirmation of tenure of 1 cottage and 1 acre, fine 9s., 9 Aug. 1348, HD 87a.

Crane, Reynold, son of Reynold, default, 14 Oct. 1348, HD 85a.

Crane, Roger, creditor v. Simon and Cecily Mous, 8 Dec. 1334, HD 84; bought 1 rood, at the mill of Burghall, from Adam Charle, 28 March 1335, HD 84; trespass v. Bartholomew le Miller, 11 Sept. 1337, SC 2 193/1; creditor v. Bartholomew le Miller, 11 Sept. 1337, SC 2 193/1; trespass v. Robert le Smith, 12 Oct. 1342, SC 2 193/1; trespass v. Richard atte Bakhous, 12 Oct. 1342, SC 2 193/1; false claim v. Richard atte Bakhous, 17 Dec. 1343, SC 2 193/1; bought 1 rood, next to the Clynt, from Mabilia Peper, 17 Dec. 1343, SC 2 193/1; bought 1 rood from Margaret Peper, 15 April 1345, SC 2 193/1; land plea v. Richard atte Bakhous, 15 April 1345, SC 2 193/1; was granted by his father John Crane a cottage and 1 acre 1 rood, 22 July 1347, HD 85a; took lease of 1 rood, next to the lord's mill, from Alice le Souter, 5 years term, 22 July 1347, HD 85a; creditor, not prosecuting his plaint v. Richard Blakeman, 8 April 1349, HD 85a; trespass v. Alice Dersy, 8 April 1348, HD 85a; for common suit, 28 May 1350, SC 2 193/1; sold with Thomas Crane a cottage with 1/2 rood to William de Shereford, 28 May 1350, SC 2 193/1; was granted tenure of 4 acres, formerly held by Cecily Dollow, 28 May 1350, SC 2 193/1; capital pledge, 22 July 1350, HD 87a.

Crane, Thomas, dispensed with suit of court until Michaelmas, 20 Jan. 1347, HD 86; was granted a cottage by his grand father John Crane, 22 July 1347, HD 85; did *hamsoken* v. Mariota Crane who raised hue and cry justly, 22 July 1347, HD 85; debtor v. Thomas Silk, 14 Oct. 1348, HD 85a; default, 14 Oct. 1348, HD 85a; debtor v. Simon Silk, 14 Oct. 1348, HD 85a; order of attachment in debt pleas v. Thomas and Simon Silk, 10 Dec. 1348, HD 85a; debtor v. Simon Silk who did not prosecute his plaint, 31 March 1349, SC 2 193/1; fealty, 31 March 1349, SC 2 193/1; for common suit, 28 May 1350, SC 2 193/1; sold a cottage and 1/2 rood, with Roger Crane, to William de Shereford, 28 May 1350, SC 2 193/1.

Craske, Adam, trespass v. Reynald Crane, 6 May 1333, HD 84; trespass v. John Andrew, 6 May 1333, HD 84; order to attach to answer John Andrew in trespass plea, 1 July 1333, HD 84; not prosecuting v. Reynald Crane in trespass plea, 1 July 1333, HD 84; died, order to keep in lord's hand his tenement until heir came forward, 4 Nov. 1334, HD 84.

Craske, Geoffrey, made illegal path, 22 July 1332, HD 82.

Craske, John, default, pauper, debtor v. Simon Burgoine, order to come to answer at next court, 3 July 1332, HD 82; failure to glean, 12 Oct. 1342, SC 2 193/1; died, order of distraint of his heir for homage and fealty, 15 Oct. 1349, HD 83.

Craske, Margery, sold 1/2 acre, at Eggemere Scote, to Peter de Langham, 21 Oct. 1334, HD 84.

Craske, Matilda, ale fine, 22 July 1337, HD 86.

Craske, Muriel, withheld grain, 22 July 1332, HD 82.

Creake, Abbot of, trespass v. lord with sheep, 17 Dec. 1343, SC 2 193/1.

Creake (Crek), Albert de, trespass v. lord with sheep, order of distraint, 12 Oct. 1342, SC 2 193/1.

Creake (Creyk), Adam son of Bartholomew, bought 1 rood from Beatrice Huberd, 27 March 1346, HD 86.

Crome, Alice, false quarrel v. Adam Cage, 17 Dec. 1343, SC 2 193/1.

Crome, Andrew, default, 29 Sept. 1337, SC 2 193/1.

Crome, Geoffrey, debt plea v. Rosa Bulwer, 3 July 1332, HD 82; debtor v. James Becces, 22 July 1332, HD 82.

Crome, Lawrence, order of distraint for fealty, 3 July 1332, HD 82; default, 22 July 1332, HD 82; dispensed with suit of court until Michaelmas, 25 Jan. 1334, HD 84; bought 1/4 rood, in Northgate, from Roger le Slopere, 25 Jan. 1334, HD 84; bought 1 rood, above Willelond, from Roger le Slopere, 8 Dec. 1334, HD 84; default, 22 July 1337, HD 86.

Crome, Margaret, bread fine, regrater of bread, 22 July 1332, HD 82.

Crome, Thomas, did not use the lord's mill, 4 June 1344, SC 2 193/1.

Cros, Simon at, default, 22 July 1332, HD 82; debtor v. James Becces, 1 July 1333, HD 84; not prosecution of plaint in debt plea v. James Becces, 22 June 1334, HD 84; ale fine, 22 July 1334, HD 84; default, 22 July 1334, HD 84; default, 22 July 1337, HD 86; not in tithing, 22 July 1347, 10 Dec. 1348.

Crouch, William, ale taster, 22 July 1350, HD 87a.

Croude, John, default, 8 April 1348, HD 85a; debtor v. Richard Speller, 11 Dec. 1348, HD 85a; oath of fealty, 31 March 1349, SC 2 193/1.

Croude, Roger, claimed as closest heir to succession of 41/2 acres of deceased John Joudy, paid relief 32d., 22 July 1350, HD 87a.

Crundel, John atte, debt plea v. Peter Meyr, 28 Dec. 1342, SC 2 193/1; made illegal path beyond land of William Curthun, 22 July 1347, HD 85a.

Cursun (Curthoun), Gilbert, heir of Helewise (le) Meyre for a messuage and 3 roods, 16 Nov. 1345, HD 83.

Cursun (Curthoun), William, bought 1 rood from Agnes Reynald, 3 July 1332, HD 82; bought 3/4 rood, at Shipmancros, from Agnes Raven, 3 July 1332, HD 82; order of distraint for fealty, 1346, HD 86; order of distraint for homage and fealty for 2 acres, 15 Oct. 1349, HD 83; capital pledge, 22 July 1350, HD 87a; ale taster, 22 July 1350; plaintiff in trespass and transgression plea v. Gilbert Neel, 26 Nov. 1350, HD 87a.

Dale (de la, atte), Caterine daughter of Clement, dispensed with suit of court, 12 Oct. 1342, SC 2 193/1.

Dale (de la, atte), Clement, for neglect of suit of court, 1 Nov. 1334, HD 84.

Dale (de la, atte), Clarice, bought 3 roods from Bartholomew Colin, 25 Jan. 1334, HD 84; dispensed with suit of court until feast of Mary Magdalen, 8 Jan. 1336, HD 85a; dispensed with suit of court until Michaelmas, 13 Dec. 1336, SC 2 193/1; dispensed with suit of court for 1 year, 11 Sept. 1337, SC 2 193/1; default, 25 Sept. 1337, SC 2 193/1.

Dale (de la, atte), John, withheld grain, 22 July 1332, HD 82; default, 6 May 1333, HD 84; did not use the lord's mill, 23 May 1334, HD 84; did not use lord's mill, 11 Dec. 1335, HD 85a; order to keep in lord's hand 3 roods and answer about rent, 12 Oct. 1342, 17 Dec. 1343, 4 Jan. 1344, SC 2 193/1; died, order to keep in lord's hand 3 acres and answer about rent, 15 April 1345, SC 2 193/1.

Dalling, Geoffrey de and wife Mariota, order to keep in lord's hand a cottage and 1 rood sold to William de Stodeye because Mariota did not know her right, 6 April 1342, SC 2 193/1; confirmation of sale, 28 Dec. 1342, SC 2 193/1.

Dam, John atte, son of Thomas, oath of fealty, after court 6 Dec. 1346, HD 86.

Dam, Thomas atte, fealty for 3 acres 1 rood held by the rod, 15 Oct. 1349, HD 86.

Daulin (Daulyn, Dollon), Cecily, held land above Seagatewey, 17 Dec. 1743, SC 2 193/1; her 4 acres holding, vacant, granted by lord to Roger Crane, 28 May 1350, SC 2 193/1.

Daulin (Daulyn, Dollon), John, agreement in trespass plea v. John le Smith, 3 July 1332, HD 82; default, held land which owed office of collector, 6 April 1342, SC 2 193/1; debtor v. John Bulwer, order to levy 8d., 6 April 1342, SC 2 193/1; trespass v. lord, fine 1d., 12 Oct. 1342, SC 2 193/1.

Daulin (Daulyn, Dollon), William, default, 6 May 1333, HD 84; default, 8 Dec. 1334; took lease of 3 roods, at Stathe gate, from John Asty, 10 years term, 28 March 1335, HD 84; took lease of 1 acre, at Langefurlong, 8 years term, from Margaret Slopere, 28 March 1335, HD 84; made illegal path, 22 July 1347, HD 85a.

Daure, Matilda, ale fine, 22 July 1334, HD 84.

Debet, Sibyl, sold 1 rood to John le Wrighte, 8 April 1348, HD 85a; sold 1 rood, near the croft of John Mey, to John Mey, 8 April 1348, HD 85a; sold 1 rood, at church gate, to John son of Adam Silk, 9 Aug. 1348, HD 87a.

Dering, Adam, sold 1 rood, at Wykenlond, to Benedict de Bestone, 4 Nov. 1334, HD 85.

Dering, Alice, daughter of Geoffrey, minor, did not come to court, order to take in lord's hand 1 rood held by father, 15 Oct. 1349, HD 83.

Dering, Gilbert, agreement in trespass plea with Caterine Marchal, 23 May 1334, HD 84; for common suit, 18 Jan. 1335, HD 85.

Dering, Geoffrey, defendant in trespass plea v. John Marchall, 23 May 1334, HD 84; paid rent 1d., 1341–42 *circa*, HD 83; creditor v. Harvey Buleman, 12 Oct. 1342, SC 2 193/1; debt plea v. Harvey Buleman who is ordered to be at next court, 17 Dec. 1343, SC 2 193/1; took from the lord 1 rood by the rod, 4 Dec. 1342, HD 83; order to seize 1 rood held by Geoffrey when he died, because no heir came forward, 6 Dec. 1346, HD 86; as Alice, daughter and closest heir, was minor and did not come forward, order to keep 1 rood in lord's hand, 15 Oct. 1349, HD 83.

Dersy, Alice, ale fine, 22 July 1334, HD 84; with sisters Matilda and Joan paid heriot 27d. and made fealty after death of father, Walter, for a messuage and 9 acres, 28 March 1335, HD 84; default for 1 *precaria* in autumn, 11 Sept. 1337, SC 2 193/1; plaintiff in trespass case v. Roger Crane, 8 April 1348, HD 85a; granted lease of 1 1/2 acres to Richard Speller, 6 years term, 8 April 1348, HD 85a; granted lease of 1/2 rood to John de Shereford, 8 years term, 8 April 1348, HD 85; granted lease of 1 acre to the Abbot of West Dereham, 14 Oct. 1348, HD 85; paid marriage licence to wed William Mariot, 10 Dec. 1348, HD 85a.

Dersy, Joan, default, 1334, HD 84; with sisters Alice and Matilda paid heriot 27d. and made fealty after death of Walter, her father, for a messuage and 9 acres, 28 March 1335, HD 84; bought a cottage to Robert Eliot, 22 July 1347, HD 85a; not in tithing, 22 July 1347, HD 85a; default, 8 April 1348, HD 85a; not in tithing, 10 Dec. 1348, HD 85a; for common suit, 31 March

1349, SC 2 193/1; default, 28 May 1350, SC 2 193/1; default, 22 July 1350, SC 2 193/1.

Dersy, Margaret, debtor v. William le Souter, 15 April 1345, SC 2 193/1; debtor v. Goda Hukster, 15 April 1345, SC 2 193/1; debtor v. Robert Herward of Burnham, summons for Margaret who did not come, 15 April 1345, SC 2 193/1; sold a messuage and 5 roods to Ralph de Burgh, 28 May 1350, SC 2 193/1.

Dersy, Matilda, agreement with Isabel de Barsham who granted and quitclaimed all her dower rights in tenements owned by her deceased husband to Matilda, 6 May 1333, HD 84; sold 1/2 rood to Richard atte Bakhous, 4 June 1344, SC 2 193/1; with sisters Alice and Joan paid heriot 27d. and made fealty after death of father, Walter, for a messuage and 9 acres, 28 March 1335, HD 84.

Dersy, Walter, order of distraint for fealty, 3 July 1332, HD 82; agreement in debt plea with William Fot, 25 Jan. 1334, HD 84; bond man, died intestate, seized of a messuage and 9 acres, heirs were his 3 daughters, Alice, Matilda and Joan, 28 March 1335, HD 84.

Deye, Ralph, defendant in debt plea v. James Becces, 3 March 1334, HD 84; order of distraint to return a coat of the value of 18d., 23 May 1334, HD 84; default, 22 July 1334, HD 84.

Deye, Richard, default, 3 July 1332, HD 82; debtor v. Simon Burgoine, order to come for answer, 22 July 1332, HD 82.

Deye, Robert, default, 22 July 1337, HD 86.

Deye, Thomas, debtor v. Robert de Hindringham, 8 April 1348, HD 85a.

Digge, Ralph, debtor v. James Becces, order to have better pledges for answer, 6 May 1333, 1 July 1333, HD 84.

Digge, Roger, default, 22 July 1332; creditor v. Richard Marchal, 25 Jan. 1334, 23 May 1334, HD 84; order to attach Richard Marchal to answer Roger in debt plea, 21 Oct. 1334, HD 84.

Dewaghe, Richard, agreement with Agnes Briche, 6 April 1342, SC 2 193/1.

Doreward, Harvey, bought 1/2 acre from Gilbert and Cecily Kele, 28 May 1350, SC2 193/1; assault with bloodshed v. John Kele, 22 July 1350, HD 87a.

Doreward, John, held 1 acre, 3 Dec. 1339, HD 83.

Doreward, Richard, held 1 acre, 3 Dec. 1339, HD 83.

Dousing, Agnes, failure to glean, 12 Oct. 1342, SC 2 193/1.

Drake, John, false claim v. Henry Speller, 16 Feb. 1337, SC 2 193/1; creditor v. William Huberd, 16 Feb. 1337, SC 2 193/1; withheld rent 3d.

Drove, Beatrice atte, bought 11/2 roods from Mabel Peper, 12 Oct. 1342, SC 2 193/1.

Drove, John atte, default, 11 Sept. 1337, SC 2 193/1; default, 10 June 1346, HD 86.

Dunbow, Roger, default, 1 Nov. 1334, HD 84.

Dusmer, Agnes, default, 22 June 1334, HD 84.

Edmund, – , vicar, default, 4 Nov. 1334, HD 85a.

Edwy, Gilbert, bought 1 rood from Richard atte Bakhous, 4 June 1344, SC 2 193/1; default, 14 Oct. 1348, HD 85a.

Edwy, Robert, default, 22 July 1334, HD 84.

Edwy, William, for fealty, 3 July 1332, HD 82.

Edrych, John, bought 1 rood from Matilda Sveyn, 28 Dec. 1342, SC 2 193/1.

Eliot, Robert, debtor v. Simon Mous, order of distraint, 3 July 1332, 22 July 1332, HD 82; sold a cottage to Joan Dersy, 22 July 1347, HD 85a; essoin for Geoffrey Pennyng, 31 March 1349, SC 2 193/1.

Eliot, Thomas, default, 22 June 1334, HD 84; default, 8 Dec. 1334, HD 84; default, 29 Sept. 1337, SC 2 193/1; default in labour services, 12 Oct. 1342, SC 2 193/1; default, 12 Oct. 1342, SC 2 193/1; default, 15 April 1345, SC 2 193/1; default, 10 June 1346, HD 86; default, 14 Oct. 1348, HD 85a.

Elsi, John, order of distraint for fealty, 6 April 1342, SC 2 193/1; default, 6 April 1342, SC 2 193/1; defendant in trespass plea v. Peter Meyre, order of distraint for answer, 6 April 1342, SC 2 193/1; order of distraint for fealty, 28 Dec. 1342, SC 2 193/1.

Elverich, Helewise, died, seized of 1/2 acre and 1/2 rood, heir her cousin John who was minor, order to keep in lord's hand, 6 Dec. 1346, HD 86.

Elverich, heirs of Gilbert, tenant of 1 rood, 1 July 1333, HD 86; default, 25 Jan. 1334, 23 May 1334, 22 June 1334, 1 Nov. 1334, HD 84.

Elverich, John, minor, heir and cousin of Helewise Elverich for 1/2 acre and 1/2 rood kept in lord's hand, 6 Dec. 1346, HD 86; order to seize John, minor, 7 July 1350, HD 83.

Elverich, John, died, held a messuage with 11/2 acres, heir was Richard, his brother, 14 years old, his other holding of 1 acre and 1 rood, in Lonadowe, to be kept in Lord's hand, 6 Dec. 1346, HD 86.

Elverich, Matilda, order of distraint for fealty, 1346, HD 86; order of distraint for homage and fealty, 15 Oct. 1349, HD 83.

Elverich, Richard, heir of John, his brother, at 14 years old, for a messuage 11/2 acres, and 1 acre 1 rood in Lonadowe, 6 Dec. 1346, HD 86; not in tithing, 22 July 1350, HD 87a; custody and marriage portion of Richard purchased from lord by John Geyste, 22 July 1350, HD 87a.

Elverich, Roger, capital pledge, 22 July 1337, HD 86; died, heir his son John, minor, order to seize in lord's hand all tenement held in socage, and also the body of John 1346, HD 86.

Elwan, John, for common suit, 15 April 1345, SC 2 193/1; for common suit, 20 Jan. 1347, HD 86.

Elwan, Thomas, default, 6 May 1333, HD 84; default, 25 Jan. 1334, HD 84; creditor v. Harvey Lode, 4 June 1344, SC 2 193/1; creditor v. Harvey Lode, 22 July 1347, HD 85a.

Ernald, Agnes, died, had a free tenure, heir, first daughter who was of age and paid relief, 9 Dec. 1348, HD 83.

Erneys, Cecily, ale fine, 22 July 1334, HD 84; debtor (with Robert Erneys, her son) v. Geoffrey Bulwer, chaplain, of 3 quarters of barley, payment term next Michaelmas, 13 Dec. 1336, SC 2 193/1; debtor v. Robert Andrew, of 40s., 2 terms of 1 mark in arrears, 13 Dec. 1336, SC 2 193/1; agreement in debt plea with John Crane, 10 Dec. 1336, SC 2 193/1; defendant in trespass plea v. John Crane, order of summons to appear at next court, 29 Sept. 1337, SC 2 193/1; conceded 11/2 acres at farm to John and Thomas de Caldwell, 17 Dec. 1343, SC 2 193/1; granted lease of 1 acre, 3 years term, to Martin de Erpingham, 22 July 1347, HD 85a.

Erneys, John, debt plea v. Thomas de Caldwell, 17 Dec. 1343, SC 2 193/1; debtor (with Robert Erneys, his brother) v. Mariota Crane, of 5s., 20 Jan. 1347, HD 86; not in tithing, 22 July 1347, HD 85a.

Erneys, Robert, debtor (with Cecily, his mother) v. Geoffrey Bulwer, 13 Dec. 1336, SC 2 193/1; order of distraint with parcener Agnes de Bilney for fealty, 1346, HD 86; held $2^{1}/_2$ acres for service of 13 days per annum, and also 1 acre, in Northcroft, for 1d. per annum, 6 Dec. 1346, HD 86; debtor (with John, his brother) v. Mariota Crane, 20 Jan. 1347, HD 86; capital pledge, 22 July 1350, HD 87a.

Erpingham, Martin de, took lease of 1 acre from Cecily Erneys, 22 July 1347, HD 85a.

Erpingham, Roger and wife Agnes, order of distraint for services and customary dues owed to the lord for 1 cottage in Burgate held by the rod bought from John Cat, 8 Dec. 1341, 4 Dec. 1342, HD 83.

Esser, Roger, for common suit, 18 Jan. 1335, HD 85.

Esser, Thomas, not prosecuting plea v. Alice Alger, 28 Dec. 1342, SC 2 193/1; bought $1/_2$ acre from Alice Alger, 28 Dec. 1342, SC 2 193/1; default, 10 June 1346, HD 86; trespass plea v. John le Wrighte, 20 Jan. 1347, HD 86; agreement in trespass plea with John le Wrighte, 8 April 1348, HD 85a; bought $1/_2$ rood from William le Souter, 9 Dec. 1348, HD 83.

Estrild, Geoffrey, died, seized of a messuage and $1/_2$ acre $1/_2$ rood, heirs, sons Stephen and Thomas, 28 Dec. 1342, SC 2 193/1.

Estrild, Stephen, son and heir of Geoffrey, 28 Dec. 1342, SC 2 193/1.

Estrild, Thomas, son and heir of Geoffrey, 20 Dec. 1342, SC 2 193/1.

Evechlord, Matilda, withheld grain, 22 July 1332, HD 82.

Everard, Roger, granted lease, without licence, of $1^{1}/_4$ roods to John Crane who took away its crop of barley, 23 May 1334, HD 84; default, 4 Nov. 1334, HD 85.

Fairweder, Peter and wife Leticia, sold a plot of land to Simon Smith, 23 May 1334, HD 85; granted lease, without licence, of $1^{1}/_2$ roods, in Hillergate, to Matilda daughter of Geoffrey, 23 May 1334, HD 85; sold a plot of land (50ft. on 23ft., angle of messuage) to Harvey Miller and his wife Alice, 23 May 1334, HD 85; for common suit, 18 Jan. 1335, HD 85.

Fasone, Edmund, mainpast, made illegal path to Townesend, 22 July 1337, HD 86.

Flour, Maye, ale fine, regrater of bread and ale, 22 July 1337, HD 86.

Fot, William, agreement in debt plea with Walter Dersy, 25 Jan. 1334, HD 84.

Fox, John, creditor v. Reynald Spileman, 1 July 1333, HD 84.

Fox, Sibyl, bought $1/_2$ rood and $1/_4$ rood, in Estgate croft, from Harvey Miller, 18 Jan. 1335, HD 85.

Foxley, Alexander de, order of distraint for fealty, 3 July 1332, HD 82; default, 29 Sept. 1337, SC 2 193/1; did not use lord's mill, 4 June 1334, SC 2 193/1; default, 27 March 1346, 10 June 1346, HD 86; default, 14 Oct. 1348, HD 85a; for fealty, 31 March 1349, SC 2 193/1.

Fuller, William le, debt plea v. Peter de Langham, inquisition ordered, 6 May 1333, HD 84; debtor v. Roger le Reeve, maintain seizures and seize more until answer, 6 May 1333, 1 July 1333, HD 84; creditor v. John de Horning, order of attachment of John for answer, 1 July 1333, 28 March 1334, 22 June 1334, 1 Nov. 1334, HD 84.

Galoun, Robert, free tenant, oath of fealty, after Dec. 1346, HD 86.

Gateley, – , vicar of, default, 8 Jan. 1335, HD 85.

Geoffrey, Matilda daughter of, bought 1 1/2 roods from Peter Fairweder, 23 May 1334, HD 85.

Gerveys, Simon, default, 22 July 1350, HD 87a.

Geyste, John, capital pledge, 22 July 1350, HD 87a; purchased from lord custody and marriage of Richard Elverich until he is of age, 5s., 22 July 1350, HD 87a.

Gilberd, Berta, default, 28 Dec. 1342, SC 2 193/1.

Godecok, Cecily, withheld grain, 22 July 1332, HD 82; for common suit, 10 Dec. 1348, HD 85a.

Godecok, Margaret, withheld grain, 22 July 1332, HD 82; creditor v. John Lamb, order of attachment for answer, 6 May 1333, HD 84.

Godwyne, Ida, land claim, order to keep in lord's hand 6 acres claimed as free tenure, 22 July 1332, HD 82; default, 8 Dec. 1334, HD 84; did not use lord's mill, 11 Dec. 1335, HD 85a; default, 1 *precaria* in autumn, 11 Sept. 1337, SC 2 193/1; did not use lord's mill, order to levy multure for the miller, 10 June 1346, HD 86; did not use lord's mill, 20 Jan. 1347, HD 86; agreement with Roger Smith in debt plea.

Godwyne, Matilda, widow of Roger Godwyne, held 3 roods, at Leyrpitte, with William Godwyne, 24 April 1332, HD 83.

Godwyne, William, succeeded to 1/2 rood, at Robbescroft end, after death of his brother Reynald, 27 April 1332, HD 83; held, with Matilda, widow of Roger Godwyne, 3 roods, and made fealty, 27 April 1332, HD 83; order of distraint for fealty, 3 July 1332, 22 July 1332.

Golde, Helewise, creditor (with Simon Silk), v. John Mey, 10 Dec. 1348, HD 85a.

Golias, Geoffrey, trespass, failure to glean, 12 Oct. 1342, SC 2 193/1; contempt of court, 15 Nov. 1343, HD 83.

Golias, Matilda, daughter of Geoffrey, default, 15 Nov. 1343, HD 83; default, 1346, HD 86.

Grace, John de, order of distraint for fealty, 3 July 1332, 22 July 1332; HD 82.

Greys (Grys), Bartholomew, default, 25 Jan. 1334, 23 May 1334, 22 June 1334, HD 84; order of distraint for fealty, tenant of a cottage, 12 Oct. 1342, 17 Dec. 1343, SC 2 193/1; did not use lord's mill, order to levy multure for the miller, 10 June 1346, HD 86.

Greys (Grys), William, paid 2d. rent, 6 April 1342, SC 2 193/1; order to appear, at next court, to certify holding and services, 15 April 1345, SC 2 193/1.

Grigges, Adam, essoin in debt plea for Alice Huberd v. Isabel de Barsham, 23 May 1334, HD 84.

Griston, nephew and heir of Robert de, order of distraint to answer about default, 28 March 1335, HD 84.

Griston, Thomas de, debtor v. Benedict le Shipwright of Great Yarmouth, summons, order of attachment for answer, 14 Oct. 1348, 10 Dec. 1348, 31 March 1349, SC 2 193/1; debtor v. Benedict le Shipwright of Great Yarmouth, acquitted, creditor not prosecuting, 28 May 1350, SC 2 193/1.

Gunnok, William, default, 3 July 1332, HD 82.

Gunthorpe, John, pledge in debt plea for Isabel de Barsham v. William and Alice Huberd, 23 May 1334, HD 84.

Gurle, Alice, for *gersuma* and default, 10 Nov. 1335, HD 83.

Gurle, Agnes, paid heriot for 1/2 rood, 12 Nov. 1333, HD 83.

Gurle, Gilbert, bond man, 31 March 1333, HD 83.

Hacks, William, dispensed with suit of court until feast of Mary Magdalen, 8 Jan. 1335, HD 85a; did not use lord's mill, 11 Dec. 1335, HD 85a.

Hagae, William, made illegal path to Townesend, 22 July 1337, HD 86.

Haghene, Sewal, for common suit, 4 Nov. 1334, HD 85.

Haldeyn, Edmund, housebreaking (*hamsoken*) v. Roger atte Hil, 22 July 1332, HD 82; made illegal path over land of Andrew Underclynt at the Clynt, 22 July 1332, HD 82; not in tithing, 10 Dec. 1334, HD 85a; default, 29 Sept. 1337, SC 2 193/1; not in tithing, 22 July 1347, HD 85a.

Haldeyn, Harvey, not in tithing, 22 July 1332, HD 82.

Haldeyn, William, prosecution pledge in debt plea Geoffrey Dering v. Harvey Buleman, 12 Oct. 1342, SC 2 193/1.

Hales, John de, default, 2 July 1337, HD 86.

Halman, Thomas, debtor v. Richard Blakeman, 13 Dec. 1336, SC 2 193/1.

Hammond, Alice, sold 1/2 acre 1/2 rood to Alice le Wrighte, 3 July 1332, HD 82; sold 1 rood to Alice le Wrighte, at Hegh Skamlond, 28 March 1335, HD 84.

Hammond, Walter, chaplain, order of distraint to show title for holding 11/2 roods, at Dalehil, 24 April 1332, HD 83.

Hammond, William, quarrel v. Sarra le Clerk, 29 Sept. 1337, SC 2 193/1.

Happisburgh, John de, order of distraint for fealty, 3 July 1332, 22 July 1332, HD 82; not in tithing, 22 July 1332, HD 82; default, 6 May 1333, HD 84; order to seize, failed all services, 8 Jan. 1336, HD 85a; default, 6 April 1342, SC 2 193/1.

Happisburgh, Roger de, order of distraint for fealty, 1346; made fealty for a cottage with a croft containing 1/2 rood, 9 Dec. 1348, HD 83; order of distraint for homage and fealty, 15 Oct. 1349, HD 83.

Hardwick, Bartholomew de, son and heir of Thomas, minor, heriot paid for 2 acres, 1 Nov. 1334, HD 84.

Hardwick, Ralph de, dispensed with suit of court until next Saint Michael, 14 Oct. 1348, HD 85a.

Hardwick, Robert de, son and heir of Thomas, minor, heriot paid for 2 acres, 1 Nov. 1334, HD 84.

Hardwick, Thomas de, died, 2 sons and heirs, held 2 acres, 1 Nov. 1332, HD 84.

Hare, Sewal, essoin for Peter de Langham, 18 Jan. 1335, HD 85.

Hawkin, Margaret, did not use lord's mill, 23 May 1334, HD 84; did not use lord's mill, 11 Dec. 1335, HD 84.

Haybone, John, essoin for Sewal Haghene, 4 Nov. 1334, HD 85.

Hayward, Geoffrey, son of William, default, 21 Oct. 1334, HD 84; default, 29 Sept. 1337, SC 2 193/1; for common suit, 15 April 1345, SC 2 193/1; default, 15 April 1345, SC 2 193/1; dispensed with suit of court until next Michaelmas, 14 Oct. 1348, HD 85a.

Hayward, John le, prosecution pledge in debt plea Edmund Pilch v. Simon Silk, 5 Oct. 1349, SC 2 193/1; failed to attach Thomas de Griston for answer Benedict le Shipwright, 5 Oct. 1349, SC 2 193/1.

Hayward, William, essoin for Geoffrey, his son, 15 April 1345, SC 2 193/1.

Hecheman, Isabel, creditor v. Robert Keynot, for levy of 17d., 11 Sept. 1337, SC 2 193/1; sold 1 rood to Richard Speller, 15 April 1345, SC 2 193/1.

Hecheman, Matilda, for leyrwite, 12 Oct. 1342, SC 2 193/1.

Heire, Andrew le, bought several pieces and tenements from Geoffrey de Walsingham, 5 Oct. 1349, SC 2 193/1; sold all his land, 7 acres, to Peter de Binham, 28 May 1350, SC 2 193/1.

Heire (Eyr), Geoffrey le, default, 13 Dec. 1336, SC 2 193/1; dispensed with suit of court until Michaelmas, 27 March 1346, HD 86.

Heire, Simon le and wife Helewise, default, 22 June 1334, 8 Dec. 1334, HD 84; sold 1 acre 1/2 rood to Richard atte Bakhous, 8 April 1348, HD 85a.

Henry, Richard, order to keep in lord's hand 1 1/2 roods for rent and services, 6 April 1342, SC 2 193/1.

Henry, William, debtor v. Emma Asty, order of attachment for answer, 16 Feb. 1337, SC 2 193/1, 22 July 1337, HD 86; debtor v. Emma Asty, order of attachment for answer, 10 June 1346, HD 86; default, 8 April 1348, HD 85a.

Hereward, John, mainpast of the Abbot of West Dereham, made illegal path with cows, 22 July 1334, HD 84.

Hereward, Robert, of Burnham, creditor v. Margaret Dersy, 15 April 1345, SC 2 193/1.

Hereward, Sewal, creditor v. Simon and Cecily Mous, 11 Dec. 1335, HD 85a; creditor v. Thomas le Northerne, 11 Dec. 1335, HD 85a; non prosecuting plaint v. Thomas le Northerne, 13 Dec. 1336, SC 2 193/1; non prosecuting plaint v. Simon Mous and his pledges, 11 Sept. 1337, SC 2 193/1; day given for debt plea v. Thomas le Northerne, order to be at next court, 29 Sept. 1337, SC 2 193/1.

Herman, John, bought 1 1/2 roods with charter from William le Souter, order of distraint for exhibit of charter, and fealty, 9 Dec. 1348, HD 83.

Heverington, Alice de, sold, without licence, 1 acre and 3 roods, order to keep in lord's hand and answer about revenues, 6 April 1342, SC 2 193/1.

Hil, Agnes atte, daughter and heir of Cecily, for 3 roods, made fealty, 4 June 1344, SC 2 193/1.

Hil, Alice atte, daughter and heir of Cecily, for 3 roods, made fealty, 4 June 1344, SC 2 193/1.

Hil, Bartholomew atte, order of distraint for fealty, 3 July 1332, 22 July 1332, HD 82.

Hil, Cecily atte, died, held 3 roods, 3 daughters and heirs, Agnes, Alice, Helewise, 4 June 1344, SC 2 193/1.

Hil, Gilbert atte, died, held 2 1/2 acres, son and heir, Roger, 23 May 1334, HD 84.

Hil, Helewise atte, daughter and heir of Cecily, for 3 roods, made fealty, 4 June 1344, SC 2 193/1.

Hil, John atte, default, 22 July 1332, HD 82; default, 22 July 1334, HD 84; bought a messuage with 5 acres from Roger le Smith, 5 Oct. 1349, SC 2 193/1.

Hil, Margaret atte, sold a cottage 1 rood to Bartholomew le Miller, 4 June 1344, SC 2 193/1.

Hil, Robert atte, default, 22 July 1334, HD 84; default, 4 June 1344, SC 2 193/1.

Hil, Roger atte, son of Gilbert, marriage without licence, 3 July 1332, HD 82; order to seize revenue of quarter of rye for 1 rood, 3 July 1332, HD 82; default, 22 July 1332, HD 82; heir of Gilbert for 2 1/2 acres, paid heriot 32d., 23 May 1334, HD 84.

Hil, Roger atte, son of Bartholomew, made illegal path to land of Beatrice atte Drove, 22 July 1334, HD 84; sold 1/2 rood, in Estfield, to John Beneyt, 17 Dec. 1343, SC 2 193/1; sold 1 rood to Roger le Smith, 4 June 1344, SC 2 193/1; made fealty, 31 March 1349, SC 2 193/1.

Hil, Thomas atte, default, 22 July 1334, HD 84; default, 11 Sept. 1337, SC 2 193/1; debtor v. John Crane, order of distraint for answer at next court, 29 Sept. 1337, SC 2 193/1; sold 1 rood to Richard and Rose atte Bakhous, 4 June 1344, SC 2 193/1.

Hildemere, Adam de, essoin for Agnes Bulwer, 22 June 1334, HD 84.

Hindringham, Joan de, widow of William, bought 1 rood from John de Hindringham, her son, 17 Dec. 1343, SC 2 193/1; debtor v. Bartholomew Bernard de Wighton, 22 July 1347, HD 85a.

Hindringham, John de, son of Gilbert, defendant in trespass plea v. John Mey, order to be at next court for answer, 11 Sept. 1337, 29 Sept. 1337, SC 2 193/1.

Hindringham, John de, son of Robert, heir of a messuage and 1 acre, paid heriot 32d. and made fealty, 31 March 1349, SC 2 193/1.

Hindringham, John de, son of William, sold 1/2 rood to Joan de Hindringham, 17 Dec. 1334, SC 2 193/1; not in tithing, 10 Dec. 1345, HD 85a; default, 27 March 1346, HD 86; default, 10 June 1346, HD 86; not in tithing, 22 July 1347, HD 85a.

Hindringham, Richard de, son of William, not in tithing, 22 July 1332, HD 82; breaking a coffer and theft of objects of wreck, order of distraint, 15 April 1345, SC 2 193/1; breaking a coffer and theft of objects of wreck, 20 Jan. 1347, HD 86, 9 Aug. 1348, HD 87a, 14 Oct. 1348, HD 85a; order of distraint for breaking a coffer and theft of objects of wreck, 31 March 1349, SC 2 193/1.

Hindringham, Robert de, creditor v. Thomas le Deye, 8 April 1348, HD 85a; died, held a messuage and 1 acre, son and heir John paid heriot 32d., 31 March 1349, SC 2 193/1.

Hindringham, William de, breaking a coffer and theft of objects of wreck, 4 June 1344, SC 2 193/1; default, 22 July 1350, HD 85a.

Hoddes, Agnes, debtor v. Muriel Casche, owed her 3s. 7d. on the market, order to levy, 4 Dec. 1342, HD 83.

Hoddes, John, creditor v. Alice Otes and Isabel Payn, order of distraint of Isabel, 22 July 1337, HD 86.

Hoddes, Matilda, died, held 11/2 roods, order to keep in lord's hand until heir comes forward, 1 July 1333, HD 84.

Hoddes, Thomas, granted by lord tenement formerly of William Rutele, 1346, HD 86.

Hoker, Richard, trespass with cattle, 26 Nov. 1350, HD 87a.

Holkham, Geoffrey de, of Walsingham, messor 1341–42, accounts rendered and settled with an obligatory note of 20 marks to the lord, 4 June 1344, SC 2 193/1.

Hopman, Gilbert, tenant of Cecily Parson, 6 April 1342, SC 2 193/1.

Horning, Alice de, order to keep in lord's hand 1 acre 3 roods, sold without licence, 28 Dec. 1342, SC 2 193/1.

Horning, John de, debtor v. William le Fuller, order to come for answer, 1 July 1333, HD 84; order to attach for answer, 25 Jan. 1334, 23 May 1334, 22 June 1335, HD 85, 21 Oct. 1334, 1 Nov. 1334, 28 March 1335, HD 84;

plaintiff in trespass plea v. Roger le Thakster, 22 June 1334, 22 July 1334, HD 84; non prosecuting plaint v. Roger le Thakster, 21 Oct. 1334, HD 84; order of distraint for fealty, 6 April 1342, SC 2 193/1; default, 6 April 1342, SC 2 193/1; order of distraint for fealty, 28 Dec. 1342, SC 2 193/1; default, 28 Dec. 1342, SC 2 193/1.

Howgate, Bartholomew de, son of Margery and Richard, made illegal path beyond land of Richard Neel, at Westfeld, with Robert atte Church, 22 July 1334, HD 84; paid rent 24d., 1341–42 *circa*, HD 83; sold by charter 1 rood held by the rod to Nicholas Andrew, 6 Dec. 1346, HD 86; held 1 acre in tenement Yudekil owing office of messor, 9 Dec. 1348, HD 83; died, held a messuage and 6 acres 1 rood by the rod, heir Cecily, sister, fine 24d., 15 Oct. 1349, HD 83.

Howgate, Cecily de, *nativa domini*, order to seize in lord's hand a messuage and 3 acres held by the rod and answer about revenues, and body of Cecily who left lord's fief, 1346, HD 86; sister and heir of Bartholomew for 6 acres 1 rood, made fealty, 15 Oct. 1349, HD 83; for *gersuma*, 22d., 7 July 1350, HD 83.

Howgate, heirs of Clarice de, dower land, 1 acre 1/2 rood seized in lord's hand until heir came forward, 3 Dec. 1339, HD 83; 1 acre occupied without licence, order to answer about revenue, 1 Dec. 1340, HD 83.

Howgate, Constance de, paid rent 24d. with John de Howgate, 1341–42 *circa*, HD 83.

Howgate, John de, paid rent 24d. with Constance, 1341–42 *circa*, HD 83; contempt of court, 15 Nov. 1343, HD 83; order to attach about breaking a coffer and theft of objects of wreck, 4 June 1344, 15 April 1345, SC 2 193/1, 20 Jan. 1347, HD 86, 9 Aug. 1348, HD 87a, 14 Oct. 1348, HD 85a; messor elect, 15 Nov. 1344, HD 83; failure to perform office of messor, 18 Nov. 1345, HD 83; messor, 1346, HD 86; did not repair 2 dilapidated houses, 6 Dec. 1346, HD 86; withheld 1 day in autumn, 20 Oct. 1347, HD 83; held 1 acre in tenement Yudekil, 9 Dec. 1348, HD 83; default, 15 Oct. 1349, HD 83; messor elect, 15 Oct. 1349, HD 83; default, 22 July 1350, HD 87a.

Howgate, Thomas de, default, 27 March 1346, HD 86.

Huberd, Beatrice, debtor v. Isabel de Barsham, 6 May 1333, HD 84; default, 6 May 1333, HD 84; debtor v. Roger le Smith, 23 May 1334, HD 84; did not use lord's mill, 23 May 1334, HD 84; agreement in debt plea v. Roger le Smith, 22 June 1334, HD 84; default, 22 June 1334, HD 84; sold 1 rood to Agnes le Ro, 15 April 1345, SC 2 193/1; sold 1 rood to Adam, son of Bartholomew de Creyk, 27 March 1346, HD 86.

Huberd, Richard, son of William, not in tithing, 22 July 1334, HD 84; default, 22 July 1337, HD 86; not in tithing, 22 July 1341, HD 85; creditor v. Harvey Buleman, 12 Oct. 1342, 17 Dec. 1343, SC 2 193/1; not in tithing, 10 Dec. 1348, HD 85a.

Huberd, William, order of distraint for fealty, 3 July 1332, HD 82; defendant in detention of chattels plea v. Richard Speller, non prosecution of plaint, 22 July 1332, HD 82; contempt of court, 25 Jan. 1334, HD 84; dispensed with suit of court, 25 Jan. 1334, HD 84; debtor v. Isabel de Barsham, 23 May 1334, 22 June 1334, 21 Oct. 1334, HD 84; agreement with John Mey, 25 March 1335, HD 84; debtor v. Simon Cony, 13 Dec. 1336, SC 2 193/1; default, 13 Dec. 1336, SC 2 193/1; debtor, in arrears of repayment, v. John

Drake, 16 Feb. 1337, SC 2 193/1; ale fine, 22 July 1337, HD 86; made illegal path to Townesend, 22 July 1337, HD 86; default, 22 July 1337, 29 Sept. 1337, SC 2 193/1; agreement in debt plea v. James, servant of Walter Bulwer, 4 June 1344, SC 2 193/1; granted lease, without licence, of 1/2 acre to Thomas Balteys, 12 years term, 4 June 1344, SC 2 193/1; order to keep in lord's hand 1/2 acre granted in lease to Thomas Balteys, for 12 years, 15 April 1345, SC 2 193/1; not in tithing, 22 July 1347, HD 85; sold 1/2 acre in Wellgate to Thomas Balteys, 8 April 1348, HD 85a; sold 11/2 roods, in Northfeld, to Richard Speller, 8 April 1348, HD 85a; default, 8 April 1348, HD 85a; for common suit, 14 Oct. 1348, HD 85a; granted lease of 1 acre, at Blakelond, to Richard Speller, 10 Dec. 1348, HD 85a.

Hugh, – , chaplain of the parish of Holkham, creditor v. Thomas de Caldwell, 12 Oct. 1342, SC 2 193/1; non prosecution of plaint v. Thomas de Caldwell, 17 Dec. 1343, SC 2 193/1.

Hugh, Geoffrey son of, contempt of suit, 1 Nov. 1334, HD 84.

Hugh, William son of, contempt of suit, 1 Nov. 1334, HD 84.

Hukster, Goda, creditor v. Margaret Dersy, 15 April 1345, SC 2 193/1.

Hute, William, ale fine, 22 July 1332, HD 82.

Hute, Richard, son of William, not in tithing, 22 July 1332, HD 82.

Idesson, Hugh, regrater of bread and ale, 22 July 1337, HD 86.

Idesson, William, not in tithing, 10 Dec. 1348, HD 85a.

Jagge, Thomas, creditor v. Robert Buleman, order to attach 2 sheep and more, 4 June 1344, SC 2 193/1; creditor v. Thomas le Baye, 8 April 1348, HD 85a; trespass plea v. John Brekepotte, agreement, 28 May 1350, SC 2 193/1; capital pledge, 22 July 1350, HD 87a; ale fine, 22 July 1350, HD 87a.

Jakes, John, dispensed with suit of court until feast of Mary Magdalen, 8 Jan. 1336, HD 85a.

Jakes, Matilda, default, 18 Jan. 1335, HD 85.

James, servant of Walter Bulwer, agreement with William Huberd in debt plea, 4 June 1344, SC 2 193/1.

Jay, Alice, heir with sister Helewise of 2 acres, 11 Dec. 1335, HD 85a; sold a cottage, 30ft. long and 20ft. wide, to William and Alice Randolph, 13 Dec. 1336, SC 2 193/1; failed to glean, 12 Oct. 1342, SC 2 193/1.

Jay, Cecily, sold a plot of land containing 60ft. in length and 40ft. in width to Margaret Crane, 8 Jan. 1336, HD 85.

Jay, Helewise, sold with Alice, her sister, a cottage (30ft. 20ft.) to William and Alice Randolph, 13 Dec. 1336, SC 2 193/1.

Jernemouth, John de, for fealty, 3 July 1332, HD 82; default, 6 May 1333, HD 84; dispensed with suit of court, 25 Jan. 1334, HD 84; did not use lord's mill, 11 Dec. 1335, HD 85a; default, 29 Sept. 1337, SC 2 193/1; dispensed with suit of court, 12 Oct. 1342, SC 2 193/1.

Jerneys, John, not in tithing, 10 Dec. 1348, HD 85a.

Jobyn, Richard, creditor v. John Asty, non prosecution of plaint, 4 June 1344, SC 2 193/1.

Joudy, Adam, default, 6 April 1342, SC 2 193/1; withheld rent 9d., 6 April 1342, SC 2 193/1.

Joudy, Agnes, bought a messuage from John Joudy, 22 July 1347, HD 85a; assize of ale, 22 July 1347, HD 85a; debtor v. William le Somynour, 14 Oct. 1348, HD 85a; default, 14 Oct. 1348, HD 85a; ale fine, 10 Dec. 1348, HD 85a.

Joudy, John, capital pledge, 22 July 1334, HD 84; capital pledge, 22 July 1337, HD 86; agreement in debt plea with Richard Blakeman, messor, 22 July 1347, HD 85a; sold a messuage to Agnes Joudy, 22 July 1347, HD 85a; died, held 4½ acres, closest heir Roger Croude, paid 32d. entry fine, 22 July 1350, HD 87a.

Joudy, Matilda, trespass plea v. Simon Rok, 28 Dec. 1342, SC 2 193/1; debtor v. Richard Boald, order of distraint for answer, 28 Dec. 1342, SC 2 193/1; bought 3 acres from Reynald Crane, without licence, 9 Aug. 1348, HD 87a.

Joule, Godeman and wife Amice, paid rent 10d., 1341–42 *circa*, HD 83; bought ½ rood from Richard Yudekil, at Cleylond, 8 Dec. 1341, HD 83; withheld *precarie*, 4 Dec. 1342, HD 83; held 3 roods with a portion of messuage in the tenement of the heirs of Northgate owing office of messor, 20 Oct. 1347, HD 83; held ½ rood in tenement Yudekil owing office of messor, 9 Dec. 1348, HD 83.

Kele, Gilbert and wife Cecily, sold 1 rood to William de Shereford, 28 May 1350, SC 2 193/1; sold ½ acre to Harvey Doreward, 28 May 1350, SC 2 193/1; granted lease, without licence, of 1 rood, for 5 crops, to Gilbert Stamp, order to seize, 28 May 1350, SC 2 193/1; default, 22 July 1350, HD 87a.

Kele, John, assault by Harvey Doreward who drew blood justly, 22 July 1350, HD 87a; not in tithing, HD 87a.

Kendale, Robert de, default, 8 April 1348, HD 85a; for common suit, 31 March 1349, SC 2 193/1; default, 28 May 1350, SC 2 193/1; default, 22 July 1350, HD 87a.

Kettlestone, Robert de, bought a messuage with croft containing 1½ roods in Northgate from John le Wrighte, 3 July 1332, HD 82; took lease of ½ acre, at Cathil, from Agnes Colyn, 4 years term, 25 Jan. 1334, HD 84; capital pledge, 22 July 1334, HD 84; failure of pledging, 11 Dec. 1335, HD 84; capital pledge, 22 July 1337, HD 86; bought ½ acre from Hugh and Matilda le Souter, 11 Sept. 1337, SC 2 193/1; bought 1 rood from Margaret le Slopere, 11 Sept. 1337, SC 2 193/1; bought 1 rood from Agnes Colyn, 4 June 1344, SC 2 193/1; for common suit, 15 April 1345, SC 2 193/1; order to keep in lord's hand 1 rood purchased from Agnes Colyn, 15 April 1345, SC 2 193/1; did not have his men in his tithing (Payn White, William Ideeson, John son of William de Hindringham), 10 Dec. 1348, HD 85a.

Kettlestone, William de, default, 8 April 1348, HD 85a; essoin for Richard atte Bakhous, 14 Oct. 1348, HD 85a.

Keynot, Robert and wife Agnes, creditor v. Simon Mous, 6 May 1333, HD 84; not prosecuting his plaint in trespass plea v. Matilda Charle, 1 July 1333, HD 84; debtor v. Isabel Hecheman, 11 Sept. 1337, SC 2 193/1; bought from Richard Yudekil ½ acre, at Bondescroft, 8 Dec. 1341, HD 83; bought from Richard Yudekil 1 rood, next to tenement of Bartholomew de Howgate, 8 Dec. 1341, HD 83; messor elect for 1342–3 as co-parcener of tenement Yudekil, 8 Dec. 1342, HD 83; plaintiff in trespass plea v. William de Barney, 22 July 1347, HD 85a; not in tithing, 22 July 1347, HD 85a; withheld 2 days in autumn, 15 Oct. 1347, HD 83; default, 20 Oct. 1347, HD 83; plaintiff in theft plea v. John de Howgate, 9 Dec. 1348, HD 83; defendant in offence (transgression) v. Constance Charle, 9 Dec. 1348, HD 83; withheld 1 day in autumn, 9 Dec. 1348, HD 83; messor designated for 1348–49 as co-parcener of tenement Yudekil with Godeman Joule,

Bartholomew and John de Howgate, 9 Dec. 1348, HD 83; not in tithing, 10 Dec. 1348, HD 85a; default, 22 July 1350, HD 87a.

Kittour, Gilbert, defendant in trespass plea v. Richard atte Bakhous, 31 March 1349, SC 2 193/1.

Knight, Alice, died, held 3½ acres, order to seize in lord's hand, 1 messuage 1 acre were transferred in court to husband Henry, 23 May 1334, HD 85.

Knight, Henry, husband of Alice, default, 18 Jan. 1335, HD 85; was granted a messuage with 1 acre from wife's holding, 23 May 1335, HD 85.

Knight, Robert, creditor, not prosecuting his plaint in debt plea v. Thomas, prior of Peterstone, 11 Sept. 1337, SC 2 193/1; withheld 1 *precaria*, 4 Dec. 1342, HD 83.

King, William, default, 22 July 1337, HD 86.

Kintende, heirs of Richard, withheld grain, 22 July 1332, HD 82.

Lacy, Agnes, granted lease, without licence, 1 rood, at Lambhillbottom, to John (le) Meyre, order to seize in lord's hand, 28 March 1335, HD 84.

Lakeman, Richard, held 1½ roods, at Rusteshowe, and made fealty, 24 April 1332, HD 83.

Lamkin, Cecily, died, held a cottage with a courtyard, order to keep in lord's hand until heir came, 23 May 1334, HD 85; heir, Richard, brother of Cecily, paid heriot 12d. for the cottage, 4 Nov. 1334, HD 85.

Lamkin, Richard, brother of Cecily, and heir for a cottage with a courtyard, 4 Nov. 1334, HD 85.

Lamkin, Margery, for common suit, 23 May 1334, HD 85.

Laner, John, default, 28 March 1335, HD 84.

Langham, Peter de and wife Helewise, in debt plea v. William le Fuller, inquisition ordered, 6 May 1333, HD 84; debtor v. Richard Blakeman, order to come for answer, 6 May 1333, HD 84; took lease, without licence, of 5 roods from John Asty, order to seize, 1 July 1333, HD 84; default, 23 May 1334, HD 84; capital pledge, 22 July 1334, HD 84; bought ½ acre, at Eggemere scote, from Margery Craske, 21 Oct. 1334, HD 84; afferator, 21 Oct. 1334, HD 84; bought 1¼ roods from Peter and Lecia atte Bek, in 2 pieces, at Lambritbotome and at Hagges, 4 Nov. 1334, HD 85; for common suit, 18 Jan. 1335, HD 85; bought, without licence, 1 acre, at Wadelond, from John and Eustace Crane, 28 March 1335, HD 84; capital pledge, 22 July 1337, HD 86; raised fold before time, 22 July 1337, HD 86; defendant in trespass plea v. Bartholomew Carpe, plaint not prosecuted, 11 Sept. 1337, SC 2 193/1; default, order of distraint not executed by messor, 3 Dec. 1339, HD 83; messor, did not perform office, 8 Dec. 1341, HD 83; default, 8 Dec. 1341, HD 83; bought ½ acre and ½ rood from Adam Meson, 6 April 1342, SC 2 193/1.

Langham, Robert de, failed to come for warranty, 20 Jan. 1347, HD 86.

Langley, – de, dispensed with suit of court until next Michaelmas, 14 Oct. 1348, HD 85.

Leman, Alice, marriage licence, 14d., 4 Nov. 1334, HD 85.

Leman, Caterine, widow of Roger, debtor, agreement in debt plea v. Simon Rok, 4 June 1344, SC 2 193/1; made *hamsoken*, with John Crane, on John Shortebar, 22 July 1347, HD 85a; ale fine, 22 Jul. 1347, HD 87a; ale fine, 10 Dec. 1348, HD 85a; ale fine, 22 July 1350, HD 87a.

Leman, Mariot, ale fine, 22 July 1332, HD 82; ale fine, 22 July 1334, HD 84.

Lenn, John de, dispensed with suit of court for 1 year, 22 July 1332, HD 82.

Lettyward, Geoffrey, withheld grain, 22 July 1332, HD 82.

Likesalt, John, default, 21 Oct. 1334, HD 84.

Likesalt, Thomas, 6 May 1333, HD 84.

Lindseye, Robert, default, 6 April 1342, 28 Dec. 1342, SC 2 193/1.

Lode, Harvey, default, 22 July 1332, HD 82; default, 6 May 1333, HD 84; default, 22 June 1334, HD 84; default, 22 July 1334, HD 84; default, 22 July 1337, HD 86; debtor v. Thomas Elwan, 4 June 1344, SC 2 193/1; default, 27 March 1346, HD 86; did not use lord's mill, 20 Jan. 1347, HD 86; inquisition established that Harvey Lode owed 8s. 6d. to Thomas Elwan, order to repay with 12d. damages, 22 July 1347, HD 85a; default, 8 April 1348, HD 85a; for common suit, 14 Oct. 1348, HD 85a: default, 22 July 1350, HD 87a.

Lode, John, pledge in debt plea Harvey Lode v. Thomas Elwan, 4 June 1344, SC 2 193/1.

Lomb, Adam, default, 14 Oct. 1348, HD 85a; for common suit, 31 March 1349, SC 2 193/1; default, 28 May 1350, SC 2 193/1; default, 22 July 1350, HD 87a.

Lomb, John, default, order of distraint for fealty, 3 July 1332, 22 July 1332, HD 82; default, 6 May 1333, HD 84; debtor v. Mariot Godecok, order to come for answer, 6 May 1333, HD 84; debtor v. Muriel Casche, order that she recovered 4s. 5d., 25 Jan. 1334, HD 84; default, 22 July 1334, HD 84; did not use lord's mill, 11 Dec. 1335, HD 85a; withheld all services, order to seize until, 8 Jan. 1336, HD 85a; made illegal path with others beyond land of William Curthun, 22 July 1347, HD 85a; for common suit, 14 Oct. 1348, HD 85a; for common suit, 31 March 1349, SC 2 193/1, default, 28 May 1350, SC 1 193/2, 22 July 1350, HD 87a.

Longe, Henry le, creditor v. John de Bilney, order of distraint of John de Bilney for answer, 11 Dec. 1335, HD 85a.

Longe, Peter le, chaplain, creditor v. Richard Marchal, 3 March 1334, HD 84; order to have Richard Marchal with 8 pledges to answer Peter le Longe, 22 June 1334, HD 84; agreement in debt plea v. Richard Marchal, 21 Oct. 1334, HD 84; essoin in debt plea Robert de Berwick v. James Becces, 8 Jan. 1336, HD 85.

Lorys, Mary, victim of *hamsoken* by Emma Asty, 22 July 1350, HD 87a.

Love, Thomas, fealty, 31 March 1349, SC 2 193/1.

Ludman, Cecily, order of distraint for fealty, 1346, HD 86.

Lydeky, Harvey, default, 22 July 1337, HD 86.

Manneyre, Harvey, default, 25 Sept. 1337, SC 2 193/1.

Mannyng, John, made fealty, held 6 acres, at Howgate, 24 Nov. 1349, HD 83.

Marchal, Alice, sold 3 roods to Thomas de Thornham, 9 Dec. 1348, HD 83.

Marchal, Caterine, agreement in plea of trespass with Gilbert Dering, 23 May 1334, HD 84.

Marchal, Christian, order of distraint for homage and fealty, 1346, HD 86, 15 Oct. 1349, HD 83.

Marchal, Joan, plaintiff in trespass plea v. Gilbert Dering, 23 May 1334, HD 84.

Marchal, Richard, default, 22 July 1332, HD 82; ale fine, 22 July 1332, HD 82; debtor v. Roger Dymes, order of distraint for answer, 25 Jan. 1334, HD 84; debtor v. Peter le Longe, chaplain, order to hold seizures of value 20d., 3

March 1334, 23 May 1334, HD 84; ale fine, 22 July 1334, HD 84; default, 22 July 1334, HD 84; agreement with Peter le Longe, chaplain, 21 Oct. 1334, HD 84; debtor v. Roger Dymes, order of attachment for answer, 1 Nov. 1334, HD 84; debtor v. John Mey, 1 Dec. 1334, 28 March 1335, HD 84; recognized debts v. Roger Dymes and v. John Mey, 28 March 1335, HD 84; default, 22 July 1337, HD 86.

Marchal, Sabina, trespass v. lord, 12 Oct. 1342, SC 2 193/1.

Margery, John, held 3 roods and a portion of messuage in tenement of heirs of Northgate responsible for the office of messor, 20 Oct. 1347, HD 83; default, 8 April HD 85a; default, 14 Oct. 1348, HD 85a; for common suit, 31 March 1349, SC 2 193/1.

Marham, John de, mainpast of the Abbot of West Dereham, made illegal path with sheep over lord's land, 15 April 1345, SC 2 193/1.

Mariot, William, died, held a messuage with croft 1 acre, heirs minors, 6 Dec. 1346, HD 86; order of distraint heirs of William Mariot, 15 Oct. 1349, HD 83.

Mariot, William, essoin in debt plea Simon Silk v. Thomas Maynild, 20 Jan. 1347, HD 86; married Alice Dersy, 10 Dec. 1348, HD 85a; essoin for Ralph Soper, 31 March 1349, SC 2 193/1.

Mason, William, order of distraint for theft of objects (3 cords) of wreck, summons for next court, 20 Jan. 1347, HD 86, 22 July 1347, HD 85a, 8 April 1348, HD 85a, 9 Aug. 1348, HD 87a, 14 Oct. 1348, HD 85a, 10 Dec. 1348, HD 85a, 31 March 1349, SC 2 193/1, 15 April 1349, SC 2 193/1.

Massingham, Harvey de, paid rent, 6 April 1342, SC 2 193/1; took lease of 2 1/2 acres from John de Caldwell (and John Mey), 5 years term, 17 Dec. 1343, SC 2 193/1; took lease of 1 1/2 acres from John de Caldwell (and Cecily Erneys), 17 Dec. 1343, SC 2 193/1.

Matilda, William son of, essoin for Robert de Kettlestone, 15 April 1345, SC 2 193/1.

Maynard, John, order of distraint for fealty, 3 July 1332, HD 82; withheld grain, 22 July 1332, HD 82; default, 22 June 1334, HD 84; took lease of 1 1/2 roods, at Hillergatecroft, from Peter and Lecia atte Bek, 4 years term, 4 Nov. 1334, HD 85; default, 4 June 1337, SC 2 193/1; default, 4 June 1344, SC 2 193/1; for common suit, 15 April 1345, SC 2 193/1; did not use lord's mill, 20 Jan. 1347, HD 85; for common suit, 15 April 1345, SC 2 193/1; default, 14 Oct. 1348, HD 85a; fealty, 31 March 1349, SC 2 193/1; default, 22 July 1350, HD 87a.

Maynild, John, debtor v. Simon Silk, 27 Jan. 1347, HD 86; default, 8 April 1348, HD 85a.

Maynild, Thomas, creditor v. Simon Silk, order to collect 7s. 3d., and 3d. damages from Simon, 20 Jan. 1347, HD 85a.

Meson, Adam and wife Alice, sold 1/2 acre and 1/2 rood to Peter de Langham, 6 April 1342, SC 2 193/1; withheld 2d., SC 2 193/1.

Mey, John, agreement in trespass plea with John le Smith (junior), 3 July 1332, HD 82; afferator, 3 July 1332, 22 July 1332, HD 82; afferator, 3 July 1332, 22 July 1332, HD 82; capital pledge, 22 July 1332, HD 82; ale taster, 22 July 1332, HD 82; raised a fold unfairly, 22 July 1332, HD 82; afferator elect, 6 May 1333, HD 84; plaintiff v. Andrew Underclynt, 43d. damages, 25 Jan. 1334, HD 84; afferator, 25 Jan. 1334, 23 May 1334, HD 84; bought 3 roods from Matilda, wife of Hugh le Souter, 23 May 1334, HD 84; creditor v.

Simon atte Cros, non prosecution of plaint, 22 June 1334, HD 84; capital pledge, 22 July 1334, HD 84; afferator, 22 June 1334, HD 84; fined as pledge for Walter Bulwer, non prosecution of plaint v. Richard Blakeman in plea of novel disseisin, 22 July 1334, HD 84; failed to control assize as ale taster, 22 July 1334, HD 84; afferator, 22 July 1334, HD 84; raised a fold before time, 22 July 1334, HD 84; bought 1 acre 1 rood, at Kirchescroft, from Margery daughter of Geoffrey de Sharrington, 21 Oct. 1334, HD 84; bought 1/2 rood from Bartholomew Coltyng, 1 Nov. 1334, HD 84; failed to comply with requirements of office of messor, contempt of court, 8 Dec. 1334, HD 84; creditor v. Richard Marchal, 8 Dec. 1334, HD 84; agreement in debt plea v. Richard Marchal, 28 March 1335, HD 84; failure in pledging, 11 Dec. 1335, HD 85a; failed to carry duties of office, 11 Dec. 1335, HD 85a; capital pledge, 22 July 1337, HD 86; raised fold before time, 22 July 1337, HD 86; hue and cry v. Roger le Thakster, 22 July 1337, HD 86; damages to pasture of lord, 22 July 1337, HD 86; agreement in debt plea v. John Albere of Creake, 11 Sept. 1337, SC 2 193/1; agreement in debt plea v. Simon Mous, 29 Sept. 1337, SC 2 193/1; default as juror, 6 April 1342, SC 2 193/1; withheld rent, 6 April 1342, SC 2 193/1; bought 1 rood from Mariot Slopere and Beatrice, her daughter, 9 Aug. 1342, HD 87a; default, 28 Dec. 1342, SC 2 193/1; sold, without licence, 1 1/4 roods to John Speller, order to keep in lord's hand, 12 Oct. 1342, SC 2 193/1; afferator, 12 Oct. 1342, SC 2 193/1; granted at farm 2 1/2 acres to Thomas and John de Caldwell, 17 Dec. 1343, SC 2 193/1; plaintiff in trespass plea v. William de Stodeye, 4 June 1344, SC 2 193/1; creditor v. Lawrence Skinner, non prosecution of plaint, 4 June 1344, SC 2 193/1; sold 1 rood to John Speller, 4 June 1344, SC 2 193/1; for common suit, 15 April 1345, SC 2 193/1; sold 2 roods to Bartholomew le Miller, 15 April 1345, SC 2 193/1; for common suit, 20 Jan. 1347, HD 86; failure to carry office of ale taster, 22 July 1347, HD 85a; afferator, 22 July 1347, HD 85a; creditor v. Margaret, widow of Thomas Coupere, 8 April 1348, HD 85a; sold 1 1/2 roods to Roger de Bilney, 8 April 1348, HD 85a: bought 1 rood from Sibyl Debet, 8 April 1348, HD 85a; creditor v. Simon Silk and Helewise Golde, 10 Dec. 1348, HD 85a; sold 1 acre to John Brid, 10 Dec. 1348, HD 85a; failed to carry duties of ale taster, 10 Dec. 1348, HD 85a; debtor v. Simon and Helewise Silk, plaint not prosecuted, acquitted, 31 March 1349, SC 2 193/1; debtor v. John le Wrighte, 4s. 10d. agreement for repayment next Saint Michael, 31 March 1349, SC 2 193/1; sold 3 roods to Edmund Pynch, 5 Oct, 1349, SC 2 193/1.

Mey, Sibyl, wife of John, ale fine, 22 July 1347, HD 85a; ale fine, 10 Dec. 1348, HD 85a.

Meydegong, Richard, took lease of 1 rood from John Mey, 15 April 1345, SC 2 193/1; bought 1/2 rood from Helewise Quyn, 15 April 1345, SC 2 193/1; creditor v. John Asty, 8 April 1348, HD 85a; creditor v. Richard Blakeman, 8 April 1348, HD 85a, 9 Aug. 1348, HD 87a.

Meyre, Helewise (le), ale fine, 22 July 1332, HD 82; withheld grain, 22 July 1332, HD 82; ale fine, 22 July 1334, HD 84; ale fine, 22 July 1337, HD 86; default of tenants of Helewise (le) Meyre, 1 Dec. 1340, HD 83; died, held a messuage with 3 roods, heir John, her son, held also a messuage with 3 roods of which Gilbert Curthun is heir, 16 Nov. 1345, HD 83.

Meyre, John (le), default, 6 May 1333, HD 83; default, 1 Nov. 1334, HD 84; took lease of 1 rood, without licence, at Lambshilbotome, from Agnes Lacy, 28 March 1335, HD 84; default, 6 April 1342, SC 2 193/1; withheld rent 2d., 6 April 1342, SC 2 193/1; died, held a messuage and a croft, heir son Peter, 6 Dec. 1346, HD 86.

Meyre, Peter (senior), pledge in debt plea Henry Speller v. Gilbert le Souter, 25 Jan. 1334, HD 84; pledge in trespass plea Joan Marchal v. Gilbert Dering, 23 May 1334, HD 84; defendant in trespass plea v. Bartholomew Carpe, 11 Sept. 1337, 29 Sept. 1337, SC 2 193/1; debtor v. John atte Crundel, 28 Dec. 1342, SC 2 193/1; false quarrel, 28 Dec. 1342, SC 2 193/1; for common suit, 22 July 1347, HD 85a; made fealty for 1 cottage held in socage, 15 Oct. 1349, HD 83; raised fold out of time, 22 July 1350, HD 87a; plaintiff in trespass plea v. Gilbert Neel, order to collect 6s. 8d. from Gilbert for Peter, 26 Nov. 1350, HD 87a.

Meyre, Peter, son of John, minor, settled unfairly in a messuage and croft seized after death of John, his father, as he was under age, 6 Dec. 1346, HD 86; order to seize Peter, minor son of John (le) Meyre, with tenements held, 7 July 1350, HD 83.

Meyre, Thomas, not in tithing, 22 July 1350, HD 87a.

Meyre, William, creditor v. Roger le Reve, day given, 6 May 1333, HD 82; agreement in debt plea v. Roger le Reve and Cecily, his wife, 1 July 1333, HD 84.

Middleton, Mathew de and wife Matilda, default, held 1/2 acre 1/2 rood, 6 Dec. 1346, HD 86.

Mileham, John de, mainpast of the Abbot of West Dereham, made illegal path with sheep, 15 April 1345, SC 2 193/1.

Miller (Molner), Bartholomew le, default, 22 July 1332, bought 1/2 rood, at Wellgate, from John Sweyn, 25 Jan. 1334, HD 84; took lease of 1 rood from Harvey, his brother, 4 years term, 4 Nov. 1334, HD 84; bought 1 rood from Richard Swerde, 8 Jan. 1336, HD 85a; sold a messuage and 1/2 acre to Adam Cage and Alice, his wife, 13 Dec. 1336, SC 2 193/1; defendant in trespass plea v. Reynald Crane, owed 3 stones of corn as damages, order to collect, 11 Sept. 1337, SC 2 193/1; debtor (with John Mey) v. John Albere of Creake, agreement, 11 Sept. 1337, SC 2 193/1; agreement in debt plea v. Simon Mous, 29 Sept. 1337, SC 2 193/1; creditor v. John Acke, 6 April 1342, SC 2 193/1; non prosecution of plaint v. John Acke in debt plea, 6 April 1342, SC 2 193/1; bought, without licence, 2 roods from John Mey, order to keep in lord's hand, 12 Oct. 1342, SC 2 193/1; bought, without licence, 2 roods from John Mey, order to keep in lord's hand, 17 Dec. 1343, SC 2 193/1; bought 1 rood, at Seagateway, from Simon and Cecily Mous, 17 Dec. 1343, SC 2 193/1; bought 1/2 acre, at Langefurlong, from Beatrice, daughter of Richard le Slopere, 17 Dec. 1343, SC 2 193/1; attorney for Thomas Elwan (creditor) in debt plea v. Harvey Lode, 4 June 1344, SC 2 193/1; sold a messuage and 3 acres to Geoffrey and Matilda, 4 June 1344, SC 2 193/1; bought a cottage with 1 rood from Margaret daughter of Cecily atte Hil, 4 June 1344, SC 2 193/1; bought 2 roods from John Mey, 15 April 1345, SC 2 193/1; defendant in trespass plea v. John Speller, 15 April 1345, SC 2 193/1; bought 1 acre 1 rood from Margaret Peper, 15 April 1345, SC 2 193/1; bought, without licence, a plot of land, at the Stathe, from Alice atte Hil, order to seize, 1346, HD 86; afferator, 22 July 1347, HD 87a; afferator, 22 July 1347, HD 85a; afferator, 16 Dec. 1348, HD 85a; bought 1/2 acre 1/2 rood, in several pieces, 11/2 roods at the end of Robert de Kettlestone's croft and 1 rood at Scamlond, from Margaret Mous, 31 March 1349, SC 2 193/1; plea, at the Hundred Court, v. Roger le Smith, 31 March 1349, SC 2 193/1; pledge for prosecution in debt plea Helen Snele (creditor) v. Simon Silk, 28 May 1350, SC 2 193/1.

Miller (Molner), Edmund le, neglect of suit of court, 1 Nov. 1334, HD 84; debtor v. Richard Blakeman, 11 Dec. 1335, HD 84; false claim of Richard Blakeman in debt plea, Edmund acquitted, 8 Jan. 1336, HD 85a; default, 22 July 1337, HD 86; dispensed with suit of court, for 1 year, 11 Sept. 1337, SC 2 193/1.

Miller (Molner), Harvey, brother of Bartholomew, and wife Alice, granted lease of 1 rood to Bartholomew, his brother, 4 years term, 4 Nov. 1334, HD 85; bought a plot of land (50ft. by 23ft.) from Peter and Lecia Fairweder, 4 Nov. 1334, HD 85; sold 1/2 rood and 1/4 of 1/2 rood, in Estgate croft, to Sibyl Fox, 18 Jan. 1335, HD 85.

Miller (Molner), Thomas le, failure of pledging, 17 Dec. 1343, SC 2 193/1; sold a cottage to Beatrice Schiphorte, 28 May 1350, SC 2 193/1.

Miller (Molner), Walter, for injurious gesture in full court, 20 Jan. 1347, HD 86; agreement in trespass case with Matilda Seburg, 22 July 1347, HD 85a.

Moine, Martin, default as juror, 6 April 1342, SC 2 193/1; withheld rent 2d. ob., 6 April 1342, SC 2 193/1; essoin in debt plea John atte Crundel v. Peter Meyre, 28 Dec. 1342, SC 2 193/1; made illegal path, 22 July 1347, HD 85a.

Mondes, John, fealty, 31 March 1349, SC 2 193/1.

Mosewell, John de and wife Agnes, debtor v. Geoffrey Saundre, order of distraint to be at next court, 12 Oct. 1342, SC 2 193/1.

Mous, Cecily, wife of Simon Mous, ale fine, 22 July 1332, HD 82; ale fine, 22 July 1334, HD 84; ale fine, 22 July 1337, HD 86.

Mous, John, not in tithing, 22 July 1332, HD 84.

Mous, Margaret, sold 1/2 acre 1/2 rood (11/2 roods at the end of Robert de Kettlestone's croft, and 1 rood at Scamlond) to Bartholomew le Miller, 31 March 1349, SC 2 193/1.

Mous, Simon and wife Cecily, debtor v. Thomas Storm, order of distraint for answer, 3 July 1332, HD 82; creditor v. Rosa Bulwer, 3 July 1332, HD 82; agreement with William son of Alice in plea of transgression, 3 July 1332, HD 82; order of distraint in debt plea v. Thomas Storm, 22 July 1332, HD 82; withheld grain, 22 July 1332, HD 82; debtor v. Robert Keynot, 6 May 1333, HD 84; debtor v. Yve, son of John Roger, order to have better pledges, 6 May 1333, HD 84; agreement with Roger de Berwick in debt plea, 1 July 1333, HD 84; plea of detention of chattels v. John Bulwer, 25 Jan. 1334, 3 March 1334, 23 May 1334, HD 84; defendant in trespass plea v. Richard Blakeman, 22 July 1334, 1 Nov. 1334, HD 84; debtor v. Richard Blakeman, order of attachment for answer, 8 Dec. 1334, HD 84; debtor v. Roger Crane, order of attachment for answer, 8 Dec. 1334, HD 84; debtor v. Sewal Hereward, 11 Sept. 1335, HD 85a; order of distraint for next court, 11 Dec. 1335, HD 85a; debtor v. Richard son of Ralph Henry, chaplain, 11 Dec. 1335, HD 85a; did not use lord's mill, 11 Dec. 1335, HD 85a; order of distraint for next court to answer John Mey, 8 Jan. 1336, HD 85a; in debt plea v. Sewal Hereward, non prosecution of plaint, 11 Sept. 1337, SC 2

193/1; debtor v. James, chaplain of Northcreyk, recognized debt of 17s. in association with Walter Bulwer, 11 Sept. 1337, SC 2 193/1; agreement in debt plea with John Mey, 29 Sept. 1337, SC 2 193/1; sold 1 rood, at Seagateway, next to tenement of Cecily Dollow, to Bartholomew le Miller, 17 Dec. 1343, SC 2 193/1.

Muriold, John, default, 6 April 1342, SC 2 193/1; did not use lord's mill, 20 Jan. 1347, HD 86.

Nath, John, of Wells, agreement with lord after damages made to the land by his cattle, 26 Nov. 1350, HD 87a.

Neel, Caterine, allowed by the steward to withdraw her quarrel, 11 Dec. 1335, HD 85a; took lease of a messuage from John Asty, 15 April 1345, SC 2 193/1; made illegal path with sheep, 15 April 1345, SC 2 193/1; trespass with pigs in lord's meadow, 15 April 1345, SC 2 193/1.

Neel, Gilbert, defendant in trespass plea v. John Aynild, order of attachment for next court, 22 July 1350, HD 87a; damages made by the mainpast of Gilbert in lord's corn, 22 July 1350, HD 87a; defendant in trespass plea v. William Curthoun, 26 Nov. 1350, HD 87a; defendant in trespass plea v. Peter Meyre, 26 Nov. 1350, HD 87a; order to collect 6s. 8d. for damages to be paid to Peter Meyre, 26 Nov. 1350, HD 87a; defendant in trespass plea v. John Speller, chaplain, order to attach Gilbert for next court, 26 Nov. 1350, HD 87a.

Nore, Richard, creditor, not prosecuting his plaint v. John Speller, 4 June 1344, SC 2 193/1.

Northerne, Thomas le, son of Richard, not prosecuting his plaint v. William Gunnok in debt plea, 3 July 1332, HD 82; agreement with Roger Ode in debt plea, 3 March 1334, HD 84; debtor v. Sewal Hereward, 11 Dec. 1335, HD 85a; order of distraint to answer Sewal Hereward in debt plea, 8 Jan. 1336, HD 85; did not come to answer Sewal Hereward, 11 Sept. 1337, SC 2 193/1; essoin for William le Wake, 12 Oct. 1342, SC 2 193/1; essoin for Henry Camplioun, 31 March 1349, SC 2 193/1.

Northgate, Agnes de, daughter of Thomas, heir of Roger de Northgate, her uncle, of 1 acre shared with 3 cousins, Amice, Cecily and Helewise, 1 Dec. 1340, HD 83; paid rent 9d., c.1341–42, HD 83.

Northgate, Cecily de, daughter of Richard, heir of Roger de Northgate, her uncle, of 1 acre shared with 3 cousins, Agnes, Amice and Helewise, 1 Dec. 1340, HD 83; default, 4 Dec. 1342, HD 83; sold 1 acre 3 1/2 roods in several pieces to William de Barney, 15 Nov. 1343, HD 83.

Northwynd, Cecily, ale and bread fines, 22 July 1347, HD 85a; ale and bread fines, 10 Dec. 1348, HD 85a.

Ode, Robert, capital pledge, 22 July 1337, HD 86; raised fold before time, 22 July 1337, HD 86.

Ode, Roger, capital pledge, 21 July 1332, HD 82; agreement in debt plea v. Muriel Casche, 3 March 1334, HD 84; agreement in debt plea v. Thomas le Northerne, 3 March 1334, HD 84; afferator, 3 March 1334, 22 July 1334, HD 84; raised fold before time, 22 July 1334, HD 84; debtor v. Robert Andrew, 11 Dec. 1335, HD 85a; agreement in debt plea v. Robert Andrew, repayment of 28s. 8d. scheduled for next Christmas, 8 Jan. 1336, HD 85a.

Olney, Alice de, defendant in trespass plea v. Richard Blakeman, 22 June 1334, HD 84; order to attach Alice for answer in trespass plea v. Richard Blakeman, 22 July 1334, HD 84; victim of *hamsoken* (house breaking) by Richard Blakeman, 22 July 1334, HD 84; order to attach for answer in trespass plea v. Richard Blakeman, 1 Nov. 1334, HD 84; default, 8 April 1348, HD 85a.

Osbern, Walter, default as juror, 6 April 1342, SC 2 193/1.

Osmund, William, trespass with sheep in the lord's marsh, 22 July 1347, HD 85a.

Otes, Alice, daughter of Hugh, agreement with Agnes Bulwer over seizure of a cow, 3 July 1332, HD 82; ale fine, 22 July 1332, HD 82; ale fine, 22 July 1332, HD 82; ale fine, 22 July 1334, HD 84; ale fine 22 July 1337, HD 86; defendant with Isabel Payn in debt plea v. John Hoddes, order of distraint of Isabel, 22 July 1337, HD 86; bought 1/2 rood from Richard Yudekil, 4 Dec. 1342, HD 83; ale fine, 22 July 1347, HD 85a; ale fine, 10 Dec. 1348, HD 85a; ale fine, 22 July 1350, HD 87a.

Otes, Beatrice, default, 3 July 1332, HD 82; dispensed with suit of court for 1 year, 11 Sept. 1337, SC 2 193/1; default, 12 Oct. 1342, SC 2 193/1.

Otes, John, default, 22 July 1350, HD 87a.

Otes, Matilda, daughter of Alice, bought with her mother 1/2 rood from Richard Yudekil, 4 Dec. 1342, HD 83.

Page, William, pledge for William de Barney in debt plea v. Richard Speller, 31 March 1349, SC 2 193/1.

Parmelay, Godman, for common suit, 4 Nov. 1334, HD 85.

Parmelay, John, granted a cottage to Lucy, his daughter, who granted it back for all his life with a reversion clause, 22 July 1332, HD 82; withheld grain, 22 July 1332, HD 82; for common suit, 4 Nov. 1334, HD 85; made illegal path to Townesend, 22 July 1336, HD 86.

Parmelay, Lucy, ceded back for life to her father, John, a cottage with a reversion clause, 22 July 1332, HD 82.

Palmer, Henry, chaplain, 12 Oct. 1342, SC 2 193/1.

Palmer, Thomas, of Burnham Norton, default, 16 Feb. 1337, 11 Sept. 1337, 29 Sept. 1337, 4 June 1344, SC 2 193/1; default, 27 March 1346, 10 June 1346, HD 86; default, 28 May 1350, SC 2 193/1; 22 July 1350, HD 87a.

Parson, Cecily, came to court to pay rents and services of all her tenants, 6 April 1342, SC 2 193/1.

Paye, John, essoin in debt plea, John Skinner v. Richard Boald, 28 Dec. 1342, SC 2 193/1.

Paye, William, damage in corn field of the lord with his horses, 22 July 1347, HD 85a; damage in corn field of the lord with his horses, 10 Dec. 1348, HD 85a.

Payn, Isabel, debtor v. John Hoddes, order of distraint of Isabel, 22 July 1337, HD 86; sold with Matilda Payn 1 acre, in South Field, to Gilbert Aldefader, 31 March 1349, SC 2 193/1.

Payn, Matilda, made leyrwite 15 April 1345, SC 2 193/1; sold with Isabel Payn 1 acre in South Field to Gilbert Aldefader, 31 March 1349, SC 2 193/1.

Payn, Richard, trespass with pigs in lord's meadow, 15 April 1345, SC 2 193/1; made illegal path beyond land of William Curthon, 22 July 1347, HD 85a; took away a cow from the park for assesment, by the agent of the King, of the 15th, 22 July 1347, HD 85a.

Pees, William, not in tithing, 22 July 1347, HD 85; not in tithing, 10 Dec. 1348, HD 85a.

Pellypar, John, defendant in trespass plea v. Thomas de Thornham, non prosecution of plaint, 15 April 1345, SC 2 193/1.

Pennyng, Geoffrey, bought 2 acres from Cecily Erneys, order to keep in lord's hand, 4 June 1344, 15 April 1345, SC 2 193/1; debtor v. Simon Silk, order to collect 4s. due to Simon, 14 Oct. 1348, 10 Dec. 1348, HD 85a; default, 28 May 1350, SC 2 193/1.

Pennyng, John, default, 22 July 1350, HD 87a.

Pentney, William de, essoin for trespass plea William de Stodeye v. John Mey, 4 June 1344, SC 2 193/1.

Peper, Mabel, sold 1½ roods, in Chercheseld, to Beatrice atte Drove, 12 Oct. 1342, SC 2 193/1; sold 1 rood, next to the Clynt, to Roger Crane, 17 Dec. 1343, SC 2 193/1; sold ½ acre, in Adowgate, to Gilbert Aldefader, 20 Jan. 1347, HD 86.

Peper, Margaret, debtor v. Muriel Casche, failed to repay 12d., order to collect 12d., 12 Oct. 1342, SC 2 193/1; trespass v. Muriel Casche, 12 Oct. 1342, SC 2 193/1; sold 1 rood to Roger Crane, 15 April 1345, SC 2 193/1; sold 1 acre 1 rood to Bartholomew le Miller, 15 April 1345, SC 2 193/1.

Peterstone, Prior of, order of distraint for fealty, 3 July 1332, HD 82; debtor v. Robert Proppe, non prosecution of plaint, 6 May 1333, 1 July 1333, HD 84; default, 23 May 1334, HD 85; for common suit, 24 March 1337, HD 84; debtor v. Robert Knight, non prosecution of plaint, 11 Sept. 1337, SC 2 193/1; damages in pasture of lord, 22 July 1337, HD 86; order to distrain the new Prior for fealty, 3 Dec. 1339, HD 83; order of distraint for fealty, 1 Dec. 1340, HD 83; order of distraint for fealty, 8 Dec. 1341, HD 83; creditor v. Richard Speller, agreement in debt plea, 4 June 1344, SC 2 193/1; order of distraint for fealty, 1346, HD 86; default, 9 Dec. 1348, HD 83; order of distraint for fealty, 15 Oct. 1349, HD 83.

Pilch, Edmund, creditor v. Simon Silk, 5 Oct. 1349, SC 2 193/1; bought 3 roods, in mortgage, from John Mey, 5 Oct. 1349; order to attach Simon Silk to answer Edmund, 28 May 1350, SC 2 193/1; agreement in debt plea, Simon Silk recognized debt of 2s., 22 July 1350, HD 87a; trespass with cattle, 23 Nov. 1350, HD 87a.

Pink, William, essoin for Harvey Yudekil, 28 May 1350, SC 2 193/1; bought 3 roods from Robert Keynot, to hold by the rod, 7 July 1350, HD 83.

Pontaye, Agnes, debtor v. John Crane, order to collect 12d., 4 June 1344, SC 2 193/1.

Pope, Harvey, creditor v. Mariota Slopere, 11 Dec. 1335, HD 85a; creditor, non prosecution of plaint v. Mariota Slopere in debt plea, 8 Jan. 1336, HD 85a; agreement in debt plea v. Richard Blakeman, 8 Jan. 1336, HD 85a; creditor v. Adam Tyson, 6 April 1342, SC 2 193/1; order to distrain Adam Tyson to answer Harvey in debt plea, 28 Dec. 1342, SC 2 193/1; plaintiff in transgression plea v. William Smodding, 14 Oct. 1348, HD 85a; agreement in transgression plea v. William Smodding, 10 Dec. 1384, HD 85a; default, 28 May 1350, SC 2 193/1; capital pledge, 22 July 1350.

Pope, Simon, died, held half a cottage, no heir came forward, order to keep in lord's hand, 8 April 1348, HD 85a.

Praywen, Edmund, default, order of distraint for fealty, 3 July 1332, dispensed with suit of court until next Saint Michael, 1 Nov. 1334, HD 84; dispensed with suit of court until feast of Mary Magdalen, 8 Jan. 1336, HD 85a; default for 1 *precaria* in autumn, 11 Sept. 1337, SC 2 193/1; default, 11 Sept. 1337, SC 2 193/1.

Presterson, Helewise, ale fine, 22 July 1337, HD 86.

Presterson, Thomas, ale and bread fine, regrater of bread and ale, 22 July 1332, HD 82; regrater of bread and ale, 22 July 1334, HD 84; not in tithing, 22 July 1337, HD 86.

Proppe, Robert, creditor v. Prior de Peterstone, order to attach the Prior for answer, 6 May 1333, HD 84; non prosecution of plaint v. the Prior of Peterstone, in debt plea, 1 July 1333, HD 84.

Pye, John and wife Hilda, debtor v. Nicholas and Agnes de Barsham, order to collect 7d. for keeping 2 bushels of barley, 6 April 1342, SC 2 193/1.

Pygg, Simon, fealty for tenure of several tenements, 15d. services per annum, and 3 suits of court, 26 Nov. 1350, HD 87a.

Qwyne, Helewise, sold 2 roods to Helen Cat, 4 June 1344, SC 2 193/1; sold 1/2 rood to Richard Meydegong, 15 April 1345, SC 2 193/1; sold 1 rood to John and Margaret Speller, 20 Jan. 1347, HD 86; sold 1/2 acre, in Burgatescroft, to John and Margaret Speller, 8 April 1348, HD 85a.

Qwyne, Payn, capital pledge, 22 July 1350, HD 87a.

Qwyne, Thomas, default, 29 Sept. 1337, SC 2 193/1; default, 15 April 1345, SC 2 193/1; default, 20 June 1346, HD 86; did not use lord's mill, 20 Jan. 1347, HD 86; default, 8 April 1348, HD 85a; default, 14 Oct. 1348, HD 85a; default, 22 July 1350, HD 87a.

Ram, Peter, chaplain, of Stiffkey, creditor, represented by attorney Henry le Clerk, v. Richard Blakeman, summons for Richard to be at next court, 9 Aug. 1348, 14 Oct. 1348, HD 85a; agreement in debt plea with Richard Blakeman about payment of 8s. (4s. at Pentecost, 4s. at Michaelmas), 31 March 1349, SC 2 193/1.

Randolph, William and wife Alice, default, 22 July 1332, HD 82; default, 22 July 1334, HD 84; default, 8 Dec. 1334, HD 84; bought a cottage from Helewise and Alice Jay, 13 Dec. 1336, SC 2 193/1; failed to glean, 12 Oct. 1342, SC 2 193/1; default, 14 Oct. 1348, HD 85a; fealty, 31 March 1349, SC 2 193/1.

Raven, Agnes, sold 3/4 rood, at Shipmancros, to William Curthoun, 3 July 1332, HD 82.

Redelyn, Richard de, trespass with sheep on lord's land, order of distraint, 12 Oct. 1342, SC 2 193/1.

Reedham, Richard de, trespass with sheep on lord's land, 17 Dec. 1343, SC 2 193/1.

Renpage, John, did not use lord's mill, 20 Jan. 1347, HD 86.

Repps, Roger de, baker, withheld grain, 22 July 1332, HD 82; bread fine, 22 July 1332, HD 82; capital pledge, 22 July 1332, HD 82; his mainpast, Sewal, made illegal path, 22 July 1332, HD 82; capital pledge, 22 July 1334, HD 84; as baker, bread fine, 22 July 1334, HD 84; capital pledge, 22 July 1337, HD 86; as baker, bread fine, 22 July 1337, HD 86.

Reeve, Roger le and wife Cecily, debtor v. William Meyre, day given without essoin, 6 May 1333, HD 84; creditor v. William le Fuller, order to distrain William for answer, 6 May 1333, HD 84; afferator, 6 May 1333, HD 84; agreement with William Meyre in debt plea, 1 July 1333, HD 84; order of distraint of William le Fuller for answer in debt plea, 1 July 1333, HD 84; afferator, 23 March 1334, 8 Dec. 1334, HD 84.

Reynald, Agnes, sold 1 rood, at Lambshill, to William Curthoun, 3 July 1332, HD 82.

Reynald, Thomas, creditor, agreement in debt plea with Mariota Underclynt, 25 Jan. 1334, HD 84; default, 6 April 1342, SC 2 193/1; withheld rent, 6 April 1342, SC 2 193/1; default, 28 Dec. 1342, SC 2 193/1.

Reynes, Emma, died, held 1/2 acre, order to distrain heir, William le Souter, 8 Dec. 1341, HD 83.

Ro, Agnes le, bought 1 rood from Beatrice Huberd, 15 April 1345, SC 2 193/1.

Robert, –, mainpast of Matilda Charle, made illegal path with sheep from Howgate to the hill, 22 July 1334, HD 84.

Robert, –, the physician, of Burnham, creditor v. John de Bilney, 22 July 1332, HD 82.

Roger, –, son of Emma, order of distraint for fealty, 1346, HD 86; order of distraint for homage and fealty, 15 Oct. 1349, HD 83.

Rok, Simon, trespass v. Matilda Joudy, 28 Dec. 1342, SC 2 193/1; failed to pay Matilda Joudy, order to collect, 28 Dec. 1342, SC 2 193/1; creditor in debt plea v. Caterine Leman, 4 June 1344, SC 2 193/1; for common suit, 15 April 1345, SC 2 193/1; for common suit, 14 Oct. 1348, HD 85a; fealty, 31 March 1349, SC 2 193/1.

Rolond, Harvey, default, 22 July 1332, HD 82; default, 22 July 1334, HD 84; regrater of ale, 22 July 1337, HD 86.

Rolond, John, default, 22 July 1350, HD 87a.

Roper, Simon, failed to glean, 12 Oct. 1342, SC 2 193/1; essoin for Thomas Coupere, 15 April 1345, SC 2 193/1.

Rotele, Christian, responsible for office of messor, 4 Nov. 1334, HD 83; collector (Sept. 1334–Sept. 1335), 10 Nov. 1335, HD 83.

Rotele, John, order to take in lord's hand a messuage and 4 acres held, by the rod, for withholding of services and customary dues, 1346, HD 86; elected and sworn in as messor, 6 Dec. 1346, HD 86; withheld 1 day in autumn, 20 Oct. 1347, HD 83; default, 7 July 1350, HD 83.

Runton, Ralph de, default, 6 April 1342, SC 2 193/1; default, 28 Dec. 1342, SC 2 193/1.

Rust, John, put corn out of villeinage, 1 Nov. 1334, HD 84.

Rust, Martin, held a cottage with 1/2 acre now in lord's hand, timber and roofing of house recently destroyed worth 12d., services 20d., 8 Dec. 1334, HD 84.

Ryburgh, Gervase de, ale taster, 22 July 1332, HD 82; sold 11/2 acres and 1/2 rood in 7 pieces to John le Smith, 22 June 1334, HD 84; ale taster, 22 July 1334, HD 84; afferator, 22 July 1334, HD 84; granted lease of 1 rood to John Blakeman, at Dalebrest, 4 years term, 28 March 1335, HD 84; prosecution pledge in debt pleas, Robert Andrew v. John de Bilney and Geoffrey Bulwer v. Robert and Cecily Erneys, 3 Dec. 1336, SC 2 193/1; essoin for Simon Burgoine v. John Crane in debt plea, 12 Oct. 1342, SC 2 193/1.

Sabe (Sabbe), May, regrater of ale, 22 July 1350, HD 87a.

Sabe (Sabbe), Stephen, failed to glean, 12 Oct. 1342, SC 2 193/1.

Saundre, Geoffrey and wife Alice, creditor v. John and Agnes de Mosewell, order to distrain John and Agnes for answer, at next court, 12 Oct. 1342, SC 2 193/1; debtor v. Simon Burgoine, failed in repayment, order to collect 1 bushel barley for Simon, 17 Dec. 1343, SC 2 193/1; did not use lord's mill, 4 June 1344, SC 2 193/1; executor of the will of John Crane senior, 20 Jan. 1347, HD 86; creditor as executor with Mariota Crane v. Richard Blakeman, order to collect 5s., 20 Jan. 1347, HD 86; creditor as executor with Mariota Crane v. Robert and John Erneys, order to collect 5s., 20 Jan. 1347, HD 86; false quarrel v. Robert and John Erneys, 20 Jan. 1347, HD 86; capital pledge, fined for not having William and Richard Huberd in his tithing, 22 July 1347, HD 85a; granted lease of 1 acre to William Bengamyn, of Walsingham, 9 years term, 8 April 1348, HD 85; attorney for William le Somynour, 14 Oct. 1348, HD 85a; capital pledge, fined for not having William and Richard Huberd in his tithing, 10 Dec. 1348, HD 85a; took on a messuage and 3 roods from lord, land formerly to Alice le Souter, 28 May 1350, SC 2 193/1; took on a messuage 1/2 rood from lord, 28 May 1350, SC 2 193/1; capital pledge, 22 July 1350, SC 2 193/1; pledge in the purchase by John Geyste of the marriage and custody of Richard Elverich, 22 July 1350, HD 87a.

Saundre, John, messor, attorney for John Crane, 22 July 1347, HD 85a; afferator, 22 July 1347, HD 85a; afferator, 10 Dec. 1348, HD 85a.

Sharrington, Geoffrey de, order of distraint for fealty, 3 July 1332, HD 82; creditor v. Henry de Shropham, 1 July 1333, HD 84; died, held 1 acre 1 rood, heir, daughter, Margery, heriot 32d., 25 Jan. 1334, HD 84.

Sharrington, Margery de, daughter and heir of Geoffrey, for 1 acre 1 rood, paid heriot 32d. and made fealty, 25 Jan. 1334, HD 84; default, 22 June 1334, HD 84; sold 1 acre 1 rood, in Kirches croft, to John Mey, 21 Oct. 1334, HD 84.

Schosman, heir of, sold 1 rood to Richard Swerde, 8 Jan. 1336, HD 85a.

Scot, Benedict, of Horning, not distrained by messor, default, 3 Dec. 1339, HD 83.

Seburg, Matilda, quarrel with Walter le Miller, inquisition proved quarrel false, Walter acquitted, 20 Jan. 1347, HD 86; agreement with Walter le Miller, 22 July 1347, HD 85a.

Sewal,–, mainpast of Roger de Repps, made illegal path, 22 July 1332, HD 82.

Sewell, John, debtor v. Geoffrey Saundre, order to attach for answer, better pledges, 17 Dec. 1343, SC 2 193/1.

Shepherd, Henry, not in tithing, 22 July 1350, HD 87a.

Shereford, John de and wife Matilda, bought 1/2 rood from Margaret Slopere, 20 Jan., 1347, HD 86; bought 1/4 rood from Margaret Slopere and Beatrice, her daughter, 8 April 1348, HD 85; took lease of 1/2 rood from Alice Dersy, 8 years term, 8 April 1348, HD 85; bought a cottage from Margaret Slopere and her daughter, 10 Dec. 1348, HD 85; bought a cottage with 1/2 rood from Roger and Thomas Crane, 28 May 1350, SC 2 193/1; bought 1 rood from Gilbert and Cecily de Kele, 28 May 1350, SC 2 193/1.

Shiphorte, Beatrice, bought a cottage from Thomas le Miller, 28 May 1350, SC 2 193/1.

Shipwright, Benedict, son of Benedict le, of Yarmouth, creditor v. Thomas de Griston, 14 Oct. 1348, 10 Dec. 1348, HD 85a; order to attach Thomas de Griston in debt plea, 31 March 1349, SC 2 193/1; non prosecution of plaint v. Thomas de Griston in debt plea, 28 May 1350, SC 2 193/1.

Shortebar, John, victim of *hamsoken* by John Crane and Caterine Leman, raised hue and cry justly on John Crane, 22 July 1347, HD 85a.

Shropham, Henry de, debtor v. Geoffrey de Sharrington, 1 July 1333, HD 84.

Silk, Adam, default, order of distraint for fealty, 3 July 1332, HD 82; not in tithing, 22 July 1334, HD 84; did not use lord's mill, 11 Dec. 1135, HD 85a; debtor, to reimburse sum of 6s. 8d., 11 Dec. 1335, HD 85a; default, 14 Oct. 1348, HD 85a; fealty, 31 March 1349, SC 2 193/1.

Silk, Helewise, creditor v. John Mey, non prosecution of plaint, 31 March 1349, SC 2 193/1.

Silk, John, son of Adam, default, 22 July 1332, HD 82; default, 22 July 1334, HD 84; bought a cottage in Nornescroft, order of distraint for fealty, 16 Nov. 1344, 18 Nov. 1345, 20 Oct. 1347, HD 83; order to attach for answer about breaking a coffer and taking objects of 'wreck', 4 June 1344, 15 April 1345, 31 March 1349, SC 2 193/1; bought 1 rood, at Church gate, from Sibyl Debet, 8 April 1348, HD 85a; summons for next court to answer lord about theft of 3 cords of 'wreck', 14 Oct. 1348, HD 87a; default, 28 May 1350, SC 2 193/1.

Silk, Richard, pledge for Adam Silk in debt plea, 11 Dec. 1135, HD 85a.

Silk, Simon, debtor v. Thomas Maynild, order to collect 7s. 3d., and 3d. damages for Thomas, 20 Jan. 1347, HD 86; creditor v. Geoffrey Pennyng, order to collect 48d. for Simon, 10 Dec. 1348, HD 85a; false quarrel v. Geoffrey Pennyng, 10 Dec. 1348, HD 85a; creditor v. Thomas Crane, 14 Oct. 1348, HD 85a; false quarrel v. John Mey (with Helewise Golde), 10 Dec. 1348, HD 85a; for common suit, 31 March 1349, SC 2 193/1; non prosecution of plaint v. Thomas Crane in debt plea, 31 March 1349, SC 2 193/1; bought a messuage and 3 acres from Matilda Burgoine, 5 Oct. 1349, SC 2 193/1; debtor v. Edmund Pilch, agreement over debt of 2s., 22 July 1350, HD 87a; debtor v. Edmund Pilch, order to collect 3s. 4d. for second debt, 22 July 1350, HD 87a; debtor v. Helen Snele, order to collect 6s. 10d. for Helen, 22 July 1350, HD 87a; capital pledge, 22 July 1350, HD 87a.

Silk, Thomas, son of Adam, order to attach to come to next court about breaking a coffer and taking objects of 'wreck', 20 Jan. 1347, HD 86, 8 April 1348, 14 Oct. 1348, 10 Dec. 1348, HD 85a; creditor v. Thomas Crane, better pledges, 14 Oct. 1348, 10 Dec. 1348, HD 85a; order to attach about breaking a coffer of 'wreck', 31 March 1349, SC 2 193/1.

Simon, Matilda daughter of, sold 1/2 rood to William de Stodeye, 6 April 1342, SC 2 193/1.

Skerd, Richard, default, 29 Sept. 1337, SC 2 193/1.

Skinner, John, creditor v. Richard Boald, 28 Dec. 1342, SC 2 193/1.

Skinner, Lawrence, default, 22 July 1337, HD 86; default, 12 Oct. 1342, SC 2 193/1; debtor v. John Mey, non prosecution of plaint, acquitted, 4 June 1344, SC 2 193/1; sold 1 rood to Richard atte Bakhous, 4 June 1344, SC 2 193/1; default, 4 June 1344, SC 2 193/1; order to keep in lord's hand 1 rood sold to Richard Bakhous, 15 April 1345, SC 2 193/1; default, 10 June 1346, HD 86; agreement in debt plea with Adam Cage, 22 July 1347, HD 85a.

Skinner, Robert, not in tithing, 22 July 1332, HD 82; not in tithing, 22 July 1344, HD 84.

Slopere, Alice, ale fine, 22 July 1332, HD 82; ale fine, 22 July 1334, HD 84.

Slopere, Beatrice, default, 1 Nov. 1334, HD 84; sold 1/2 acre, at Langefurlong, next to land of Alice Brown, to Bartholomew le Miller, 17 Dec. 1343, SC 2 193/1.

Slopere, Helewise, daughter and heir of Roger, for a messuage and 4 acres, heriot 2s. 8d., 11 Dec. 1335, HD 85; withheld all services, order to seize, 8 Jan. 1336, HD 85a; married a free man, 10 Dec. 1348, HD 85a.

Slopere, Margaret, payment of *gersuma*, 2s. 8d., 1 Nov. 1334, HD 84; was granted a messuage from parents, Roger and Alice, with 3 acres, and gave it back to them for life, 8 Dec. 1334, HD 84; granted lease of 1 acre, at Langefurlong, to William Dollon, 8 years term, 28 March 1335, HD 84; debtor v. Harvey Pope, 11 Dec. 1335, HD 84; in debt plea v. Harvey Pope, non prosecution of plaint, 8 Jan. 1336, HD 85a; sold 1 rood to Reynald Crane, 8 Jan. 1336, HD 85; granted lease, without licence, of 1 rood, order to seize, 16 Feb. 1337, SC 2 193/1; childwyte, 32d., 11 Sept. 1337, SC 2 193/1; sold 1/2 rood to John de Shereford, 20 Jan. 1347, HD 86; sold 1/4 rood to John de Shereford, 8 April 1348, HD 85a; sold a cottage to John de Shereford, 10 Dec. 1348, HD 85a.

Slopere, Roger and wife Alice, sold 1/4 rood, in Northgate, to Lawrence Crome, 25 Jan. 1334, HD 84; sold 1 rood, above Willelond, to Lawrence Crome, 8 Dec. 1334, HD 84; granted to Margaret, their daughter, a messuage and 3 acres which were given back to hold for life, 8 Dec. 1334, HD 84.

Slopere, Roger, died, held a messuage and 4 acres, heir, daughter Helewise, heriot, 2s. 8d., 11 Dec. 1335, HD 85a.

Slopere, Roger, damaged lord's land, order to repair before Easter, *sub poena* 6s. 8d., 20 Jan. 1347, HD 86.

Smith, John le (senior), trespass v. Rose Bulwer, 3 July 1332, HD 82; land plea v. Muriel Casche, order to seize 1 acre and 3 roods claimed by Muriel, summons for next court, 3 July 1332, HD 82; defendant in trespass plea v. Richard and Cecily de Stanton, 3 July 1332, 22 July 1332, HD 82; capital pledge, 22 July 1332, HD 82; bought 1 1/2 acres and 1/2 rood, in 7 pieces, from Gervase de Ryburgh, 22 June 1334, HD 84; capital pledge, 22 July, 1334, HD 84; default, 21 Oct. 1334, 9 Dec. 1334, HD 84; sold a messuage 2 acres and 3 roods to Reynald Crane who gave it back to John and his wife Alice, 8 Jan. 1336, HD 85a; capital pledge, 22 July 1337, HD 86.

Smith, John le (junior), agreement in trespass plea with John Daulyn, 3 July 1332, HD 82; died, held 8 acres, order to seize until son and heir, Roger, came forward, 16 Feb. 1337, SC 2 193/1.

Smith, Robert le, defendant in trespass plea v. Roger Crane, order to attach for 2 bushels barley, 12 Oct. 1342, SC 2 193/1; failed to glean, 12 Oct. 1342, SC 2 193/1.

Smith, Roger le, son of John junior, default, 22 July 1332, HD 82; creditor v. Beatrice Huberd, 23 May 1334, HD 84; agreement with Beatrice Huberd in debt plea, 22 June 1334; heir of John le Smith, father, for 8 acres, 16 Feb. 1337, SC 2 193/1; withheld a *precaria* in autumn, 11 Sept. 1337, SC 2 193/1; debtor v. Reynald Crane, 4 June 1344, SC 2 193/1; agreement with William de Barney, in trespass plea, 4 June 1344, SC 2 193/1; bought 1 rood from Roger atte Hil, 4 June 1344, SC 2 193/1; did not use lord's mill, 20 Jan. 1347, HD 86; agreement in trespass plea with John Crane, 22 July

1347, HD 85a; agreement with Ida Godwine, in trespass plea, 22 July 1347, HD 85a; capital pledge, did not have Edmund Haldeyn and Simon atte Cros in his tithing, 22 July 1347, HD 85a; default, 8 April 1348, HD 85a; for common suit, 14 Oct. 1348, HD 85a; capital pledge, did not have Edmund Haldeyn and Simon atte Cros in his tithing, 10 Dec. 1348, HD 85a; plea in Hundred Court v. Bartholomew le Miller, 31 March 1349, SC 2 193/1; sold a messuage and 5 acres to John atte Hil, 5 Oct. 1349, SC 2 193/1.

Smith, Simon le, at the Stathe, withheld grain, 22 July 1332, HD 82; bought a plot of land, 40ft. by 40ft. next to his messuage, from Peter Fairweder, 23 May 1334, HD 85; default, 1 Nov. 1334, HD 84; default, 20 Dec. 1342, SC 2 193/1.

Smith, William le, essoin for John Parmelay, 4 Nov. 1334, HD 85; essoin for Gilbert Dering, 18 Jan. 1335, HD 85.

Smodding, William, plaintiff in trespass plea v. Harvey Pope, 14 Oct. 1348, HD 85a; agreement with Harvey Pope in trespass plea, 10 Dec. 1348, HD 85a.

Snele, Helen, creditor v. Simon Silk, order to have Simon at next court, 28 May 1350, SC 2 193/1; creditor v. Simon Silk, order to collect 6s. 10d. for Helen, 22 July 1350, HD 85a.

Somynour, William le, order to seize a messuage with 1 acre bought from John Aynild, 6 Dec. 1346, HD 86; creditor v. Agnes Joudy, William represented by attorneys, Robert of Arenburgh and Geoffrey Saundre, 14 Oct. 1348, HD 85a; took, without licence, 1 1/2 acres on lease from John Asty, 3 years term from last Michaelmas, order to seize in lord's hand, 14 Oct. 1348, HD 85a.

Soper, Harvey le, dispensed with suit of court for 1 year, 11 Sept. 1337, SC 2 193/1.

Soper, Hugh le, bought 1/2 rood, north of William Wake's croft, from Eustace and John Crane, 24 March 1337, HD 86; essoin in trespass case Matilda Joudy v. Simon Rok, 28 Dec. 1342, SC 2 193/1.

Soper, Ralph le, for common suit, 15 April 1345, SC 2 193/1; default, 8 April 1348, HD 85a; for common suit, 22 July 1348, 14 Oct. 1348, HD 85a; for common suit, 31 March 1349, SC 2 193/1.

Souter (Sutor), Alice le, granted lease of 1 rood, next to the lord's mill, from Roger Crane, 5 years term from next Michaelmas, 22 July 1347, HD 85a; held a messuage and 3 roods which Geoffrey Saundre took from lord, 28 May 1350, SC 2 193/1.

Souter (Sutor), Gilbert le, debtor v. Henry Speller, 25 Jan. 1334, HD 84; in debt plea v. Henry Speller, order to have better pledges, 3 March 1334, HD 84; agreement in debt plea with Henry Speller, 23 May 1334, HD 84; creditor v. John Asty, 22 July 1347, HD 85a.

Souter (Sutor), Hugh le and wife Matilda, withheld grain, 22 July 1332, HD 82; sold 1/2 acre to Robert de Kettlestone, 11 Sept. 1337, SC 2 193/1; withheld rent, 6 April 1342, SC 2 193/1.

Souter (Sutor), Matilda, wife of Hugh le, sold 3 roods, at Tykylyng, to John Mey, 23 May 1334, HD 84.

Souter (Sutor), William le, heir of Emma Reynes for 1/2 acre, made fealty, 8 Dec. 1341, HD 83; creditor v. Margaret Dersy, 15 April 1345, SC 2 193/1; sold 1 1/2 roods to John Herman, with charter, 9 Dec. 1348, HD 83; sold 1/2 rood to Thomas Esser, 9 Dec. 1348, HD 83.

Speller, Berta (le), default, 10 Nov. 1335, HD 83; held 1 acre as dower land, part of
     Roger de Northgate succession, 1 Dec. 1340, HD 83.
Speller, Henry, default, 22 July 1332, HD 82; default, 6 May 1333, HD 84; creditor
     v. Gilbert le Souter, 25 Jan. 1334, HD 84; agreement with Gilbert le Souter,
     23 May 1334, HD 84; default, 22 July 1334, HD 84; plaintiff in false claim
     v. John Drake, 16 Feb. 1337, SC 2 193/1; default as juror, 16 Feb. 1337,
     SC 2 193/1; default, withheld rent 8d., 6 April 1342, SC 2 193/1; creditor
     (5s.) v. William de Barney, 4 June 1344, SC 2 193/1; defendant in trespass
     v. John le Wrighte, 14 Oct. 1348, HD 85a; agreement with John le Wrighte
     in trespass plea, 10 Dec. 1348, HD 85a; debtor v. John Speller, order to
     attach for next court, 31 March 1349, SC 2 193/1.
Speller, John, chaplain, default, order of distraint for fealty, 3 July 1332, HD 82;
     default, withheld grain, 22 July 1332, HD 82; in land plea v. Agnes
     Treweman, non prosecution of plaint, 6 May 1333, HD 82; plaintiff in
     trespass plea v. Andrew Underclynt, should recover 21d., 25 Jan. 1334, HD
     84; default, 13 Dec. 1337, SC 2 193/1; took 8 acres 1/2 rood on lease from
     Richard Blakeman, 5 years term, 16 Feb. 1337, SC 2 193/1; took 1 1/2 acres
     on lease from John and Eustace Crane, 16 Feb. 1337, SC 2 193/1; default as
     juror, 6 April 1342, SC 2 193/1; bought, without licence, 1 rood from John
     Mey, order to keep in lord's hand, 12 Oct. 1342, SC 2 193/1; for common
     suit, 17 Dec. 1343, SC 2 193/1; bought, without licence, 1 1/4 roods from
     John Mey, order to keep in lord's hand, 17 Dec. 1343, SC 2 193/1; creditor
     v. William and Beatrice Charle, order to collect 6s. and 6d. damages, 4 June
     1344, SC 2 193/1; debtor v. Richard Nore, non prosecution of plaint, 4 June
     1344, SC 2 193/1; bought 1 rood from John Mey, 4 June 1344, SC 2 193/1;
     did not use the lord's mill, 15 April 1345, SC 2 193/1; plaintiff in trespass
     plea v. Bartholomew le Miller, 15 April 1345, SC 2 193/1; order to keep in
     lord's hand a horse seized from John Speller, for fealty, relief and arrears, 6
     Dec. 1346, HD 86; did not use the lord's mill, 20 Jan. 1347, HD 86; bought
     1 rood from Helewise Quyn, 20 Jan. 1347, HD 86; creditor v. John Aynild,
     about contracts, goods and accounts between them, 40d., 20 July 1347, HD
     85a; bought 1/2 acre, in Burgatescroft, from Helewise Quyn, 8 April 1348,
     HD 85a; creditor v. Roger Bulwer, order to collect 24d. from John, 10 Dec.
     1348, HD 85a; creditor v. Henry Speller, 31 March 1349, SC 2 193/1; plea
     out of manor court v. William de Barney and Henry Speller, 31 March
     1349, SC 2 193/1; sold 4 acres 3 roods to John, son of Simon Speller, with
     reversion clause, 28 May 1350, SC 2 193/1; plaintiff in plea of trespass v.
     Gilbert Neel, 26 Nov. 1350, HD 87a.
Speller, John, son of John, not in tithing, 22 July 1350, HD 87a.
Speller, John, son of Simon, bought 4 acres 3 roods from John Speller, chaplain,
     with a reversion clause if he had no heir, 28 May 1350, SC 2 193/1.
Speller, Richard, non prosecution of plaint v. William Huberd in possession of
     chattels plea, 22 July 1332, HD 82; ale fine, 22 July 1332, HD 82; ale fine,
     22 July 1334, HD 84; default, 8 Dec. 1334, HD 84; dispensed with suit of
     court for 1 year, 11 Sept. 1337, SC 2 193/1; ale fine, 22 July 1337, HD 86;
     agreement in debt plea v. Prior of Peterstone, 4 June 1344, SC 2 193/1;
     agreement in debt plea v. Simon Conyn, 4 June 1344, SC 2 193/1; debtor,
     agreement in debt plea v. Robert de Stanford of Blakeney, 4 June 1344, SC
     2 193/1; did not use lord's mill, 4 June 1344, SC 2 193/1; plaintiff in

trespass plea v. Richard atte Bakhous, 15 April 1345, SC 2 193/1; bought 1 rood from Isabel Hecheman, 18 April 1345, SC 2 193/1; bought 1½ roods from William Huberd, 8 April 1348, HD 85a; took 1½ acres on lease from Alice Dersy, 6 years term, from last Michaelmas, 8 April 1348, HD 85a; took 1½ acres on lease from William de Barney, 6 years term, from last Michaelmas, 8 April 1348, HD 85a; took 3 roods on lease from William de Barney, 8 years term, 8 April 1348, HD 85a; took 1 acre on lease, at Blakelond, from William Huberd, 12 years term, 10 Dec. 1348, HD 85a; creditor v. John Croude, order to collect 10d. for Richard, 10 Dec. 1348, HD 85a; creditor v. William de Barney, 10 Dec. 1348, HD 85a; creditor v. William de Barney, 31 March 1349, SC 2 193/1; plaintiff in other courts v. William de Barney and Henry Speller, in association with John Speller, order to attach, 31 March 1349, SC 2 193/1.

Spileman, Reynald, defendant in debt plea v. John Fox, order to come for answer, 1 July 1333, HD 84.

Springall, Adam, default, 22 July 1332, HD 82; default, 22 July 1334, HD 84.

Stamp, William, took 1 rood on lease, without licence, from Gilbert Kele, for 5 crops, 28 May 1350, SC 2 193/1; default, 28 May 1350, SC 2 193/1; default, 22 July 1350, HD 87a.

Stanford, Robert de, of Blakeney, agreement with Richard Speller in debt plea, 4 June 1344, SC 2 193/1.

Stapel, William, fealty, 31 March, 1349, SC 2 193/1.

Stanton (Steynton), Richard de and wife Cecily, trespass plea v. John le Smith (senior), order to withhold 2 sheep or more for answer to John le Smith in trespass plea, 3 July 1332, 22 July 1332, HD 82.

Stirtup, John and wife Cecily, defendant in trespass plea v. Helewise Stirtup, order to attach John and Cecily, 23 May 1334, HD 84; agreement in trespass plea v. Helewise Stirtup, 23 May 1334, HD 84; default, 22 July 1337, HD 86; default, 29 Sept. 1337, SC 2 193/1; default 4 June 1344, SC 2 193/1; sold 1½ roods, in South Field, to Alice Aynild and her daughter Matilda, 8 April 1348, HD 85a.

Stirtup, Cecily, wife of John, made *hamsoken* v. Helewise Stirtup, 22 July 1334, HD 84.

Stirtup, Helewise, plaintiff v. John and Cecily Stirtup in trespass plea, agreement, 23 May 1334, HD 84; victim of *hamsoken* by Cecily Stirtup, 22 July 1334, HD 84.

Stody, William de, bought a cottage and 1 rood from Geoffrey and Mariota de Dalling, without licence, order to keep in lord's hand, 6 April 1342, 28 Dec. 1342, SC 2 193/1; bought ½ rood from Andrew atte Clynt, 6 April 1342, SC 2 193/1; bought ½ rood from Matilda, daughter of Simon, 6 April 1342, SC 2 193/1; plaintiff in trespass plea v. John Mey, 4 June 1344, SC 2 193/1; took 1½ roods on lease from Gervase de Ryburgh, 15 April 1345, SC 2 193/1.

Stone, William at, capital pledge, 22 July 1350, HD 87a; made *hamsoken* on wife of John Kele, 22 July 1350, HD 87a; trespass with pigs in lord's pasture, 22 July 1350, HD 87a.

Storm, Thomas, creditor v. Simon Mous, 3 July 1332, HD 82; non prosecution of plaint v. Simon Mous in debt plea, 22 July 1332, HD 82.

Surlingham, Henry de, dispensed with suit of court until Michaelmas, 25 Jan. 1334, HD 84; dispensed with suit of court until next Michaelmas, 1 Nov. 1334, HD 84; with son, Simon, bought 1 rood, north of lord's mill, from Agnes Aleyn, 24 March 1337, HD 86.

Swerd, Andrew, default, 15 April 1345, SC 2 193/1; default, 27 March 1346, HD 86.

Swerd, Richard, sold 1 rood to Bartholomew le Miller, 8 Jan. 1336, HD 85a.

Swet, Agnes, default, 6 April 1342, SC 2 193/1.

Sweyn, John, sold 1/2 rood, at Wellgate, to Bartholomew le Miller, out of court, 25 Jan. 1334, HD 84.

Sweyn, Matilda, order of distraint for fealty, 3 July 1332, HD 82; default, sold 1 rood to John Edrych, 11 Sept. 1337, SC 2 193/1.

Sweyn, Thomas, withheld grain, 22 July 1332, HD 82.

Taylour, John, order of distraint to answer about breaking a coffer of 'wreck', 4 June 1344, 15 April 1345, SC 2 193/1.

Tebbe, Edmund, creditor, non prosecution of plaint v. Agnes Treweman, 3 July 1332, HD 82.

Thakster, Richard le, made illegal path beyond croft of Carpe, 22 July 1334, HD 84.

Thakster, Roger le, of Boughton, debtor v. Robert son of Thomas, order to attach for answer, 23 May 1334, 22 June 1334, HD 84; defendant in trespass plea v. John de Horning, 22 June 1334, 22 July 1334, HD 84; ale fine, 22 July 1334, HD 84; in trespass plea John de Horning not prosecuting his plaint v. Roger, 21 Oct. 1334, HD 84; John Mey raised hue and cry justly against Roger, 22 July 1337, HD 86.

Thakster, Thomas le, bought 1 rood from Thomas atte Hil, 15 April 1345, SC 2 193/1.

Thomas, Simon, order to attach for answer about breaking a coffer of 'wreck', and be at next court, 4 June 1342, SC 2 193/1.

Thomas, Robert son of, creditor v. Roger le Thakster, 23 May 1334, 22 June 1334, HD 84; non prosecution of plaint v. Roger le Thakster in debt plea, 22 July 1334, HD 84; default, 22 July 1337.

Thomas, William son of, capital pledge, 22 July 1334, HD 84; paid rent for tenement of Andrew Rotur, 6 April 1342, SC 2 193/1.

Thornham, Thomas de, in trespass plea not prosecuting his plaint v. John Pellypar, 15 April, 1345 SC 2 193/1; bought 3 roods, by charter, from Alice Marchal, 9 Dec. 1348, HD 83.

Thurbern, Amabel, for marriage licence, 6d., 25 Jan. 1334, HD 84.

Tidy, John, withheld grain, 22 July 1332, HD 82.

Tobers, Joan, creditor for 43s. 9d., 22 July 1332, HD 82.

Tobill, William, servant of Agnes de Bilney, trespass with pigs in lord's corn, 22 July 1350, HD 87a.

Treweman, Agnes, debtor v. Isabel Tober, 22 July 1332, HD 82; non prosecution of plaint in land plea v. John Speller, 6 May 1333, HD 84.

Tyson, Adam, default as juror, 6 April 1342, SC 2 193/1; debtor v. Harvey Pope, 6 April 1342, 28 Dec. 1342, order to distrain Adam, 28 Dec. 1342, SC 2 193/1.

Underclynt (atte Clynt), Andrew, marriage without licence, 3 July 1332, HD 82; made illegal path, 22 July 1332, HD 82; defendant in trespass plea v. John Mey, 25 Jan. 1334, HD 84; defendant in trespass plea v. John Speller, order to collect 21d. for John, 25 Jan. 1334, HD 84; John, his mainpast, made illegal path beyond land of Beatrice atte Drove, 22 July 1334, HD 84; default, 28 March 1335, HD 84; did not use lord's mill, 11 Dec. 1335, HD 85a; made illegal path to Townesend, 22 July 1337, HD 86; sold 1/2 rood to William de Stodeye, 6 April 1342, SC 2 193/1; default, 6 April 1342, SC 2 193/1; did not use lord's mill, 10 June 1346, HD 86.

Underclynt (atte Clynt), Mariota, agreement with Thomas Reynald in debt plea, 25 Jan. 1334, HD 84.

Valet, Alice, ale fine, 22 July 1337, HD 86.

Valet, Harvey, sold 11/2 roods, at Wellgate, to Alice Calwere, out of court, 3 July 1332, HD 82; order of distraint for fealty, 3 July 1332, HD 82; withheld grain, 22 July 1332, HD 82; order of distraint for fealty, 22 July 1332, HD 82; default, 8 April 1348, HD 85a.

Valet, Sayene, wife of Harvey, ale fine, 22 July 1337, HD 86.

Vans, Margaret, regrater of bread, bread fine, 22 July 1347, HD 85a; bread fine, 10 Dec. 1348, HD 85a.

Vans, Reynald, made illegal path beyond land of William Curthun, 22 July 1342, HD 85a.

Vicar, Thomas le, essoin in debt plea James Becces v. Reynald Crane, 4 June 1344, SC 2 193/1; for common suit, 15 April 1345, SC 2 193/1; attorney for Thomas and Simon Silk in debt plea v. Thomas Crane, 14 Oct. 1348, HD 85a; attorney for John Adwald, of Waterden v. William Mariot, 31 March 1349, SC 2 193/1.

Wake, Godwin, order of distraint for fealty, 1346, HD 86; for common suit, 20 Jan. 1347, HD 86; essoin for William Wake, 31 March 1349, SC 2 193/1; order of distraint for fealty, 15 Oct. 1349, HD 83; not in tithing, 22 July 1350, HD 87a.

Wake, Richard, not in tithing, 22 July 1332, HD 82.

Wake, Thomas, chaplain, order of distraint for fealty, 15 Oct. 1349, HD 83; his mainpast made trespass in lord's corn, 22 July 1350, HD 87a.

Wake, William, attorney for Agnes Bulwer v. Walter Bulwer in plea of assize of novel disseisin, 22 July 1334, HD 84; sold 21/2 acres to Roger Ode, 6 Dec. 1346, HD 86; for common suit, 12 Oct. 1342, SC 2 193/1; for common suit, 20 Jan. 1347, HD 86; trespass with pigs in lord's pasture, 15 April 1345, SC 2 193/1; for common suit, 31 March 1349, SC 2 193/1.

Walker, Alice, sister and heir of Margaret for half a cottage, 1 Nov. 1334, HD 84.

Walker, Margaret, paid a marriage licence, 6d., 25 Jan. 1334, HD 84; died, held half a cottage, heir Alice, her sister, who did not come to claim it, order to take in lord's hand, 1 Nov. 1334, HD 84.

Walsingham, Amis de, held, at Gibbesgate, 1 rood, order to distrain for fealty, 24 April 1332, HD 83; order to keep in lord's hand 1 rood, at Gibbesgate, for services and rents due, 24 April 1332, HD 83; fined with the whole homage, 31 March 1333, HD 83; default, 10 Nov. 1335, HD 83.

Walsingham, Geoffrey de, for common suit, essoin by John de Walsingham, 17 Dec. 1343, SC 2 193/1; sold several pieces and tenements to Andrew le Eyr, 5 Oct. 1349, SC 2 193/1; sold all his holding, 7 acres, to Peter de Binham, 28 May 1350, SC 2 193/1.

Walsingham, John de, essoin for Geoffrey de Walsingham,, 17 Dec. 1343, SC 2 193/1; made illegal path with sheep, 15 April 1345, SC 2 193/1.

Walsingham, Prior of, order to take in lord's hand, at Lazareswong, 1 rood given on lease to Richard Blakeman, 10 Nov. 1335, HD 83; raised fold before time, 22 July 1337, HD 86; made illegal path to the Grange, 22 July 1350, HD 87a.

Walsingham, Thomas de, essoin in land plea Richard atte Bakhous v. Roger Crane, 15 April 1345, SC 2 193/1.

Walter, Thomas, damages to lord's land with his cattle, 26 Nov. 1350, HD 87.

Warham, Bartholomew de, essoin in trespass plea Roger le Thakster v. John de Horning, 22 July 1334, HD 84; essoin for Prior of Peterstone, 24 March 1334, HD 86.

Warham, John de, debtor v. James Becces, better pledges, 3 July 1332, HD 82.

Warin, Alice daughter of, was granted a piece of land by father, Warin, 20 Jan. 1347, HD 86.

Wast, Robert, pledge for William Huberd, 25 Jan. 1334, HD 84.

West Dereham, Abbot of, raised a fold before time, 22 July 1337, HD 86; raised 3 folds with nuisance, order to attach the abbot to be at next court to answer lord, 15 April 1345, SC 2 193/1; trespass with pigs in lord's meadow, 15 April 1345, SC 2 193/1; made illegal path through lord's land to Claylondhende, 22 July 1350, HD 87a; made illegal path through the lord's grange to the church, 22 July 1350, HD 87a.

West Dereham, Adam of (Brother), made illegal path beyond the lord's land to Townesend, 22 July 1334, HD 84; made illegal path to Townesend, 22 July 1337, HD 86.

Whine, Thomas, default, 6 May 1333, HD 84; default, 25 Jan. 1334, HD 84; default, 8 Dec. 1334, HD 84.

Whine, William, capital pledge, 3 July 1332, HD 82.

Whitbred, Agnes, order to distrain for fealty, 3 July 1332, 22 July 1332, HD 82.

Whitbred, Harvey, sold 3 acres to John de Bilney, without licence, order to keep in lord's hand, 11 Dec. 1335, HD 85a.

White, Geoffrey, dispensed with suit of court until Michaelmas, 25 Jan. 1334, HD 84; ale fine, 22 July 1337, HD 86; essoin for Robert White, 31 March 1349, SC 2 193/1; for common suit, 28 May 1350, SC 2 193/1.

White, Gilbert, died, held a cottage 1/4 rood, order to seize in lord's hand until heir came forward, 6 May 1333, HD 84.

White, John, pledge for prosecution in debt plea Richard Blakeman v. Edmund le Miller, 11 Dec. 1335, HD 85; for common suit, 26 Nov. 1350, HD 87a.

White, Matilda, ale fine, 22 July 1332, HD 82.

White, Payn, dispensed with suit of court until Michaelmas, 25 Jan. 1334, HD 84; default, 22 July 1337, HD 86; not in tithing, 10 Dec. 1348, HD 85a; for common suit, 31 March 1349, SC 2 193/1; essoin for John White, 26 Nov. 1350, HD 87a.

White, Robert, dispensed with suit of court until Michaelmas, 25 Jan. 1334, HD 84; default, 22 July 1334; dispensed with suit of court until Michaelmas, 1 Nov. 1334, HD 84; did not use lord's mill, order to collect multure for the miller, 10 June 1346, HD 86; for injurious gesture in court, 20 Jan. 1347, HD 86; for common suit, 31 March 1349, SC 2 193/1.

Wighton, Adam de, essoin in debt plea William son of Thomas v. Roger Thakster, 22 June 1334, HD 84.

William, John son of, default, 11 Sept. 1337, SC 2 193/1; default, 22 July 1350, HD 87a.

William, Matilda, wife of Thomas son of, regrater of ale, 22 July 1337, HD 86.

William, Thomas son of, agreement with Bartholomew Colting in trespass plea, 22 July 1332, HD 82; victim of assault and bloodshed by Bartholomew Colting, 22 July 1332, HD 82; plaintiff in trespass plea v. Matilda Charle, 6 May 1333, HD 84; bought 1 rood from James Becces, 24 March 1337, HD 86.

William, – , parson of Holkham, default, 3 July 1332, 22 July 1332, HD 82; order to distrain for fealty, 22 July 1332, HD 82; sold a tenement to John Andrew, 6 May 1333, HD 84.

Winter, Richard, essoin for John Lombe, 14 Oct. 1348, HD 85a.

Wodehil, Harvey, default, 22 July 1332, HD 82.

Wolner, John, bought 1/2 acre from Peter Cori, 26 Nov. 1350, HD 87a.

Wrighte, Alice le, daughter of John, was granted tenure of 1/2 acre 1/2 rood, at Nineacres and Claylond, 3 July 1332, HD 82; withheld grain, 22 July 1332, HD 82; ale fine, 22 July 1332, HD 82; bought 1 rood, at Heghskamlond, from Alice Hammond, 28 March 1335, HD 84.

Wrighte, John le, sold a messuage and a croft with 11/2 roods, in Northgate, to Robert de Kettlestone, 3 July 1332, HD 82; withheld grain, 22 July 1332, HD 82; capital pledge, 22 July 1332, HD 82; defendant in trespass plea v. Richard Blakeman, 22 June 1334, HD 84; agreement with Richard Blakeman in trespass plea, 21 Oct. 1334, HD 84; took on lease, without licence, a piece of land for Bartholomew Colting, 21 Oct. 1334, HD 84; creditor v. Richard Marchal, 8 Dec. 1334, HD 84; default as juror, 6 April 1342, SC 2 193/1; plaintiff in trespass plea v. Thomas Esser, 20 Jan. 1347, HD 86; agreement in trespass plea with Thomas Esser, 8 April 1348, HD 85a; bought 1/2 rood from Sibyl Debet, 8 April 1348, HD 85a; plaintiff in trespass plea v. Henry Speller, 14 Oct. 1348, HD 85a; agreement with Henry Speller in trespass plea, 10 Dec. 1348, HD 85a; creditor v. John Mey, agreement over payment of sum of 4s. 10d., next payment at Michaelmas *sub poena* 10s., 31 March 1349, SC 2 193/1.

Wrighte, Ralph le, son and heir of John, order to seize Ralph, minor son of John le Wrighte and land held from lord, 7 July 1350, HD 83.

Wrighte, Richard le, withheld grain, 22 July 1332, HD 82.

Wrighte, Robert le, essoin for Richard Blakeman, 31 March 1349, SC 2 193/1.

Wrighte, Roger le, his servant, Geoffrey, made an illegal path to the church, 22 July 1334, HD 84; default as juror, 6 April 1342, SC 2 193/1.

Yudekil, Harvey, order of distraint for fealty, 3 July 1332, 22 July 1332, HD 82; dispensed with suit of court until next Michaelmas, 3 March 1334, HD 84; default, 22 July 1334, HD 84; dispensed with suit of court, 1 Nov. 1334, HD 84; default, 14 Oct. 1348, HD 85a; for common suit, 28 May 1350, SC 2 193/1; default, 22 July 1350, HD 87a.

Yudekil, Richard, sold 1/2 rood, at Claylond, to Godeman Joule and Amice, his wife, 8 Dec. 1341, HD 83; sold 1/2 acre, at Bondescroft, to Robert Keynot, 8 Dec. 1341, HD 83; sold 1 rood, next to land of Bartholomew de Howgate, to Robert Keynot, 8 Dec. 1341, HD 83; sold 1/2 rood to Alice, daughter of Hugh Otes, and her daughter Matilda, with reversion clause, 4 Dec. 1342, HD 83.

Yve, Roger, son of John, creditor v. Simon Mous, 6 May 1333, HD 84.

SIXTEEN HOLKHAM FAMILIES

ASTY

In 1272–3 William Asty held of Burghall 3½ roods, portion of the disintegrated 13 acre tenement of Bishop and Wulfrun and also 1½ roods, portion of the 12 acre tenement called Dusing. William, Cecily and Adam Asty and Ralph held shortly afterwards what had been William Whitbred's 3 acres. He paid 7d., then worth 1d., ¼d. wardsea, 14 boon works in autumn at the lord's board worth 14d. and thrashed for 8 days (worth 4d.), rendering all the other services which William Asketel rendered except spreading dung, viz. 1 day's carriage in autumn worth 3d., 1 boon work with the plough (worth 6d.), weeding 1½ days worth ¾d. and going twice to the pond (HD 4, 4a). The Astys are interesting though none of them was rich enough to qualify for inclusion with the 53 taxpayers named in 1332–3.[7] In 1334 John Asty had a cottage at the Stathe 40 ft long, on 23 March, and on 22 July he paid a heriot on the death of his brother Walter (HD 84). On 24 March 1337 he surrendered the cottage for the use of Gilbert Eldefader, Helewise his wife, and their brood (HD 86).[8] Various lettings from Walter and to and from John are mentioned in the Burghall court rolls of 1333–5. Emma Asty with her brood was granted a cottage by her brother Walter on 23 March 1334. John Asty appears in pleas of debt and trespass like many of his neighbours in 1333–4, but in 1350 Emma was not only a regrator but also broke into the house of Mary Jonys (HD 87a). John's relationship to Richard and Thomas Asty is unknown. For John Asty as a tenant (1332–47), see Prosopography *supra*. Eventually the family produced a capital pledge, John Asty, on 22 July 1407 (HD 97); but in 1358 Alice daughter of William Asty and her sister Emma, had fled and Robert Asty, villein, had fled with Richard and Harvey Asty and they were to be seized (HD 89). Simon Asty surrendered ½ acre for Matilda Aynild and her brood on 15 March 1358. He too was a regrator (22 July 1358). Mary Chapman was to answer him for debt on 6 April 1364 (HD 85a).

AYNILD

The brothers John and Gilbert Aynild, occasionally with their brother Adam witness many of our deeds. Gilbert's house was broken into and robbed (*Cal. Patent*, 1281–92, p. 400). His last appearance is with both brothers in 1303 (HP 1045), but the name of John, often found in 1294–6, recurs throughout the fourteenth century. John was one of the privileged possessors of a fold (1306, HD 22a, Fo. 1v no. 1 by

---

7   PRO E 179/149/9 m. 32, printed *supra*. There are more than twice as many different names in the Burghall court rolls (HD 82) for the same year as in the tax roll. But no less than 21 names in the tax roll are not found in the court rolls in spite of Zvi Razi's belief that at least at Halesowen men are almost fully represented, Cf. *Life, Marriage and Death in a Medieval Parish: Economy, Society and Demography in Halesowen 1270–1400*, Cambridge 1980, pp. 25–6. On the use of manorial court records as a source for demography, see the controversy: Larry Poos and Richard Smith, "Legal windows onto Historical Populations"?, 'Recent research on the Demography and the manor court in Medieval England', *Law and History Review*, 2, 1984, pp. 128–52; Zvi Razi, 'The Use of Manorial Court Rolls in Demographyc Analysis: A reconsideration', *Law and History Review*, 3, 1985, pp. 191–200; Larry Poos and Richard Smith, "Shades still on the window": 'A reply to Zvi Razi', *Law and History Review*, 3, 1986, pp 409–29; Zvi Razi, 'The Demographic Transparency of Manorial Court Rolls', *Law and History Review*, 5, 1987, pp. 524–35.

8   Eldefader's successor William surrendered it with ½ rood villein land for use of William Stampe and his brood, 22 July 1351. The entry fee was 3s. 4d., HD 87a.

lease of Walter Hakun), but unlike Adam who pays 16d., he is not assessed for tax in 1332–3. It is remarkable that John and Gilbert seldom witness the same document. John made a grant to Gilbert Neel of land which he had recently acquired (HD 22a, Fo. 11v no. 144 and Fo. 22 no. 237). He granted other land to William le Somynour for which he was distrained (6 December 1346, HD 86) and was distrained for homage at the Neel manor court on 15 October 1349 (HD 83). He does not appear as a tenant of Burghall in 1332–5 (HD 82, 84, 85a) or of Hillhall about 1360 (HD 51). Adam's assessment was the same as that of Simon Mous and John Mey. He farmed 1½ roods in Flaxlond let by John Asty (28 March 1335, HD 84). Sixty-five years later his namesake's sheep damaged the rye and oats of the lord of Burghall (28 February 1400, HD 97). John Aynild rescued a horse from the *messor* in 1352. He had a messuage of Neel, once Wake, at the Stathe. In 1390 Gilbert had a collapsed house of Hillhall at Crosgate. The name Aynild vanishes after 1400. Henry Silk possessed John's house at the Stathe (1427–8, HD 114) which was subsequently described as empty (HD 194). John's various opponents in court included the aggressive Gilbert Neel for trespass (1350, HD 87a) and John Calwere (17 May 1356, HD 86) and Simon Asty for debt. He had a daughter Matilda who defaulted at court (14 May 1346, HD 81) for whom Simon Asty surrendered ½ acre (15 March 1354, HD 87a). She was one of the regrators of bread in Wells court rolls (Wells Document 2). The Aynild trio were outstanding as witnesses and tenants.

BALTEYS

Thomas Balteys was on the Holkham shipping inquiry in 1336–7 when he himself had a fishing boat of 12 tons called 'La Skardeyn' moored at Wells-next-the-Sea.[9] He was much the largest tenant of Hillhall in the decade after the Black Death paying 8s. 10d. out of 26s. 9¼d. which the 42 tenants traditionally paid, as well as 4 bushels of corn (compared with the Abbot of Creake's 1½ bushels). He was interested in wool as well as fish and corn and at the 22 July 1358 Burghall leet was found to have commoned with sheep in several pastures wrongly (HD 89). On 22 July 1367 the leet found that he had destroyed Holkham common with sheep (HD 85a). He was guilty of similar offences in 1346–7 in Wells. He was a capital pledge and served on an inquiry there into a wreck (Wells Document 2). The name Balteys does not occur in the Burghall court rolls of 1332–3 (HD 82) or 1335 (HD 84, 85A) but he essoined at the court of 20 June 1347 (HD 86) and is in default there on 16 March 1353 (HD 87A). The name does not occur in the tax roll for Holkham in 1332–3. This absence may be due to the fact that he lived at Wells, as appeared when he died, a free tenant, leaving an heir who was of age according to a Hillhall court of 1380. *Tenementum Balteys*, concentrated mostly in Stathe Field, is often mentioned in fifteenth-century Hillhall court rolls. This tenement was held freely of Hillhall but owed (and detained) *precaria* in autumn to Burghall (24 September 1374, 25 September 1375, HD 91). Several other people called Balteys (or Balteyn) are mentioned. Agnes was the sister of Nicholas Godcok (1372, HD 85A). Geoffrey owed suit to Burghall (1 November 1334, HD 84). The relationship of William Balteys, *capellanus*, to Thomas is unknown (11 January 1366, HD 85a). His son aged two died in 1383 seised of William's land in Wells, held of Hillhall.

---

9   PRO C. 47 Misc. Bundle 2 File 25/18, printed *supra*.

BILNEY

Except for Richard Neel, John Billey or Bilney was the largest taxpayer at Holkham in 1332–3. His father Roger de Bilney was a tenant of Geoffrey le Bret and witnessed three charters. John is mentioned as the holder of adjoining land in eight feoffments so his holdings would not have been inconsiderable, but his wealth lay mainly at sea. He was sworn to inquire into the maritime resources of Holkham when service abroad was required, and it appeared that he was owner and master of no fewer than three vessels, *La Haga*, of 20 tons, *La Katerine* also of 20 tons and *La Plente* of 12 tons. John is not a conspicuous figure in the court rolls and others of his surname were few, though there was a dom. Walter in 1349 and an Agnes in 1350 (HD 87a). The name seems to have died out at Holkham. John de Bilney, however, was often enough available on shore to be a very frequent witness. The court rolls also mention Helewise, Roger, Walter and William de Bilney between 1330 and 1350 as tenants.

BULWER

John Bulwer of Holkham, Richard and Walter never occur as grantors or recipients in our deeds, perhaps because the farming crisis of 1315 had not led them to dispose of land during the decades when Richard Neel was buying pieces that became available; but John sometimes holds adjoining land and is often a witness. They all occur in court rolls with Agnes, Roger, Walter and Simon. Agnes alone represents the family in the 1332–3 taxation , paying 12d. like Bartholomew le Miller and three others. She was John's widow (HD 84). She and Rose Bulman were villeins withholding grain on 22 July 1337 when Simon Bulwer had the same offence condoned (HD 82). She served as a pledge for Simon and Cecily Mous and one of her suits was against Robert Andrew about a bond for 36s. HD 84). John Bulwer jun. sued Mous on 25 January 1334 for detention of cattle. His daughter Margaret was married without licence (HD 84). Richard le Bulwer granted half a messuage and 20 acres which Richard Blakeman and Agnes his wife held in dower for life reverting to Bulwer with remainder to Blakeman and his brood (HD 84). A later John was immensely active between 1377 and 1385. His cows were among those which damaged New Close of Hillhall in 1381 and on 22 December 1404 he cut down an ash tree worth 20d. (HD 97). Laurence Bulwer was sworn into tithing on 22 July 1356 (HD 86). Walter Bulwer, *capellanus*, sought admission on 25 January 1334 and was granted 3 acres 1 rood with his brood for 40d. fine on 3 March 1334 (HD 84). Thirty years later he surrendered to his brother John his messuage on 25 June 1364 (HD 85).

BURGOINE

Godman Burgoine or Le Burgoyne held twelve acres of Burghall in 1272–3 on conditions which included payment of wardsea (1/2d.), 2 hens, 2d woodload, 6 autumn boon works worth 6d., a boon work with a plough at the lord's board if he had horse, a day's corn carriage if he had a horse (worth 1d.), weeding for 3 days worth 11/2d., 2 journeys to the pond (1d.), carrying the lord's writ (or 1d.) twice (worth 4d.) and if the lord visits the vill the provision at his departure of a horse for 12 leagues – total 3s. 3d. (HD 4). The tenement was thereafter apparently divided between three heirs, Roger, Simon and Thomas (HD 4a), but the name Godman persisted in the family for sixty years. Later, in the taxation of 1332–3, a second Godman Burgoine was assessed at 22d., the same as Robert Keynot, an obscurer person. Godman was capital pledge in 1327, 1334 and 1337 (HD 84 and 82). Another Burgoine, Simon, paid 2s. tax, the same as Edmund Haldeyn who was also obscure. Simon was capital pledge in 1334 and 1337 (HD 86 and 82) and a pledge in many cases between 1332 and 1337. Both

were among the more prominent suitors at the leet though both paid less than the
average tax. They were evidently co-heirs for they sought admission together on 25
January 1334 to 4 acres at Whitewong and were both given entry with their broods
for a 12d. fine on 3 March 1334 (HD 84). Our documents also refer to John and
Thomas son of William Burgoine, but notices of the family, have not been found in
the second half of the century. Godman's son Thomas was a villein of Burghall and
fell in mercy for marrying without a licence (HD 86). Matilda Burgoine was a brewer
who failed to have a measure on 3 July 1333 (HD 84) and was fined for breaking the
assise of ale on 22 July 1337 (HD 84).

CALWERE

Beside sixteen references in our documents to Bartholomew they refer to his wife
Seyeua and five other Calweres including one *capellanus*, Thomas (HD 45); but
Bartholomew is the only one named among the taxpayers of 1332-3. He had 6s. 8d.,
the same as John Speller, well above the average. He held land in the NE quarter of
the parish (HD 22a, Fo. 23v no. 249). His son was Gilbert (HD 22a, Fo. 23v no.
249). Gilbert Calwere held land in the NE and SE quarters of the parish. The pigs of
Thomas were damaging the lord of Burghall's meadow on 26 November 1350 (HD
87a). He broke into Peter Cory's house and injured a horse; he was vicar of
'Sidesete' in 1356 (HD 86). On 17 May 1356 a John Calwere was in mercy 3d. for
not prosecuting John Aynild in a plea for debt and on 1 July 1356 he owed Simon
Silk for two bushels of barley worth 8d. (HD 86). William Calwere and Thomas were
tenants of Hillhall and Tobers paying 12d. and 4d. respectively (HD 87a). William
destroyed a warren on 14 November 1356 taking a hare with his dog on 14
November 1356 (HD 86). Forty years on he was a capital pledge and was taking
hares in Burghall warren – unless the offender was a younger namesake following in
his footsteps. He failed to pay a Scottish merchant for malt from Newcastle, a
surprising import in a barley growing area. Margaret Calwere broke the assise of ale
on 22 July 1352. She detained two boon works owed to Burghall on 24 September
1367, when William detained one (HD 85). She married John Silk and owed the
service of *messor* to Burghall in 1384. In 1393 and 1397 Walter Calwere's 12 acre
tenement was elected *prepositus* of Burghall. In 1381 Adam, like many others in the
time of *rumor*, had his beasts damaging the meadow and barley of the hated lord of
Hillhall, John of Holkham. But for Adam this was nothing very new. On 26 March
1367 he had damaged the lord's several marshes with his sheep and on 22 July 1367
he had rescued his horse from the lord of Burghall's bailiff and blocked Kirkway. He
detained 9s. 8d. from Simon Silk. A Bartholomew le Calwere de 'Helcham' with his
wife Hawise, occurs in an obit roll of the hospital of St. Mary Magdalen, Gaywood,
printed by Dorothy Owen among the records of Bishop's Lynn (no. 85) and dated as
earlier than 1296. They and seven other Holkham people may have been included as
benefactors – presumably they gave small pieces of land which were later
consolidated to form 'Magdalen Piece', an enclave of five acres on the west side of
the avenue which Coke of Norfolk acquired by exchange for land at Gaywood. As
Warin de Montchesney is in the obit roll, the lands may have been part of his fee
granted in free alms before his rental was made.

CARPENTER

In 1272–3 Adam le Carpenter held 10 acres and 1 messuage for 13½d. under Bartholomew de Burgate among the free tenants of Geoffrey le Bret whose estate later became the nucleus of Neel Manor (HD 22a, Fos. 27–29v no. 253). Adam's tenement was however yielding 2s. on 24 September 1314 when Peter le Bret son of Geoffrey granted the rent to William Wake as it had been paid by Gilbert le Carpenter on that tenement and was then held by Roger de Foxley (HD 22a, Fo. 6 no. 74). Gilbert is described as the son of Adam le Carpenter of Holkham on 1 March 1311, when he was taken for robbing Geoffrey Nogun of Warham of 6s. 5d. in silver and cloth worth 1/2 mark in Wighton Linges, but was acquitted.[10] It is unknown whether Geoffrey, John, Matthew and Roger, the other carpenters mentioned in the Neel Cartulary, were trade rivals bearers or a common surname. John le Carpenter of Holkham was also accused of crime, aiding William Pipelot in stealing three quarters of barley from the land of the Abbot of West Dereham.[11] In the taxation of 1332–3 John le Carpenter paid 2s., and Roger le Carpenter paid 4s. and Robert le Carpenter 8s. As there are several instances in the court rolls of the bodily removal of houses, one to Wells and one to Neel Manor, it may well be that carpenters at Holkham made wooden frames for houses. Adam was the son of Bartholomew and Agnes was the daughter of Matthew (Cf. HD 8 and 22a, Fo. 11v no. 141).

CRANE

In the taxation of 1332–3 Gilbert Crane paid 8d., John Crane paid 18d. and Reynold Crane paid 4s. One out of every thirteen taxpayers was called Crane, and the richest one's assessment exceeded the average, but only by 3¼d. The Speller's were wealthier, but were the only other family to have more than one representative on the subsidy roll. Their predecessor Elias Crane, married to Rose, daughter of Sibyl Buleman, was dead by 11 May 1322 when she made a grant (HD 22a, Fo. 15 no. 176 and HD 30).[12] Many Bulmans occur, with capital pledges among them in the 1390s, but none is in the roll. John Crane removed barley without licence (23 March 1324, HD 84) and put corn outside the villeinage (1 November 1334, HD 84), removing a sheaf from the lord's manor (11 December 1335, HD 85a). He had left a widow, Mariota, and a son, by 20 January 1347 (HD 86). John was son of Gilbert and had a brother Eustace. The brothers had entry (with their broods) in three acres when Gilbert died (20 March 1333, HD 84) and they sold land without licence (28 March 1335, HD 84). John was an affeerer on 8 December 1334 having failed to do his duty as *messor* of Burghall on 1 November 1334. He was collector from 28 March 1335 and served as capital pledge with Reynold Crane in 1337. Between 1352 and 1372 Roger and Thomas Crane were often capital pledges, often together, and thereafter Thomas served in 1378 and 1380 after Roger had died leaving his daughter Matilda 6 villein acres as his heir while his widow Joan had a third as dower. Roger had pleas of debt with Simon and Cecily Mous on 1 November 1334 (HD 84) and with John Aynild on 17 May 1356 (HD 86). Three sheep of Thomas were taken to make him answer a plea of debt on 12 December 1371 (HD 84a). Reynold surrendered a cottage and 1 acre on 16 October 1348 (HD 87a). His flock damaged Adam Craske's wheat on 6 May 1333 (HD 87a). No Crane occurs in a Hillhall rental of about 1360 (HD

---

10   B. Hanawalt, ed., *Crime in East Anglia in the Fourteenth Century, Norfolk Gaol Delivery Rolls, 1307–16* Norfolk Record Society, xliv, 1976, no. 223.
11   *Id.*, no. 93.
12   The seal has a squirrel with an inscription.

51), but in 1394 *tenementum Crane* was elected *prepositus* of Burghall. Margaret Crane was a regrator of bread on 22 July 1334. She held in villeinage and married without licence, 1 November 1334 (HD 84). Christina Crane made an illegal track over the lord of Burghall's meadow called Lytlemedow, 22 July 1358 (HD 89).

CRASKE

(2) Ralph atte Gateshende =	Margery	=	William Craske (1)
of Brisley	grantor as		of Holkham
grantor in 1329	Craske widow		recipient in 11.
HD 22a, nos. 5, 9	1327 HD 22a,		one dated 1283
	nos. 158, 189		
	as Gateshende,		
	widow, 1330,		
	HD 22a, no. 76		

	Adam Craske	=	Joan
	grantor in 8		grantor in 1336
	charters 1318–33		HD 22a, Fo. 15 no. 170.

John and Thomas Craske also occur in the deeds. Adam and Margery each use two different seals. The Craske family declined in importance at Holkham. Towards the end of the thirteenth century William Craske had appeared regularly among the dozen or so local worthies most often named in lists of witnesses but the name has not been noted as a capital pledge in the court rolls of the next century so far as they survive at Holkham. Adam Craske of Holkham was acquitted of aiding William Pipelot in the theft of two bushels of malt worth 14d.[13] Adam and John appear in Burghall court roll of 1332–3 (HD 82), but only Adam appears in the tax roll of that year paying perhaps 18d. (but the reading is unclear), 32). Were they victims of the bad times of 1315–22?[14] One rood of Adam's wheat was eaten by Reynold Crane's sheep, while he himself trespassed on John Andrew on 6 May and 1 July 1333 (HD 84). On 21 October 1334 (HD 84), Margery Craske granted 12 acres to Peter de Langham (and his brood) assessed at as much as 8s in 1332–3 (HD 82). Matilda occurs on 22 July 1337 (HD 86), and Roger essoins at Burghall court in 1377. Outside Holkham the Craske's continued and on 29 December 1389 John Goddysman and others received a messuage and a croft from John Craske described as of Snitterby (Lincs.), (HP 1377).

HAMMOND

Simon son of Hamo of Holkham, also called Simon Hammond, received land in no less than 50 deeds in the Neel Cartulary, out of the 149 old grants which precede those to the Neels. Twenty-five original grants to Simon survive. These are mostly from Geoffrey son of Peter le Bret, John son of Geoffrey le Bret and John son of Adam le Bret between 1294 and 1296 but one from Geoffrey le Bret is as early as 24 December 1293 and none of the ones from John son of Adam le Bret are before 12 December 1295. An undated grant from Geoffrey le Bret (HP 1029) might be as early

---

13   *Crime in East Anglia in the Fourteenth-Century, op. cit.* no. 93.
14   Ian Kershaw, 'The Great famine and Agrarian Crisis in England 1315–22', *Past and Present*, vol. 59, May 1973, p. 38, (citing A.C. Chibnall, *Sherington*, 1965, pp. 121, 131–3): there were three times as many charters in 1315–26 locally as in preceding and following decades.

as about 1284. Other grantors in original charters are Gilbert de Bintry, Gilbert son of John Brown, Walter Hakun, Gilbert son of William Nicol and Bartholomew de Burgate. These are in chronological order beginning with undated ones which *could* be as early as the 1270's and concluding on 27 October 1299. Most of Simon's acquisitions are stated to have been granted in return for sums of money which are sometimes specified. Quantities of land are not always stated but grants are of 1/2 rood, 11/2 roods, 1/2 acre, 11/2 acres, 7 roods but there is one piece of 6 acres (HP 1032) and the largest, costing 46s. is 15 acres 3 roods in 8 pieces (HP 1011). One piece of undefined area cost 11s. (HP 998) and another 22s. (HP 997), 11/2 acres and 1/2 rood was 13s. (HP 1023) but 11/2 acres 1 rood was 5 marks (HP 1029). 7 roods was 31/2 marks (HP 1027) or 4 marks (HP 1031), 1/2 rood was 10s. (HP 1041) and 21/2 acres was 21/2 marks (HP 1022). Nine of these documents mention Simon's wife Cecily. Simon's son William granted eleven pieces of land on 13 April 1313 (HD 22a, Fo. 8v no. 105) and Walter de Helweton perpetual vicar of Holkham, who regranted them on 15 October 1313 to William son of Robert de Dunwich of Walsingham (HD 22a, Fo. 8v no. 106). They had another son, Adam, sometimes called son of Simon and sometimes Hamund or even, like his father, son of Hamo. In 1316 Adam granted to Richard and Caterine Neel 7 acres and 11/2 roods, with 33 acres and the liberty of a fold and Gilbert Gurle and Eluina Daleman serfs (HD 22a, Fo. 21v no. 230). In 1315 they had already received a piece of 3 acres from Joan widow of Henry Hammond of North Barsham (HP 1053) confirmed a week later by William and Hamo sons of Henry (HP 1054). Simon had another son John (HD 22a, Fo. 8 no. 101) who had a sheepfold (HD 22a, Fo. 1v no. 1). There was a younger Cecily, daughter of Agnes who made another small grant to the Neels in 1332 (HD 22a, Fo. 13 no. 155). Agnes was the stepmother of Cecily, the wife of Simon atte Cruche (HD 22a, Fo. 13v no. 157). Adam made some grants (HP 1047 and 1050) not to Caterine Neel but to William son of Robert de Dunwich of Walsingham in 1314. These and a grant to him the same year by John Atte Falgate de Burnham and Cecily his wife (HP 1048) are included in the cartulary. Presumably the land granted came to the Neels. Could Caterine wife of Richard Neel have been an heiress of Robert de Dunwich of Walsingham? Did he move from Hindringham to Walsingham? The seal of Adam Hammond bore a squirrel (HP 1047), a device more suitable for his father the acquisitive Simon, or for Richard Neel. Simon, generally called son of Simon, is called son of Hammond in HD 22a, Fo. 4 no. 40. In HD 22a, Fo. 3v no. 30, and Fo. 10 nos. 121 and 126, he is called Simon Hammond or Hamund (HD 10). Perhaps the name Hammond is connected with Hamo Mundi (HD 2). Among thirteenth century inscribed tombstones in Holkham church which have been broken in the past and mended wrongly so as to distort the inscriptions are those of Bret and Hammond. One is 'Anneys de Br[et]ham La Feme [d]e Adam Hamund' (Fiche 3: F9) and the other one reads 'Simund Hamund git ici deu...'.

MILLER

Bartholomew le Miller appears as a grantee in 1294–6 and as a grantor in deeds of 1315 (HD 22a, Fo. 18v no. 198, HP 1055)[15] and 1316 (HD 22a, Fo. 17v no. 188, and HP 1057). In 1332–3 he paid 12d. tax, well-below the average assessment. In 1335–6 he had a grant from a brother Henry – perhaps they were grandsons of Hugh le Miller, an earlier tenant of Burghall (HD 4, 4a, and HD 22a, Fos. 31–34v no. 255). Bartholomew held no land of Hillhall (HD 51), but often occur in Burghall court

---

15   Grantee in HP 1014 and 1035 and HD 22a, Fo. 11 nos. 133–4.

rolls. Like many others he paid on entry for himself and his brood (25 Jan. 1334, HD 86). His various suits included ones for debt (v. Simon Silk) (7 June 1359, HD 85a) and trespass (v. Simon Grigges), (14 Nov. 1356, HD 86). An unusual claim for debt against him was for 6s. 8d. which was Helewise Hemming unsuccessfully alleged he owed to her as his concubine on 6 April 1372 (HD 85a). On 22 July 1368 he was found to have retained a Burghall court roll lent to him by the *prepositus*, perhaps a testimony to his literacy. The Burghall roll of 4 November 1368 gives details of the component pieces of 19 acres additional to a tenement of 48 acres granted to him by the lord.[16] In 1378, his daughter, Matilda Crane was admitted as tenant, in 1385 his daughter, wife of William Kele, paid 2 s. 6 d. heriot as heir, and in 1387 his son and heir did not come to claim admission after his death. No distinction has been observed between senior and junior bearers of his name, though there must have been Bartholomew in more than one generation. He is sometimes called *atte milne*, but there were several mills at Holkham despite the nineteenth century legend that it had been a barren waste with no corn. It is not known which was his. It could not have been that of Hillhall or indeed of Burghall for he refused to grind at the lord of Burghall's mill on 28 March 1368 (HD 85a). Could it have been Wakesmill or even a private mill of his own? He was prominent enough to be a capital pledge on 26 July 1352 though he was not a regular one like William Curzon, Robert Erneys or Harvey Pope.

NEEL

Gilbert Neel of Burnham was the second son of Richard and Caterine Neel, the founders of the Neel estate, and the heir of his elder brother Thomas Neel. Their pedigree is HD 22a, Fo. 30 no. 254. His first court was held on 15 October 1349 after the death of Thomas (See Neel Pedigree, Appendix 2). As a grantee on 9 August 1344 (HD 22a, Fo. 15v no. 178, HP 1099) he was resident at Burnham (presumably Burnham Norton like his father). He was investing money for trade in 1345 and 1346 (HP 1100–1). In 1350 his calves were damaging the corn of the lord of Burghall (HD 87a). He figured in numerous disputes, mostly debt and trespass, and was fined for not serving as a capital pledge (22 July 1364, HD 85a). He vexed John Tobul in the archdeacon's court and made an illegal track across the court of Thomas Cat, as his servant did in the croft of Richard de Geyst (22 July 1366). He took eleven geese from the vicar. His numerous opponents included Bartholomew le Miller and William le Somynour, and his controversial moat perhaps reflects not only his aggressiveness but a move to the Neel manor house (1356). At his death, Gilbert was holding by military service for half a knight's fee and two suits of court. It was later found that at his death his son Thomas Neel II was aged 20 years 45 weeks and 3 days (courts of 22 July and 24 September 1375 for Burghall, HD 91). It is Gilbert's archive which Edmund Lucas organised in HD 22a in 1414–15 as husband of his youngest daughter and ultimate heir, Mary. A sixteenth-century lawyer who made a 'breviate of the court rolls' of Burghall summed him up as 'ever in sutes quarelling and fighting' (HD 469), could this have been an early piece of work of Chief Justice Coke for Lady Anne Gresham? She was lady of Burghall and Sir Edward spent

---

16   (HD 85a). Of Walter Bulwer's former tenement, Bartholomew le Miller held by charter 11 acres which owed the office of *prepositus* and 6 which owed the office of *messor*. He also occupied 19 acres of various tenements in the lord's hands for lack of tenants, i.e. tenements Carpe, Fairman, Rotele, Roger Smith and Alice Cage, John Crane, Paye, Richard atte Bakhous, Robert Erneys, Slopere once Randolf, Crane and Cecily Horn.

Christmas at her house at Osterley when she died. Gilbert's widow Isabel later married John de Lyng (HD 77 of 1393), who was writer of a Neel terrier of the time of Richard II according to a court roll of 1449 (HD 149a). Their elder daughter Margaret followed her mother in marrying a Lyng, Thomas (*Cal. Close* 1381–5, pp. 544–5). Like her mother she remarried – John de Quarles (HD 78) and perhaps John Waylond, indefatigable transcriber of documents and local administrator, for she is called Margaret Waylond in 1430 (HD 22a, Fo. 37v no. 258, Copy of the last presentation of Letheringsett).

NORTHERNE AND ITS HEIRS THE NEWGATES

In 1332–3 Thomas Le Northerne was assessed at 2 s., well below the average, twice as much as Bartholomew le Miller and only one-sixth as much as Richard Neel. Like his father Richard, Thomas was often among those enrolled in lists of witnesses. Richard had been one of those privileged to have a fold in 1306 (HD 22a, Fo. 1v no. 1).[17] He obtained it of Bartholomew de Burgate who held under Denise de Montchesney, of the manor of Burghall (HD 22a, Fos. 27–29 no. 253), but the Northerns were also tenants of Hillhall (HD 51). Richard occurs as a witness for over thirty years, from about 1291 (HP 1023) to 1323 (HD 51), and Thomas for over forty, from 1303 (HP 1054) to 1347 (HD 31). Richard and Thomas witness together in 1312 (HP 1003) and 1322 (HP 1005). In 1336–7 Thomas Northerne was a juror on the inquiry into Holkham shipping and had a house near the shore (HP 1102). Thomas made a grant to Caterine Neel as a widow in 1335 (HP 1085, HD 22a, Fo. 16v no. 187) of a place in Burgate, following it up the next year with 33 1/2 acres scattered in forty-two pieces apparently all in the northern fields mostly the Stathe Field, adding one acre and 3 roods held for life by Ela wife of Bartholomew de Burgate, probably a Northerne. His seal bore an *agnus dei* suitable for a family whose pastoral enterprise was eventually to draw the censure of the *Domesday of Inclosure* in 1517.[18] Thomas's great charter was not only cited by William Wake in 1336 (HP 1092) but is quoted in a Neel manor court roll of 22 October 1449 (HD 194a) as evidence for the title of 34 acres and 1 rood of Thomas's granddaughter Juliana Patryk and her son John Newgate, who conveyed four score acres of marsh with a sheepfold and 50 acres of arable to John's son Thomas on 4 January 1461 (HD 145). In 1546 Edmund Newgate's estate consisted of 44 pieces in Stathe Field, 11 pieces in Church Field and only 8 pieces in South Field (HD 296). His pedigree is in a monumental inscription in the church and in the Visitation of Norfolk in 1664 (Harleian Society, 86, 1934, pp. 143–4). Could the name Northerne allude, not to a migration from the north, but to a concentration of land in the northern part of the parish? John Coke acquired the inheritance in Holkham of Edmund Newgate, gent., in 1659, reaching to the low tide mark. Thomas le Northerne was connected through the marriage of Ela with her husband Bartholomew de Burgate, and also perhaps with William Wake (HP 1092, HD 22a, Fo. 14 no. 163).

---

17   Richard was granted the tenements and bodies of the four children of John, son of Hyde with their broods on 19 Dec. 1294 by John son of Geoffrey le Bret, HD 22a, Fo. 10v no. 132. Perhaps he is the same as Richard le Norne who paid 11 1/2d. rent at Easter and 61/2d at Michaelmas in Geoffrey le Bret's rental of c. 1293–4, HD 11.

18   I.S. Leadam, *The Inquisition of 1517. Inclosures and Evictions*, Pt. II, *T.R.H.S.* NS, VII, 1893, p. 180. John Newgate devoted 30 acres of arable to pasture.

SILK

In 1272–3 the Holkham feodary shows that John Silk held 4 acres of Bartholomew de Burgate's holding of Geoffrey le Bret (later Neel Manor) and 19 acres and 1 fold of Ralph Hakun of Tosny's fee (later Hillhall). The latter is analysed in HD 75 Fo. 30v–32 in 1467/8. John Silk was one of those with the lowest assessment and the only one of his surname among the 53 taxpayers of 1332–3. Three John Silks occur in our documents. The first was the father of Adam, William and Gilbert (HP 1041 and 1045) and Ada (HD 14). Adam was in conflict with Olaf Ivari, merchant of Norway, over the import of specified lengths and breadths of timber in 1302 ordered in Holkham Town, thus involving the King of Norway in three years' ineffective correspondence with Edward I.[19] Could the surname be regarded as a metonym for the costly oriental fabric? Adam's sons John and Thomas took goods from a wreck in 1347 (HD 86, 87a, 85) and in 1388 a later John had to deliver le Clement of St. Andrews with its wool, hide, fells, and blanket.[20] Adam and Gilbert cannot be distinguished from namesakes who were sons of William and brothers of a John Silk of Holkham who cannot be always separated from a namesake who was son of Geoffrey and a brother William. Richard Silk had a twelve-ton ship 'La Charité'. Some of these Silks had successors who grew up to be active in the decades after the Black Death. Thomas Silk had John le Wright's croft and tenement in 1366 – could it be Silk's croft marked by the old coast line in the 1590 map? (HD 85a). He paid 6d rent to Hillhall compared with John's 14 1/2d. (HD 51). He was arrested for letting from custody the men from Scottish ships with John de Holkham an unpopular public figure and lord of Holkham who was hunted by rebels and escaped by sea under cover of darkness in 1381.[21] There were several called John, Thomas or Richard, and marriage connections with Calweres and Essers. Some daughters paid chevage as villeins by blood, but one Thomas who held by villein tenure was the son of a John whom John of Holkham had set free (Hillhall roll 1399). A colourful character most often mentioned was Simon, a capital pledge in 1352 and sometimes aletaster. He rescued sheep in 1366, detained barley in 1356, made an illegal cart track in 1372 when he detained an autumn boon work, refused to use the lord's mill in 1370, made

---

19   Cal. Patent 1301–1307 (1898), p. 183, m. 46d, 26 Nov. 1302, reading: 'The like, at the request of H, King of Norway, to William Haward and John le Breton on complaint by Olaf Iveri, merchant of Norway, that whereas he made an agreement at the town of Holcham, Co. Norfolk, with Adam Silk of that town, to load a ship in Norway with logs of a specified length and breadth, and send them to the said town, for which the said Adam was to pay Olaf a specified sum upon the latter's return to Holkham; although Adam received logs to the value of £ 147 8s., he has only payd £ 40 thereof, and refuses to pay the residue. They are to hear the pleadings of both parties according to merchant law, and if necessary to make enquiry by jury of the towns of Lenne, Blakeneye and Holcham, and other good men of the County of Norfolk. By K. on the information of J. de Benestede.' Cf. PRO, Lists and Indexes v. List of Ancient Correspondence, Chancery and Exchequer (revised), p. 292, Correspondence vol. 19, nos. 174 and 175. Alexander Bugge, in Diplomatorium Norvegicum, xix, i, 460; A. Bugge, 'Studier over de Norske byershandel og seltstyre', Norsk hist. Tidsskr., tillnegshefte til 1898, 197; A. Bugge, ed., Oldbreve til Kundskap om Norges indre og ytre forhold, Sprog, Sleylter, seder Lovginning og rettergang i middelalderen doktstykker vedrorende Norges forbindelse med de Britiske Oer (forste bind), Nittende Samling forste halvdel, Kristiano 1910; W. Purchas, Some History of Wells-next-the sea and district, 1965, p. 24.

20   Cal. Close, Richard II, vol. iii, 1385–9, p. 401.

21   C. Oman, The Great Revolt of 1381, 1906, pp. 113–4; Edgar Powell, The Rising of 1381 in East Anglia, 1896, p. 135.

tenement Burgonye waste and cast down a barn in 1367 when he had his horse in the lord's corn. He took a swan on the lord's fee in 1352, in 1364 he had kept 1/2 acre concealed for eight years, he detained cattle in 1375 and he withdrew from the lord's court without leave in 1377. He was collector in 1380[22] and arrested a Burnham man who had robbed the Abbot of West Dereham's house and stolen his horses at Holkham *tempore rumoris*, but Geoffrey Lyster pardoned the offender.[23]

SPELLER

John Speller was a pledge of Edmund le Miller on 1 November 1334 (HD 84). He was a villein who withheld his grain (22 July 1337, HD 82) and failed to use Burghall mill (20 January 1347, HD 86) according to the court at which he was admitted with his wife Margaret and his brood. He was among the six richest Holkham taxpayers in 1332–3 and in 1337–8 was master and owner of 2 ships, the 'Christofer' and 'La Welyfair' of 20 and 12 tons. In 1350 John was not in a tithing (HD 87a). For John and Richard Speller as tenants see *supra*. In 1332–3 there was a second taxpayer called Speller. Richard Speller's assessment was 4s. compared with John's 6s. 8d. He was owner and master of the ship Nicholas of 12 tons. There were a succession of John Speller, presumably father and son, between whom it is hard to distinguish. In 1364 there is a John Speller *capellanus* (HD 85a). John Speller junior was a pledge and had to pay Andrew Underklynt for damage by trespass (25 January 1334, HD 84). A rather late John Speller junior often failed to come as a capital pledge in 1366 (HD 85) though he (or his namesake) served in 1383–5. In 1390–1 the then John Speller senior and junior (married to a Newgate) made separate grants of different pieces of land, all so far as identifiable in the North Fields) to John Grigges of Wells (Hillhall Book, HD 75). Buildings which they held included a cottage outside the lord's bondage in Northgate (1382–3) held of Hillhall, a villein messuage at the Stathe let for 5 years in 1378 (also Hillhall) and a villein messuage in Crosgate let for 2 years in 1398. In 1386–90 he was ordered at the Hillhall court to repair his house. On 26 March 1367 the Burghall court (HD 85a) found that John Speller junior had removed from the lord's bondage two windows worth 12d. so he was in mercy 6d. In 1387 he held a messuage with one free acre of Burghall.

---

22   His bailiff's accounts for 1380 and 1381 for Hillhall as HD 65, 68.
23   A. Réville, *Le Soulèvement des travailleurs d'Angleterre en 1381*, 1898, pp. 89, 119, citing PRO Assize Rolls.

Pedigrees of Bret, Neel and
Montchesney Families

Sources:

Brets of Neel Manor: Holkham Documents, Holkham Papers, Norfolk Fines, *Curia Regis* Rolls, *Cal. Patent* Rolls.

Brets of Tobers: Holkham Documents, Holkham Papers, Cart. of Walsingham, Cart. of Dereham.

Neel Pedigree: Holkham Documents, Holkham Papers, Norwich Consistory Court.

Kin of Denise de Montchesney: GEC Peerage, Farrer, *Rotuli de Dominabus 1185* (ed. J.H. Round), F.M. Powicke, *Stephen Langton* (1928) and *Henry III and the Lord Edward* (1947).

The three Lucas Wills (1391, 1435, 1447)

> The three following wills provide additional information to the Neel pedigree transcribed by Edmund Lucas in the Neel Cartulary, HD 22a, Fo. 30 no. 254. They concern three generations of the Lucas family: Roland Lucas (1391), his son Edmund (1435) and his grandson Thomas (1447).

Will of Roland Lucas of East Dereham, Thursday 22 June 1391

> NCC, Harsyk Fo. 146, 22 June 1391, prob. 10 July 1391

In Dei nomine Amen Ego Rollandus Lucas de Estderham die Jovis ante festum Nativitatis Sancti Johannis Baptiste Anno domini millesimo cccmo nonagesimo primo condo testamentum meum in hunc modum In primis [commendo] animam meam Deo omnipotenti beate Marie Virgini et omnibus sanctis sui et corpus meum ad sepeliendum in cimiterio ecclesie Sancti Nicholai in Estderham ex parte australi Item lego fabricacioni ecclesie predicte xvj s. Item lego Johanni de Qwarles unam jupam talarim stragulatam et furratam. Et omnia alia bona mea mobilia et immobilia mea ubicumque fuerunt inventa do et lego Edmundo et Ricardo filiis executoribus meis Dat. die loco et anno prenominatis.

Will of Edmund Lucas of Holkham, Monday 25 April 1435

> NCC, Surflete Fo. 185v, 25 April 1435, prob. 17 Nov. 1435

<Testamentum Edmundi Lucas de Holkham defuncti>
In Dei nomine Amen. Anno Domini millesimo ccccmo xxxvto in festo Sancti Marci

evangeliste. Ego Edmundus Lucas de Holkham compos mentis et sane memorie condo
testamentum meum in hunc modum In primis lego animam Deo omnipotenti beate
Marie et omnibus Sanctis corpus .. ecclesiastice sepulture de Holkham predicta. Item
lego summo altari ecclesie de Holkham viii d. Item lego fabrice ejusdem ecclesie ij s.
vj d. Item lego lumini aratri iiij d. Residuum omnium bonorum meorum non
legatorum do et lego Marie Lucas uxori mea Stephano Lucas et Ricardo Lucas clerico
filiis meis quosquidem ordino facio et constituo meos executores per presentem Dat.
die et anno domini supradictis.

Will of Thomas Lucas of Holkham, Saturday 25 February 1447

 NCC, Fo. 133 Wilbey, 25 Feb. 1447, ultima voluntas 7 March 1447, prob. 20 April
 1447.

<Testamentum Thomas Lucas armigeri de Holkham>
In Dei nomine anno vicesimo quinto die mensis Februarij de domini millesimo cccc
xlvito Ego Thomas Lucas de Holkham armiger compos mentis cum bona existens
memoria condo testamentum meum in hunc modum. In primis commendo animam
meam Deo omnipotenti beate Marie cum omnibus Sanctis corpus quod sepeliendum in
ecclesia Sancte Withburge de Holkham predicta in Capella Sancti Thome martyri
juxta matrem meam. Item lego summo altari ecclesie ejusdem vj s. viij d. Item lego
fabrice ejusdem ecclesie xl s. Item lego diversis quatuor luminibus scilicet Aratri, le
Rowell, Sancte Withburge et Sancti Christofori vj s. viii d. equis portionibus. Item
lego Stephano fratre meo optimam togam meam pannalatam et optimam et optimum
equum meum. Item lego Domino Ricardo fratre meo Rectore de Horningtoft unum
equum bayodum unum pallium cum lanario. Residuum vero omnium bonorum et
catallorum meorum mobilium non legatorum do et lego Etheldrede uxori mee quam
ordino et constituo executorem meum principalem et Ricardum Lucas Rectorem de
Horningtoft fratrem meum ac Dominum Galfridum Coly vicarium ecclesie parrochiale
de Holkham dicte Etheldrede uxori et executrice mea associatos consiliarios et
conductores et Willelmum Ruchewode armigerum supervisorem eorumdem ut ipsa
cum consilio eorumdem ordinat et disponat pro anima mea et pro animabus parentum
et benefactorum meorum prout melius viderit sibi Deo placere et anima mea prodesse.
In cujus rei testimonium huic presenti testamento sigillum meum apposui. Datum die
loco et anno domini supradicto.

Last Will of Thomas Lucas of Holkham, Tuesday 7 March 1447

<Ultima voluntas ejusdem>
Haec est ultima voluntas mei Thome Lucas de Holkham armigeri sano mente facta
die martis modo proxima ante festum Sancti Gregorij pape anno Domini millesimo
ccccmo xlvito et anno regni Regis Henrici sexti post conquestum vicesimo quinto. In
primo volo ante omnia quod omnia et singula debita mea plenarie persolvantur. Item
volo quod omnia in testamento meo contenta legata et assignata sint plenarie per
executores meos et persolvantur. Item volo quod Etheldreda uxor mea habeat et
possideat sibi et assignatis suis omnia et singula bona mea et catalla mobilia utensilia
et vesturas terrarum prout illa prius legata ac in testamento meo assignata et contenta.
Item volo quod tota vestura crescens et tretura per istum annum instantem super
omnes terras meas in Holkham seminatas et seminandas cujuscumque generis fuerunt
dividatae inter ipsam Etheldredam uxorem meam et me ita quod medietas dicte

vesture recipiatur per executores meos et distribuatur pro anima mea et ad exequandum presentem meam voluntatem proviso tunc quod omnia onera misia et exponentia circa easdem inter nos eque supportantur. Item volo et lego fabrice et sustentationi ecclesie de Horningtoft vi s. viii d. Item volo et lego summo altari ejusdem ecclesie iij s. iiij d. Item volo et lego ecclesie Sancti Petri de Wesenham vj s. viij d. Item volo habere presbiterum ydoneum et honestum ad celebrandum pro anima mea et parentum meorum in ecclesia de Holkham per unum annum duraturum aut per duos annos si possit fieri post legata et assignata executa mea et debita mea persoluta. Item volo quod Etheldreda uxor mea habeat totum manerium meum in Holkham Surlingham et Sweynesthorp scilicet cum advocacione ecclesie Sancti Andree de Leryngsete et cum omnibus pertinentibus eidem manerio spectantibus ac etiam totum manerium meum vocatum Kypton in villa de Wesenham et Raynham cum omnibus redditibus homagiis serviciis et pertinenciis eisdem maneriis spectantibus quovismodo ad totum terminum minoris etatis Elizabethe filie mee ad persolvendum et exequendum presentem voluntatem et testamentum meum perimplendum. Ita quod cum dicta Elizabeth ad legitimam etatem pervenerit habeat medietatem predicti manerij de Kypton cum suis pertinentibus in villa de Wesenham et Raynham tenendum sibi et heredibus de corpore suo legitime procreatis et exemptam de capitalibus dominis feodorum illorum per servicia inde debita et de jure consueta. Item volo quod Etheldreda uxor mea habeat alteram medietatem dicti manerij vocati Kypton tunc partum et totum manerium de Holkham Surlingham et Sweynesthorp cum advocacione predicta ad totam vitam suam tenendum de capitalibus dominis feodorum illorum per servicia inde debita et de jure consueta. Item volo quod post decessum dicte Etheldrede uxoris mee omnia et singula predicta maneria de Holkham Surlingham et Sweynesthorp Wesenham et Raynham una cum advocacione ecclesie predicte et cum omnibus et singulis pertinentibus suis integre remaneantur dicta Elizabeth filia mea habendum et tenendum sibi et heredibus de corpore suo legitime procreatis et procreandis de capitalibus dominis feodorum illorum per servicia inde debita et de jure consueta. Et si contingat prefata Elizabeth sine herede de corpore suo legitime procreato obierit tunc volo quod omnia predicta maneria cum advocacione predicta ac cum omnibus pertinentibus suis integre remaneant Stephano Lucas fratre meo habendum et tenendum sibi et heredibus de corpore suo legitime procreatis de capitalibus dominis feodorum illorum per servicia inde debita et de jure consueta. Et si contingat dictum Stephanum sine herede de corpore suo procreato legitime obire tunc volo quod omnia predicta maneria cum advocacione predicta cum pertinentibus suis integre remaneant Ricardo Lucas fratre meo habendum et tenendum sibi et heredibus suis de corpore suo legitime procreatis de capitalibus dominis feodorum illorum per servicia inde debita et de jure consueta. Et si contingat ipsum Ricardum sine herede de corpore suo legitime extunc volo quod omnia et singula maneria predicta cum advocacione ecclesie predicte et cum omnibus suis pertinentibus rectis heredibus mei predicti Thome Lucas integre remaneant habendum et tenendum dictis heredibus et assignatis suis de capitalibus dominis feodorum illorum per servicia inde debita et de jure consueta in perpetuum per presentem. In cujus rei testimonio nunc presentis mee ultime voluntatis sigillum meum apposui. Data apud Holkham predicto die anno supradicto.

BRET OF NEEL MANOR

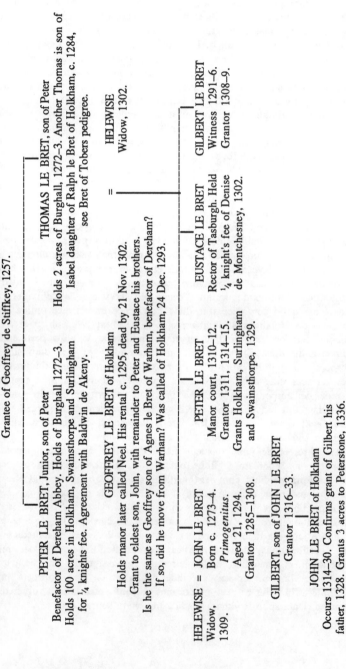

PETER LE BRET, Senior
On 7 Oct. 1198 Peter son of Geoffrey granted Vincent the Clerk 42 acres for 6 marks and 2½ marks to his wife. He obtained 40 acres in Holkham and 40s. rent in Holkham and Surlingham from Peter de Stiffkey, 1213–15. Grantee of Geoffrey de Stiffkey, 1257.

THOMAS LE BRET, son of Peter
Holds 2 acres of Burghall, 1272–3. Another Thomas is son of Isabel daughter of Ralph le Bret of Holkham, c. 1284, see Bret of Tobers pedigree.

HELEWISE
Widow, 1302.

PETER LE BRET, Junior, son of Peter
Benefactor of Dereham Abbey. Holds of Burghall 1272–3. Holds 100 acres in Holkham, Swainsthorpe and Surlingham for ¼ knights fee. Agreement with Baldwin de Akeny.

GEOFFREY LE BRET of Holkham
Holds manor later called Neel. His rental c. 1295, dead by 21 Nov. 1302. Grant to eldest son, John, with remainder to Peter and Eustace his brothers. Is he the same as Geoffrey son of Agnes le Bret of Warham, benefactor of Dereham? If so, did he move from Warham? Was called of Holkham, 24 Dec. 1293.

EUSTACE LE BRET
Rector of Tasburgh. Held ¼ knight's fee of Denise de Montchesney, 1302.

GILBERT LE BRET
Witness 1291–6. Grantor 1308–9.

PETER LE BRET
Manor court, 1310–12. Grantor 1311, 1314–15. Grants Holkham, Surlingham and Swainsthorpe, 1329.

HELEWISE = JOHN LE BRET
Widow, 1309. Born c. 1273–4. *Primogenitus.* Aged 21, 1294. Grantor 1285–1308.

GILBERT, son of JOHN LE BRET
Grantor 1316–33.

JOHN LE BRET of Holkham
Occurs 1314–30. Confirms grant of Gilbert his father, 1328. Grants 3 acres to Peterstone, 1336.

BRET OF TOBERS

RALPH LE BRET of Holkham
Is Ralph le Bret father of Adam the landholder mentioned in grant to William Prior of Walsingham?

ISABEL
Was her father Ralph le Bret the same as Ralph le Bret the father of Adam?

THOMAS
Witness, c. 1284. Evidently distinguished from Thomas le Bret the son of Peter who held 2 acres of Burghall manor.

ADAM LE BRET
Son of Ralph. Granted 7 roods free land to Angerus abbot of Dereham for 16d. p.a. Messuage held of Adam, granted by Thomas With to Prior of Walsingham.

ADAM LE BRET, grantor
Son of Adam. Benefactor of Dereham Abbey. Called Adam le Bret, junior. Confirms ½ acre given to Walsingham by Thomas With of Holkham, Chaplain.

JOHN LE BRET
Witness, c. 1274–96.
Holds of Roger Brown of Arundel fee annotated as Tobers by E. Lucas in Holkham Feodary, 1279–80. Grantor, 1321.

JOHN LE BRET
Lord of Tobers manor before its inclusion in Hillhall manor (1331–2). Grantor, 1330. The last Bret to be lord of Tobers.

NEEL PEDIGREE

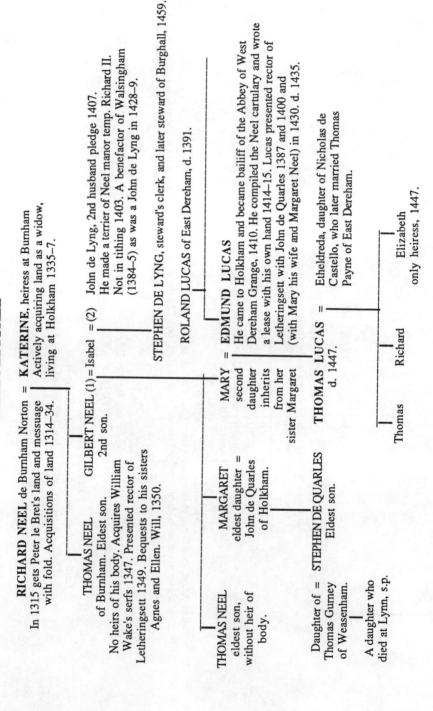

RICHARD NEEL de Burnham Norton = KATERINE, heiress at Burnham
In 1315 gets Peter le Bret's land and messuage with fold. Acquisitions of land 1314–34.
Actively acquiring land as a widow, living at Holkham 1335–7.

THOMAS NEEL of Burnham. Eldest son. No heirs of his body. Acquires William Wake's serfs 1347. Presented rector of Letheringsett 1349. Bequests to his sisters Agnes and Ellen. Will, 1350.

GILBERT NEEL (1) = Isabel = (2) John de Lyng, 2nd husband pledge 1407.
2nd son.

(2) John de Lyng, 2nd husband pledge 1407. He made a terrier of Neel manor temp. Richard II. Not in tithing 1403. A benefactor of Walsingham (1384–5) as was a John de Lyng in 1428–9.

STEPHEN DE LYNG, steward's clerk, and later steward of Burghall, 1459.

ROLAND LUCAS of East Dereham, d. 1391.

MARY = EDMUND LUCAS
second daughter inherits from her sister Margaret

He came to Holkham and became bailiff of the Abbey of West Dereham Grange, 1410. He compiled the Neel cartulary and wrote a lease with his own hand 1414–15. Lucas presented rector of Letheringsett with John de Quarles 1387 and 1400 and (with Mary his wife and Margaret Neel) in 1430. d. 1435.

MARGARET eldest daughter = John de Quarles of Holkham.

THOMAS NEEL eldest son, without heir of body.

Daughter of = STEPHEN DE QUARLES
Thomas Gurney of Weasenham.
Eldest son.

A daughter who died at Lynn, s.p.

THOMAS LUCAS = Etheldreda, daughter of Nicholas de Castello, who later married Thomas Payne of East Dereham.
d. 1447.

Thomas

Richard

Elizabeth only heiress, 1447.

KIN OF DENISE DE MONTCHESNEY

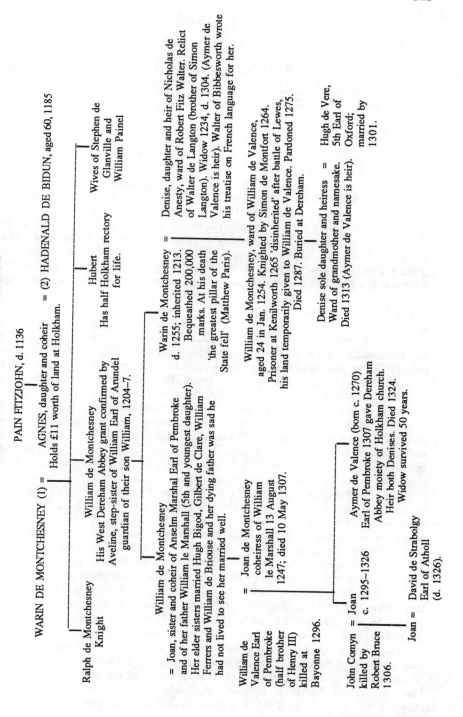

PAIN FITZJOHN, d. 1136

WARIN DE MONTCHESNEY (1) = AGNES, daughter and coheir = (2) HADENALD DE BIDUN, aged 60, 1185
Holds £11 worth of land at Holkham.

Ralph de Montchesney
Knight

William de Montchesney
His West Dereham Abbey grant confirmed by
Aveline, step-sister of William Earl of Arundel
guardian of their son William, 1204-7.

Hubert
Has half Holkham rectory
for life.

Wives of Stephen de
Glanville and
William Painel

William de Montchesney
= Joan, sister and coheir of Anselm Marshal Earl of Pembroke
and of her father William le Marshall (5th and youngest daughter).
Her elder sisters married Hugh Bigod, Gilbert de Clare, William
Ferrers and William de Briouse and her dying father was sad he
had not lived to see her married well.

Warin de Montchesney
d. 1255; inherited 1213.
Bequeathed 200,000
marks. At his death
'the greatest pillar of the
State fell' (Matthew Paris).

Denise, daughter and heir of Nicholas de
Anesty, ward of Robert Fitz Walter. Relict
of Walter de Langton (brother of Simon
Langton). Widow 1234, d. 1304. (Aymer de
Valence is heir). Walter of Bibbesworth wrote
his treatise on French language for her.

William de
Valence Earl
of Pembroke
(half brother
of Henry III)
killed at
Bayonne 1296.

= Joan de Montchesney
coheiress of William
le Marshall 13 August
1247; died 10 May 1307.

William de Montchesney, ward of William de Valence,
aged 24 in Jan. 1254. Knighted by Simon de Montfort 1264.
Prisoner at Kenilworth 1265 'disinherited' after battle of Lewes,
his land temporarily given to William de Valence. Pardoned 1275.
Died 1287. Buried at Dereham.

Denise sole daughter and heiress =
Ward of grandmother and namesake.
Died 1313 (Aymer de Valence is heir).

Hugh de Vere,
5th Earl of
Oxford;
married by
1301.

Aymer de Valence (born c. 1270)
Earl of Pembroke 1307 gave Dereham
Abbey moiety of Holkham church.
Heir both Denises. Died 1324.
Widow survived 50 years.

John Comyn = Joan
killed by   c. 1295–1326
Robert Bruce
1306.

Joan = David de Strabolgy
       Earl of Atholl
       (d. 1326).

Commentaries on the Feodary of Holkham

A faded version on paper in HD 6 is derived from West Dereham Abbey, for it concludes with a note about the Abbey's half of the church at Holkham followed by six and a half pages summarising thirty charters mostly relating to the church. Like the West Dereham Cartulary it lacks sub-titles and its text contains many of the same idiosyncracies. Both the Dereham and the Lucas version are alike in listing the five free tenants of Burton Lazars ignored elsewhere; but the Dereham version is not interested in the free tenants of Geoffrey le Bret who naturally appear in the Neel Cartulary, though it is largely based upon it. Both versions ignore Ralph Hakun's suit at the half-yearly courts of Denise de Montchesney (Burghall). There are five versions described as transcribed by John Waylond though some are clearly later copies. These are HD 5a, 5b, 71 and 120. Waylond was extremely active in the estate business of several Holkham manors. It is not known how he may be related to that Waylond whose surname was taken by Edmund Lucas's sister-in-law Margaret, the eldest daughter of Gilbert and Isabel Neel of HD 22a, Fo. 30 no. 254 and Fo. 37v no. 258. HD 5b contains a terrier for Peterstone and Burnham for 1471-2, so presumably was made then for Peterstone. A book of rentals by Waylond, HD 120, presumably belongs to Burghall as it describes Walsingham, Burghall and Peterstone property at Holkham in 1439-40. The scribe of HD 71 may have been unfamiliar with the locality as he entitles Peterstone Palston. The text printed is that of Edmund Lucas. In HD 55 the title is '*In feodario hundredi de Northgrenehowe continetur vt inferius patet*'. The order and text of HD 55 has more affinity with the transcripts of Lucas and Dereham than with that of John Waylond. Its unique title is a significant indication of the archetype. HD 5b follows the text of the Feodary with details of tenants in Northgate, the accounts of John Iring *messor* for 1392/3, a terrier of Peterstone for Burnham Overy, 1471/2, and a terrier of Peterstone for Holkham Fields in the same year. In HD 71 and 120 a Wighton rental follows the Feodary. The signature of Dame Anne Gresham occurs in HD 120, a book of eight rentals, suggesting that this copy of the Feodary belonged to her manor of Burghall rather than to Wighton. Walsingham Priory would also have had a copy of the Feodary but that has not been found among those at Holkham; for it would be identifiable readily, as on the dorse was written a copy of the inquisition of 1308 about sheep folds (HD 22a, Fo. 1v no. 1). For according to a statement in the Walsingham Cartulary (BL Ms. Cotton Nero E VII, Fo. 55), *Ista inquisicio patet in feodario super dorsum eiusdem in principio*, and this seems not to be at Holkham. It appears however that the Walsingham copy of the Feodary is perhaps not any of the copies found at Holkham, unless indeed the Priory had two. For on a Peterstone terrier (on which John Waylond of Holkham made pen trials) there occurs a quotation from a Feodary of the Hundred of North Greenhoe, then in the hands of the Prior of Walsingham. This reads: *Terre Prioris de Petraston in Holkham vt patet per rotulum Feodarij Hundredi de Grenhowe quod est in manibus Prioris de Walsingham. Prior de Petra tenet terras quondam Radulphi Noioun videlicet xxiij sokemannos qui tenent in villenagio. vj^xx. acras terre et xij acras terre cum suis mesuagiis et idem tenet iij coterellos qui tenent in villenagio iiij acras terre cum cotagiis. Idem prior tenet terras quondam Iohannis Goldwyn de feodo Noioun videlicet j mesuagium et xl acras terre et j faldam et reddebat pro xiij dicto Noioun .v. s. iiij d. Iohanne Sylke tenet de predicto Noioun iij acras terre et .j. rodam et reddit per annum j d. Idem Prior tenet de Feodo Hakeney modo. T. Grigg' de Well' . xl . acras terre et j faldam et reddit per annum dicto Thome iiij s . x d. ob.*

Commentary I

Geoffrey de Lusignan, son of Henry III's half brother, Geoffrey de Lusignan.
He was ward of John d'Harcourt and his wife Joan in 1272/3. John d'Harcourt was married to Joan de Nodariis, widow of Roger and mother of Roger. Cf. *Cal. Inq. Misc.* vol. iii no. 473, 2 May 1298. Wighton was an 'ancient demesne' manor. Henry III gave it to his son Edward who gave it to Geoffrey de Lusignan. *Rot. Hund.* 483. Matthew Paris describes the arrival in 1251 of Geoffrey's father, Geoffrey, with his brothers William de Valence and Ailmer Bishop of Winchester. Helen Cam cites Wighton as an example of an 'ancient demesne' manor in the *Hundred and the Hundred Rolls*, 1963, p. 196.

Commentary II

A Wighton rental indicating locations of tenements in 1456–7 is in HD 71 and HD 120 following the text of the Feodary. This includes 26 acres of the Abbot of West Dereham, a messuage of John Newgate at the Stathe, a messuage there once of John Speller, Alice Seger's curtilage called Norman and one once Cordell's at Eastgate, Thomas Smyth shipman's messuage at Crossgate, the messuage of Robert de Bregge once of John Mey next Newgate's at the Stathe, the messuage of John Torold chandler (once Henry Asty's formerly Edmund Patryk's) at the Stathe, Thomas Esser's messuage at the Stathe, part of Geoffrey Coly's messuage in Crossgate, Thomas Clerke's messuage at the Stathe, Geoffrey Porter's messuages at the Stathe, William Bulman's messuage at the Stathe, Thomas Gunthorpe's messuage, Robert Koo's messuage at the Stathe (once Henry Silk's), John Haltre's messuage at the Stathe, the messuage of John Aldous's heirs at Crossgate, parcel of Thomas Martyn's messuage, Henry Mere's messuage (once John Torold's), William Geyton's curtilage at Crossgate besides many small pieces of land and 3 cottages and messuages held by base tenure. See also Commentary XXIV.

Commentary III

Prior de Peterston tenet in Holcham et Styuekye dimidium feodum Militis de domina Philippa Regina Anglie de Manerio de Wighton et illa de Rege in Capite, cf. *Feudal Aids 1284–1431,* vol. iii, p. 547 (dated 1346). A terrier and rental of Peterstone's Feodum Noion is in HD 22a, Fos. 55–55v no. 267 for 1456–7, made shortly after the annexation of Peterstone's lands to Walsingham Priory in 1449. This describes only eleven holdings of land of which the largest is only five roods. All but one (which is in two pieces) consist of single pieces of land. There are two pieces in Crossgate and no reference to messuages or cottages. HD 129 is a Peterstone terrier of 1452–3, a book of 20 leaves made by John Waylond and describing lands *in Bondagio de*

Peterstone quondam Iohannis Noiun (or *Nogeons*). It gives much more detail. Some of the tenants were also tenants of Hillhall and of Burghall. On 2 September 1538 the Prior of Walsingham (as owner of Peterstone's lands) let Goldingscrofte, later in the hands of John Newgate and William Waylond, for 15s. p.a. to Thomas Pepys. This was not part of the 130 acres of pasture and 80 acres of arable anciently called Peterstone land for which the bailiff of the manor of Peterstone rendered account the following year, HD 280.

Commentary IV

Thomas d'Akeny, 1275, 1302, 1315 (pilgrimages of Sir James), Ch. Moor, *Knights of Edward I*, 1929–32, 5 vols., A–E, p. 261; John (like William de Montchesney) was in the retinue of Richard of Cornwall in 1257 at his coronation as king of the Romans but N. Denholm-Young could not trace him, *Richard of Cornwall*, 1947, p. 91.

Commentary V

A terret is one of the two rings by which the leash is attached to the jesses of the hawk in falconry, OED.

Commentary VI

Roger de Tosny III de Conches had a grant from Henry II in 1157–8 of 100 solidates of land in Holkham. He died soon after 29 Dec. 1208. His heirs still had the 100 solidates in 1218 and 1219. GEC, *Peerage*, 12, 764; Pipe Roll, 4 Henry II (1157/8), p. 125; Pipe Roll, 11 John (1209/10), p. 41; J.H. Round, ed., *Rotuli de Dominabus*, p. 77 no. 4. Holkham no longer has the charter witnessed by Roger son of Ralph and his mother, Margaret, which General Wrottesley reported to J.H. Round. It is not recorded among letters from George Wrottesley to Round in London University Library, Institute of Historical Research Ms. 694. See also Ida de Tosny and d'Akeny, VCH *Oxon.*, v. 137–8.

Commentary VII

Hillhall accounts include the profits of the market. References to the market place occur. In the Hillhall Book (HD 75, Fo. 3) Thomas d'Akeny's sokemen held 110 (not 130) acres. There were only nine customary tenements of 6 acres each owing the office of *messor* in 1467–8 but there were 42 free tenants.

Commentary VIII

For Creake's lands see *Cart. of Creake*, nos. 175–203 where *Utgong* is misread as *le Uegong*. Of the 491/2 acres of Creake 46 may be the subject of a final concord. Cf. Appendix 5, no. 18. In it, following a plea of warranty, Reginald son of Geoffrey of Holkham recognised 46 acres as the abbey's right by gift of Reginald and gave a further 21/2 acres in Utgon' and an acre near Adam le Bret's mill. The cartulary shows that this mill was in Sut[h]gate. The rent was 9s. 111/2d. *p.a.* – 30d. at Christmas, Easter and St. John Baptist's day and 91/2 for all suit and service. The Hillhall Book describes in 1467–8 the abbot's free tenement of 44 acres 3 roods (held by military service of the Tosny fee) in detail, HD 75, Fo. 14v. In 1428 the rent of 9s. 6d. and 11/2 bushells of corn covered 48 acres and 2 cottages, HD 115.

Commentary IX

Harvey Bulman was one of twelve jurors inquiring into services due to Thomas d'Akeny, HD 22a, Fo. 12 no. 150. He was not only an under-tenant of Hillhall but also of Burghall, for he held 2 acres for 4d. of the ubiquitous Bartholomew de Burgate. His name is sometimes wrongly written Henry. Harvey occurs in court rolls as late as 1337, HD 84 and HD 86. His surname flourished locally in the fourteenth and fifteenth centuries persisting into the sixteenth. Harvey son of Thomas Bulman of Holme occurs in a final concord of 1281 recovering 12 acres in Holkham and Burnham for 4s. 1d. rent *p.a.* from William Reynald and Cecily his wife for 100s. Cf. Appendix 5, no. 24. In 1317–18 Creake Abbey obtained from William Bulman his Holkham land in exchange for a messuage and 55 acres 3 rods in 35 pieces at Quarles, BD O, Fo. 19.

Commentary X

The Hillhall Book describes in detail an estate of 19 acres and a free fold held by military service of the Tosny fee acquired by Robert Koo in right of his wife the widow of Henry Silk the successor of John Silk, HD 75, Fo. 30v. This cites John's final concord of 1278 with Ralph Hakun. Cf. Appendix 5, no 23. In 1428 the tenant of the land and fold granted by Hakun was Margaret Silk once Thomas Silk and afterwards John Silk her husband, HD 115.

Commentary XI

In the free rental of Burghall in HD 120, Fo. 3v (also HD 124) the location of the Peterstone lands are not defined in such detail as is given in the free rental of Hillhall in HD 75. In addition to this 2s. 2d. rent Peterstone paid Burghall in 1439–40, 2d. and another 2d. for lands once of Ralph Ryborth, Nicholas Brown and Robert Bulman respectively. Terriers of Peterstone for 1427–8 and 1456–7 are HD 114 and HD 22a, Fo. 53 no. 265. HD 5b may have belonged to Peterstone for it includes Peterstone terriers for Burnham Overy and Holkham, 1471–2. Some of Peterstone's lands in Holkham did not belong to the priory in the thirteenth century but were obtained from the Abbot of Creake in exchange for land in Quarles in 1314–15. These are described in BD O, a survey of the lands of the Prior of Walsingham. The Priory of Walsingham later obtained the lands of Peterstone.

Commentary XII

In 1302 Walter Hakun of Holkham had one sixteenth of a knight's fee of the Honor of Arundel. In 1324 Ralph Hakun was the tenant, Farrer, i, p. 109. The one sixteenth part of a knight's fee held by Ralph Hakun or Hacoun is mentioned as held of the barony of Montchesney in an inquisition on the death of Aymer de Valence, Earl of Pembroke in 1324 and of that of his successor David de Strabolgy, Earl of Atholl, in 1326 when his son David was found in 1327 to be next heir, aged 20, *Cal. IPM* , vi, no. 518, p. 333 and no. 759, p. 482. During the Atholl minority Hakun held of Walter de Manny, HD 19a and *Feudal Aids 1284–1431*, vol. iii, 547.

Commentary XIII

John Silk held a larger estate of Hakun of the fee of Tosny (above). The composition of that 19 acres received with a fold is analysed in a rental of Robert Koo (free tenant of Hillhall), who obtained it as the husband of Katerine the former wife of Henry Silk, John's successor, in 1467–8, HD 75, Fos. 30v–32. John obtained it by a final concord of 1278 which mentions Baldwin d'Akeny. Cf. Appendix 5, no. 23.

Commentary XIV

Robert Fuller is also mentioned below in the account of the 12 acres which Geoffrey Godwyne holds of Geoffrey de Hindringham. Fuller was also a tenant of Hillhall and Wighton in the mid fifteenth century. A Burghall rental of 1439–40 in HD 120 describes Fuller's land, once Brice's, 6 acres of the tenement of Geoffrey Godwyne, adding the information that it was liable for the office of *messor*. The 6 acres of Geoffrey Godwyne paying 13d., two hens and a carriage duty worth 6d. are also mentioned in HD 4. They seem to be identifiable in a Burghall rental of 1424, HD 113, paid by William Oxenford for tenement Bryce, cf. HD 120. John Bryce's tenement was described as late of John Godwyne when a heriot of 2s. 8d. was paid on the admission of Bryce's heir, Katerine wife of William Fuller and daughter of his daughter Joan, HD 97. Fuller's son was called William Fuller *alias* Oxford, HD 75.

Commentary XV

In 1243 Robert II de Tattershall obtained the Honor of Buckenham (which included Holkham) through Maud the eldest of the co-heirs of Hugh d'Aubigny, Earl of Arundel (d. 1243). He died in 1249, his son Robert II died in 1273, his grandson Robert IV died in 1298. His grandson Robert VI died a childless minor, a royal ward, in 1306 leaving his aunts heirs. Thomas de Cailly, son of his aunt Emma and Adam de Cailly, inherited Buckenham in 1306 when aged 24 and died in 1356, I.J. Sanders, *English Baronies, a study of their origin and descent 1086–1327*, 1960, p. 70; Farrer, pp. 384–5; *Feudal Aids*, iii, p. 456; *Cal. IPM*, iv, no. 163, p. 103; no. 391, p. 258. In 1324 Thomas de Cailly held 5½ knight's fees in thirteen Norfolk parishes out of 11½ knight's fees which Aymer de Valence, Earl of Pembroke, held of the inheritance of Robert de Tattershall, *Cal. IPM*, vi, no. 487, p. 287.

Commentary XVI

Walsingham held 46 acres by military service of the fee of Tobers, granted by Ralph son of Silvester in HD 3, described in detail in HD 75, Fo. 13 and 155, Fo. 8v (Hillhall Book). In the Walsingham Cartulary Ralph son of Silvester's grant is 32 acres of arable and 25 acres of marsh, BL Ms. Cotton Nero E VII. This was of the fee of Adam le Bret with 6 acres of the fee of Gerard de Noyon and 6 acres of the fee of the Abbot of Viterbo. Adam son of Ralph le Bret confirmed this, *ibid.* no. ciii as did Robert son of William of Walsingham, Ralph's nephew, *ibid.* no. civ. The cartulary contains many small grants. The Hillhall Book describes Ralph's grant as 46 acres, including 7 acres, inclosed in the Lyng and Walsingham Grange, HD 75, Fo. 13. It names the lord of Tobers Manor before it was incorporated into Hillhall. It indicates which Hillhall freeholders hold land by knight service of Tobers and where, but holdings had been much fragmented. It names former holders but holdings had been subject to so much reconstitution by 1467–8 that identification with those of the lay free tenants of John le Bret is rendered perhaps impossible.

Commentary XVII

A survey of folds in 1306, HD 22a, Fo. 1v no. 1, distinguishes between Walsingham's common fold in the fields and Ling and that next the salt marsh. For the latter see Hakun's free tenants above. Tobers manor house lay to the east of Hillhall manor house on Wighton way by the modern Tubbins Wood. The arms of Tobers were a canting pair of bears according to a note accompanying a list of the lords. A terrier of Tobers Manor of about 1375 is HD 63.

Commentary XVIII

There is an undated grant of a house to John Brain of Holkham from Geoffrey son of William de Hindringham in HD 22a, Fo. 9 no. 108. William of Hindringham makes grants to Richard Neel in HD 22a, Fos. 18 no. 196 and 23 no. 247, in 1315 and 1320.

Commentary XIX

Mary Neville, lady of Middleham (Yorks), was great-grand-niece of Alan, Count of Richmond. She married Robert Neville, son of the lord of Raby, co-heir of her father, Ranulph (died 1270). She died in 1320.

Commentary XX

HD 138 contains copies of Robert Fuller's five title deeds to the land and fold granted by William son of Hamo de Hindringham to Geoffrey, son of William Godwine of Holkham. William father of Geoffrey had it of Bartholomew, son of Walter of Wighton. Fuller was also called Robert Oxford of Holkham.

Commentary XXI

Vewters Manor in Burnham Overy had appurtenances in Holkham. This entry occupies the same position in HD 6 (with which Edmund Lucas would have been familiar as bailiff of Huncrondale). In HD 5a, 5b, 71 and 120 it follows the fee of John le Bret (Tobers Manor) also held of Tattershall and the fee of Clare (the brothers of St. Lazars). John le Veutre held in Holkham one 16th part of a knight's fee of Robert de Tattershall, *Feudal Aids 1284–1431*, vol. iii, p. 547. William le Veutre once held it (cf. W. Farrer, *Honors and Knight's Fees*, vol. iii, 109). Richard Hoo was lord in the 16th century. The manor passed via a daughter of Peter Lombard to Horace Walpole. In 1408/9, Pomfret's manor was taken out of Vewters and went to the college of Holy Trinity, Pontefract, Yorks., also called Knolles alms house. Many of the early documents went to PRO and are among Ancient Deeds. A 'Pomfrett dragge' of 1451–2 is HD 281. Vewter Manor was dismembered in 1379/80. Thomas Grigges hoped to exchange many pieces of land with Pomfret, HD 75, Fo. 108. The Hillhall Book refers to the land of the college of Pomfret as being once of Robert Knolles, HD 75, Fo. 4v. William de Calthorpe held land of the heirs of Tattershall in Burnham as did John Veutre, *Feudal Aids 1284–1431*, vol. iii, p. 517, but perhaps Vewter's land at Holkham included the 24 acres and 2 roods described in the terrier of William de Calthorpe in HD 22a, Fo. 35 no. 256. It comprised 39 small pieces of which all except two lay in the South Field especially in its central and western furlongs towards the Burnham Thorpe boundary. The terrier did not include an 18 acre field in the Southwestern corner of the parish called 'Sir Phillippe Parker's xviij acres' in the 1590 map. Elizabeth, daughter and heir of Philip de Calthorpe married Henry Parker of Erwarton, Suffolk and later William Wodehouse Esq. In 1449 William de Calthorpe also farmed 98¹/₂ acres in the South Field of Peterstone Priory (HD 194 Nogeon's court).

Commentary XXII

The Honor of Clare lay in nine counties. The Earl of Gloucester's tenants in Norfolk, Suffolk and Essex only attended the court of Clare, cf. rolls printed by Warren Ault in *Court Rolls of the Abbey of Ramsey and of the Honor of Clare*, 1928, pp. 75–110. The Master of Burton Lazars held a quarter of two knight's fees in free alms by gift of the Earl of Gloucester, *Rot. Hund.*, i, 1812, p. 483. The Hospital of Burton Lazars, Leics., was the chief Lazar house in England and owned Chosele Manor and Wyndham. This item is between Peter le Veutre and Feodum Richemond in HD 71. The Book of Edmund Newgate (HD 296) describes every piece of land in the South Field in 1549: pieces belonging to Burton Lazars were ¹/₂ acre in Longlands, 1¹/₂ acres in Middlefurlong, two ¹/₂ acres in Steynhill, ¹/₂ acre in Gunnyngswong, ¹/₂ acre in Shortland, ¹/₂ rood in Lethirpitway, ¹/₂ rood in Creakegate, 3, 5 and 7 roods at Thorpeheads.

Commentary XXIII

There is a detailed rental in the Hillhall Book of Thomas Grigges' tenement of Gunores in Bacon's fee, renewed 1482–3, HD 75, Fo. 80v and HD 155, Fo. 46. Thomas Bacon holds in Holkham and Cockthorpe half a knight's fee of Hugh Bardolf and Hugh Bardolf holds of the Bishop of Norwich in 1302, *Feudal Aids 1280–1431*, vol. iii, p. 420. The Bardolf of Wormegay were an important Norfolk family. In 1330, after the death of Thomas Bardolf, William Wake was found to hold 50 acres for a fourth part of a knight's fee; *Cal. IPM*, vol. vii, no. 243, p. 174. References occur to Wake's mill, marsh, croft and sty, not far from the Stathe. On the death of William Bardolf of Wormegay in 1386 an inquisition in 1389 showed that at Holkham he had a fourth part of a knight's fee held by Richard Smyth, *Cal. IPM*, vol. xvi, no. 816, p. 315. In 1419–20 John Speller paid 2s. 6d. a year for this 15 acres, held in right of Mariora his wife, to John Gunnor (tenant of Burghall), HD 111. There were 3 acres in Cotecrofte, 3¹/₂ in Mershgrene, 1 in Longfurlong and 3 in Wellgate and elsewhere in the North Field. John Gunnor held 3 acres at Ryngemanslond which rendered castleguard to the Bishop of Norwich in 1453 (cited in John Sewale's terrier, HD 120).

Commentary XXIV

Various fifteenth century ministers' accounts include Wighton, see PRO, *Lists and Indexes*, vol. v, *Ministers' and receivers' accounts*, p. 26. A Wighton rental follows the Feodary in HD 71 and 120. It is for 1456–7. This suggests that the writer of HD 71 and 120 had a particular interest in Wighton, a fact which makes the omission of the fee of Hubert de Wighton seem strange. After *Feodum de Kerebrok*, the Wighton rental HD 71 and 120 contain an item not in HD 22a: *Prior de Petrastone tenet de Humfrido de Wythun quondam Bartholomei Orchard xiij acras terre Et reddit dicto Humfrido xvj [s.] et iacet in Warham*. Warham is written in the left margin. Geoffrey de Hindringham held land of Humphrey de Wighton of the fee of Richmond, see above.

Commentary XXV

The Earl of Clare founded a commandery of the Templars at Carbrooke in 1173. This was transferred to the Hospitallers. As a preceptory of the Hospitallers it was used as a sort of almshouse. Cf. J.H.F. Brabner, *Gazetteer* and D. Knowles and N. Hadcock, *Medieval Religious Houses in England and Wales*, 1953, pp. 241, 261. In 1302 Baldwin de Maners held one fee in Great Carbrooke of Denise de Montchesney of the Honor of Clare, *Feudal Aids* cited by Farrer, i, p. 109. In 1253 Warin de Montchesney obtained free warren in Holkham, Carbrooke and elsewhere, *Cal. of Charter Rolls*, cited by Farrer, i, p. 107. An inquisition on the death of Denise de Montchesney, widow of Hugh de Vere, in 1314, showed that her holdings included the manor of Carbrooke (extent given) held of Gilbert de Clare, Earl of Gloucester, by service of 1/8 knight's fee, *Cal. IPM*, vi, no. 475, p. 269. In 1424 the Prior of Walsingham held a salt marsh of Burghall for 4d., HD 113.

Commentary XXVI

The Earl Warenne, important in Normandy and Surrey, held in addition to Castle Acre many lordships in Norfolk. They included many manors later associated with the estate of Chief Justice Coke, viz. Lexham, Weasenham and Kempstone in Launditch, Tittleshall, Kettlestone, Waterden, Fulmerston, Croxton and Creake in Gallow, and Holkham and Egmere in North Greenhoe. These 24 acres may be those granted to Walsingham by Thorald le Bretun and Aveline his wife held in villeinage by Ralph Hidekil and other villeins with their broods, BL Ms. Cotton Nero E VII, Fo. 48. This Walsingham Cartulary contains many Holkham grants but unfortunately without lists of witnesses. Thorald's grant is the subject of a final concord of 1245 (cf. Appendix 5, no. 17), five years before the grant of one Ralph son of Silvester (HD 3 and HD 75 Fo. 13, also in BL Ms. Cotton Nero E VII) of 32 acres with 25 acres of marsh confirmed by Adam le Bret and Robert son of William of Walsingham, nos. ciii, civ). As a free tenant of Ralph Hakun the prior has 41 acres of marsh above (Fo. 27v). The Clare family were benefactors of Walsingham, Dugdale, *Monasticon*, vi, pt. 1, pp. 70–1. Peterstone was subordinate to Walsingham and was wholly annexed to it in 1449. As parcel of Walsingham it was wholly annexed to the bishopric of Norwich by Edward VI, Dugdale, *loc.cit.* Walsingham terriers in the Neel Cartulary are no. 257, Fos. 36v–38, of perhaps 1414–15. and no. 264, Fos. 51–52v, of 1456–7. Cf. 'Book of Walsingham rental' included in HD 120 and Hillhall rental, HD 75 and 155 for 1467–8. The best collection of terriers of Peterstone and Walsingham is in BD O. In 1306 Walsingham has one of the nine common folds in the fields and waste and Everard le Caly has one 'Cotesfold' between Clynt and Hadehow held by Humphrey David and parceners, HD 22a, Fo. 1v no. 1.

Commentary XXVII

In HD 6 the note about the church is followed by six and a half pages of summaries of grants to West Dereham Abbey, keeping the order in which transcripts of these charters are arranged in the Dereham Cartulary, BL, Ms. Add. 46353. For the division of Holkham church between the White Canons of West Dereham and the Cistercian abbey of Viterbo, for the recovery of the portion of the latter by Aymer de Valence, Earl of Pembroke (and successor as lord of Burghall of William de Montchesney), for the appropriation by West Dereham of the whole rectory and for subsequent disputes with Viterbo, see sources cited by H. Colvin, *The White Canons of England*, 1951, p. 134. The only surviving bailiff's account of West Dereham at Holkham is for 1366, HD 53. The Bishop of Norwich granted to West Dereham the reunited vicarage of Holkham on 21 March 1347, copy in HD 43. The church is dedicated to St. Withburga, the youngest daughter of Anna, King of the East Angles and sister of Etheldreda. She lived as a solitary at Holkham and later at East Dereham. Legend says she was fed by a doe. See references cited by D.H. Farmer, *The Oxford Dictionary of Saints*, 1982. She died in about 743. The earliest terrier is 'The Abbot of Dereham's dragge in Holkham Fylde', c. 1542, HD 284. The land was scattered in the western half of the parish. The abbot's grange was at Honcrondale, now the site of the Model Farm, but called the Parsonage (i.e. Rectory farm not the vicarage) in the sixteenth and seventeenth centuries.

Topography of Holkham

1250–1350

The area covered by the parish of Holkham and the fields and fiefs of medieval Holkham is illustrated here by our map *Holkham Fields, 1250–1350* and corresponds to approximately 4,000 acres. Brabner's Gazetteer mentions the figure of 4,000 acres for Holkham, while Kelly's Dictionary (1912) gives 4,618 acres, which include the area of the tidal marshes reclaimed in the modern period, 1720–1860. The *Gazetteer of the British Isles* (John Bartholomew, 1966) mentions 4,717 acres. The present park within its walls covers about 3,000 acres. The Coke estates in Norfolk amounted to 42,000 acres in the nineteenth century, but at the death of the fourth Earl of Leicester (1949), 17,000 acres were sold, and they now amount to 25,000 acres, including land in the Burnhams and in Castle Acre. The present Holkham estate, including land in Warham, Burnham (Peterstone) and the foreshore amounts to 5,000 acres.

The existence of a map of Holkham of 1590 has long been known and was used by Gray,[24] but it was made for the lord of one manor as a result of a dispute over foldcourses. The text of the cartouche reads as follows:[25] 'The Description of the Lordeshippe or mannor of Holkeham as the same lyethe within the meetes and boundes in the Countie of Norfolke beinge a percelle of the possessions of dame Anne Gresham widdowe made by Thomas Clerke of Stamforde Saincte Martines in the Countye of Northton. gent., and measured at xvj foote vj to the perche in the presence by the testimonye and upon the othes of the tenn[ts] . of the same manor in the monethe of September in the xxxijteth yeare of the raigne of Elyzabethe &c. A$^{\circ}$. DNI . 1590.' The map is not concerned with arable strips or, generally, the names of furlongs. It marks on it many roads, but not all. The 1590 map is surprisingly accurate. Its compiler, Thomas Clerke of Stamford, left his instruments to Thomas Langdon, the compiler of the famous All Souls and Corpus Christi maps at Oxford.[26]

A topographical gazetteer arranged alphabetically was made in the early fifteenth century in the hand of Edmund Lucas of East Dereham, HD 22a, Fos. 41–50v no. 260. He came to Holkham to manage the estate of the Abbot of West Dereham and married Mary Neel who inherited Neel Manor. We have made a larger gazetteer with identifications of locations to illustrate the microtoponomy of Holkham. Lucas was concerned with the dates when Neel Manor parcels of land were acquired in each furlong. Our aim has been to make a detailed map of medieval Holkham based on the superimposition of the 1590 map onto an Ordnance Survey map. Mr. Ralph Goldsmith, a retired local farmer and local historian has helped us much with the technical difficulties of relating the 1590 map and the Ordnance Survey map. The Norfolk archaeological unit and Mrs. Eleanor Beard of the Oxford archaeological unit have given valuable cartographical help.

---

24 H.L. Gray, *The English Field Systems*, 1915, new ed. 1959, pp. 326–31.
25 See illustration in frontispiece.
26 Cf. P. Eden, 'Three Elizabethan Estate Surveyors: Peter Kempe, Thomas Clerke and Thomas Langdon', 1983.

Several places have alternative names. Some names were used for different areas in different parts of the parish. So much information is available that it cannot all be presented on a map of a smaller scale than the map of 1590. For certain parts of the parish it is possible, thanks to sixteenth century Field Books, to locate individual strips when they are bounded by a road or parish boundary; but there are some areas where the furlongs become wider or narrower or the strips change direction and we have not yet sufficient data for detailed cartographical representation. Mr. Dickerson of the forestry department has, in recent years, taken us to see various large pits, rendered invisible to air photography by the growth of trees. Many of these are marked on a map made for Coke of Norfolk before he began to encourage marling on an increased scale and more pits were dug for exploitation. But the court rolls show that marl was dug and carted for sale as early as the fifteenth century, and microtoponymy indicates even earlier use of marling. Many pits (often called crundles), and barrows (called hows), had names and were used as landmarks in the Middle Ages.

All the lands in the whole of the South Field are described with the names of their occupants in 1549 in the terrier of Edmund Newgate, HD 296. These are listed to read beginning at the south and working northwards and starting in the eastern side of the arable where it is bounded by the *bruara*, heath or Lyng. The first great furlong described runs northwards towards Wightongate from Peterstone's 12 acres which is marked on the 1590 map. It is called Lyngsti. West of this runs Middlefurlong and then, further west again, Lamberhillheads. In 1549 the furlong next to the Lyng contained parcels of three roods and of five acres belonging to Neel Manor. The five acres occur in terriers of Neel Manor lands, but Lyngsyde is not mentioned in the documents of 1250–1350. Further west near Branchcrundel is a great pit at the junction of Gibbesgate and the Egmere road. It lies just north of the road from Creake to Wells near Galloweshowe. This landmark is first mentioned in 1315 in a Peterstone terrier (BD 28). It was by a corner called Galouescoote at Lyngeside in 1467.

The map of 1590 marks in all, and more than all, the roads and tracks mentioned in the documents of 1250–1350, except Dalegate and the path from the Abbot of West Dereham's barn to the church. This map gives the names of places mentioned in the documents in their original spellings. A few which do not occur in 1250–1350, but only in later documents, are also added in brackets because of their importance as landmarks and the frequency with which they occur in the post 1350 court rolls, rentals and terriers. The drawings of Tudor houses have been retained from the 1590 map, despite the anachronism. There were many more houses in 1250–1350 than those drawn, especially in Holkham Eastgate. This map does not cover the northern portion of the parish separated from the seashore by dunes called the 'meals', and by the salt marshes. The course of the tidal channels which intersected these before John Coke's mid-seventeenth century embankment is unknown; but a vanished channel ran directly northward towards the sea. This continued on the axis of the present lake, until an embankment was made about 1720, across the marshes at the head of Holkham Gap with its accompanying rectilinear dykes.

MAP 1

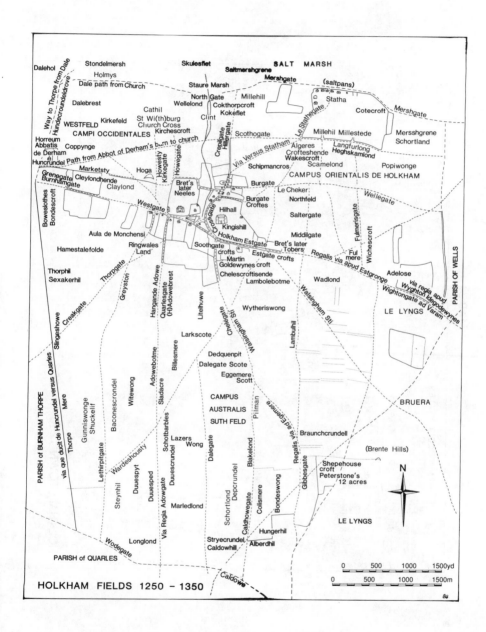

HOLKHAM FIELDS 1250 – 1350

MAP 2

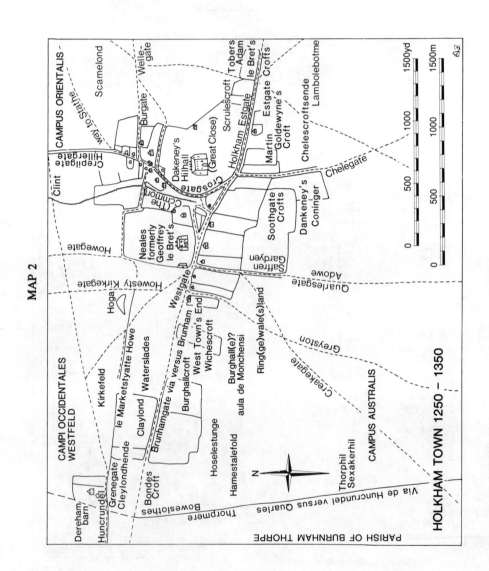

HOLKHAM TOWN 1250 – 1350

THE AREA BOUNDARIES

1. The old coast line in the north (followed by the coast road except at the north end of the lake where T.W. Coke thrust it towards the sea further than nature intended. The park wall was washed away in 1953.).
2. The road from Burnham to Walsingham outside T.W. Coke's extended park wall on the south.
3. The Burnham Thorpe boundary formed by the Roman Road which is clearly shown on air photographs by the lines of hedgerows stretching away to the south.
4. The Wells parish boundary marked by the Long Rood or Meer in the west. The boundary in the south-east is less simple than appears, for the line of the Creake-Wells road has been altered to enlarge the park and straighten the road.

FIXED POINTS OF REFERENCE

Apart from the four chief area boundaries already discussed fixed points are:

1. The Burgh, an iron age earthwork. The surrounding (eastern) portion of the marshes was the first of three portions to be reclaimed by two predecessors and the successor of T.W. Coke. It was called Burghall Manor marsh.
2. The Howe, a high natural mound north-east of the 19th century kitchen garden.
3. The Church, a sea mark for sailors, situated on high ground equidistant between three settlements, but not itself (as W.G. Hoskins naturally but wrongly stated) in a village destroyed when the park was made. See Appendix 3, commentary XXVII.
4. The lane on the east side of the ancient house at Holkham Staithe. It took a curving course northwards from an almost vanished tidal creek.
5. The narrow and deep portion of the artificial lake flanked by steep slopes anciently called the Clynt Breasts.
6. The Golden Gates built by the 2nd Earl of Leicester where the old road from Burnham to Wighton crosses the road from Wells to Fakenham.
7. The Lodge on the road to Burnham. The course of the drive to the house has been changed by T.W. Coke. It used to head straight from Burnham to Wighton.
8. Huncrundale or the old Parsonage, T.W. Coke's New Inn is the 2nd Earl of Leicester's Model Farm.

LOST LANDMARKS

1. Documents suggest that Littlehowe, which gave its name to a furlong, was in the western part of Obelisk Wood. It does not survive unless it lies beneath the Temple or possibly the Obelisk on the skyline.
2. Gallowhowe was in the south-east portion of the park, presumably in an elevated situation beside a road for the benefit of passers-by. There must have been access to the hill from the town. It would have been a prominent landmark beside the boundary between the foldcourses of Wheatleys (Hillhall Manor) and Peterstone which was in the same area running westwards from Branthill, surely made use of it. The road from the town was called Gibbesgate, perhaps meaning Gibbet's road. The passers-by would be going between Holkham and Egmere or Walsingham or travelling between Creake and Wells.

3.   A 'toot' was a lookout place. 'Tutsia' (pronounced tootsy) clump was planted
      round a deep pit called Branchcrundel just at the junction of Gibbesgate way
      and Egmere Scoot. The names of other clumps are recent corruptions: Billy
      Button's became Billy Butlin's clump, after the name of an organiser of
      holiday camps.

TOPOGRAPHICAL UNCERTAINTIES

Later unprinted documents allow the localisation on the map, with greater or less
precision, of the chief places mentioned in the documents. All spellings in the map
are those of 1250–1350. A few important names which happen not to occur in our
early documents are added in brackets. The following toponyms are not marked for
lack of evidence: Kirkdele and Kirklond (arable near the church), Calislond, Feldhous,
Hardy's gate (*porta Mabilie Hardy*), perhaps one of a row of messuages in Westgate,
crofts called after Gobwaye (or Goldwine), Brunle, James, Payns and Stowe (some
perhaps in Holkham Town, the Staithe or Eastgate), and small pieces of land, with
their individual names: Moltysaker (by Caldowegate), Mundsiesaker, Sennigranesaker,
Seyntemarialvaker and Tokeshalfaker. Later references do not illuminate two
landmarks, Vesthowe and Shugeshowe, possibly the remains of barrows obliterated by
14th century ploughing.

Some names like Hamestale may occur in several places. The Dalegate was a track
often mentioned and running roughly along the line of the 18th century avenue; but
Dalebrest is near the north west corner of the park above the Dalehole which is
approached from the church by what late medieval documents called Dalesti along the
line of the coast road. Scamlond occurs in both the East and West Fields; and
Skokelif, towards the eastern side of South Field seems to relate to different parts of
the area and is marked on the map accordingly. Shortlands were numerous: abutting
in the east on Caldowegate (HD 22a, Fo. 17 no. 188) and abutting in the south on
Scothowgate (HD 22a, Fo. 16v no. 187). Later documents contribute another, abutting
in the west on Chelisgate (HD 296, Fos. 8–8v) at Strumpethill (HD 135). Another
was at Sexacrehyll (HD 296, Fo. 19v). Another abutted on Lethirpittgate in the west
(HD 111, HD 243) or East (HD 120, Fo. 24v and HD 136). 'Sc.s... botme' may be
connected with Scrulescroft. Sculesflet was a channel through the northern part of the
marshes next Walsingham marsh (BL Ms. Cotton Nero E VII, Fo. 51v, no. cxxi).
Evidence for particular locations is given in Edmund Lucas' alphabetical gazetteer of
the places mentioned in Neel charters (HD 22a, Fos. 41–50v no. 260 printed *supra*).
Locations of others marked on the map are derived from various later documents of
which there is an unpublished gazetteer. The map of 1590 marks every road
mentioned, except Dalegate, Wardehowsti and Duuesty. The latter was presumably le
Dowesty on the east side of the Mill Hill of Burghall (HD 120, Fo. 9 and HD 136) at
Restyngstede near the Staithe.

AMBIGUITIES OF NAMES

There are two Saffron Closes, two Chequers, several Middlefurlongs. Burgate Way
(Burgate Furlong preserves its name) is not heading towards the Burgh in the marshes
or towards the location of Burghall manor house southwest of the town on the
southside of the road to Burnham. It looks as if Hillhall may have been intended and
may originally have been another 'Burgh'. Dalegate ran north and south
approximately on the line of the eighteenth century avenue but it is not marked on the
1590 map, perhaps because it was not a royal road which demarcated the foldcourses

with which the map was primarily concerned. The name is not to be confused with the Dalesti running towards the Dale Hole in the northwest corner of the parish which is marked on the 1590 map.

MEDIEVAL AND MODERN LANDSCAPE

On the south side of the Common Marsh Field was East Field, later called the Staithe – it was divided from Wells by the Long Rood. The map of 1590 names a number of roads – Crepplegate, the way from Holkham Town to Staithe, the way from Staithe to Wells and a way leading to Wells in addition to Wellgate Way (also called Burgate Way or Brymbylldykewaye), Staithgate meare, Staithgate Waye and Lacyes meare. Many documents refer to Crossgate in Holkham Town at right angles to the southern end of Crepplegate. The map marks Great Tubberdes which preserves the name of Tobers manor house at the south east end of Hillhall or Wheatley's Great Close. The high ground south of the Staithe was called Mouse Hill, corresponding to Cat Hill by the church. There was a Clynte Breste in the eastern as on the western side of a former arm of the sea which is now the deepest (or seaward) part of the lake. At Adelose or AldeloseWong were Allows and Lingside furlongs. Much of Edmund Newgate's land lay in Staithe Field and it seems that rotation of crops was possible within Staithe Field independently of furlongs to the south and west. Burgate Croft, Staithe Crofts (or the Whinclose) and Silk's Croft were apparently divided up into the strips of different occupiers like any of the other furlongs. Shipmanscross, the Restingstead and the Fish-House do not occur in 1250–1350 documents. The West Field or Kirk Field is normally called Church Field. In 1572 there is a description of 23 furlongs into which it was then divided. The barn of the Abbot of West Dereham is there called the Site of the Rector (HD 355). In the map of 1590 along the western and northern sides of Church Field run Dale Waye and Dale Stighe, north of the latter is Marsh Furlong. The site of the Abbot of West Dereham's barn is called Huncrundale. On the northwest corner is Dale Hole (at the western extremity of a 50ft. contour). Half-way between Dale Hole and Huncrundale is a huge pit, now outside the park, with a lime-kiln, the predecessor of which was mentioned in a Burghall court roll of 22 July 1452 (HD 194). It lay in Dalefurlong called in 1590 Lymekiln Furlong, not to be confused with Calkpit Furlong between Clynte Breste and Neel manor house. Gonnors Croft marked in 1590 as west of Neel manor house and a furlong south of Howe Hill was the name of the first *quarentena* described in the Church Field terrier of 1572 (abutting on Burnhamgate and running as far west as Dalegateway and the Abbot of West Dereham's grange). The South Field was divided from the West (Church) and East (Staithe) Fields by the road which led (until it was closed in the early 1720s) from Burnham to Wighton. The South Field was considerably larger than both of the others together, and occasionally there is distinction between the South-east Field (1451–2, HD 128) and the Southwest Field (1696, HD 937). The latter included Dalegate furlong, marked by the line of the avenue. In the Southwest Field at the western end of Burnhamgate stretched Burnhamgate Furlong, Podyngsty and, Boweslothes. Where Dalegate runs south, and before rising, descends towards the present Obelisk Wood lay Dalegate Bottom. The 1590 map marks Gonningswong.

The relation of the map to modern Holkham is simplest on the west side where the park wall and Burnham Thorpe parish boundary follows the Roman road, but, north of Huncrundale (now Model Farm), the present park wall slants away to the north-east towards the sea leaving Dalewaye on its outside. It bisects Lymekiln furlong and leaves the lime-kiln outside the park, in the large pit which has been increasing for at least six centuries. On the north the Dale styghe (the approach to the deep Dale hole from the East) and the way from Staithe to Wells follow the undisturbed contour of the pre-medieval coast line, except at the northern head of the eighteenth-century lake. Here Coke of Norfolk diverted the coast road to reach a point 500 yards nearer the sea to allow of the creation of a fashionable curve at the end of the lake which his great uncle had made, and of fish stews. The northern park wall between the almshouses and Wells Lodge follows the line of Scottowgate along the ridge where the 1st Earl of Leicester planted a protective belt of trees against winds from the North Pole. This hides the marshes and the sea which once formed the northern horizon. The eastern boundary followed Wells parish boundary southwards down 'the long roode'. Coke of Norfolk and his son made park extensions on former heathland in the Wighton direction, reaching first to Samuel Wyatt's Palmer's Lodge and eventually to the American Gardens, and Golden Gates. The south-east boundary was extended and the present park wall follows a line several hundred yards south of the old way from Creake to Wells further away from the gallows on which roads from Holkham Town and the Staithe used to converge beside a deep pit called Branchcrundel. The southern park boundary follows the line of the way from Burnham to Walsingham called Woodgate way, and accordingly remains unchanged. In the centre of the park, William Kent's Obelisk rises on a high point 200 yards SE. of the junction of Cheeles Gate way with a way from Creake and the Roman road to Staithe. Due south of it the present South Lodge stands on Woodgate way at West Caldow, and due north of it, the centre of Holkham Hall, not far from the north east corner of medieval Hillhall. The avenue largely follows the course of Dalegate, which is often mentioned as a landmark; it is not marked in the 1590 map, presumably because it was not a royal road or foldcourse boundary.

The modern kitchen garden has Howe Hill outside its north eastern corner. The street which curves northward to the coast road at the Staithe is the lane which now bounds the garden on the east side of the ancient house. The Victoria Hotel is in the north-east corner of Silk croft. Coke of Norfolk's 'Great barn' stands in Bramlond. The way from Burnham to Staithe can still in part be traced along the length of Willow clump, which was presumably largely developed out of its hedgerows by Coke of Norfolk; and in air photographs under the water of the artificial lake. The present drive to the Hall from the Burnham Lodge makes a detour well to the south of the medieval Burnham gate, and at the widest point is separated from it by Deep Clump − the north east sector of this clump formed the western half of a large enclosure belonging to Burghall. Burghall manor house, the ancient house of Montchesney, early fell into decay and perhaps stood in the north eastern portion of the site of the present wood until about the middle of the thirteenth century.

PHYSICAL FEATURES

High Ground. Most of the elevated land in Holkham parish gave its name to landmarks called hills, though some hardly qualify as such to a stranger's eye. North of the church the land above the marshes is Cat Hill, matched in the eastern half of the parish by Mouse Hill on the contour which is followed by the park wall. One of the manor houses at the southern end of the present lake, at the southwest corner of the present Palladian mansion was Hillhall. In the western and eastern halves of the 18th century Obelisk Wood were Sommereshill and Strumpetshill. On the western parish boundary was Sixacrehill, Thorphill or Whinhill (now Lucarhill) and to north east and east of the South Field were Bondescrofthill and Lamberhill. In the south-western part of the great South Field were Skotbarblehill (called Skarborough Hill by 1554 in HD 274, Fo. 33 and now perpetuated in 'Scarborough Clump'). To its south west was Steynhill. By the south eastern border of the park was Hungerhill and Alverdhill, and beyond its bounds Branthill, the name still borne by a farm founded by 1750. Of comparative significance the Staithe Field towards the Wells boundary had Alleleueshyll, Aldershille and Houndhill in Burgate by Nesfield's pleasure ground. A map of 1781 conveniently marks slopes by hachures.

Low Ground. A deep depression at the north west corner of the parish is still called Dalehole. The coast road approaching it from the east was called Dalesti and the road from the south was called the Dalewaye. This is not to be confused with Dalegate which followed approximately the line of the avenue to Dalegate Bottom on the south side of the Obelisk Hill. Adowegate ran north and south on the west side of Dalegate and was more important as a road. The low ground which it traversed was called Adowbotme. It is possible that Somershilbottom which abutted west of Dalgateway (HD 155, Fo. 30v) was only an alternative name for the northern part of Dalegate Bottom. The steep slopes of the depression which divided the North Field (and is now the lake) were called Clyntbrests. Dalebreste was by the Daleway not by Dalegate, and gave its name (in use for five centuries) to a furlong on the west side of Church Field by the ancient lime pit (HD 355, Fo. 3). Another declivity on the edge of Obelisk Hill gave the name to Hangandeadowe.

Barrows or tumuli. The church stands on a very prominent knoll which renders the church tower a sea mark for mariners, but it does not give rise to a name. The next most prominent mound, south of the church outside the north-east corner of the 19th century extension to the kitchen garden is still called the Howe. By contrast a barrow at or near William Kent's Temple in the Obelisk Wood was called Littlehowe. Adhowe gate may have been so called because it headed towards the Howe. Caldhowe, by the southern entrance to the park, may recall the bleakness of its position (near Hungerhill). Gallowhowe is discussed *infra* 'Gibbesgate'. Slyngeshowe was on the Burnham Thorpe boundary, (the Roman Road). Scottowgate leading along the northern park boundary to Wells does not recall the Norfolk village Scottow but, like it, a howe where a 'Scot' was buried. Warldhowesty led to a Howe at Quarles (perhaps near the Triumphal Arch).

Pits. There are many deep pits, some may be of natural glacial origin, some may be 18th or 19th century marlpits, others may have been made at various dates for the extraction of marl, flint, chalk for making lime, clay for bricks, stone or gravel. These pits, like *tumuli*, served as landmarks and had names. The positions of Letherpits, Deadqueenspit, Hunclecrondel Kilnpit and Braunchcrundel are precisely localised. Others, like Salterscrundel and Depecrundel, Cuntcrundel, Shiterscrundel, Steynhilcrundel, Dunnesped, Stricrundell and Baconscrundel can be approximately localised but some (Bramliscrundell, Devenepit, Wifecrundel) cannot be pinpointed. Only two references have been found to Erlcro(u)ndell. It is fortunate that before Coke of Norfolk's celebrated encouragement of marling, the Hanoverian surveyor H.A. Biederman completed in 1781 a map which showed the crundels (or pits with irregular contours) already in existence. Unfortunately, he gave no names. The planting of clumps of trees for game and landscape improvement concealed such agriculturally difficult areas from modern air photographs. Many pits survive. Some near the Roman road might have been first started when it was built.

SALT MARSHES AND SALT PRODUCTION

Until the mid-fourteenth century Northern Europe obtained its supplies of salt from indigenous sources, and from then onwards supplies came increasingly from salines in France.[27] This was due partly to the Gascon political connection and partly to the greater warmth of a more southerly climate. The counties where there were most salines recorded in Domesday Book were Sussex, Norfolk and Lincolnshire. The importance of production at Bishop's Lynn is discussed by Dorothy Owen who described the great build-up of waste material on which houses could be built.[28] The absence of any reference to a saline at Holkham in Domesday Book suggests that any production on its extensive level shore was relatively insignificant and so presumably the product was mainly used locally for herring in the fish-house in August and September soon after it was caught, while curing pigs after slaughter in December would also require brine. The direction of a road called Saltergate[29] leading due south suggests that at least some salt went to parishes inland. The weather became colder and wetter after 1300 and would have hindered the production of 'whyte Salte made by force of the sonne in England'[30] and would have necessitated what Robert Hitchcock describes in 1580 as 'Salte houses standying upon the coaste of Englande that makes Salte by sething [boiling] of salt Sea Water'. Production at Holkham would have been wholly impossible after the construction of the dyke of 1720. The fuel used in 18th century Holkham brick kilns was whins of which toponyms testify to the widespread growth. Fast burning brushwood was also used at Lüneburg and would have yielded at Holkham a small grained salt.[31] Piles of salt left to dry after evaporation at Calpe (Alicante) look like heaps of snow, and it is curious to note that after Saltergate has surmounted the slope up from the coast road it passes an area called 'Snow' in which some of the plots of land were occupied by the Newgate family which also held the saltings right down to the tide line. Local demand meant the survival at Cley of a small rectangular saltpan, such as Georgius Agricola illustrates in De Re Metallica (1556) so late that it is shown on a nineteenth century Ordnance map on the seaward side of the coast road.

27   A.R. Bridbury, England and the Salt Trade in the Later Middle Ages, 1955, p. vii.
28   D.M. Owen, The Making of King's Lynn, 1984, pp. 5–12.
29   The earliest written reference to Saltergate is 14 Nov. 1356 (HD 86) after which it occurs often.
30   A.R. Bridbury, op. cit., p. 16, citing document of c. 1453–61.
31   Ibid., p. 22.

ADELOSE

Adelose lay next to the field of Wells (HD 476) next to Longemere (HD 155, Fo. 22v) or Longrode (HP 1141), a very long strip which formed the eastern boundary of the Staithe Field of Holkham. On its south it reached Le Lynge (HD 155, Fo. 46) or the heath (*Bruera*) and the road to Wighton (HP 1083). There was a furlong called Adelosewonge which included Downecrundell at le Snow in the North Field in 1477–8 (HD 75, Fo. 85). The area was sometimes called East Field (HD 155, Fo. 28v). Arable strips abutted on Wightonway towards the south. They are especially often mentioned in the terriers of Hillhall as well as of Neel. In the late 15th century Hillhall let some at farm (5 roods at Crondellond at Adelose). Adelose is not marked in the map of 1590, perhaps because it does not occur in Burghall Manor records and that map was made for the lady of Burghall. The name might possibly mean old barrows (Aldelose). It abutted on Alleleueshyll' (HD 22a, Fo. 22v no. 239).

ADOWE

Adow is spelt in many ways, with or without, an initial or medial H and final E. The name is qualified by a preliminary Short, Long or Hangande and with a final bottom, brest, crundel, gate, heads or way, spelt in a multitude of ways. Adowgate was a synonym for Quarlesgate or Warlesgate (HD 128 and 296, Fo. 13). It traversed the great South Field heading from the Howe at the northwest corner of the present kitchen garden south towards the parish of Quarles in which lies the Triumphal Arch. It ran approximately parallel to the Roman road which formed the Burnham Thorpe boundary away to the west and the present avenue which approximates to a way called Dalegate on its east, not marked in the 1590 map. Adowgate passed Longlands and the lane which approaches Longlands from the north approximates to Adowgate which is thus the only medieval road in the park of which the line has survived eighteenth and nineteenth century landscape gardening and agricultural improvement. As well as being frequently mentioned in descriptions of abuttals and in the Neel Cartulary, it often occurs in the terriers and rentals of Burghall Manor, Hillhall Manor as well as of Peterstone and Walsingham Priories and the West Dereham Abbey Cartulary (BL, Ms. Add. 46353, Fo. 264v) and the terriers of individuals like Geoffrey Coly (1456, HD 135) and Edmund Newgate (1549, HD 296, Fo. 13). The latter lists all the strips, lands starting from the south and proceeding northwards. In 1484 (HD 199) Edmund Edyman ploughed over the royal way to the nuisance of travellers and was bound to desist under penalty of 12d. Adowebottom was lower ground west and south-west of the present Obelisk Wood. Parts of Billesmere, Longlands, Larkscote and Longadow were in Adowebottom (HD 22a, Fo. 53; HD 296, Fos. 11, 13, 14). Part lay west of Adoweway, which was called Northende How or Northadow (HD 205, Fo. 10v; HD 22a, Fos. 52, 52v, 55; HD 300). Adowebreast was the slope west of the Obelisk Wood, and Adowehefdes a headland running north and south through the middle of the South Field, with lands on its east and west sides. The headlands at the head of arable strips, where the plough turned and the ploughshare was cleared, formed a bank of earth. The light sandy loam of the headlands of Adowe were eroded after the layout of the fields was altered during the creation of the park, as were other headlands running north and south at intervals of about a furlong on either side. Their vestiges could still be detected recently in the form of slight rises in the surface of the eighteenth-century road which cut across them at right angles on its westward course from the Avenue at the southern foot of Obelisk Wood. Approximately parallel to Adowehefdes, Longlands Furlong ran the whole lengh of the South Field from Peterstone's 22 acres in the south to Westgate in the north. Shortadowe strips abutted on Adehowgate (HD 300), a croft of 3 acres 3½ roods at Schortadowe with a fold (HD 22a, Fo. 21v). Shortadowe lay next to Ryngmanslond Furlong to the west near Creykgate (HD 296, Fo. 17v). Longadowe was a furlong in the South Field, abutting on Adowegate, *alias* Adoweye, on the west side (HD 22a, Fo. 36v, HD 111, HD 128, HD 300, HD 795 and HD 840). In 1665 it was called 'Longaddfurlong'. Billesmere, Adowebottom and Larkscote seem to be names of component parts of it.

ALGERESCROFTESHENDE

'A place called Algers .. in the Staithe Field' (HD 765) abutting on Algers, was 'upon a waie leading from Holkham Staithe to Lamberhill towards the west and Bullwere Meere towards the east' (HD 765). One of the six acre tenements of Hillhall was called Algers (HD 52), presumably after the personal name of an early tenant, which also survives at Algarskirk in Lincolnshire. W. Rye cited Algar as among Scandinavian personal names still to be found in Norfolk (*Scandinavian names*, 1916). It abutted east on Staithegatemere (HD 114) and the common way leading from Brymbyldyke to the Staithe (HD 52). It was directly west of Bulswersmere (HD 296, Fo. 25) and north of Welgate (HD 116 and HD 120, Fo. 9v). It abutted west on Lacy's mere or Lasaysmer (HD 71 and 120, on 1590 map). Burghall had villein land here (HD 120, Fo. 8, HD 136). Wighton (HD 71 and 120) and Peterstone (HD 114) also had strips here. In 1467 a fold of Hillhall abutting on Bulwersmer in the east was called Algersgate, but anciently Blakelond (HD 155, Fo. 119), a name which also occurs in the South Field. This fold was originally given to John Silk by Ralph Hakun of Holkham (1288/9) who had it by gift of Thomas son of Baldwin d'Akeny (HD 115). References to Algerescrofteshende have not been noted outside the Neel Cartulary.

BACONESCRUNDEL

'Crundell' signifies a pit with an irregular outline. Like other pits this one served as a landmark and occurs in fourteenth century documents in the Neel Cartulary. A map made soon after Coke of Norfolk inherited Holkham marks in the pits which were already there but it does not indicate their names. Edmund Newgate's terrier of 1549 (HD 296, Fo. 16v) shows that Middlefurlong in the South Field passed *Baconscrundell'* north of Stonyhill and south of Ryngmanslondbottom, Shortadowebottom and (Q)warleshowsty. Its west head abutted on Wardhowsty (HD 111). It lay at Wharleshowe or Wharledowe (HD 75, Fo. 61v).

BILLESMERE

Bellesmere, Billesmere, Billismere, Billsmer, Byllesmer, Byllmere or Byllysmere is the name of a furlong which occurs from about 1295 (HD 11) until Thomas Coke rationalised the fields in order to make his avenue possible (HD 1086). It lay along the eastern side of Quarlesgate (HD 22a, Fos. 3v, 47 and 53). Its strips are described as abutting on Adowegate on the west in terriers of Walsingham and Peterstone priories (HD 22a, Fos. 51v and 53). There were 94 strips in Billesmere totalling 102 acres 3½ roods. It extended from the large fields of Peterstone, Neel Manor and Walsingham (of 16, 6 and 7 acres respectively) on the southern parish boundary as far north as Southgatecrofts on the south side of Holkham Town in the north. A detailed description in 1549 in Edmund Newgate's terrier (HD 296) shows that on its western side it ran along Adowgate *alias* Warlesgate (the road to Quarles) and on its eastern side it passed Skotbarbylhill, Larkeskote, and Adowbottom. It included 2½ acres called Byllesmere pytts, 3 roods called Le Wynns belonging to Hillhall, 13 acres of Neel Manor, 1 acre with a crundel (pit) in the middle, and 1½ acres of Burghall towards Whitwong pitte, and 1 acre of Edmund Waylond with a gravel pit. South of Skotbarbylhill where Hillhall with Gunnors had 13 acres and 1 rood, and at the northern end were several pieces of an acre or larger; but the central portion of the furlong consisted mostly of very small parcel. Another furlong, described in equal detail, separated Billesmere from Dalegate way in the east. Edmund Newgate's terrier shows that in 1549 the greater portion of the South Field, except towards its southern end, consisted of arable strips. This is not indicated by the map of 1590 which locates the ways traversing it from south to north but which only indicates the few particular ones which belonged to Burghall. Along the western side of Billesmere ran Longland furlong.

BLACKLAND

Blackland, also called North, South, and East Blacklond lay in the South Field to the east of Caldowesty or Caldowegate. Strips in Estblacklond called Frerbusk (later Ferrybush) abutted on Caldowegate in the west (HD 22a, Fo. 55). The way running north and south along the east head of Blacklond was Blakelondway (HD 71 and HD 120). Strips at Blacklond abutted in the east on Chelesgate (HD 819).

BONDESCROFT

Bondescroft in South Field abutted towards the west on Thorpheds, i.e. the Roman Road which forms the parish boundary (HD 120, Fo. 9v), but is described as abutting on the royal road on the west in 1318/9 (HD 22a, Fo. 14v no. 165) and at Puddyngsty in 1456 (HD 135). The name *bondi* originally meant a peasant proprietor in Old Norse. It declined in status to mean an unfree tenant. Some of the land was free and some villein (HD 22a, Fo. 45 no. 262). Land here belonged to Burghall (HD 120, Fo. 9v), Hillhall (HD 201), William de Calthorpe (HD 22a, Fo. 35 no. 256), Foxley Manor (HD 22a, Fo. 48v no. 260), Walsingham (HD 22a, Fo. 52v no. 264) and Neel Manor (HD 22a, Fo. 14v no. 165 and Fo. 16 no. 184, some belonging to W. Hakun's fee and some to Caly's fee in 1330 (HD 81), Clarice de Howgate and the Abbot of West Dereham (HD 79). Bondescroft is not the same as Bondeswong which was a furlong (HD 296, Fo. 5v), which abutted E. on Gibbesgate (HD 22a, Fo. 3 no. 28) or Egmersti (HD 129, pp. 9 and 24) and adjoined Frebuske (HD 205). Allusions occur to Estbondescroft, Westbondescroft and Bondescrofthil[l] (HD 22a, Fo. 45 no. 262). This was a furlong (HD 81) outside its foldcourse, south of Hallebusk and abutting east on Hallecroftende (HD 201). Bondeswong was a furlong of 53 acres in the South Field running to the north from the 80 acres of Burghall and Bramlond (HD 296, Fo. 5). Next to Frerbush (Ferrybush) in the west, its head abutted on Gibbesgate (HD 205).

BOWESLOTHES

Boweslothes lay in the South Field on the south side of Burnhamgate, the royal road leading west (HD 22, HD 52), and outside the sheep fold (HD 201).

BRAMLOND

Bramlond was an area in the South Field. Lands there of Walsingham and Peterstone (of 1/2 roods each) abutted in the west on Chelisgate, *alias* Walsinghamgate (HD 22a, Fo. 51 no. 264 and Fo. 53 no. 265) but other land there abutted on it in the east. Wighton had 3 roods between those of Walsingham (HD 243) and Neel Manor on their south and north (HD 243). Hillhall also had land there, 3 acres held by Neel Manor by military service and some in tenement Wulsy. Some of Hillhall's land abutted on either side of the royal road to Egmere from Holkham (HD 115). The name is one of the four medieval names at Holkham to survive, which it does in the form of Broom Close (c. 1720). This lies near the Great Barn and its survival may have been aided by the fact that it lay outside the boundary of the original park of Thomas Coke and thus, like Longlands, retained the vestiges of medieval topography for a generation longer than the area near the Hall. The name suggests the growth of brooms or whins, but in the late fourteenth century 1/2 acres of Hillhall here was let for 5 years for a barley rent of 6 bushells (HD 76). The Newgate terrier of 1549 (HD 296, Fos. 5 and 6) describes all the strips on the west side of Gibbesgate running northwards (with Caldehowgate on its west) from the 80 acres of pasture of Burghall. This great furlong comprised 53 acres (Bondeswong), and Bramlond occupied its northern end. A distinction was made between North, South, East, and West Bramlond. The latter was identical with Collymeer (HD 201) or Colesmere in Bramlond which lay along the east side south of Egmerskote (HD 155, Fo. 16). Towards the north, Neel Manor had 3 roods called Longacre.

BRUERA

The heath or wasteland is called by the synonyms *Bruera, the Bruary* (HD 71 and 120), the *comunis bruera*, or *Le Lyng* (HD 22a, Fo. 51 no. 264 and HD 75 describing Walsingham Grange). Lyng is the Old Norse for heather and the nature of the soil suggested the creation of 'the American Garden' here in the mid-nineteenth century between Palmers Lodge and the Golden Gate, outside which lay in 1467 le Entree in Le Lynge (HD 155). It lay on the E and S sides of Holkham Fields towards Wells-next-the-Sea and Wighton. The adjoining parts of Holkham included Fulmere, Wadlond, Wechecroft, Aldelose, Linghevedes (Walsingham Cartulary, BL Ms. Cotton Nero E VII, Fo. 54v, nos. cxi, cxli). Walsingham Priory had 7 acres (next 12 acres land of Burghall) which formed an island in the Lyng called Whight Ollands (HD 205, shown on 1590 map). The holders of 27 pieces of land on the west of the Lyng are listed from south to north in the terrier of Edmund Newgate of 1549 (HD 296, Fo. 12v). The most southerly was 12 acres of Peterstone, the largest was 14 acres of Gunnor, 61/2 acres of Hillhall and 5 acres each of the Abbot of West Dereham and Neel Manor. Burghall had 4 pieces all under 1 acre, Hillhall had 5 and Walsingham had 2. Five others had one or two pieces each. At right angles to these pieces were ones abutting in the northern side of the way to Wighton. Lyngsti was the name of the path leading from Eastgate (17 Oct. 1410, HD 97). Strips of Wighton and Burghall lay across it (HD 71 and 120). It lay a furlong south of 'Estgatewaye' leading to Wighton (HD 155, Fo. 30). Strips in Lyngsyde abutted towards the south on the 'common way from Wighton to Holkham' in the North Field (1538–9, HD 382) or on the common Bruera (19 March, 1472, HD 195). It formed the eastern boundary of the East Field.

BURNHAMGATE

Brunham or Burnham Gate or Way (Weye) was the name of the royal road from Warham and Wighton and passed through Holkham Town under the southern extension of the artificial lake and proceeded towards Burnham Market. This road was cut by Thomas Coke as it passed too close to the old manor house of Hillhall which he replaced with Holkham Hall, and bisected the small park which he laid out around it. Many pieces of land abutted upon Burnhamgate and it was also the name of a furlong (HD 1086). The royal road is sometimes called Westgate (HD 155) and sometimes simply 'The Way'. Westounneshend lay on the side of Burnhamgate (HD 22a, Fo. 3v nos. 36 and 39; HD 155, Fos. 38–39 and HD 111). It did not follow the same line as the present drive to West Lodge, but ran along the southern edge of Gardiner's cottage, due straight. Its present course is not straight and passes further south. It is the product of landscaping by Coke of Norfolk after the southern end of the lake had been given a fashionable curve and Thomas Coke's kitchen garden, gardener's house, steward's house and dovecote had been removed as had been the medieval houses which preceded them. Lands of Neel Manor, Peterstone, Burghall and Hillhall lay to the west of the town at Boweslothes, abutted on Burnhamgate towards the north and Thorpmere (west), HD 22a, Fo. 53 no. 265. They would have lain across the line of the present drive where it approaches S. Wyatt's West Lodge. Westgate lay at the northern termination of a great furlong called Longlands which ran along the west side of Adowgate (HD 296, Fo. 15). In Westgate were the messuages of a number of free tenants of Peterstone (HD 300), which, in 1427–8, was 'the streete namit of the Prior of Peterstone' (HD 114). Westgatecroft lay towards the gate of Borough Hall (HD 120 and 136).

BRYMBYLDYKE

Brymbyldyke was a synonym of Wellsgate, 'a highway called Brimbledikeway', leading from Holkham to Wells (HD 782).

BULWERMERE

Strips at Bulwermere abutted on Wellsway: in the eastern side by a headland at Algers, in the west on the way from Holkham Staithe to Lamberhill (HD 52, HD 765). It was situated above Scothowgate (HD 119B).

BURGATE

Burgate in Staithe Field or North Field lay to the east and north-east of Hillhall and its great close it was bounded by two royal roads, vanished since the eighteenth century, called Burgateway, leading from Wells to Holkham on the north, and Wightonway, leading via Holkham to Burnham Market on the south. The site is now covered by Nesfield's mid-nineteenth century Pleasure Ground. The name, which also occurs at Canterbury, is associated with the word for a fortified enclosure, but does not relate to 'the Burgh', an iron age earthwork in the marshes, or the manor of Burghall. Halle Mille stood at Burgate croft in 1334 (HD 84). Burgate was divided into small pieces, some villein, some free, held by a number of tenants. Bartholomew de Burgate, a prominent personality in the thirteenth century, may have lived here for there were messuages with buildings and crofts here (HD 22a, Fo. 6 nos. 71, 73 and HP 1039). Walsingham had 5 roods in Burgate between two houses (BL Ms. Cotton Nero E VII, Fo. 52). As early as 22 July 1358 there were fruitless complaints at the

Burghall Hall Court of Ralph Wryth continuing to choke up a well at Burgatescroft (HD 89). The tenement of Matthew de Burgate was elected to fill the office of *messor* for Hillhall on 1 Dec. 1390 (HD 93, no. 17), but this tenement is not among those reported as liable in later documents. Burgate, one of several acres called Towncroft, which included a messuage surrendered by Robert Mason for the use of William Sabbe in Burghall manor court as late as 10 Dec 1566 (HD 171, Fo. 12v). One of the buildings with a one acre croft, held by Thomas Gunthorpe of Hillhall (mentioned in 1449, HD 194a) had vanished by 1467 (HD 155, Fo. 17v). A messuage of 9 x 61/2 perches next Alexander de Burgate's had a building in 1319 which ceased to stand in the next century, perhaps including a cottage held from Neel Manor by Roger de Erpingham (1341, HD 83). The map of 1590 shows a furlong called Burgate on the east side of the close in which the old manor house of Hillhall (or Wheatley) and the modern Holkham Hall stands. On the north side of Burgate ran a royal road called Burgate way (HD 155 Fo. 17v), called a lane in 1695 (HD 923). Some of Burgate was called Chekerland or Chetelond of Wighton (HD 300).

CALDOWE

A long track, sometimes called Caldousty (HD 22a, Fo. 3v no. 39) or Caldowey (HD 120, fo. 6), running north and south through the South Field with strips abutting upon each side of it. Those on its east are called Colle(s)mere (HD 22a, Fo. 15 no. 171). It lay to the east of Dalegate (HD 22a, Fo. 8 no. 98). It passed a pit called Depecrundel (HD 120, Fo. 6v). One of the foldcourses in the early eighteenth century was called Caldowe foldcourse, otherwise Longlands foldcourse, otherwise Ashyards course (HD 1086). It was said in 1634 to belong to the manor of Peterstone and was for 225 sheep, but actually it belonged to Burghall and was not mentioned in the terriers of Peterstone (HD 1093), though about 1469–70 it was said to contain 80 acres parcel of Peterstone and fed 800 sheep (HD 346). Anne Gresham's book of rentals called it 114 acres 3 roods pertaining to Peterstone (HD 300). In 1584 the right of Burghall foldage called Caldow otherwise Holkham Lynge was maintained by the farmers John and Thomas Pepys (PRO, DL 44/250). The Lyngfolde abutted west on Caldowegate (HD 155, Fo. 36). Alternative names in 1467 were Eggemergate (HD 155, Fo. 13) and Blakelondhevedes (HD 155, Fo. 33). These were its ancient names (HD 128). Eggemerscote (HD 202) and Frebuske abutted west upon it (HD 201) and east on Gibbesgate (HD 155, Fo. 33). Blacklond or Blakelondhevedes abutted east upon it (HD 155, Fo. 35). Caldowegate was the name of a furlong which began in the south with 15 acres of Peterstone at High Caldowe and abutted to the east on Caldowgate thereafter called Blakelondheved. The strips are listed in 1549 (HD 296, Fo. 9). The western side of the southern end is Hungerhill (HD 22a, Fo. 16 no. 185) on the eastern side is Caldhowe (the cold tumulus).

CATHILL

Cathill designated a furlong with strips running from east to west, abutting on Wellelond north of the church and south of Dalesty or Daleway, the coast road. Catescroft (or Cootescroft or Ketcroft) was the name of 5 acres belonging to Walsingham Priory next to le Salt Merch in the east between 'le Merch' (Walsingham Marsh) to the north and Dalestye to the south (HD 22a, Fos. 39, 52). But it designated also a furlong in the Staithe Field with 9 strips (HD 296, Fo. 23).

CHEELESGATE

Also called Walsinghamgate, Cheelesgate was leading south-south-west from Holkham Town, from the junction of Crossgate and Wighton way (south of Hillhall). To the north of the present Obelisk Wood it traversed Bramlond and at the south-east corner of the present wood it diverged at Egmerescoot, with Caldowegate on the west and Lamberhillway in the east, each side of Ferrybush Closes and the arable strips of Bondeswong. In the south Caldowegate and Lamberhillway cross each side of Hunger Hill and the 'Fourscore acres' of Burghall, to meet the way from Burnham to Walsingham at East Caldowe in the south-east corner of Holkham parish. Though this was pasture, there were arable strips on both sides along most of its length. The part running through the present wood was a furlong called Strumpettshyll with 18 parallel strips in 1549 (HD 296, Fo. 8). Chelesgate was called 'Kingshighway' (HD 1267) and also 'Hollowway' (HD 948) in the seventeenth century.

CHEKER

There were two Chekers; that most frequently mentioned was in North Field or Staithe Field or Burgate. The other was in South Field at Frebush (HD 75, HP 1266), but 1/2 acre in Wechcroft and 1/2 acres at Clynt were also called Chekerlond (HD 120) and 4 acres next to the common marsh (HD 119b). It is sometimes called Chekerlond or Chetelond of Wighton. The chief Chekerland abutted west on Hillhall land at Toberscroft (HD 75). Le Cheker above Toberescrofte abutted in the south on the royal road to Wighton called Estgateweye (HD 155, Fo. 27v). Four acres in Le Cheker lay in the end part of Le Marketewey (HD 93, no. 1). The location is shown in the map of c. 1725. The name is connected with the exchequer or counting house of Wighton (HD 75), but at the Lyngesyde was 1 acre called Cheetelond of this manor (i.e. Hillhall, HD 155, Fo. 30), which seems to contrast, two leaves later, with land at Gybbesgate called Cheetelond of Wighton (HD 155, Fo. 32v).

CHURCH FIELD

The Church Field occupied the north-west corner of Holkham parish, from the Saltmarsh in the north to Burnhamgate in the south, as far east as the Clint. In the Latin Holkham Documents it is called *Campus Occidentalis de Holkham*.

CLEYLOND

Cleylond Furlong was part of a belt of brick earth in Church Field between Huncrondel (now Model Farm) and the Howe. It included the late 18th century kitchen garden (now the Garden Centre) and was otherwise known as Waterslades (HD 11). It lay parallel to Burnham Gate (in the south) and its strips abutted on the Marketwey in the north (HD 120). The south heads abutted on the way towards Hundcrundell'. A path connected Hundcrundell and the church (HD 155, Fo. 39v). 'Nyneacres' was in Cleylond in 1467 (HD 155, Fo. 39v) but counted as a separate furlong in 1467–8 (HD 75) between Cleylond and Coppynge (HD 155, Fo. 40). This abutted on Le Dalgate (HD 22a, Fo. 53 no. 265) by the western parish boundary. Estcleilond occurs in HD 22a, Fo. 39 no. 259 and Fos., 42 and 43 no. 260. The eastern boundary of Watyrslade was the common way from Westgate to the church (HD 111, HD 155, Fo. 39). It extended to the north of Le Howe (HD 155, Fo. 39). Estcleilond or Est Cleylond is mentioned in HD 22a, Fo. 39 no. 259 and Fos. 42 and 43 no. 260. Numerous references to strips in Cleylond occur, but these are the only

ones found in its eastern part. The manor house of the Neel lay to the east of
Cleylond and the grange of the Abbot of West Dereham (Huncrondel, now Model
Farm, lying away to the west). It is perhaps significant that Fo. 39 concerns an
exchange of 1 rood acquired by Gilbert Neel from the Abbot, while Fos. 42 and 43
concern a piece of 1/2 acres abutting on the croft of Katerine Neel, widow of Richard
Neel. It looks as if Richard's successors were continuing to round off their main
house (to which their father had not himself originally moved from Burnham) at the
expense of the eastern (i.e. adjoining) head of the adjoining furlong. The Neel
Cartulary mentions Cleygraves, i.e. clay pits; the plot granted by Ralph Colt to John
son of Richard the smith abutted with its west head on the royal road to Quarles at
Cleygraves (HD 22a, Fo. 3v no. 38). In 1665 land at Old Claypit Furlong abutted on
Adowegate in the east, but was located further west in 1690. Leatherpitway had come
to be called Claypitway (HD 943). There were new clay pits dug by the end of the
seventeenth century, and a large clay pit is marked at Skotbarbilhill (map of 1781).

CLYNT

The name Klint signifies a hard rock projecting on the side of a hill or river. It is of
Old Norse or Danish origin. At Holkham the word Clynt apparently at first meant the
high lands flanking the watery depression between them, for an early surname is that
of Bartholomew and Andrew Underclynt (HD 22a, Fos. 31–34 no. 255, and HD 84 of
1334). The Clynt came to be the name of a depression between high banks (le
Clyntebreste, HD 201) dividing Church Field and Staithe Field. It was fed by seven
springs at its southern end and flowed into a tidal creek at its northern end. The
damming of this by Thomas Coke in 1727 and the extensions at each end by T.W.
Coke formed the present lake. In the 16th century the Clynt was the name of a
common between the church and the Staithe (PRO DL 44/350). Three arable furlongs
between the Clynt and the church bore its name in the sixteenth century. On its
eastern side, meadows lay between it and a narrow track called Cripplegate which ran
parallel to it from the present Hall to the Monument. The strips in these furlongs
(numbered 17, 18 and 19) are enumerated in a terrier of Church Field of 1572 (HD
955). This arable was also called Le Clynt (HD 71 and 120). Before the lake was
formed there were ponds and a small common at its southern end, and a watermill
(later superseded by various windmills) at what was once its northern end. It was
traversed from E. to W. by roads. These led from the Staithe to the church via
Northgate near the Clynt and from Wells-next-the-Sea to Burnham Market. At
Northgate there dwelt a shipbuilder called John le Wrighte (1335–41, HD 82) and a
shipowner called John Speller (1384, HD 93). This, the coast road, ran further south
than at the present time, keeping to the contour till T.W. Coke extended the park
northwards. This coast road crossed the water by a bridge called Le Clynt Bridge
(HD 355). To the north 'the Pryor of Walsingham holdeth xl acres of marsh and vj
acres of arable land lying at Clynte in Northgate whereof the Sowth hedd abutteth
upon the waye leading from Holkham Stath towards the dale and the payment by yere
ij s. ij d.'. (1427–8, HD 300). This is bisected by the present coast road. The old
coast road was called Dalesty.

COLLESMERE

Collesmere was the alternative name for South Bramlond in 1467–8 (HD 75 and HD
155, Fo. 16v). It was a furlong running southwest through the present Obelisk Wood
on the east side of the Obelisk. Collymeer is described as in Bramlond (HD 155, Fo.

12v, 30v; HD 201). This toponym was obsolete by 1549 (HD 296) and is last noted in 1468 (HD 156 and 187). It lay to the east of Caldhowegate (HD 22a, Fo. 15 no. 171). Calesdigate on which its west head abutted (HD 22a, Fo. 2 no. 6 and HP 1079). It is also described as abutting towards the west on the road from Holkham to Egmere (HD 22a, Fo. 2v no. 16 and HP 1037), for Caldowegate was anciently called Eggemergate (HD 155, Fo. 30v). Peterstone had 1/2 roods of villein land in Collesmere (HD 22a, Fo. 54v no. 266; HD 205; HD 300). This is apparently the same as the 1/2 roods of Noion's fee described in the Wighton rental (HD 71 and 120) as held by Thomas Clerke in 1456/7 once by Thomas Chosyll' and formerly by William Brystymber. *Col* is an Old English personal name.

COPPYNGE

Coppynge was situated in the West Field or Church Field (HD 296, Fo. 26) at the northern end of Bartholomew of Burgate's 'Hamestalfolde', a sheep fold which extended to Creykgate (HD 22a, Fo. 1v).

CREAKEGATE

The road from Holkham Town to Burnham Thorpe and Creake across the north western portion of the South Field was 'Crekgate alias Thorpgate' (HD 470, Fo. 1). It is often called Creyksty in early documents (HD 22a, Fo. 1 no. 1) and Crekewey (HD 128) or Crekegateway (HD 171, Fo. 28), in later ones Creykgate ran on the east side of the Hallegate (HD 116, cf. HD 300) of the Hall of Mounchansi (Montchesney), the manor house of Burghall which had vanished by the sixteenth century. A furlong called Cryekegate lay in Le Middelforlonge of the South Field adjoining the southern boundary of Merlawescrofte in Westgate: Edmund Newgate's terrier of 1549 (HD 296, Fo. 20v) lists its 39 strips starting with 7 roods lying athwart Creykgate due west of Sixacrehill in Gonnyngswong (now called Lucar Hill on the Burnham Thorpe boundary). Neel Manor then had four pieces, none larger than 1/2 acres, although its holdings originally included one of four acres (HD 22a, Fo. 3v no. 36 and Fo. 9v no. 115). In 1549 the Abbot of West Dereham had two pieces, one of 1/2 acre and one of 1 rood. These were separated from each other by two pieces of 3 roods, but in the Dereham Cartulary (BL, Ms. Add 46353, Fos. 263 and 260) the abbey was given 1/2 roods adjoining some existing property. The Prior of Walsingham's land (mentioned in HD 22a, Fos. 3v no. 30, 11v no. 147, 52v no. 264 and HD 305 Fo. 10v) had disappeared by 1549. Whether or not tenants were trying to acquire adjoining strips, it seems that lords of manors were not making great efforts to consolidate holdings. None of the strips in Creykgate belonged to Peterstone in 1549, but in the eighteenth century consolidation in this area at the time of piecemeal enclosure was largely into the lands of Peterstone. In a court roll of 1 Aug. 1495 (HD 195) Peterstone had 3 roods between lands of Burton Lazars. In 1549 the lands of Burton Lazars were divided by 1 rood belonging to Hillhall.

CRIPPLEGATE

The map of 1590 shows Cripplegate running northwards from Holkham Town to the site of the 19th-century monument. Arable strips abutted on it on either side (HD 22a, Fo. 54v, HD 212). There were houses on the southern end in 1630 (HD 1259). In 1660 it was described as 'at the Staithefield next Crossgate' (HD 814, 815).

CROSSGATE

The west part of the site of Hillhall lay in a street called Crossegate (1639, HD 659) linked with Wells by Wellegatewaye (1465, HD 156) and by a path to the way from Wighton to Burnham (1439–40, HD 120). Land at the north end of Crossegate abutted towards the west on Crepylgate and on the meadow of Burghall which is now beneath the lake (1517, HD 228). This was Crossegateshead (HD 120, Fo. 5 and HD 136). There were many cottages and messuages and inhabited plots called Cros(se)gatecroft(e)s. Not all the property in 'the street called Crossgate' (1464, HD 1146) was Hillhall's, though Hillhall's tenants are detailed (1467, HD 155, Fo. 4, 5, 21v, 27). It abutted on Hemplond (1439–40, HD 120). The earliest references are to a cottage and an unauthorised short-cut in a Neel manor court of 22 July 1332 (HD 82). Burghall court rolls of 21 March 1352 (HD 87a) and 22 July 1356 (HD 86) mention a quarter of rood and two tenants ploughing over their common boundary. The pinfold of Hillhall had Hillhall on the south, the road on the west and Thomas Webster's messuage in the north (25 July 1428, HD 115). It was on the east side of Crossegatewey with the messuage, garden and dovecote of Geoffrey Coly, clerk, on the west (1456, HD 135) between the Common More in the south and west and Thomas Smith's messuage in the north. Further north lay Crossegate Well by Thomas Webster's messuage between royal roads to the west and south and a common lane with a pightle of Neel Manor in the north (1439–40, HD 120, Fo. 3). Crossegate or Crossegatewaie was a royal road (HD 155, Fo. 21v, 27). One cottage of Hillhall was 30 x 12ft (HD 93). On the south of Burgatewey or Marketwey, 1362, HD 52) a cottage called Standards of 1/2 rood (1454–5, HD 202) was held by military service from Tobers (HD 75, Fo. 3v). Though devastated in 1403 (HD 92) it was repaired and various occupants are known (HD 52, 73 Fo. 3v, 115, 155). Wighton as well as Tobers had rents in Crossgate, but their records are not available for 1250–1350. After Tobers was united with Hillhall the earliest known tenant of Standards was Agnes Gayton (1362, HD 52).

DALEGATE

Dalegate was a track running parallel to Quarlesway (Long Adow) in the west and Caldowegate, Blacklandheads and Cheelesway in the east. The strips abutting on them, each side of it, are listed from south to north in 1549 (HD 296). At right angles to these, where the land dips towards the north, lay Dalegate Bottom (7 acres, 1 rood), with its 7 strips reading from east to west (HD 296, Fo. 11v) reaching to Deadqueenspit furlong (on the south of the present Obelisk Wood) and bounded in the west by Dalegatewey (HD 795). Dalegate was a *communis via* (in 1451–2), HD 128, but is not marked in the 1590 map, perhaps because that map seems to be mainly concerned with a dispute about foldcourses and Dalegate was not a foldcourse boundary. There it was divided from Caldehowgate by the distance of a one acre strip (HD 22a, Fo. 10v no. 129, Fo. 14v no. 168 and Fo. 18 no. 196). Between the two tracks lay Depcrundel (HD 111), which may possibly have been an early marlpit. Early improvement of some of the soil by the medieval precursors of Coke of Norfolk is suggested by the name of an area on the other side of Dalegate (i.e. towards Longlands) called Marlond (HD 22a, Fo. 17v no. 189 and Fos. 42v and 46v no. 260). This was no less than 12 acres of Neel Manor called Mareldewong (HD 128) bounded on the south by Wodegateweye, the road along the present southern boundary of the park. About 1390 Hillhall leased 10 acres at Dalegate for a barley rent, 3 combs, 6 bushels (HD 76). One area abutting on Dalegate (sometimes called

Dalegateway) towards the east was called Pilman (HD 22a, Fo. 53 no. 264). Some Neel Manor land at Dalegate was held of Hillhall (d'Akeny fee). At the southern end of Dalegate furlong on the present park boundary was the 16 acres of Walsingham Priory called Overouttergonge. At its northern end was Southgatecroftys (HD 296, Fo. 10v). There were 37 strips on the southside of Dalegate Bottom which contained only seven. At the western end of the valley called Dalegate Bottom (1467, HD 155, Fo. 13) was a five-acre piece of pasture belonging to the hospital of St. Mary Magdalen of Bishop's Lynn (HD 287) called Mawdalence pece and early consolidated from small benefactions. The exact location of this land, an enclave in his great farm eventually eliminated through exchange by Coke of Norfolk, is indicated in a map c. 1725 marking the newly planted avenue. The hospital's land abuts on Dalgate on the east in HD 128 and is divided by Skotbarble from Adehowgate on the west (BD 0, no. 7, Fo. 9 (33)). Dalebreast lay *super Lymekyln* (HD 300). It was also called Holmus or Holmys (HD 120, Fo. 3v and HD 124). Arable strips abutted there on Dalweg (HD 205 and HD 22a, Fo. 52v).

DALEHOLE

Le Dale is the Dale Hole which lies on the edge of the marshes in the chalk escarpment outside the northwest corner of the present park, approached along the coast road by Dalesti (HD 22a, Fo. 52v no. 264) from the church in the east and by Daleway from the south outside the park wall from Model Farm (HD 22a, Fo. 52v no. 264). Dalegate meant the way towards Dalehole. In the Middle Ages it did not go there directly, for it stopped at Holkham Town and was linked to Dalesti and Daleway by the Church wey or Burnhamgate.

DEDQUENESPIT

This pit is the one below the south-east margin of the Obelisk Wood. It gave its name to a furlong. The second syllable has no royal connotation and the locality is called Dedwyvvespitte in a Peterstone court roll of 1 August 1489, (HD 195). A similar name occurs in Quarles parish – Dedequenesgrave (Peterstone terrier, HD 300). At Holkham the name of the furlong survives until the mid-eighteenth century (HD 1086) when it was incorporated into Thomas Coke's park near its then southern edge which lay in a fold of low ground serving to conceal William Kent's lodges (since destroyed) from the eyes of anyone proceeding northwards from Kent's Triumphal Arch to Kent's Obelisk. Along this depression was Dalegate Bottom, and along this ran a road from Burnham Thorpe to Wells employed by Thomas Coke to by-pass the area around his new Holkham Hall, when he obtained permission to close the central stretch of the main road from Burnham to Wighton. Dedquenespit furlong is described as bounded in the west by Dalegateway (Hillhall terrier HD 155, Fo. 34v). It lay next Dalegate Bottom (HD 296, Fo. 11v) on its northern side. Nearby lay Pilman on the north, an alternative name for the place where the road leading from Holkham towards the south divided at a fork also called Egmerskote (1665, HD 840; 1452-3, HD 129). Dedquenepit lay to the north of Magdalen Piece in the northern end of a furlong called Dalgate where the land slopes downwards towards the north, before the ascent to the 18th century Obelisk Wood. Magdalen Piece is exactly located on a map of the 1720s. It is not the lowest part of the declivity in the 'valley called Dalegatebotom' (1467, HD 155, Fo. 13), but it is described itself as in Dalgat Bottome in 1548 (HD 287). In HD 22a, Fo. 8 no. 101, Dedquenepit is described as reaching as far west as Adowgate (which is further west than Dalegate) and (in Fo.

36v) it adjoins land in Adowebotme. In no. 246, land there abuts east on Elsiscot' –
perhaps a rare early synonym for Egmerescote, for the name has only been noted
once after the 1350s (1449, HD 194). The extent of the land connotated by the word
apparently varied at different dates like Longlands.

DEEPCRUNDEL

This pit is the most northerly of four marked on the east side of Caldowegate,
between Blacklond and Egmerescoot (HD 296, Fo. 10).

DOVECOTE

William de Calthorpe had a messuage under le Doffehous next to the path leading
towards the church (HD 22a, Fo. 35v no. 256). Peterstone had 1/2 rood in
Dovehowsecroft at Howegate, also in the Church Field (HD 300). But the octagonal
dovehouse illustrated by Brettingham lay further south, beyond the Burnham to
Wighton road (map of 1788/9). John Gunnor had a messuage called Duffowyard with
an adjacent croft on Howgate royal road in the east on the corner of the royal road to
Burnham in the south (1419–20, HD 111).

DUUESPIT

Duuecrundel lay on the royal road in a furlong called Adowe (HD 22a, Fo. 11v no.
142). A crundell is a pit and in Shortadowebottom land abutting on Adowgate was
described as opposite Adowecrundell, otherwise called Dowecrundell (HD 155, Fo.
36). These are apparently all the same which suggests that the 2 minims which form
the third letter of the name Duuescrundel should be indeed a u, not an n. Duuspet or
Duuespeit (HD 81) or Duuespyt (HD 22a, Fo. 4 no. 46) seems to be other names for
the same place. The west head of 2 acres and 1 rood there abutted on Lethirpitthefdes
(HD 22a, Fo. 9v no. 112) or on a path of similar name (HD 22a, Fo. 4v no. 47). The
positions of Lethirpits and Adowgate are marked in the map of 1590. Between the
two there is a large pit. The west head of Duuesped is described (HD 22a, Fo. 10 no.
121) as abutting on Gonyeswong, a name which applied not only to the area on the
southwest corner of the present park marked in the 1590 map, but to the land
reaching along the Burnham Thorpe boundary, from there far to the north (HD 296,
Fo. 21v). Whether or not this pit was identical with, or only in the vicinity of,
Steynhilcrundel (HD 22a, Fo. 5v no. 68 and Fo. 9v no. 114), it is possible that
Duuspet was part of that locality later called Steynhill furlong, a name (HD 296, Fo.
18) which was applied to the whole area (521/2 acres, 1 rood) along the east side of
Letherpythewey (*alias* Greyston) as far north as Burnhamgate near the northern edge
of the South Field.

DUUSTY

The third letter of this name is a *u* not an *n*, for it is sometimes spelt Douwesty (HD
22a, Fo. 18v no. 201; HD 197). The name occurs seldom. This suggest that it may be
no more than an alternative form of Adowgate or Adowwey.

EDISCROSSE

The north end of the lane at Edescross abutted on the royal road to Wighton (HD
22a, Fo. 51). In 1451–2 Edescroft (called Ediscroft in HD 119) was situated south of
Wyghtongate in Southhestfeld (HD 128).

EGMEREGATE

The common path from the Staithe to Egmere (HD 200) ran straight south along Lamberhillway to converge with the 'commonway from Holkham to Egmere', which veered east at Egmerescoot (or Pilman) near East Bramlond (south-east of Obelisk Wood) out of Cheelesgate, to diverge from Caldowegate and cut the Creake-Wells road at East Caldowe.

ELSISCOTE

The 'cottage of Elsy' was situated in Dedquenespit Furlong (HD 22a, Fos. 3 no. 25 and 23 no. 246).

ENDAKER

Endaker, Hendaker or Tendaker was at Greyston (HD 22a, Fo. 36 no. 257) or Hey Greyston' (HD 129) at the south end of Gonnyngeswong furlong (HD 296, Fo. 21v) abutting on Lethirpitgate on the west (HD 129) and east (HD 22a, Fo. 36 no. 257). On its west lay Thorpheveds and on its south lay Calthorpe's 18 acres (HD 296, Fo. 21 v). It is possible that the two minims should be read as *u* not *n* if the names is the same as Heuedaker in the Dereham Cartulary (BL, Ms. Add 46353, Fo. 266 no. xxiv) but this seems to be further north as it abuts east on Crekgate.

EASTGATE

Holkham Estgate (HP 1151) lay along the road from Burnham to Wighton, like Holkham Westgate. Estgateweye extended as far west as Chelesgatewaye which formed the western boundary of Estgatecroft (HD 155, Fo. 10). Estgate extended to Lambehilsti (HD 22a, Fo. 55 no. 266), further east than the northern end of Gibbesgate (HD 155, Fo. 30). By 1590 the map shows that the northern side of the Wighton road was included in the great close of Hillhall. At the south-east corner of this lay Tobers croft, called after a manor which had become united with Hillhall. Tobers croft was also called E(s)tgatecroftes (HD 296, Fo. 6v) and lay at the northern end of Wethereswonge furlong. Land at Ediscrosse, on the edge of the heath, is once described at Estgate (HD 155, Fo. 30), but this is unusual. In Estgate was land of Hillhall Manor of old called Marketstedlond (HD 155, Fo. 10). Estgate was both the name of a royal road (HD 155, Fo. 21), passing Le Martwestelond, a street in the town of Holkham (1609, HD 481) and of a furlong in 1617/8 (HP 1250) which lay on the south side of 'le Drovewaye leading from Wighton to Burnham Market' (HP 1240), though it also applied to land on its north side (HD 296, Fo. 25) but Estgate is described as in South Field (HD 119b). The road is called Estgatewaye in 1467 (HD 155, Fo. 9 and 10), evidently in contrast to Estgate the furlong. There was a cross there and houses belonging to Peterstone Priory (HD 205 and 300) and Hillhall (HD 202). Houses lay in the northern side of the road on land now occupied by the South Terrace; in 1465 an empty messuage of Hillhall was occupied by John Waylond who had to show his title (HD 196a). That of Walter Tolle was on a plot 3 perches 8 ft long by 42 ft wide (HD 481). The path leading from the Staithe to Egmere, which was the boundary of Burgate, may have been the same as the boundary called Estgate Mere (HP 1266, HD 71 and 120). To the west of this lay 'Trewpagecrofteshende at Estgate' (HD 129, 195, 300 and 481). In 1372 Gilbert Neel was found to have uprooted a boundary between his land and that of Burghall (HD 85a).

FELDHOUS

Feldhous can also be spelt Feldhowes or Feildhus (HD 22a, Fos. 8, 9 nos. 105, 106; HD 81; HD 81) Evidently it was the name of a furlong which became obsolete and cannot be located.

FREBUSKE

This furlong, later called Ferrybush, was situated in the South Field (HD 201). Its eastern head abutted on Gibbesgate (HD 22a, Fo. 51v). Next to Bondeswong (HD 205, Fo. 9), its western head abutted on Caldowegate (HD 22a, Fo. 55v). It also abutted on Blakelond Hedds on 'Heved West' (HD 281, HD 296, Fo. 26v). One of two places called le Cheker was at Frebuske (HD 296, Fo. 7v). It contained a headland of strips at Bramlond (HMD 647–8, 1266). South Blakelond lay at Frebuske on the east side of Caldehowgate (HD 128).

FULMERSGATE

This name has only been found in HD 22a, Fo. 2v nos. 17, 18 and Fo. 16 no. 186, so it evidently soon fell into disuse. The land there lay near the royal road, which generally, but not necessarily, means the royal road from Wighton to Burnham. Fulmer may mean the marsh with many birds. This could allude to the common at the south end of the lake, and not to some special part of the coastal salt marshes. As there was arable at Fulmerescroft end on the north side of Fulmerscroft (HD 22a, Fo. 16v no. 187) a road may have passed along the south side of the croft. Fulmeresgate presumably ran north and south to join this road. This situation could have been on the north side of the way to Wighton near the entry to the Ling. If so, Fulmere could have related to some ill-drained land such as is elsewhere called a *spong*. Land at Fulmersgate abuts on the royal road between two other pieces of land in HD 22a, Fo. 2v no. 17. It is possible that the name does not have the topographical meaning suggested above but is linked with Robert Fulmer, like the name Hardys gate. Peterstone had 2 1/2 acres 'at Fullmere nighe Estgronge' (HD 300, Fo. 35v). Estgronge was the grange of Walsingham at the point where the road to Wighton left the arable to enter the Lyng.

GIBBESGATE

Just as Markesty gets called Marketsty (HD 22a, Fo. 13v no. 160) it is possible that Gibbesgate meant Gibbetsgate. It was a long road leading across the South Field from Holkham Town. It converged with a road from the Staithe alongside a large pit called Braunchcrundel (now Tutsia Clump). The word crundel means a pit but the name is applied to an area of 11 1/2 acres on the east of Gybbesgate (HD 201, Fo. 31v). On slightly elevated ground, south of the pit, within easy sight of the old Wells-Creake road, was Gallowhowe (HD 93, no. 23), just south of the road junction (Gallowscote or Galouescote, HD 119B, HD 120, Fo. 31v). Scoote means a corner, as in Egmerescoote. A *cultura* called Lambulbotme (HD 37) lay below the plateau on which the nineteenth century reservoir between the Burnham-Wighton road in the north and the Creake road on the south, on the western edge of which Coke of Norfolk was to build his Great Barn and which was called Lamberhil. The lands on it abutted on Gibbesgate to the west. Lambirhilsti approached the Burnham-Wighton road a furlong to the west (HD 205, Fo. 8v). The point where Gibbesgate reached the Wighton road was at Tobers (HD 22a, Fo. 51 no. 264), now remembered in the name

Tubbins Wood, but originally a separate manor which became united with Hillhall to its west. Its northern end was sometimes called Northgebbsgate and Under Lamburhill'. Gibbesgate ran through the area called East Bramlond abutting on Lamberhillhevedes in the east (HD 201, Fo. 32). Lamberhillhevedes is sometimes synonymous with Gibbesgate and sometimes is a furlong to the east (HD 75, Fo. 50v and 54v). Eastgybbesgate is also mentioned. At its extreme northern end lay Estgate Crofts alias Toberscroft (HD 296, Fo. 6v) and next to it West Gibbesgate furlong, Wederwong or Wetherwong, Witherwong. This consists of 27 strips totalling 28 acres, 1 rood in 1549 (HD 296, Fo. 6v) when only 1/2 acres belonged to Neel Manor. Gibbesgate was the eastern boundary of a sheepcourse which went as far west as Adowe, which was therefore called a 'common mere' (HD 155, Fo. 30). Galowescote lay on the east side of Gibbesgate opposite to Bondeswong (53 acres, 36 strips described in HD 296, Fo. 5v), Freebush or Ferybush and Egmeregate *alias* Caldowegate *alias* Blacklandheads were alternative names for Gybbesgate (HD 135; HD 22a, Fo. 55 no. 266 and HD 155, Fo. 131v). *p At its southern end lay the great piece of Burghall called Four Score Acres.

GODEWYNE

HD 22a gives no indication of the whereabouts of the croft of Martin Goldewine (HD 22a, Fo. 15 no. 172 and Fo. 18v no. 202), except that the east head of the latter abutted on the croft of John Silk (HD 28). It is not clear whether it was the same as Godewyne's croft (HD 22a, Fo. 35v no. 256) or whether Martin had the same land as Ida (HD 22a, Fo. 39 no. 259) or John Goldewyne (HD 22a, Fo. 44 no. 260). In the fifteenth century Wighton's Goldewyne's croft abutted on Le Saltmershe (HD 71 and 120) but Peterstone's was in Norwestkerkstyle (HD 129), but this may have been next Goldewynnescroft abutting on the saltmarsh (HD 114). It could not have been the same as Goodyngscroft which lay west of the foldcourse boundary, Cheelesgate, near Dalgateskote in 1549 (HD 296), for this would have been in the South Field. This could not have been the same as Neel Manor's Nine Acres at Goldwenscroft (HD 22a, Fo. 54 no. 265) which was far too large an area. Possibly there were several Goldewynescrofts for in 1470 some land at Goldewenyscroft, a piece of three roods, had an east head abutting on Le Dowesty (HD 197a) like Burghall Mill Hill (HD 120, Fo. 9; HD 136 and HD 197a).

GONDESHEFTLOND

Gondesheftlond was the name of a piece of 5 roods (headland) of Neel Manor (HD 22a, Fo. 16v no. 187). It is also mentioned in Lucas's Gazetteer (HD 22a, Fo. 44). It could be the same piece of 5 roods belonging to Neel Manor listed in 1549, situated between two pieces belonging to Hillhall Manor in Gonnyngeswong Furlong, which lay along the east side of the Burnham Thorpe boundary (the roman road of the Ordnance Survey Map), called Thorpeheveds (HD 296, Fo. 21v).

GONYESWONG

Two furlongs called Gonyeswong stretched along the eastern side of Holkham extending as far north as Burnham Gate Furlong and Town Crofts. One abutted west on Thorpehevedes, the Burnham Thorpe parish boundary having in its southwest corner an 18 acre field of Calthorpe, 10 acres of Burghall and 6 acres of Peterstone (HD 296, Fo. 21v). The other abutted east on Letherpytts and Greyston (HD 296, Fos. 19 and 20) and ended near Burghalstede. This furlong contains 9 strips of Hillhall, 7 of Walsingham Priory, 6 of the Abbot of West Dereham and of Burghall, 5 of Peterstone Priory, 4 of Neel Manor and Burton Lazars, 3 of Pomfret and Calthorpe and 10 is divided among 8 individual tenants. The second furlong starts with 12 acres of Burghall called Gunnyngswong, 9 of Neel and 5 and 6 roods of Walsingham and Neel respectively called Letherpits. When the strips reach the area opposite 'Sexacres Hill' (now Lucar's Hill), the furlong gets progressively shorter, and there is a small furlong called Shortlond (set at right angles) on its west. In addition to the familiar names of occupiers of strips, 1 rood belonged to the Gild of St. Withburga. The Abbot of West Dereham had 8 more (total 14) – his grange was on the west side of the present park. Walsingham had 9 more pieces (16 altogether – more than occur in the Walsingham terrier. This figure might possibly be swollen with lands which originally belonged to Creake Abbey). Neel Manor had 10 more pieces (14 in all, more than occur in the cartulary). Burghall had 14 more pieces (20 in all, a large number, perhaps of significance in view of the proximity of its manor house, contrasting with Hillhall's contribution of 2 to its total of 11). The heads of these lands were called Gondeshefdlond or Gondeseflond (HD 22a, Fo. 16v no. 187). Land in the east of Thorphefds is described in a Peterstone terrier of 1470–1 as at Skokly Botham or Guneswonge (HD 300, no. 11 Fo. 25v).

GREENGATE

A way on the north side onto which strips abut (HD 22a, Fo. 2v no. 8; Fo. 4 no. 41; Fo. 14 no. 160 and Fo. 20 no. 216). It passes Cleylond (HD 22a, Fo. 14 no. 160). Other strips abut on its south side as in HD 22a, Fo. 7 no. 89 and Fo. 8 no. 99. In 1686 it is called Greenway, running on the south side of 'Brist Furlong'. This seems to be in Mouse Hill Furlong, north of Wellgate Way in map of c. 1724, where one of several strips on the south of Greenway abutts on Mouse Hillway to the east. In HD 1101 Greenway is a continuation of Sanders Lane (marked in the map of c. 1724) and divides Coneyhall or Hillhall foldcourse from the Staithe or Newgate Foldcourse. A reference occurs to another Greeneway in Peterstone terrier (HD 300), evidently in the South Field. This looks like an alternative name for Dalegateway or another way running parallel to it, such as Quarles Way from the depression south of the Obelisk Wood to the present South Lodge.

GREYSTON

Greiston or Greyston in South Field generally came to be called Gravestonwey (HD 171, Fo. 29; HD 471, Fo. 14v) or Gravestone Furlong (HD 840) in the sixteenth and seventeenth centuries. Lethirpyttwey was a synonym for Greystonhevedes (HD 155, Fo. 37). In 1690 it was called Claypitway (HD 915). It ran the whole length of South Field parallel to Thorpheads on the west and Adowegate on its east, but there seems to have also been an area of the same name of nearly 110 acres in one piece in Churchefeld in the northern side of the royal way called Burnhamgate, near Cleylond (HD 155, Fo. 37). Adowgate lay only one furlong distant from Lethergraves (HD 205, Fo. 9v). Land called Greyston abutted both in the east and west side of Lethirpitgate (HD 22a, Fos. 36, 36v no. 257) which was a synonym for Greystonhevedes (HD 155, Fos. 37, 37v). Some of this was let for 2 bushels of barley an acre by Neel Manor in 12 1388–9 (HD 22a, Fo. 38 no. 259). Some Neel Manor land at Greiston was alternatively described as at Warledehousty (HD 22a, Fo. 38 no. 259). Other land abutting on Letherpitgate was at Rengemanslond (HD 120) and, in 1452–3, below the Hallewalle of Burghall (HD 128) and (abutting west) at Shortlond (HD 243).

Leatherpit is marked on the map of 1590. To the west of Lethirpittes lay Neel Manor's 14 acres called Gonyeswong (HD 22a, Fo. 38 no. 259) let in 1388–9 for a corn rent. Lethirpittshyll with whynnes or firez abutted east on Ledirpithil (HD 205, Fo. 10) and land at Ryngmenlond (HD 120, Fo. 1v) at Skocly and Shortlond abutted west (HD 111). Four dozen strips comprising 52½ acres called Steynhill ran along the west side reaching from Peterstone's 7 acres near Longlands in the south to Burnhamgate furlong in the north (HD 296, Fo. 18).

HALL

The vanished manor house of Burghall was called *Aula de Monchensy* (Montchesney) in the Neel Cartulary (HD 22a, Fo. 1v no. 1). Near the royal road from Holkham Town towards Creake a strip abutted on Hallegate in the east (HD 22a, Fos. 35 and 36). A strip at Hallcroftend abutted on 'le Hall' in the east (HD 71, HD 120). There were strips next to Halleyerd and the way of Halleyerd (HD 22a, Fo. 38). Strips at Hallegate abutted on Creykgate in the east and west (HD 116, HD 128). The word Kreykegate is glossed Hallgate in the Neel Cartulary (HD 22a, Fo. 52v).

HAMESTALEFOLDE

Hamestalefolde was the name of a sheep fold between Thorpemere, Creykgate and Coppynge (HD 22a, Fo. 1v, 1306). Hamstallande, Hamstalond or Hamestalonde was a headland in the Church Field (HD 300, Hd 305, Fo. 22).

HANGANDE ADOWE

Hangandehadow was part of the long road called [H]adowe or Quarlesgate which ran the whole length of the South Field from north to south. It skirted the steep flank of what is now called the Obelisk Wood in the map of c. 1725, and curved to follow the contour although it is marked as running quite straight in the map of 1590. This section was doubtless the part described as 'hanging'. It abutted on Ryngemanneslond (HD 22a, Fo. 36v no. 257), which lay near the crofts at the north end of Adow on the south side of the ribbon development along the Burnham road of the part of Holkham Town called Holkham Westgate.

HARDY'S GATE

Half an acre of Hardy's gate was villein land of Neel Manor (HD 22a, Fo. 45 no. 262). It is anglicized as Hardiesgate in a note of agenda arising from a manor court in 1330 (HD 81). It was then called after Hardy although he had already ceased to be the owner by then of Croft Hardy; later surviving terriers and court rolls have not yielded examples of its continued use. It is variously described as of the fee of W. Hakun and of the fee of Geoffrey le Bret.

HEVEDLONDLOND

Hevedlondlond designated a piece of land on the north side of the way called Grenegate (HD 22a, Fos. 2 and 4). Another Heflondlond is the same as Wellelond near Kirkesty (HD 22a, Fo. 39v).

HEYCALDOWE

Heycaldowe was an area at the southern extremity of the present park, east of South Lodges, at the end of the furlong which abutted in the east and west side of Caldowgate,. Here, at Wodegate lay 16 acres of Peterstone Priory (HD 22a, Fo. 53v).

HOLKHAM HEADS

On the west side of Holkham parish and of Holkham Park, Thorpfeld (Burnham Thorpfield) abutted on Holkham heds (HD 22a, Fo 52v). Thorpfeelde abutted on Holkham hevdes (HD 300). The westernmost furlong in Holkham parish (Gonyeswong) is described in turn as abutting on Thorpeheads.

HOLKHAM TOWN

Holkham Town or Village was situated on the royal road from Burnham to Wighton, part of which were called Holkham Westgate and Holkham Eastgate, and at right angles to which were Howgate, Southgate and Northgate (in the eastern side of the present lake). In the centre lay Crossgate, where there was, perhaps, a market place. The largest houses were Neel manor house beside the way to the church, and Hillhall, formerly called Wheatley's or Coneyhall, near the south-west corner of the present mansion. 'Peterstone street' was a group of dwellings, perhaps in Westgate, where Shityrblastylane ran, according to HD 300, Fo. 30v.

HOLMYS

Holmys was one of the fifteen sheep folds which existed in 1306. It ran in the fields between Hundecronndeldrove and Millehil and the royal road (HD 22a, Fo. 1v). Holmus was situated at Dalebrest (HD 124). This lay near Daleway (HD 22a, Fo. 52v), which may have been another name for Hundecroundeldrove, running towards the saltmarshes from the present Model Farm.

HUNDECRUNDEL

Hundecrundel was the site of the Abbot of West Dereham's Grange in medieval Holkham, which became the site of T.W. Coke's New Inn and the present Model Farm. An Adam de Hundecrundel occurs in 1332–3 (HD 82). It is shown as an isolated farmhouse in the map of 1590. The Neel Cartulary (HD 22a, Fo. 38) mentions strips in Huncrundellond. Hundecroundeldrove (perhaps the same as Dalway) was the boundary of a sheep fold (HD 22a, Fo. 1v). Huncrundallweye, Huncrundelwey in the Church Field passes le Skoote, Huncrundell Skote or Huncrundyleskote (HD 296, Fo. 22v). It was a *stadium* to the north of Huncrundell, containing 17 strips. Alternative names occur: 'Huncrundel, otherwise the North, otherwise the Borough Hall Foldcourse' (HD 1086, HD 1101). Land next to Huncrundelmer abutted in the south on the common way leading to Huncrundel (HD 111, 1419–20). Neel Manor had no strip there.

HUGGE

Le Hugge is a large steep mound now called the Howe situated on the south side of Church Field outside the north-east corner of the nineteenth century extension of Coke of Norfolk's kitchen garden (now the garden centre). In a Peterstone court roll of 19 March 1472 (HD 195) Le Hugge is called *alias* Lordesmylhill. A piece of common on which a well was improperly dug was called Hugg (HD 195). Various crofts, e.g. Craskescrofte, lay on its south; one common way went past it westwards to Burnham and another northwards to the church (HD 300). The way from the Parsonage (Huncrundel by present Model Farm) towards Howhill skirted 'parsonage furlonge' in 1643 (HD 957) formerly called Cleylond. The way from Burnham continued eastwards across the present lake to Crosgate under the name of Le Howewey (HD 461 and HD 465). Parallel to, and further east than the 'common way from Westgate to Holkham church', was another link called Howestye (HD 465).

HUNGERHILL

Hungerhill lay in the south-eastern section of the relatively high land now occupied by the present park. It was on the west side of Caldowegate (HD 22a, Fo. 16 no. 185) which ran northwards through the length of the South Field on the eastern side of the present avenue: the first element of the name is fairly common in field names to denote poor pasturage or crops, but is often very difficult to distinguish from *langra*, the word for a slope. At Holkham the name has not been noted later than 1456–7 in a Peterstone terrier (HD 22a, Fo. 53v no. 265).

HUSULESTUNGE

Other than HD 296 no reference has been found in the terriers and rentals to Huselestunge. Neel Manor land there abutted on Thorpegate. Another name for this was Crekgate (HD 470). It would have been not far from Sexakerhill (now Lucars Hill, HD 22a, Fo. 21v no. 233). The last syllable may allude to the shape of the land. Neel Manor had 4 strips in 'Creykegate in Le Middelforlonge' described in 1549 (HD 296, Fo. 20v) which do not seem to have been odd in shape. But there was apparently one parcel which had a tapering shape there: 'Burghall 3 roods with le Gorr'.

LAMBHILL

Lamberhilhevedes was at the western head of strips which lay in the eastern edge of the South Field (north and south of each other) at Lyngsty (HD 135). It was at the western head of strips abutting upon Gybbesgate (HD 135). Lamberhill itself lay west of Lamberhilhevedes and east of Gybbesgate (HD 135) above which it stood (HD 155, Fo. 30v). Lamberhilhefdes was at the western extremity not of the first but of the second furlong from the east at Lyngsty (HD 119B). Two acres there in two pieces were let for 5 bushels of barley rent in 1380 for 5 years (HD 93). It was connected with Holkham Staithe by a way which ran parallel to, and a furlong west of, Bullewer Meere (HD 765). The continuation south of this way towards Egmere was called Lamberhilsti (HD 22a, Fo. 51 no. 264) or Lamburrowewaie, on which abutted Lamburrowehille furlong (HD 681). In contrast to a furlong called Lamboroughhille (HD 481), a furlong on lower ground was called Lambulbotme (HD 22a, Fo. 4v no. 50). This had strips on both sides, some abutting on Gibbesgate towards the east (HD 22a, Fo. 18v no. 200). Part was called Brettslond (HD 22a, Fo. 53v no. 265). Hillhall let 5 roods in Lambhilbotme for 4 years for a rent of 2 1/2 bushels of barley about 1390 (HD 76). Lambulbotme was a *cultura* on low ground either at the north or south side of Lambhill (HD 37). The eastern heads of strips there abutted on Gibbesgate (HD 22a, Fo. 18v).

LARKESCOTE

'Lark's Cottage' was situated in the South Field, in Byllesmere Furlong, south of Adowebottom (HD 296, Fo. 14). Described as a furlong (HD 22a, Fo. 8v), it abutted on Adowegate in the west (HD 205).

LAZARESWONG

Lazareswong was the name of a piece of land belonging to the lazaret ('Lazer' of Mary Magdalen of Lynn which abutted on Dalegete in the east. The strip next to it was glossed 'Skottbarbilhill' (HD 22a, Fo. 51v). It lay west of the Avenue and its position is marked on the map of 1724. It was acquired by exchange from the 'Poor of Lynn' by T.W. Coke. He also acquired rights in Holkham of Chosele Manor of Burton Lazars (Leics.). Magdalen piece (5 acres) is marked on the map of 1724 and was described in 1545 as 'at Dalegatebottom'. It lay just south of a low quadrangular area, where at first no trees were planted along the Avenue. In the west it extended to Adowegate.

LEATHERPIT

The map of 1590 marks Leatherpit north of Longlands. Strips abutted on the path which bore its name on both sides, even as far north as Creyksty (HD 22a, Fo. 3 no. 26). This is Burnham Thorpe way which cuts across Litherpitway as they both approach Holkham Town. Lethirpithevdes (i.e. headlands) was called a way, *super semitam que vocatur Lethirpitheveds*, (HD 22a, Fo. 9v no. 112). The Neel Cartulary mentions Leatherpit often (HD 22a, Fos. 6v no. 80, 16 no. 186, 38 no. 259, 45v no. 262 and 53 no. 260). The alternative forms, Lethirgraves, Leyrgraves or Leygraves are also mentioned in the Neel documents (HD 22a, Fos. 8v no. 105, 24 no. 252, 35 no. 256, 46 no. 260, 51v no. 264 and HD 81), and in the Walsingham Terrier (HD 205, Fo. 9v). A constellation of pits is marked on the map of 1590. It is unknown whether these pits acquired their name from an early use for tanning, dating from a period when oak trees may have been more plentiful at Holkham than they were before the wholesale tree planting in the 18th century. Then the nearest tanner operated in Wighton parish. Letherpitgate and Lethirpitweye were synonyms for Greyston way. An alternative form with 'pits' instead of 'graves' occurs in HD 22a, Fo. 6v no. 80; Fo. 16 no. 186; Fo. 38 no. 259; 45v no. 262 and 53 no. 260. For further details see the note on Greystone.

LITELHOWE

Litelhowe lay in what became Thomas Coke's new wood around his new Obelisk. The barrow, as a landmark, may have been on one of the highest points, either the site of the Obelisk itself or of William Kent's Temple. The Temple was built on the highest point reached by projecting a line up the centre of the low ground of which the northern end was a maritime creek called the Clynt. This was dammed by Thomas Coke to form the nucleus of the present lake, wrongly attributed by Pevsner and his followers to Capability Brown. The word Letilhou may have begun as the name of a tumulus, small compared with Howehill, but it is usually used as the name of a furlong surviving into the sixteenth and seventeenth centuries. It seems that Littlehowehill is not identical with Strumpettshill (on Shortlond which abutted west on Chelisgate) whereas Litelhowe abutted E. on Chelisgate (Hillhall terrier of 1486/7 HD 155, Fo. 34). The name Lytelhowehill in William de Calthorpe's terrier, HD 22a, Fo. 35v no. 256, suggests a summit. A Walsingham terrier of 1457-8 gives Sladacre as a synonym for Letylhouhede, but HD 22a, Fo. 7v no. 97 and HP 1047 questions the identity in the thirteenth century of Litelhowe and Sladaker which are given as the locations of two separate pieces. Sladacre included much more than Lytelhowehill. In 1467-8 Sladacre abuts E. on Littlehoweheveds (HD 75). Sladaker is often mentioned. It was a vast furlong stretching from Southgatecrofts in the north the whole length of the South Field and was sometimes called Billesmer. Its numerous component lands are described in Edmund Newgate's terrier of 1549 (HD 296, Fos. 12–13), which also describes Strumpettshyll on Fo.8. A Neel Manor feodary of 1388–9 suggests that Litelhowe is the name of a way (HD 22a, Fo. 38v no. 259). Land at Letylow is described as abutting on Dalgate and called Pilman (1456–7, HD 22a, Fo. 53 no. 265) so it looks as if the way was either what is often called Dalgate or a balk at the other end of the ploughed lands. In a Hillhall court roll of 1 Dec. 1473 (HD 196a) 1/2 acres of peas, at W. end of Lytelhow are Hanggangadough'. This makes the Temple seem a more probable site than the Obelisk, if it was a tumulus sited on a skyline. Littlehoweheds in HD 300, Fo. 24, is used as the Elizabethan equivalent of *Dalgat' vocat' Pilman* in HD 22a, Fo. 53 no. 265.

LONGACRE

There was a furlong called Longacre in the South Field, described in the Newgate Terrier as 'situated at the north end of Longland furlong' (HD 249, Fo. 9). The name also applied to an acre belonging to Neel Manor at the north end of a furlong abutting in the north-west on Caldowegate and its northern extension Chelisgate, described as 'at Chelysgate' (HD 22a, Fo. 53; HD 296). Next to it, to the north, lay a rood called Strumpet, or a furlong called Strumpettshyl, *alias* Shortlond, which abutted in the west on Chelisgate (HD 22a, Fo. 39v; HD 296, Fo. 8). Longaker was a headland lying to the north, above North Bramlond (HD 128).

LONGFURLONG

The strips of Longfurlong abutted north on Scottowgate and ran east towards Wells through the Staithe Field (HD 187, Fo. 17). Some strips abutted on Egmeresty in the east (HD 300) and Brymbledykewey (HD 296, Fo. 24v). Longlands represented an area bounded by the way from Burnham to Walsingham, along the south boundary of Holkham parish and between Gravestone heads in the west, leading north past Leatherpits to the west and Adow or Quarles way to the east, as marked on the map of 1590. In the 18th century a farm was built on it, and in the 19th century estate-works workshops. The name was extended to denote a *stadium* comprising, in 1549, 76 strips, mostly small except for the 7 acres of the Abbot of West Dereham, the 7 acres of the priory of Peterstone, Hillhall's 3 1/2 acres, Neel's 6 acres, Gunnor's 9 acres and Burghall's 3 acres. It seems that the word Longlands does not allude to the length of the furrows, but to the extent of the furlong. In the 18th century there was a foldcourse called Caldowe foldcourse, otherwise Longlands foldcourse, otherwise Ashyards foldcourse (HD 1086), and Longlands wong (i.e. furlong) could be applied to land abutting as far east as Gibbesgate (HD 205, Fo. 9). The word Longlands now applies to the group of buildings round the estate workshop, but it has been used to include New Holkham, and even perhaps the Great Barn.

LYNGS

The common lynge was the name of an area of acid soil with heathy vegetation to the east and south of the arable lands of Holkham. Part of it was in Wells parish and part in Holkham. Much of it was incorporated into the park by the 2nd Earl of Leicester who made an American Garden characterised by rhododendrons, azaleas and wellingtonias suited to the ground between Samuel Wyatt's Palmer's Lodge outside the eastern confines of Thomas Coke's original park and the Golden Gates where the old road to Warham cuts the 'Dry Road' from Wells to Fakenham. In Latin documents the area is generally called *bruera* though the Lyngs are so called in a court roll of 1277 (HD 14). Near 'le entree in le Lynge' (mentioned in 1467, HD 155) five roods near the road from Burnham to Wighton were linked with Le Grange of Walsingham Gronge (HD 205) which is called *regalis via que ducit apud Estgronge* (HD 22a, Fo. 16v no. 187). Though not mentioned in our printed documents, the 5 roods at Le Lyngesyde called Walsinghamgronghe in fact formed part of the grant made by Ralph son of Silvester to Walsingham Priory (HD 3 amplified in HD 75 Fo. 13). This grant also mentions 7 acres in Le Lynge in a place called Whytpeece or White Oolond which is shown adjoining 12 enclosed acres of Burghall in the map of 1590. Arable strips of Aldelose furlong in the East or Staithe Field abutted on the *bruera* and the way to Wighton (and Warham) on the south (HD 22a, Fo. 22v no. 239, HP 1083). Wadlondes abutted on it in the east (HD 22a, Fo. 5 no. 61 and Fo. 5v no. 63). South of this way lay the big South Field. Its most easterly furlong next to the Ling contained 27 pieces of land ending in the south with a 12 acre close of Peterstone and including 14 acres of Gunnore (HD 296, Fo. 2v). The 1590 map shows the bounds of four strips of Burghall. In 1584 the Queen owned as of Wighton Manor the Holkham common on the south of Holkham called the Common Ling (PRO, DL 44/356). It was 100 or more acres of waste adjoining Wighton Common and Field and crossed by the Wells-Creake road. Grigges or Hillhall sheep grazed the north part and Caldow (later Wheatley's) sheep grazed the south part. On 29 October 1416 encroachment by ploughing was attempted (HD 479) and on 21 March 1486 Thomas Porter was found to have illegally erected a fold in le Southfeld in Le Lyngfold of Hillhall (HD 199a).

MARKESTY

Markesty atte Howe lay on the north side of Tuffehowe or Rustelhowe (HD 22a, Fos. 13v no. 160 and 49). A strip at Rustes abutted on 'Markesty at le Howe' in 1451–2 (HD 128). Strips in the Church Field abutted on its north side (HD 52) and a rood of Hillhall Manor lay across 'le Markesty' (HD 201). In 1650 Markettsty is a *quarantena* (HD 763). North of Marketwey lay, in 1456–7, Mekelhowe, the large mound north-west of the kitchen garden (HD 120). There was a market place at Holkham itself. This is not mentioned in the Neel Cartulary, but existed in the 14th and 15th centuries. The Prior of Peterstone had one of various messuages there (HD 300). Properties there abutted on the royal road from Burnham to Wighton in the south (HD 115), but others abutted in the north as well as the south, with the Lyng to their east (HD 281, 1538–9).

MARLOND

Two acres of land in one piece abutted on Dalegate in the east, in 1327 (HD 22a, Fo. 46v no. 260). Peterstone also had 5 acres called Marlond (HD 22a, Fo. 5 no. 57) Peterstone's land adjoined Neel's Marlond in the north and there was more land of Richard Neel on its south (HD 22a, Fo. 17v no. 189). In discussing names like Marled Piece in Shropshire Foxall remarks that 'the marling of light, sandy soils had been practised in pre-Roman times, but was revived by improvers of the 17th and 18th centuries'.[32] Many scattered medieval references to marling occur and Rodney Hilton indicated that an extra effort in marling may not have been a clear sign of

---

32   H.D.G. Foxall, *Shropshire Field-Names*, Shropshire Archaeological Soc., Shrewsbury, p. 35. Pliny understood the practice.

improved farming but of an attempt to keep yields up to a previous level.[33] Widespread marling at Holkham by Coke of Norfolk might raise the suspicion that almost any large pit might have been one of his marlpits. Fortunately a map was made soon after he inherited Holkham, and this marks in many pits existing already at that time. Many such pits (not all made for marl) had names and served as landmarks in medieval documents. The use of the name Marllond in the early 14th century suggests that the practice was then revived. The extraction of marl proceeded commercially a century later and Peter Blake's servant was presented in the Burghall manor court for making a pit and extracting marl without permission (HD 194). Possibly near Claypits, Mareldewong lay on the north side of Wodegatewey to the west of Dalegate.

MILLESTEDE

There are scattered references to a surprisingly large number of different mills at Holkham in the records of different manors. We count eight windmills here and a water-mill. So far as these worked simultaneously their individual capacities must have been somewhat limited. The land at Millestede must have been subdivided as Neel Manor had there only 1/2 roods of the fee of Geoffrey le Bret in 1330 (HD 81). Neel Manor had a Mill Hill in 1451–2 above Stathgate (HD 128). The Mill Hill of Burghall was near the way from Wells to Burnham (HD 450 and 541). This is the same as the mill of the Earl of Atholl (HD 76 and HD 115) and perhaps as Burghalle Myllehyll next to the way leading towards the Hugge in 1428 (HD 115). It is curious that among the tenants who failed to have their corn ground at Burghall mill, as they should have done, the name of Bartholomew le Miller appears (28 March 1368, HD 85a). Wakesmillehill was in Northgate (HD 243) near le Dalesti (HD 22a, Fo. 39 no. 259), that is to say on the ground which rises along the southern edge of the marshes. Hillhall had a Mill Hill in Estgatecroft (HD 355, Fo. 27), i.e. on the land lying to the east of the present mansion near the old road to Wighton. There was also a Towne Milhill (HD 450, 451) on the high ground south of Holkham town near the later ice-house. 'Ye Wynd Mylle at Holkham' abutted on Scottogatewey' (north) (HP 1179) on the ridge on which the almshouses and northern park wall are built. A map of c. 1725 has a field name which suggests that a windmill then or recently stood to the east of the site of Coke of Norfolk's monument on the high ground above the marshes south of Samuel Wyatt's model 'Rose Cottages'. A windmill house was mentioned in 1753 (audit book) which could have been one on the road to Wells on land of Wells Manor (Wells Document 619 of 1729). A windmill in one of the North Fields was held of Hoo Manor in 1552 (HD 460 and HD 470). Silkmillecroft was north of Hillhall's Mill Hill near le Dufhowse (HD 155, Fo. 20). In the thirteenth century Burghall had a watermill and millpond, presumably at the outfall of the Clynt water (HD 4). This plethora of mills is an interesting footnote on the legend that no corn grew in the district before Coke of Norfolk or at least before his great uncle, Thomas Coke, Earl of Leicester (1697–1759). Modern Holkham has no mill.

MUNDIESAKER

Mundiesaker was the name of a piece of land of 1 acre 1 rood included with many others to form an estate of 331/2 acres (HD 22a, Fo. 16v no. 187). Thomas son of

---

33   R.H. Hilton, *The English Peasantry in the Later Middle Ages*, 1975, p. 184., citing J.Z. Titow, *English Rural Society 1200–1350*, 1969, pp. 52–3.

Richard le Northerne, granted it to Katerine, widow of Richard Neel of Burnham, on 30 April 1336. Edmund Lucas includes this 'acre' in his Gazetteer. Later references to this name have not been found and it may have fallen out of use earlier than others. It is therefore impossible to locate it. It might have been *Mondayland*, held on condition of rendering work to the lord on Mondays.

NORTHGATE

Northgate Furlong contained strips abutting on le Saltemarsche in the north and Dalestye in the south, i.e. along the coast road (HD 296, Fo. 26). One strip of five roods abutting on Saltemerse was called Cokthorpecroft (HD 22a, Fo. 48v). Another was as large as 6 acres, but most were of one acre or less (HD 52). Acremyll lay there, as did John Grigges's barn and Walsingham's 6 acres of arable land called Cotescrofte, '6 acres of arable land lying at Northegate were the marsh in the northe parte and the comon scite on the south parte and is called Cotescrofte' (HD 300).

NORTHPILMAN

Adam son of William Craske of Holkham gave Richard and Caterine Neel one rood at Northpilman in 1328 (HD 22a, Fo. 19 no. 207). Apart from the reference to this in Edmund Lucas's Gazetteer no other references to the name have been noted. Pilman, Pilleman or Pylman was a furlong abutting to the east on Dalegate at Letyihow (HD 22a, Fo. 53 no. 264). The west head of Pilman abutted on Qwarlesgate (HD 22a, Fo. 19v no. 214, and Gazetteer). Land here was also described as at Egmereskote (HD 22a, Fo. 52 no. 264). Deadqueenspytte furlong abutted upon it in the north in 1549 (HD 296, Fo. 11v). Littlehowheds in HD 300, Fo. 24 is used as the Elizabethan equivalent of *Dalgat' vocat' Pilman* in HD 22a, Fo. 53 no. 264.

PEDELOND

Pedelond lay in the South Field, just south of Wightongate where it approaches the Lyng. At the north end of Middle Furlong, Neel Manor had half an acre at Wadelond, *alias* Pedelond (HD 22a, Fo. 39). It was bounded in the east by Idescroft and in the west by Lamberhillway comprising 6 acres 1/2 rood in six strips abutting north and south, but there were nine more strips called Podeslond Furlong, apparently to the west of Lammerhill way and east of one of the two places called Wechecroft. See Wadelond *infra*.

PODYNGSTY

Podyngsty was situated in the South Field west of Thorpehefdes, its strips running from north to south (HD 22a, Fos. 36, 52v and HD 1198). It lay outside the foldcourse (HD 201). It adjoined Thorpeheads and was situated at the northern end of Gonnyngeswong Furlong, i.e. on the south side of Burnham gate near the present West Lodge (HD 296, Fo. 22). Le Pynfold or pound of Hillhall Manor to the east of the royal road called Crosgatewey, east of the messuage, garden and dovecote of Geoffrey Coly, clerk, is not mentioned in HD 22a (1456, HD 135).

POPIWONG

The south head of one of the strips of Popiwong abutted on a way which was not Wighton, but Wellegateway (HD 22a, Fo. 16v no. 187; HD 135). It lay at Stathegatemere (HD 202). Marked as Popilwong on the map of 1590.

QUARLESGATE

This was a royal road running southwards from Holkham Town to Quarles (HD 128), a parish on the south side of Holkham, which includes William Kent's Triumphal Arch. Upon it abutted west and east heads of the furlongs called Pilman (HD 22a, Fo. 15 no. 175 and Fo. 19v no. 214) and 214) and Billesmere (HD 22a, Fo. 3 no. 27). The west head of land at Scotbarbles abutted upon it (1428, HD 115), on it also abutted the eastern head of Qwythewong (HD 22a, Fo. 15v no. 179) and Wodgate (1456-7, HD 22a, Fo. 53v no. 264). Fourteenth century references have not been found to Wythtwonge Pytte, which occurs in 1592 (HD 409), and may be the same as Magnum le Crondell at Wodegate mentioned in 1436-7 (HD 119b). The approximate line of Quarlesgate or Adowegate is still followed by the present farm road leading northwards from the estate workshops at Longlands. This passes near a large pit, which may be the one thus named lying to the west of Scarborough Lodge. 'Adowgate, otherwise called *ab antiquo* Wharlesgate' ran along the side of Byllesmere furlong from south to north passing Skotbabylhyll, le Wynnes, a crundell, Whitwongpitte, Larkeskote, Adowebottom and Gravellpit until it finally reached Southgatecrofts (HD 296, Fo. 13v). It was a common way (HD 22a, Fo. 13 no. 153) or royal road (HD 22a, Fo. 3 no. 27; Fo. 10 no. 120; Fo. 15v no. 179 and Fo. 48v no. 260). Quarleshow was a barrow near Lederpytts on which the western head abutted (HD 22a, Fo. 53). See Warledhousty, *infra*.

QUICHEGIFT

The north head of a strip at Quichegift abutted on a way which was called Grenegate (HD 22a, Fo. 7 no 89). Of the two ways of this name this would have been the one in Mousehill Furlong (in Staithe Field), for the one in the South Field ran north and south.

RESTINGSTEAD

Restingstead lay in the Staithe Field in Long Furlong between Brymbledykewey (Wellsgate) and Wakescroft (HD 296, Fo. 24v). It was described as 'in le Stathe Field at Dowesty and near Gatsend' (HD 71; HD 135; HD 120).

RINGEWARESLOND

Ryngewareslond was divided by the length of a furrow from Hadowgate on the east (HD 22a, Fo. 3v no. 35). The east head of land here abutted on Crekgate (HD 22a, Fo. 4v nos. 49 and 54 and Fo. 20 no. 219) and the west head of some strips abutted on Letherpitgate (HP 1051) or Letherpitway (1439-40, HD 120, Fo. 1v). It also extended the other side of Letherpyttway, its east head has abuttals also on it (HD 22a, Fo. 53 no. 264 and HD 118, 1451-2). In this furlong there were three sets of strips, two of them running parallel to the roads, instead of as usual, at right angles to them. The strips in 1549 are described in HD 296, Fo. 17v. Ryngmanslond bottom lay to the west of Shortadowebottom and Warlehowsty *alias* Gravepitway along some low ground (HD 296, Fo. 17v). This was at the northern end of Steynhyll furlong and Middlefurlong on its east (HD 296, Fo. 18); and at the southern end of Bondescroft and Hevedlond (c. 1380, HD 63). Thorpheued lay to the east (HD 296, Fo. 18). Land at Hangeande Hadow (on the west side of the 18th century Obelisk Wood) abuts on Ryngemanneslond (HD 22a, Fo. 36v no. 257).

ROTELESCROFT

Rotelescroft designated the tenement of Rutele with a croft. Neel Manor had villein land there; 1½ rood lay fallow as it was not occupied (HD 22a, Fos. 39, 39v, 45).

SAFFREN GARDEYNE

John Waylond's messuage (2½ acres) in Southgate abutting on the royal road (from Burnham to Wighton) in the north and on land of John Waylond, called Saffrengardeyne in the west, HD 22a, Fo. 48v no. 260. Walsingham was famous for saffron (used for the golden yellow dye of wool cloth) and the beds needed considerable care. An acre in Church Field, north-east of the church was planted with saffron in 1612 (Misc. Document 1233). Edmund Dowdie grew saffron, 1615 (Misc. Document 1239). Saffron Closes in South Field are marked in the map of c. 1724.

SALT MARSH

'All the common of Holkham of the north side of Holkham is called the common Salt Marsh. It belongs to the Queen as to the manor of Holkham'. Mersh Furlong and land 'at le Stath' at Kekethorpp' abutted on Salt Marsh (1584, PRO DL 44/350). On Salt Marsh abutted 5 acres called Rammyngspece at Cokethorpp (HD 212), lands at Catescroftes and Dalstye (HD 205, Fo. 11), Poyntel, a 6 acre tenement at Norgate (HD 52). There were also messuages at le Stathe adjoining those of Willam Bulman and Geoffrey Porter. The messuages of Goldewyne, Edmund and John Elvereche, Robert Gonnor, Thomas Gunthorp on le Stath abutted on Salt Marsh (HD 71, HD 120, 1457–8). Neel Manor lands at Bondmaniscrofts abutted on Salt Marsh at Saltmershgrene: '*apud Saltmershgrene in croftis et abuttat super Salsum Mariscum et fuit mesuagium Ide nativi domini*' (HD 22a, Fo. 45v).

SALTERSGATE

The north head of Saltersgate abuts on Wellgate (HD 22a, Fo. 16 no. 187, also Wighton rental, 1456–7, HD 71 and 120). Strips in Saltersgate are also described as abutting north, on Brymbylldyk' way in the same Wighton rental, and in 'Pomfrett Dragge' of 1538–9 (HD 281). In the latter, one furlong abuts on the common way from Wighton to Holkham. The furlong is named after Saltersgatewey which ran southwards from saltpans in the marshes, but the way is much less often mentioned than the furlong because strips in Staithe Field abutted north and south not east and west. Accordingly in Newgate's terrier of 1549 (HD 296, Fo. 25), one of his strips lies between a strip on the west and Saltergatewey in the east. It abutted in the north on a pit called Salterscrundell, possibly the pit used by villagers within living memory as a rubbish dump. The name Salterscrundel occurs very often and land there abuts north on the royal road called Welgate furlong (1486–7, HD 155, Fo. 42v), so the name may have sometimes meant the whole furlong.

SCAMLOND

Lands in Scamlond in the Staithe or East Field abutted on the lands of other persons to east and west and not upon any named road or track (HD 22a, Fo. 21v no. 232 and Fo. 23v no. 249). The north head of a strip abutted on Scothowgate in HD 22a, Fo. 23v no. 249 as in Hillhall rental of 1467 (HD 155, Fo. 22v). This describes Scamlond as next Popywonge (marked in the 1590 map) and abutting on the royal road called Wellegatewaye. Another Scamlond was in Le Chirchefield (HD 22a, Fo. 2

no. 5 and HP 1077). Both are mentioned in one document, a Hillhall terrier of 1454–5 (HD 201).

SCOTBARBLES

Scotbarbles is a name which survives in the corrupted form Scarborough Clump, now applied to a wider area reaching from the park boundary on the west almost to the avenue in the east. Neel Manor land there abutted in the west on Quarlesgate (HD 115) or Adowgate (HD 111, 120, 128, 243). The east head abutted on Lazerslond (HD 22a, Fo. 48v no. 260) and in a Peterstone terrier (HD 22a, Fo. 53 no. 265) is said to abut on Le Adowgate as if it extended both sides of that royal road. Lazerslond de Lenia (i.e. Magdalen Piece, HD 127) is a fuller name for land in the east side of Skotbarble dividing it from Adehowgate (BD 0 no. 7 Fo. 9 (33) which is marked on the map of c. 1725. It is called Land of Lazar' Marie Magdalene (HD 128), a name which differentiates it from scattered lands of the hospital of Burton Lazars in Leicestershire pertaining to its manor of Chossells, a benefaction from William d'Aubigny before 1146, bought out by T.W. Coke. As at Steynhill there were whins at Skotbarblehill (HD 128, 155 and 201). This was the name of a furlong in 1554–5 (HD 274). In it there was one crundell, perhaps the pit north of Scarborough Lodge and one of the Leatherpits. If they were connected with tanning, the area in the 12th century may have had many more old trees than it had in the 18th century before the planting programmes of Thomas and T.W. Coke.

SCOTHOWGATE

This road ran between parallel sets of lands with their north and south heads abutting on it e.g. north heads (HD 22a, Fo. 2 no. 4; Fo. 16v no. 187 and Fo. 22 no. 237), and south heads (HD 22a, Fo. 7 no. 83 and HP 1046). These comprised Schortland (HD 22a, Fo. 17v no. 188) and Longfurlong (HD 97). Shortfurlong abutted on Scothowgate (south) (HD 71). Strips in Longfurlong abutted north on Scothowgate (1406, HD 97; 1439–40, HD 120, also HD 71). On its south side lay Le Millehill of Burghall (1467, HD 155) and Schipmanscros (1428, HD 115). This was in the Staithe Field with the royal road towards the shore on its west. Hallmyll was next Scothowgate in the south (HD 71, 120). The name still flourished in the late 17th century and Scottogate way is marked in a map of Wells of 1668 (Holkham map 2/12). Land at a pit called Cuntecrundell abutted south on Scothowgate (1476, HD 155, Fo. 17v).

SCRULESCROFT

A piece of this name abutted on Holkham Estgate, where its southern head abutted on the royal road to Wighton, and its northern head on the 'land which formerly belonged to Richard Fraunceys' (HD 22a, Fo. 5 no. 62).

SCUCKELIF

Some land here abutted in the west (HD 79; HD 111) and some land in the east (HD 22a, Fo. 36 no. 257 and 52 no. 264; HD 120 Fo. 10 and HD 136) on Lethirpittes or Lethirgate. A list of strips in Gonnyngeswong furlong suggests that Skokely and Skokely bottom was about a furlong east of the Burnham Thorpe border on the west side of Greyston (HD 296, Fo. 21v–22). In 'Skokelybottom lay lez Cleypytts' (HD 128) on the east of Thorpheveds. There are large and deep pits on the east side of the Burnham Thorpe boundary of which one could be 'le Crundell' belonging to Hillhall in Skokelybotom (HD 155, Fo. 37v). Another name for Skocly was Hye Greyston

abutting east upon Wharledowesty and west upon Lethirpytteweye (HD 155, Fo. 37v).
Pieces of land here were often less than one acre in size, but Peterstone had a piece
as large as six acres (HD 22a, Fo. 53v no. 265). One piece in Schukkelif given to
Walsingham was sufficiently far north to abut with its eastern head on Creakegate
(Walsingham Cartulary, BL Ms. Cotton Nero E VII, no. cxxviii). Land in the east of
Thorphefds is described in a Peterstone terrier of 1470–1 as at 'Skokly bothom or
Guneswong' (HD 300, Fo. 25v no. 11).

SEXACRES

Sixacres or Sexacres lay between Hadowgate in the east and Ryngewareslond in the
west (HD 22a, Fos. 3v no 35, 9v no. 116). It was not the same as Gunnor's 7 acres
in Gunnungg's Wong called 'Sexacrehyll', which adjoined Thorpeheads and is
probably Lucas Hill (HD 296, Fo. 19v). Neel Manor had villein roods at both
Sexacres and Sexakerhil (HD 22a, Fo. 45). Peterstone had another 6 acres near 4
acres at Heycaldow, abutting in the west on the Way, and 6 acres at Skokelyffebotum
(HD 22a, Fo. 53v). Peterstone's 6 acres in Estcaldehow were called Stryte Crundel in
1547 (HD 296, Fo. 7v).

SHIPMANCROSS

Strips at Shipmancross abutted in the east on Shepeman weye (HD 71; HD 120).

SHITERSCRUNDEL

The northern head of a strip in Chyterscrendel abutted on the crofts of Robert
Dockyng (HD 22a, Fo. 55; HD 205, Fo. 22).

SHORTLAND

There were several places of this name: 1) The eastern head of one Shortland abuts
on Caldowegate (HD 22a, Fo. 17v no. 188). This is Heycaldehow in the Neel terrier
of 1451–2 (HD 128); 2) Another Shortland has a furlong stretching from between the
Wells parish boundary in the east and Staithegatemere to the west, abutting on
Scothowgate in the south; on its north was Le Mershe Furlong. Its south head abuts
on Scothowgate (HD 22a, Fo. 11v no. 141). On the east it reached Wells (1436–7,
HD 117b). A sixteenth century field book (HD 371) of Staithe Field enumerates all
the strips in Shortland. It lies next Le Longmere next to the land of the lord of Wells
and abuts south on Scothowgate. This cannot be the Shortland in Staithe Field next
Brymbildyk (1490–1, HD 155, Fo. 42); 3) In Geoffrey Coly's terrier of 1456 (HD
135) and in Newgate's terrier of 1549 Shortland is a synonym for Strumpettshyll in
the South Field abutting west on Chelisgate (HD 296, Fos. 8–8v); 4) A furlong near
Sexacrehyll (i.e. Lucarhill) in Gunnyngswong furlong (on the Burnham Thorpe
boundary, HD 296, Fo. 9v). This may be the same as a Shortland abutting on
Letherpytway east (1456–7, HD 120, Fo. 24v). But a Shortland abuts west on
Lethirpitweye (1419–20, HD 111a; 1456–7, HD 22a, Fo. 38 no. 259), and it abuts N.
on Lethirpitgate in a Burghall rental of 1439–40 (HD 120, Fo. 10 and HD 136).

SHUGESHOWE

Shugeshowe was an unidentified barrow, where Walter de Helwetone, perpetual vicar
of Holkham, was granted a strip of land by William son of Simon Hamo in 1313
(HD 22a, Fo. 8v no. 105). The name became obsolete.

SILK'S CROFT

Henry Anger of Holkham sold 1 1/2 rood abutting on the croft of John Silk to Richard and Katerine Neel on 22 March 1318 (HD 22a, Fo. 18v no. 202). Thomas Gunthorp held 1/2 acre at the end of the croft of Henry Sylke. Henry Coo holds a messuage 'once Henry Sylk's next le Stath' with a croft of 1 acre and 1 rood abutting on le Staithe in the north (HD 71, HD 120). Henry Silk's messuage and croft was also described as 'with its southern end abutting on the King's Highway' (HD 300). 'Sylke croftes' is marked east of a settlement at the Staithe on the map of 1590.

SLADACRE

'Shladeacre' or 'Sladaker' was, in 1296, the name of a furlong (HD 13; HD 22a, Fo. 7v no. 93). Its western head abutted on Hadhoweheved or Adoweheftes and Longeadowe (HD 12, 1295; HD 22a, Fo. 36v). The eastern heads of the strips abutted on land of Peterstone Priory (HD 12; HD 13; HD 22a, Fo. 7 nos. 93–97). Some abutted on Littlehowe or Lytillhowheveds in the east (HD 300; HD 128). Sladeacre Furlong lay between Dalgate in the east and Byllylmer (Quarlesgate) in the west and abutted on Dalegateway in the east. It stretched from Southgatecroftys in the north to Overoughtgong at the southern end of the South Field (HD 296, Fo. 12).

SLYNGESHOWE

Slyngeshowe was in the South Field and abutted on Thorpheveds in the west (HD 111, HD 128), leading towards Huncrundel (HD 155, Fo. 37v). It would have lain on slightly elevated ground on the east side of the Roman road which formed the Burnham Thorpe boundary (HD 111, HD 128, HD 155, Fo. 37v) and may have been surmounted by a barrow. It abutted on Lethirpitway on the west (HD 155, Fo. 37v). The reference to Huncrundell (the site of the mid-nineteenth century Model Farm) suggests that Slyngeshow was not towards the more distant, or southern, end of Thorpheveds. Perhaps Slyngeshowe was an ancient name for Lucar's Hill which perpetuates the name of Lucas, the early fifteenth century lord of Neel Manor. If so it seems to be the same as Sexakerhil. Slyngeshowe consisted of a series of small pieces (1 acre 1 rood or 5 roods, 1 acre and 3 roods). Some belonged to Neel Manor and some to Hillhall.

SOMERESHILL

Two acres at Somereshil were mentioned in the terrier of William de Calthorpe (HD 22a, Fo. 35). The furlong was situated in the South Field (HD 201). Somerhill Furlong may have been located between Longadowe Furlong and Egmerescote *alias* Pilman (HD 840). Somereshillbottom abutted on Pilman in the west. In the east it abutted on Common way, *alias* Dalegate (HD 128).

SOUTH FIELD

The largest of the three Holkham fields, South Field occupied the half of Holkham Park on the south side of the old road from Burnham to Wighton. It ran straight from the West Lodge past the garden of 'Garden Cottage', somewhat north of the present circuitous course of the drive towards Burnham. It included Lambullbotme, Wytheryswong, Gibbesgate and the royal road to Egmere and Adowegate (HD 22a, Fo. 2v and Fo. 53). Caldowe lay at its southern tip. Its southern boundary was the way from Burnham to Walsingham. On its eastern side a path called Lyngsty divided it from the Lynge. Its western boundary, marked 'Roman Road' on the Ordnance Survey Map, was the Burnham Thorpe parish boundary called 'Thorpe Heavdes' (Map of 1590). Parallel to this ran 'Graveston way', 'Longa Adowe' *alias* 'Quarles waye', Dalegate way, Chelesgate way, called, further south, 'Blacke land heavedes' and, yet further south, Caldowegate, then Lammerhill way, called Gibbesgate further south. Between these lay long *stadium* abutting on the crofts and strips which abutted on the Burnham to Wighton way. In the Holkham Documents it is called, in Latin, 'Campus Australis de Holkham'.

SOUTHGATE

The exact position is obscure and there may have been a way called Southgate on both the north and the south sides of the Burnham to Wighton road. John Weylond's messuage of 2 1/2 acres lay betweeen Thomas Weylond's former messuage to the east and John Weylond's Saffrongardeyne. This abutted in the north on the royal road (presumably the Burnham to Wighton road), but enclosures in Holkham Southgate are also found in le Chirchefeld (HD 201). In 1590 Waylands lay between Neel and Hillhall manor lands, and another messuage held by John Weylond as free tenent of Peterstone was in Westgate (HD 300). Possibly Southgate denoted the way due south from the church, called 'the churche pathe', which passed the west side of Neel manor house. After crossing the Burnham to Wighton road it is called 'longe Adowe *alias* Quarles way' on the map of 1590. Sladeacre Furlong, between Byllylmer and Dalgate, reached Southgate croftys at its northern end and abutted in the east on Daleacre (HD 296, Fo. 12). Byllesmere Furlong, abutting in the west on Adowgate *alias* Warlesgate, ended in the north at Sowgatecrofts (HD 296, Fo. 14v).

STAITHE

A settlement separate from Holkham Town grew up on the old coast line and was called the Staithe, or landing place. Cottages are mentioned there in the Burghall court rolls of 23 March 1334 (HD 84) and 24 March 1337 (HD 86). Of these, Asty's was 40 ft. long. In the fifteenth century references to messuages and cottages at Staithe are legion. Peterstone court rolls between 1452 and 1605 often mention a barn measuring 60 x 36 ft which had passed from the Meres to John Thorold, a chandler, in 1452 and thence to the Gunthorpes. It abutted on the royal road. In 1439 Peterstone's court was held in a cottage, but William Bulman spitefully sealed the door (HD 194). Silk's messuage abutted north between the saltmarsh to the north and the royal road to the south (1439–40, HD 120, Fo. 5). Restyngstede lay in a field south of a road from Staithe to the church called Staithegate (1408, HD 106). One messuage lay next 'le communem le Lane' in the east abutting on the royal road in the north (1439–40, HD 120, Fo. 5). The Silks had a mill and a dove-house (1467, HD 155, Fo. 20). The Staithe, Marsh or Newgate's foldcourses stretched from 'The Meels next the Sea' as far south as a straight line formed by Sanders Lane and Green Road i.e. between the West Lodge and the old Wells lodge (c. 1721, HD 1101). The ancient house retains its original ground plan and the north wall, made of flint and narrow rough bricks. It is a long house only presenting a small upper window suitable for a look-out, towards the North Sea. The Northerne family (thirteenth to fifteenth century) had a house near the shore, perhaps on the site for the Newgates were its heirs (HD 194) and John Coke bought this chief mansion house with Wagstaffe's and Gunthorp's adjoining from Edmund Newgate of Holkham, gent., next to the High Street in the east and the salt marsh in the north (HD 1276). In 1599 it included the fish-house, then used as a milk-house, a malt- house, with a little house and a table and then a swine-yard and swines croft. These adjoined each other from north to south and lay on the east side of the yard (HD 450 and 451). In 1452–3 John Newgate's messuage was called Le Fysshop (HD 129) and in 1456–7 Le Fisshehouse (HD 71 and 120). On 4 January 1730/1 an inventory of the contents of each room of Geoffrey Porter (NRO, ANW/23/IN/58/1729/31) corresponds to a detailed plan of Stathe Farm, as the ancient house of Newgate was then called, after Thomas Coke had consolidated the lands into rectangular fields outside his new park pale (Fiche 3: E13 and F14) The second Earl of Leicester transformed the Staithe into a model Victorian estate village, with new house, red neo-Tudor chimneys from his brick-works for the ancient house, creepers on the walls and a reading room and a school. His curate, Alexander Napier, prepared the minds of the people for change.

STAITHE FIELD

The East Field of Holkham stretched from the common marsh in the north to Wightongate in the south, and from the depression of the future lake in the west to the Wells boundary in the east (HD 300). A pit called 'saltarscrundel' was a landmark (HD 22a, Fo. 52v). While HD 296 (1549) gave details of every furlong in the South Field, it only describes 'le Marishe Furlong' in the Staithe Field. This stretched from Holkham Staithe as far as the Wells boundary, with strips abutting north and south (HD 296, Fo. 51). Parallel to the coast road, according to the map of 1590, were three ways running from east to west. 'The way from Burnham to Staithe' ran along the southern boundary of the 'Stathecrofts' and continued towards Wells-next-the-Sea as Scottowgateway, forming the northern park boundary. Nearly half way from there to 'the waye leading from Holkham to Wighton called Wighton gate' ran 'the way leading from Holkham to Welles called Wellgate way'. This was often called Brymbeldykegate. Four ways linked this with Scottowgateway: the 'waye from Holkham Towne to Stathe' (Stathegateway), Lacyes meare (probably Saltergate), the Staithegate, which became the eastern boundary of the old park, and the Wells-next-the-Sea parish boundary. South of Wellgatewaye, several ways connected it with Wighton gate. The most westerly of these headed towards Quarles, the next headed via Lamehill towards Egmere. Lacyes meare and Staithegate led towards the Lynge, Wighton and Warham. Algers, Shipmanscross and Edescross were in the Staithe Field. In the Holkham Documents it is called, in Latin, 'Campus Orientalis de Holkham'.

STANDARDS

Standards was the name of a cottage situated at Crossgate, abutting on Burgate in the north (HD 52; HD 115; HD 202).

STEYNHILL

This long furlong extends from the furlong called Burnhamgate in the north as far south as Peterstone's 7 acres at Longland, parallel to Middlefurlong in the east and Letherpyttewey *alias* Greystoneheved (or Warldhowesti) in the west. All its lands (521/2 acres and 1 rood) in 1549 are described in the Book of Edmund Newgate (HD 296, Fos. 18, 18v). Part of it was called Steynhilcrundel (HD 22a, Fo. 5v no. 68) and this contained a great pit at its southern end. It is uncertain which of several pits in the south-east portion of the parish this is. There are several pits along the eastern side of the Roman road, tempting one to wonder whether they could have originally yielded hard core for that road, when it was first made or improved. One was called

Calcrundel in 1451–2 (HD 128). Steynhill was separated from the Roman Road which forms the Burnham Thorpe parish boundary by a furlong called Goneyeswong, a name applied to an area reaching much further north than is suggested by the 1590 map. The hill of Steynhill lay southwest of Lucar Hill and hachures on Biederman's map made in the early days of Coke of Norfolk indicate its morphology better than the widely spaced contours of the Ordnance Survey map. Below it was Stanhyllbottom (HD 274, Fo. 3). Steynhill was not far from Longlands and in the late 15th century part was occupied by whins (HD 55, Fo. 37). In 1549 Steynhill's 48 separate strips were divided among 19 occupiers. Six belonged to Walsingham and Neel Manor each, four to Burghall, West Dereham Abbey, Hillhall and Gunnor's and 3 to Calthorpe. Peterstone had only two but they comprised 7 acres 3 roods. These adjoined Quarles where Peterstone acquired land.

STOWECROFT *(not located)*

Stowecroft contained strips of land belonging to, and perhaps near, the church of St Wytburga, the parish church of Holkham (HD 22a, Fo. 7v nos. 91, 92).

STRICRUNDEL

Stricrundel was the name of a piece of land also designated as Est Bramlond and Fulmiskere. It was situated north of East Caldow, to the west of Caldehowgate (HD 71; HD 120; HD 296, Fo. 7v).

STRUMPETSHILL

Strumpetshill lay near an acre called Longaker. A road in this furlong abutted on Walsingham weye in the west. Strumpetshyll, a synonym of Shortlond, abutted in the west on Chelisgate, once called Walsingham way, with 18 strips on part of the site of the present Obelisk Wood (HD 296, Fo. 8).

TENDAKER

Tendacre abutted on Lethirpitgate at Greyston in the east, according to the Neel Cartulary, 'At Hey Greystone it abutted on Lethirpitgate' (HD 22a, Fo. 36 no. 257). According to the Newgate Terrier, another strip lay between it and Thorpheveds in the west (HD 296, Fo. 21v).

THORPEGATE

Thorpegate is a name used in HD 22a, Fo. 13v no 157; Fo. 19 no. 206 and Fo. 21v no. 233 for what is more often called Creykgate, as if traffic to Creake were more important than traffic to Burnham Thorpe. It skirted Sexakerhil (HD 22a, Fo. 21v no. 233) or Six acres, now called Lucar Hill – a corruption of the surname of Edmund Lucas.

THORPEMERE

The boundary between Holkham and Burnham Thorpe follows a Roman road heading, like the Peddar's Way, from Castle Acre to the North Sea coast. It served as a boundary for one of the Holkham sheep-runs (HD 22a, Fo. 1v no. 1) and as the eastern boundary of arable land at Holkham (HD 22a Fo. 18v no. 199). The Roman road is clearly visible proceeding southwards in air photographs along a line marked by the hedgerows of field boundaries; but alterations in water channels and the accumulation of sand brought to this part of the coast from further south, has caused the disappearance of the port to which the Roman road must have led. It must have been near the Dale hole at the eastern extremity of a ridge which follows the 50 ft. contour line. Roads to Walsingham, Wighton, Burnham and Wells mattered to Holkham, but traffic inland down the Roman road ceased. It is never mentioned as a royal road in Holkham documents. It served as a parish boundary, and, as such, is mentioned; but nearly every reference to it is by the name of Thorpheads (or generally Thorphefdes or Thorpheavds) – the point at which the furrows of Burnham Thorpe ended and the ploughs were turned – and as such it is marked on the 1590 map. The other side of the boundary, the name used in Burnham Thorpe was, naturally, Holkham Heved (PRO *Ancient deeds*, 10611, 10612). Thorpehill was the same as Sixacres or Lucas hill on the Burnham Thorpe boundary. A rare name, it is more often called Qwynhil or Whinhill.

TOBERSCROFT

Toberscroft, *alias* Estgate croftes, was situated in the northern end of Wethereswonge Furlong (HD 296, Fo. 6v). Bondlands lay in Tobersgate 'nigh a messuage of Margaret Priest' in the west, with its southern head abutting on the King's Highway (HD 300). According to the map of 1590, Stathgate divided Little and Great Tubberds at its junction with Wightongate. It then forked: the way to Walsingham ran south-east, and an unnamed way (Gibbesgate ?) ran south-west to Cheales gate.

WADELOND

Wadelond was a furlong (HD 22a, Fo. 23 no. 243) abutting east on the Heath (HD 22a, Fo. 20v no. 223) or Common Lynge (HD 840), north on Wightongate, and west on Lamberhillway (HD 13). The name suggests the cultivation of woad for blue dye. Pedelond was an alternative name (HD 22a, Fo. 39 no. 259). It is more often spelt Podesland. It lay at the northern end of the Middlefurlong which ran northwards under Lamberhyll from Galoweshowe (1549, HD 295, Fo. 3v). It is mentioned as late as 1665 in a sale from William Gaseley to John Coke (HD 840).

WALSINGHAMGATE

Walsingham gate, *alias* Chelegate, passes Depcrundel north of Egmerskote (HD 296, Fo. 10). It was the name of a furlong athwart the way leading towards Walsingham (HD 22a, Fo. 35). Illegal paths were made with carts over land belonging to Neel Manor at Walsinghamgate (HD 82, 1332-3). There were 5 roods called Walsyngham Grange recorded at Lyngside between lands of Burghall Manor: the eastern head abutted on *Bruera* (the Lyng) and the western head on Robert Fuller's land (HD 22a, Fo. 51). A strip of Idescroft next Walsingham Grange abutted on Wyghtongate in the north (HD 296, Fo. 3). As for Walsingham marsh, the map of 1590 shows the Walsingham part of the salt marsh situated between Burghall marsh to the west and the common marsh to the east (Newgate marsh). In 1270-9 Walsingham Priory held of Denise de Montchesney 41 acres as a free tenant there, and 10 acres next le Dyp Hyrne from Bartholomew of Burgate, who himself held of the Knights Hospitallers of Carbrooke 21 acres of marsh (HD 5). A Peterstone terrier describes a Walsingham holding of 80 acres of marsh in two separate halves of 40 acres and 6 acres of arable land, one lying at Northgate 'nere the Marsh in the north parte and the comon site on the south parte and ys called Cotecrofte...', the other 'lying at Qynte is Northgate whereof the south hedd abbuteth upon the waye leading from Holkham Stathe towards the dale...' (HD 300). (See Salt Marsh, *supra*)

WARLDHOUSTY

This name means the path which leads (south) to Warleshowe, i.e. the tumulus at Quarles. Land abutted on Lethirpytgate in the west and Wardehoosty in the east (1451–2, HD 128). This may have been the land at Warldhowh' granted to Richard and Katerine Neel (HD 22a, Fo. 14v no. 166) and mentioned in the Feodary of Gilbert Neel of 1388–9 at Warledhousty (HD 22a, Fo. 38v no. 259; Fo. 45, no. 260 and HD 81). The Hillhall terrier of 1423–4 (HD 155, Fo. 36) shows that land lay athwart Wharlehowesty and that Wharleshowe was otherwise called Baconscrundell. Land at Bakonescrundel or Baconescrundel is granted in HD 22a, Fo. 8v no. 105 and Fo. 16 no. 186. This is the name of a pit in Le Myddyllfurlong somewhat north of Stonyhill and south of Qwarleshowsty (HD 296, Fo. 16). John Gunnor in 1419–20 (HD 111) has 3 roods called Baconyscrundel next to the heirs of Gilbert Neel in the north, with the west head abutting on Wardhowsty. Strips did not abut upon Warldhousty or run parallel to it, but ran athwart it (HD 22a, Fo. 36v no. 257; HD 155, Fo. 145). The Hillhall terrier shows that Baconscrundell lay next it and had given its name to a *stadium*.

WELLGATE

Wellgate was the name of the direct inland road from Holkham Town to Wells and also of a furlong which lay between it and Wightongate in the south. Wellgate furlong is mentioned as late as 1687 (HD 878) in the period when the piecemeal enclosure of the lands was soon to be much accelerated – 1720–30. The strips abutted on Wellgate towards the north (HD 162) forming a furlong sometimes called Saltergate (HD 22a, Fo. 16v no. 187). Welgate was north of Salterscrundell (Robert Dockyng's terrier of 1456–7, HD 222). Other strips abutted southwards upon it (*id.*) and formed a furlong called Popiwong (*id.*). Also on the north side of Wellgate (but further west) was Alger (HD 116). Land in Wellgate is described in 1436–7 as abutting north on Wellgatewey (HD 119); some of this land was called Le Snow (Hillhall terrier of 1436–7, HD 119b). The Hillhall terrier of 1486–7 (HD 155, Fo. 28) shows that this lay at Welleskote – a corner where the road to the Staithe went northwards. Le Snow ran from the Wells boundary called Le Longmere and ran as far west as Stagatemere, which also terminated Popywong below Myddel Skamlond in the north (HD 371/4). Wellgateway was a royal road in Hillhall rental of 1486–7 (HD 155, Fo. 28). Strips in this area survived until Thomas Coke reorganised the area to concentrate in his own hands the land south of his new park paling at Scothowgate and they are accordingly marked in a detailed map of the mid-1720s. After his boundary changes another map shows that all the land of Staithe farm had become concentrated outside his park. Thomas Coke's creation of the lake submerged the central portion of this link between Burnham and Wells and none of the existing roads follow any part of its course.

WELLELOND

Wellelond was a piece of land also called Hefdlondlond. It lay next to the Kirkesty (HD 22a, Fo. 29v no. 253). This was a path past the church at Cat Hill which lay north of the church (HD 22a, Fo. 20v no. 223, cf. map of 1590). Wellelond was at the west head of the land of Geoffrey Coly, the vicar, at Cat Hill (HD 135). It seems to have been near the junction of the droveway past the church from the marshes and the coast road, for a Walsingham terrier describes certain land as south of the marsh at North Cat Hill, abutting west on Lucas's land called Wellond (HD 22a, Fo. 52v no. 264). A rood at Cat Hill called le Wellond is described as in Northgate furlong (HD 155, Fo. 39v). This Wellelond is not to be confused with a tenement called Wellond's marked on the Elizabethan map of 1590 between the manor houses of Neel Manor and Wheatley (i.e. Hillhall) where Thomas Clerke (the cartographer) made a pound for Burghall in 1592 on the common moor (Wighton deed 103).

WESTGATE

The road west from Holkham Town towards Burnham had houses on each side. The names Westgate and Burnhamgate are partly interchangeable, but Burnham Gate extended further east than Westouwnesende (HD 22a, Fo. 52v), and Westgate included the houses in Holkham Town at least as far as Adowegate, *alias* Quarlesgate at the northern end of Longlands Furlong (HD 296, Fo. 52v). In 1419–20 John Gunnor had a messuage and croft in Westgate, abutting on the royal road in the south, and another messuage and croft, also abutting on the royal road, called Duffoweyend (HD 111). In 1549 Merlowescroft in Westgate lay at the end of the strips of a *stadium* called Creykgate in the Middlefurlonge (HD 296, Fo. 20v). Neel Manor's 1½ roods in Westgatecroft, with 1 rood at its northern head situated in Wychecroft, presumably lay west of Gunnor's Croft in the Church Field (HD 22a, Fo. 39).

WETHERESWONG

Wethereswong *stadium* (or furlong) is terminated in the north by Estgate croftes *alias* Tobers Croft (HD 296, Fo. 6v). It lay west of the furlong which abutted on the east side of Lamberhill and went straight through to west Gibbesgate *stadium* past East Gybbgate. The map of *c.* 1724 shows a 'Weatherswong Close' east of Obelisk Wood. A strip in Wytherswong abutted on East Gybbesgate (HD 22a, Fo. 2v).

WHITE OLLANDS

White Ollands was the name of Walsingham's 7 acres in le Lyng next to the land of Burghall in the west, with common heath on all sides (HD 205). The position is marked on the map of 1590, where Burghall's portion is 12 acres. Its south-east corner touched the Creake to Wells way, while its eastern side ran near the Wells parish boundary. The heath was bounded by Wightongate in the north and Walsingham way in the south.

WHITEWONG

About 1272–5 arable at Witewonge is described as abutting on Haddoghate to the west (HP 1001). But the land on the other side of Adowegate which abutted upon it to the east was regarded as in the same *wong* or furlong (HD 22a, Fo. 15v no. 179; HD 120, Fo. 10 and HD 111). A map of c. 1725 suggests that clay was dug in this neighbourhood. This seems to have started by the sixteenth century because references occur in 1524 and 1592 to Wythtwonge pytte (HD 194a and HD 409). This furlong is not the same as Wetherwong, Witherwong or Wedyswong which lay further east abutting on Gibbesgate and reaching as far north as Estgatecroftes *alias* Toberscroft (HD 136, Fo. 6v) with its 28 acres. Wetherwong is marked on a map of c. 1725, after which these names do not survive the reorganisation of the land of Holkham into rectangular fields. Whitwongpitte is described as in Billesmere furlong, east of

Adowgate *alias* Warlesgate between Skotbarbylhill in the south and Larkeskote and Adowbottom in the north (HD 296, Fo. 13v), and it may be the same as Magnum le Crondell at Wodegate mentioned in 1436–7 (HD 119b).

WICHESCROFT

Wichescroft was the name of a rood at the northern head of Westgatecroft (HD 22a, Fo 39). There were strips abutting north and south in le Churcheffeld (HD 296, Fo. 26). Another Wechecrofte lay in the South Field west of Lodelond, south of Wighton way. It was apparently situated towards the northern end of strips which abutted on Lamberhylleheved (HD 296, Fo. 5).

WIGHTONGATE

Because of the feudal dominance of Wighton and the economic significance of Burnham Market, the royal road between them was an important link, with its medieval ribbon development at the south end of the present lake. (Here a recent survey found that in its centre there were seven springs.) The road cut straight across the parish until its middle portion was wholly diverted (1722) and thoroughly blocked (1725) after the return of Thomas Coke from his Grand Tour in 1719, as at Killerton in Devon and Ambrosden in Oxfordshire. T. Coke of Holkham was determined to form a park and eventually a new house, which would have been incommoded by it. Accordingly, he obtained approval after an *Inquisition Quod Damnum* in Chancery to turn the road past the old house as far as a 'great gravel pit' on the edge of the Heath. The new alternative road was constructed out of sight of the house on the far side of the high ground where Thomas Coke planted the wood with the Temple and Obelisk on the skyline. Across the old road Thomas Coke built a walled kitchen garden, a gardener's house, a steward's house, and he submerged some 100 yards beneath an artificial 'canal' south of the present 19th century terrace. All these obstructions have now gone, but with them has gone the old road beneath them. Coke of Norfolk, in his turn, transformed the western end of the road to Burnham to 'improve' the appearance of the approach to the Hall. Wightongate had formed the boundary between South Field and the two North Fields called after the church and the Staithe. At the eastern end of Wightongate, at the entry between the Holkham arable and the Lyng, stood 'Walsyngham gronge' (on the west of Idescross), with its southern head abutting on the royal way to Wighton (HD 115). In view of the celebrated lack of trees in the 'barren waste' at Holkham which Thomas Coke and Coke of Norfolk transformed in turn, it is interesting to note a complaint about boughs overhanging the road in a Burghall court roll of 1562 (HD 171, Fo. 2a). As well as in the east of the parish, the Lyng lay to the south of some of the royal road to Wighton (HD 22a, Fo. 46 no. 260). Towards Burnham and towards Wighton the west and east end of this road were often called Westgate and Eastgate.

WODEGATE

This name may be a significant warning against assuming that the absence of timber growing in the early 18th century on the area of the present park had prevailed in the period when this place name arose. Woodgate was the name of the road from Burnham to Walsingham. It is marked on the 1590 map. It runs outside the southwestern portion of the park wall, without any change in its line. For the roads outside the park preserved their ancient identities, and were not periodically altered in the interests of the latest revolution of landscape gardening. It is not to be confused with a place at Skotbarbylhille called Wodegatewey (1457, HD 194) for it forms the southern parish boundary of Holkham and, like the Roman road which runs northwards from it along the heads of Burnham Thorpe's ploughlands it may well have existed even before the parish came into existence, and have been used like it as a convenient boundary on the landward side from very early times. At Woodgate Hillhall had land with *Magnum le Crondell* (HD 119b). This pit is not identified. On the north side of it there were large fields of 6, 7 and 16 acres (1549, HD 296, Fo. 13) contrasting with the small strips nearer the crofts of the village. Adowgate, *alias* Warlesgate, connected Holkham with Quarles to the south and the southwesterly continuation of the road was called by the people of Quarles, Holchamgate (HD 2). Unlike the Roman road there was probably no made surface, as on 22 July 1372, the servants of the Abbot of Creake encroached upon it in ploughing (HD 85a). The area was called Caldhowe, perhaps alluding to a cold, wind-swept tumulus. It is unknown how near Quarles Howe lay to William Kent's Triumphal Arch which was built outside Holkham parish and, indeed, outside the original Coke estate; see Warldhousty *supra*.

WYNHILL

This furlong was situated on the west side of the South Field near Lucas Hill next Thorphefdes (HD 22a, Fo. 38 no. 259). The western head of land there abutted on Thorpheds (HD 119b; HD 1238). It is not to be confused with le Qwhyrmes on the other side of the parish, which abutted on the 'common Lyngg' (HD 111). Whins or furze also give place names at Calwers Whynnes, lez Whynnes on Skotbarblehill, Lambirhilqvyn, Maygodes Whynnes, Whin Close or Great Whin Close. Whynhill to the east of Thorpheads is spelt thus in 1615 (HD 1238). Whins were used for the kilns that made bricks for Holkham Hall. Other, unnamed, patches of whins occur in furlongs with Lyng to the east and Wighton way to the south, or on the side of Wighton way further west (HD 296, Fos. 3 and 3v), and at Bondescrofthill (HD 128).

SOURCES FOR HOLKHAM TOPOGRAPHY POST 1350
Terriers and Maps

A The eight most significant later terriers

These form the basis of the second volume of *Lordship and Landscape in Norfolk*, 1350–1600:

(1) The Hillhall Book, HD 75 and 155. Fiche 1: E10 and F12.

(2) The Peterstone and Walsingham Book, HD 205 (defective), Fiche 1: F13; and 3: F12. HD 300 (complete, Tudor English translation). Burnham Document O (complete), Fiche 3: F11. This contains most of the documents in the Neel Cartulary, HD 22a, which are not printed here.

(3) Edmund Newgate's Field Book, 1549, HD 296, describing not only Newgate's lands in the Staithe Field, but lands of all occupiers in the South Field. It reads from south to north and from east to west. Fiche 1: G1 and 2; Fiche 3: F1 strips along Le Lyng with others written at right-angles to show direction like a map; Gonnyngs wong, lands along Burnham Thorpe boundary.

(4) The Dereham terrier, HD 284, Fiche 1: F14.

(5) The Burghall Book, HD 120, Fiche 1: F10, made by John Waylond, later belonged to Lady Anne Gresham.

(6) Holkham terrier, HD 349, shortly before 1560. This includes details of furlongs in Church Field after South Field. Lands of Burghall and Hillhall are abbreviated B and H, Fiche 3: F2, area with Burnham boundary (west), Huncrundel (south) and the marsh (north).

(7) Church Field Terrier, HD 355, describing all lands in 24 furlongs, made by William Wheatley, gent. and others, 1572. Still speaks of Abbot of West Dereham. Fiche 3: F3, Gunnerscrofte, reading westwards from Neel Manor, abbutting south on road from Burnham to Wighton.

(8) Field book of Staithe Field and North Field, HD 371, dated about 1580 by H.A. Davidson actually about 1480, Fiche 3: F14, lands in Marsh furlong.

B The most significant maps[34]

(1) The Holkham map of 1590 by Thomas Clerke of Stamford, Ms. 771 Rack n° 2/1.[35] Fiche 3: F4 and 3: F5, detail of title, 1590 and detail of central portion showing Holkham Town with church, Howe Hill, Neel and Wheatley (Hillhall) manor houses, the Clynt and the Staithe. The original is touched with watercolour and blue indicates water and glass in the windows of the larger houses. Fiche 3: F5, above: St. Withburga's church before restorations by the 1st Earl of Leicester's widow Margaret, Dowager Countess of Leicester (1767) and that of the 2nd Earl's first wife Juliana (1869); below: Neel and Wheatley (Hillhall) manor houses. Mr. Manser is one of the

---

34   See also W.O Hassall, 'Views from the Holkham Windows' in *Tribute to an Antiquary, Essays presented to Marc Fitch*, ed. by E. Emmison and Roy Stephens, 1976, pp. 305–319.

35   The call numbers for the maps are in the process of being replaced by new ones.

last owners of Neel Manor. Chief Justice Coke bought this for his fourth son John. Fiche 3: F5, the map as a whole with the chief roads and tracks (except Dalegate) foldcourses and furlongs. The map of 1590 was made by Thomas Clerke steward of Anne Gresham, widow of Sir Thomas and lady of Burghall Manor, in connection with a dispute over foldcourses. Thomas Clerke left his instruments to Thomas Langdon, maker of the maps at All Souls and Corpus Christi College, Oxford. Clarke came from Stamford St. Martin, i.e. Thomas Cecil's manor by Burleigh House. Cecil was Chief Justice Coke's father-in-law. Coke was staying at Osterley when Ann Gresham died there. The map, Holkham Ms. 771, measures 100.5 x 68.0 in. The number of dwellings at what is now the southern head of the lake had been larger in the early fourteenth century, according to a rental of Peterstone. The road from Burnham to Wighton through Westgate, was closed in 1722. The number and position of messuages may have been originally dictated by the fact that there are seven springs which feed the lake. Wheatley is the manor which had been called Hillhall and was renamed after its late sixteenth century lord. Newly-inherited wealth enabled improvements to be made under the Protectorate and after the Restoration the Hearth Tax showed that Wheatley Manor had 34 hearths, having it seems been recently enlarged. It then served as *venue* for county gatherings. In the north east corner is the Staithe through which runs the road from Holkham Town to the coast. This road survives as the lane still remaining on the east side of the ancient house, of which the north wall is the only medieval vestige to survive. A streak of blue indicates water in the Clynte. According to a terrier of 1577 a bridge crossed it at the north end of Burghall's acre meadow called Le Rede at the south end of which ran le Causeye next to the *forum* of Holkham (AD 355). South of Le Rede was a small Common between Neel and Wheatley. Along the northern side of the map the coast roads follows the modern route except where it crossed the Clynt. At that point the modern road follows a more northerly line made by Coke of Norfolk below the ancient coast line. At this point his park wall was breached by the flood in 1953. This would be a natural place for the watermill of Burghall, later superseded by windmills. Burghall manor house had long disappeared and the Gresham's predecessor's the Boleyns' had administered it from Blickling Hall through a local bailiff. Chief Justice Coke, having bought Neel Manor for his younger son, who married the heiress of Hillhall, later acquired Burghall.

(2) In Fiche 3: E6 and E7 is a detail kindly photographed by Leopold Schmidt from the original of a working map used by George Appleyard, 1721 until 1728 (Rack no called *palimpsest map*. 2/1A). It is not possible to get a satisfactory reproduction but the much used original reveals erasure of medieval village, fields and roads, the creation of the lake, Obelisk Wood, vistas and avenues inside Thomas Coke's new park pale. The scale is 18 inches to 1 mile or 1:3520. It was made after the reclamation of New Marsh (1720), marking (erased) the old Burnham-Wighton road beneath T. Coke's new kitchen garden, for which permission to divert was obtained on 24 June 1722 (PRO, C.202/109/2). The roads through Holkham Town were dug up in 1725–6. The Obelisk Wood was planted in 1727 when an alternative road was paled. The Clynt was dammed in 1727 causing the new lake to flood various fields and roads. The site of the Temple (built 1731–2) is shown where the axis of the lake cuts the skyline on the south. The initials of tenants of newly enclosed fields were inserted in 1728–9 followed by areas of plots. No cottage survived on the north of the Hall or the east of the kitchen garden. The wood was taken in hand in 1728 when the avenue was made. The initial C is earlier than 1729 when W. Leeds succeeded to E.

Cremer's tenancy. Details (Fiche 3: E6, E7 and E11) show the centre, the southern head of the lake and the southern part of the parish. The whole original map measured 256.5 x 193.0 cm.

(3)   Holkham after the destruction of Holkham Town and the creation of Thomas Coke's park is well documented. A small simplified map for display measuring 86.5 x 61.0 cm. in brown, decorated with water colour and gold, with 'A Scale of 40 Gunters Chains' (11.2 cm) is on Fiche 3: D2: 'Holkham in the County of Norfolk the seat of the Rt. Hon. Thos. Earl of Leicester' dates the map as between 1744 and 1759 (Rack no. 2/4). His stables beyond the lake (built in 1758–60) are absent. The map records the achievement of Thomas Coke and the old park as Capability Brown would have found it under the Dowager Countess of Leicester (1700–1775). The road from Burnham to Wighton, which bounded the medieval South Field, is covered by a kitchen garden and ornamental canal (which survived until about 1800). Its line is shown but has since been modified. The alternative model is south of Obelisk Wood. Holkham Town has gone. A few oblong strips survive between the roads to the church, but outside the park, where alone hedgerows are shown, the medieval furlongs have been divided into rectangular closes, but the divisions between the furlongs still survive – except along the artificially created parallel sides of the avenue between the recently grown Obelisk Wood and the Triumphal Arch outside the parish on the south (in Quarles). The medieval climate and maritime background has been transformed by the growth of a belt of trees to break the winds from the north Pole, and conceal the marshes and sand dunes, though the sea was still visible from the south windows of the *piano nobile* when newly-built in the mid-eighteenth century. The solitary great house inspired Thomas Coke to remark that he was 'giant in giant castle and I have eaten up all my neighbours'. Jacobean Hillhall or Wheatleys had been linked by a passage to the south west wing for it had still been in use while the Hall was being built. Perhaps when the Wheatleys were building their Tudor manor house, the d'Akeny's Hillhall (which stood on a knoll), had been left temporarily standing on a neighbouring site, near the south western wing of the present Hall. Old stone work in a cellar under the northwestern or Strangers' wing might be a vestige of an outbuilding, and the Old Hall with its kitchen hall and spare chambers was linked to William Kent's new western (or family) wing while building operations proceeded.

(4)   A map of Holkham by H.A. Biederman (of Hanover) was commissioned by T.W. Coke on inheriting Holkham (Rack no. 2/5). It shows the state of the park in the decade after Capability Brown's visit. It is dated 1776 and was reduced by him for inclusion in a bound volume of plans, 1781. See Fiche 3: C2. This map marks by hachures changes in declivity better than the contour lines of the Ordnance survey. It marks the positions of many pits which are concealed by subsequent tree planting from aerial photography. Coke of Norfolk became famous for the amount of marling undertaken in subsequent decades and it is useful to know which pits existed before his activities, for these pits, like barrows, served as landmarks in the medieval documents in which they are called crundels. The map shows the topography before Coke of Norfolk had made many alterations in the line of roads and in the contours of the lake, and before the planting of woods, belts of trees and clumps, which had been inaugurated in the 1720s by Thomas Coke, reached a crescendo.

(5)   Map of 1778–9 with Plan of the Staithe (Rack no. 2/161) (Fiche 3: C14). Detail of a large map made in 1778–9 (as revealed in the names of the tenants in the marshes) shows the Staithe as it was before it was completely replanned and rebuilt

by Coke of Norfolk and his son. The original map measures no less than 414 x 130–140 cm. It is tinted in watercolour. The central portion of the map marks a series of plots (numbered 308–314) running along the line of the old way from Burnham to Wighton between new garden in the north and the north-eastern part of the Obelisk Wood on the south. These rectangular pieces fronting on what had been the south side of the road were the crofts of villeins, perhaps those called East Bondyscrofts. There are two earlier representations of the Staithe, one as early as 1590 (Fiche 3: F4 and F5) but they are not so clear and detailed. References in medieval documents to dwellings at the Staithe are numerous. With the disappearance of the sea the name Staithe has become obsolete. The settlement, as it is today, looks like the model Victorian estate village which it became, but W.G. Hoskins erred in giving his authority to the erroneous idea that there was no early settlement here and that it was artificially created to house people turned out of the 'lost' village near the Hall.

(6)   Holkham Park as altered by T.W. Coke, 1843, (Rack no. 2/7) is illustrated on Fiche 3: B1–5, 14 and C1. The similarity with modern air photographs, owing to the dark clumps and belts of trees around the periphery is striking. The air photographs show the present planned verdure of this area, of which over a quarter, about 1,000 out of 3,000 acres of the park, is wooded. Medieval Holkham had few trees, and timber was imported from Scandinavia. Features on this map which were already prominent throughout the Middle Ages are the church, the Howe, the Roman road along the western parish boundary with Burnham Thorpe, a straight depression up the axis of the lake, a hill in the centre of the park crowned by an eighteenth century wood with vistas converging on the Temple and Obelisk, the main road along the southern boundary, and the old coast line along the southern edge of the marshes. Various pits in the South Field are surrounded by trees. T.W. Coke's New Inn (later replaced by Model Farm) marks Hundecrundel just north of the road from Burnham. T.W. Coke's kitchen garden south of the Howe indicates the site of Gunnors. Fashionable curves at the ends of the lake mark extensions beyond the old coast road in the north and the site of Holkham Westgate in the south. The clumps on the lawn north of the Hall do not indicate sites of old pits but are a beautification by William Kent. Burgate lay below a new Pleasure Ground in the east of the Hall. The wooded area in the east of the park is the Lyng or *bruera* unsuitable for arable. Longlands is an eighteenth century farm isolated among new enclosures and later made into large steam-powered workshops just west of the southern end of the trees of the avenue. The northern termination of these trees (since extended by rows of ilex clumps) marks the eastern edge of the consolidated medieval estate of the Hospital of St. Mary Magdalen in Bishop's Lynn. The obit roll of the hospital (founded in 1146–74) names some fifteen benefactors associated with Holkham. The five acres of pasture let to Nicholas Newgate in Dalgate Bottome in 1545 for 30 years for 2s. 6d. (HD 287) had probably been originally obtained in exchange for small scattered parcels originally given by Roger Chele, Bartholomew le Calwere of Holkham and Mary his wife, Roger and Alice Blakeman of Holkham and others perhaps encouraged by Brother Thomas of Holkham. Coke obtained it in exchange for land nearer the hospital at Gaywood. The obit roll is printed by Dorothy M. Owen, *The Making of King's Lynn*, 1984, nos. 84 and 85. The Great Barn (south-east of Obelisk Wood) and Longlands lie in Thomas William Coke's (1754–1842) great southerly extension of Thomas Coke's (1697–1759) embryonic park over lands he had enclosed.

APPENDIX 5

Feet of Fines relating to Holkham
in the Public Record Office: 1198–1406

NOTE: The starting point for our list is Walter Rye's[36] *Short Calendar* published in 1885 and 1886. The PRO class mark for all the items in the following series is CP 25 (1). We have selected all fines broadly related to Holkham and to individuals holding land in Holkham.

[1]	1 Oct. 1198	William son of Wido versus Peter de Holkham, in Burnham *Case 153, File 8 no. 183.* Dodwell, *Fines*, 1952, no. 103.[37]
[2]	7 Oct. 1198	Peter son of Geoffrey de Holkham v. Vincent, clerk of Surlingham, in Surlingham *Case 153, File 9 no. 224.* Dodwell, *Fines*, 1952, no. 140.
[3]	8 Aug. 1206	Alan son of Simon de Wighton v. Abbot and Convent of West Dereham, in Holkham *Case 154, File 26 no. 360.* Dodwell, *Fines*, 1956, no. 95.[38]
[4]	12 Aug. 1206	William de Holkham v. Peter de Bodham and Helewise de Bodham *Case 154, File 26 no. 340.* Dodwell, *Fines*, 1956, no. 98.
[5]	20 Jan. 1209	William son of Hugh v. Wido de Verdun and William de Holkham, in Saxlingham *Case 154, File 29 no. 413.* Dodwell, *Fines*, 1956, no. 151.
[6]	3 Feb. 1222	Ralph le Bret v. Peter de Grimston, in Burnham *Case 155, File 39 no. 145.*
[7]	9 Sept. 1222	Ralph le Bret v. Gilbert de Titchwell, in Titchwell *Case 155, File 39 no. 148.*
[8]	9 Sept. 1222	Ralph le Bret v. Nicholas de Docking, in Docking *Case 155, File 39 no. 136.*

---

36 Rye, W., *A Short Calendar of the Feet of Fines for Norfolk in the Reigns of Richard I, John, Henry III and Edward I*, Pt. I, Norwich, 1885. Pp. 1–218; idem, *A Short Calendar of the Feet of Fines for Norfolk, Comprising the Fines of the Reigns of Edward II, Edward III, Richard II, Henry IV, Henry V, Henry VI, Edward IV and Richard III*, Pt. II, Norwich, 1886. Pp. 219–502.

37 B. Dodwell, ed. *Feet of Fines for the County of Norfolk for the 10th Year of the Reign of King Richard the First, 1198–99, and for the First Four Years of the Reign of King John, 1199–1202*, PRS, n.s., 27, London, 1952.

38 B. Dodwell, ed., *Feet and Fines of the County of Norfolk for the Reign of King John, 1201–1215*, PRS, n.s., 32, London, 1956.

[9]   19 June 1228   Peter le Bret v. Jordan de Mundham, in Surlingham
                        Case 155, File 45 no. 290.

[10]   6 June 1228   Geoffrey le Bret v. Ralph son of Stephen and William and
                        Hugh, his brothers, in Warham
                        Case 155, File 48 no. 375.

[11]   26 June 1228   Bertram de Holkham v. Robert son of Hugh, in
                        Hindringham
                        Case 155, File 48 no. 369.

[12]   26 June 1228   Bertram de Holkham v. Thomas son of Peter, in Holkham
                        Case 155, File 42 no. 220.

[13]   26 July 1228   Bertram de Holkham v. Thomas son of Peter, in Holkham
                        Case 155, File 44 no. 265.

[14]   11 June 1228   Thomas de Holkham v. Warin de Montchesney, in
                        Holkham
                        Case 155, File 46 no. 320.

[15]   4 Oct. 1234   Bartholomew son of Vincent v. Peter le Bret, by Thomas le
                        Bret, in Holkham
                        Case 156, File 53 no 477.

[16]   24 Oct. 1234   Robert Burgelium v. Geoffrey le Bret, whom Alured
                        Hunred calls to warrant, in Great Snoring, and whom
                        James de Snoring calls to warrant, also in Great Snoring
                        Case 156, File 52 no. 455.

[17]   18 Nov. 1245   William, Prior of Walsingham by Brother Alan del
                        Orchard, his canon, v. Thorald le Breton and Aveline his
                        wife, in Holkham and Parva Walsingham
                        Case 157, File 70 no. 901.

[18]   1 June 1247   William, Abbot of Creake v. Reginald son of Geoffrey de
                        Holkham, by Geoffrey de Scluley, in Holkham
                        Case 157, File 70 no. 904.

[19]   24. April 1248 Hugh de Cressi, by Brother Henry de Norwich v. Ralph
                        d'Akeny, in Holkham
                        Case 157, File 71 no. 945.

[20]   25 Nov. 1250   William, Prior of Walsingham, by Brother Alan del
                        Orchard, his canon, v. Ralph son of Silvester of
                        Walsingham
                        Case 157, File 80 no. 1159 (printed supra: HD 3).

[21]   20 Jan. 1256   Reginald de Walton and Agnes his wife, Adam de Warham
                        and Alice his wife, Richard de Fulmodestone and Margaret
                        his wife v. William, Abbot of Creake in Holkham
                        (endorsed: *William de Grauntcourt apponit clamium suum
                        eo quod Ricardus de Fulmodestone villanus suum* (sic) *est)*
                        Case 158, File 84 no. 1271.

[22] 29 Apr. 1257 Geoffrey de Stiffkey v. Peter le Bret, in Holkham
Case 158, File 88 no. 1360.

[23] 8 Jul. 1278 John Silk of Holkham v. Ralph Hakun of Holkham, in
Holkham (Baldwin d'Akeny mentioned)
Case 159, File 108 no. 130.

[24] 15 June 1281 Harvey son of Thomas Buleman of Holme v. William
Renaud and Cecily his wife, in Holkham and Burnham
Case 159, File 111 no. 203.

[25] 25 June 1303 William son of Roger de Waterden v. William Renaud of
Burnham and Cecily his wife, in Burnham and Holkham
Case 161, File 119 no. 894.

[26] 19 Nov. 1311 Matilda, widow of John atte Falgate of Burnham Norton,
and Simon son of Richard Neel v. Richard son of John of
Assheneye, in Burnham Norton and Burnham Westgate
Case 162, File 127 no. 227.

[27] 9 June 1314 Edmund Athelwald of South Creake and [Margery] his
wife v. Ranulf Homay of South Creake, chaplain, and
Hugh atte Welle of South Creake, Quarles, Burnham
Thorpe, Burnham St Andrew, Burnham Sutton, Burnham St
Clement, Holkham, Egmere and Siderstone
Case 162, File 130 no. 393.

[28] 9 June 1314 Simon Brake of Brandiston v. Thomas de Snetterton and
Beatrice his wife, in Hunstanton, Magna Ringstead, Parva
Ringstead, Holm, Burnham, Holkham and Creake (Richard
atte Howe, Simon Dodeman of Raynham, James atte Mille
of Burnham, Richard Page of Burnham, Thomas son of
said Richard app. clam.)
Case 162, File 130 no. 395.

[29] 20 Jan. 1316 Richard Neel of Burnham and Katerine his wife v. John
son of Harvey Underburgh of Burnham and Cecily his
wife, in Holkham (Cecily daughter of Adam Hamond, and
Cecily sister of the said Cecily app. clam.)
Case 162, File 132 no. 500.

[30] 24 Apr. 1317 John Reyner v. Richard Silk and Cecily his wife, in
Holkham
Case 163, File 134 no 584.

[31] 28 Oct. 1318 The Prior of the Austin Order's convent of Peterstone v.
William Bulman of Holkham and Cecily his wife, in
Quarles
Case 163, File 136 no 688.

[32] 13. June 1322 Ralph Grigges of Wells-next-the-Sea v. John de Aston and
Petronilla his wife, in Wells-next-the-Sea and Holkham
Case 163, File 140 no. 883.

[33] 20 Jan. 1329 William de Calthorpe and Isabel his wife v. John de Ridlington, parson of the church of St Edmund of Burnham Westgate, John de Thursford and Walter de Waleford of the manors of Sithingge and Burnham Thorpe, and lands in Burnham Thorpe, Burnham Westgate, Burnham Sutton, Burnham Norton, Holkham and the advowsons of the churches of St Peter of Burnham Thorpe and St Edmund of Burnham Westgate
Case 164, File 146 no. 105.

[34] 6 Oct. 1329 Richard Ede of South Creake and Alice his wife v. Richard Neel of Burnham in South Creake and Waterden
Case 164, File 145 no. 92.

[35] 7 Oct. 1330 Richard Neel of Burnham and Katerine his wife, and Thomas son of Edward of Snetterton and Matilda his wife v. Roger Bretoun and Alice his wife, in Hunstanton, Magna Ringstead, Parva Ringstead and Holm-next-the-Sea
Case 164, File 146 no. 130.

[36] 13 June 1333 Richard Neel of Burnham and Katerine his wife and John son of the said Richard v. Paul Underburgh of Burnham and John son of Richard le Smyth, chaplain, in Burnham Westgate, Burnham Norton, Burnham Sutton, Burnham Overy, Burnham St Andrew, Burnham St Edmund and Depdale
Case 164, File 149 no. 300.

[37] 9 Feb. 1341 Thomas de Lacy v. John Sage and Joan his wife, in Holkham
Case 165, File 154 no. 539 (printed supra: HD 41).

[38] 27 Jan. 1344 William Mariot of Hindringham v. John de Mosewell and Amice his wife, in Holkham and Thorpe *juxta Burnham*
Case 165, File 157 no. 678.

[39] 19 Apr. 1366 John de Holkham v. William de Kelsey and Elizabeth his wife, in Holm, Hunstanton and Magna Ringstead
Case 167, File 168 no. 1243.

[40] 19 Apr. 1366 William de Rougham, William Hestyng and John de Holkham v. John Bastle and Sybil his wife, in Holm, Hunstanton and Magna Ringstead
Case 167, file 169 no. 1254.

[41] 29 Oct. 1368 John Leche of Egmere, clerk, John of Halteclo of Syderstone and John Richeman, chaplain, v. Edmund Crede and Leticia his wife, and Matilda daughter of Simon Chamberleyn, in Burnham and Holkham
Case 167, File 171 no. 1363.

[42]   20 Jan. 1369   Thomas Clerk of Cley-next-the-Sea and Matilda his wife v.
                          Robert Galun of Holkham and Agatha his wife and
                          Thomas Dortour and Alice his wife, in Cley-next-the-Sea
                          Case 167, File 172 no. 1401.

[43]   3 Nov. 1369   John Leche of Egmere, clerk, John de Halteclo of
                          Syderstone, and John Richeman, chaplain, v. Joan daughter
                          of Simon Chamberleyn, in Burnham and Holkham
                          Case 167, File 171 no. 1392.

[44]   3 Nov. 1370   Nicholas de Chosele v. John de Holkham and Katerine his
                          wife, in Holkham
                          Case 167, File 172 no. 1438.

[45]   19 June 1373   William Curszoun of Barford, Reginald de Eccles, Edmund
                          Gurnay, John de Holkham, William Berard, John de
                          Foxley, Roger de Barningham and Robert Curszoun of
                          Bintry, of the manor of Folsham called Swanton, and in
                          Norwich, Folsham, Bintry, Geyst, Gestweyt, Thursford,
                          Sparham and the advowson of Thursford
                          Case 167, File 174 no. 1512.

[46]   27 Jan. 1378   John de Wolferton, parson of the church of Harpley, John
                          Horning, parson of the church of Magna Snoring, William
                          Ellerton, parson of the church of Thursford, John de
                          Holkham and Simon Baret v. John Aleyn of Bliburgh and
                          Joan his wife, of the manor of Bedingham
                          Case 168, File 176 no. 13.

[47]   27 Jan. 1381   John de Holkham, John son of Reginald de Eccles and
                          Martin de Taverham v. William de Cailly, chivaler, and
                          Alice his wife, of the manor of Ouby
                          Case 168, File 176, no. 49.

[48]   20 June 1406   John Felbrigge, clerk, [Thomas] Tournay of Weasenham,
                          John Silk and John Bulwere of Holkham v. John de
                          Quarles of Holkham and Margaret [Neel] his wife, in
                          Weasenham, Raynham and half the manor of Kypton
                          (Weasenham)
                          Case 168, File 183 no. 66.

List of Documents

reproduced in Fiches 1, 2 and 3

Fiche 1: A

Fiche 1: B

Fiche 1: C

1   HD 22a, Fos. 36–37, Terre Prioris de Walsingham in Holkham dimisse
    Edmundo Lucas (1414–15), not printed.

2   HD 22a, Fo. 37v, Copy of Presentation of Letheringsett (23 April 1430).

3   HD 22a, Fo. 38, Terrier of Gilbert Neel (1388–9), not printed.

4   HD 22a, Fo. 42, Edmund Lucas's Gazetteer (C), Creykgate

5   HD 22a, Fo. 44v, Edmund Lucas's Gazetteer (H), Hosolestunge and *Terra
    Solidata per nativos in manibus Gilberti Neel.*

6   HD 22a, Fo. 47, Edmund Lucas's Gazetteer (N), [North Pilman] and *Dominium
    Petri le Bret.*

7   HD 22a, Fo. 51, Terrier of the Prior of Walsingham, renewed by John Waylond
    (1456–7), not printed.

8   HD 22a, Fo. 53, Terrier of Peterstone (1456–7), not printed.

9   HD 22a, Fo. 54v, Rental of Peterstone (not dated), not printed.

10 HD 22a, Fo. 55, Rental of Peterstone (*Feodum Noion*) (not dated).

11 HD 22b, Grant from John, son of Geoffrey le Bret of Holkham to Simon, son
    of Hamo of Holkham (24 Dec. 1293).

12 HD 23, Grant from Godeman Sutor of Holkham to Margery, widow of William
    Craske of Holkham (21 Feb. 1309).

13 HD 24, Grant from Helewise, widow of John le Bret of Holkham, to Gilbert
    her son (4 May 1309).

14 HD 25, Grant from Roger Chele of Holkham to William of Walsingham (6
    Dec. 1315).

Fiche 1: D

1   HD 26, Grant from William Silk of Holkham to Richard Neel of Burnham and
    Caterine his wife (23 Dec. 1315).

2   HD 27, Grant from Roger Hewerard of Holkham to Richard Neel of Burnham
    and Katerine his wife (17 May 1317).

3   HD 28, Grant from Henry Anger of Holkham and Isabel his wife to Richard
    Neel of Burnham and Katerine his wife (22 Mar. 1318).

4   HD 29, Letter of Attorney from Adam, son of William Craske of Holkham, to
    Thomas, son of William Grene, chaplain of South Creake (25 Sept. 1327).

5   HD 30, Grant from Rose, widow of Elias Crane of Holkham, to Richard Neel
    of Burnham and Katerine his wife (11 May 1322).

6   HD 31, Grant from John, son of Thomas Leffe of Holkham, to John, son of
    William Renaud of Burnham (21 Aug. 1323).

7   HD 32, Letter of Attorney from William Roteney of Walsingham to Martin
    Rust of Holkham to give seisin to Richard Neel of Burnham and Caterine his
    wife (4 Nov. 1323).

8   HD 33, Grant from Margery, widow of William Craske of Holkham, to Richard
    Neel of Burnham and Caterine his wife (20 Dec. 1327).

9   HD 34, Letter of Attorney from Margery, widow of William Craske of
    Holkham, to Adam her son to give seisin to Richard Neel of Burnham and
    Caterine his wife (20 Dec. 1327).

10 HD 35, Confirmation from John le Bret of Holkham to Walter de Mundene,
    vicar of Holkham (6 May 1328).

11   HD 36, Grant from William Curthun of Holkham to William Craske of Holkham [c. 1291–8].
12   HD 37, Grant from Walter de Mundene, vicar of Holkham, and Alice his sister to William of Heveringlond, rector of Holkham, and Robert of Knapton, chaplain (23 Oct. 1330).
13   HD 38, Grant from Simon atte Cros of Holkham to Katerine, widow of Richard Neel (20 Nov. 1336).
14   HD 40, Certificate from John de Cromhale, subescheator (10 Mar. 1338).

Fiche 1: E
1   HD 41, Final Concord, John Sage to Thomas de Lacy (9 Feb. 1341).
2   HD 42, Grant from William, son of John Goldwyne of Holkham, to Walter Osbern of Holkham (30 May 1342).
3   HD 44, Acquittance by the Official of the Archdeacon of Norwich of administration of the will of Thomas Neel (1 Mar. 1350).
4   HD 45, Hillhall Manor hayward's account (Sept. 1349–Sept. 1350).
5   HD 46, Hillhall Manor hayward's account (Sept. 1350–Sept. 1351).
6   HD 47, Hillhall Manor hayward's account (fragment) (Sept. 1351–Sept. 1352).
7   HD 70, Terrier of Gilbert Neel (1383–4), not printed.
8   HD 70, Terrier of Gilbert Neel (1383–4), not printed.
9   Feodary of Holkham of 1279, transcribed by John Waylond
10   HD 75, HD 155, Lords of the manor of Hillhall and of Bret-Tobers in Holkkham, from Hillhall Book.
11   HD 79 Court of Richard Neel (22 Dec. 1322).
12   HD 80, select cases in Borough Hall and Wighton leets about sheepfolds and shipwrecks, not printed.
13   HD 81, (part of), Tenements bought by Richard and Caterine Neel from William Roteney (c. 1329).
14   HD 82, First Court of Richard Neel and others after lease of Burghall by David de Strabolgy, Earl of Atholl (3 July 1332).

Fiche 1: F
1   HD 83 List of Neel Manor tenants on narrow strip, not printed.
2   HD 84 Account of John Mey, collector, not printed.
3   HD 85 Court Roll of Holkham Noyon (Peterstone) 23 May 1334. Not printed
4   HD 85a, Walter de Manny's court Leet (Borough Hall) (1347–8), not printed.
5   HD 86, (do), not printed.
6   HD 87, Walter de Manny's court Leet (Borough Hall) (1339–40), not printed.
7   HD 87a, Walter de Manny's court Leet (Borough Hall) (1339–40), not printed.
8   HD 118, Triangular document of 1318, not printed.
9   HD 112, Lease from Edmund Lucas of East Dereham to Nicholas Buntyng of Holkham of 100 acres with inventory of tools, stock and furniture at Neel manor house (29 Sept. 1419), not printed.
10   HD 120 Burghall Book, 1439, made by John Waylond, includes feodary (1273) with autograph of Anne Gresham, lady of Burghall, not printed.
11   HD 138 Descent to 1459 of land held by Geoffrey, son of William Godwyne, not printed.
12   HD 155, Hillhall Book, complementing HD 75 with list of lords.

13   HD 205 no. VIIa, Fos. 15–15v and Burnham Document 0, Rental of Peterstone
      in Holkham (1337).
14   HD 284, West Dereham Abbey terrier (1542), not printed.

Fiche 1: G

1   HD 296, Edmund Newgate's Fieldbook (1549), Fo. 2v, 3, South Fields, not
      printed.
2   HD 296, Edmund Newgate's Fieldbook (1549), Fos. 4v, 5, South Field, not
      printed.
3   HP 995. Grant from Geoffrey, son of Peter le Bret of Holkham, to Simon, son
      of Hamo of Holkham [c. 1294–6].
4   HP 996. Grant from Geoffrey, son of Peter le Bret of Holkham, to Simon, son
      of Hamo of Holkham [c. 1294–6].
5   HP 997. Grant from Gilbert, son of John Brun of Holkham, to Simon, son of
      Hamo of Holkham [c. 1283–93].
6   HP 998. Grant from John, son of Gilbert of Bintry, to Simon, son of Hamo of
      Holkham [c. 1283–93].
7   HP 999. Grant from Richard, son of Ralph Goldwyne of Holkham, to William,
      son of Geoffrey Silk of Holkham [c. 1270].
8   HP 1000. Grant from Thomas, son of Harvey Leffe of Holkham, to William the
      clerk of Holkham [c. 1283–93].
9   HP 1001. Grant from Thomas, son of David Man of Holkham, to Henry his
      brother [c. 1272–4].
10   HP 1002. Confirmation from Peter, son of Geoffrey le Bret of Holkham, of
      grants from his father and brother John to Robert, son of Emma of Holkham (5
      Dec. 1311).
11   HP 1003. Grant from Thomas Likesalt and Caterine his wife of Holkham to
      Bartholomew Calwere of Holkham (31 Oct. 1312).
12   HP 1004. Grant from Adam, son of William Craske of Holkham, to Richard
      Neel of Burnham and Caterine his wife (12 Apr. 1318).
13   HP 1005. Grant from Bartholomew, son of Robert of Holkham, to Richard Neel
      of Burnham and Katerine his wife (20 Aug. 1322).
14   HP 1006. Grant from John, son of Geoffrey le Bret of Holkham, to Richard de
      Barking, rector of half Egmere (5 Sept. 1293).

Fiche 2: A

1   Table of Contents of Fiche 2
2   HP 1007. Grant from Walter Hakun of Holkham to Simon Hamund of
      Holkham (17 Mar. 1294).
3   HP 1008. Grant from John, son of Geoffrey le Bret of Holkham, to Simon
      Hamund of Holkham (17 Mar. 1294).
4   HP 1009. Grant from Geoffrey le Bret of Holkham to Simon Hamund of
      Holkham (24 Dec. 1293).
5   HP 1010. Quitclaim from John, son of Geoffrey le Bret of Holkham, to Simon,
      son of Hamo of Holkham (18 Dec. 1294).
6   HP 1011. Grant from John, son of Geoffrey le Bret of Holkham, to Simon, son
      of Hamo of Holkham (30 Apr. 1295).

7   HP 1012. Quitclaim from John, son of Geoffrey le Bret of Holkham, to Humphrey David of Holkham (5 June 1295).

8   HP 1013. Grant from Roger le Norne of Holkham to Simon, son of Hamo of Holkham (27 June 1295).

9   HP 1014. Grant from Everard Underhowe of Holkham to Bartholomew the Miller of Holkham (20 July 1295).

10   HP 1015. Quitclaim from John, son of Geoffrey le Bret of Holkham, to Simon Hamund of Holkham (15 Oct. 1295).

11   HP 1016. Grant from John, son of Geoffrey le Bret of Holkham, to Simon Hamund of Holkham (12 Dec. 1295).

12   HP 1017. Quitclaim from John, son of Adam le Bret of Holkham, to Simon Hamund of Holkham (24 Dec. 1295).

13   HP 1018. Grant from John, son of Geoffrey le Bret of Holkham, to Simon, son of Hamo of Holkham (16 Feb. 1296).

14   HP 1019. Grant from John, son of Geoffrey le Bret of Holkham, to Simon Hamund of Holkham (14 Mar. 1296).

Fiche 2: B

1   HP 1020. Grant from John, son of Geoffrey le Bret of Holkham, to Bartholomew, son of William le Marschall of Holkham (29 Nov. 1294).

2   HP 1021. Quitclaim from John, son of Geoffrey le Bret of Holkham, to Nicholas, son of Aveline of Little Witchingham (25 July 1298).

3   HP 1022. Grant from Bartholomew de Burgate of Holkham to Simon Hamund of Holkham (27 Oct. 1299).

4   HP 1023. Grant from William Bulleman of Holkham to Simon Hamund of Holkham [c. 1291–3].

5   HP 1024. Grant from John, son of Warin de Walsingham, to Bartholomew, son of William le Marschall of Holkham (2 Oct. 1294).

6   HP 1025. Grant from Geoffrey, son of Peter le Bret of Holkham, to John, son of Geoffrey Silk of Holkham [c. 1284].

7   HP 1026. Grant from Thomas, son of John of Holkham, to Bartholomew, son of Stephen of Holkham [c. 1291–1300].

8   HP 1027. Grant from Geoffrey, son of Peter le Bret of Holkham, to Simon, son of Hamo of Holkham [c. 1294–6].

9   HP 1028. Grant from Geoffrey, son of Peter le Bret of Holkham, to Simon, son of Hamo of Holkham [c. 1294–6].

10   HP 1029. Grant from Geoffrey le Bret of Holkham to Simon, son of Hamo of Holkham [c. 1283–93].

11   HP 1030. Grant from Geoffrey, son of Peter le Bret of Holkham, to Simon Hamund of Holkham and Cecily his wife [c. 1294].

12   HP 1031. Grant from Geoffrey, son of Peter le Bret of Holkham, to Simon, son of Hamo of Holkham [c. 1294–5].

13   HP 1032. Grant from John, son of Geoffrey le Bret of Holkham, to Simon Hamund of Holkham and Cecily his wife [c. 1294–6].

14   HP 1033. Grant from John, son of Geoffrey le Bret of Holkham, to Simon Hamund of Holkham [c. 1291–3].

Fiche 2: C

1   HP 1034. Grant from John, son of Geoffrey le Bret of Holkham, to Simon Hamund of Holkham [c. 1294–6].

2   HP 1035. Grant from John, son of Adam le Bret of Holkham, to Bartholomew le Miller of Holkham [c. 1294–6].

3   HP 1036. Grant from Isabel, daughter of Ralph le Bret, with the assent of her son Thomas in her widowhood to William Craske of Holkham [c. 1284].

4   HP 1037. Confirmation from Thomas, son of Isabel, daughter of Ralph le Bret of Holkham, to Wiliam Craske of Holkham [c. 1284].

5   HP 1038. Grant from Everard, son of Everard le Caly of Holkham, to William Craske of Holkham [c. 1284].

6   HP 1039. Grant from Robert le Heire of Merston to William Cursun and Agnes le Heire, his daughter, of 3 acres of land in Holkham as dowry [c. 1284].

7   HP 1040. Grant from William, son of Bartholomew Mariot of Holkham, to Richard his brother [c. 1284].

8   HP 1041. Grant from Gilbert, son of William Nichol of Holkham, to Simon, son of Hamo of Holkham [c. 1294–6].

9   HP 1042. Grant from Ralph, son of Thouey Powel of Holkham, to Simon, son of Charles del Hil of Holkham [c. 1270].

10   HP 1043. Grant from John, son of Geoffrey le Bret of Holkham, to Simon, son of Hamo of Holkham [c. 1294–6].

11   HP 1044. Quitclaim from Helewise, widow of Geoffrey le Bret, to John de Fallegate of Burnham and Cecily his wife of Holkham (21 Nov. 1302).

12   HP 1045. Quitclaim from Bartholomew de Burgate of Holkham to Richard le Northerne of Holkham (13 Sept. 1303).

13   HP 1046. Grant from Thomas Selone of Wells and Matilda his wife to Bartholomew Caluere of Holkham (9 May 1304).

14   HP 1047. Grant from Adam Hamund of Holkham to William, son of Robert de Dunwich of Walsingham (1 Feb. 1314).

Fiche 2: D

1   HP 1048. Grant from John atte Falgate de Burnham and Cecily his wife to William, son of Robert de Dunwich of Walsingham (13 Apr. 1314).

2   HP 1049. Quitclaim from Adam, son of Simon Hamond of Holkham, to William, son of Robert de Dunwich of Walsingham (14 Apr. 1314).

3   HP 1050. Grant from Adam Hamond of Holkham to William, son of Robert de Dunwich of Walsingham (24 June 1314).

4   HP 1051. Grant from Adam, son of Simon Hamond of Holkham, to Richard Neel of Burnham and Caterine his wife (5 Nov. 1314).

5   HP 1052. Grant from Martin Goldwyne of Holkham to William, son of Robert de Dunwich of Walsingham (3 May 1315).

6   HP 1053. Grant from Joan, widow of Henry Hamond of North Barsham, to Richard Neel of Burnham and Caterine his wife (1 July 1315).

7   HP 1054. Quitclaim from William and Hamo, sons of Henry Hamond of North Barsham to Richard Neel of Burnham and Caterine his wife (15 July 1315).

8   HP 1055. Grant from Bartholomew le Muner of Holkham to Richard Neel of Burnham and Caterine his wife (1 Aug. 1315).

9   HP 1056. Quitclaim from William Silk of Holkham to Richard Neel of Burnham and Caterine his wife (9 Mar. 1316).

10 HP 1057. Letter of Attorney from Bartholomew le Miller of Holkham to Martin Rust of Holkham to give seisin to Richard Neel of Burnham and Caterine his wife (12 Apr. 1316.).

11 HP 1058. Grant from William Silk of Holkham to Gilbert his son (3 Oct. 1316).

12 HP 1059. Grant from William the smith of Gresham and Emma his wife to Richard Neel and Katerine his wife (7 July 1317).

13 HP 1060. Grant from John, son of William Silk of Holkham, to Richard Neel of Burnham and Katerine his wife (22 Nov. 1317).

14 HP 1062. Grant from Bartholomew, son of William le Marchale of Holkham, to Richard Neel of Burnham and Katerine his wife (20 Jan. 1318).

Fiche 2: E

1 HP 1063. Grant from Adam, son of William Craske of Holkham, to Richard Neel of Burnham and Katerine his wife (13 Dec. 1318).

2 HP 1064. Grant from Gilbert, son of William Silk of Holkham, to Richard Neel of Burnham (25 Feb. 1320).

3 HP 1065. Grant from Adam Craske of Holkham to Richard Neel of Burnham and Katerine his wife (5 Oct. 1319).

4 HP 1066. Grant from Humphrey, son of David and Amice his wife of Holkham, to William Craske of Holkham [c. 1284].

5 HP 1067. Quitclaim from William de Gresham to Richard Neel of Burnham and Katerine his wife [c. 1300].

6 HP 1068. Grant from Roger Marchal of Holkham to Richard Neel of Burnham and Katerine his wife [c. 1319].

7 HP 1069. Letter of Attorney from Roger Marchal of Holkham to Thomas Large of South Creake to give seisin to Richard Neel of Burnham and Katerine his wife [c. 1319].

8 HP 1070. Grant from Gilbert, son of John Silk of Holkham, to Richard Neel of Burnham (3 March 1320).

9 HP 1071. Grant from Gilbert, son of John Silk of Holkham, to Thomas le Northerne of Holkham (22 Oct. 1321).

10 HP 1072. Grant from Adam, son of William Craske of Holkham, to Richard Neel and Katerine his wife of Burnham Norton (1 May 1323).

11 HP 1073. Quitclaim from Margery Craske of Holkham to her son Adam of her dower (28 Sept. 1326).

12 HP 1074. Letter of Attorney from Adam, son of William Craske of Holkham, to Thomas, son of William Grene of South Creake, chaplain, to give seisin to Richard Neel of Burnham and Caterine his wife (14 Oct. 1326).

13 HP 1075. Grant from Adam, son of William Craske of Holkham, to Richard Neel of Burnham and Caterine his wife (29 Oct. 1326).

14 HP 1076. Grant from Adam Craske of Holkham to Richard Neel of Burnham and Caterine his wife (6 June 1329).

Fiche 2: F

1 HP 1077. Grant from Ralph, son of William a le Gateshende of Brisley, and Margaret his wife to Simon Mous of Kettlestone and Cecily his wife (27 Nov. 1329).

2   HP 1078. Grant from Lovegold and Alice, daughters of Richard Payn of
       Holkham, to William Roteney of Holkham (29 May 1317).
3   HP 1079. Grant from John, son of John Bret of Holkham, to William of
       Heveringlond and Robert of Knapton, chaplains (6 Feb. 1330).
4   HP 1080. Indenture between David de Strabolgy Earl of Atholl and Richard
       Neel of Burnham, Gilbert Burgeys of Titchwell, Henry Burgeys of same and
       William of Waterden (30 May 1332).
5   HP 1081. Letter of Attorney from Adam Craske of Holkham to John Mey of
       Holkham to give seisin to Richard Neel of Burnham and Katerine his wife (18
       June 1333).
6   HP 1082. Grant from Simon Mous of Kettlestone and Cecily his wife to
       Caterine, widow of Richard Neel of Burnham (9 Feb. 1336).
7   HP 1083. Grant from Simon, son of William Eyr of Merston, to Katerine,
       widow of Richard Neel of Burnham (11 July 1335).
8   HP 1084. Grant from Simon Mous of Kettlestone and Cecily his wife to
       Caterine, widow of Richard Neel of Burnham (9 Feb. 1336).
9   HP 1085. Grant from Thomas le Northerne of Holkham to Katerine, widow of
       Richard Neel of Burnham (11 Nov. 1335).
10   HP 1086. Grant from Ralph le Deye and Agnes his wife of Holkham to
       Caterine, widow of Richard Neel of Burnham (20 Nov. 1335).
11   HP 1087. Grant from Thomas, son of Richard le Northerne of Holkham, to
       Caterine, widow of Richard Neel of Burnham (18 Jan. 1336).
12   HP 1088. Grant from Ralph le Deye and Agnes his wife of Holkham to
       Caterine, widow of Richard Neel of Burnham (20 Apr. 1336).
13   HP 1089. Quitclaim from Simon atte Cros and Cecily his wife of Holkham to
       Caterine, widow of Richard Neel of Holkham (20 Apr. 1336).
14   HP 1090. Letter of Attorney from Thomas, son of Richard le Northerne of
       Holkham, to Peter Longe of Burnham, chaplain, to give seisin to Caterine,
       widow of Richard Neel of Burnham (30 Apr. 1336).

Fiche 2: G

1   HP 1091. Grant from Thomas, son of Richard le Northerne of Holkham, to
       Caterine, widow of Richard Neel of Burnham (20 July 1336).
2   HP 1092. Confirmation from William Wake of Holkham to Caterine, widow of
       Richard Neel of Burnham (22 July 1336).
3   HP 1093. Quitclaim from Simon atte Cros and Cecily his wife of Holkham to
       Katerine Neel of Holkham (12 Mar. 1337).
4   HP 1094. Letter of Attorney from Simon atte Cros and Cecily his wife of
       Holkham for Thomas Wake, chaplain, to give seisin to Caterine, widow of
       Richard Neel (2 June 1337).
5   HP 1095. Bond from Thomas, son of Richard le Northerne of Holkham, to
       Katerine, widow of Richard Neel (19 July 1337).
6   HP 1096. Defeasance of bond between Thomas, son of Richard le Northerne,
       and Katerine, widow of Richard Neel (19 July 1337).
7   HP 1097. Grant from Lawrence Bending of Holkham to Lawrence Skinner of
       Holkham (28 Apr. 1339).
8   HP 1098. Bond from Caterine, widow of Richard Neel of Burnham, to Thomas
       Neel her son (26 Sept. 1339).

9   HP 1099. Grant from Lawrence Skinner of Holkham to Gilbert Neel of
      Burnham (9 Aug. 1344).
10   HP 1100. Bond from William de Barney dwelling in Holkham to Gilbert Neel
      of Burnham (2 Oct. 1345).
11   HP 1101. Bond from Benedict Scot of Horning dwelling in Holkham to Gilbert
      Neel of Burnham (17 Aug. 1347).
12   HP 1102. Quitclaim from Gilbert Calwere of Holkham to John Calwere his
      brother (13 June 1347).
13   HP 1103. Grant from Ralph Colt of Holkham to John, son of Richard the smith
      [c. 1284].
14   HP 3808. Will of Thomas Neel of Burnham (20 Feb. 1350; Prob. 1 Mar. 1350).

Fiche 3: A
Twentieth-Century Holkham

Nine details from Ordnance maps, 1906, working copy with Ms. notes, 1962–7.
Details from a map of 1590 and early names from various documents are entered in
Ms.

1   Detail NW portion, Church Field with lake on east and road from Burnham on
      S. tracks converge towards Huncrundel (Model Farm, G.A. Dean, architect).
2   Detail SW portion, SW part of South Field with Avenue on E. Four tracks run
      North towards North Sea.
3   Central Portion. Tracks in north converge towards Huncrundale.
4   Smaller scale. Holkham town, the Hall, western part of Stathe Field, South
      Field.
5   Detail, South and South East of Obelisk Wood including Great Barn.
6   North central section with church, north end of lake, Stathe. The railway station
      with private waiting room for Coke family, 1866–1953 (destroyed by sea). The
      2nd Earl allowed no room for a siding for visitor's carriages here, but he
      allowed a siding in the Peterstone brick works. Note: West Norfolk railway
      running through marshes.
7   South section, with road from Burnham to Walsingham.
8   West Boundary with Church Field and South West field.
9   East central section with Hall and Obelisk Wood. Pleasure Ground and
      American Garden (near S. Wyatt's Palmers Lodge and Golden Gate) by W.A.
      Nesfield 1851, I. New terrace has Charles Raymond Smith's 'Perseus' (later
      called 'George and Dragon').
10   NE detail, way from Stathe to Wells on N. Way to Wighton on S.

Five Cambridge University aerial photographs 1962–7
      by permission of Director of Aerial Photographs.

11   Aerial view. Roman road running north towards marshes and sea on west
      boundary of Holkham, Cambridge AJI 48.
12   *ditto*. Avenue running through Triumphal arch to Obelisk, aligned on centre of
      Hall and monument northwards towards sea. Cambridge AEZ 87.
13   *ditto*. Sea, sand, nineteenth century wind break of Corsican pines, and the
      marshes with park showing Coke of Norfolk's second extension of lake
      breaking the belt of trees along northern boundary. Cambridge ARO 56

14   *ditto.* Park showing Creake (near) and Wells (distant) from which roads leading
      to Holkham are broken short at park boundaries. Note greater preponderance of
      trees in the park compared with surrounding country. Cambridge ATR 42.

Fiche 3: B

1   Aerial view. Church, Lake, the Hall (with Pleasure Ground beyond) and Wells
      boundary, in distance. Cambridge AMU 85.

Changes under the second Earl of Leicester, 1842–1910

2   NW portion of Holkham, 1843, map made on T.W. Coke's death showing park
      wall (1833–9) enclosing park extension, road diversion and northward extension
      of lake (1788–9), S. Wyatt's West Lodge (1780), New Inn (1786–8), kitchen
      gardens (1780-6) with S. Wyatt's vinery (1804–5), Church Lodge (1787). In
      1953 tidal surge destroyed park wall projecting onto seaward side of old coast
      road.

3   Model Farm (1852–3), from G.A. Dean, *A series of selected designs for
      selected country residences... etc. which have been erected for... the Earl of
      Leicester,* reproduced by permission of the curators of the Bodleian Library,
      Oxford. (Previously 'Hondecrondale', cf. 3: E2).

4   SW section of Holkham, 1843, Note trees lining T. Coke's curving park
      boundary NW of Obelisk Wood, absence of trees along northern half of
      Avenue, and survival of vistas through wood. West of Longlands (S. Wyatt,
      1792–8) park includes extension of 1790 where Burnham Thorpe boundary
      meets Burnham road. SE of Longlands S. Wyatt's New Holkham (1792–5),
      Great Barn (1790).

5   Map of 1843, reduced from original for reproduction on tin trays. Numbers (too
      small to appear) relate to a handsomely bound key. East of the house is a
      pleasure ground by John Sandys II (1872–9). John Sandys I (with forty staff in
      1788) planted most of the belts and clumps for T.W. Coke, keeping an annual
      record, 1781–1804.

6   Ordnance map, 1866. West Norfolk Railway (1866–1953) crossed Lady Ann's
      Drive (1847). Victoria Hotel (1838–9). Village 'beautified' (1854). Golden gates
      (1851). G.A. Dean's Longland workshops (1855–6). Groups of ilex recently
      planted along northern half of Avenue. Most vistas in Obelisk Wood gone.
      Terraces, fountains, table and office added around house and Pleasure ground
      transformed by W. Burn and W.A. Nesfield (1849–57).

7   Path to Temple, made by 5th Earl. Picture in Temple niche by Miss Audrey
      Earle of Burnham Market. Vistas originally converging on Temple were
      completely blocked. Home of three families (1851 census). The 5th Earl
      reopened vista down lake over marshes and dunes to sea and made an
      approach, curving for privacy.

8   The Avenue leading to Obelisk on skyline. The dip in the ground, once
      'Dalegate Bottom' concealed W. Kent's South Lodges. *Ditto,* by Miss Audrey
      Earle.

9   Ilex on eastern edge of Obelisk Wood, planted by T. Coke (1721). Drawing by
      Hon. Cory Lyons. Cf. W.O. Hassall, 'Ilexes at Holkham', *Garden History, The
      Journal of the Garden History Society,* vol. vi, no. 1, Spring 1978, p. 58.
      Acorns were said to have been used to pack imported classical sculpture.

10   Stable (1758–60) on west side of lake shortly before, removal beyond Hall, 1854. The Lodge was originally at south end of Lake before it was enlarged.

11   Above: Holkham Hall south front. The terrace runs along the north side of the old road from Burnham to Wighton which formed the boundary of the South Field. Photograph by Professor Yoko Miyoshi.

Below: Bank with old hedgerow tree, marking old road (cut by formation of lake) from Holkham to Wells. Photograph by Professor Yoko Miyoshi.

12   Thomas William Coke, 2nd Earl of Leicester (1822–1909), by Hon. John Collier (property of a grandson, Major Richard Coke, Weasenham Hall, Norfolk). The sandhills with marram grass bound 580 acres of salt-marsh, reclaimed 1852–78, and were planted with a windbreak of Corsican pines.

13   Samuel Bone, Park-Keeper, 1883, Deer-Keeper 1865. 'Bones Belt', west of Church, is called after him. He occupied Church Lodge, the only lodge by W. Kent to survive park extensions.

14   NW section, map of 1843. Shows West Fleet, the marsh reclaimed in 1857–9. Land on north of coast road opposite the ancient house, the former tidal channel (until Sea bank was made in 1720–2) is divided into cottage gardens.

Fiche 3: C

1   Inset from map of 1843. Holkham village, formerly 'the Stathe', before the Second Earl 'beautified' it (1845). Approach to almshouse gate (S.S. Teulon, 1848) not yet straightened.

Coke of Norfolk's Changes at Holkham, 1776–1842

2   Map by H.A. Biederman, 1781, showing whole parish. T. Coke's park boundary is ignored. Some fields on east and west boundaries are already planted with trees. Ancient pits are marked. Hachures indicate slopes.

3   Another map as above, but a new road across the NW corner of the present park cuts across, and rolls back, the rectangular closes between the road to Burnham and the coast road. Photograph by Leopold Schmidt.

4   Above: detail of map on paper of 1778–9 showing table and T. Coke's kitchen garden at SW corner of lake, linked by Serpentine river to canal below south front. East of lawn and canal is a pleasure ground. Between the Serpentine river and the SW wing is Brettingham's steward's house. In lower right corner are vestiges of Eastgate crofts and (W) of rectangular kitchen garden, the remains of Neel manor house.

Below: Tithe award map of 1839, showing same area after removal of garden, canal and pleasure ground, and addition of curve to end of lake. T.W. Coke's new garden is further west, and his new pleasure ground is east of the house.

5   H. Repton's views.

Above: improved lake, showing boat; and

Below: crazy cottage, perhaps the hermitage. Redbook, 1789, Ms. 772.

6   Above: North front by W. Watts.

Below: South front by W. Watts

7   Above: T. Weaver, T.W. Coke with his sheep, 1806. Church tower and South
        Front visible beyond trees.
        Below: Repton's ferry over lake. Redbook, 1789, Ms. 772.
8   T.W. Coke's monument. *The Illustrated London News*, August 16 1845, p. 112.
        On site of Kent's North Lodges.
9   Clumps on north lawn as designed by Kent. North Lodges beyond belt of trees.
        Map of 1778/9, made after Capability Brown had tidied environs of house and
        T.W. Coke had inherited. Before visits of Repton and Eames and removal of T.
        Coke's walled kitchen garden to make way for extension of lake.
10   Redrawing of approach to North Lodges, removed to clear site of monument.
11   Obelisk Wood, showing vistas converging on Temple and Obelisk. Map of
        1778/9. Such vistas were old-fashioned but remained unchanged until after
        1843.
12   Young T.W. Coke by Thomas Gainsborough (d. 1788).
13   Francis Blaikie (1824) by Chester Harding. As T.W. Coke's agent (1816–32) he
        recorded his daily business in letter books. These concern all Coke's estates,
        not only Holkham. He was under-gardener at Dalkeith Palace, a departmental
        head at Kew and Lord Chesterfield's agent at Bradley, Derbyshire, before
        coming to Holkham in preference to Woburn. He retired to Melrose
        (monumental inscription).
14   Plan of Stathe, 1778/9, detail from survey by T. Wyatt, dated by names of
        tenants listed in General Estate deed 77 compared with rentals in Audit books.

Fiche 3: D

1   Detail of Biederman's map showing SE portion of parish with enclosure
        hedges. SW of house trees at right angles to line of old road to Wighton
        indicate former hedgerows of Eastgate crofts. In addition to Obelisk Wood and
        windbreak on northern edge of park there is recent planting in direction of
        Wells. Photograph by Leopold Schmidt.

Completion of Thomas Coke's Park

2   Lord Leicester's display map, 1754–9. Original park boundary surrounded by
        recent rectangular enclosures. Burnham-Wighton road replaced by straight road
        on southern boundary avenue heads due north.
3   T. Wyatt, map, 1778/9, with field boundaries before park extension by T.W.
        Coke. Contemporary simplification from very large and detailed map.
4   W. entrance to old park and E. Lodges, from M. Brettingham, by W. Kent,
        moved by Samuel Wyatt further towards Burnham and Warham. A Kent
        fireplace was moved to Palmer's lodge, later replaced by Golden Gates.
5   Views of lake as first formed, straight, 1744. From plates made later by J.
        Wedgwood from Empress Catherine's 'Frog Service'. From photograph by
        Aurora publishing house, Nos. 1190 and 1191 in G. Williamson, Catalogue,
        1909. By permission of the Director of the Hermitage Museum, St Petersburg.
        The outflow went due north originally under a bridge.
6   Temple on axis of lake from M. Brettingham and Hon. Cory Lyons. The 2nd
        Earl removed the statues from niches to oblige the tenants. The 5th Earl

inserted pictures by Audrey Earle. Bricks made in 1730 from near kiln at Burnham North, only 2 inches thick to present miniature scale.

7 Engraving from lost portrait by C.F. Zincke showing T. Coke after he became Earl (1744) with S. front completed with two towers (1749).

8 W. Kent's N. and S. Lodges from M. Brettingham. N. Lodges were destroyed to clear site of T.W. Coke's monument as farmer 1845. S. Lodge lay concealed in low ground and was removed when T.W. Coke extended park southward.

9 Obelisk and Garden seat, from M. Brettingham. Sculptures by Peter Scheemaker, 1743, went, after the seat was destroyed, to a doorway in Burnham Overy by leave of 2nd Earl. The Obelisk ('1729' actually 1730–2) was at highest point on axis of park running from the Triumphal Arch through the marble Hall and Monument, due north.

10 Section of North Lodge, from M. Brettingham.

11 Environs of Hall, 1754–9. The parallel hedges, on plan of the *cour d'honneur* of Versailles, were removed – perhaps the only remaining trace of Capability Brown's visits, 1762–4. Photograph by Leopold Schmidt.

12 Triumphal Arch, from M. Brettingham. G. Vertue disliked W. Kent's pyramids at sides. They were removed by 1835. J. Lees-Milne thought they had unfortunately never been built.

13 Above: proposed building on chalk cliff in Church Wood, probably excavated when John Coke senior made first dam to reclaim salt marsh, 1659, after inheriting the Grand Estate in 1653.
Below: Arch gate to garden and Seat in Orangery, from M. Brettingham. This garden lay under the south end of the lake and was made (across the recently closed Burnham road) by T. Coke, 1727. It was moved further from Hall by T.W. Coke, 1782, on land newly taken in hand, to make the curve in S. end of lake possible. On site of medieval Holkham town (Westgate).

14 Viscount Coke by A. Casali, with N. front (before addition of porch by 2nd Earl). His death in 1753, aged 34, made Lord Leicester's nephew (born Wenman Roberts) his heir and led Lord Leicester to accelerate building the Hall to complete it, regardless of debts.

Fiche 3: E

1 Map, 1754–9, detail with New Marshes reclaimed from sea by Nathaniel Kinderley for T. Coke, 1720, after return from Grand Tour and marriage, 1719. Lands in Stathe Field had been largely consolidated by Grigges of Hillhall and the Newgates before 1500. Thomas Coke kept Stathe farm lands outside his new park pale. Photograph by Leopold Schmidt.

Enclosure of farms and creation of park on axis of avenue and new hall by T. Coke after embankment of 1720–2.

2 Key to plan of Parsonage (once grange of Dereham Abbey), 'Hondecrondale' farm, 1728.

3 Plan of William Leeds 'Honclecrondale', later S. Wyatt's New Inn (1786–8).

4. Henry Knatt's farm, once Neel manor house, with fields outside new park.

5 Consolidated fields of Peterstone Farm, the barn is still largely a medieval vestige of Priory.

6   Centre of palimpsest working map, 18 in. to 1 mile, used in 1720's. Photograph by Leopold Schmidt.

7   Detail of *ditto* with lake superimposed and Wighton-Burnham road erased. Photograph by Leopold Schmidt.

8   W. Kent drawings. Above: formal clumps on N. Lawn;
     Below: formal water, hedges and pavilions below south front (below). Horace Walpole disliked being 'dragged to see clumps at Holkham' and Kent's passion for 'sticking a dozen trees here and there till a lawn looks like the ten of spades' (1743).

9   Extract from Norfolk map, 1731, with sea on north, to show neighbouring rival seats of Sir Robert Walpole (Houghton), Lord Townshend (Rainham) and Lord Lovel (Holkham) in the adjoining Hundreds of Brothercross, North Greenhoe and Gallow. Formal avenues are shown at Holkham, but the Wighton-Burnham road is marked on the original though it had in fact gone.

10   Longlands Farm. In 1733 the tenant was promised that inclosures would be done in 2 years. Longland is one of few medieval toponyms to survive Holkham enclosures. Samuel Wyatt enlarged it with fashionable white bricks and mathematical tiles. G.A. Dean's estate workshops with steam engine (1855–6) retained the name.

11   Palimpsest map of SE portion of area. Avenue with straight lines superimposed on curving medieval tracks. Further out the old lines of the roads are retained. New field boundaries for Longlands tally with 3: E10. The avenue was aligned due north, pointing outwards through the centre of the proposed hall.

12   William Kent's drawings. Above: Triumphal arch in highest point in line with Obelisk and house centre. T.W. Coke removed the pyramids. It stood on land leased from Christ's college, Cambridge, to whom it had passed from Creake abbey.
     Below: projects for the seat on the mount, built in 1743, and for pool, formerly south of the house with west end pool formerly below south terrace. The pavilions which cast refection survived the hedges which they terminate until the accession of Coke of Norfolk. The hedges reached to the Obelisk Wood.

13   Map of Stathe Farm. The plan corresponds to a contemporary inventory which shows that the tenant kept a ship at Wells (Richard Porter's inventory, 4 Jan. 1730/1, NRO ANW/23/In/58/1729/31)

14   Fold-courses, c. 1722–4. Map shows new bank (1721–2) and Wighton road (dug up 1725). Huncrundle *alias* Borough Hall (top left). The Stathe *alias* Newgates (top right). Coneyhall *alias* Hillhall (right centre). Longlands *alias* Caldowe (bottom). The Old Creek or Delph leads north to Borough Channel from the Clynt or Broad Water, dividing the foldcourses on East and West which both straddle the contour line between the marshes and high land. Holkham town and Homestall (centre) straddles Wighton Road. Hillhall is represented by a hill (drawn upside down). In south, Longlands *alias* Ashyards *alias* Caldowe foldcourse has Quarles and Wighton on south and Coney Hall *alias* Hillhall foldcourse on the East. Cf. HD 22a, Fo. 1 no. 1.

Fiche 3: F
Sixteenth and Seventeenth Century

1   Gunnyngswong Furlong, lands along western (or Burnham Thorpe) parish boundary beginning with Calthorpe's 18 acres in the south and reading northwards towards Burnham Gate. In 1590 Calthorpe's is called: *S Phillippe Parkers xiiij ac.* SW corner of Holkham, HD 296, Fo. 21v.

2   Lands in NE corner of Holkham arable with marsh on North, HD 349.

3   Gunnerscrofte lands on north of old road to Burnham from Neel Manor (West), HD 355, Fo. 2.

4   Title and centres of population, with church and Clynt, 1590, Ms. 771, details.

5   Above: Church;
Below: manor houses of Neel and Hillhall, 1590, Ms. 771, details.

6   Church after lake was made, but before trees grew tall and hid it. Portrait by A. Casali of Henry Coke, who never owned or occupied Holkham. One of nine portraits, mostly imaginary ones of ancestors, painted at Holkham in 1757.

7   Nicholas Stone, monument of Meriel Wheatley (d. 1636) with ancestors and children. Heiress of Hillhall, wife of Chief Justice Coke's fourth son John (1590–1661), the first Coke to live at Holkham, a Cromwellian, whose male heir John died unmarried in 1670. Photograph by Mrs. F.C. Howlett.

8   Circular thatched roof of oldest part of icehouse, enlarged by T. Coke and given neo-Tudor entrance by 2nd Earl. Photograph by Professor Yoko Miyoshi.

9   One of five thirteenth-century monumental slabs: *Anneys de Bretham. Feme de Adam Hamund git ici.* Photograph by Professor Yoko Miyoshi.

10   Map of 1590 showing roads. Superimposed on Ordnance map, this gave framework of map of medieval Holkham.

11   Terrier of 140½ acres in 71 pieces, of Peterstone, from BD O, Fo. 16v.

12   Terrier of 140½ acres in 71 pieces, scattered lands of Peterstone Priory, 1314–15, in HD 205 no. VIIa, Fo. 15.

13   Portrait of the founder of the Coke family fortune, Chief Justice Coke, as Attorney General, 1593, d. 1633. He first bought Neel Manor as nucleus of Coke estate at Holkham (for his son John) and arranged marriage with heiress of Hillhall (3: F7). Attributed to C. Jonson. His legal earnings bought 'The Great Estate' in many counties for male heirs of his body and estates for each son. Eventually through lack of male heirs of various sons the estate was reunited in the hands of Thomas Coke who built Holkham. He and his heirs (descended from his sister) subsidised Holkham and its park by sales of remote properties.

14   Lands in Marsh furlong from Stathe Field terrier, c. 1480, HD 371, Fo. 1. When enclosed by T. Coke these became rectangular fields of Stathe Farm outside his new park pale. NE corner of Holkham arable.

Fiche 3: G
Fourteen seals (six of Brets), 1300–50

1   Stags head cabossed: Helewise widow of John le Bret, 1309, HD 24

2   Fleur-de-Lys: Isabel daughter of Ralph le Bret, 1284, HP 1036

3   Vesica, cross potence with St. Andrew's Cross: John, son of Adam le Bret, 1295, HP 1017

4   Vesica, a bird: John, son of Geoffrey le Bret of Holkham, 1296, HP 1018
5   Flower or star with eight petals or points: John son of Geoffrey le Bret, c. 1291–3, HP 1033
6   Flower or star with eight petals or points: John son of Geoffrey le Bret, 1294, HD 10
7   Six pointed star: Bartholomew de Burgate, 1299, HP 1022
8   Squirrel: Rose widow of Elias Crane, 1322, HD 30
9   Ship: Adam Craske, 1333, HP 1081
10   Fleur-de-lys on back of quadruped passant: Margery, widow of William Craske, 1327, HD 33
11   Oval, St. Andrew: Simon atte Cros,1336, HP 1084
12   Face in profile: Bartholomew, son of Robert, 1322, HP 1005
13   Ship: Gilbert Silk, 1321, HP 1071
14   Armorial: David de Strabolgy, Earl of Atholl, 1332, HP 1080

INDICES

INDEX OF PERSONS

References are to pages of the edition, and not to numbered documents. All names are standardized and indexed either by topographic surname or by patronymic surname. In their absence, first names only are used. 'De' or 'of' are not alphabetized. We have translated all first names and surnames. Thus 'Faber' or 'Cocus' appear as (the) Smith or (the) Cook, and 'Galfridus' and 'Johannes' appear as Geoffrey and John. Variants in the spelling of some surnames have been recorded where the connection is not obvious.

INDEX OF PLACES

Included here are place names of Norfolk and elsewhere together with the field names and landmarks of Holkham. Some Burnham field names are distinguished by the addition of (B). Elements of the modern landscape of Holkham are distinguished by (M). A few variant spellings of Holkham medieval field names and landmarks are included, but the full range of these variants is to be found in the topographical gazetteer in Appendix 4. References are to the page numbers of the edition.

INDEX OF SELECT SUBJECTS

The subjects in this index are grouped under the headings listed below.

AGRICULTURE

LANDSCAPE

b4   Holkham Park

American gardens, 540, 546, 563
Avenue, 538–41, 543–4, 553, 561–2, 565, 569, 581–3
Boundaries, park, 537, 539–40, 553, 565, 573, 576, 578, 581
Canal, ornamental canal, 538, 574, 578, 582
Brick kiln, 542
Brickworks, 573
Garden centre, 549
Gardener's cottage, 547
Golden gates, 537, 540, 546, 563
Great barn, 540, 546, 556
Holkham Hall, 54, 540 and *passim*
   Kitchen wing, 3–4
   Strangers wing, 4
   Terrace, 578
Holkham Park, 15, 26, 54, 207, 295, 327, 492, 533, 537–41, 543, 546–7, 550, 552–4, 558, 560–1, 563, 576, 578, 582–3
– Extension of, 540
Kent's lodge, 553
Kitchen gardens, 437, 537, 540–1, 543, 547, 549, 560, 564, 578, 581–3
Lake, 25, 31, 179, 343, 534, 537, 539–41, 547, 550, 552, 556, 560, 562, 573, 576, 578, 581–3
Lodge, 537
Model farm, 72, 532, 537, 539, 549–50, 553, 560, 571, 583
Model estate village, 573, 583
Monument, 550–1, 565
New Inn, 537, 560, 583
Obelisk, 537, 540, 550, 553, 562–3, 578, 583
– Wood, 537, 539–41, 543, 549–50, 552–3, 558–9, 567–8, 575, 578, 581–3
Old parsonage, 537
Pale *see* Boundaries, park
Palmer's lodge, 563
Parsonage *see* Rectory farm
Rectory, 34, 532
Rectory farm, 116
South lodge, 540, 558–9
Springs, 578, 581
Stables, 4, 582
Stathe Farm, 452
Steward's house, 547
Temple, 537, 541, 562–3, 578, 581, 583
Triumphal arch, 541, 543, 553, 567, 579, 582
Wells lodge, 540, 573
West lodge (Burnham lodge), 540, 547, 566, 573
Workshops, 567

JURISDICTION

c1   Lordship

Armorial seals, 42, 426
Arms, 32
Dubbing, 29, 87
Falconry, 29, 216, 526
Frankalmoin, 27, 33, 42, 64–6, 69–72, 219, 221, 509, 530
Holding, seigneurial, 39
Honor (Arundel), 30, 32, 220, 527
   (Buckenham), 221, 528
   (Clare), 33, 530, 531
   (Richmond), 27, 32
   (Warenne), 33, 223
Lordship, 19, 28, 41, 96, 293, 551

Collective, 38
Divided, 26, 36, 38, 40–1
Lay, 7, 11, 19, 27, 35
Manor, 39, 168, 261, 265, 519
Manorial office, 50, 56–7, 92, 303, 305, 323, 326, 329
   Structure, 25–6, 28–9, 35–6, 38, 42
Primogeniture, 72, 231
Soke, 75, 132
   Forinsec soke, 139, 147, 160–1, 351–3, 367, 392
   Sokemen, 27–9, 36, 215–16, 334, 525–6
Sub-infeudation, 9, 27, 29, 34, 39–43
Tenant-in-chief (*capitalis dominus*), 28, 30, 32, 38–41, 215 and *passim*

c5   Seigneurial documents

c6   Royal jurisdiction

SOCIAL STRUCTURE

d1   Royal officers

d2   Manorial officers

d3   Knights and freeholders

d7 Women